POETRY:
AN INTRODUCTION

POETRY:
AN INTRODUCTION

Second Edition

MICHAEL MEYER

University of Connecticut

BEDFORD BOOKS  BOSTON

For Bedford Books

President and Publisher: Charles H. Christensen
General Manager and Associate Publisher: Joan E. Feinberg
Managing Editor: Elizabeth M. Schaaf
Developmental Editor: Alanya L. Harter
Editorial Assistant: Aron Keesbury
Production Editor: Sherri Frank
Production Assistant: Deborah Baker
Copyeditor: Pamela Thomson
Text Design: Sandra Rigney, The Book Department, Inc.
Cover Design: Hannus Design Associates
Cover Art: In the Garden at Villiers-le-Bel, 1889, by Childe Hassam. Private Collection.
    Photograph courtesy of the collector.
Composition: Stratford Publishing Services
Printing and Binding: Haddon Craftsman, Inc.

Library of Congress Catalog Card Number: 97–72374

For information, write: Bedford Books, 75 Arlington Street, Boston, MA 02116
(617–426–7440)

ISBN: 0–312–14835–6

Acknowledgments

Diane Ackerman. "A Fine, a Private Place" from *Jaguar of Sweet Laughter* by Diane Ackerman. Copyright © 1991 by Diane Ackerman. Reprinted by permission of Random House, Inc. "On What Poetry Is Not–and Is" from "White Lanterns" in *The Writer and Her Work*, edited by Janet Sternburg (1991). Reprinted by permission of Diane Ackerman.

Anna Akhmatova. "Dedication" from *Anna Akhmatova: Selected Poems*, trans. Richard McKane. Copyright © 1967 by Richard McKane, Blookdaxe Books, Ltd.

Claribel Alegría. "I Am Mirror" from *Sobrevito* by Claribel Alegría. Reprinted by permission of the author.

Elizabeth Alexander. "Harlem Birthday Party" from *Ploughshares,* Spring 1996, vol. 22, no. 1, pp. 6-8. Reprinted by permission of the author.

Julia Alvarez. "Woman's Work" from *Homecoming: New and Collected Poems,* NAL/Dutton, 1996.

A. R. Ammons. "Coward" from *Diversifications* by A. R. Ammons. Copyright © 1975 by A. R. Ammons. Reprinted by permission of W. W. Norton & Co., Inc.

Charles R. Anderson. "Eroticism in 'Wild Nights — Wild Nights!'" from *Emily Dickinson's Poetry: Stairway of Surprise,* Holt, Rhinehart, and Winston, 1960. Reprinted with permission of the author.

Maya Angelou. "Africa" from *Oh Pray My Wings Are Gonna Fit Me Well* by Maya Angelou. Copyright © 1975 by Maya Angelou. Reprinted by permission of Random House, Inc.

Katerina Angheláki-Rooke. "Jealousy" from *Daughters of Sappho: Contemporary Greek Women Poets.* Ed. and trans. Rae Dalven. Associated University Presses, Fairleigh Dickinson UP, 1994. Reprinted with permission of Associated University Presses.

Richard Armour. "Going to Extremes" from *Light Amour* by Richard Armour. Reprinted by permission of Kathleen Armour.

John Ashbery. "Paradoxes and Oxymorons" from *Shadow Train* (New York: Viking Press and Penguin Books, 1981). Copyright © John Ashbery, 1980, 1981. Reprinted by permission.

Margaret Atwood. "Bored" and "February" from *Morning in the Burned House.* Copyright © 1995 by Margaret Atwood. Reprinted by permission of Houghton Mifflin Company and McClelland & Stewart, Inc, The Canadian Publishers. All rights reserved. "you fit into me" from *Power Politics* by Margaret Atwood (Toronto: House of Anansi Press, 1971). Reprinted with permission of Stoddard Publishing Co., Limited, Canada.

W.H. Auden. "Musée des Beaux Arts" and "The Unknown Citizen" from *W.H. Auden: Collected Poems* by W.H. Auden, ed. by Edward Mendelson. Copyright © 1940 and renewed 1968 by W.H. Auden. Reprinted by permission of Faber & Faber Ltd.

Jimmy Santiago Baca. "Green Chile" by Jimmy Santiago Baca, from *Black Mesa Poems.* Copyright © 1989 by Jimmy Santiago Baca. Reprinted by permission of New Directions Publishing Corp.

Acknowledgments and copyrights are continued at the back of the book on pages 642–647, which constitute an extension of the copyright page. It is a violation of the law to reproduce these selections by any means whatsoever without the written permission of the copyright holder.

Preface for Instructors

Poetry: An Introduction, Second Edition, is drawn from the widely adopted *Bedford Introduction to Literature.* This second edition of *Poetry* has many distinctive features that have already been class-tested in hundreds of literature courses and carefully revised over four editions. With its balance of classic and contemporary, traditional, and multicultural works, along with its in-depth treatment of selected poets, provocative secondary materials, and its pervasive concern with critical reading, thinking, and writing, *Poetry* addresses all the requirements of the contemporary poetry course. *Poetry: An Introduction* reflects the assumptions that understanding enhances the enjoyment of literature and that reading literature offers a valuable and unique means of apprehending life in its richness and diversity. The book also reflects the hope that the selections included will encourage students to become lifelong readers of imaginative literature. Designed to accommodate a variety of teaching styles, this rich collection of 442 poems (157 of them new) represents a wide range of periods, nationalities, ethnicities, and voices. Each selection has been carefully chosen for its appeal to students today and for its usefulness in demonstrating the effects, significance, and pleasures of poetry.

Poetry: An Introduction, Second Edition, is designed for the introductory poetry course as it is taught today, which varies — from school to school and from instructor to instructor — more than ever before. Even the traditional course emphasizing the elements of poetry and a broad range of works from the Western canon is changing in response to important developments in literary studies and, more generally, in higher education and in American society. The course is now viewed by many teachers as an opportunity to supplement classics of Western literature with the work of writers previously excluded from the traditional canon. Increasingly, it now also serves as an introduction to the discipline of literary study, a challenging development which brings to the undergraduate classroom important trends in literary theory and provocative new readings of both familiar and unfamiliar texts. Finally, introduction to poetry is now frequently taught as a second course in composition in which the critical thinking and writing that students do are as important as the reading that they do. The second edition of *Poetry: An Introduction* responds to these developments with distinctive features that address the needs of instructors who teach a traditional course but who are also concerned about canonical issues, literary theory, and writing about literature.

Selected Major Authors Treated in Depth

The book includes an extensive selection of poems, thirty-nine by Emily Dickinson, nineteen by Robert Frost, and — new to this edition — twenty-seven by Langston Hughes. Substantial introductions provide useful biographical and critical information about each of these important writers. A selection of "Perspectives" — excerpts from letters, journals, and critical commentaries — follows each writer's works to provide a context for discussion and writing. "Considerations for Critical Thinking and Writing" follow both selections and "Perspectives"; these questions for discussion or writing encourage critical thinking and provide stimulating opportunities for student essays.

In addition, "Two Complementary Critical Readings" on a particular work by each of the three major authors offer students examples of the variety of approaches they can take in reading and writing about poetry. The two readings on Dickinson, for instance, focus on the eroticism of "Wild Nights — Wild Nights!" and its relationship to nineteenth-century popular sensationalist literature. By reading commentaries from two critics who argue competing ideas about one text or who illuminate different aspects of that text, students can see immediately that there is no single way to read a work of literature, an important and necessary step for learning how to formulate their own critical approaches in their essays.

Albums of Contemporary and World Literature

An album of contemporary selections offers some of the most interesting and lively poems published in the last decade or so, including works by Deborah Garrison, Robert Hass, Jane Hirshfield, Linda Hogan, Yusef Komunyakaa, and Ronald Wallace. Biographical information about the album authors is included in the text to introduce instructors and students to these important but, perhaps, unfamiliar writers. Moreover, many contemporary poets are included throughout *Poetry*.

In addition, an album of world literature offers students a sampling of poems from other cultures, including the work of Claribel Alegría (Salvadoran), Faiz Ahmed Faiz (Pakistani), Xu Gang (Chinese), Wole Soyinka (Nigerian), Wislawa Szymborska (Polish), and Tomas Transtromer (Swedish), among others. Over a third of the poems in this edition are by women and minority writers and writers from other cultures. Related to the multicultural emphasis of *Poetry* is a new feature in Chapter 2, "Word Choice, Word Order, and Tone." A new section on poetry in translation provides different translations of several poems that help students to understand the significance of a translator's choices concerning diction and tone. These poems in translation encourage students to explore the nuances of poetic language as well as larger issues related to translation.

"Connections to Other Selections" consist of questions that link the selections in the albums of contemporary and world literature to more traditional selections in the text. For example, Linda Hogan's "Hunger" is linked with Emily Dickinson's "'Heaven' — is what I cannot reach!" and Wole Soyinka's "Future Plans" is connected to Dylan Thomas's "The Hand That Signed the Paper." These questions provide engaging writing opportunities and provocative topics for class discussion. "Connections to Other Selections" questions also appear after many of the works in the chapters on the elements of poetry.

Perspectives on Literature

"Perspectives" — journal notes, letters, classic and contemporary theoretical essays, interviews, and student responses — have proven to be extremely useful for class discussion and student writing. These seventy "Perspectives" (fifteen new) are included in six different places in the text: in Chapter 14 devoted to "Perspectives on Poetry"; in the chapters treating major authors in depth; in a chapter-length collection in "A Critical Case Study" on T. S. Eliot's "The Love Song of J. Alfred Prufrock"; at the end of Chapter 15, on literary theory; and, finally, throughout the text's discussion chapters. Individual "Perspectives" in these chapters follow the works to which they refer and, in many cases, discuss a poem in terms of the element of literature for which it serves as an illustration to teach students how to think critically and write effectively about poetry.

Focus on Critical Reading and Thinking

To further encourage critical reading and thinking, a discussion of how to read imaginative literature appears in Chapter 1. This offers practical advice about the kinds of questions active readers ask themselves as they read poetry. In addition, Chapter 15, "Critical Strategies for Reading," deepens the introductory discussions of active reading by focusing on the different reading strategies employed by contemporary literary theorists. This chapter, which can be assigned at any point in the course, introduces students to eight major contemporary theoretical approaches — formalist, biographical, psychological, historical, sociological (including Marxist and feminist strategies), mythological, reader-response, and deconstructionist. In brief examples the approaches are applied in analyzing Robert Frost's "Mending Wall," as well as other works, so that students will have a sense of how to use these strategies in their own reading and writing. A selected bibliography for the approaches and a set of "Perspectives" by contemporary literary critics conclude this unique chapter.

Although the emphasis in this text is on critical reading and understanding rather than on critical terminology, terms such as *symbol, irony,* and *metaphor* are defined and illustrated to equip students with a basic working vocabulary for discussing and writing about poetry. When first defined in the text, these terms appear in boldface type. An "Index of Terms" appears inside the back cover of the book for easy reference. Also, a new "Glossary of Literary Terms" provides concise explanations of more than 200 terms central to the study of poetry.

Writing about Poetry

The book's concern with helping students write about poetry is pervasive. The second edition of *Poetry: An Introduction* is especially suited for courses in which writing in response to literature is a central component. Three chapters cover every step of the writing process — from generating topics to documenting sources — and offer advice on different kinds of writing assignments. Two extensive chapters — "Reading and Writing" and "The Literary Research Paper" — discuss and illustrate the writing process while offering models of the different types of papers usually assigned in an introductory course, including explication, analysis, and comparison-contrast. A detailed chapter on the literary research paper, with a student model (documented in the MLA style), provides the necessary information for finding, evaluating, and documenting sources.

In addition, a new chapter — "Writing about Poetry" — focuses on genre-specific writing assignments, with questions for responsive reading and writing along with a sample student paper. New to this edition are "Questions for Writing about an Author in Depth" that accompany several poems by Emily Dickinson and help students to develop a coherent critical strategy for writing about one or more poems by the same author. This unit is illustrated by a sample paper. The book includes a total of seven sample papers (increased from four in the first edition) that provide concrete, accessible models for a wide range of assignments. Also new to this edition is a chapter on taking essay examinations for literature courses. Finally, a new quick-reference chart of all the writing-about-literature features is provided on the front endpapers of the book to help students (and instructors) find the writing advice they need. In sum, this new and expanded coverage offers a comprehensive overview of writing about literature.

Connections between "Popular" and "Literary" Culture

Poetry: An Introduction, Second Edition, draws carefully on examples from popular culture to explain the elements of poetry, inviting students to make connections between what they already know and what they will encounter in subsequent selections. Comparisons between popular culture and more canonical literary selections offer excellent writing opportunities, and suggestions are provided after each popular culture example. The examples include greeting card verse and contemporary song lyrics, such as Bruce Springsteen's "Streets of Philadelphia" and Queen Latifah's "The Evil That Men Do."

Resources for Teaching *Poetry: An Introduction*

This thorough and practical instructor's manual — about 300 pages long — discusses every selection, suggests answers to the questions posed in the text, provides suggestions for connections to other selections, and includes teaching tips from instructors who have taught from previous editions. The manual also offers commentary and writing assignments for the collection of poems in Chapter 13. It includes biographical information for many authors whose backgrounds are not discussed in the text and offers selected bibliographies for authors treated in depth. Finally, the manual provides a list of selections linked by "Connections" questions, an appendix, "Suggested Thematic Units for Discussion and Writing," including questions, and an annotated list of videos, films, and recordings related to the works of literature in the text.

Classic and Contemporary Poems

An audiotape of poetry selections from the book is available to instructors who adopt the second edition of *Poetry: An Introduction*. Poems linked by "Connections to Other Selections" questions are read together to offer an added resource for class discussion. In addition, the tape features the work of poets treated in depth (Dickinson, Frost, and Hughes); poems that serve as good examples of the elements of poetry discussed in the book; and, finally, a rich selection of classic and contemporary poems.

Acknowledgments

This book has benefited from the ideas, suggestions, and corrections of scores of careful readers who helped transform various stages of an evolving manuscript into a finished book and into subsequent editions. I remain grateful to those I have thanked in prefaces of *The Bedford Introduction to Literature,* particularly Robert Wallace of Case Western Reserve University. I would also like to give special thanks to Ronald Wallace of the University of Wisconsin and William Henry Louis of Mary Washington College. In addition, many instructors who have used *The Bedford Introduction to Literature* responded to a questionnaire on the book. For their valuable comments and advice I am grateful to Timothy Dow Adams, West Virginia University; Ronald H. Bayes, St. Andrews Presbyterian College; Denny Berthiaume, Foothill College; W. K. Buckley, Indiana University Northwest; Sandra Cookson, Canisius College; Spencer Edmunds, Elon College; Jerome Garger, Lane Community College; Carol Harding, Western Oregon State College; Robert McIlvaine, Slippery Rock University; John Orr, Fullerton College; Robert Regan, University of Pennsylvania; Michael Steinman, Nassau Community College; and Edward Zimmerman, Canisius College.

I am also indebted to those who cheerfully answered questions and generously provided miscellaneous bits of information. What might have seemed to them like inconsequential conversations turned out to be important leads. Among these friends and colleagues are Raymond Anselment, Ann Charters, Irving Cummings, William Curtin, Herbert Goldstone, Margaret Higonnet, Patrick Hogan, Lee Jacobus, Greta Little, George Monteiro, Brenda Murphy, Joel Myerson, Thomas Recchio, William Sheidley, Milton Stern, Kenneth Wilson, and the dedicated reference librarians at the Homer Babbidge Library, University of Connecticut.

I continue to be grateful for what I have learned from teaching my students and for the many student papers I have received over the years that I have used in various forms to serve as good and accessible models of student writing. I am particularly indebted to Quentin Miller for his excellent work on the second edition of *Resources for Teaching Poetry: An Introduction*.

At Bedford Books, my debts once again require more time to acknowledge than the deadline allows. Charles H. Christensen and Joan Feinberg initiated this project and launched it with their intelligence, energy, and sound advice. Karen Henry and Kathy Retan tirelessly steered earlier editions of *The Bedford Introduction to Literature* through rough as well as becalmed moments; their work was as first-rate as it was essential. Alanya Harter flawlessly carried on that tradition as developmental editor for this second edition; her savvy and quick takes made this project a pleasure. Aron Keesbury oversaw *Resources for Teaching Poetry: An Introduction* with clear-headed intelligence as well as enthusiasm. Moreover, he deftly arranged permissions. The difficult tasks of production were skillfully managed by Sherri Frank. (I also thank Deborah Baker for her assistance with these tasks.) Pamela Thomson provided careful copyediting, and Janet Cocker and Cynthia Hastings did more than meticulous proofreading. I thank all of the people at Bedford Books — including Amanda Bristow, Donna Lee Dennison, Susan Pace, and Stephanie Westnedge — who helped to make this formidable project a manageable one.

Finally, I am grateful to my sons Timothy and Matthew for all kinds of help, but mostly I'm just grateful they're my sons. And for making all the difference, I thank my wife, Regina Barreca.

Brief Contents

Contents

8.   Poetic Forms   204

POETRY:
AN INTRODUCTION

Introduction: Reading Imaginative Literature

THE NATURE OF LITERATURE

Literature does not lend itself to a single tidy definition, because the making of it over the centuries has been as complex, unwieldy, and natural as life itself. Is literature everything that is written, from ancient prayers to graffiti? Does it include songs and stories that were not written down until many years after they were recited? Does literature include the television scripts from *Seinfeld* as well as Shakespeare's *King Lear?* Is literature only that which has permanent value and continues to move people? Must literature be true or beautiful or moral? Should it be socially useful?

Although these kinds of questions are not conclusively answered in this book, they are implicitly raised by the poems included here. No definition of literature, particularly a brief one, is likely to satisfy everyone, because definitions tend to weaken and require qualification when confronted by the uniqueness of individual works. In this context it is worth recalling Herman Melville's humorous use of a definition of a whale in *Moby-Dick* (1851). In the course of the novel Melville presents his imaginative and symbolic whale as inscrutable, but he begins with a quotation from Georges Cuvier, a French naturalist who defines a whale in his nineteenth-century study *The Animal Kingdom* this way: "The whale is a mammiferous animal without hind feet." Cuvier's description is technically correct, of course, but there is little wisdom in it. Melville understood that the reality of the whale (which he describes as the "ungraspable phantom of life") cannot be caught by isolated facts. If the full meaning of the whale is to be understood, it must be sought on the open sea of experience, where the whale itself is, rather than in exclusionary definitions. Facts and definitions are helpful; however, they do not always reveal the whole truth.

Despite Melville's reminder that a definition can be too limiting and even comical, it is useful for our purposes to describe literature as a fiction consisting of carefully arranged words designed to stir the imagination. Stories, poems, and plays are fictional. They are made up — imagined — even when based on actual historic events. Such imaginative writing differs from other kinds of writing because its purpose is not primarily to transmit facts or ideas.

Imaginative literature is a source more of pleasure than of information, and we read it for basically the same reasons we listen to music or view a dance: enjoyment, delight, and satisfaction. Like other art forms, imaginative literature offers pleasure and usually attempts to convey a perspective, mood, feeling, or experience. Writers transform the facts the world provides — people, places, and objects — into experiences that suggest meanings.

Consider, for example, the difference between the following factual description of a snake and a poem on the same subject. Here is *Webster's Ninth New Collegiate Dictionary* definition:

> any of numerous limbless scaled reptiles (suborder Serpentes or Ophidia) with a long tapering body and with salivary glands often modified to produce venom which is injected through grooved or tubular fangs.

Contrast this matter-of-fact definition with Emily Dickinson's poetic evocation of a snake in "A narrow Fellow in the Grass":

> A narrow Fellow in the Grass
> Occasionally rides —
> You may have met Him — did you not
> His notice sudden is —
>
> The Grass divides as with a Comb —   5
> A spotted shaft is seen —
> And then it closes at your feet
> And opens further on —
>
> He likes a Boggy Acre
> A floor too cool for Corn —   10
> Yet when a Boy, and Barefoot —
> I more than once at Noon
> Have passed, I thought, a Whip lash
> Unbraiding in the Sun
> When stooping to secure it   15
> It wrinkled, and was gone —
>
> Several of Nature's People
> I know, and they know me —
> I feel for them a transport
> Of cordiality —   20
>
> But never met this Fellow
> Attended, or alone
> Without a tighter breathing
> And Zero at the Bone —

The dictionary provides a succinct, anatomical description of what a snake is, whereas Dickinson's poem suggests what a snake can mean. The definition offers facts; the poem offers an experience. The dictionary would probably allow someone who had never seen a snake to sketch one with reasonable accuracy. The poem also provides some vivid subjective descriptions — for example, the snake dividing the grass "as with a Comb" — yet it offers more than a picture of serpentine movements. The poem conveys the ambivalence many people have about snakes — the kind of feeling, for example, so evident on the faces of visitors viewing the snakes at a zoo. In the poem there is both a fascination with and a horror of what might be called snakehood; this combination of feelings has been coiled in most of us since Adam and Eve.

That "narrow Fellow" so cordially introduced by way of a riddle (the word *snake* is never used in the poem) is, by the final stanza, revealed as a snake in the grass. In between, Dickinson uses language expressively to convey her meaning. For instance, in the line "His notice sudden is," listen to the *s*-sound in each word and note how the verb *is* unexpectedly appears at the end, making the snake's hissing presence all the more "sudden." And anyone who has ever been surprised by a snake knows the "tighter breathing / And Zero at the Bone" that Dickinson evokes so successfully by the rhythm of her word choices and line breaks. Perhaps even more significant, Dickinson's poem allows those who have never encountered a snake to imagine such an experience.

A good deal more could be said about the numbing fear that undercuts the affection for nature at the beginning of this poem, but the point here is that imaginative literature gives us not so much the full, factual proportions of the world as some of its experiences and meanings. Instead of defining the world, literature encourages us to try it out in our imaginations.

THE VALUE OF LITERATURE

Mark Twain once shrewdly observed that a person who chooses not to read has no advantage over a person who is unable to read. In industrialized societies today, however, the question is not who reads, because nearly everyone can and does, but what is read. Why should anyone spend precious time with literature when there is so much reading material available that provides useful information about everything from the daily news to personal computers? Why should a literary artist's imagination compete for attention that could be spent on the firm realities that constitute everyday life? In fact, national best-seller lists much less often include collections of stories, poems, or plays than they do cookbooks and, not surprisingly, diet books. Although such fare may be filling, it doesn't stay with you. Most people have other appetites too.

Certainly one of the most important values of literature is that it nourishes our emotional lives. An effective literary work may seem to speak directly to us, especially if we are ripe for it. The inner life that good writers reveal in their characters often gives us glimpses of some portion of ourselves. We can be moved to laugh, cry, tremble, dream, ponder, shriek, or rage with a character by simply turning a page instead of turning our lives upside down. Although the experience itself is imagined, the emotion is real. That's why the final chapters of a good adventure novel can make a reader's heart race as much as a 100-yard dash or why the repressed love of Hester

Prynne in *The Scarlet Letter* by Nathaniel Hawthorne is painful to a sympathetic reader. Human emotions speak a universal language regardless of when or where a work was written.

In addition to appealing to our emotions, literature broadens our perspectives on the world. Most of the people we meet are pretty much like ourselves, and what we can see of the world even in a lifetime is astonishingly limited. Literature allows us to move beyond the inevitable boundaries of our own lives and culture because it introduces us to people different from ourselves, places remote from our neighborhoods, and times other than our own. Reading makes us more aware of life's possibilities as well as its subtleties and ambiguities. Put simply, people who read literature experience more life and have a keener sense of a common human identity than those who do not. It is true, of course, that many people go through life without reading imaginative literature, but that is a loss rather than a gain. They may find themselves troubled by the same kinds of questions that reveal Daisy Buchanan's restless, vague discontentment in F. Scott Fitzgerald's *The Great Gatsby:* "What'll we do with ourselves this afternoon?" cried Daisy, "and the day after that, and the next thirty years?"

Sometimes students mistakenly associate literature more with school than with life. Accustomed to reading it to write a paper or pass an examination, students may perceive such reading as a chore instead of a pleasurable opportunity, something considerably less important than studying for the "practical" courses that prepare them for a career. The study of literature, however, is also practical, because it engages you in the kinds of problem solving important in a variety of fields, from philosophy to science and technology. The interpretation of literary texts requires you to deal with uncertainties, value judgments, and emotions; these are unavoidable aspects of life.

People who make the most significant contributions to their professions — whether in business, engineering, teaching, or some other area — tend to be challenged rather than threatened by multiple possibilities. Instead of retreating to the way things have always been done, they bring freshness and creativity to their work. F. Scott Fitzgerald once astutely described the "test of a first-rate intelligence" as "the ability to hold two opposed ideas in the mind at the same time, and still retain the ability to function." People with such intelligence know how to read situations, shape questions, interpret details, and evaluate competing points of view. Equipped with a healthy respect for facts, they also understand the value of pursuing hunches and exercising their imaginations. Reading literature encourages a suppleness of mind that is helpful in any discipline or work.

Once the requirements for your degree are completed, what ultimately matters are not the courses listed on your transcript but the sensibilities and habits of mind that you bring to your work, friends, family, and, indeed, the rest of your life. A healthy economy changes and grows with the times; people do too if they are prepared for more than simply filling a job description. The range and variety of life that literature affords can help you to interpret your own experiences and the world in which you live.

To discover the insights that literature reveals requires careful reading

and sensitivity. One purpose of a college introduction to literature is to culti-
vate the analytic skills necessary for reading well. Class discussions often help
establish a dialogue with a work that perhaps otherwise would not speak to
you. Analytic skills can also be developed by writing about what you read.
Writing is an effective means of clarifying your responses and ideas, because
it requires you to account for the author's use of language as well as your
own. This book is based on two premises: that reading literature is pleasurable and that the more sensitively a work is read and understood by thinking,
talking, or writing about it, the more pleasurable the experience of it is.

Understanding its basic elements — such as point of view, symbol,
theme, tone, irony, and so on — is a prerequisite to an informed appreciation
of literature. This kind of understanding allows you to perceive more in a literary work in much the same way that a spectator at a tennis match sees more
if he or she understands the rules and conventions of the game. But literature
is not simply a spectator sport. The analytic skills that open up literature also
have their uses when you watch a television program or film and, more
important, when you attempt to sort out the significance of the people,
places, and events that constitute your own life. Literature enhances and
sharpens your perceptions. What could be more lastingly practical as well as
satisfying?

THE CHANGING LITERARY CANON

Perhaps the best reading is that which creates some kind of change in us:
we see more clearly; we're alert to nuances; we ask questions that previously
didn't occur to us. Henry David Thoreau had that sort of reading in mind
when he remarked in *Walden* that the books he valued most were those that
caused him to date "a new era in his life from the reading." Readers are sometimes changed by literature, but it is also worth noting that the life of a literary work can also be affected by its readers. Melville's *Moby-Dick,* for
example, was not valued as a classic until the 1920s, when critics rescued the
novel from the obscurity of being cataloged in many libraries (including
Yale's) not under fiction but under cetology, the study of whales. Indeed,
many writers contemporary to Melville who were important and popular in
the nineteenth century — William Cullen Bryant, Henry Wadsworth Longfel-
low, and James Russell Lowell, to name a few — are now mostly unread; their
names appear more often on elementary schools built early in this century
than in anthologies. Clearly, literary reputations and what is valued as great
literature change over time and in the eyes of readers.

Such changes have accelerated during the past thirty years as the literary
canon — those works considered by scholars, critics, and teachers to be
the most important to read and study — has undergone a significant series
of shifts. Writers who previously were overlooked, undervalued, neglected, or
studiously ignored have been brought into focus in an effort to create a more
diverse literary canon, one that recognizes the contributions of the many
cultures that make up American society. Since the 1960s, for example, some

critics have reassessed writings by women who had been left out of the standard literary traditions dominated by male writers. Many more female writers
are now read alongside the male writers who traditionally populated literary
history. This kind of enlargement of the canon also resulted from another
reform movement of the 1960s. The civil rights movement sensitized literary
critics to the political, moral, and aesthetic necessity of rediscovering African
American literature, and more recently Asian and Hispanic writers have been
making their way into the canon. Moreover, on a broader scale the canon is
being revised and enlarged to include the works of writers from parts of the
world other than the West, a development that reflects the changing values,
concerns, and complexities of the past decade, when literary landscapes have
shifted as dramatically as the political boundaries of Eastern Europe and what
was once the Soviet Union.

No semester's reading list — or anthology — can adequately or accurately echo all the new voices competing to be heard as part of the main-
stream literary canon, but recent efforts to open up the canon attempt to
sensitize readers to the voices of women, minorities, and writers from all over
the world. This development has not occurred without its urgent advocates or
passionate dissenters. It's no surprise that issues about race, gender, and class
often get people off the fence and on their feet (these controversies are discussed further in Chapter 15, "Critical Strategies for Reading"). Although what
we regard as literature — whether it's called great, classic, or canonical —
continues to generate debate, there is no question that such controversy will
continue to reflect readers' values as well as the writers they admire.

POETRY

1. Reading Poetry

READING POETRY RESPONSIVELY

Perhaps the best way to begin reading poetry responsively is not to allow yourself to be intimidated by it. Come to it, initially at least, the way you might listen to a song on the radio. You probably listen to a song several times before you hear it all, before you have a sense of how it works, where it's going, and how it gets there. You don't worry about analyzing a song when you listen to it, even though after repeated experiences with it you know and anticipate a favorite part and know, on some level, why it works for you. Give yourself a chance to respond to poetry. The hardest work has already been done by the poet, so all you need to do at the start is listen for the pleasure produced by the poet's arrangement of words.

Try reading the following poem aloud. Read it aloud before you read it silently. You may stumble once or twice, but you'll make sense of it if you pay attention to its punctuation and don't stop at the end of every line where there is no punctuation. The title gives you an initial sense of what the poem is about.

MARGE PIERCY (b. 1936)
The Secretary Chant   1973

My hips are a desk.
From my ears hang
chains of paper clips.
Rubber bands form my hair.
My breasts are wells of mimeograph ink.   5
My feet bear casters.
Buzz. Click.
My head is a badly organized file.
My head is a switchboard
where crossed lines crackle.   10

Press my fingers
and in my eyes appear
credit and debit.
Zing. Tinkle.
My navel is a reject button.   15
From my mouth issue canceled reams.
Swollen, heavy, rectangular
I am about to be delivered
of a baby
Xerox machine.   20
File me under W
because I wonce
was
a woman.

What is your response to this secretary's chant? The point is simple
enough — she feels dehumanized by her office functions — but the pleasures
are manifold. Piercy makes the speaker's voice sound mechanical by using
short bursts of sound and by having her make repetitive, flat, matter-of-fact
statements ("My breasts . . . My feet . . . My head . . . My navel"). "The Secretary Chant" makes a serious statement about how such women are reduced
to functionaries. The point is made, however, with humor since we are asked
to visualize the misappropriation of the secretary's body — her identity —
as it is transformed into little more than a piece of office equipment,
which seems to be breaking down in the final lines, when we learn that she
"wonce / was / a woman." Is there the slightest hint of something subversive
in this misspelling of "wonce"? Maybe so, but the humor is clear enough, particularly if you try to make a drawing of what this dehumanized secretary has
become.

The next poem creates a different kind of mood. Think about the title,
"Those Winter Sundays," before you begin reading the poem. What associations do you have with winter Sundays? What emotions does the phrase
evoke in you?

ROBERT HAYDEN (1913-1980)
Those Winter Sundays   1962

Sundays too my father got up early
and put his clothes on in the blueblack cold,
then with cracked hands that ached
from labor in the weekday weather made
banked fires blaze. No one ever thanked him.   5

I'd wake and hear the cold splintering, breaking.
When the rooms were warm, he'd call,
and slowly I would rise and dress,
fearing the chronic angers of that house,

Speaking indifferently to him,
who had driven out the cold
and polished my good shoes as well.
What did I know, what did I know
of love's austere and lonely offices?

Does the poem match the feelings you have about winter Sundays? Either way your response can be useful in reading the poem. For most of us Sundays are days at home; they might be cozy and pleasant experiences or they might be dull and depressing. Whatever they are, Sundays are more evocative than, say, Tuesdays. Hayden uses that response to call forth a sense of missed opportunity in the poem. The person who reflects on those winter Sundays didn't know until much later how much he had to thank his father for "love's austere and lonely offices." This is a poem about a cold past and a present reverence for his father — elements brought together by the phrase "Winter Sundays." *His* father? You may have noticed that the poem doesn't use a masculine pronoun; hence the voice could be a woman's. Does the sex of the voice make any difference to your reading? Would it make any difference about which details are included or what language is used?

What is most important about your initial readings of a poem is that you ask questions. If you read responsively, you'll find yourself asking all kinds of questions about the words, descriptions, sounds, and structures of a poem. The specifics of those questions will be generated by the particular poem. We don't, for example, ask how humor is achieved in "Those Winter Sundays" because there is none, but it is worth asking what kind of tone is established by the description of "the chronic angers of that house." The remaining chapters in this part will help you to formulate and answer questions about a variety of specific elements in poetry, such as speaker, image, metaphor, symbol, rhyme, and rhythm. For the moment, however, read the following poem several times and note your response at different points in the poem. Then write down a half dozen or so questions about what produces your response to the poem. To answer questions, it's best to know first what the questions are, and that's what the rest of this chapter is about.

JOHN UPDIKE (b. 1932)
Dog's Death

1969

She must have been kicked unseen or brushed by a car.
Too young to know much, she was beginning to learn
To use the newspapers spread on the kitchen floor
And to win, wetting there, the words, "Good dog! Good dog!"

We thought her shy malaise was a shot reaction.   5
The autopsy disclosed a rupture in her liver.
As we teased her with play, blood was filling her skin
And her heart was learning to lie down forever.

Monday morning, as the children were noisily fed
And sent to school, she crawled beneath the youngest's bed. 10
We found her twisted and limp but still alive.
In the car to the vet's, on my lap, she tried

To bite my hand and died. I stroked her warm fur
And my wife called in a voice imperious with tears.
Though surrounded by love that would have upheld her, 15
Nevertheless she sank and, stiffening, disappeared.

Back home, we found that in the night her frame,
Drawing near to dissolution, had endured the shame
Of diarrhoea and had dragged across the floor
To a newspaper carelessly left there. *Good dog*. 20

Here's a simple question to get started with your own questions: what would its effect have been if Updike had titled the poem "Good Dog" instead of "Dog's Death"?

THE PLEASURE OF WORDS

The impulse to create and appreciate poetry is as basic to human experience as language itself. Although no one can point to the precise origins of poetry, it is one of the most ancient of the arts, because it has existed ever since human beings discovered pleasure in language. The tribal ceremonies of peoples without written language suggest that the earliest primitive cultures incorporated rhythmic patterns of words into their rituals. These chants, very likely accompanied by the music of a simple beat and the dance of a measured step, expressed what people regarded as significant and memorable in their lives. They echoed the concerns of the chanters and the listeners by chronicling acts of bravery, fearsome foes, natural disasters, mysterious events, births, deaths, and whatever else brought people pain or pleasure, bewilderment or revelation. Later cultures, such as the ancient Greeks, made poetry an integral part of religion.

Thus, from its very beginnings, poetry has been associated with what has mattered most to people. These concerns — whether natural or supernatural — can, of course, be expressed without vivid images, rhythmic patterns, and pleasing sounds, but human beings have always sensed a magic in words that goes beyond rational, logical understanding. Poetry is not simply a method of communication; it is a unique experience in itself.

What is special about poetry? What makes it valuable? Why should we read it? How is reading it different from reading prose? To begin with, poetry pervades our world in a variety of forms, ranging from advertising jingles to song lyrics. These may seem to be a long way from the chants heard around a primitive camp fire, but they serve some of the same purposes. Like poems printed in a magazine or book, primitive chants, catchy jingles, and popular songs attempt to stir the imagination through the carefully measured use of words.

Although reading poetry usually makes more demands than does the kind of reading used to skim a magazine or newspaper, the appreciation of poetry comes naturally enough to anyone who enjoys playing with words. Play is an important element of poetry. Consider, for example, how the following words appeal to the children who gleefully chant them in playgrounds.

> I scream, you scream
> We all scream
> For ice cream.

These lines are an exuberant evocation of the joy of ice cream. Indeed, chanting the words turns out to be as pleasurable as eating ice cream. In poetry, the expression of the idea is as important as the idea expressed.

But is "I scream ..." poetry? Some poets and literary critics would say that it certainly is one kind of poem, because the children who chant it experience some of the pleasures of poetry in its measured beat and repeated sounds. However, other poets and critics would define poetry more narrowly and insist, for a variety of reasons (some of which are included among the definitions in Chapter 14), that this isn't true poetry but merely *doggerel,* a term used for lines whose subject matter is trite and whose rhythm and sounds are monotonously heavy-handed.

Although probably no one would argue that "I scream ..." is a great poem, it does contain some poetic elements that appeal, at the very least, to children. Does that make it poetry? The answer depends on one's definition, but poetry has a way of breaking loose from definitions. Because there are nearly as many definitions of poetry as there are poets, Edwin Arlington Robinson's succinct observations are useful: "poetry has two outstanding characteristics. One is that it is undefinable. The other is that it is eventually unmistakable."

This comment places more emphasis on how a poem affects a reader than on how a poem is defined. By characterizing poetry as "undefinable," Robinson acknowledges that it can include many different purposes, subjects, emotions, styles, and forms. What effect does the following poem have on you?

WILLIAM HATHAWAY (b. 1944)
Oh, Oh

1982

My girl and I amble a country lane,
moo cows chomping daisies, our own
sweet saliva green with grass stems.
"Look, look," she says at the crossing,
"the choo-choo's light is on." And sure   5
enough, right smack dab in the middle
of maple dappled summer sunlight
is the lit headlight — so funny.
An arm waves to us from the black window.
We wave gaily to the arm. "When I hear   10

trains at night I dream of being president,"
I say dreamily. "And me first lady," she
says loyally. So when the last boxcars,
named after wonderful, faraway places,
and the caboose chuckle by we look   15
eagerly to the road ahead. And there,
poised and growling, are fifty Hell's Angels.

Hathaway's poem serves as a convenient reminder that poetry can be full of surprises. Even on a first reading there is no mistaking the emotional reversal created by the last few words of this poem. With the exception of the final line, the poem's language conjures up an idyllic picture of a young couple taking a pleasant walk down a country lane. Contented as "moo cows," they taste the sweetness of the grass, hear peaceful country sounds, and are dazzled by "dappled summer sunlight." Their future together seems to be all optimism as they anticipate "wonderful, faraway places" and the "road ahead." Full of confidence, this couple, like the reader, is unprepared for the shock to come. When we see those "fifty Hell's Angels," we are confronted with something like a bucket of cold water in the face.

But even though our expectations are abruptly and powerfully reversed, we are finally invited to view the entire episode from a safe distance — the distance provided by the delightful humor in this poem. After all, how seriously can we take a poem that is titled "Oh, Oh"? The poet has his way with us, but we are brought in on the joke too. The terror takes on comic proportions as the innocent couple is confronted by no fewer than *fifty* Hell's Angels. This is the kind of raucous overkill that informs a short animated film produced some years ago titled *Bambi Meets Godzilla:* you might not have seen it, but you know how it ends. The poem's good humor comes through when we realize how pathetically inadequate the response of "Oh, Oh" is to the circumstances.

As you can see, reading a description of what happens in a poem is not the same as experiencing a poem. The exuberance of "I scream . . ." and the surprise of Hathaway's "Oh, Oh" are in the hearing or reading rather than in the retelling. A *paraphrase* is a prose restatement of the central ideas of a poem in your own language. Consider the difference between the following poem and the paraphrase that follows it. What is missing from the paraphrase?

ROBERT FRANCIS (1901–1987)
Catch   1950

Two boys uncoached are tossing a poem together,
Overhand, underhand, backhand, sleight of hand, every hand,
Teasing with attitudes, latitudes, interludes, altitudes,
High, make him fly off the ground for it, low, make him stoop,
Make him scoop it up, make him as-almost-as-possible miss it,   5
Fast, let him sting from it, now, now fool him slowly,

Anything, everything tricky, risky, nonchalant,
Anything under the sun to outwit the prosy,
Over the tree and the long sweet cadence down,
Over his head, make him scramble to pick up the meaning,   10
And now, like a posy, a pretty one plump in his hands.

Paraphrase: A poet's relationship to a reader is similar to a game of catch. The poem, like a ball, should be pitched in a variety of ways to challenge and create interest. Boredom and predictability must be avoided if the game is to be engaging and satisfying.

A paraphrase can help us achieve a clearer understanding of a poem, but, unlike a poem, it misses all the sport and fun. It is the poem that "out-wit[s] the prosy," because the poem serves as an example of what it suggests poetry should be. Moreover, the two players — the poet and the reader — are "uncoached." They know how the game is played, but their expectations do not preclude spontaneity and creativity or their ability to surprise and be surprised. The solid pleasure of the workout — of reading poetry — is the satisfaction derived from exercising your imagination and intellect.

That pleasure is worth emphasizing. Poetry uses language to move and delight even when it includes a cast of fifty Hell's Angels. The pleasure is in having the poem work its spell on us. For that to happen, it is best to relax and enjoy poetry rather than worrying about definitions of it. Pay attention to what the poet throws you. We read poems for emotional and intellectual discovery — to feel and to experience something about the world and ourselves. The ideas in poetry — what can be paraphrased in prose — are important, but the real value of a poem consists in the words that work their magic by allowing us to feel, see, and be more than we were before. Perhaps the best way to approach a poem is similar to what Francis's "Catch" implies: expect to be surprised; stay on your toes; and concentrate on the delivery.

A SAMPLE ANALYSIS:
TOSSING METAPHORS TOGETHER IN "CATCH"

The following sample paper on Robert Francis's "Catch" was written in response to an assignment that asked the students to discuss the use of metaphor in the poem. Notice that Chris Leggett's paper is clearly focused and well organized. His discussion of the use of metaphor in the poem stays on track from beginning to end without any detours concerning unrelated topics (for a definition of *metaphor,* see p. 109). His title draws on the central metaphor of the poem, and he organizes the paper around four key words used in the poem: "attitudes, latitudes, interludes, [and] altitudes." These constitute the heart of the paper's four substantive paragraphs, and they are effectively framed by introductory and concluding paragraphs. Moreover, the transitions between paragraphs clearly indicate that the author was not merely tossing a paper together.

Chris Leggett

Professor Lyles

English 203-1·

November 9, 19--

Tossing Metaphors Together in "Catch"

The word "catch" is an attention getter. It usually means something is about to be hurled at someone, and that he or she is expected to catch it. "Catch" can also signal a challenge to another player if the toss is purposefully difficult. Robert Francis, in his poem "Catch," uses the extended metaphor of two boys playing catch to explore the considerations a poet makes when "tossing a poem together." Line 3 of "Catch" enumerates these considerations metaphorically as "attitudes, latitudes, interludes, [and] altitudes." While regular prose is typically straightforward and easily understood, poetry usually takes great effort to understand and appreciate. To exemplify this, Francis presents the reader not with a normal game of catch with the ball flying back and forth in a repetitive and predictable fashion, but with a physically challenging game in which one must concentrate, scramble, and exert oneself to catch the ball, as one must stretch the intellect to truly grasp a poem.

The first consideration mentioned by Francis is attitude. Attitude, when applied to the game of catch, indicates the ball's pitch in flight, upward, downward, or straight. It could also describe the players' attitudes toward each other or toward the game in general. Below this literal level lies attitude's meaning in relation to poetry. Attitude in this case represents a poem's tone. A poet may "tease with attitude" by experimenting with different tones to achieve the desired mood. The underlying tone of "Catch" is a playful one, set and reinforced

by the use of a game. This playfulness is further reinforced by such words and phrases as "teasing," "outwit,"
and "fool him."

Considered also in the metaphorical game of catch is
latitude, which, when applied to the game, suggests the
range the object may be thrown, how high, how low, or how
far. Poetic latitude, along similar lines, concerns a
poem's breadth, or the scope of topic. Taken one level
further, latitude suggests freedom from normal restraints
or limitations, indicating the ability to go outside the
norm to find originality of expression. The entire game
of catch described in Francis's poem reaches outside the
normal expectations of something being merely tossed back
and forth in a predictable manner. The ball is thrown in
almost every conceivable fashion, "overhand, underhand
. . . every hand." Other terms describing the throws, such
as "tricky," "risky," "fast," "slowly," and "anything
under the sun," express endless latitude for avoiding predictability in Francis's game of catch and metaphorically
in writing poetry.

During a game of catch the ball may be thrown at different intervals, establishing a steady rhythm or a broken, irregular one. Other intervening features, such as
the field being played on or the weather, could also
affect the game. These features of the game are alluded
to in the poem by the use of the word "interludes."
"Interlude" in the poetic sense represents the poem's
form, which can similarly establish or diminish rhythm or
enhance meaning. Lines 6 and 9 respectively show a broken
and a flowing rhythm. Line 6 begins rapidly as a hard
toss that stings the catcher's hand is described. The
rhythm of the line is immediately slowed, however, by the
word "now" followed by a comma, followed by the rest of

the line. In contrast, line 9 flows smoothly as the
reader visualizes the ball flying over the tree and sailing downward. The words chosen for this line function
perfectly. The phrase "the long sweet cadence down"
establishes a sweet rhythm that reads smoothly and rolls
off the tongue easily. The choice of diction not only
affects the poem's rhythmic flow but also establishes
through connotative language the various levels at which
the poem can be understood, represented in "Catch" as
altitude.

    While "altitude" when referring to the game of catch
means how high an object is thrown, in poetry it could
refer to the level of diction, lofty or down-to-earth,
formal or informal. It suggests also the levels at which
a poem can be comprehended, the literal as well as the
interpretive. In Francis's game of catch the ball is
thrown high to make the player reach, or low to make him
stoop, or over his head to make him scramble, implying
that the player should have to exert himself to catch it.
So too, then, should the reader of poetry put great effort
into understanding the full meaning of a poem. Francis
exemplifies this consideration in writing poetry not only
by giving "Catch" an enjoyable literal meaning concerning
the game of catch, but also a rich metaphorical meaning--
reflecting the process of writing poetry. Francis uses
several phrases and words with multiple meanings. The
phrase "tossing a poem together" can be understood as
tossing something back and forth or the process of constructing a poem. While "prosy" suggests prose itself, it
also means the mundane or the ordinary. In the poem's
final line the word "posy" of course represents a flower,
while it is also a variant of the word "poesy," meaning
poetry, or the practice of composing poetry.

Francis effectively describes several considerations to be taken in writing poetry in order to "outwit the prosy." His use of the extended metaphor in "Catch" shows that a poem must be unique, able to be comprehended on multiple levels, and a challenge to the reader. The various rhythms in the lines of "Catch" exemplify the ideas they express. While achieving an enjoyable poem on the literal level, Francis has also achieved a rich metaphorical meaning. The poem offers a good workout both physically and intellectually.

Before beginning your own writing assignment on poetry, you should review Chapter 10, "Writing about Poetry," and Chapter 16, "Reading and Writing," which provides a step-by-step overview of how to choose a topic, develop a thesis, and organize various types of writing assignments. If you are using outside sources in your paper, you should make sure that you are familiar with the conventional documentation procedures described in Chapter 17, "The Literary Research Paper."

WOLE SOYINKA (b. 1934)
Telephone Conversation   1960

The price seemed reasonable, location
Indifferent. The landlady swore she lived
Off premises. Nothing remained
But self-confession. "Madam," I warned,
"I hate a wasted journey — I am African."   5
Silence. Silenced transmission of
Pressurized good-breeding. Voice, when it came,
Lipstick coated, long gold-rolled
Cigarette-holder pipped. Caught I was, foully.
"HOW DARK?" . . . I had not misheard . . . "ARE YOU LIGHT   10
OR VERY DARK?" Button B. Button A. Stench
Of rancid breath of public hide-and-speak.
Red booth. Red pillar-box. Red double-tiered
Omnibus squelching tar. It *was* real! Shamed
By ill-mannered silence, surrender   15

Pushed dumbfoundment to beg simplification.
Considerate she was, varying the emphasis —
"ARE YOU DARK? OR VERY LIGHT?" Revelation came.
"You mean — like plain or milk chocolate?"
Her assent was clinical, crushing in its light   20
Impersonality. Rapidly, wave-length adjusted,
I chose. "West African sepia" — and as afterthought,
"Down in my passport." Silence for spectroscopic
Flight of fancy, till truthfulness clanged her accent
Hard on the mouthpiece. "WHAT'S THAT?" conceding   25
"DON'T KNOW WHAT THAT IS." "Like brunette."
"THAT'S DARK, ISN'T IT?" "Not altogether.
Facially, I am brunette, but madam, you should see
The rest of me. Palm of my hand, soles of my feet
Are a peroxide blonde. Friction, caused —   30
Foolishly madam — by sitting down, has turned
My bottom raven black — One moment madam!" — sensing
Her receiver rearing on the thunderclap
About my ears — "Madam," I pleaded, "wouldn't you rather
See for yourself?"   35

The conversation that we hear in this traditional English telephone box evokes serious racial tensions as well as a humorous treatment of them; the benighted tradition represented by the landlady seems to be no match for the speaker's satiric wit.

Poets often remind us that beauty can be found in unexpected places. What is it that Elizabeth Bishop finds so beautiful about the "battered" fish she describes in the following poem?

ELIZABETH BISHOP (1911–1979)
The Fish

1946

I caught a tremendous fish
and held him beside the boat
half out of water, with my hook
fast in a corner of his mouth.
He didn't fight.   5
He hadn't fought at all.
He hung a grunting weight,
battered and venerable
and homely. Here and there
his brown skin hung in strips   10
like ancient wall-paper,
and its pattern of darker brown
was like wall-paper:
shapes like full-blown roses
stained and lost through age.   15

He was speckled with barnacles,
fine rosettes of lime,
and infested
with tiny white sea-lice,
and underneath two or three   20
rags of green weed hung down.
While his gills were breathing in
the terrible oxygen
— the frightening gills,
fresh and crisp with blood,   25
that can cut so badly —
I thought of the coarse white flesh
packed in like feathers,
the big bones and the little bones,
the dramatic reds and blacks   30
of his shiny entrails,
and the pink swim-bladder
like a big peony.
I looked into his eyes
which were far larger than mine   35
but shallower, and yellowed,
the irises backed and packed
with tarnished tinfoil
seen through the lenses
of old scratched isinglass.   40
They shifted a little, but not
to return my stare.
— It was more like the tipping
of an object toward the light.
I admired his sullen face,   45
the mechanism of his jaw,
and then I saw
that from his lower lip
— if you could call it a lip —
grim, wet, and weapon-like,   50
hung five old pieces of fish-line,
or four and a wire leader
with the swivel still attached,
with all their five big hooks
grown firmly in his mouth.   55
A green line, frayed at the end
where he broke it, two heavier lines,
and a fine black thread
still crimped from the strain and snap
when it broke and he got away.   60
Like medals with their ribbons
frayed and wavering,
a five-haired beard of wisdom
trailing from his aching jaw.
I stared and stared   65
and victory filled up

the little rented boat,
from the pool of bilge
where oil had spread a rainbow
around the rusted engine
to the bailer rusted orange,
the sun-cracked thwarts,
the oarlocks on their strings,
the gunnels — until everything
was rainbow, rainbow, rainbow!
And I let the fish go.

70

75

Considerations for Critical Thinking and Writing

1. Which lines in this poem provide especially vivid details of the fish? What makes these descriptions effective?
2. How is the fish characterized? Is it simply a weak victim because it "didn't fight"?
3. Comment on lines 65–76. In what sense has "victory filled up" the boat, given that the speaker finally lets the fish go?

The speaker in Bishop's "The Fish" ends on a triumphantly joyful note. The *speaker* is the voice used by the author in the poem; like the narrator in a work of fiction, the speaker is often a created identity rather than the author's actual self. The two should not automatically be equated. Contrast the attitude toward life of the speaker in "The Fish" with that of the speaker in the following poem.

PHILIP LARKIN (1922–1985)
A Study of Reading Habits

1964

When getting my nose in a book
Cured most things short of school,
It was worth ruining my eyes
To know I could still keep cool,
And deal out the old right hook
To dirty dogs twice my size.

5

Later, with inch-thick specs,
Evil was just my lark:
Me and my cloak and fangs
Had ripping times in the dark.
The women I clubbed with sex!
I broke them up like meringues.

10

Don't read much now: the dude
Who lets the girl down before
The hero arrives, the chap
Who's yellow and keeps the store,
Seem far too familiar. Get stewed:
Books are a load of crap.

15

What the speaker sees and describes in "The Fish" is close if not identical to Bishop's own vision and voice. The joyful response to the fish is clearly shared by the speaker and the poet, between whom there is little or no distance. In "A Study of Reading Habits," however, Larkin distances himself from a speaker whose sensibilities he does not wholly share. The poet — and many readers — might identify with the reading habits described by the speaker in the first twelve lines, but Larkin uses the last six lines to criticize the speaker's attitude toward life as well as reading. The speaker recalls in lines 1–6 how as a schoolboy he identified with the hero, whose virtuous strength always triumphed over "dirty dogs," and in lines 7–12 he recounts how his schoolboy fantasies were transformed by adolescence into a fascination with violence and sex. This description of early reading habits is pleasantly amusing, because many readers of popular fiction will probably recall having moved through similar stages, but at the end of the poem the speaker provides more information about himself than he intends to.

As an adult the speaker has lost interest in reading, because it is no longer an escape from his own disappointed life. Instead of identifying with heroes or villains, he finds himself identifying with minor characters who are irresponsible and cowardly. Reading is now a reminder of his failures, so he turns to alcohol. His solution, to "Get stewed," because "Books are a load of crap," is obviously self-destructive. The speaker is ultimately exposed by Larkin as someone who never grew beyond fantasies. Getting drunk is consistent with the speaker's immature reading habits. Unlike the speaker, the poet understands that life is often distorted by escapist fantasies, whether through a steady diet of popular fiction or through alcohol. The speaker in this poem, then, is not Larkin but a created identity whose voice is filled with disillusionment and delusion.

The problem with Larkin's speaker is that he misreads books as well as his own life. Reading means nothing to him unless it serves as an escape from himself. It is not surprising that Larkin has him read fiction rather than poetry, because poetry places an especially heavy emphasis on language. Fiction, indeed any kind of writing, including essays and drama, relies on carefully chosen and arranged words, but poetry does so to an even greater extent. Notice, for example, how Larkin's deft use of trite expressions and slang characterizes the speaker so that his language reveals nearly as much about his dreary life as what he says. Larkin's speaker would have no use for poetry.

What is "unmistakable" in poetry (to use Robinson's term again) is its intense, concentrated use of language — its emphasis on individual words to convey meanings, experiences, emotions, and effects. Poets never simply process words; they savor them. Words in poems frequently create their own tastes, textures, scents, sounds, and shapes. They often seem more sensuous than ordinary language, and readers usually sense that a word has been hefted before making its way into a poem. Although poems are crafted differently from the ways a painting, sculpture, or musical composition is created, in each form of art the creator delights in the medium. Poetry is carefully orchestrated so that the words work together as elements in a structure to sustain close, repeated readings. The words are chosen to interact with one another to create the maximum desired effect, whether the purpose is to capture a mood or feeling, create a vivid experience, express a point of view, narrate a story, or portray a character.

Here is a poem that looks quite different from most *verse,* a term used for lines composed in a measured rhythmical pattern, which are often, but not necessarily, rhymed.

ROBERT MORGAN (b. 1944)
Mountain Graveyard   1979

for the author of "Slow Owls"

Spore Prose

stone	notes
slate	tales
sacred	cedars
heart	earth
asleep	please
hated	death

Though unconventional in its appearance, this is unmistakably poetry because of its concentrated use of language. The poem demonstrates how serious play with words can lead to some remarkable discoveries. At first glance "Mountain Graveyard" may seem intimidating. What, after all, does this list of words add up to? How is it in any sense a poetic use of language? But if the words are examined closely, it is not difficult to see how they work. The wordplay here is literally in the form of a game. Morgan uses a series of *anagrams* (words made from the letters of other words, such as *read* and *dare*) to evoke feelings about death. "Mountain Graveyard" is one of several poems that Morgan has called "Spore Prose" (another anagram) because he finds in individual words the seeds of poetry. He wrote the poem in honor of the fiftieth birthday of another poet, Jonathan Williams, the author of "Slow Owls," whose title is also an anagram.

The title, "Mountain Graveyard," indicates the poem's setting, which is also the context in which the individual words in the poem interact to provide a larger meaning. Morgan's discovery of the words on the stones of a graveyard is more than just clever. The observations he makes among the silent graves go beyond the curious pleasure a reader experiences in finding the words *sacred cedars,* referring to evergreens common in cemeteries, to consist of the same letters. The surprise and delight of realizing the connection between heart and earth is tempered by the more sober recognition that everyone's story ultimately ends in the ground. The hope that the dead are merely asleep is expressed with a plea that is answered grimly by a hatred of death's finality.

Little is told in this poem. There is no way of knowing who is buried or who is looking at the graves, but the emotions of sadness, hope, and pain are unmistakable — and are conveyed in fewer than half the words of this sentence. Morgan takes words that initially appear to be a dead, prosaic list and energizes their meanings through imaginative juxtapositions.

The following poem also involves a startling discovery about words. With the peculiar title "l(a," the poem cannot be read aloud, so there is no sound, but is there sense, a *theme,* a central idea or meaning, in the poem?

E. E. CUMMINGS (1894–1962)
l(a
1958

l(a

le
af
fa

ll

s)
one
l

iness

Considerations for Critical Thinking and Writing

1. Discuss the connection between what appears inside and outside the parentheses in this poem.
2. What does Cummings draw attention to by breaking up the words? How do this strategy and the poem's overall shape contribute to its theme?
3. Which seems more important in this poem — what is expressed, or the way it is expressed?

Although "Mountain Graveyard" and "l(a" do not resemble the kind of verse that readers might recognize immediately as poetry on a page, both are actually a very common type of poem, called the *lyric*, usually a brief poem that expresses the personal emotions and thoughts of a single speaker. Lyrics are often written in the first person but sometimes — as in "Spore Prose" and "l(a" — no speaker is specified. Lyrics present a subjective mood, emotion, or idea. Very often they are about love or death, but almost any subject or experience that evokes some intense emotional response can be found in lyrics. In addition to brevity and emotional intensity, lyrics are also frequently characterized by their musical qualities. The word *lyric* derives from the Greek word *lyre,* meaning a musical instrument that originally accompanied the singing of a lyric. Lyric poems can be organized in a variety of ways, such as the sonnet, elegy, and ode (see Chapter 8), but it is enough to point out here that lyrics are an extremely popular kind of poetry with writers and readers.

The following anonymous lyric was found in a sixteenth-century manuscript.

ANONYMOUS
Western Wind

c. 1500

Western wind, when wilt thou blow,
The small rain down can rain?
Christ, if my love were in my arms,
And I in my bed again!

This speaker's intense longing for his lover is characteristic of lyric poetry. He impatiently addresses the western wind that brings spring to England and could make it possible for him to be reunited with the woman he loves. We do not know the details of these lovers' lives, because this poem focuses on the speaker's emotion. We do not learn why the lovers are apart or if they will be together again. We don't even know if the speaker is a man. But those issues are not really important. The poetry gives us a feeling rather than a story.

A poem that tells a story is called a **narrative poem.** Narrative poetry may be short or very long. An **epic,** for example, is a long narrative poem on a serious subject chronicling heroic deeds and important events. Among the most famous epics are Homer's *Iliad* and *Odyssey,* the Old English *Beowulf,* Dante's *Divine Comedy,* and John Milton's *Paradise Lost*. More typically, however, narrative poems are considerably shorter, such as the following poem, which tells the story of a child's memory of her father.

REGINA BARRECA (b. 1957)
Nighttime Fires

1986

When I was five in Louisville
we drove to see nighttime fires. Piled seven of us,
all pajamas and running noses, into the Olds,
drove fast toward smoke. It was after my father
lost his job, so not getting up in the morning   5
gave him time: awake past midnight, he read old newspapers
with no news, tried crosswords until he split the pencil
between his teeth, mad. When he heard
the wolf whine of the siren, he woke my mother,
and she pushed and shoved   10
us all into waking. Once roused we longed for burnt wood

and a smell of flames high into the pines. My old man liked
driving to rich neighborhoods best, swearing in a good mood
as he followed fire engines that snaked like dragons
and split the silent streets. It was festival, carnival.   15

If there were a Cadillac or any car
in a curved driveway, my father smiled a smile
from a secret, brittle heart.
His face lit up in the heat given off by destruction
like something was being made, or was being set right.   20
I bent my head back to see where sparks
ate up the sky. My father who never held us
would take my hand and point to falling cinders that
covered the ground like snow, or, excited, show us
the swollen collapse of a staircase. My mother   25
watched my father, not the house. She was happy
only when we were ready to go, when it was finally over
and nothing else could burn.
Driving home, she would sleep in the front seat
as we huddled behind. I could see his quiet face in the   30
rearview mirror, eyes like hallways filled with smoke.

This narrative poem could have been a short story if the poet had wanted to say more about the "brittle heart" of this unemployed man whose daughter so vividly remembers the desperate pleasure he took in watching fire consume other people's property. Indeed, a reading of Faulkner's short story "Barn Burning" suggests how such a character can be further developed and how his child responds to him. The similarities between Faulkner's angry character and the poem's father, whose "eyes [are] like hallways filled with smoke," are coincidental, but the characters' sense of "something . . . being set right" by flames is worth comparing. Although we do not know everything about this man and his family, we have a much firmer sense of their story than we do of the story of the couple in "Western Wind."

Although narrative poetry is still written, short stories and novels have largely replaced the long narrative poem. Lyric poems tend to be the predominant type of poetry today. Regardless of whether a poem is a narrative or a lyric, however, the strategies for reading it are somewhat different from those for reading prose. Try these suggestions for approaching poetry.

SUGGESTIONS FOR APPROACHING POETRY

1. Assume that it will be necessary to read a poem more than once. Give yourself a chance to become familiar with what the poem has to offer. Like a piece of music, a poem becomes more pleasurable with each encounter.
2. Do pay attention to the title; it will often provide a helpful context for the poem and serve as an introduction to it. Larkin's "A Study of Reading Habits" is precisely what its title describes.

3. As you read the poem for the first time, avoid becoming entangled in words or lines that you don't understand. Instead, give yourself a chance to take in the entire poem before attempting to resolve problems encountered along the way.

4. On a second reading, identify any words or passages that you don't understand. Look up words you don't know; these might include names, places, historical and mythical references, or anything else that is unfamiliar to you.

5. Read the poem aloud (or perhaps have a friend read it to you). You'll probably discover that some puzzling passages suddenly fall into place when you hear them. You'll find that nothing helps, though, if the poem is read in an artificial, exaggerated manner. Read in as natural a voice as possible, with slight pauses at line breaks. Silent reading is preferable to imposing a te-tumpty-te-tum reading on a good poem.

6. Read the punctuation. Poems use punctuation marks — in addition to the space on the page — as signals for readers. Be especially careful not to assume that the end of a line marks the end of a sentence, unless it is concluded by punctuation. Consider, for example, the opening lines of Hathaway's "Oh, Oh."

> My girl and I amble a country lane,
> moo cows chomping daisies, our own
> sweet saliva green with grass stems.

Line 2 makes little or no sense if a reader stops after "own." Keeping track of the subjects and verbs will help you find your way among the sentences.

7. Paraphrase the poem to determine whether you understand what happens in it. As you work through each line of the poem, a paraphrase will help you to see which words or passages need further attention.

8. Try to get a sense of who is speaking and what the setting or situation is. Don't assume that the speaker is the author; often it is a created character.

9. Assume that each element in the poem has a purpose. Try to explain how the elements of the poem work together.

10. Be generous. Be willing to entertain perspectives, values, experiences, and subjects that you might not agree with or approve. Even if baseball bores you, you should be able to comprehend its imaginative use in Francis's "Catch."

11. Try developing a coherent approach to the poem that helps you to shape a discussion of the text. See Chapter 15, "Critical Strategies for Reading," to review formalist, biographical, historical, psychological, feminist, and other possible critical approaches.

12. Don't expect to produce a definitive reading. Many poems do not resolve all the ideas, issues, or tensions in them, and so it is not

always possible to drive their meaning into an absolute corner. Your reading will explore rather than define the poem. Poems are not trophies to be stuffed and mounted. They're usually more elusive. And don't be afraid that a close reading will damage the poem. Poems aren't hurt when we analyze them; instead, they come alive as we experience them and put into words what we discover through them.

A list of more specific questions using the literary terms and concepts discussed in the following chapters begins on page 248. That list, like the suggestions just made, raises issues and questions that can help you to read just about any poem closely. These strategies should be a useful means for getting inside poems to understand how they work. Furthermore, because reading poetry inevitably increases sensitivity to language, you're likely to find yourself a better reader of words in any form — whether in a novel, a newspaper editorial, an advertisement, a political speech, or a conversation — after having studied poetry. In short, many of the reading skills that make poetry accessible also open up the world you inhabit.

You'll probably find some poems amusing or sad, some fierce or tender, and some fascinating or dull. You may find, too, some poems that will get inside you. Their kinds of insights — the poet's and yours — are what Emily Dickinson had in mind when she defined poetry this way: "If I read a book and it makes my whole body so cold no fire can ever warm me, I know that it is poetry. If I feel physically as if the top of my head were taken off, I know that it is poetry." Dickinson's response may be more intense than most — poetry was, after all, at the center of her life — but you too might find yourself moved by poems in unexpected ways. In any case, as Edwin Arlington Robinson knew, poetry is, to an alert and sensitive reader, "eventually unmistakable."

POETRY IN POPULAR FORMS

Before you try out these strategies for reading on a few more poems, it is worth acknowledging that the verse that enjoys the widest readership appears not in collections, magazines, or even anthologies for students, but in greeting cards. A significant amount of the personal daily mail delivered in the United States consists of greeting cards. That represents millions of lines of verse going by us on the street and in planes over our heads. These verses share some similarities with the poetry included in this anthology, but there are also important differences that indicate the need for reading serious poetry closely rather than casually.

The popularity of greeting cards is easy to explain: just as many of us have neither the time nor the talent to make gifts for birthdays, weddings, anniversaries, graduations, Valentine's Day, Mother's Day, and other holidays, we are unlikely to write personal messages when cards conveniently say them for us. Although impersonal, cards are efficient and convey an important message no matter what the occasion for them: I care. These greetings are rarely serious poetry; they are not written to be. Nevertheless, they demonstrate the impulse in our culture to generate and receive poetry.

In a handbook for greeting-card free-lancers, a writer and past editor of such verse began with this advice:

> Once you determine what you want to say — and in this regard it is best to stick to one basic idea — you must choose your words to do several things at the same time:
>
> 1. Your idea must be expressed as a complete idea; it must have a beginning, a middle, and an end.
> 2. There must be coherence in your verse. Every line must be linked logically and smoothly with its neighbors.
> 3. Your expressions . . . must be conversational. High-flown language rarely comes off successfully in greeting card writing.
> 4. You must write with emphasis — and something else: enthusiasm. It's necessary to create interest in that all-important first line. From that point on, writing your verse is a matter of developing your idea and bringing it to a peak of emphasis in the last line. Occasionally you will find that you have shot your wad too early in the verse, and whatever you say after that point sounds like an afterthought.
> 5. You must do all of the above and at the same time make everything come out right in the meter-and-rhyme department.[1]

This advice is followed by a list of approximately fifty of the most frequently used rhyme sounds accompanied by rhyming words, such as *love, of, above* for the sound *uv*. The point of these prescriptions is that the verse must be written so that it is immediately accessible — consumable — by both the buyer and the recipient. Writers of these cards are expected to avoid any complexity.

Compare the following greeting-card verse with the poem that comes after it. "Magic of Love," by Helen Farries, has been a longtime favorite in a major greeting-card company's "wedding line"; with different endings it has been used also in valentines and friendship cards.

HELEN FARRIES
Magic of Love

date unknown

There's a wonderful gift that can give you a lift,
It's a blessing from heaven above!
It can comfort and bless, it can bring happiness —
It's the wonderful MAGIC OF LOVE!

Like a star in the night, it can keep your faith bright,   5
Like the sun, it can warm your hearts, too —
It's a gift you can give every day that you live,
And when given, it comes back to you!

[1]Chris Fitzgerald, "Conventional Verse: The Sentimental Favorite," *The Greeting Card Writer's Handbook,* ed. H. Joseph Chadwick (Cincinnati: Writer's Digest, 1975): 13, 17.

When love lights the way, there is joy in the day
And all troubles are lighter to bear,   10
Love is gentle and kind, and through love you will find
There's an answer to your every prayer!

May it never depart from your two loving hearts,
May you treasure this gift from above —
You will find if you do, all your dreams will come true,   15
In the wonderful MAGIC OF LOVE!

JOHN FREDERICK NIMS (b. 1913)
Love Poem   1947

My clumsiest dear, whose hands shipwreck vases,
At whose quick touch all glasses chip and ring,
Whose palms are bulls in china, burs in linen,
And have no cunning with any soft thing

Except all ill-at-ease fidgeting people: 5
The refugee uncertain at the door
You make at home; deftly you steady
The drunk clambering on his undulant floor.

Unpredictable dear, the taxi drivers' terror,
Shrinking from far headlights pale as a dime   10
Yet leaping before red apoplectic streetcars —
Misfit in any space. And never on time.

A wrench in clocks and the solar system. Only
With words and people and love you move at ease.
In traffic of wit expertly maneuver   15
And keep us, all devotion, at your knees.

Forgetting your coffee spreading on our flannel,
Your lipstick grinning on our coat,
So gaily in love's unbreakable heaven
Our souls on glory of spilt bourbon float.   20

Be with me, darling, early and late. Smash glasses —
I will study wry music for your sake.
For should your hands drop white and empty
All the toys of the world would break.

Considerations for Critical Thinking and Writing

1. Read these two works aloud. Characterize their differences.
2. To what extent does the advice to would-be greeting-card writers apply to each work?
3. Compare the two speakers. Which do you find more appealing? Why?
4. How does Nims's description of love differ from Farries's?

In contrast to poetry, which transfigures and expresses an emotion or experience through an original use of language, the verse in "Magic of Love" relies on **clichés,** ideas or expressions that have become tired and trite from overuse, such as describing love as "a blessing from heaven above." Clichés anesthetize readers instead of alerting them to the possibility of fresh perceptions. They are used to draw out **stock responses,** predictable, conventional reactions to language, characters, symbols, or situations; God, heaven, the flag, motherhood, hearts, puppies, and peace are some often-used objects of stock responses. Advertisers manufacture careers from this sort of business.

Clichés and stock responses are two of the major ingredients of sentimentality in literature. **Sentimentality** exploits the reader by inducing responses that exceed what the situation warrants. This pejorative term should not be confused with *sentiment,* which is synonymous with *emotion* or *feeling.* Sentimentality cons readers into falling for the mass murderer who is devoted to stray cats, and it requires that we not think twice about what we're feeling, because those tears shed for the little old lady, the rage aimed at the vicious enemy soldier, and the longing for the simple virtues of poverty might disappear under the slightest scrutiny. The experience of sentimentality is not unlike biting into a swirl of cotton candy; it's momentarily sweet but wholly insubstantial.

Clichés, stock responses, and sentimentality are generally the hallmarks of weak writing. Poetry — the kind that is unmistakable — achieves freshness, vitality, and genuine emotion that sharpen our perceptions of life.

Although the most widely read verse is found in greeting cards, the most widely *heard* poetry appears in song lyrics. Not all songs are poetic, but a good many share the same effects and qualities as poems. Consider these lyrics by Bruce Springsteen about Philadelphia, the "City of Brotherly Love."

BRUCE SPRINGSTEEN (b. 1949)
Streets of Philadelphia   1993

I was bruised and battered and I couldn't tell
What I felt
I was unrecognizable to myself
I saw my reflection in a window I didn't know
My own face   5
Oh brother are you gonna leave me
Wastin' away
On the streets of Philadelphia

I walked the avenue till my legs felt like stone
I heard the voices of friends vanished and gone   10
At night I could hear the blood in my veins
Black and whispering as the rain
On the streets of Philadelphia

Ain't no angel gonna greet me
It's just you and I my friend
My clothes don't fit me no more
I walked a thousand miles
Just to slip this skin

15

The night has fallen, I'm lyin' awake
I can feel myself fading away
So receive me brother with your faithless kiss
Or will we leave each other alone like this
On the streets of Philadelphia

20

Considerations for Critical Thinking and Writing

1. Characterize Philadelphia in this song lyric. What sort of life is described by the speaker? Which images seem especially evocative to you?
2. Why is there almost no punctuation in these lines? How do you make sense of the lines in the absence of conventional punctuation?
3. What kind of mood is evoked by the language of this song? How does your reading of "Streets of Philadelphia" compare with listening to Springsteen singing it (available on his *Greatest Hits,* a Columbia CD)?
4. Explain whether you think this song can be accurately called a narrative poem.

QUEEN LATIFAH (b. 1970)
The Evil That Men Do

1989

You asked, I came
So behold the Queen
Let's add a little sense to the scene
I'm livin' positive
Not out here knocked up

5

But the lines are so dangerous
I oughta be locked up
This rhyme doesn't require prime time
I'm just sharin' thoughts in mind
Back again because I knew you wanted it

10

From the Latifah with the Queen in front of it
Droppin' bombs, you're up in arms and puzzled
The lines will flow like fluid while you guzzle
You slip, I'll drop you on a BDP-produced track
From KRS to be exact

15

It's a Flavor Unit quest that today has me speakin'
'Cause it's knowledge I'm seekin'
Enough about myself, I think it's time that I tell you
About the Evil That Men Do

Situations, reality, what a concept

20

Nothin' ever seems to stay in step
So today here is a message for my sisters and brothers

Here are some things I want to cover
A woman strives for a better life
But who the hell cares   25
Because she's livin' on welfare
The government can't come up with a decent housin' plan
So she's in no man's land
It's a sucker who tells you you're equal
(You don't need 'em   30
Johannesburg cries for freedom)
We the people hold these truths to be self-evident
(But there's no response from the president)
Someone's livin' the good life tax-free
'Cause some poor girl can't find   35
A way to be crack-free
And that's just part of the message
I thought I had to send you
About the Evil That Men Do

Tell me, don't you think it's a shame   40
When someone can put a quarter in a video game
But when a homeless person approaches you on the street
You can't treat him the same
It's time to teach the deaf, the dumb, the blind
That black on black crime only shackles and binds   45
You to a doom, a fate worse than death
But there's still time left
To stop puttin' your conscience on cease
And bring about some type of peace
Not only in your heart but also in your mind   50
It will benefit all mankind
Then there will be one thing
That will never stop you
And it's the Evil That Men Do

Considerations for Critical Thinking and Writing

1. Describe the "message for my sisters and brothers" in this rap song (line 22).
2. Comment on the effects of the rhymes. How do they help the lines "flow like fluid"? (line 13).
3. This song's title is taken from III. ii. of Shakespeare's play *Julius Caesar:*

   > Friends, Romans, countrymen, lend me your ears;
   > I come to bury Caesar, not to praise him.
   > The evil that men do lives after them,
   > The good is oft interred with their bones.

   How does knowing the context of Queen Latifah's title enrich your understanding of the poem?

Connection to Another Selection

1. Compare the world described in this song with that presented in "Streets of Philadelphia" (p. 32).

PERSPECTIVE

ROBERT FRANCIS (1901–1987)
On "Hard" Poetry   1965

When Robert Frost said he liked poems hard he could scarcely have meant he liked them difficult. If he had meant difficult he would have said he didn't like them easy. What he said was that he didn't like them soft.

Poems can be soft in several ways. They can be soft in form (invertebrate). They can be soft in thought and feeling (sentimental). They can be soft with excess verbiage. Frost used to advise [writers] to squeeze the water out of a poem. He liked poems dry. What is dry tends to be hard, and what is hard is always dry, except perhaps on the outside.

Yet though hardness here does not mean difficulty, some difficulty naturally goes with hardness. A hard poem may not be hard to read but is hard to write. Not too hard, preferably. Not so hard to write that there is no flow in the writer. But hard enough for the growing poem to meet with some healthy resistance. Frost often found this healthy resistance in a tight rhyme scheme and strict meter. There are other ways of getting good resistance, of course.

And in the reader too, a hard poem will bring some difficulty. Preferably not too much. Not enough difficulty to completely baffle him. Ideally a hard poem should not be too hard to make sense of, but hard to exhaust its meaning and its beauty.

"What I care about is the hardness of the poems. I don't like them soft, I want them to be little pebbles, but placed where they won't dislodge easily. And I'd like them to be little pebbles of precious stone — precious, or semiprecious" (interview with John Ciardi, *Saturday Review*, March 21, 1959).

Here is hard prose talking about hard poetry. Frost was never shrewder or more illuminating. Here, as well as in anything else he ever said, is his flavor.

What contemporary of his can you imagine saying this or anything like it?

In 1843 Emerson jotted in his journal: "Hard clouds and hard expressions, and hard manners, I love."

From *The Satirical Rogue on Poetry*

Considerations for Critical Thinking and Writing

1. What is the distinction between "hard" and "soft" poetry?
2. Given Francis's brief essay and his poem "Catch" (p. 14), write a review of Helen Farries's "Magic of Love" (p. 30) as you think Francis would.
3. Explain whether you would characterize Bruce Springsteen's "Streets of Philadelphia" (p. 32) as hard or soft.

ALICE WALKER (b. 1944)
a woman is not a potted plant   1991

A WOMAN IS NOT
A POTTED PLANT

her roots bound
to the confines
of her house   5

a woman is not
a potted plant
her leaves trimmed
to the contours
of her sex   10

a woman is not
a potted plant
her branches
espaliered
against the fences   15
of her race
her country
her mother
her man

her trained blossom   20
turning
this way
& that
to follow
the sun   25
of whoever feeds
and waters
her

a woman
is wilderness   30
unbounded
holding the future
between each breath
walking the earth
only because   35
she is free
and not creepervine
or tree.

Nor even honeysuckle
or bee.   40

Considerations for Critical Thinking and Writing

1. According to the speaker, how do the properties of a potted plant inappropriately describe a woman?
2. What *is* a woman, according to the speaker? What is the effect of defining her primarily by what she is not?
3. Describe the meaning and effect of the poem's final two lines.

Connection to Another Selection

1. Compare Walker's take on female identity in this poem with Piercy's in "The Secretary Chant" (p. 9)? How are their conceptions similar? Different?

WYATT PRUNTY (b. 1947)
Elderly Lady Crossing on Green   1993

And give her no scouts doing their one good deed
Or sentimental cards to wish her well
During Christmas time or gallstone time —
Because there was a time, she'd like to tell,

She drove a loaded V8 powerglide   5
And would have run you flat as paint
To make the light before it turned on her,
Make it as she watched you faint

When looking up you saw her bearing down
Eyes locking you between the wheel and dash,   10
And you either scrambled back where you belonged
Or jaywalked to eternity, blown out like trash

Behind the grease spot where she braked on you . . . .
Never widow, wife, mother, or a bride,
And nothing up ahead she's looking for   15
But asphalt, the dotted line, the other side,

The way she's done a million times before,
With nothing in her brief to tell you more
Than she's a small tug on the tidal swell
Of her own sustaining notion that she's doing well.   20

Considerations for Critical Thinking and Writing

1. How does the description of the elderly lady in the poem undercut your expectations about her created by the title? Explain whether or not you think this is a sentimental poem.
2. In what ways is this elderly woman "doing well" (line 20)? Does the poem suggest any ways in which she's not?
3. Describe the effect produced by the first line's beginning with "And . . .". Why is this a fitting introduction to this elderly lady?

Connection to Another Selection

1. Write an essay comparing the humor in this poem with that of Hathaway's "Oh, Oh" (p. 13).

ALBERTO RÍOS (b. 1952)
Seniors   1985

William cut a hole in his Levi's pocket
so he could flop himself out in class
behind the girls so the other guys
could see and shit what guts we all said.
All Konga wanted to do over and over   5
was the rubber band trick, but he showed
everyone how, so nobody wanted to see
anymore and one day he cried, just cried
until his parents took him away forever.
Maya had a Hotpoint refrigerator standing   10
in his living room, just for his family to show
anybody who came that they could afford it.

Me, I got a French kiss, finally, in the catholic
darkness, my tongue's farthest half vacationing
loudly in another mouth like a man in Bermudas,   15
and my body jumped against a flagstone wall,
I could feel it through her thin, almost
nonexistent body: I had, at that moment, that moment,
a hot girl on a summer night, the best of all
the things we tried to do. Well, she   20
let me kiss her, anyway, all over.

Or it was just a flagstone wall
with a flaw in the stone, an understanding cavity
for burning young men with smooth dreams —
the true circumstance is gone, the true   25
circumstances about us all then
are gone. But when I kissed her, all water,
she would close her eyes, and they into somewhere
would disappear. Whether she was there
or not, I remember her, clearly, and she moves   30
around the room, sometimes, until I sleep.

I have lain on the desert in watch
low in the back of a pick-up truck
for nothing in particular, for stars, for
the things behind stars, and nothing comes   35
more than the moment: always now, here in a truck,
the moment again to dream of making love and sweat,
this time to a woman, or even to all of them

in some allowable way, to those boys, then,
who couldn't cry, to the girls before they were   40
women, to friends, me on my back, the sky over me
pressing its simple weight into her body
on me, into the bodies of them all, on me.

Considerations for Critical Thinking and Writing

1. Comment on the use of slang in the poem. How does it serve to characterize the speaker?
2. How does language of the final stanza differ from that of the first stanza? To what purpose?
3. Write an essay that discusses the speaker's attitudes toward sex and life. How are they related?

Connections to Other Selections

1. Compare the treatment of sex in this poem with that in Sharon Olds's "Sex without Love" (p. 68).
2. Think about "Seniors" as a kind of love poem and compare the speaker's voice here with the one in T. S. Eliot's "The Love Song of J. Alfred Prufrock" (p. 371). How are these two voices used to evoke different cultures? Of what value is love in these cultures?

MARY JO SALTER (b. 1954)
Welcome to Hiroshima   1985

is what you first see, stepping off the train:
a billboard brought to you in living English
by Toshiba Electric. While a channel
silent in the TV of the brain

projects those flickering re-runs of a cloud   5
that brims its risen columnful like beer
and, spilling over, hangs its foamy head,
you feel a thirst for history: what year

it started to be safe to breathe the air,
and when to drink the blood and scum afloat   10
on the Ohta River. But no, the water's clear,
they pour it for your morning cup of tea

in one of the countless sunny coffee shops
whose plastic dioramas advertise
mutations of cuisine behind the glass: 15
a pancake sandwich; a pizza someone tops

with a maraschino cherry. Passing by
the Peace Park's floral hypocenter (where

how bravely, or with what mistaken cheer,
humanity erased its own erasure),   20

you enter the memorial museum
and through more glass are served, as on a dish
of blistered grass, three mannequins. Like gloves
a mother clips to coatsleeves, strings of flesh

hang from their fingertips; or as if tied   25
to recall a duty for us, *Reverence*
the dead whose mourners too shall soon be dead,
but all commemoration's swallowed up

in questions of bad taste, how re-created
horror mocks the grim original,   30
and thinking at last *They should have left it all*
you stop. This is the wristwatch of a child.

Jammed on the moment's impact, resolute
to communicate some message, although mute,
it gestures with its hands at eight-fifteen   35
and eight-fifteen and eight-fifteen again

while tables of statistics on the wall
update the news by calling on a roll
of tape, death gummed on death, and in the case
adjacent, an exhibit under glass   40

is glass itself: a shard the bomb slammed in
a woman's arm at eight-fifteen, but some
three decades on — as if to make it plain
hope's only as renewable as pain,

and as if all the unsung   45
debasements of the past may one day come
rising to the surface once again —
worked its filthy way out like a tongue.

Considerations for Critical Thinking and Writing

1. Describe the scene set by the first five stanzas. Is the speaker in "Welcome to Hiroshima" feeling welcome? Welcoming the reader?

2. How is the commemoration of the atomic bombing of Hiroshima "swallowed up in questions of bad taste" (lines 28–29) in this poem? Pick out specific images, and describe your reaction to them.

3. Do the speaker's emotions change through the course of the poem? Explain whether or not you think this is a hopeful or pessimistic poem.

Connection to Another Selection

1. Write an essay comparing Salter's treatment of the commemoration of Hiroshima with Denise Levertov's in "Gathered at the River" (p. 233).

JOHN DONNE (1572-1631)
The Sun Rising

c. 1633

Busy old fool, unruly sun,
    Why dost thou thus,
Through windows, and through curtains, call on us?
Must to thy motions lovers' seasons run?
    Saucy pedantic wretch, go chide   5
    Late schoolboys, and sour prentices,
  Go tell court-huntsmen that the king will ride,
  Call country ants° to harvest offices;   *farm workers*
Love, all alike, no season knows, nor clime,
Nor hours, days, months, which are the rags of time.   10

    Thy beams, so reverend and strong
    Why shouldst thou think?
I could eclipse and cloud them with a wink,
But that I would not lose her sight so long:
    If her eyes have not blinded thine,   15
    Look, and tomorrow late, tell me
  Whether both the Indias° of spice and mine   *East and West Indies*
  Be where thou left'st them, or lie here with me.
Ask for those kings whom thou saw'st yesterday,
And thou shalt hear, all here in one bed lay.   20

    She is all states, and all princes I,
    Nothing else is.
Princes do but play us; compared to this,
All honor's mimic, all wealth alchemy.
    Thou, sun, art half as happy as we,   25
    In that the world's contracted thus;
  Thine age asks ease, and since thy duties be
  To warm the world, that's done in warming us.
Shine here to us, and thou art every where;
This bed thy center° is, these walls thy sphere.   *of orbit* 30

Considerations for Critical Thinking and Writing

1. What is the situation in this poem? Why is the speaker angry with the sun? What does he urge the sun to do in the first stanza?
2. What claims does the speaker make about the power of love in stanzas 2 and 3? What does he mean when he says, "Shine here to us, and thou art every where"?
3. Are any of the speaker's exaggerations in any sense true? How?

Connection to Another Selection

1. Compare this lyric poem with Richard Wilbur's "A Late Aubade" (p. 60). What similarities do you find in the ideas and emotions expressed in each?

LI HO (791-817)

A Beautiful Girl Combs Her Hair

date unknown

TRANSLATED BY DAVID YOUNG

Awake at dawn
she's dreaming
by cool silk curtains

fragrance of spilling hair
half sandalwood, half aloes   5

windlass creaking at the well
singing jade

the lotus blossom wakes, refreshed

her mirror
two phoenixes   10
a pool of autumn light

standing on the ivory bed
loosening her hair
watching the mirror

one long coil, aromatic silk   15
a cloud down to the floor

drop the jade comb — no sound

delicate fingers
pushing the coils into place
color of raven feathers   20

shining blue-black stuff
the jewelled comb will hardly hold it

spring wind makes me restless
her slovenly beauty upsets me

eighteen and her hair's so thick   25
she wears herself out fixing it!

she's finished now
the whole arrangement in place

in a cloud-patterned skirt
she walks with even steps   30
a wild goose on the sand

turns away without a word
where is she off to?

down the steps to break a spray of
    cherry blossoms   35

Considerations for Critical Thinking and Writing

1. How does the speaker use sensuous language to create a vivid picture of the girl?
2. What are the speaker's feelings toward the girl? Do they remain the same throughout the poem?
3. Why would it be difficult to capture the essence of this poem in a paraphrase?

Connections to Other Selections

1. Compare the description of hair in this poem with that in Cathy Song's "The White Porch" (p. 104). What significant similarities do you find?
2. Write an essay that explores the differing portraits in this poem and in Sylvia Plath's "Mirror" (p. 118). Which portrait is more interesting to you? Explain why.

ROBERT HASS (b. 1941)
Happiness

1996

Because yesterday morning from the steamy window
we saw a pair of red foxes across the creek
eating the last windfall apples in the rain —
they looked up at us with their green eyes
long enough to symbolize the wakefulness of living things   5
and then went back to eating —

and because this morning
when she went into the gazebo with her black pen and yellow pad
to coax an inquisitive soul
from what she thinks of as the reluctance of matter,   10
I drove into town to drink tea in the cafe
and write notes in a journal — mist rose from the bay
like the luminous and indefinite aspect of intention,
and a small flock of tundra swans
for the second winter in a row were feeding on new grass   15
in the soaked fields; they symbolize mystery, I suppose,
they are also called whistling swans, are very white,
and their eyes are black —

and because the tea steamed in front of me,
and the notebook, turned to a new page,   20
was blank except for a faint blue idea of order,
I wrote: *happiness! it is December, very cold,*
we woke early this morning,
and lay in bed kissing,
our eyes squinched up like bats.   25

Considerations for Critical Thinking and Writing

1. What kinds of experiences contribute to the speaker's happiness? Describe the person speaking.

2. Try writing a paraphrase of "Happiness." What happens to the poem when it's changed to prose? What accounts for these changes?

3. As Hass has done, define happiness or a moment in which you felt that emotion, in poetry or prose.

Connection to Another Selection

1. Write an essay that compares and contrasts "Happiness" with Emily Dickinson's "I like a look of Agony" (p. 266). Do they both succeed in capturing an emotion? What message do you take away from each?

MILLER WILLIAMS (b. 1930)
Excuse Me

1992

Give me just a second before you start.
Let's agree on what you're reading here.
Let's call it a poem, a poem being an act
of language meant to hold its own exceptions,
which you therefore read with a double mind,   5
accepting and rejecting what you find.

If part of what you find is what you brought,
let's call this reading a poem, one of the games
imaginations play when they meet.
If you suspect you may not have the wit   10
to face the other player, one to one,
then you can be a deconstructionist
and make believe the other doesn't exist,
though that will be like sitting on one end
of a seesaw in summer, wishing you had a friend.   15

Considerations for Critical Thinking and Writing

1. How does the speaker define a poem (lines 3–6)? Do you agree?

2. What is a deconstructionist (line 12)? Read the section on deconstructionist criticism (p. 543). What do you think is the speaker's attitude toward deconstructionists?

3. Discuss the significance of the title. How does it affect the tone of the poem?

2. Word Choice, Word Order, and Tone

DICTION

Like all good writers, poets are keenly aware of *diction,* their choice of words. Poets, however, choose words especially carefully, because the words in poems call attention to themselves. Characters, actions, settings, and symbols may appear in a poem, but in the foreground, before all else, is the poem's language. Also, poems are usually briefer than other forms of writing. A few inappropriate words in a two-hundred-page novel (which would have about 100,000 words) create fewer problems than they would in a 100-word poem. Functioning in a compressed atmosphere, the words in a poem must convey meanings gracefully and economically. Readers therefore have to be alert to the ways in which those meanings are released.

Although poetic language is often more intensely charged than ordinary speech, the words used in poetry are not necessarily different from everyday speech. Inexperienced readers may sometimes assume that language must be high-flown and out of date to be included in a poem: instead of reading about a boy "enjoying a swim," they expect to read about a boy "disporting with pliant arm o'er a glassy wave." During the eighteenth century this kind of *poetic diction* — the use of elevated language over ordinary language — was highly valued in English poetry, but since the nineteenth century poets have generally overridden the distinctions that were once made between words used in everyday speech and those used in poetry. Today all levels of diction can be found in poetry.

A poet, like any writer, has several levels of diction from which to choose; they range from formal to middle to informal. *Formal diction* consists of a dignified, impersonal, and elevated use of language. Notice, for example, the formality of Thomas Hardy's description of the sunken luxury liner *Titanic* in this stanza from "The Convergence of the Twain" (the entire poem appears on p. 65):

> In a solitude of the sea
> Deep from human vanity,
> And the Pride of Life that planned her, stilly couches she.

There is nothing casual or relaxed about these lines. Hardy's use of *stilly*, meaning "quietly" or "calmly," is purely literary; the word rarely, if ever, turns up in everyday English.

The language used in Richard Wilbur's "A Late Aubade" (p. 60) represents a less formal level of diction; the speaker uses a ***middle diction*** spoken by most educated people. Consider how Wilbur's speaker tells his lover what she might be doing instead of being with him.

> You could be sitting now in a carrel
> Turning some liver-spotted page,
> Or rising in an elevator-cage
> Toward Ladies' Apparel.

The speaker elegantly enumerates his lover's unattractive alternatives to being with him — reading old books in a library or shopping in a department store — but the wit of his description lessens its formality.

Informal diction is evident in Larkin's "A Study of Reading Habits" (p. 22). The speaker's account of his early reading is presented ***colloquially***, in a conversational manner that in this instance includes slang expressions not used by the culture at large.

> When getting my nose in a book
> Cured most things short of school,
> It was worth ruining my eyes
> To know I could still keep cool,
> And deal out the old right hook
> To dirty dogs twice my size.

This level of diction is clearly not that of Hardy's or Wilbur's speakers.

Poets may also draw on another form of informal diction, called ***dialect***. Dialects are spoken by definable groups of people from a particular geographic region, economic group, or social class. New England dialects are often heard in Robert Frost's poems, for example. Gwendolyn Brooks employs a black dialect in "We Real Cool" (p. 70) to characterize a group of pool players. Another form of diction related to particular groups is ***jargon***, a category of language defined by a trade or profession. Sociologists, photographers, carpenters, baseball players, and dentists, for example, all use words that are specific to their fields. E. E. Cummings manages to get quite a lot of mileage out of automobile jargon in "she being Brand" (p. 49).

Many levels of diction are available to poets. The variety of diction to be found in poetry is enormous, and that is how it should be. No language is foreign to poetry, because it is possible to imagine any human voice as the speaker of a poem. When we say a poem is formal, informal, or somewhere in between, we are making a descriptive statement rather than an evaluative one. What matters in a poem is not only which words are used but how they are used.

DENOTATIONS AND CONNOTATIONS

One important way that the meaning of a word is communicated in a poem is through sound: snakes *hiss,* saws *buzz.* This and other matters related to sound are discussed in Chapter 6. Individual words also convey meanings through denotations and connotations. **Denotations are the literal, dictionary meanings of a word.** For example, *bird* denotes a feathered animal with wings (other denotations for the same word include a shuttlecock, an airplane, or an odd person), but in addition to its denotative meanings, *bird* also carries **connotations,** associations and implications that go beyond a word's literal meanings. Connotations derive from how the word has been used and the associations people make with it. Therefore, the connotations of *bird* might include fragility, vulnerability, altitude, the sky, or freedom, depending on the context in which the word is used. Consider also how different the connotations are for the following types of birds: hawk, dove, penguin, pigeon, chicken, peacock, duck, crow, turkey, gull, owl, goose, coot, and vulture. These words have long been used to refer to types of people as well as birds. They are rich in connotative meanings.

Connotations derive their resonance from a person's experiences with a word. Those experiences may not always be the same, especially when the people having them are in different times and places. *Theater,* for instance, was once associated with depravity, disease, and sin, whereas today the word usually evokes some sense of high culture and perhaps visions of elegant opulence. In several ethnic communities in the United States many people would find *squid* appetizing, but elsewhere the word is likely to produce negative connotations. Readers must recognize, then, that words written in other times and places may have unexpected connotations. Annotations usually help in these matters, which is why it makes sense to pay attention to them when they are available.

Ordinarily, though, the language of poetry is accessible, even when the circumstances of the reader and the poet are different. Although connotative language may be used subtly, it mostly draws on associations experienced by many people. Poets rely on widely shared associations rather than the idiosyncratic response that an individual might have to a word. Someone who has received a severe burn from a fireplace accident may associate the word *hearth* with intense pain instead of home and family life, but that reader must not allow a personal experience to undermine the response the poet intends to evoke. Connotative meanings are usually public meanings.

Perhaps this can be seen most clearly in advertising, where language is also used primarily to convey moods and feelings rather than information. For instance, our recent efforts to get in shape have created a collective consciousness that advertisers have capitalized on successfully. Knowing that we want to be slender or lean or slim (not spare or scrawny and certainly not gaunt), advertisers have created a new word to describe beers, wines, sodas, cheeses, canned fruits, and other products that tend to overload what used to be called sweatclothes and sneakers. The word is *lite.* The assumed denotative meaning of *lite* is low in calories, but as close readers of ingredient labels know, some *lites* are heavier than regularly prepared products. There can be no doubt about the connotative meaning of *lite,* however. Whatever is *lite* cannot hurt you; less is more. Even the word is lighter than *light;* there is no unnecessary droopy *g* or plump *h. Lite* is a brilliantly manufactured use of connotation.

Connotative meanings are valuable because they allow poets to be economical and suggestive simultaneously. In this way emotions and attitudes are carefully woven into the texture of the poem's language. Read the following poem and pay close attention to the connotative meanings of its words.

RANDALL JARRELL (1914-1965)
The Death of the Ball Turret Gunner 1945

From my mother's sleep I fell into the State
And I hunched in its belly till my wet fur froze.
Six miles from earth, loosed from its dream of life,
I woke to black flack and the nightmare fighters.
When I died they washed me out of the turret with a hose.

The title of this poem establishes the setting and the speaker's situation. Like the setting of a short story, the setting of a poem is important when the time and place influence what happens. "The Death of the Ball Turret Gunner" is set in the midst of a war and, more specifically, in a ball turret — a Plexiglas sphere housing machine guns on the underside of a bomber. The speaker's situation obviously places him in extreme danger; indeed, his fate is announced in the title.

Although the poem is written in the first-person singular, its speaker is clearly not the poet. Jarrell uses a _**persona**_, a speaker created by the poet. In this poem the persona is a disembodied voice that makes the gunner's story all the more powerful. What is his story? A paraphrase might read something like this:

> After I was born, I grew up to find myself at war, cramped into the turret of a bomber's belly some 31,000 feet above the ground. Below me were exploding shells from antiaircraft guns and attacking fighter planes. I was killed, but the bomber returned to base, where my remains were cleaned out of the turret so the next man could take my place.

This paraphrase is accurate, but its language is much less suggestive than the poem's. The first line of the poem has the speaker emerge from his "mother's sleep," the anesthetized sleep of her giving birth. The phrase also suggests the comfort, warmth, and security he knew as a child. This safety was left behind when he "fell," a verb that evokes the danger and involuntary movement associated with his subsequent "State" (*fell* also echoes, perhaps, the fall from innocence to experience related in the Bible).

Several dictionary definitions appear for the noun *state;* it can denote a territorial unit, the power and authority of a government, a person's social status, or a person's emotional or physical condition. The context provided by the rest of the poem makes clear that "State" has several denotative meanings here: because it is capitalized it certainly refers to the violent world of a government at war, but it also refers to the gunner's vulnerable status as well as his physical and emotional condition. By having "State" carry more than one meaning, Jarrell has created an intentional ambiguity. *Ambiguity* allows for two or more simultaneous interpretations of a word, phrase, action, or situation, all of which can be supported by the context of a work. Through his ambiguous use of "State," Jarrell connects the horrors of war not just to bombers and gunners but to the governments that control them.

Related to this ambiguity is the connotative meaning of "State" in the poem. The context demands that the word be read with a negative charge. The word is not used with patriotic pride but to suggest an anonymous, impersonal "State" that kills rather than nurtures the life in its "belly." The state's "belly" is a bomber, and the gunner is "hunched" like a fetus in the cramped turret, where, in contrast to the warmth of his mother's womb, everything is frozen, even the "wet fur" of his flight jacket (newborn infants have wet fur too). The gunner is not just 31,000 feet from the ground but "six miles from earth." *Six miles* has roughly the same denotative meaning as 31,000 feet, but Jarrell knew that the connotative meaning of *six miles* makes the speaker's position seem even more remote and frightening.

When the gunner is born into the violent world of war, he finds himself waking up to a "nightmare" that is all too real. The poem's final line is grimly understated, but it hits the reader with the force of an exploding shell: what the State-bomber-turret gives birth to is a gruesome death that is merely one of an endless series. It may be tempting to reduce the theme of this poem to the idea that "war is hell"; but Jarrell's target is more specific. He implicates the "State," which routinely executes such violence, and he does so without preaching or hysterical denunciations. Instead, his use of language conveys his theme subtly and powerfully. Consider how this next poem uses connotative meanings to express its theme.

how much does diction matter?

E. E. CUMMINGS (1894–1962)
she being Brand

1926

she being Brand

-new;and you
know consequently a

little stiff i was
careful of her and(having

thoroughly oiled the universal
joint tested my gas felt of
her radiator made sure her springs were O.

K.)i went right to it flooded-the-carburetor cranked her

up,slipped the
clutch(and then somehow got into reverse she
kicked what
the hell)next
minute i was back in neutral tried and

again slo-wly;bare,ly nudg. ing (my

lev-er Right-
oh and her gears being in
A 1 shape passed
from low through
second-in-to-high like
greasedlightning) just as we turned the corner of Divinity

avenue i touched the accelerator and give

her the juice,good

                (it

was the first ride and believe i we was
happy to see how nice she acted right up to
the last minute coming back down by the Public
Gardens i slammed on

the
internalexpanding
&
externalcontracting
brakes Bothatonce and

brought allofher tremB
-ling
to a:dead.

stand-
;Still)

Considerations for Critical Thinking and Writing

1. How does Cummings's arrangement of the words on the page help you to read this poem aloud? What does the poem describe?
2. What ambiguities in language does the poem ride on? At what point were you first aware of these double meanings?
3. Explain why you think the poem is primarily serious or humorous.
4. Find some advertisements for convertibles or sports cars in magazines and read them closely. What similarities do you find in the use of connotative language in them and in Cummings's poem? Write a brief essay explaining how language is used to convey the theme of one of the advertisements and the poem.

WORD ORDER

Meanings in poems are conveyed not only by denotations and connotations but also by the poet's arrangement of words into phrases, clauses, and sentences to achieve particular effects. The ordering of words into meaningful verbal patterns is called *syntax.* A poet can manipulate the syntax of a line to place emphasis on a word; this is especially apparent when a poet varies normal word order. In Dickinson's "A narrow Fellow in the Grass" (p. 2), for example, the speaker says about the snake that "His notice sudden is." Ordinarily, that would be expressed as "his notice is sudden." By placing the verb *is* unexpectedly at the end of the line, Dickinson creates the sense of surprise we feel when we suddenly come upon a snake. Dickinson's inversion of the standard word order also makes the final sound of the line a hissing *is.*

Cummings uses one long sentence in "she being Brand" to take the reader on a ride that begins with a false start but accelerates quickly before coming to a halt. The jargon creates an exuberantly humorous mood that is helped along by the poem's syntax. How do Cummings's ordering of words and sentence structure reinforce the meaning of the lines?

TONE

Tone is the writer's attitude toward the subject, the mood created by all the elements in the poem. Writing, like speech, may be characterized as serious or light, sad or happy, private or public, angry or affectionate, bitter or nostalgic, or any other attitudes and feelings that human beings experience. In Jarrell's "The Death of the Ball Turret Gunner," the tone is clearly serious; the voice in the poem even sounds dead. Listen again to the persona's final words: "When I died they washed me out of the turret with a hose." The brutal, restrained matter-of-factness of this line is effective because the reader is called on to supply the appropriate anger and despair, a strategy that makes those emotions all the more convincing.

Consider how tone is used to convey meaning in the next poem, inspired by the poet's contemplating how island life has changed.

DEREK WALCOTT (b. 1930)
The Virgins

1976

Down the dead streets of sun-stoned Frederiksted,°
the first free port to die for tourism,
strolling at funeral pace, I am reminded
of life not lost to the American dream;
but my small-islander's simplicities   5

1 *Frederiksted:* A duty-free port in St. Croix, one of the American Virgin Islands.

can't better our new empire's civilized
exchange of cameras, watches, perfumes, brandies
for the good life, so cheaply underpriced
that only the crime rate is on the rise
in streets blighted with sun, stone arches   10
and plazas blown dry by the hysteria
of rumor. A condominium drowns
in vacancy; its bargains are dusted,
but only a jeweled housefly drones
over the bargains. The roulettes spin   15
rustily to the wind — the vigorous trade
that every morning would begin afresh
by revving up green water round the pierhead
heading for where the banks of silver thresh.

Considerations for Critical Thinking and Writing

1. In what sense are the streets of Frederiksted dead? In what sense alive? Pick out
   the images of death and life and discuss how they work together.
2. What is the speaker's attitude toward the "American dream"? How is it defined?
3. Discuss the diction of lines 16–19. (You might want to look up "trade wind.")
   How do the last four lines contrast with the first fifteen? What is your final impression of trade?

RUTH FAINLIGHT (b. 1931)
Flower Feet   1989

(SILK SHOES IN THE WHITWORTH ART GALLERY,
MANCHESTER, ENGLAND)

Real women's feet wore these objects
that look like toys or spectacle cases stitched
from bands of coral, jade, and apricot silk
embroidered with twined sprays of flowers.
Those hearts, tongues, crescents, and disks, leather   5
shapes an inch across, are the soles of shoes
no wider or longer than the span of my ankle.

If the feet had been cut off and the raw stumps
thrust inside the openings, surely
it could not hurt more than broken toes, twisted   10
back and bandaged tight. An old woman,
leaning on a cane outside her door
in a Chinese village, smiled to tell how
she fought and cried, how when she stood on points
of pain that gnawed like fire, nurse and mother   15
praised her tottering walk on flower feet.

Her friends nodded, glad the times had changed.
Otherwise, they would have crippled their daughters.

Considerations for Critical Thinking and Writing

1. Why did the Chinese bind women's feet?
2. How is the speaker's description of the process of binding feet in lines 8–16 different from the description of the shoes in lines 1–7?
3. Describe the poem's tone. Does it remain the same throughout the poem or does it change? Explain your response.

Connections to Other Selections

1. How is the speaker's perspective on tradition and custom in this poem similar to that in Robert Frost's "Mending Wall" (p. 304)?
2. The final line of this poem is startling. Why? How is it similar in its strategy to James Merrill's "Casual Wear" (p. 147)?

The next work is a ***dramatic monologue,*** a type of poem in which a character — the speaker — addresses a silent audience in such a way as to reveal unintentionally some aspect of his or her temperament or personality. What tone is created by Machan's use of a persona?

KATHARYN HOWD MACHAN (b. 1952)
Hazel Tells LaVerne   1976

last night
im cleanin out my
howard johnsons ladies room
when all of a sudden
up pops this frog   5
musta come from the sewer
swimmin aroun an tryin ta
climb up the sida the bowl
so i goes ta flushm down
but sohelpmegod he starts talkin   10
bout a golden ball
an how i can be a princess
me a princess
well my mouth drops
all the way to the floor   15
an he says
kiss me just kiss me
once on the nose
well i screams
ya little green pervert   20

an i hitsm with my mop
an has ta flush
the toilet down three times
me
a princess

25

Considerations for Critical Thinking and Writing

1. What do you imagine the situation and setting are for this poem?
2. What creates the poem's humor? How does Hazel's use of language reveal her personality? Is her treatment of the frog consistent with her character?
3. Although it has no punctuation, this poem is easy to follow. How does the arrangement of the lines organize Hazel's speech for clarity and emphasis?
4. What is the theme? Is it conveyed through denotative or connotative language?
5. Write what you think might be LaVerne's reply to Hazel. First, write LaVerne's response as a series of ordinary sentences, and then try editing and organizing them into poetic lines.

Connection to Another Selection

1. Although Robert Browning's "My Last Duchess" (p. 150) is a more complex poem than Machan's, both use dramatic monologues to reveal character. How are the strategies in each poem similar?

MARTÍN ESPADA (b. 1957)
Latin Night at the Pawnshop

1987

Chelsea, Massachusetts
Christmas, 1987

The apparition of a salsa band
gleaming in the Liberty Loan
pawnshop window:

Golden trumpet,
silver trombone,
congas, maracas, tambourine,
all with price tags dangling
like the city morgue ticket
on a dead man's toe.

Considerations for Critical Thinking and Writing

1. What kind of tone is created by the poet's word choice and by the rhythm of the poem?
2. Does it matter that this apparition occurs on Christmas night? Why or why not?
3. What do you think is the central point of this poem?

How do the speaker's attitude and tone change during the course of this next poem?

MAXINE KUMIN (b. 1925)
Woodchucks

Gassing the woodchucks didn't turn out right.
The knockout bomb from the Feed and Grain Exchange
was featured as merciful, quick at the bone
and the case we had against them was airtight,
both exits shoehorned shut with puddingstone,°   5
but they had a sub-sub-basement out of range.

Next morning they turned up again, no worse
for the cyanide than we for our cigarettes
and state-store Scotch, all of us up to scratch.
They brought down the marigolds as a matter of course   10
and then took over the vegetable patch
nipping the broccoli shoots, beheading the carrots.

The food from our mouths, I said, righteously thrilling
to the feel of the .22, the bullets' neat noses.
I, a lapsed pacifist fallen from grace   15
puffed with Darwinian° pieties for killing,
now drew a bead on the littlest woodchuck's face.
He died down in the everbearing roses.

Ten minutes later I dropped the mother. She
flipflopped in the air and fell, her needle teeth   20
still hooked in a leaf of early Swiss chard.
Another baby next. O one-two-three
the murderer inside me rose up hard,
the hawkeye killer came on stage forthwith.

There's one chuck left. Old wily fellow, he keeps   25
me cocked and ready day after day after day.
All night I hunt his humped-up form. I dream
I sight along the barrel in my sleep.
If only they'd all consented to die unseen
gassed underground the quiet Nazi way.   30

5 *puddingstone:* Pebbles cemented together.   16 *Darwinian:* Charles Darwin (1809–1882), an English naturalist associated with the ideas of evolution and natural selection.

Considerations for Critical Thinking and Writing

1. How does the word *airtight* help create the tone of the first stanza?
2. How does the speaker's attitude toward the woodchucks change in the second stanza? How does that affect the tone in lines 13–24?

3. What competing emotions are present in the speaker's descriptions of the wood-chucks' activities and the descriptions of killing them?
4. Given that "Gassing" begins the poem, why does the speaker withhold the description of the woodchucks being "gassed underground the quiet Nazi way" until the final line?
5. Explain how line 15 suggests, along with the final stanza, the theme of the poem.

DICTION AND TONE IN FOUR LOVE POEMS

The first three of these love poems share the same basic situation and theme: a male speaker addresses a female (in the first poem it is a type of female) urging that love should not be delayed because time is short. This theme is as familiar in poetry as it is in life. In Latin this tradition is known as *carpe diem,* "seize the day." Notice how the poets' diction helps create a distinctive tone in each poem, even though the subject matter and central ideas are similar (although not identical) in all three.

ROBERT HERRICK (1591–1674)
To the Virgins, to Make Much of Time   1648

Gather ye rose-buds while ye may,
  Old Time is still a-flying;
And this same flower that smiles today,
  Tomorrow will be dying.

The glorious lamp of heaven, the sun,   5
  The higher he's a-getting,
The sooner will his race be run,
  And nearer he's to setting.

That age is best which is the first,
  When youth and blood are warmer;   10
But being spent, the worse, and worst
  Times still succeed the former.

Then be not coy, but use your time,
  And while ye may, go marry;
For having lost but once your prime,   15
  You may for ever tarry.

Considerations for Critical Thinking and Writing

1. Would there be any change in meaning if the title of this poem were "To Young Women, to Make Much of Time"? Do you think the poem can apply to young men too?

2. What do the virgins have in common with the flowers (lines 1–4) and the course of the day (5–8)?
3. How does the speaker develop his argument? What will happen to the virgins if they don't "marry"? Paraphrase the poem.
4. What is the tone of the speaker's advice?

The next poem was also written in the seventeenth century, but it includes some words that have changed in usage and meaning over the past three hundred years. The title of Marvell's "To His Coy Mistress" requires some explanation. *Mistress* does not refer to a married man's illicit lover but to a woman who is loved and courted — a sweetheart. Marvell uses *coy* to describe a woman who is reserved and shy rather than coquettish or flirtatious. Often such shifts in meanings over time are explained in the notes that accompany reprintings of poems. You should keep in mind, however, that it is helpful to have a reasonably thick dictionary available when you are reading poetry. The most thorough is the *Oxford English Dictionary* (*OED*), which provides histories of words. The *OED* is a multivolume leviathan, but there are other useful unabridged dictionaries and desk dictionaries.

Knowing its original meaning can also enrich your understanding of why a contemporary poet chooses a particular word. Elizabeth Bishop begins "The Fish" (p. 20) this way: "I caught a tremendous fish." We know immediately in this context that *tremendous* means very large. In addition, given that the speaker clearly admires the fish in the lines that follow, we might even understand *tremendous* in the colloquial sense of wonderful and extraordinary. But a dictionary gives us some further relevant insights. Because, by the end of the poem, we see the speaker thoroughly moved as a result of the encounter with the fish ("everything / was rainbow, rainbow, rainbow!"), the dictionary's additional information about the history of *tremendous* shows why it is the perfect adjective to introduce the fish. The word comes from the Latin *tremere* (to tremble) and therefore once meant "such as to make one tremble." That is precisely how the speaker is at the end of the poem: deeply affected and trembling. Knowing the origin of *tremendous* gives us the full heft of the poet's word choice.

Although some of the language in "To His Coy Mistress" requires annotations for the modern reader, this poem continues to serve as a powerful reminder that time is a formidable foe, even for lovers.

ANDREW MARVELL (1621–1678)
To His Coy Mistress   1681

Had we but world enough, and time,
This coyness, lady, were no crime.
We would sit down, and think which way

To walk, and pass our long love's day.
Thou by the Indian Ganges'° side   5
Shouldst rubies find; I by the tide
Of Humber° would complain.° I would   *write love songs*
Love you ten years before the Flood,
And you should, if you please, refuse
Till the conversion of the Jews.   10
My vegetable love should grow°
Vaster than empires, and more slow;
An hundred years should go to praise
Thine eyes and on thy forehead gaze,
Two hundred to adore each breast,   15
But thirty thousand to the rest:
An age at least to every part,
And the last age should show your heart.
For, lady, you deserve this state,
Nor would I love at lower rate.   20
    But at my back I always hear
Time's wingèd chariot hurrying near;
And yonder all before us lie
Deserts of vast eternity.
Thy beauty shall no more be found,   25
Nor in thy marble vault shall sound
My echoing song; then worms shall try
That long preserved virginity,
And your quaint honor turn to dust,
And into ashes all my lust.   30
The grave's a fine and private place,
But none, I think, do there embrace.
    Now, therefore, while the youthful hue
Sits on thy skin like morning dew,
And while thy willing soul transpires°   *breathes forth*   35
At every pore with instant fires,
Now let us sport us while we may,
And now, like amorous birds of prey,
Rather at once our time devour
Than languish in his slow-chapped° power.   *slow-jawed*   40
Let us roll all our strength and all
Our sweetness up into one ball,
And tear our pleasures with rough strife
Thorough° the iron gates of life.   *through*
Thus, though we cannot make our sun   45
Stand still, yet we will make him run.

5 *Ganges:* A river in India sacred to the Hindus.   7 *Humber:* A river that flows through Marvell's
native town, Hull.   11 *My vegetable love . . . grow:* A slow, unconscious growth.

— how important is historical/social context?

Considerations for Critical Thinking and Writing

1. This poem is divided into a three-part argument. Briefly summarize each section:
   if (lines 1–20), but (21–32), therefore (33–46).

2. What is the speaker's tone in lines 1–20? How much time would he spend ador-
   ing his mistress? Is he sincere? How does he expect his mistress to respond to
   these lines?
3. How does the speaker's tone change beginning with line 21? What is his view of
   time in lines 21–32? What does this description do to the lush and leisurely sense
   of time in lines 1–20? How do you think his mistress would react to lines 21–32?
4. In the final lines of Herrick's "To the Virgins, to Make Much of Time" (p. 56), the
   speaker urges the virgins to "go marry." What does Marvell's speaker urge in lines
   33–46? How is the pace of these lines (notice the verbs) different from that of the
   first twenty lines of the poem?
5. This poem is sometimes read as a vigorous but simple celebration of flesh. Is
   there more to the theme than that?

PERSPECTIVE

BERNARD DUYFHUIZEN (b. 1953)
"To His Coy Mistress": On How a Female Might Respond   1988

Clearly a female reader of "To His Coy Mistress" might have trouble identifying with the poem's speaker; therefore, her first response would be to identify with the listener-in-the-poem, the eternally silent Coy Mistress. In such a
reading she is likely to recognize that she has heard this kind of line before
although maybe not with the same intensity and insistence. Moreover, she is
likely to (re)experience the unsettling emotions that such an egoistic assault on
her virginal autonomy would provoke. She will also see differently, even by
contemporary standards, the plot beyond closure, the possible consequences —
both physical and social — that the Mistress will encounter. Lastly, she is likely
to be angered by this poem, by her marginalization in an argument that seeks
to overpower the core of her being.

From "Textual Harassment of Marvell's Coy Mistress:
The Institutionalization of Masculine Criticism,"
College English, April 1988

Considerations for Critical Thinking and Writing

1. Explain whether you find convincing Duyfhuizen's description of a female's
   potential response to the poem. How does his description compare with your
   own response?
2. Characterize the silent mistress of the poem. How do you think the speaker treats
   her? What do his language and tone suggest about his relationship to her?
3. Does the fact that this description of a female response is written by a man make
   any difference in your assessment of it? Explain why or why not.

The third in this series of *carpe diem* poems is a twentieth-century work.
The language of Wilbur's "A Late Aubade" is more immediately accessible
than that of Marvell's "To His Coy Mistress"; a dictionary will quickly identify
any words unfamiliar to a reader, including the allusion to Arnold Schoenberg, the composer, in line 11. An ***allusion*** is a brief reference to a person,

place, thing, event, or idea in history or literature. Allusive words, like connotative words, are both suggestive and economical; poets use allusions to conjure up biblical authority, scenes from Shakespeare's plays, historic figures, wars, great love stories, and anything else that might serve to deepen and enrich their own work. The speaker in "A Late Aubade" makes an allusion that an ordinary dictionary won't explain. He tells his lover: "I need not rehearse / The rosebuds-theme of centuries of verse." True to his word, he says no more about this for her or the reader. The lines refer, of course, to the *carpe diem* theme as found familiarly in Herrick's "To the Virgins, to Make Much of Time." Wilbur assumes that his reader will understand the allusion.

Allusions imply reading and cultural experiences shared by the poet and reader. Literate audiences once had more in common than they do today because more people had similar economic, social, and educational backgrounds. But a judicious use of specialized dictionaries, encyclopedias, and other reference tools can help you decipher allusions that grow out of this body of experience. (See page 602 for a list of useful reference works for students of literature.) As you read more, you'll be able to make connections based on your own experiences with literature. In a sense, allusions make available what other human beings have deemed worth remembering, and that is certainly an economical way of supplementing and enhancing your own experience.

Wilbur's version of the *carpe diem* theme follows. What strikes you as particularly modern about it?

RICHARD WILBUR (b. 1921)

A Late Aubade

1968

You could be sitting now in a carrel
Turning some liver-spotted page,
Or rising in an elevator-cage
Toward Ladies' Apparel.

You could be planting a raucous bed   5
Of salvia, in rubber gloves,
Or lunching through a screed of someone's loves
With pitying head,

Or making some unhappy setter
Heel, or listening to a bleak   10
Lecture on Schoenberg's serial technique.
Isn't this better?

Think of all the time you are not
Wasting, and would not care to waste,
Such things, thank God, not being to your taste.   15
Think what a lot

hmm.

Of time, by woman's reckoning,
You've saved, and so may spend on this,
You who had rather lie in bed and kiss
Than anything.   20

It's almost noon, you say? If so,
Time flies, and I need not rehearse
The rosebuds-theme of centuries of verse.
If you *must* go,

Wait for a while, then slip downstairs   25
And bring us up some chilled white wine,
And some blue cheese, and crackers, and some fine
Ruddy-skinned pears.

Considerations for Critical Thinking and Writing

1. An *aubade* is a song about lovers parting at dawn, but in this "late aubade," "It's almost noon." Is there another way of reading the adjective *late* in the title?
2. How does the speaker's diction characterize both him and his lover? What sort of lives do they live? What does the casual allusion to Herrick's poem (line 23) reveal about them?
3. What is the effect of using "liver-spotted page," "elevator-cage," "raucous bed," "screed," "unhappy setter," and "bleak / Lecture" to describe the woman's activities?

Connections to Other Selections

1. How does the man's argument in "A Late Aubade" differ from the speakers' in Herrick's and Marvell's poems? Which of the three arguments do you find most convincing?
2. Explain how the tone of each poem is suited to its theme.

   This fourth love poem is by a woman. Listen to the speaker's voice. Does it sound different from the way the men speak in the previous three poems?

DIANE ACKERMAN (b. 1948)
A Fine, a Private Place   1983

He took her one day
under the blue horizon
where long sea fingers
parted like beads
hitched in the doorway   5
of an opium den,
and canyons mazed the deep
reef with hollows,
cul-de-sacs, and narrow boudoirs,
and had to ask twice   10

before she understood
his stroking her arm
with a marine feather
slobbery as aloe pulp
was wooing, or saw the octopus   15
in his swimsuit
stretch one tentacle
and ripple its silky bag.

While bubbles rose
like globs of mercury,   20
they made love
mask to mask, floating
with oceans of air between them,
she his sea-geisha
in an orange kimono   25
of belts and vests,
her lacquered hair waving,
as Indigo Hamlets
tattooed the vista,
and sunlight   30
cut through the water,
twisting its knives
into corridors of light.

His sandy hair
and sea-blue eyes,   35
his kelp-thin waist
and chest ribbed wider
than a sandbar
where muscles domed
clear and taut as shells   40
(freckled cowries,
flat, brawny scallops
the color of dawn),
his sea-battered hands
gripping her thighs   45
like tawny starfish
and drawing her close
as a pirate vessel
to let her board:
who was this she loved?   50

Overhead, sponges
sweating raw color
jutted from a coral arch,
Clown Wrasses°   *brightly colored tropical fish*
hovered like fireworks,   55
and somewhere an abalone opened
its silver wings.
Part of a lusty dream
under aspic, her hips rolled
like a Spanish galleon,   60

her eyes swam
and chest began to heave.
Gasps melted on the tide.
Knowing she would soon be
breathless as her tank,   65
he pumped his brine
deep within her,
letting sea water drive it
through petals
delicate as anemone veils   70
to the dark purpose
of a conch-shaped womb.
An ear to her loins
would have heard the sea roar.

When panting ebbed,   75
and he signaled *Okay?*
as lovers have asked,
land or waterbound
since time heaved ho,
he led her to safety: 80
shallower realms,
heading back toward
the boat's even keel,
though ocean still petted her
cell by cell, murmuring   85
along her legs and neck,
caressing her
with pale, endless arms.

Later, she thought often
of that blue boudoir,   90
pillow-soft and filled
with cascading light,
where together
they'd made a bell
that dumbly clanged   95
beneath the waves
and minutes lurched
like mountain goats.
She could still see
the quilted mosaics   100
that were fish
twitching spangles overhead,
still feel the ocean
inside and out, turning her
evolution around.   105

She thought of it miles
and fathoms away, often,
at odd moments: watching
the minnow snowflakes
dip against the windowframe,   110

holding a sponge
idly under tap-gush,
sinking her teeth
into the cleft
of a voluptuous peach.   115

Considerations for Critical Thinking and Writing

1. Read Marvell's "To His Coy Mistress" (p. 57). To what in Marvell's poem does Ackerman's title allude? Explain how the allusion to Marvell is crucial to understanding Ackerman's poem.
2. Comment on the descriptive passages of "A Fine, a Private Place." Which images seem especially vivid to you? How do they contribute to the poem's meanings?
3. What are the speaker's reflections on her experience in lines 106–115? What echoes of Marvell do you hear in these lines?

Connections to Other Selections

1. Write an essay comparing the tone of Ackerman's poem with that of Marvell's "To His Coy Mistress" (p.57). To what extent are the central ideas in the poems similar?
2. Compare the speaker's voice in Ackerman's poem with the voice you imagine for the coy mistress in Marvell's poem.

POEMS FOR FURTHER STUDY

MARGARET ATWOOD (b. 1939)
Bored   1995

All those times I was bored
out of my mind. Holding the log
while he sawed it. Holding
the string while he measured, boards,
distances between things, or pounded   5
stakes into the ground for rows and rows
of lettuces and beets, which I then (bored)
weeded. Or sat in the back
of the car, or sat still in boats,
sat, sat, while at the prow, stern, wheel   10
he drove, steered, paddled. It
wasn't even boredom, it was looking,
looking hard and up close at the small
details. Myopia. The worn gunwales,
the intricate twill of the seat   15
cover. The acid crumbs of loam, the granular
pink rock, its igneous veins, the sea-fans
of dry moss, the blackish and then the greying
bristles on the back of his neck.

Sometimes he would whistle, sometimes   20
I would. The boring rhythm of doing
things over and over, carrying
the wood, drying
the dishes. Such minutiae. It's what
the animals spend most of their time at,   25
ferrying the sand, grain by grain, from their tunnels,
shuffling the leaves in their burrows. He pointed
such things out, and I would look
at the whorled texture of his square finger, earth under
the nail. Why do I remember it as sunnier   30
all the time then, although it more often
rained, and more birdsong?
I could hardly wait to get
the hell out of there to
anywhere else. Perhaps though   35
boredom is happier. It is for dogs or
groundhogs. Now I wouldn't be bored.
Now I would know too much.
Now I would know.

Considerations for Critical Thinking and Writing

1. Atwood has described this poem as one of several about her father and his death. Is it possible to determine that "he" is the speaker's father from the details of the poem? Explain whether or not you think it matters who "he" is.
2. Play with the possible meanings of the word "bored" and its variations in the poem. What function does the repetition of the word serve?
3. What does the speaker "know" at the end of the poem that she didn't before?

Connection to Another Selection

1. Write an essay on the speaker's attitude toward the father in this poem and in Hayden's "Those Winter Sundays" (p. 10).

THOMAS HARDY (1840–1928)
The Convergence of the Twain   1912

Lines on the Loss of the "Titanic"°

I

      In a solitude of the sea
      Deep from human vanity,
And the Pride of Life that planned her, stilly couches she.

Titanic: A luxurious ocean liner, reputed to be unsinkable, which sank after hitting an iceberg on its maiden voyage in 1912. Only a third of the 2,200 passengers survived.

II

        Steel chambers, late the pyres
        Of her salamandrine fires,°   5
Cold currents thrid,° and turn to rhythmic tidal lyres.   *thread*

III

        Over the mirrors meant
        To glass the opulent
The sea-worm crawls — grotesque, slimed, dumb, indifferent.

IV

        Jewels in joy designed   10
        To ravish the sensuous mind
Lie lightless, all their sparkles bleared and black and blind.

V

        Dim moon-eyed fishes near
        Gaze at the gilded gear
And query: "What does this vaingloriousness down here?"   15

VI

        Well: while was fashioning
        This creature of cleaving wing,
The Immanent Will that stirs and urges everything

VII

        Prepared a sinister mate
        For her — so gaily great —   20
A Shape of Ice, for the time far and dissociate.

VIII

        And as the smart ship grew
        In stature, grace, and hue,
In shadowy silent distance grew the Iceberg too.

IX

        Alien they seemed to be: 25
        No mortal eye could see
The intimate welding of their later history,

X

        Or sign that they were bent
        By paths coincident
On being anon twin halves of one august event,   30

XI

        Till the Spinner of the Years
        Said "Now!" And each one hears,
And consummation comes, and jars two hemispheres.

---

5 *salamandrine fires:* Salamanders were, according to legend, able to survive fire; hence, the ship's fires burned even though under water.

Considerations for Critical Thinking and Writing

1. How do the words used to describe the ship in this poem reveal the speaker's attitude toward the *Titanic?*
2. The diction of the poem suggests that the *Titanic* and the iceberg participate in something like an arranged marriage. What specific words imply this?
3. Who or what causes the disaster? Does the speaker assign responsibility?

DAVID R. SLAVITT (b. 1935)
Titanic   1983

Who does not love the *Titanic?*
If they sold passage tomorrow for that same crossing,
who would not buy?

To go down . . . We all go down, mostly
alone. But with crowds of people, friends, servants,   5
well fed, with music, with lights! Ah!

And the world, shocked, mourns, as it ought to do
and almost never does. There will be the books and movies
to remind our grandchildren who we were
and how we died, and give them a good cry.   10

Not so bad, after all. The cold
water is anesthetic and very quick.
The cries on all sides must be a comfort.

We all go: only a few, first-class.

Considerations for Critical Thinking and Writing

1. What, according to the speaker in this poem, is so compelling about the *Titanic?*
2. Discuss the speaker's tone. Why would it be inaccurate to describe it as solemn and mournful?
3. What is the effect of the poem's final line? What emotions does it produce in you?

Connections to Other Selections

1. How does "Titanic" differ in its attitude toward opulence from "The Convergence of the Twain" (p. 65)?
2. Which poem, "Titanic" or "The Convergence of the Twain," is more emotionally satisfying to you? Explain why.
3. Compare the speakers' tones in "Titanic" and "The Convergence of the Twain."
4. Hardy wrote his poem in 1912, the year the *Titanic* went down, but Slavitt wrote his more than seventy years later. How do you think Slavitt's poem would have been received if it had been published in 1912? Write an essay explaining why you think what you do.

SHARON OLDS (b. 1942)

Sex without Love   1984

How do they do it, the ones who make love
without love? Beautiful as dancers,
gliding over each other like ice skaters
over the ice, fingers hooked
inside each other's bodies, faces   5
red as steak, wine, wet as the
children at birth whose mothers are going to
give them away. How do they come to the
come to the   come to the   God   come to the
still waters, and not love   10
the one who came there with them, light
rising slowly as steam off their joined
skin? These are the true religious,
the purists, the pros, the ones who will not
accept a false Messiah, love the   15
priest instead of the God. They do not
mistake the lover for their own pleasure,
they are like great runners: they know they are alone
with the road surface, the cold, the wind,
the fit of their shoes, their over-all cardio-   20
vascular health — just factors, like the partner
in the bed, and not the truth, which is the
single body alone in the universe
against its own best time.

Considerations for Critical Thinking and Writing

1. What is the nature of the question asked by the speaker in the poem's first two
   lines? What is being asked here?
2. What is the effect of describing the lovers as athletes? How do these descriptions
   and phrases reveal the speaker's tone toward the lovers?
3. To what extent does the title suggest the central meaning of this poem? Try to
   create some alternative titles that are equally descriptive.

Connections to Other Selections

1. How does the treatment of sex and love in Olds's poem compare with that in
   Cummings's "she being Brand" (p. 49)?
2. Just as Olds describes sex without love, she implies a definition of love in this
   poem. Consider whether the lovers in Wilbur's "A Late Aubade" (p. 60) fall within
   Olds's definition.

JOHN KEATS (1795–1821)

Ode on a Grecian Urn

1819

I

Thou still unravished bride of quietness,
   Thou foster-child of silence and slow time,
Sylvan° historian, who canst thus express
   A flowery tale more sweetly than our rhyme:
What leaf-fringed legend haunts about thy shape   5
   Of deities or mortals, or of both,
      In Tempe or the dales of Arcady?°
What men or gods are these? What maidens loath?
    What mad pursuit? What struggle to escape?
      What pipes and timbrels? What wild ecstasy?   10

II

Heard melodies are sweet, but those unheard
   Are sweeter; therefore, ye soft pipes, play on;
Not to the sensual ear, but, more endeared,
   Pipe to the spirit ditties of no tone:
Fair youth, beneath the trees, thou canst not leave   15
   Thy song, nor ever can those trees be bare;
      Bold Lover, never, never canst thou kiss,
Though winning near the goal — yet, do not grieve;
    She cannot fade, though thou hast not thy bliss,
      For ever wilt thou love, and she be fair!   20

III

Ah, happy, happy boughs! that cannot shed
   Your leaves, nor ever bid the Spring adieu;
And, happy melodist, unwearièd,
   For ever piping songs for ever new;
More happy love! more happy, happy love!   25
   For ever warm and still to be enjoyed,
      For ever panting, and for ever young;
All breathing human passion far above,
    That leaves a heart high-sorrowful and cloyed,
      A burning forehead, and a parching tongue.   30

IV

Who are these coming to the sacrifice?
   To what green altar, O mysterious priest,
Lead'st thou that heifer lowing at the skies,
   And all her silken flanks with garlands drest?
What little town by river or sea shore,   35
   Or mountain-built with peaceful citadel,
      Is emptied of this folk, this pious morn?

---

3 *Sylvan:* Rustic. The urn is decorated with a forest scene.   7 *Tempe, Arcady:* Beautiful rural valleys in Greece.

And, little town, thy streets for evermore
   Will silent be; and not a soul to tell
      Why thou art desolate, can e'er return.   40

V

O Attic° shape! Fair attitude! with brede°
Of marble men and maidens overwrought,
With forest branches and the trodden weed;
   Thou, silent form, dost tease us out of thought
As doth eternity: Cold Pastoral!   45
   When old age shall this generation waste,
      Thou shalt remain, in midst of other woe
Than ours, a friend to man, to whom thou say'st,
   Beauty is truth, truth beauty — that is all
      Ye know on earth, and all ye need to know.   50

41 *Attic:* Possessing classic Athenian simplicity; *brede:* Design.

Considerations for Critical Thinking and Writing

1. What does the speaker's diction reveal about his attitude toward the urn in this ode? Does his view develop or change?
2. How is the happiness in stanza III related to the assertion in lines 11–12 that "Heard melodies are sweet, but those unheard / Are sweeter"?
3. What is the difference between the world depicted on the urn and the speaker's world?
4. What do lines 49–50 suggest about the relation of art to life? Why is the urn described as a "Cold Pastoral" (line 45)?
5. Which world does the speaker seem to prefer, the urn's or his own?
6. Describe the overall tone of the poem.

Connections to Other Selections

1. Write an essay comparing the view of time in this ode with that in Marvell's "To His Coy Mistress" (p. 57). Pay particular attention to the connotative language in each poem.
2. Discuss the treatment and meaning of love in this ode and in Richard Wilbur's "Love Calls Us to the Things of This World" (p. 465).
3. Compare the tone and attitude toward life in this ode with those in John Keats's "To Autumn" (p. 102).

GWENDOLYN BROOKS (b. 1917)
We Real Cool   1960

The Pool Players.
Seven at the Golden Shovel.

We real cool. We
Left school. We

Lurk late. We
Strike straight. We   5

Sing sin. We
Thin gin. We

Jazz June. We
Die soon.   10

Considerations for Critical Thinking and Writing

1. How does the speech of the pool players in this poem help to characterize them?
   What is the effect of the pronouns coming at the ends of the lines? How would
   the poem sound if the pronouns came at the beginnings of lines?
2. What is the author's attitude toward the players? Is there a change in tone in the
   last line?
3. How is the pool hall's name related to the rest of the poem and its theme?

MARILYN BOWERING (b. 1949)
Wishing Africa   1980

There's never enough whiskey or rain
when the blood is thin and white,
but oh it was beautiful,
the wind delicate as Queen Anne's lace,
only wild with insects   5
breeding the sponge-green veldt,
and bands of white butterflies
slapping the acacia.
The women's bodies were variable as coral
and men carried snakes on staves.   10

It would do me no good
to go back,
I am threaded
with pale veins,
I am full with dying   15
and ordinary;
but oh if there was a way
of wishing Africa.

When there was planting,
when there was harvesting,   20
I was not far behind
those who first
opened the ground.
I stitched in seed,
I grew meat in the earth's blond side.   25
I did it all with little bloody stitches.
What red there was in me

I let out there.
The sun stayed forever
then was gone.   30

I am scented with virus,
I breed flowers for the ochre
my skin was.
There is no sex in it.
I am white as a geisha,   35
my roots indiscriminate
since my bones gave way.
It is a small, personal pruning
that keeps me.
I had a soul,   40
and remember how it hurt
to be greedy and eat.

Considerations for Critical Thinking and Writing

1. Explain how the word choice in this poem creates a sensual tone.
2. Trace the connotative meanings (both traditional and untraditional) of the color white throughout the poem.
3. What values does the speaker associate with Africa? How are those values contrasted with the speaker's present life?

Connections to Other Selections

1. What does the use of sensuality in this poem and in Ackerman's "A Fine, a Private Place" (p. 61) reveal about the speaker in each poem?
2. In an essay compare the themes of "Wishing Africa" and Rainer Maria Rilke's "The Panther" (p. 99).

D. H. LAWRENCE (1885-1930)
The English Are So Nice!   1932

The English are so nice
So awfully nice
They are the nicest people in the world.

And what's more, they're very nice about being nice
About your being nice as well!   5
If you're not nice they soon make you feel it.

Americans and French and Germans and so on
They're all very well
But they're not *really* nice, you know.
They're not nice in *our* sense of the word, are they now?   10

That's why one doesn't have to take them seriously.
We must be nice to them, of course,

Of course, naturally.
But it doesn't really matter what you say to them,
They don't really understand   15
You can just say anything to them:
Be nice, you know, just nice
But you must never take them seriously, they wouldn't understand,
Just be nice, you know! oh, fairly nice,
Not too nice of course, they take advantage   20
But nice enough, just nice enough
To let them feel they're not quite as nice as they might be.

Considerations for Critical Thinking and Writing

1. What is the effect of the repetition of the word "nice"?
2. What does "nice" ordinarily mean? What does it come to mean in this poem?
3. Describe the speaker's tone and style. What does he really think of the English? Does he deliver his message in a nice way?

Connection to Another Selection

1. Write an essay that compares and contrasts the English in this poem with the way they're presented in Langston Hughes's "The English" (p. 348).

IRA SADOFF (b. 1945)
Nazis   1989

Thank God they're all gone
except for one or two in Clinton Maine
who come home from work
at Scott Paper or Diamond Match
to make a few crank calls   5
to the only Jew in New England
they can find

These make-shift students of history
whose catalogue of facts include
every Jew who gave a dollar   10
to elect the current governor
every Jew who'd sell this country out
to the insatiable Israeli state

I know exactly how they feel
when they say they want to smash my face   15

Someone's cheated them
they want to know who it is
they want to know who makes them beg
It's true Let's Be Fair

it's tough for almost everyone
I exaggerate the facts
to make a point

20

Just when I thought I could walk to the market
just when Jean the check-out girl
asks me how many cords of wood I chopped
and wishes me a Happy Easter
as if I've lived here all my life

25

Just when I can walk into the bank
and nod at the tellers who know my name
where I work who lived in my house in 1832
who know to the penny the amount
of my tiny Jewish bank account

30

Just when I'm sure we can all live together
and I can dine in their saltbox dining rooms
with the melancholy painting of Christ
on the wall their only consolation
just when I can borrow my neighbor's ladder
to repair one of the holes in my roof

35

I pick up the phone
and listen to my instructions

40

I see the town now from the right perspective
the gunner in the glass bubble
of his fighter plane shadowing the tiny man
with the shopping bag and pointy nose
his overcoat two sizes too large for him
skulking from one doorway to the next
trying to make his own way home

45

I can see he's not one of us

Considerations for Critical Thinking and Writing

1. Characterize the "make-shift students of history" described by the speaker. Why do they behave as they do?
2. Why do you think the speaker says "I know exactly how they feel / when they say they want to smash my face" (lines 14–15)?
3. What is the effect of the poem's being set in New England rather than, say, New York City?
4. Describe the shift in tone that begins with line 41. How do the final eight lines complicate the poem?

Connections to Other Selections

1. Compare and contrast the treatment of Nazis in Sadoff's poem with that in Sylvia Plath's "Daddy" (p. 442).
2. Write an essay on the effects of prejudice in "Nazis" and in Soyinka's "Telephone Conversation" (p. 19). How does prejudice affect the self-concept of the speaker in each work?

LOUIS SIMPSON (b. 1923)
In the Suburbs

1963

There's no way out.
You were born to waste your life.
You were born to this middleclass life

As others before you
Were born to walk in procession
To the temple, singing.

Considerations for Critical Thinking and Writing

1. Why is the title of this poem especially significant?
2. What does the repetition in lines 2–3 suggest?
3. Discuss the possible connotative meanings of lines 5 and 6. Who are the "others before you"?

Connection to Another Selection

1. Write an essay on suburban life based on this poem and John Ciardi's "Suburban" (p. 148).

A NOTE ON READING TRANSLATIONS

Sometimes translation can inadvertently be a comic business. Consider, for example, the discovery made by John Steinbeck's wife, Elaine, when in a Yokohama bookstore she asked for a copy of her husband's famous novel *The Grapes of Wrath* and learned that it had been translated into Japanese as *Angry Raisins*. Close but no cigar (perhaps translated as: Nearby, yet no smoke). As amusing as that *Angry Raisins* title is, it teaches an important lesson about the significance of a poet's or a translator's choices when crafting a poem: a powerful piece moves us through diction and tone, both built word by careful word. Translations are frequently regarded as merely vehicular, a way to arrive at the original work. It is, of course, the original work — its spirit, style, and meaning — that most readers expect to find in a translation. Even so, it is important to understand that a translation is *by nature* different from the original — and that despite that difference, a fine translation can be an important part of the journey and become part of the literary landscape itself. Reading a translation of a poem is not the same as reading the original, but neither is watching two different performances of *Hamlet*. The translator provides a reading of the poem in much the same way that a director shapes the play. Each interprets the text from a unique perspective.

Basically, there are two distinct approaches to translation: literal translations and adaptations. A literal translation sets out to create a word-for-word equivalent that is absolutely faithful to the original. As simple and direct as this method may sound, literal translations are nearly impossible over extended passages because of the structural differences between languages. Moreover, the meaning of a single word in one language may not exist in another language, or it may require a phrase, clause, or entire sentence to capture its implications. Adaptations of works offer broader, more open-ended approaches to translation. Unlike a literal translation, an adaptation moves beyond denotative meanings in an attempt to capture the spirit of a work so that its idioms, dialects, slang, and other conventions are recreated in the language of the translation.

The question we ask of an adaptation should not be "Is this exactly how the original reads?" Instead, we ask "Is this an insightful, graceful rendering worth reading?" To translate poetry it is not enough to know the language of the original; it is also necessary that the translator be a poet. A translated poem is more than a collation of decisions based on dictionaries and grammars; it must also be poetry. However undefinable poetry may be, it is unmistakable in its intense use of language. Poems are not merely translated; they are savored.

Here are two translations of "Juventud" written by the Chilean poet Pablo Neruda. Read through the Spanish version first even if you don't know Spanish so that you have a sense of what the translators worked through to create their poems. Pay particular attention to the way in which diction and word order help to create the tone in each of the translations.

PABLO NERUDA (1904–1973)
Juventud   1942

Un perfume como una ácida espada
de ciruelas en un camino,
los besos del azúcar en los dientes,
las gotas vitales resbalando en los dedos,
la dulce pulpa erótica,   5
las eras, los pajares, los incitantes
sitios secretos de las casas anchas,
los colchones dormidos en el pasado, el agrio valle verde
mirado desde arriba, desde el vidrio escondido:
toda la adolescencia mojándose y ardiendo   10
como una lámpara derribada en la lluvia.

Youth   1942
TRANSLATED BY ROBERT BLY (1971)

An odor like an acid sword made
of plum branches along the road,
the kisses like sugar in the teeth,
the drops of life slipping on the fingertips,

the sweet sexual fruit,
the yards, the haystacks, the inviting
rooms hidden in the deep houses,
the mattresses sleeping in the past, the savage green
     valley
seen from above, from the hidden window:
adolescence all sputtering and burning
like a lamp turned over in the rain.

      5

      10

Youth   1942

TRANSLATED BY JACK SCHMITT (1991)

A perfume like an acid plum
sword on a road,
sugary kisses on the teeth,
vital drops trickling down the fingers,
sweet erotic pulp,
threshing floors, haystacks, inciting
secret hideaways in spacious houses,
mattresses asleep in the past, the pungent green
     valley
seen from above, from the hidden window:
all adolescence becoming wet and burning
like a lantern tipped in the rain.

      5

      10

Considerations for Critical Thinking and Writing

1. Consult a Spanish dictionary and write a word-for-word translation of "Juventud" into English. Which lines are particularly difficult to translate? How does your translation compare with Bly's and Schmitt's? Explain why one of the two translations is closest to the original Spanish.
2. Compare the diction and images in the Bly and Schmitt translations and explain which you think is more effective. Explain why, for example, you find Bly's "sweet sexual fruit" or Schmitt's "sweet erotic pulp" more effective.

    The following two translations of "The Joy of Writing" by Wislawa Szymborska, a contemporary Polish writer awarded the Nobel Prize in Literature in 1996, offer an opportunity to compare subtle differences in translations.

WISLAWA SZYMBORSKA (b. 1923)

The Joy of Writing 1967

TRANSLATED BY MAGNUS J. KRYNSKI AND ROBERT A. MAGUIRE (1981)

Where through the written forest runs that written doe?
Is it to drink from the written water,
which will copy her gentle mouth like carbon paper?
Why does she raise her head, is it something she hears?
Poised on four fragile legs borrowed from truth   5
she pricks up her ears under my fingers.
Stillness — this word also rustles across the paper
and parts
the branches brought forth by the word "forest."

Above the blank page lurking, set to spring   10
are letters that may compose themselves all wrong,
besieging sentences
from which there is no rescue.

In a drop of ink there's a goodly reserve
of huntsmen with eyes squinting to take aim,   15
ready to dash down the steep pen,
surround the doe and level their guns.

They forget that this is not real life.
Other laws, black on white, here hold sway.
The twinkling of an eye will last as long as I wish,   20
will consent to be divided into small eternities
full of bullets stopped in flight.
Forever, if I command it, nothing will happen here.
Against my will no leaf will fall
nor blade of grass bend under the full stop of a hoof.   25

Is there then such a world
over which I rule sole and absolute?
A time I bind with chains of signs?
An existence perpetuated at my command?

The joy of writing.
The power of preserving.   30
The revenge of a mortal hand.

The Joy of Writing 1967

TRANSLATED BY STANISLAW BARAŃCZAK AND CLARE CAVANAGH (1995)

Why does this written doe bound through these
     written woods?
For a drink of written water from a spring

whose surface will xerox her soft muzzle?
Why does she lift her head; does she hear something? 5
Perched on four slim legs borrowed from the truth,
she pricks up her ears beneath my fingertips.
Silence — this word also rustles across the page
and parts of boughs
that have sprouted from the word "woods." 10

Lying in wait, set to pounce on the blank page,
are letters up to no good,
clutches of clauses so subordinate
they'll never let her get away.

Each drop of ink contains a fair supply 15
of hunters, equipped with squinting eyes behind their sights,
prepared to swarm the sloping pen at any moment,
surround the doe, and slowly aim their guns.

They forget that what's here isn't life.
Other laws, black on white, obtain. 20
The twinkling of an eye will take as long as I say,
and will, if I wish, divide into tiny eternities,
full of bullets stopped in mid-flight.
Not a thing will ever happen unless I say so.
Without my blessing, not a leaf will fall, 25
not a blade of grass will bend beneath that little hoof's full stop.

Is there then a world
where I rule absolutely on fate?
A time I bind with chains of signs?
An existence become endless at my bidding? 30

The joy of writing.
The power of preserving.
Revenge of a mortal hand.

Considerations for Critical Thinking and Writing

1. What are the major differences between these two translations? Are they significant differences? Explain how these differences affect your reading of the poem.
2. Which poem do you prefer? Explain your response by making specific references
   to the two translations.
3. Try rewriting the first stanza while retaining its essential meaning.

Four Translations of a Poem By Sappho

Sappho, born about 630 B.C. and a native of the Greek island of Lesbos,
is the author of a hymn to Aphrodite, the Goddess of love and beauty in
Greek myth. The four translations that follow suggest how widely translations
can differ from one another. The first, by Henry T. Wharton, is intended to be
a literal prose translation of the original Greek.

SAPPHO (c. 630 B.C.–c. 570 B.C.)

Immortal Aphrodite of the broidered throne

TRANSLATED BY HENRY T. WHARTON (1885)

Immortal Aphrodite of the broidered throne, daughter of Zeus, weaver of wiles, I pray thee break not my spirit with anguish and distress, O Queen. But come hither, if ever before thou didst hear my voice afar, and listen, and leaving thy father's golden house camest with chariot yoked, and fair fleet sparrows drew thee, flapping fast their wings around the dark earth, from heaven through mid sky. Quickly arrived they; and thou, blessed one, smiling with immortal countenance, didst ask What now is befallen me, and Why now I call, and What I in my mad heart most desire to see. 'What Beauty now wouldst thou draw to love thee? Who wrongs thee, Sappho? For even if she flies she shall soon follow, and if she rejects gifts shall yet give, and if she loves not shall soon love, however loth.' Come, I pray thee, now too, and release me from cruel cares; and all that my heart desires to accomplish, accomplish thou, and be thyself my ally.

Beautiful-throned, immortal Aphrodite

TRANSLATED BY T. W. HIGGINSON (1871)

Beautiful-throned, immortal Aphrodite,
Daughter of Zeus, beguiler, I implore thee,
Weigh me not down with weariness and anguish
  O Thou most holy!

Come to me now, if ever thou in kindness   5
Hearkenedst my words, — and often hast thou
  hearkened —
Heeding, and coming from the mansions golden
  Of thy great Father,

Yoking thy chariot, borne by the most lovely   10
Consecrated birds, with dusky-tinted pinions,
Waving swift wings from utmost heights of
  heaven
   Through the mid-ether;

Swiftly they vanished, leaving thee, O goddess,   15
Smiling, with face immortal in its beauty,
Asking why I grieved, and why in utter longing
  I had dared call thee;

Asking what I sought, thus hopeless in desiring,
Wildered in brain, and spreading nets of   20
  passion —
Alas, for whom? and saidst thou, "Who has
  harmed thee?
   "O my poor Sappho!

"Though now he flies, ere long he shall pursue
            thee;
"Fearing thy gifts, he too in turn shall bring
            them;
"Loveless to-day, to-morrow he shall woo thee,
            "Though thou shouldst spurn him."

Thus seek me now, O holy Aphrodite!
Save me from anguish; give me all I ask for,
Gifts at thy hand; and thine shall be the glory,
            Sacred protector!

Invocation to Aphrodite

TRANSLATED BY RICHARD LATTIMORE (1955)

Throned in splendor, deathless, O Aphrodite,
child of Zeus, charm-fashioner, I entreat you
not with griefs and bitternesses to break my
            spirit, O goddess;

standing by me rather, if once before now
far away you heard, when I called upon you,
left your father's dwelling place and descended,
            yoking the golden

chariot to sparrows, who fairly drew you
down in speed aslant the black world, the bright
trembling at the heart to the pulse of countless
            fluttering wingbeats.

Swiftly then they came, and you, blessed lady,
smiling on me out of immortal beauty,
asked me what affliction was on me, why I
            called thus upon you,

what beyond all else I would have befall my
tortured heart: "Whom then would you have Per-
            suasion
force to serve desire in your heart? Who is it,
            Sappho, that hurt you?

Though she now escape you, she soon will follow;
though she take not gifts from you, she will give
            them:
though she love not, yet she will surely love you
            even unwilling."

In such guise come even again and set me
free from doubt and sorrow; accomplish all those
things my heart desires to be done; appear and
            stand at my shoulder.

5

10

15

20

25

30

Artfully adorned Aphrodite, deathless

TRANSLATED BY JIM POWELL (1993)

Artfully adorned Aphrodite, deathless
child of Zeus and weaver of wiles I beg you
please don't hurt me, don't overcome my spirit,
    goddess, with longing,

but come here, if ever at other moments   5
hearing these my words from afar you listened
and responded: leaving your father's house, all
    golden, you came then,

hitching up your chariot: lovely sparrows
drew you quickly over the dark earth, whirling   10
on fine beating wings from the heights of heaven
    down through the sky and

instantly arrived — and then O my blessed
goddess with a smile on your deathless face you
asked me what the matter was *this* time, what I   15
    called you for this time,

what I now most wanted to happen in my
raving heart: "Whom *this* time should I persuade to
lead you back again to her love? Who *now*, oh
    Sappho, who wrongs you?
                                                                        20

If she flees you now, she will soon pursue you;
if she won't accept what you give, she'll give it;
if she doesn't love you, she'll love you soon now,
    even unwilling."

Come to me again, and release me from this
want past bearing. All that my heart desires to   25
happen — make it happen. And stand beside me,
    goddess, my ally.

Considerations for Critical Thinking and Writing

1. Explain which translation seems closest to Wharton's prose version.
2. Discuss the images and metaphors in Higginson's and Lattimore's versions. Which version is more appealing to you? Explain why.
3. How does Powell's use of language clearly make his version the most contemporary of the translations?

3. Images

POETRY'S APPEAL TO THE SENSES

A poet, to borrow a phrase from Henry James, is one of those on whom nothing is lost. Poets take in the world and give us impressions of what they experience through images. An *image* is language that addresses the senses. The most common images in poetry are visual; they provide verbal pictures of the poets' encounters — real or imagined — with the world. But poets also create images that appeal to our other senses. Richard Wilbur arouses several senses when he has the speaker in "A Late Aubade" gently urge his lover to linger in bed with him instead of getting on with her daily routines and obligations.

> Wait for a while, then slip downstairs
> And bring us up some chilled white wine,
> And some blue cheese, and crackers, and some fine
> Ruddy-skinned pears.

These images are simultaneously tempting and satisfying. We don't have to literally touch that cold, clear glass of wine (or will it come in a green bottle beaded with moisture?) or smell the cheese or taste the crackers to appreciate this vivid blend of colors, textures, tastes, and fragrances.

Images give us the physical world to experience in our imaginations. Some poems, like the following one, are written to do just that; they make no comment about what they describe.

WILLIAM CARLOS WILLIAMS (1883-1963)
Poem

1934

As the cat
climbed over
the top of

the jamcloset
first the right
forefoot

5

carefully
then the hind
stepped down

into the pit of
the empty
flowerpot

This poem defies paraphrase because it is all an image of agile movement. No statement is made about the movement; the title, "Poem" — really no title — signals Williams's refusal to comment on the movements. To impose a meaning on the poem, we'd probably have to knock over the flowerpot.

We experience the image in Williams's "Poem" more clearly because of how the sentence is organized into lines and groups of lines, or stanzas. Consider how differently the sentence is read if it is arranged as prose.

> As the cat climbed over the top of the jamcloset, first the right forefoot carefully then the hind stepped down into the pit of the empty flowerpot.

The poem's line and stanza division transforms what is essentially an awkward prose sentence into a rhythmic verbal picture. Especially when the poem is read aloud, this line and stanza division allows us to feel the image we see. Even the lack of a period at the end suggests that the cat is only pausing.

Images frequently do more than offer only sensory impressions, however. They also convey emotions and moods, as in the following lyric.

BONNIE JACOBSON (b. 1933)
On Being Served Apples

1989

Apples in a deep blue dish
        are the shadows of nuns

Apples in a basket
        are warm red moons on Indian women

Apples in a white bowl
        are virgins waiting in snow

Beware of apples on an orange plate:
        they are the anger of wives

The four images of apples in this poem suggest a range of emotions. How would you describe these emotions? How does the meaning of the apples change depending upon the context in which they are served? In this poem we are given more than just images of the world selected by the poet; we are also given her feelings about them.

What mood is established in this next poem's view of Civil War troops moving across a river?

WALT WHITMAN (1819-1892)
Cavalry Crossing a Ford

1865

A line in long array where they wind betwixt green islands,
They take a serpentine course, their arms flash in the sun — hark to the
    musical clank,
Behold the silvery river, in it the splashing horses loitering stop to drink,
Behold the brown-faced men, each group, each person, a picture, the
    negligent rest on the saddles,
Some emerge on the opposite bank, others are just entering the ford — while,
Scarlet and blue and snowy white,
The guidon flags flutter gaily in the wind.

Considerations for Critical Thinking and Writing

1. What effect do the colors and sounds have in establishing the mood of this poem?
2. How would the poem's mood have been changed if Whitman had used *look* or *see* instead of *behold* (lines 3–4)?
3. Where is the speaker as he observes this troop movement?
4. Does *serpentine* in line 2 have an evil connotation in this poem? Explain your answer.

Whitman seems to capture momentarily all the troop's actions, and through carefully chosen, suggestive details — really very few — he succeeds in making "each group, each person, a picture." Specific details, even when few are provided, give us the impression that we see the entire picture; it is as if those are the details we would remember if we had viewed the scene ourselves. Notice too that the movement of the "line in long array" is emphasized by the continuous winding syntax of the poem's lengthy lines.

Movement is also central to the next poem, in which action and motion are created through carefully chosen verbs.

DAVID SOLWAY (b. 1941)
Windsurfing

1993

It rides upon the wrinkled hide
of water, like the upturned hull
of a small canoe or kayak
waiting to be righted — yet its law
is opposite to that of boats,   5
it floats upon its breastbone and
brings whatever spine there is to light.
A thin shaft is slotted into place.
Then a puffed right-angle of wind

pushes it forward, out into the bay,   10
where suddenly it glitters into speed,
tilts, knifes up, and for the moment's
nothing but a slim projectile
of cambered fiberglass,
peeling the crests.   15

               The man's
clamped to the mast, taut as a guywire.
Part of the sleek apparatus
he controls, immaculate nerve
of balance, plunge and curvet,   20
he clinches all component movements
into single motion.
It bucks, stalls, shudders, yaws, and dips
its hissing sides beneath the surface
that sustains it, tensing   25
into muscle that nude ellipse
of lunging appetite and power.

And now the mechanism's wholly
dolphin, springing toward its prey
of spume and beaded sunlight,   30
tossing spray, and hits the vertex
of the wide, salt glare of distance,
and reverses.

             Back it comes through
a screen of particles,   35
scalloped out of water, shimmer
and reflection, the wind snapping
and lashing it homeward,
shearing the curve of the wave,
breaking the spell of the caught breath   40
and articulate play of sinew, to enter
the haven of the breakwater
and settle in a rush of silence.

Now the crossing drifts
in the husk of its wake   45
and nothing's the same again
as, gliding elegantly on a film of water,
the man guides
his brash, obedient legend
into shore.   50

Considerations for Critical Thinking and Writing

1. Draw a circle around the verbs that seem especially effective in conveying a strong sense of motion and explain why they are effective.
2. How is the man made to seem to be one with his board and sail?
3. How does the rhythm of the poem change beginning with line 45?

Connections to Other Selections

1. Consider the effects of the images in "Windsurfing" and Ho's "A Beautiful Girl Combs Her Hair" (p. 42). In an essay explain how these images produce emotional responses in you.
2. Compare the descriptions in "Windsurfing" and Bishop's "The Fish" (p. 20). How does each poet appeal to your senses to describe windsurfing and fishing?

"Windsurfing" is awash with images of speed, fluidity, and power. Even the calming aftermath of the breakwater is described as a "rush of silence," adding to the sense of motion that is detailed and expanded throughout the poem.

Poets choose details the way they choose the words to present those details: only telling ones will do. Consider the images Theodore Roethke uses in "Root Cellar."

THEODORE ROETHKE (1908–1963)
Root Cellar
1948

Nothing would sleep in that cellar, dank as a ditch,
Bulbs broke out of boxes hunting for chinks in the dark,
Shoots dangled and drooped,
Lolling obscenely from mildewed crates,
Hung down long yellow evil necks, like tropical snakes.   5
And what a congress of stinks! *a formal assembly or mtg. to discuss problems*
Roots ripe as old bait,
Pulpy stems, rank, silo-rich,
Leaf-mold, manure, lime, piled against slippery planks.
Nothing would give up life: 10
Even the dirt kept breathing a small breath.

Considerations for Critical Thinking and Writing

1. What senses are engaged by the images in this poem? Is the poem simply a series of sensations, or do the detailed images make some kind of point about the root cellar?
2. What controls the choice of details in the poem? Why isn't there, for example, a rusty shovel leaning against a dirt wall or a worn gardener's glove atop one of the crates?
3. Look up *congress* in a dictionary for its denotative meanings. Explain why "congress of stinks" is especially appropriate given the nature of the rest of the poem's imagery.
4. What single line in the poem suggests a theme?

The tone of the images and mood of the speaker are consistent in Roethke's "Root Cellar." In Matthew Arnold's "Dover Beach," however, they shift as the theme is developed.

MATTHEW ARNOLD (1822–1888)
Dover Beach

1867

The sea is calm tonight.
The tide is full, the moon lies fair
Upon the straits; — on the French coast the light
Gleams and is gone; the cliffs of England stand,
Glimmering and vast, out in the tranquil bay.   5
Come to the window, sweet is the night-air!
Only, from the long line of spray
Where the sea meets the moon-blanched land,
Listen! you hear the grating roar
Of pebbles which the waves draw back, and fling,   10
At their return, up the high strand,
Begin, and cease, and then again begin,
With tremulous cadence slow, and bring
The eternal note of sadness in.

Sophocles long ago   15
Heard it on the Aegean, and it brought
Into his mind the turbid ebb and flow
Of human misery;° we
Find also in the sound a thought,
Hearing it by this distant northern sea.   20

The Sea of Faith
Was once, too, at the full, and round earth's shore
Lay like the folds of a bright girdle furled.
But now I only hear
Its melancholy, long, withdrawing roar,   25
Retreating, to the breath
Of the night-wind, down the vast edges drear
And naked shingles° of the world.   *pebble beaches*

Ah, love, let us be true
To one another! for the world, which seems   30
To lie before us like a land of dreams,
So various, so beautiful, so new,
Hath really neither joy, nor love, nor light,
Nor certitude, nor peace, nor help for pain;
And we are here as on a darkling plain   35
Swept with confused alarms of struggle and flight,
Where ignorant armies clash by night.

15–18 *Sophocles long ago . . . misery:* In *Antigone*, lines 656–677, Sophocles likens the disasters that beset the house of Oedipus to a "mounting tide."

Considerations for Critical Thinking and Writing

1. Contrast the images in lines 4–8 and 9–13. How do they reveal the speaker's mood? To whom is he speaking?

2. What is the cause of the "sadness" in line 14? What is the speaker's response to the ebbing "Sea of Faith"? Is there anything to replace his sense of loss?

3. What details of the beach seem related to the ideas in the poem? How is the sea used differently in lines 1–14 and lines 21–28?

4. Describe the differences in tone between lines 1–8 and 35–37. What has caused the change?

Connections to Other Selections

1. Explain how the images in Wilfred Owen's "Dulce et Decorum Est" (p. 93) develop further the ideas and sentiments suggested by Arnold's final line concerning "ignorant armies clash[ing] by night."

2. Contrast Arnold's images with those of Anthony Hecht in his parody "The Dover Bitch" (p. 417). How do Hecht's images create a very different mood from that of "Dover Beach"?

Consider the poetic appetite for images displayed in the celebration of chile peppers in the following passionate poem.

JIMMY SANTIAGO BACA (b. 1952)
Green Chile

1989

I prefer red chile over my eggs
and potatoes for breakfast.
Red chile *ristras°* decorate my door,   *a braided string of peppers*
dry on my roof, and hang from eaves.
They lend open-air vegetable stands   5
historical grandeur, and gently swing
with an air of festive welcome.
I can hear them talking in the wind,
haggard, yellowing, crisp, rasping
tongues of old men, licking the breeze.   10

        But grandmother loves green chile.
When I visit her,
she holds the green chile pepper
in her wrinkled hands.
Ah, voluptuous, masculine,   15
an air of authority and youth simmers
from its swan-neck stem, tapering to a flowery
collar, fermenting resinous spice.
A well-dressed gentleman at the door
my grandmother takes sensuously in her hand,   20
rubbing its firm glossed sides,
caressing the oily rubbery serpent,
with mouth-watering fulfillment,
fondling its curves with gentle fingers.

Its bearing magnificent and taut   25
as flanks of a tiger in mid-leap,
she thrusts her blade into
and cuts it open, with lust
on her hot mouth, sweating over the stove,
bandanna round her forehead,   30
mysterious passion on her face
and she serves me green chile con carne
between soft warm leaves of corn tortillas,
with beans and rice — her sacrifice
to her little prince.   35
I slurp from my plate
with last bit of tortilla, my mouth burns
and I hiss and drink a tall glass of cold water.

All over New Mexico, sunburned men and women
drive rickety trucks stuffed with gunny-sacks   40
of green chile, from Belen, Veguita, Willard, Estancia,
San Antonio y Socorro, from fields
to roadside stands, you see them roasting green chile
in screen-sided homemade barrels, and for a dollar a bag,
we relive this old, beautiful ritual again and again.   45

Considerations for Critical Thinking and Writing

1. How do the different images the speaker uses to describe red and green chile
   serve to draw a distinction between the two?
2. What kinds of images are used to describe the grandmother's preparation of
   green chile? What is the effect of those images?
3. Try writing a description — in poetry or prose — that uses vivid images to evoke
   a powerful response (either positive or negative) to a particular food.

POEMS FOR FURTHER STUDY

SEAMUS HEANEY (b. 1939)
The Pitchfork   1991

Of all implements, the pitchfork was the one
That came near to an imagined perfection:
When he tightened his raised hand and aimed with it,
It felt like a javelin, accurate and light.

So whether he played the warrior or the athlete   5
Or worked in earnest in the chaff and sweat,
He loved its grain of tapering, dark-flecked ash
Grown satiny from its own natural polish.

Riveted steel, turned timber, burnish, grain,
Smoothness, straightness, roundness, length and sheen.   10
Sweat-cured, sharpened, balanced, tested, fitted.
The springiness, the clip and dart of it.

And then when he thought of probes that reached the
     farthest,
He would see the shaft of a pitchfork sailing past   15
Evenly, imperturbably through space,
Its prongs starlit and absolutely soundless —

But has learned at last to follow that simple lead
Past its own aim, out to an other side
Where perfection — or nearness to it — is imagined   20
Not in the aiming but the opening hand.

Considerations for Critical Thinking and Writing

1. How do the images make this pitchfork more than merely one of many "implements"?
2. In what ways does the pitchfork change through the course of the poem?
3. Explain what the speaker means by "imagined perfection" (line 2 and again in the
   last stanza).
4. What does the thrower of the pitchfork learn in lines 13–16?

Connection to Another Selection

1. Pitchforks and green chile do not have much in common, but the images used to
   describe the pitchfork in this poem and the chile in Jimmy Santiago Baca's "Green
   Chile" invest significance in these otherwise ordinary objects. Write an essay that
   discusses how the images in these two poems give these objects qualities that are
   not inherent in either pitchforks or chile.

H. D.
[HILDA DOOLITTLE] (1886–1961)
Heat   1916

O wind, rend open the heat,
cut apart the heat,
rend it to tatters.

Fruit cannot drop
through this thick air —   5
fruit cannot fall into heat
that presses up and blunts
the points of pears
and rounds the grapes.

Cut the heat —   10
plough through it,
turning it on either side
of your path.

Considerations for Critical Thinking and Writing

1. What physical properties are associated with heat in this poem?
2. Explain the effect of the description of fruit in lines 4–9.
3. Why is the image of the cutting plow especially effective in lines 10–13?

TIMOTHY STEELE (b. 1948)
An Aubade   1986

As she is showering, I wake to see
A shine of earrings on the bedside stand,
A single yellow sheet which, over me,
Has folds as intricate as drapery
In paintings from some fine old master's hand.   5

The pillow which, in dozing, I embraced
Retains the salty sweetness of her skin;
I sense her smooth back, buttocks, belly, waist,
The leggy warmth which spread and gently laced
Around my legs and loins, and drew me in.   10

I stretch and curl about a bit and hear her
Singing among the water's hiss and race.
Gradually the early light makes clearer
The perfume bottles by the dresser's mirror,
The silver flashlight, standing on its face,   15

Which shares the corner of the dresser with
An ivy spilling tendrils from a cup.
And so content am I, I can forgive
Pleasure for being brief and fugitive.
I'll stretch some more, but postpone getting up   20

Until she finishes her shower and dries
(Now this and now that foot placed on a chair)
Her fineboned ankles, and her calves and thighs,
The pink full nipples of her breasts, and ties
Her towel up, turban-style, about her hair.   25

Considerations for Critical Thinking and Writing

1. Characterize the poem's speaker. What does his use of language reveal about him?
2. How does this poem fit the definition of an aubade?
3. What do you think is the central point of this poem?
4. Is this a *carpe diem* poem? Explain why or why not.

Connections to Other Selections

1. How does the tone of Steele's poem compare with Wilbur's "A Late Aubade" (p. 60)? Explain why you prefer one over the other.
2. Write an essay that compares and contrasts the speaker/observer in "An Aubade" with that of Joan Murray's "Play-By-Play" (p. 502).

WILLIAM BLAKE (1757–1827)
London   1794

I wander through each chartered° street,   *defined by law*
Near where the chartered Thames does flow,
And mark in every face I meet
Marks of weakness, marks of woe.

In every cry of every man,   5
In every Infant's cry of fear,
In every voice, in every ban,
The mind-forged manacles I hear.

How the Chimney-sweeper's cry
Every black'ning Church appalls;   10
And the hapless Soldier's sigh
Runs in blood down Palace walls.

But most through midnight streets I hear
How the youthful Harlot's curse
Blasts the new-born Infant's tear,   15
And blights with plagues the Marriage hearse.

Considerations for Critical Thinking and Writing

1. How do the visual images in this poem suggest a feeling of being trapped?
2. What is the predominant sound heard in the poem?
3. What is the meaning of line 8? What is the cause of the problems that the speaker sees and hears in London? Does the speaker suggest additional causes?
4. The image in lines 11–12 cannot be read literally. Comment on its effectiveness.
5. How does Blake's use of denotative and connotative language enrich this poem's meaning?
6. An earlier version of Blake's last stanza appeared this way:

   > But most the midnight harlot's curse
   > From every dismal street I hear,
   > Weaves around the marriage hearse
   > And blasts the new-born infant's tear.

   Examine carefully the differences between the two versions. How do Blake's revisions affect his picture of London life? Which version do you think is more effective? Why?

WILFRED OWEN (1893–1918)
Dulce et Decorum Est   WWI   1920

Bent double, like old beggars under sacks,
Knock-kneed, coughing like hags, we cursed through sludge,
Till on the haunting flares we turned our backs,
And towards our distant rest began to trudge.

Men marched asleep. Many had lost their boots,   5
But limped on, blood-shod. All went lame, all blind;
Drunk with fatigue; deaf even to the hoots
Of gas-shells dropping softly behind.

Gas! GAS! Quick, boys! — An ecstasy of fumbling,
Fitting the clumsy helmets just in time,   10
But someone still was yelling out and stumbling
And flound'ring like a man in fire or lime. —
Dim through the misty panes and thick green light,
As under a green sea, I saw him drowning.

In all my dreams before my helpless sight   15
He plunges at me, guttering, choking, drowning.

If in some smothering dreams, you too could pace
Behind the wagon that we flung him in,
And watch the white eyes writhing in his face,
His hanging face, like a devil's sick of sin,   20
If you could hear, at every jolt, the blood
Come gargling from the froth-corrupted lungs
Bitter as the cud
Of vile, incurable sores on innocent tongues, —
My friend, you would not tell with such high zest   25
To children ardent for some desperate glory,
The old lie: *Dulce et decorum est*
Pro patria mori.

Considerations for Critical Thinking and Writing

1. The Latin quotation in lines 27–28 is from Horace: "It is sweet and fitting to die for one's country." Owen served as a British soldier during World War I and was killed. Is this poem unpatriotic? What is its purpose?
2. Which images in the poem are most vivid? To which senses do they speak?
3. Describe the speaker's tone. What is his relationship to his audience?
4. How are the images of the soldiers in this poem different from the images that typically appear in recruiting posters?

WISLAWA SZYMBORSKA (b. 1923)
End and Beginning   1993

TRANSLATED BY JOSEPH BRODSKY

After each war
somebody has to clear up
put things in order
by itself it won't happen.

Somebody's got to push   5
rubble to the highway shoulder

making way
for the carts filled up with corpses.

Someone might trudge
through muck and ashes,
sofa springs,
splintered glass
and blood-soaked rugs.

Somebody has to haul
beams for propping a wall,
another put glass in a window
and hang the door on hinges.

This is not photogenic
and takes years.
All the cameras have left already
for another war.

Bridges are needed
also new railroad stations.
Tatters turn into sleeves
for rolling up.

Somebody, broom in hand,
still recalls how it was.
Someone whose head was not
torn away listens nodding.
But nearby already
begin to bustle those
who'll need persuasion.

Somebody still at times
digs up from under the bushes
some rusty quibble
to add it to burning refuse.

Those who knew
what this was all about
must yield to those
who know little
or less than little
essentially nothing.

In the grass that has covered
effects in causes
somebody must recline,
a stalk of rye in the teeth,
ogling the clouds.

10

15

20

25

30

35

40

45

Considerations for Critical Thinking and Writing

1. Discuss the effectiveness of the poem's images. Which seem especially vivid to you in their depiction of war?

2. How does the word *somebody* take on particularly strong meanings in this poem through repetition?

3. Discuss the effects of the final stanza. How does it differ from the preceding stanzas?
4. What do you think is the theme of the poem? How is the poem's title related to its theme?

MARGARET HOLLEY (b. 1944)
Peepers   1992

One amber inch
of blinking berry-eyed
amphibian,

four fetal fingers
on each hand,   5
a honey and mud-brown

pulse of appetite
surprised into stillness,
folded in a momentary lump

of flying bat-fish   10
ready to jump
full-tilt into anything

— the whole strength
of its struggling length
you can hold in your hand.   15

Its poetry, a raucous
refrain of pleasure
in the April-warm pools

of rain, the insistent
chorus of whistles   20
jingles through night woods,

Females! It's time!
that confident come-on
to a whole wet population

of embraces, eggs, tadpoles   25
— all head and tail,
mind darting in every direction

until the articulating torso,
Ovidian bag of bones,
results in the "mature adult":   30

a rumpled face in the mirror
still sleeping through Basho's°
awakening plop,

---

32 *Basho:* Matsuo Bashō (1644–1694), a Japanese poet most famous for his haiku. See "Under cherry trees," p. 219.

re-enchanted daily
by the comforting slop   35
of burgeoning spring woods

and all this sexual chatter,
doing its best to make
the wet and silky season

last forever. Yet   40
as you lie dreaming mid-leap,
splayed in the sheets,

the future as a kind
but relentless scientist
feels around in your flesh   45

for the nerve of surprise;
he just loves
the look of wonder on your face,

the world on your open lips
for the immensity   50
that grips you,

Oh.

Considerations for Critical Thinking and Writing

1. What is being described in lines 1–40? How does the subject shift in lines 40–52? What is the relationship between these two groups of lines?
2. The word "peepers" does not appear in the poem, but are there images that connect to the title? What does the title mean?
3. What is the effect and significance of the final line?

ELIZABETH BARRETT BROWNING (1806–1861)
Grief   1844

I tell you, hopeless grief is passionless;
That only men incredulous of despair,
Half-taught in anguish, through the midnight air
Beat upward to God's throne in loud access
Of shrieking and reproach. Full desertness,   5
In souls as countries, lieth silent-bare
Under the blanching, vertical eye-glare
Of the absolute Heavens. Deep-hearted man, express
Grief for thy Dead in silence like to death —
Most like a monumental statue set   10
In everlasting watch and moveless woe
Till itself crumble to the dust beneath.
Touch it; the marble eyelids are not wet.
If it could weep, it could arise and go.

Considerations for Critical Thinking and Writing

1. What images does Browning use to describe grief?
2. What is the effect of the poem's first words, "I tell you"? How do they serve to characterize the speaker?
3. Describe the emotional tone of this poem.

JAMES DICKEY (1923–1997)
Deer Among Cattle

1981

Here and there in the searing beam
Of my hand going through the night meadow
They all are grazing

With pins of human light in their eyes.
A wild one also is eating   5
The human grass,

Slender, graceful, domesticated
By darkness, among the bred-
for-slaughter,

Having bounded their paralyzed fence   10
And inclined his branched forehead onto
Their green frosted table,

The only live thing in this flashlight
Who can leave whenever he wishes,
Turn grass into forest,   15

Foreclose inhuman brightness from his eyes
But stands here still, unperturbed,
In their wide-open country,

The sparks from my hand in his pupils
Unmatched anywhere among cattle,   20

Grazing with them the night of the hammer
As one of their own who shall rise.

Considerations for Critical Thinking and Writing

1. What images distinguish the deer from the cattle?
2. Do the words "domesticated" and "human" have positive or negative connotations in this poem? Explain your answer.
3. Discuss the possible implications of the last two lines. You may want to consider the speaker and his role in this tableau.

Connection to Another Selection

1. Discuss the idea of confinement in "Deer Among Cattle" and Rainer Maria Rilke's "The Panther" (p. 99).

RAINER MARIA RILKE (1875-1926)

The Panther 1927

TRANSLATED BY STEPHEN MITCHELL

His vision, from the constantly passing bars,
has grown so weary that it cannot hold
anything else. It seems to him there are
a thousand bars; and behind the bars, no world.

As he paces in cramped circles, over and over,   5
the movement of his powerful soft strides
is like a ritual dance around a center
in which a mighty will stands paralyzed.

Only at times, the curtain of the pupils
lifts, quietly — . An image enters in,   10
rushes down through the tensed, arrested muscles,
plunges into the heart and is gone.

Considerations for Critical Thinking and Writing

1. What kind of "image enters in" the heart of the panther in the final stanza?
2. How are images of confinement achieved in the poem? Why doesn't Rilke describe the final image in lines 10–12?

Connection to Another Selection

1. Write an essay explaining how a sense of movement is achieved by the images and rhythms in this poem and in Dickinson's "A Bird came down the Walk — " (p. 159).

JANE KENYON (1947-1995)

The Blue Bowl 1990

Like primitives we buried the cat
with his bowl. Bare-handed
we scraped sand and gravel
back into the hole.
    They fell with a hiss   5

and thud on his side,
on his long red fur, the white feathers
between his toes, and his
long, not to say aquiline, nose.

We stood and brushed each other off.   10
There are sorrows keener than these.

Silent the rest of the day, we worked,
ate, stared, and slept. It stormed

life is
not
better
yet

all night; now it clears, and a robin
burbles from a dripping bush
like the neighbor who means well
but always says the wrong thing.

15

Considerations for Critical Thinking and Writing

1. Why do you think Kenyon titles the poem "The Blue Bowl" rather than, say, "The Cat's Bowl"?
2. What is the effect of being reminded that "There are sorrows keener than these"?
3. Why is the robin's song "the wrong thing"?

Connection to Another Selection

1. Write an essay comparing the death of this cat with the death of the dog in Updike's "Dog's Death" (p. 11). Which poem draws a more powerful response from you? Explain why.

SALLY CROFT (b. 1935)
Home-Baked Bread

1981

> *Nothing gives a household a greater sense of stability and common comfort than the aroma of cooling bread. Begin, if you like, with a loaf of whole wheat, which requires neither sifting nor kneading, and go on from there to more cunning triumphs.*
>
> *– The Joy of Cooking*

What is it she is not saying?
Cunning triumphs. It rings
of insinuation. Step into my kitchen,
I have prepared a cunning triumph
for you. Spices and herbs   5
sealed in this porcelain jar,

a treasure of my great-aunt
who sat up past midnight
in her Massachusetts bedroom
when the moon was dark. Come,   10
rest your feet. I'll make
you tea with honey and slices

of warm bread spread with peach butter.
I picked the fruit this morning
still fresh with dew. The fragrance   15
is seductive? I hoped you would say that.
See how the heat rises
when the bread opens. Come,

we'll eat together, the small flakes
have scarcely any flavor. What cunning   20

triumphs we can discover in my upstairs room
where peach trees breathe their sweetness
beside the open window and
sun lies like honey on the floor.

Considerations for Critical Thinking and Writing

1. Why does the speaker in this poem seize upon the phrase "cunning triumphs" from the *Joy of Cooking* excerpt?

2. Distinguish between the voice we hear in lines 1–3 and the second voice in lines 3–24. Who is the "you" in the poem?

3. Why is "insinuation" an especially appropriate word choice in line 3?

4. How do the images in lines 20–24 bring together all the senses evoked in the preceding lines?

5. Write a paragraph that describes the sensuous (and perhaps sensual) qualities of a food you enjoy.

CAROLYN KIZER (b. 1925)
Food for Love   1984

> *Eating is touch carried to the bitter end.*
>   – Samuel Butler II

I'm going to murder you with love;
I'm going to suffocate you with embraces;
I'm going to hug you, bone by bone,
Till you're dead all over.
Then I will dine on your delectable marrow.   5

You will become my personal Sahara;
I'll sun myself in you, then with one swallow
Drain your remaining brackish well.
With my female blade I'll carve my name
In your most aspiring palm   10
Before I chop it down.
Then I'll inhale your last oasis whole.

But in the total desert you become
You'll see me stretch, horizon to horizon,
Opulent mirage!   15
Wisteria balconies dripping cyclamen.
Vistas ablaze with crystal, laced in gold.

So you will summon each dry grain of sand
And move towards me in undulating dunes
Till you arrive at sudden ultramarine: 20
A Mediterranean to stroke your dusty shores;
Obstinate verdure, creeping inland, fast renudes
Your barrens; succulents spring up everywhere,
Surprising life! And I will be that green.

When you are fed and watered, flourishing   25
With shoots entwining trellis, dome and spire,
Till you are resurrected field in bloom,
I will devour you, my natural food,
My host, my final supper on the earth,
And you'll begin to die again.   30

Considerations for Critical Thinking and Writing

1. What's going on here? Is this a love poem? Explain why or why not.
2. What does the epigraph from Samuel Butler contribute to your understanding of the poem?
3. Contrast the speaker's relationship with her "personal Sahara" in lines 1–12 and in lines 13–30.

Connections to Other Selections

1. Write a reply to this poem — in poetry or prose — as you think the speaker of Marvell's "To His Coy Mistress" (p. 57) would respond.
2. Discuss the relationship between food and love in Kizer's poem and in "Home-Baked Bread."
3. Write an essay comparing the tone of "Food for Love" and Elaine Magarrell's "The Joy of Cooking" (p. 123).

JOHN KEATS (1795–1821)
To Autumn   1819

I
Season of mists and mellow fruitfulness,
   Close bosom-friend of the maturing sun;
Conspiring with him how to load and bless
   With fruit the vines that round the thatch-eves run;
To bend with apples the mossed cottage-trees,   5
   And fill all fruit with ripeness to the core;
     To swell the gourd, and plump the hazel shells
   With a sweet kernel; to set budding more,
And still more, later flowers for the bees,
Until they think warm days will never cease,   10
     For summer has o'er-brimmed their clammy cells.

II
Who hath not seen thee oft amid thy store?
   Sometimes whoever seeks abroad may find
Thee sitting careless on a granary floor,
   Thy hair soft-lifted by the winnowing wind;   15
Or on a half-reaped furrow sound asleep,
   Drowsed with the fume of poppies, while thy hook°   *scythe*
     Spares the next swath and all its twinèd flowers:

And sometimes like a gleaner thou dost keep
   Steady thy laden head across a brook;   20
Or by a cider-press, with patient look,
   Thou watchest the last oozings hours by hours.

III

Where are the songs of spring? Ay, where are they?
   Think not of them, thou hast thy music too, —
While barred clouds bloom the soft-dying day,   25
   And touch the stubble-plains with rosy hue;
Then in a wailful choir the small gnats mourn
   Among the river swallows,° borne aloft   *willows*
      Or sinking as the light wind lives or dies;
And full-grown lambs loud bleat from hilly bourn;°   *territory* 30
   Hedge-crickets sing; and now with treble soft
The redbreast whistles from a garden-croft,
   And gathering swallows twitter in the skies.

Considerations for Critical Thinking and Writing

1. How is autumn made to seem like a person in each stanza of this ode?
2. Which senses are most emphasized in each stanza?
3. How is the progression of time expressed in the ode?
4. How does the imagery convey tone? Which words have particularly strong connotative values?
5. What is the speaker's view of death?

Connections to Other Selections

1. Compare this poem's tone and its perspective on death with those of Robert Frost's "After Apple-Picking" (p. 309).
2. Write an essay comparing the significance of the images of "mellow fruitfulness" in "To Autumn" with that of the images of ripeness in Roethke's "Root Cellar" (p. 87). Explain how the images in each poem lead to very different feelings about the same phenomenon.

EZRA POUND (1885–1972)
In a Station of the Metro°   1913

The apparition of these faces in the crowd;
Petals on a wet, black bough.

Metro: Underground railroad in Paris.

Considerations for Critical Thinking and Writing

1. What kind of mood does the image in the second line convey?
2. Why is "apparition" a better word choice than, say, "appearance" or "sight"?

CATHY SONG (b. 1955)
The White Porch   1983

I wrap the blue towel
after washing,
around the damp
weight of hair, bulky
as a sleeping cat,   5
and sit out on the porch.
Still dripping water,
it'll be dry by supper,
by the time the dust
settles off your shoes,   10
though it's only five
past noon. Think
of the luxury: how to use
the afternoon like the stretch
of lawn spread before me.   15
There's the laundry,
sun-warm clothes at twilight,
and the mountain of beans   ⸱
in my lap. Each one,
I'll break and snap   20
thoughtfully in half.

But there is this slow arousal.
The small buttons
of my cotton blouse
are pulling away from my body.   25
I feel the strain of threads,
the swollen magnolias
heavy as a flock of birds
in the tree. Already,
the orange sponge cake   30
is rising in the oven.
I know you'll say it makes
your mouth dry
and I'll watch you
drench your slice of it   35
in canned peaches
and lick the plate clean.

So much hair, my mother
used to say, grabbing
the thick braided rope   40
in her hands while we washed
the breakfast dishes, discussing
dresses and pastries.
My mind often elsewhere
as we did the morning chores together.   45
Sometimes, a few strands

would catch in her gold ring.
I worked hard then,
anticipating the hour
when I would let the rope down   50
at night, strips of sheets,
knotted and tied,
while she slept in tight blankets.
My hair, freshly washed
like a measure of wealth,   55
like a bridal veil.
Crouching in the grass,   *poet? or? friend?*
you would wait for the signal,
for the movement of curtains
before releasing yourself   60
from the shadow of moths.
Cloth, hair and hands,
smuggling you in.

Connections to Other Selections

1. Compare the images used to describe the speaker's "slow arousal" in this poem
   with Croft's images in "Home-Baked Bread" (p. 100). What similarities do you
   see? What makes each description so effective?
2. Write an essay comparing the images of sensuality in this poem with those in
   Ho's "A Beautiful Girl Combs Her Hair" (p. 42). Which poem seems more erotic
   to you? Why?

PERSPECTIVE

T. E. HULME (1883–1917)
On the Differences between Poetry and Prose   1924

In prose as in algebra concrete things are embodied in signs or counters
which are moved about according to rules, without being visualized at all in the
process. There are in prose certain type situations and arrangements of words,
which move as automatically into certain other arrangements as do functions in
algebra. One only changes the X's and the Y's back into physical things at the
end of the process. Poetry, in one aspect at any rate, may be considered as an
effort to avoid this characteristic of prose. It is not a counter language, but a
visual concrete one. It is a compromise for a language of intuition which would
hand over sensations bodily. It always endeavors to arrest you, and to make you
continuously see a physical thing, to prevent you gliding through an abstract
process. It chooses fresh epithets and fresh metaphors, not so much because
they are new, and we are tired of the old, but because the old cease to convey
a physical thing and become abstract counters. A poet says a ship "coursed the
seas" to get a physical image, instead of the counter word "sailed." Visual meanings can only be transferred by the new bowl of metaphor; prose is an old pot
that lets them leak out. Images in verse are not mere decoration, but the very

essence of an intuitive language. Verse is a pedestrian taking you over the ground, prose — a train which delivers you at a destination.

From "Romanticism and Classicism," in *Speculations,*
edited by Herbert Read

Considerations for Critical Thinking and Writing

1. What distinctions does Hulme make between poetry and prose? Which seems to be the most important difference?
2. Write an essay that discusses Hulme's claim that poetry "is a compromise for a language of intuition which would hand over sensations bodily."

4. Figures of Speech

Figures of speech are broadly defined as a way of saying one thing in terms of something else. An overeager funeral director might, for example, be described as a vulture. Although figures of speech are indirect, they are designed to clarify, not obscure, our understanding of what they describe. Poets frequently use them because, as Emily Dickinson said, the poet's work is to "Tell all the truth but tell it slant" to capture the reader's interest and imagination. But figures of speech are not limited to poetry. Hearing them, reading them, or using them is as natural as using language itself.

Suppose that in the middle of a class discussion concerning the economic causes of World War II your history instructor introduces a series of statistics by saying, "Let's get down to brass tacks." Would anyone be likely to expect a display of brass tacks for students to examine? Of course not. To interpret the statement literally would be to wholly misunderstand the instructor's point that the time has come for a close look at the economic circumstances leading to the war. A literal response transforms the statement into the sort of hilariously bizarre material often found in a sketch by Woody Allen.

The class does not look for brass tacks, because, to put it in a nutshell, they understand that the instructor is speaking figuratively. They would understand, too, that in the preceding sentence *in a nutshell* refers to brevity and conciseness rather than to the covering of a kernel of a nut. Figurative language makes its way into our everyday speech and writing as well as into literature because it is a means of achieving color, vividness, and intensity.

Consider the difference, for example, between these two statements.

Literal: The diner strongly expressed anger at the waiter.
Figurative: The diner leaped from his table and roared at the waiter.

The second statement is more vivid because it creates a picture of ferocious anger by likening the diner to some kind of wild animal, such as a lion or tiger. By comparison, "strongly expressed anger" is neither especially strong nor especially expressive; it is flat. Not all figurative language avoids this kind of flatness, however. Figures of speech such as "getting down to brass tacks" and "in a nutshell" are clichés because they lack originality and freshness. Still, they suggest how these devices are commonly used to give language some color, even if that color is sometimes a bit faded.

There is nothing weak about William Shakespeare's use of figurative language in the following passage from *Macbeth*. Macbeth has just learned that his wife is dead, and he laments her loss as well as the course of his own life.

WILLLIAM SHAKESPEARE (1564–1616)
From Macbeth *(Act V, Scene v)* 1605–06

Tomorrow, and tomorrow, and tomorrow
Creeps in this petty pace from day to day
To the last syllable of recorded time;
And all our yesterdays have lighted fools
The way to dusty death. Out, out, brief candle! 5
Life's but a walking shadow, a poor player,
That struts and frets his hour upon the stage,
And then is heard no more. It is a tale
Told by an idiot, full of sound and fury,
Signifying nothing. 10

This passage might be summarized as "life has no meaning," but such a brief paraphrase does not take into account the figurative language that reveals the depth of Macbeth's despair and his view of the absolute meaninglessness of life. By comparing life to a "brief candle," Macbeth emphasizes the darkness and death that surround human beings. The light of life is too brief and unpredictable to be of any comfort. Indeed, life for Macbeth is a "walking shadow," futilely playing a role that is more farcical than dramatic, because life is, ultimately, a desperate story filled with pain and devoid of significance. What the figurative language provides, then, is the emotional force of Macbeth's assertion; his comparisons are disturbing because they are so apt.

The remainder of this chapter discusses some of the most important figures of speech used in poetry. A familiarity with them will help you to understand how poetry achieves its effects.

SIMILE AND METAPHOR

The two most common figures of speech are simile and metaphor. Both compare things that are ordinarily considered unlike each other. A *simile* makes an explicit comparison between two things by using words such as *like, as, than, appears,* or *seems:* "A sip of Mrs. Cook's coffee is like a punch in the stomach." The force of the simile is created by the differences between the two things compared. There would be no simile if the comparison were stated this way: "Mrs. Cook's coffee is as strong as the cafeteria's coffee." This is a literal comparison because Mrs. Cook's coffee is compared with something like it, another kind of coffee. Consider how simile is used in this poem.

MARGARET ATWOOD (b. 1939)
you fit into me

1971

you fit into me
like a hook into an eye

a fish hook
an open eye

If you blinked on a second reading, you got the point of this poem, because you recognized that the simile "like a hook into an eye" gives way to a play on words in the final two lines. There the hook and eye, no longer a pleasant domestic image of fitting closely together, become a literal, sharp fishhook and a human eye. The wordplay qualifies the simile and drastically alters the tone of this poem by creating a strong and unpleasant surprise.

A *metaphor*, like a simile, makes a comparison between two unlike things, but it does so implicitly, without words such as *like* or *as*: "Mrs. Cook's coffee is a punch in the stomach." Metaphor asserts the identity of dissimilar things. Macbeth tells us that life *is* a "brief candle," life *is* a "walking shadow," life *is* a "poor player," life *is* a "tale / Told by an idiot." Metaphor transforms people, places, objects, and ideas into whatever the poet imagines them to be, and if metaphors are effective, the reader's experience, understanding, and appreciation of what is described are enhanced. Metaphors are frequently more demanding than similes because they are not signaled by particular words. They are both subtle and powerful.

Here is a poem about presentiment, a foreboding that something terrible is about to happen.

EMILY DICKINSON (1830–1886)
Presentiment — is that long Shadow — on the lawn —

c. 1863

Presentiment — is that long Shadow — on the lawn —
Indicative that Suns go down —

The notice to the startled Grass
That Darkness — is about to pass —

The metaphors in this poem define the abstraction *presentiment*. The sense of foreboding that Dickinson expresses is identified with a particular moment, the moment when darkness is just about to envelop an otherwise tranquil ordinary scene. The speaker projects that fear onto the "startled Grass" so that it seems any life must be frightened by the approaching "Shadow" and "Darkness" — two richly connotative words associated with death. The metaphors obliquely tell us ("tell it slant" was Dickinson's motto, remember) that presentiment is related to a fear of death, and, more important, the metaphors convey the feelings which attend that idea.

Some metaphors are more subtle than others, because their comparison of terms is less explicit. Notice the difference between the following two metaphors, both of which describe a shaggy derelict refusing to leave the warmth of a hotel lobby: "He was a mule standing his ground" is a quite explicit comparison. The man is a mule; X is Y. But this metaphor is much more covert: "He brayed his refusal to leave." This second version is an *implied metaphor,* because it does not explicitly identify the man with a mule. Instead, it hints at or alludes to the mule. Braying is associated with mules and is especially appropriate in this context because of those animals' reputation for stubbornness. Implied metaphors can slip by readers, but they offer the alert reader the energy and resonance of carefully chosen, highly concentrated language.

Some poets write extended comparisons in which part or all of the poem consists of a series of related metaphors or similes. Extended metaphors are more common than extended similes. In "Catch" (p. 14), Francis creates an *extended metaphor* that compares poetry to a game of catch. The entire poem is organized around this comparison, just as all of the elements in Cummings's "she being Brand" (p. 49) are clustered around the extended comparison of a car and a woman. Because these comparisons are at work throughout the entire poem, they are called *controlling metaphors.* Extended comparisons can serve as a poem's organizing principle; they are also a reminder that in good poems metaphor and simile are not merely decorative but inseparable from what is expressed.

Notice the controlling metaphor in this poem, written by a woman whose contemporaries identified her more as a wife and mother than as a poet. Bradstreet's first volume of poetry, *The Tenth Muse,* was published by her brother-in-law in 1650 without her prior knowledge.

ANNE BRADSTREET (c. 1612–1672)
The Author to Her Book   1678

Thou ill-formed offspring of my feeble brain,
Who after birth did'st by my side remain,
Till snatched from thence by friends, less wise than true,
Who thee abroad exposed to public view;
Made thee in rags, halting, to the press to trudge,   5
Where errors were not lessened, all may judge.
At thy return my blushing was not small,
My rambling brat (in print) should mother call;
I cast thee by as one unfit for light,
Thy visage was so irksome in my sight;   10
Yet being mine own, at length affection would
Thy blemishes amend, if so I could:
I washed thy face, but more defects I saw,
And rubbing off a spot, still made a flaw.
I stretched thy joints to make thee even feet,   15

Yet still thou run'st more hobbling than is meet;
In better dress to trim thee was my mind,
But nought save homespun cloth in the house I find.
In this array, 'mongst vulgars may'st thou roam;
In critics' hands beware thou dost not come;   20
And take thy way where yet thou are not known.
If for thy Father asked, say thou had'st none;
And for thy Mother, she alas is poor,
Which caused her thus to send thee out of door.

    The extended metaphor likening her book to a child came naturally to
Bradstreet and allowed her to regard her work both critically and affection-
ately. Her conception of the book as her child creates just the right tone of
amusement, self-deprecation, and concern.
    The controlling metaphor in the following poem is identified by the title.
The game of chess these two players are engaged in is simultaneously literal
and metaphoric.

ROSARIO CASTELLANOS (1925-1974)

Chess   1988

TRANSLATED BY MAUREEN AHERN

Because we were friends and sometimes loved each other,
perhaps to add one more tie
to the many that already bound us,
we decided to play games of the mind.

We set up a board between us;   5
equally divided into pieces, values,
and possible moves.
We learned the rules, we swore to respect them,
and the match began.

We've been sitting here for centuries, meditating   10
ferociously
how to deal the one last blow that will finally
annihilate the other one forever.

Considerations for Critical Thinking and Writing

1. Why do the players decide to play chess? What is the effect of the game on their
   relationship?
2. Why is chess a particularly resonant controlling metaphor? Explain why chess is
   more evocative than, say, cards or checkers.
3. How does the poem's diction suggest tensions between the two players that go
   beyond a literal game of chess? Which lines are especially suggestive to you?
4. Do you think the players are men, women, or a man and a woman? Explain your
   response. How does the sex of the players affect your reading of the poem?

OTHER FIGURES

Perhaps the humblest figure of speech — if not one of the most familiar — is the pun. A *pun* is a play on words that relies on a word having more than one meaning or sounding like another word. For example, "A fad is in one era and out the other" is the sort of pun that produces obligatory groans. But most of us find pleasant and interesting surprises in puns. Here's one that has a slight edge to its humor.

EDMUND CONTI (b. 1929)
Pragmatist

1985

Apocalypse soon
Coming our way
Ground zero at noon
Halve a nice day.

Grimly practical under the circumstances, the pragmatist divides the familiar cheerful cliché by half. As simple as this poem is, its tone is mixed because it makes us laugh and wince at the same time.

Puns can be used to achieve serious effects as well as humorous ones. Although we may have learned to underrate puns as figures of speech, it is a mistake to underestimate their power and the frequency with which they appear in poetry. A close examination, for example, of Henry Reed's "Naming of Parts" (p. 147), Robert Frost's "Design" (p. 318), or almost any lengthy passage from a Shakespeare play will confirm the value of puns.

Synecdoche is a figure of speech in which part of something is used to signify the whole: a neighbor is a "wagging tongue" (a gossip); a criminal is placed "behind bars" (in prison). Less typically, synecdoche refers to the whole used to signify the part: "Germany invaded Poland"; "Princeton won the fencing match." Clearly, certain individuals participated in these activities, not all of Germany or Princeton. Another related figure of speech is *metonymy,* in which something closely associated with a subject is substituted for it: "She preferred the silver screen [motion pictures] to reading." "At precisely ten o'clock the paper shufflers [office workers] stopped for coffee."

Synecdoche and metonymy may overlap and are therefore sometimes difficult to distinguish. Consider this description of a disapproving minister entering a noisy tavern: "As those pursed lips came through the swinging door, the atmosphere was suddenly soured." The pursed lips signal the presence of the minister and are therefore a synecdoche, but they additionally suggest an inhibiting sense of sin and guilt that makes the bar patrons feel uncomfortable. Hence, the pursed lips are also a metonymy, since they are in this context so closely connected with religion. Although the distinction between synecdoche and metonymy can be useful, when a figure of speech overlaps categories, it is usually labeled a metonymy.

Knowing the precise term for a figure of speech is, finally, less important than responding to its use in a poem. Consider how metonymy and synecdoche convey the tone and meaning of the following poem.

DYLAN THOMAS (1914-1953)
The Hand That Signed the Paper   1936

The hand that signed the paper felled a city;
Five sovereign fingers taxed the breath,
Doubled the globe of dead and halved a country;
These five kings did a king to death.

The mighty hand leads to a sloping shoulder,   5
The finger joints are cramped with chalk;
A goose's quill has put an end to murder
That put an end to talk.

The hand that signed the treaty bred a fever,
And famine grew, and locusts came;   10
Great is the hand that holds dominion over
Man by a scribbled name.

The five kings count the dead but do not soften
The crusted wound nor stroke the brow;
A hand rules pity as a hand rules heaven;   15
Hands have no tears to flow.

The "hand" in this poem is a synecdoche for a powerful ruler, because it is a part of someone used to signify the entire person. The "goose's quill" is a metonymy that also refers to the power associated with the ruler's hand. By using these figures of speech, Thomas depersonalizes and ultimately dehumanizes the ruler. The final synecdoche tells us that "Hands have no tears to flow." It makes us see the political power behind the hand as remote and inhuman. How is the meaning of the poem enlarged when the speaker says, "A hand rules pity as a hand rules heaven"?

One of the ways writers energize the abstractions, ideas, objects, and animals that constitute their created worlds is through ***personification,*** the attribution of human characteristics to nonhuman things: temptation pursues the innocent; trees scream in the raging wind; mice conspire in the cupboard. We are not explicitly told that these things are people; instead, we are invited to see that they behave like people. Perhaps it is human vanity that makes personification a frequently used figure of speech. Whatever the reason, personification, a form of metaphor that connects the nonhuman with the human, makes the world understandable in human terms. Consider this concise example from William Blake's *The Marriage of Heaven and Hell,* a long poem that takes delight in attacking conventional morality: "Prudence is a rich ugly old maid courted by Incapacity." By personifying prudence, Blake transforms what is usually considered a virtue into a comic figure hardly worth emulating.

Often related to personification is another rhetorical figure called *apostrophe*, an address either to someone who is absent and therefore cannot hear the speaker or to something nonhuman that cannot comprehend. Apostrophe provides an opportunity for the speaker of a poem to think aloud, and often the thoughts expressed are in a formal tone. John Keats, for example, begins "Ode on a Grecian Urn" (p. 69) this way: "Thou still unravished bride of quietness." Apostrophe is frequently accompanied by intense emotion that is signaled by phrasing such as "O Life." In the right hands — such as Keats's — apostrophe can provide an intense and immediate voice in a poem, but when it is overdone or extravagant it can be ludicrous. Modern poets are more wary of apostrophe than their predecessors, because apostrophizing strikes many self-conscious twentieth-century sensibilities as too theatrical. Thus modern poets tend to avoid exaggerated situations in favor of less charged though equally meditative moments, as in this next poem, with its amusing, half-serious cosmic twist.

JANICE TOWNLEY MOORE (b. 1939)
To a Wasp

1984

You must have chortled
finding that tiny hole
in the kitchen screen. Right
into my cheese cake batter
you dived,   5
no chance to swim ashore,
no saving spoon,
the mixer whirring
your legs, wings, stinger,
churning you into such
delicious death.   10
Never mind the bright April day.
Did you not see
rising out of cumulus clouds
That fist aimed at both of us?   15

Moore's apostrophe "To a Wasp" is based on the simplest of domestic circumstances; there is almost nothing theatrical or exaggerated in the poem's tone until "That fist" in the last line, when exaggeration takes center stage. As a figure of speech exaggeration is known as *overstatement* or *hyperbole* and adds emphasis without intending to be literally true: "The teenage boy ate everything in the house." Notice how the speaker of Marvell's "To His Coy Mistress" (p. 57) exaggerates his devotion in the following overstatement.

An hundred years should go to praise
Thine eyes and on thy forehead gaze,
Two hundred to adore each breast,
But thirty thousand to the rest:

That comes to 30,500 years. What is expressed here is heightened emotion, not deception.

The speaker also uses the opposite figure of speech, _understatement,_
which says less than is intended. In the next section he sums up why he cannot take 30,500 years to express his love.

The grave's a fine and private place,
But none, I think, do there embrace.

The speaker is correct, of course, but by deliberately understating — saying "I think" when he is actually certain — he makes his point, that death will
overtake their love, all the more emphatic. Another powerful example of
understatement appears in the final line of Randall Jarrell's "The Death of the
Ball Turret Gunner" (p. 48), when the disembodied voice of the machine-
gunner describes his death in a bomber: "When I died they washed me out
of the turret with a hose."

Paradox is a statement that initially appears to be self-contradictory but
that, on closer inspection, turns out to make sense: "The pen is mightier than
the sword." In a fencing match, anyone would prefer the sword, but if the goal
is to win the hearts and minds of people, the art of persuasion can be more
compelling than swordplay. To resolve the paradox, it is necessary to discover
the sense that underlies the statement. If we see that "pen" and "sword" are
used as metonymies for writing and violence, then the paradox rings true. _Oxy-
moron_ is a condensed form of paradox in which two contradictory words are
used together. Combinations such as "sweet sorrow," "silent scream," "sad joy,"
and "cold fire" indicate the kinds of startling effects that oxymorons can produce. Paradox is useful in poetry because it arrests a reader's attention by its
seemingly stubborn refusal to make sense, and once a reader has penetrated
the paradox, it is difficult to resist a perception so well earned. Good paradoxes
are knotty pleasures. Here is a simple but effective one.

J. PATRICK LEWIS (b. 1942)
The Unkindest Cut   1993

Knives can harm you, heaven forbid;
Axes may disarm you, kid;
Guillotines are painful, but
There's nothing like a paper cut!

This quatrain is a humorous version of "the pen is mightier than the
sword." The wounds escalate to the paper cut, which paradoxically is more

damaging than even the broad blade of a guillotine. "The unkindest cut" of all (an allusion to Shakespeare's *Julius Caesar,* III.ii.188) is produced by chilling words on a page rather than cold steel, but it is more painfully fatal nonetheless.

The following poems are rich in figurative language. As you read and study them, notice how their figures of speech vivify situations, clarify ideas, intensify emotions, and engage your imagination. Although the terms for the various figures discussed in this chapter are useful for labeling the particular devices used in poetry, they should not be allowed to get in the way of your response to a poem. Don't worry about rounding up examples of figurative language. First relax and let the figures work their effects on you. Use the terms as a means of taking you further into poetry, and they will serve your reading well.

POEMS FOR FURTHER STUDY

MARGARET ATWOOD (b. 1939)
February

1995

Winter. Time to eat fat
and watch hockey. In the pewter mornings, the cat,
a black fur sausage with yellow
Houdini eyes, jumps up on the bed and tries
to get onto my head. It's his   5
way of telling whether or not I'm dead.
If I'm not, he wants to be scratched; if I am
he'll think of something. He settles
on my chest, breathing his breath
of burped-up meat and musty sofas,   10
purring like a washboard. Some other tomcat,
not yet a capon, has been spraying our front door,
declaring war. It's all about sex and territory,
which are what will finish us off
in the long run. Some cat owners around here   15
should snip a few testicles. If we wise
hominids were sensible, we'd do that too,
or eat our young, like sharks.
But it's love that does us in. Over and over
again, *He shoots, he scores!* and famine   20
crouches in the bedsheets, ambushing the pulsing
eiderdown,° and the windchill factor hits
thirty below, and pollution pours
out of our chimneys to keep us warm.
February, month of despair,   25
with a skewered heart in the centre.
I think dire thoughts, and lust for French fries

° comforter

116 Figures of Speech

with a splash of vinegar.
Cat, enough of your greedy whining
and your small pink bumhole.   30
Off my face! You're the life principle,
more or less, so get going
on a little optimism around here.
Get rid of death. Celebrate increase. Make it be spring.

Considerations for Critical Thinking and Writing

1. How do your own associations with February compare with the speaker's?
2. Explain how the poem is organized around an extended metaphor that defines winter as a "Time to eat fat / and watch hockey."
3. Explain the paradox in "it's love that does us in" (line 19).
4. What theme(s) do you find in the poem? How is the cat central to them?

SOPHIE CABOT BLACK (b. 1958)
August   1994

A doe puts her nose to sky: stark hub
Around which the second cut of hay spins
Into one direction. A man rests
Against the fence, waiting

For the last minute to turn home. By heart   5
He knows the tilt and decline of each field,
His own faulty predictions. The well
Hoards its shadow while a raw haze gluts

With harvest, with guessing rains, presses
At the temple and wrist. The pastures, tired   10
Of abiding, begin to burn. Gold takes over,
Loose, unguarded. Cows stay deep

In the chafe of underbush; reckless leaves shawl
The edges, unaware of the sap that will send them down.

Considerations for Critical Thinking and Writing

1. What tone is created by the poem's images of August?
2. How does Black's use of personification contribute to the tone?
3. Discuss what you think is the poem's theme.

Connection to Another Selection

1. Discuss the moods created in "August" and Atwood's "February." To what extent do you think each poem is successful in capturing the essence of the title's subject?

ERNEST SLYMAN (b. 1946)
Lightning Bugs

1988

In my backyard,
They burn peepholes in the night
And take snapshots of my house.

Considerations for Critical Thinking and Writing

1. Explain why the title is essential to this poem.
2. What makes the description of the lightning bugs effective? How do the second and third lines complement each other?
3. As Slyman has done, take a simple, common fact of nature and make it vivid by using a figure of speech to describe it.

SYLVIA PLATH (1932–1963)
Mirror

1963

I am silver and exact. I have no preconceptions.
Whatever I see I swallow immediately
Just as it is, unmisted by love or dislike.
I am not cruel, only truthful —
The eye of a little god, four-cornered.   5
Most of the time I meditate on the opposite wall.
It is pink, with speckles. I have looked at it so long
I think it is a part of my heart. But it flickers.
Faces and darkness separate us over and over.

Now I am a lake. A woman bends over me,   10
Searching my reaches for what she really is.
Then she turns to those liars, the candles or the moon.
I see her back, and reflect it faithfully.
She rewards me with tears and an agitation of hands.
I am important to her. She comes and goes.   15
Each morning it is her face that replaces the darkness.
In me she has drowned a young girl, and in me an old woman
Rises toward her day after day, like a terrible fish.

Considerations for Critical Thinking and Writing

1. What is the effect of the personification in this poem? How would our view of the aging woman be different if she, rather than the mirror, told her story?
2. What is the mythical allusion in "Now I am a lake" (line 10)?
3. In what sense can "candles or the moon" be regarded as "liars"? Explain this metaphor.
4. Discuss the effectiveness of the simile in the final line of the poem.

WILLIAM WORDSWORTH (1770–1850)

London, 1802

apostrophe 1802

Milton!° thou should'st be living at this hour:
England hath need of thee: she is a fen
Of stagnant waters: altar, sword, and pen, → *metonymy — associated w/ religion, war, writing*
Fireside, the heroic wealth of hall and bower,
Have forfeited their ancient English dower *relationship metaphor, religion bad*
Of inward happiness. We are selfish men;
Oh! raise us up, return to us again;
And give us manners, virtue, freedom, power.
Thy soul was like a star, and dwelt apart: → *simile*
Thou hadst a voice whose sound was like the sea: → *simile*   10
Pure as the naked heavens, majestic, free, → *metaphor*
So didst thou travel on life's common way,
In cheerful godliness; and yet thy heart } *personification*
The lowliest duties on herself did lay.

---

1 *Milton:* John Milton (1608–1674), poet, famous especially for his religious epic *Paradise Lost* and his defense of political freedom.

Considerations for Critical Thinking and Writing

1. Explain the metonymies in lines 3–6 of this poem. What is the speaker's assessment of England?
2. How would the effect of the poem be different if it were in the form of an address to Wordsworth's contemporaries rather than an apostrophe to Milton? What qualities does Wordsworth attribute to Milton by the use of figurative language?

JIM STEVENS (b. 1922)

Schizophrenia

1992

It was the house that suffered most.

It had begun with slamming doors, angry feet scuffing the carpets,
dishes slammed onto the table,
greasy stains spreading on the cloth.

Certain doors were locked at night,   5
feet stood for hours outside them,
dishes were left unwashed, the cloth
disappeared under a hardened crust.

The house came to miss the shouting voices,
the threats, the half-apologies, noisy   10
reconciliations, the sobbing that followed.

Then lines were drawn, borders established,
some rooms declared their loyalties,
keeping to themselves, keeping out the other.
The house divided against itself.   15

Seeing cracking paint, broken windows,
the front door banging in the wind,
the roof tiles flying off, one by one,
the neighbors said it was a madhouse.

It was the house that suffered most.   20

Considerations for Critical Thinking and Writing

1. What is the effect of the personification in this poem?
2. How are the people who live in the house characterized? What does their behavior reveal about them? How does the house respond to them?
3. Comment on the title. If the title were missing, what, if anything, would be missing from the poem? Explain your answer.

WALT WHITMAN (1819–1892)
A Noiseless Patient Spider   1868

A noiseless patient spider,
I mark'd where on a little promontory it stood isolated,
Mark'd how to explore the vacant vast surrounding,
It launch'd forth filament, filament, filament, out of itself,
Ever unreeling them, ever tirelessly speeding them.   5

And you O my soul where you stand,
Surrounded, detached, in measureless oceans of space,
Ceaselessly musing, venturing, throwing, seeking the spheres to connect them,
Till the bridge you will need be form'd, till the ductile anchor hold,
Till the gossamer thread you fling catch somewhere, O my soul.   10

Considerations for Critical Thinking and Writing

1. Spiders are not usually regarded as pleasant creatures. Why does the speaker in this poem liken his soul to one? What similarities are there in the poem between spider and soul? Are there any significant differences?
2. How do the images of space relate to the connections made between the speaker's soul and the spider?

Connection to Another Selection

1. Read the early version of "A Noiseless Patient Spider" printed below. Which version is more unified by its metaphors? Which do you prefer? Why? Write an essay about the change of focus from the early version to the final one.

WALT WHITMAN (1819–1892)
The Soul, reaching, throwing out for love   c. 1862

The Soul, reaching, throwing out for love,
As the spider, from some little promontory, throwing out filament after filament,
    tirelessly out of itself, that one at least may catch and form a link, a bridge,
    a connection
O I saw one passing along, saying hardly a word — yet full of love I detected
    him, by certain signs
O eyes wishfully turning! O silent eyes!
For then I thought of you o'er the world,
O latent oceans, fathomless oceans of love!
O waiting oceans of love! yearning and fervid! and of you sweet souls perhaps
    in the future, delicious and long:
But Death, unknown on the earth — ungiven, dark here, unspoken, never
    born:
You fathomless latent souls of love — you pent and unknown oceans of
    love!

JOHN DONNE (1572–1631)
A Valediction: Forbidding Mourning   1611

As virtuous men pass mildly away,
    And whisper to their souls to go,
While some of their sad friends do say,
    The breath goes now, and some say, no:

So let us melt, and make no noise,   5
    No tear-floods, nor sigh-tempests move;
'Twere profanation of our joys
    To tell the laity our love.

Moving of th' earth° brings harms and fears,   *earthquakes*
    Men reckon what it did and meant,   10
But trepidation of the spheres,°
    Though greater far, is innocent.

Dull sublunary° lovers' love
    (Whose soul is sense) cannot admit
Absence, because it doth remove   15
    Those things which elemented° it.   *composed*

But we by a love so much refined,
    That ourselves know not what it is,

---

11 *trepidation of the spheres:* According to Ptolemaic astronomy, the planets sometimes moved violently, like earthquakes, but these movements were not felt by people on earth.   13 *sublunary:* Under the moon; hence mortal and subject to change.

Inter-assured of the mind,
　　Care less, eyes, lips, and hands to miss.　　　　　　　　　　　20

Our two souls therefore, which are one,
　　Though I must go, endure not yet
A breach, but an expansion,
　　Like gold to airy thinness beat.

If they be two, they are two so　　　　　　　　　　　　　　　25
　　As stiff twin compasses are two;
Thy soul the fixed foot, makes no show
　　To move, but doth, if th' other do.

And though it in the center sit,
　　Yet when the other far doth roam,　　　　　　　　　　　30
It leans, and hearkens after it,
　　And grows erect, as that comes home.

Such wilt thou be to me, who must
　　Like th' other foot, obliquely run;
Thy firmness makes my circle just,°　　　　　　　　　　　35
　　And makes me end, where I begun.

35 *circle just:* The circle is a traditional symbol of perfection.

Considerations for Critical Thinking and Writing

1. A valediction is a farewell. Donne wrote this poem for his wife before leaving on a trip to France. What kind of "mourning" is the speaker forbidding?
2. Explain how the simile in lines 1–4 is related to the couple in lines 5–8. Who is described as dying?
3. How does the speaker contrast the couple's love to "sublunary lovers' love" (line 13)?
4. Explain the similes in lines 24 and 25–36.

LINDA PASTAN (b. 1932)
Marks　　　　　　　　　　　　　　　　　　　　　　1978

My husband gives me an A
for last night's supper,
an incomplete for my ironing,
a B plus in bed.
My son says I am average,　　　　　　　　　　　　　　5
an average mother, but if
I put my mind to it
I could improve.
My daughter believes
in Pass/Fail and tells me　　　　　　　　　　　　　　10
I pass. Wait 'til they learn
I'm dropping out.

Considerations for Critical Thinking and Writing

1. Explain the appropriateness of the controlling metaphor in this poem. How does it reveal the woman's relationship to her family?
2. Discuss the meaning of the title.
3. How does the last line serve as both the climax of the woman's story and the controlling metaphor of the poem?

"St. Louis Blues"

LUCILLE CLIFTON (b. 1936)
come home from the movies   1974

come home from the movies,
black girls and boys,
the picture be over and the screen
be cold as our neighborhood.
come home from the show,   5
don't be the show.
take off some flowers and plant them,
pick us some papers and read them,
stop making some babies and raise them.
come home from the movies   10
black girls and boys,
show our fathers how to walk like men,
they already know how to dance.

Considerations for Critical Thinking and Writing

1. What are the "movies" a metaphor for?
2. What advice does the speaker urge upon "black girls and boys"?
3. Explain the final two lines. Why do they come last?

ELAINE MAGARRELL (b. 1928)
The Joy of Cooking   1988

I have prepared my sister's tongue,
scrubbed and skinned it,
trimmed the roots, small bones, and gristle.
Carved through the hump it slices thin and neat.
Best with horseradish   5
and economical — it probably will grow back.
Next time perhaps a creole sauce
or mold of aspic?

I will have my brother's heart,
which is firm and rather dry,   10

slow cooked. It resembles muscle
more than organ meat
and needs an apple-onion stuffing
to make it interesting at all.
Although beef heart serves six   15
my brother's heart barely feeds two.
I could also have it braised
and served in sour sauce.

Considerations for Critical Thinking and Writing

1. How are the tongue and heart used to characterize the sister and brother in this poem?
2. Describe the speaker's tone. What effect does the title have on your determining the tone?

Connection to Another Selection

1. Write an essay that explains how cooking becomes a way of talking about something else in this poem and in Croft's "Home-Baked Bread" (p. 100).

STEPHEN PERRY (b. 1947)
Blue Spruce   1991

My grandfather worked in a barbershop
smelling of lotions he'd slap on your face,
hair and talc. The black razor strop

hung like the penis of an ox. He'd draw
the sharp blade in quick strokes over   5
the smooth-rough hide, and then carefully

over your face. The tiny hairs would gather
on the blade, a congregation singing
under blue spruce in winter,

a bandstand in the center of town   10
bright with instruments, alto sax, tenor
sax, tuba or sousaphone — the bright

oompah-pahs shaving the town somehow,
a bright cloth shaking the air
into flakes of silvering hair   15

floating down past the houses, the horses
pulling carriages past the town fountain,
which had frozen into a coiffure

of curly glass. My grandfather had an affair
with the girl who did their nails   20
bright pink, bright red, never blue,

perhaps as the horses clip-clopped on ice
outside his shop, his kisses
smelling of lather and new skin —

when she grew too big and round   25
with his child, with his oompah love,
with his bandstand love, with his brassy love,

and the town dropped its grace notes
of gossip and whispered hiss,
he bundled her out of town   30

with the savings which should have gone
to my mom. But how could you hate him?
My mother did, my father did,

and my grandmother, who bore his neglect.
When she was covered in sheets   35
at her last death,

he flirted with the nurses, bright
as winter birds in spruces
above a bandstand —

I'll always remember him in snow, a deep lather   40
of laughter, the picture
where he took me from my mother

and raised me high, a baby, into the bell
of his sousaphone, as if I were a note
he'd play into light —   45

Considerations for Critical Thinking and Writing

1. What are the controlling metaphors in "Blue Spruce"? How do they help to characterize the grandfather?
2. The grandfather is presented as an outrageous figure, "but how could you hate
   him" (line 32)? Do you think the speaker is successful in preventing the reader
   from hating his grandfather? Explain.
3. Write a paragraph detailing what you think the speaker means by his grandfather's "oompah love" (line 26).

ROBIN BECKER (b. 1951)
Shopping   1996

If things don't work out
I'll buy the belt
with the fashionable silver buckle
we saw on Canyon Road.
If we can't make peace   5
I'll order the leather duster and swagger
across the plaza in Santa Fe,
cross-dressing for the girls.

If you leave I'll go back
for the Navaho blanket   10
and the pawn ring, bargain
with the old woman who will know
I intend to buy.
If you pack your things,
if you undress in the bathroom,   15
if you see me for what I am,
I'll invest in the folk art mirror
with the leaping rabbits
on either side, I'll spring
for the Anasazi pot with the hole   20
in the bottom where the spirit
of the potter is said to escape
after her death.

If you say you never intended
to share your life, I'll haunt the museum   25
shops and flea markets,
I'll don the Spanish riding hat,
the buckskin gloves with fringe at the wrists,
I'll step into the cowboy boots
tanned crimson and designed to make   30
any woman feel like she owns the street.
If you never touch me again,
I'll do what my mother did
after she buried my sister:
outfitted herself in an elegant suit   35
for the rest of her life.

Considerations for Critical Thinking and Writing

1. Explain whether or not you think shopping is an extended metaphor in this poem.
2. What purpose does the speaker's imagined shopping serve for her?
3. Describe the shift in tone in lines 32–36.

Connection to Another Selection

1. In an essay examine the relationship between love and death in "Shopping" and Emily Dickinson's "The Bustle in a House" (p. 277).

PERSPECTIVE

JOHN R. SEARLE (b. 1932)
Figuring Out Metaphors   1979

If you hear somebody say, "Sally is a block of ice," or, "Sam is a pig," you are likely to assume that the speaker does not mean what he says literally, but that he is speaking metaphorically. Furthermore, you are not likely to have very much trouble figuring out what he means. If he says, "Sally is a prime number between 17 and 23," or "Bill is a barn door," you might still assume he is speaking metaphorically, but it is much harder to figure out what he means. The existence of such utterances — utterances in which the speaker means metaphorically something different from what the sentence means literally — poses a series of questions for any theory of language and communication: What is metaphor, and how does it differ from both literal and other forms of figurative utterances? Why do we use expressions metaphorically instead of saying exactly and literally what we mean? How do metaphorical utterances work, that is, how is it possible for speakers to communicate to hearers when speaking metaphorically inasmuch as they do not say what they mean? And why do some metaphors work and others do not?

From *Expression and Meaning*

Considerations for Critical Thinking and Writing

1. Searle poses a series of important questions. Write an essay that explores one of these questions, basing your discussion on the poems in this chapter.

2. Try writing a brief poem that provides a context for the line "Sally is a prime number between 17 and 23" or the line "Bill is a barn door." Your task is to create a context so that either one of these metaphoric statements is as readily understandable as "Sally is a block of ice" or "Sam is a pig." Share your poem with your classmates and explain how the line generated the poem you built around it.

5. Symbol, Allegory, and Irony

SYMBOL

A *symbol* is something that represents something else. An object, person, place, event, or action can suggest more than its literal meaning. A handshake between two world leaders might be simply a greeting, but if it is done ceremoniously before cameras, it could be a symbolic gesture signifying unity, issues resolved, and joint policies that will be followed. We live surrounded by symbols. When an eighty-thousand-dollar Mercedes-Benz comes roaring by in the fast lane, we get a quick glimpse of not only an expensive car but an entire life-style that suggests opulence, broad lawns, executive offices, and power. One of the reasons some buyers are willing to spend roughly the cost of five Chevrolets for a single Mercedes-Benz is that they are aware of the car's symbolic value. A symbol is a vehicle for two things at once: it functions as itself and it implies meanings beyond itself.

The meanings suggested by a symbol are determined by the context in which they appear. The Mercedes could symbolize very different things depending on where it was parked. Would an American political candidate be likely to appear in a Detroit blue-collar neighborhood with such a car? Probably not. Although a candidate might be able to afford the car, it would be an inappropriate symbol for someone seeking votes from all the people. As a symbol, the German-built Mercedes would backfire if voters perceived it as representing an entity partially responsible for layoffs of automobile workers or, worse, as a sign of decadence and corruption. Similarly, a huge portrait of Mao Tse-tung conveys different meanings to residents of Beijing than it would to farmers in Prairie Center, Illinois. Because symbols depend on contexts for their meaning, literary artists provide those contexts so that the reader has enough information to determine the probable range of meanings suggested by a symbol.

In the following poem the speaker describes walking at night. How is the night used symbolically?

ROBERT FROST (1874-1963)

Acquainted with the Night   1928

I have been one acquainted with the night.
I have walked out in rain — and back in rain.
I have outwalked the furthest city light.

I have looked down the saddest city lane.
I have passed by the watchman on his beat   5
And dropped my eyes, unwilling to explain.

I have stood still and stopped the sound of feet
When far away an interrupted cry
Came over houses from another street,

But not to call me back or say good-by;   10
And further still at an unearthly height
One luminary clock against the sky

Proclaimed the time was neither wrong nor right.
I have been one acquainted with the night.

In approaching this or any poem, you should read for literal meanings
first and then allow the elements of the poem to invite you to symbolic readings, if they are appropriate. Here the somber tone suggests that the lines
have symbolic meaning too. The flat matter-of-factness created by the repetition of "I have" (lines 1–5, 7, 14) understates the symbolic subject matter of
the poem, which is, finally, more about the "night" located in the speaker's
mind or soul than it is about walking away from a city and back again. The
speaker is "acquainted with the night." The importance of this phrase is
emphasized by Frost's title and by the fact that he begins and ends the poem
with it. Poets frequently use this kind of repetition to alert readers to details
that carry more than literal meanings.

The speaker in this poem has personal knowledge of the night but does
not indicate specifically what the night means. To arrive at the potential
meanings of the night in this context, it is necessary to look closely at its connotations, along with the images provided in the poem. The connotative
meanings of night suggest, for example, darkness, death, and grief. By drawing upon these connotations, Frost uses a ***conventional symbol,*** something
that is recognized by many people to represent certain ideas. Roses conven-
tionally symbolize love or beauty; laurels, fame; spring, growth; the moon,
romance. Poets often use conventional symbols to convey tone and meaning.

Frost uses the night as a conventional symbol, but he also develops it
into a ***literary*** or ***contextual symbol,*** which goes beyond traditional, public
meanings. A literary symbol cannot be summarized in a word or two. It tends
to be as elusive as experience itself. The night cannot be reduced to or
equated with darkness or death or grief, but it evokes those associations and
more. Frost took what perhaps initially appears to be an overworked, con-

ventional symbol and prevented it from becoming a cliché by deepening and extending its meaning.

The images in "Acquainted with the Night" lead to the poem's symbolic meaning. Unwilling, and perhaps unable, to explain explicitly to the watchman (and to the reader) what the night means, the speaker nevertheless conveys feelings about it. The brief images of darkness, rain, sad city lanes, the necessity for guards, the eerie sound of a distressing cry coming over rooftops, and the "luminary clock against the sky" proclaiming "the time was neither wrong nor right" all help to create a sense of anxiety in this tight-lipped speaker. Although we cannot know what unnamed personal experiences have acquainted the speaker with the night, the images suggest that whatever the night means, it is somehow associated with insomnia, loneliness, isolation, coldness, darkness, death, fear, and a sense of alienation from humanity and even time. Daylight — ordinary daytime thoughts and life itself — seems remote and unavailable in this poem. The night is literally the period from sunset to sunrise, but, more important, it is an internal state of being felt by the speaker and revealed through the images.

Frost used symbols rather than an expository essay that would explain the conditions that cause these feelings, because most readers can provide their own list of sorrows and terrors that evoke similar emotions. Through symbol, the speaker's experience is compressed and simultaneously expanded by the personal darkness that each reader brings to the poem. The suggestive nature of symbols makes them valuable for poets and evocative for readers.

ALLEGORY

Unlike expansive, suggestive symbols, *allegory* is a narration or description usually restricted to a single meaning because its events, actions, characters, settings, and objects represent specific abstractions or ideas. Although the elements in an allegory may be interesting in themselves, the emphasis tends to be on what they ultimately mean. Characters may be given names such as Hope, Pride, Youth, and Charity; they have few, if any, personal qualities beyond their abstract meanings. These personifications are a form of extended metaphor, but their meanings are severely restricted. They are not symbols because, for instance, the meaning of a character named Charity is precisely that virtue.

There is little or no room for broad speculation and exploration in allegories. If Frost had written "Acquainted with the Night" as an allegory, he might have named his speaker Loneliness and had him leave the City of Despair to walk the Streets of Emptiness, where Crime, Poverty, Fear, and other characters would define the nature of city life. The literal elements in an allegory tend to be deemphasized in favor of the message. Symbols, however, function both literally and symbolically, so that "Acquainted with the Night" is about both a walk and a sense that something is terribly wrong.

Allegory especially lends itself to ***didactic poetry***, which is designed to teach an ethical, moral, or religious lesson. Many stories, poems, and plays are concerned with values, but didactic literature is specifically created to convey a message. "Acquainted with the Night" does not impart advice or offer guidance. If the poem argued that city life is self-destructive or sinful, it would be didactic; instead, it is a lyric poem that expresses the emotions and thoughts of a single speaker.

Although allegory is often enlisted in didactic causes because it can so readily communicate abstract ideas through physical representations, not all allegories teach a lesson. Here is a poem describing a haunted palace while also establishing a consistent pattern that reveals another meaning.

EDGAR ALLAN POE (1809–1849)
The Haunted Palace   1839

I
In the greenest of our valleys,
   By good angels tenanted,
Once a fair and stately palace —
   Radiant palace — reared its head.
In the monarch Thought's dominion —   5
   It stood there!
Never seraph spread a pinion
   Over fabric half so fair.

II
Banners yellow, glorious, golden,
   On its roof did float and flow;   10
(This — all this — was in the olden
   Time long ago)
And every gentle air that dallied,
   In that sweet day,
Along the ramparts plumed and pallid,   15
   A wingèd odor went away.

III
Wanderers in that happy valley
   Through two luminous windows saw
Spirits moving musically
   To a lute's well-tunèd law,   20
Round about a throne, where sitting
   (Porphyrogene!)°   *born to purple, royal*
In state his glory well befitting,
   The ruler of the realm was seen.

IV
And all with pearl and ruby glowing   25
   Was the fair palace door,

Through which came flowing, flowing, flowing
   And sparkling evermore,
A troop of Echoes whose sweet duty
   Was but to sing,   30
In voices of surpassing beauty,
   The wit and wisdom of their king.

V
But evil things, in robes of sorrow,
   Assailed the monarch's high estate;
(Ah, let us mourn, for never morrow   35
   Shall dawn upon him, desolate!)
And, round about his home, the glory
   That blushed and bloomed
Is but a dim-remembered story
   Of the old time entombed.   40

VI
And travelers now within that valley,
   Through the red-litten windows see
Vast forms that move fantastically
   To a discordant melody;
While, like a rapid ghastly river,   45
   Through the pale door,
A hideous throng rush out forever,
   And laugh — but smile no more.

On one level this poem describes how a once happy palace is desolated by "evil things." If the reader pays close attention to the diction, however, an allegorical meaning becomes apparent on a second reading. A systematic pattern develops in the choice of words used to describe the palace, so that it comes to stand for a human mind. The palace, banners, windows, door, echoes, and throng are equated with a person's head, hair, eyes, mouth, voice, and laughter. That mind, once harmoniously ordered, is overthrown by evil, haunting thoughts that lead to the mad laughter in the poem's final lines. Once the general pattern is seen, the rest of the details fall neatly into place to strengthen the parallels between the surface description of a palace and the allegorical representation of a disordered mind.

Modern writers generally prefer symbol over allegory because they tend to be more interested in opening up the potential meanings of an experience instead of transforming it into a closed pattern of meaning. Perhaps the major difference is that while allegory may delight a reader's imagination, symbol challenges and enriches it.

IRONY

Another important resource writers use to take readers beyond literal meanings is *irony,* a technique that reveals a discrepancy between what appears to be and what is actually true. Here is a classic example in which appearances give way to the underlying reality.

EDWIN ARLINGTON ROBINSON (1869–1935)
Richard Cory 1897

Whenever Richard Cory went down town,
We people on the pavement looked at him:
He was a gentleman from sole to crown,
Clean favored, and imperially slim.

And he was always quietly arrayed, 5
And he was always human when he talked;
But still he fluttered pulses when he said,
"Good-morning," and he glittered when he walked.

And he was rich — yes, richer than a king —
And admirably schooled in every grace: 10
In fine, we thought that he was everything
To make us wish that we were in his place.

So on we worked, and waited for the light,
And went without the meat, and cursed the bread;
And Richard Cory, one calm summer night, 15
Went home and put a bullet through his head.

Richard Cory seems to have it all. Those less fortunate, the "people on the pavement," regard him as well bred, handsome, tasteful, and richly endowed with both money and grace. Until the final line of the poem, the reader, like the speaker, is charmed by Cory's good fortune, so quietly expressed in his decent, easy manner. That final, shocking line, however, shatters the appearances of Cory's life and reveals him to have been a desperately unhappy man. While everyone else assumes that Cory represented "everything" to which they aspire, the reality is that he could escape his miserable life only as a suicide. This discrepancy between what appears to be true and what actually exists is known as ***situational irony:*** what happens is entirely different from what is expected. We are not told why Cory shoots himself; instead, the irony in the poem shocks us into the recognition that appearances do not always reflect realities.

Words are also sometimes intended to be taken at other than face value. ***Verbal irony*** is saying something different from what is meant. After reading "Richard Cory," to say "That rich gentleman sure was happy" is ironic. The tone of voice would indicate that just the opposite was meant; hence, verbal irony is usually easy to detect in spoken language. In literature, however, a reader can sometimes take literally what a writer intends ironically. The remedy for this kind of misreading is to pay close attention to the poem's context. There is no formula that can detect verbal irony, but contradictory actions and statements as well as the use of understatement and overstatement can often be signals that verbal irony is present.

Consider how verbal irony is used in this poem.

KENNETH FEARING (1902–1961)
AD
1938

Wanted: Men;
Millions of men are *wanted at once* in a big new field;
New, tremendous, thrilling, great.
If you've ever been a figure in the chamber of horrors,
If you've ever escaped from a psychiatric ward,   5
If you thrill at the thought of throwing poison into wells, have heavenly visions
    of people, by the thousands, dying in flames —

You are the very man we want
We mean business and our business is *you*
Wanted: A race of brand-new men.   10

Apply: Middle Europe;
No skill needed;
No ambition required; no brains wanted and no character allowed;

Take a permanent job in the coming profession
Wages: *Death.*   15

This poem was written as Nazi troops stormed across Europe at the start of World War II. The advertisement suggests on the surface that killing is just an ordinary job, but the speaker indicates through understatement that there is nothing ordinary about the "business" of this "*coming profession.*" Fearing uses verbal irony to indicate how casually and mindlessly people are prepared to accept the horrors of war.

Consider how the next poem, by Janice Mirikitani, a third-generation Japanese American, uses a similar ironic strategy in a different context.

JANICE MIRIKITANI (b. 1942)
Recipe
1987

Round Eyes

Ingredients: scissors, Scotch magic transparent tape,
             eyeliner — water based, black.
             Optional: false eyelashes.

Cleanse face thoroughly.   5

For best results, powder entire face, including eyelids.
    (lighter shades suited to total effect desired)

With scissors, cut magic tape ⅟₁₆″ wide, ¾″–½″ long —
depending on length of eyelid.

Stick firmly onto mid–upper eyelid area   10
    (looking down into handmirror facilitates finding
    adequate surface)

If using false eyelashes, affix first on lid, folding any
excess lid over the base of eyelash with glue.

Paint black eyeliner on tape and entire lid.   15

Do not cry.

Considerations for Critical Thinking and Writing

1. What is the effect of the very specific details of this recipe?
2. Why is "false eyelashes" a particularly resonant phrase in the context of this poem?
3. Discuss your response to the poem's final line.
4. Try writing your own "recipe" in poetic lines — one that makes a commentary concerning a social issue that you feel strongly about.

Connections to Other Selections

1. Why are the formulas for an advertisement and a recipe especially suited for Fearing's and Mirikitani's respective purposes? To what extent do the ironic strategies lead to a similar tone and theme?
2. Write an essay comparing the themes in "Recipe" to those in Fainlight's "Flower Feet" (p. 52).

Like "AD," "Recipe" is a *satire,* an example of the literary art of ridiculing a folly or vice in an effort to expose or correct it. The object of satire is usually some human frailty; people, institutions, ideas, and things are all fair game for satirists. Fearing satirizes the insanity of a world mobilizing itself for war: His irony reveals the speaker's knowledge that there is nothing *"New, tremendous, thrilling,* [or] *great"* about going off to kill and be killed. The implication of the poem is that no one should respond to advertisements for war. The poem serves as a satiric corrective to those who would troop off armed with unrealistic expectations; wage war and the wages consist of death.

Dramatic irony is used when a writer allows a reader to know more about a situation than a character does. This creates a discrepancy between what a character says or thinks and what the reader knows to be true. Dramatic irony is often used to reveal character. In the following poem the speaker delivers a public speech that ironically tells us more about him than it does about the patriotic holiday he is commemorating.

E. E. CUMMINGS (1894-1962)
next to of course god america i

1926

"next to of course god america i
love you land of the pilgrims' and so forth oh
say can you see by the dawn's early my
country 'tis of centuries come and go
and are no more what of it we should worry   5
in every language even deafanddumb
thy sons acclaim your glorious name by gorry
by jingo by gee by gosh by gum
why talk of beauty what could be more beaut-
iful than these heroic happy dead   10
who rushed like lions to the roaring slaughter
they did not stop to think they died instead
then shall the voice of liberty be mute?"

He spoke. And drank rapidly a glass of water

This verbal debauch of chauvinistic clichés (notice the run-on phrases and lines) reveals that the speaker's relationship to God and country is not, as he claims, one of love. His public address suggests a hearty mindlessness that leads to "roaring slaughter" rather than to reverence or patriotism. Cummings allows the reader to see through the speaker's words to their dangerous emptiness. What the speaker means and what Cummings means are entirely different. Like Fearing's "AD," this poem is a satire that invites the reader's laughter and contempt in order to deflate the benighted attitudes expressed in it.

When a writer uses God, destiny, or fate to dash the hopes and expectations of a character or humankind in general, it is called *cosmic irony*. In "The Convergence of the Twain" (p. 65), for example, Hardy describes how "The Immanent Will" brought together the *Titanic* and a deadly iceberg. Technology and pride are no match for "the Spinner of the Years." Here's a painfully terse version of cosmic irony.

STEPHEN CRANE (1871-1900)
A Man Said to the Universe

1899

A man said to the universe:
"Sir, I exist!"
"However," replied the universe,
"The fact has not created in me
A sense of obligation."

Unlike in "The Convergence of the Twain," there is the slightest bit of humor in Crane's poem, but the joke is on us.

Irony is an important technique that allows a writer to distinguish between appearances and realities. In situational irony a discrepancy exists between what we expect to happen and what actually happens; in verbal irony a discrepancy exists between what is said and what is meant; in dramatic irony a discrepancy exists between what a character believes and what the reader knows to be true; and in cosmic irony a discrepancy exists between what a character aspires to and what universal forces provide. With each form of irony, we are invited to move beyond surface appearances and sentimental assumptions to see the complexity of experience. Irony is often used in literature to reveal a writer's perspective on matters that previously seemed settled.

POEMS FOR FURTHER STUDY

JANE KENYON (1947-1995)
Surprise   1996

He suggests pancakes at the local diner,
followed by a walk in search of mayflowers,
while friends convene at the house
bearing casseroles and a cake, their cars
pulled close along the sandy shoulders   5
of the road, where tender ferns unfurl
in the ditches, and this year's budding leaves
push last year's spectral leaves from the tips
of the twigs of the ash trees. The gathering
itself is not what astounds her, but the casual   10
accomplishment with which he has lied.

Considerations for Critical Thinking and Writing

1. Why is it especially interesting that this poem is set in the spring?
2. Consider the connotative meaning of "ash trees" (line 9). Why are they particularly appropriate?
3. Why do you suppose Kenyon uses "astounds" rather than "surprises" in line 10? Use a dictionary to help you determine the possible reasons for this choice.
4. Discuss the irony in the poem.

Connections to Other Selections

1. Write an essay on the nature of the surprises in Kenyon's poem and in Hathaway's "Oh, Oh" (p. 13). Include in your discussion a comparison of the tone and irony in each poem.
2. Compare and contrast in an essay the irony associated with the birthday parties in "Surprise" and Sharon Olds's "Rite of Passage" (p. 238).

CONRAD HILBERRY (b. 1928)

The Frying Pan 1978

My mark is my confusion.
If I believe it, I am
another long-necked girl
with the same face.
I am emptiness reflected 5
in a looking glass, a head
kept by a collar and leash,
a round belly with something
knocking to get in.

But cross the handle 10
with a short stroke
and I am Venus, the old
beauty. I am both the egg
and the pan it cooks in,
the slow heat, the miraculous 15
sun rising.

Considerations for Critical Thinking and Writing

1. Discuss the meanings of the "mark" in the first stanza. Can you think of any potential readings of it not mentioned by the speaker?
2. How is the pan transformed into an entirely different kind of symbol in the second stanza? How do the images of lines 13–16 create powerful symbolic values?
3. Discuss the significance of the poem's title.
4. The speaker of this poem is a woman, but the author is a man. Write an essay explaining whether knowing this makes any difference in your appreciation or understanding of the poem.

WILLIAM BLAKE (1757–1827)

The Sick Rose 1794

[handwritten annotation: not a conventional symbols — perception from bud to open → true]

O Rose, thou art sick!
The invisible worm
That flies in the night,
In the howling storm,

Has found out thy bed
Of crimson joy,
And his dark secret love
Does thy life destroy.

Considerations for Critical Thinking and Writing

1. How does the use of personification in this poem indicate that the speaker laments the fate of more than a rose?
2. Discuss some of the possible meanings of the rose. How does the description of the worm help to explain the rose?
3. Is this poem to be read allegorically or symbolically? Can it be read literally?

PAUL LAURENCE DUNBAR (1872–1906)
We Wear the Mask 1896

We wear the mask that grins and lies,
It hides our cheeks and shades our eyes, —
This debt we pay to human guile;
With torn and bleeding hearts we smile,
And mouth with myriad subtleties.   5

Why should the world be overwise,
In counting all our tears and sighs?
Nay, let them only see us, while
    We wear the mask.

We smile, but, O great Christ, our cries   10
To thee from tortured souls arise.
We sing, but oh the clay is vile
Beneath our feet, and long the mile;
But let the world dream otherwise,
    We wear the mask!   15

Considerations for Critical Thinking and Writing

1. What does the mask symbolize? What kind of behavior does it represent?
2. Dunbar was a black man. Does awareness of that fact affect your reading of the poem? Explain why or why not.

Connections to Other Selections

1. How might the first line of this poem be used to describe the theme of Langston Hughes's "Dinner Guest: Me" (p. 359)?
2. Write an essay on oppression as explored in "We Wear the Mask" and William Blake's "The Chimney Sweeper" (p. 152).

ROBERT BLY (b. 1926)
Snowbanks North of the House 1975

Those great sweeps of snow that stop suddenly six feet
    from the house . . .
Thoughts that go so far.

The boy gets out of high school and reads no more books;
the son stops calling home.
The mother puts down her rolling pin and makes no more
   bread.
And the wife looks at her husband one night at a party
   and loves him no more.
The energy leaves the wine, and the minister falls leaving
   the church.
It will not come closer —
the one inside moves back, and the hands touch nothing,
   and are safe.

And the father grieves for his son, and will not leave the
   room where the coffin stands;
he turns away from his wife, and she sleeps alone.

And the sea lifts and falls all night; the moon goes on
   through the unattached heavens alone.
And the toe of the shoe pivots
in the dust. . . .
The man in the black coat turns, and goes back down the
   hill.
No one knows why he came, or why he turned away, and
   did not climb the hill.

Considerations for Critical Thinking and Writing

1. How can the varying images in the poem be related to one another? What do they have in common?
2. Describe the tone produced by the images. What emotions do you experience after carefully considering the images?
3. What symbolic meanings do you think are associated with the poem's images? Describe in a paragraph what you think the poem's themes are.

Connections to Other Selections

1. "Snowbanks North of the House" is the first poem in Bly's collection titled *The Man in the Black Coat Turns* (1981), a title drawn from line 15 of the poem. In *Selected Poems* (1986) Bly explains that

   > I wanted the poems in *The Man in the Black Coat Turns* to rise out of some darkness beneath us, as when the old Norse poets fished with an ox head as bait in the ocean. We know that the poem will break water only for a moment before it sinks again, but just seeing it rise beneath the boat is enough pleasure for one day; and to know that a large thing lives down there puts us in a calm mood, lets us endure our deprived lives with more grace.

   How does Bly's observation that such a poem "lets us endure our deprived lives with more grace" shed light on "Snowbanks North of the House" and Bly's "Snowfall in the Afternoon" (p. 394)? Write an essay that details your response.
2. Compare and contrast the symbolic images in "Snowbanks North of the House" and Robert Frost's "Stopping by Woods on a Snowy Evening" (p. 314).

140 Symbol, Allegory, and Irony

WILLIAM STAFFORD (b. 1914)
Traveling through the Dark

struggle betw.
treating humans,
and other animals

1962

Traveling through the dark I found a deer
dead on the edge of the Wilson River road.
It is usually best to roll them into the canyon:
that road is narrow; to swerve might make more dead.

→ shirking responsibility
humans ya s well?
dead

By glow of the tail-light I stumbled back of the car
and stood by the heap, a doe, a recent killing;
she had stiffened already, almost cold.
I dragged her off; she was large in the belly.

partial light, uncertainty

My fingers touching her side brought me the reason —
her side was warm; her fawn lay there waiting,
alive, still, never to be born.
Beside that mountain road I hesitated.

→ taking responsibility for 10
others' action

The car aimed ahead its lowered parking lights;
under the hood purred the steady engine.
I stood in the glare of the warm exhaust turning red;
around our group I could hear the wilderness listen.

→ content

stasis

thinking of something else? 15
what's most humane?

I thought hard for us all — my only swerving —
then pushed her over the edge into the river.

→ does he have a diff.
decision to
make here?
options??

Considerations for Critical Thinking and Writing

1. Notice the description of the car in this poem: the "glow of the tail-light," the "lowered parking lights," and how the engine "purred." How do these and other details suggest symbolic meanings for the car and the "recent killing"?

2. Discuss the speaker's tone. Does the speaker seem, for example, tough, callous, kind, sentimental, confused, or confident?

3. What is the effect of the last stanza's having only two lines rather than the established four lines of the previous stanzas?

4. Discuss the appropriateness of this poem's title. In what sense has the speaker "thought hard for us all"? What are those thoughts?

5. Is this a didactic poem?

no rule of thumb,
can't be boiled down

for Stafford, a
moral choice -
is it more important / pivotal
to author rather
than reader

car = dangerous animal
on your side & method of
destruction
religious moments --
gift's in general?

ANDREW HUDGINS (b. 1951)
Seventeen

1991

Ahead of me, the dog reared on its rope,
and swayed. The pickup took a hard left turn,
and the dog tipped off the side. He scrambled, fell,
and scraped along the hot asphalt
before he tumbled back into the air.   5
I pounded on my horn and yelled. The rope
snapped and the brown dog hurtled into the weeds.

I braked, still pounding on my horn. The truck
stopped too.

10

          We met halfway, and stared
down at the shivering dog, which flinched
and moaned and tried to flick its tail.
Most of one haunch was scraped away
and both hind legs were twisted. *You stupid shit!*
I said. He squinted at me. "Well now, bud —

15

you best watch what you say to me."
I'd never cussed a grown-up man before.
I nodded. I figured on a beating. He grinned.
"You so damn worried about that ole dog,
he's yours." He strolled back to his truck,

20

gunned it, and slewed off, spraying gravel.
The dog whined harshly.

            By the road,
gnats rose waist-high as I waded through
the dry weeds, looking for a rock.

25

I knelt down by the dog — tail flick —
and slammed the rock down twice. The first
blow did the job, but I had planned for two.
My hands swept up and down again. I grabbed
the hind legs, swung twice, and heaved the dog

30

into a clump of butterfly weed and vetch.
But then I didn't know that they had names,
those roadside weeds. His truck was a blue Ford,
the dog a beagle. I was seventeen.
The gnats rose, gathered to one loose cloud,

35

then scattered through coarse orange and purple weeds.

Considerations for Critical Thinking and Writing

1. What kind of language does Hudgins use to describe the injured dog (line 1–14)? What is its effect?
2. Characterize the speaker and the driver of the pickup. What clues does the poem provide to the way each perceives the other?
3. Hudgins has described "Seventeen" as a "rite of passage." How does the title focus this idea?
4. Might killing the dog be understood as a symbolic action? Try to come up with more than one interpretation for the speaker's actions.

Connections to Other Selections

1. Write an essay that compares the speakers and themes of "Seventeen" and "Traveling through the Dark."
2. In an essay discuss the speakers' attitudes toward dogs in "Seventeen" and Ronald Wallace's "Dogs" (p. 504). What do these attitudes reveal about the speakers?

D. H. LAWRENCE (1885–1930)
Snake   1923

A snake came to my water-trough
On a hot, hot day, and I in pajamas for the heat,
To drink there.

In the deep, strange-scented shade of the great dark carob-tree
I came down the steps with my pitcher   5
And must wait, must stand and wait, for there he was at the trough before me.

He reached down from a fissure in the earth-wall in the gloom
And trailed his yellow-brown slackness soft-bellied down, over the edge of the
    stone trough
And rested his throat upon the stone bottom,
And where the water had dripped from the tap, in a small clearness,   10
He sipped with his straight mouth,
Softly drank through his straight gums, into his slack long body,
Silently.

Someone was before me at my water-trough,
And I, like a second comer, waiting.   15

He lifted his head from his drinking, as cattle do,
And looked at me vaguely, as drinking cattle do,
And flickered his two-forked tongue from his lips, and mused a moment,
And stooped and drank a little more,
Being earth-brown, earth-golden from the burning bowels of the earth   20
On the day of Sicilian July, with Etna° smoking.   *a volcano*
The voice of my education said to me
He must be killed,
For in Sicily the black, black snakes are innocent, the gold are venomous.

And voices in me said, If you were a man   25
You would take a stick and break him now, and finish him off.

But must I confess how I liked him,
How glad I was he had come like a guest in quiet, to drink at my
    water-trough
And depart peaceful, pacified, and thankless,
Into the burning bowels of this earth?   30

Was it cowardice, that I dared not kill him?
Was it perversity, that I longed to talk to him?
Was it humility, to feel so honored?
I felt so honored.

And yet those voices: 35
If you were not afraid, you would kill him!

And truly I was afraid, I was most afraid,
But even so, honored still more
That he should seek my hospitality
From out the dark door of the secret earth.   40

He drank enough
And lifted his head, dreamily, as one who has drunken,
And flickered his tongue like a forked night on the air, so black,
Seeming to lick his lips,
And looked around like a god, unseeing, into the air,   45
And slowly turned his head,
And slowly, very slowly, as if thrice adream,
Proceeded to draw his slow length curving round
And climb again the broken bank of my wall-face.

And as he put his head into that dreadful hole,   50
And as he slowly drew up, snake-easing his shoulders, and entered farther,
A sort of horror, a sort of protest against his withdrawing into that horrid
     black hole,
Deliberately going into the blackness, and slowly drawing himself after,
Overcame me now his back was turned.

I looked round, I put down my pitcher,   55
I picked up a clumsy log
And threw it at the water-trough with a clatter.

I think it did not hit him,
But suddenly that part of him that was left behind convulsed in undignified
     haste.
Writhed like lightning, and was gone   60
Into the black hole, the earth-lipped fissure in the wall-front,
At which, in the intense still noon, I stared with fascination.

And immediately I regretted it.
I thought how paltry, how vulgar, what a mean act!
I despised myself and the voices of my accursed human education.   65

And I thought of the albatross,
And I wished he would come back, my snake.

For he seemed to me again like a king,
Like a king in exile, uncrowned in the underworld,
Now due to be crowned again.   70

And so, I missed my chance with one of the lords
Of life.
And I have something to expiate;
A pettiness.

Considerations for Critical Thinking and Writing

1. Do you think Lawrence uses the snake in this poem as a conventional symbol of
   evil, or does he go beyond the traditional meanings associated with snakes? Consider the images used to describe the snake.
2. What is the "voice of my education" (line 22)? What is the conflict the speaker
   feels about the snake?
3. Identify the allusion to the albatross (line 66).
4. Explain why the speaker wishes the snake would return (lines 67–70). Why do
   you think the snake is described as "one of the lords / Of life" (71–72)?

ALDEN NOWLAN (1933–1983)
The Bull Moose

Down from the purple mist of trees on the mountain,
lurching through forests of white spruce and cedar,
stumbling through tamarack swamps,
came the bull moose
to be stopped at last by a pole-fenced pasture.   5

Too tired to turn or, perhaps, aware
there was no place left to go, he stood with the cattle.
They, scenting the musk of death, seeing his great head
like the ritual mask of a blood god, moved to the other end
of the field, and waited.   10

The neighbors heard of it, and by afternoon
cars lined the road. The children teased him
with alder switches and he gazed at them
like an old, tolerant collie. The women asked
if he could have escaped from a Fair.   15

The oldest man in the parish remembered seeing
a gelded moose yoked with an ox for plowing.
The young men snickered and tried to pour beer
down his throat, while their girl friends took their pictures.

The bull moose let them stroke his tick-ravaged flanks,   20
let them pry open his jaws with bottles, let a giggling girl
plant a little purple cap
of thistles on his head.

When the wardens came, everyone agreed it was a shame
to shoot anything so shaggy and cuddlesome.   25
He looked like the kind of pet
women put to bed with their sons.

So they held their fire. But just as the sun dropped in the river
the bull moose gathered his strength
like a scaffolded king, straightened and lifted his horns   30
so that even the wardens backed away as they raised their rifles.
When he roared, people ran to their cars. All the young men
leaned on their automobile horns as he toppled.

Considerations for Critical Thinking and Writing

1. How does the speaker present the moose and the townspeople? How are the moose and townspeople contrasted? Discuss specific lines to support your response.
2. Explain how the symbols in this poem point to a conflict between humanity and nature. What do you think the speaker's attitude toward this conflict is?
3. Read the section on mythological criticism in Chapter 15, "Critical Strategies for Reading," and write an essay on "The Bull Moose" that approaches the poem from a mythological perspective.

Nowlan / The Bull Moose **145**

Connection to Another Selection

1. In an essay compare and contrast how the animals portrayed in "The Bull Moose," Stafford's "Traveling through the Dark" (p. 141), and Lawrence's "Snake" are used as symbols.

JULIO MARZÁN (b. 1946)
Ethnic Poetry

(1994)

The ethnic poet said: "The earth is maybe
a huge maraca/ and the sun a trombone/
and life/ is to move your ass/ to slow beats."
The ethnic audience roasted a suckling pig.

The ethnic poet said: "Oh thank Goddy, Goddy/   5
I be me, my toenails curled downward/
deep, deep, deep into Mama earth."
The ethnic audience shook strands of sea shells.

The ethnic poet said: "The sun was created black/
so we should imagine light/ and also dream/   10
a walrus emerging from the broken ice."
The ethnic audience beat on sealskin drums.

The ethnic poet said: "Reproductive organs/
Eagles nesting California redwoods/
Shut up and listen to my ancestors."   15
The ethnic audience ate fried bread and honey.

The ethnic poet said: "Something there is that
doesn't love a wall/ That sends
the frozen-ground-swell under it."
The ethnic audience deeply understood humanity.   20

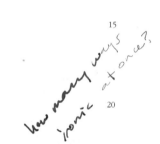

Considerations for Critical Thinking and Writing

1. What is the implicit definition of ethnic poetry in this poem?
2. The final stanza quotes lines from Robert Frost's "Mending Wall" (p. 304). Read the entire poem. Why do you think Marzán chooses these lines and this particular poem as one kind of ethnic poetry?
3. What is the poem's central irony? Pay particular attention to the final line. What is being satirized here?

Connection to Another Selection

1. Write an essay that discusses the speaker's ideas about what poetry should be in "Ethnic Poetry" and in Langston Hughes's "Formula" (p. 345).

JAMES MERRILL (1926–1995)
Casual Wear

1984

Your average tourist: Fifty. 2.3
Times married. Dressed, this year, in Ferdi Plinthbower
Originals. Odds 1 to 9
Against her strolling past the Embassy

Today at noon. Your average terrorist: 5
Twenty-five. Celibate. No use for trends,
At least in clothing. Mark, though, where it ends.
People have come forth made of colored mist

Unsmiling on one hundred million screens
To tell of his prompt phone call to the station,   10
"Claiming responsibility" — devastation
Signed with a flourish, like the dead wife's jeans.

Considerations for Critical Thinking and Writing

1. What is the effect of the statistics in this poem?
2. Describe the speaker's tone. Is it appropriate for the subject matter? Explain why or why not.
3. Comment on the ironies that emerge from the final two lines. How are the tourist and terrorist linked by the speaker's description? Explain why you think the speaker sympathizes more with the tourist or the terrorist — or with neither.

Connection to Another Selection

1. Compare the satire in this poem with that in Peter Meinke's "The ABC of Aerobics" (p. 245). What is satirized in each poem? Which satire is more pointed from your perspective?

HENRY REED (1914–1986)
Naming of Parts

1946

Today we have naming of parts. Yesterday,
We had daily cleaning. And tomorrow morning,
We shall have what to do after firing. But today,
Today we have naming of parts. Japonica
Glistens like coral in all of the neighboring gardens,   5
           And today we have naming of parts.

This is the lower sling swivel. And this
Is the upper sling swivel, whose use you will see,
When you are given your slings. And this is the piling swivel,
Which in your case you have not got. The branches   10
Hold in the gardens their silent, eloquent gestures,
           Which in our case we have not got.

This is the safety-catch, which is always released
With an easy flick of the thumb. And please do not let me
See anyone using his finger. You can do it quite easy   15
If you have any strength in your thumb. The blossoms
Are fragile and motionless, never letting anyone see
       Any of them using their finger.

And this you can see is the bolt. The purpose of this
Is to open the breech, as you see. We can slide it   20
Rapidly backwards and forwards: we call this
Easing the spring. And rapidly backwards and forwards
The early bees are assaulting and fumbling the flowers:
       They call it easing the Spring.

They call it easing the Spring: it is perfectly easy   25
If you have any strength in your thumb: like the bolt,
And the breech, and the cocking-piece, and the point of balance,
Which in our case we have not got; and the almond-blossom
Silent in all of the gardens and the bees going backwards and forwards,
       For today we have naming of parts.   30

Considerations for Critical Thinking and Writing

1. Characterize the two speakers in this poem. Identify the lines spoken by each. How do their respective lines differ in tone?
2. What is the effect of the last line of each stanza?
3. How do ambiguities and puns contribute to the poem's meaning?
4. What symbolic contrast is made between the rifle instruction and the gardens? How is this contrast ironic?

JOHN CIARDI (1916–1986)
Suburban

1978

Yesterday Mrs. Friar phoned. "Mr. Ciardi,
   how do you do?" she said. "I am sorry to say
this isn't exactly a social call. The fact is
   your dog has just deposited — forgive me —
a large repulsive object in my petunias."   5

I thought to ask, "Have you checked the rectal grooving
   for a positive I.D.?" My dog, as it happened,
was in Vermont with my son, who had gone fishing —
   if that's what one does with a girl, two cases of beer,
and a borrowed camper. I guessed I'd get no trout.   10

But why lose out on organic gold for a wise crack?
   "Yes, Mrs. Friar," I said, "I understand."
"Most kind of you," she said. "Not at all," I said.
   I went with a spade. She pointed, looking away.
"I always have loved dogs," she said, "but really!"   15

I scooped it up and bowed. "The animal of it.
  I hope this hasn't upset you, Mrs. Friar."
"Not really," she said, "but really!" I bore the turd
  across the line to my own petunias
and buried it till the glorious resurrection   20

when even these suburbs shall give up their dead.

Considerations for Critical Thinking and Writing

1. How does the speaker transform Mrs. Friar into a symbolic figure of the suburbs?
2. Why do you suppose Ciardi focuses on this particular incident to make a comment upon the suburbs? What is the speaker's attitude toward suburban life?
3. Write a one-paragraph physical description of Mrs. Friar that captures her character for you.

Connection to Another Selection

1. Compare the speakers' voices in "Suburban" and in Updike's "Dog's Death" (p. 11).

CHITRA BANERJEE DIVAKARUNI (b. 1956)
Indian Movie, New Jersey   1990

Not like the white filmstars, all rib
and gaunt cheekbone, the Indian sex-goddess
smiles plumply from behind a flowery
branch. Below her brief red skirt, her thighs
are satisfying-solid, redeeming   5
as tree trunks. She swings her hips
and the men-viewers whistle. The lover-hero
dances in to a song, his lip-sync
a little off, but no matter, we
know the words already and sing along.   10
It is safe here, the day
golden and cool so no one sweats,
roses on every bush and the Dal Lake
clean again.
                The sex-goddess switches   15
to thickened English to emphasize
a joke. We laugh and clap. Here
we need not be embarrassed by words
dropping like lead pellets into foreign ears.
The flickering movie-light   20
wipes from our faces years of America, sons
who want mohawks and refuse to run
the family store, daughters who date
on the sly.

When at the end the hero   25
dies for his friend who also
loves the sex-goddess and now can marry her,
we weep, understanding. Even the men
clear their throats to say, "What *qurbani!*°   *sacrifice*
What *dosti!*"° After, we mill around   *friendship*   30
unwilling to leave, exchange greetings
and good news: a new gold chain, a trip
to India. We do not speak
of motel raids, canceled permits, stones
thrown through glass windows, daughters and sons   35
raped by Dotbusters.°
       In this dim foyer
we can pull around us the faint, comforting smell
of incense and *pakoras,*° can arrange   *fried appetizers*
our children's marriages with hometown boys and girls,   40
open a franchise, win a million
in the mail. We can retire
in India, a yellow two-storied house
with wrought-iron gates, our own
Ambassador car. Or at least   45
move to a rich white suburb, Summerfield
or Fort Lee, with neighbors that will
talk to us. Here while the film-songs still echo
in the corridors and restrooms, we can trust
in movie truths: sacrifice, success, love and luck,   50
the America that was supposed to be.

36 *Dotbusters:* New Jersey gangs that attack Indians.

Considerations for Critical Thinking and Writing

1. Why does the speaker feel comfortable at the movies? How is the world inside
   the theater different from life outside in New Jersey?
2. Explain the differences portrayed by the speaker between life in India and life in
   New Jersey. What connotative values are associated with each location in the
   poem?
3. Discuss the irony in the final two lines.

ROBERT BROWNING (1812–1889)
My Last Duchess   1842

Ferrara°

That's my last Duchess painted on the wall,
Looking as if she were alive. I call

Ferrara: In the sixteenth century, the duke of this Italian city arranged to marry a second time after
the mysterious death of his very young first wife.

That piece a wonder, now: Frà Pandolf's° hands
Worked busily a day, and there she stands.
Will't please you sit and look at her? I said   5
"Frà Pandolf" by design, for never read
Strangers like you that pictured countenance,
The depth and passion of its earnest glance,
But to myself they turned (since none puts by
The curtain I have drawn for you, but I)   10
And seemed as they would ask me, if they durst,
How such a glance came there; so, not the first
Are you to turn and ask thus. Sir, 'twas not
Her husband's presence only, called that spot
Of joy into the Duchess' cheek: perhaps   15
Frà Pandolf chanced to say "Her mantle laps
Over my lady's wrist too much," or "Paint
Must never hope to reproduce the faint
Half-flush that dies along her throat": such stuff
Was courtesy, she thought, and cause enough   20
For calling up that spot of joy. She had
A heart — how shall I say? — too soon made glad,
Too easily impressed; she liked whate'er
She looked on, and her looks went everywhere.
Sir, 'twas all one! My favor at her breast,   25
The dropping of the daylight in the West,
The bough of cherries some officious fool
Broke in the orchard for her, the white mule
She rode with round the terrace — all and each
Would draw from her alike the approving speech,   30
Or blush, at least. She thanked men, — good! but thanked
Somehow — I know not how — as if she ranked
My gift of a nine-hundred-years-old name
With anybody's gift. Who'd stoop to blame
This sort of trifling? Even had you skill   35
In speech — which I have not — to make your will
Quite clear to such an one, and say, "Just this
Or that in you disgusts me; here you miss,
Or there exceed the mark" — and if she let
Herself be lessoned so, nor plainly set   40
Her wits to yours, forsooth, and made excuse,
— E'en then would be some stooping; and I choose
Never to stoop. Oh sir, she smiled, no doubt,
Whene'er I passed her; but who passed without
Much the same smile? This grew; I gave commands;   45
Then all smiles stopped together. There she stands
As if alive. Will't please you rise? We'll meet
The company below, then. I repeat,
The Count your master's known munificence
Is ample warrant that no just pretense   50
Of mine for dowry will be disallowed;

3 *Frà Pandolf:* A fictitious artist.

Though his fair daughter's self, as I avowed
At starting, is my object. Nay, we'll go
Together down, sir. Notice Neptune, though,
Taming a sea-horse, thought a rarity,
Which Claus of Innsbruck° cast in bronze for me!   55

56 *Claus of Innsbruck:* Also a fictitious artist.

Considerations for Critical Thinking and Writing

1. To whom is the duke addressing his remarks about the duchess in this poem? What is ironic about the situation?
2. Why was the duke unhappy with his first wife? What does this reveal about the duke? What does the poem's title suggest about his attitude toward women in general?
3. What seems to be the visitor's response (lines 53–54) to the duke's account of his first wife?
4. What do you think happened to the duchess?

Connection to Another Selection

1. Write an essay describing the ways in which the speakers of "My Last Duchess" and "Hazel Tells LaVerne" (p. 53) by Katharyn Howd Machan inadvertently reveal themselves.

WILLIAM BLAKE (1757–1827)
The Chimney Sweeper   1789

When my mother died I was very young,
And my father sold me while yet my tongue
Could scarcely cry "'weep! 'weep! 'weep! 'weep!"
So your chimneys I sweep, and in soot I sleep.

There's little Tom Dacre, who cried when his head,   5
That curled like a lamb's back, was shaved: so I said
"Hush, Tom! never mind it, for when your head's bare
You know that the soot cannot spoil your white hair."

And so he was quiet, and that very night,
As Tom was a-sleeping, he had such a sight!
That thousands of sweepers, Dick, Joe, Ned, and Jack,   10
Were all of them locked up in coffins of black.

And by came an Angel who had a bright key,
And he opened the coffins and set them all free;
Then down a green plain leaping, laughing, they run,   15
And wash in a river, and shine in the sun.

Then naked and white, all their bags left behind,
They rise upon clouds and sport in the wind;

And the Angel told Tom, if he'd be a good boy,
He'd have God for his father, and never want joy.   20

And so Tom awoke; and we rose in the dark,
And got with our bags and our brushes to work.
Though the morning was cold, Tom was happy and warm;
So if all do their duty they need not fear harm.

Considerations for Critical Thinking and Writing

1. Characterize the speaker in this poem, and describe his tone. Is his tone the same as the poet's? Consider especially lines 7–8 and 24.
2. What is the symbolic value of the dream in lines 11–20?
3. Why is irony central to the meaning of this poem?
4. Discuss the validity of this statement: "'The Chimney Sweeper' is a sentimental poem about a shameful eighteenth-century social problem; such a treatment of child abuse cannot be taken seriously."

GARY SOTO (b. 1952)
Behind Grandma's House   1985

At ten I wanted fame. I had a comb
And two Coke bottles, a tube of Bryl-creem.
I borrowed a dog, one with
Mismatched eyes and a happy tongue,
And wanted to prove I was tough   5
In the alley, kicking over trash cans,
A dull chime of tuna cans falling.
I hurled light bulbs like grenades
And men teachers held their heads,
Fingers of blood lengthening   10
On the ground. I flicked rocks at cats,
Their goofy faces spurred with foxtails.
I kicked fences. I shooed pigeons.
I broke a branch from a flowering peach
And frightened ants with a stream of spit.   15
I said "*Chale*," "In your face," and "No way
Daddy-O" to an imaginary priest
Until grandma came into the alley,
Her apron flapping in a breeze,
Her hair mussed, and said, "Let me help you,"   20
And punched me between the eyes.

Considerations for Critical Thinking and Writing

1. How does the speaker characterize himself at ten?
2. What is the central irony of this poem?
3. Though the "grandma" appears only briefly, she seems, in a sense, fully characterized. How would you describe her? Why do you think she says, "Let me help you"?

Connection to Another Selection

1. Write an essay comparing the themes of "Behind Grandma's House" and Sharon Olds's "Rite of Passage" (p. 238).

ROBERT BLY (b. 1927)
Sitting Down to Dinner 1988

Suppose a man can't find what is his.
Suppose as a boy he imagined that some demon
Forced him to live in "his room,"
And sit on "his chair" and be a child of "his parents."

That would happen each time he sat down to dinner. 5
His own birthday party belonged to someone else.
And — was it sweet potatoes that he liked? —
He should resist them. Whose plate is this?

That man would be like a lean-to attached
To a house. It doesn't have a foundation. 10
He would be helpful and hostile at the same time.
Such a person leans toward you and leans away.

Do you feel me leaning?

Considerations for Critical Thinking and Writing

1. What kind of "demon" is described in line 2?
2. How do the boy's experiences serve to shape the man, according to the speaker?
3. Discuss the symbolic values associated with "dinner" in this poem.
4. Do you feel the speaker leaning toward you or away from you? Explain your response.

Connection to Another Selection

1. In an essay consider how early childhood experiences affect adult identities in "Sitting Down to Dinner" and in Judy Page Heitzman's "The Schoolroom on the Second Floor of the Knitting Mill" (p. 498).

EZRA POUND (1885-1972)
On Symbols   1912

I believe that the proper and perfect symbol is the natural object, that if a man use "symbols" he must so use them that their symbolic function does not obtrude; so that *a* sense, and the poetic quality of the passage, is not lost to those who do not understand the symbol as such, to whom, for instance, a hawk is a hawk.

From "Prolegomena," *Poetry Review,* February 1912

Considerations for Critical Thinking and Writing

1. Discuss whether you agree with Pound that the "perfect symbol" is a "natural object" that does not insist on being read as a symbol.
2. Write an essay in which you discuss Lawrence's "Snake" (p. 143) as an example of the "perfect symbol" Pound proposes.

6. Sounds

Poems yearn to be read aloud. Much of their energy, charm, and beauty comes to life only when they are heard. Poets choose and arrange words for their sounds as well as for their meanings. Most poetry is best read with your lips, teeth, and tongue, because they serve to articulate the effects that sound may have in a poem. When a voice is breathed into a good poem, there is pleasure in the reading, the saying, and the hearing.

LISTENING TO POETRY

The earliest poetry — before writing and painting — was chanted or sung. The rhythmic quality of such oral performances served two purposes: it helped the chanting bard remember the lines and it entertained audiences with patterned sounds of language, which were sometimes accompanied by musical instruments. Poetry has always been closely related to music. Indeed, as the word suggests, lyric poetry evolved from songs. "Western Wind" (p. 26), an anonymous Middle English lyric, survived as song long before it was written down. Had Robert Frost lived in a nonliterate society, he probably would have sung some version — a very different version to be sure — of "Acquainted with the Night" (p. 129) instead of writing it down. Even though Frost creates a speaking rather than a singing voice, the speaker's anxious tone is distinctly heard in any careful reading of the poem.

Like lyrics, early narrative poems were originally part of an anonymous oral folk tradition. A **_ballad_** such as "Bonny Barbara Allan" (p. 386) told a story that was sung from one generation to the next until it was finally transcribed. Since the eighteenth century, this narrative form has sometimes been imitated by poets who write **_literary ballads_**. John Keats's "La Belle Dame sans Merci" (p. 427) is, for example, a more complex and sophisticated nineteenth-century reflection of the original ballad traditions that developed in the fifteenth century and earlier. In considering poetry as sound, we should not forget that poetry traces its beginnings to song.

These next lines exemplify poetry's continuing relation to song. What poetic elements can you find in this ballad, which was adapted by Simon and Garfunkel and became a popular antiwar song in the 1960s?

156

ANONYMOUS
Scarborough Fair

date unknown

Where are you going? To Scarborough Fair?
Parsley, sage, rosemary, and thyme,
Remember me to a bonny lass there,
For once she was a true lover of mine.

Tell her to make me a cambric shirt,   5
Parsley, sage, rosemary, and thyme,
Without any needle or thread work'd in it,
And she shall be a true lover of mine.

Tell her to wash it in yonder well,
Parsley, sage, rosemary, and thyme,   10
Where water ne'er sprung nor a drop of rain fell,
And she shall be a true lover of mine.

Tell her to plough me an acre of land,
Parsley, sage, rosemary, and thyme,
Between the sea and the salt sea strand,   15
And she shall be a true lover of mine.

Tell her to plough it with one ram's horn,
Parsley, sage, rosemary, and thyme,
And sow it all over with one peppercorn,
And she shall be a true lover of mine.   20

Tell her to reap it with a sickle of leather,
Parsley, sage, rosemary, and thyme,
And tie it all up with a tom tit's feather,
And she shall be a true lover of mine.

Tell her to gather it all in a sack,   25
Parsley, sage, rosemary, and thyme,
And carry it home on a butterfly's back,
And then she shall be a true lover of mine.

Considerations for Critical Thinking and Writing

1. What is the effect of the refrain? What do you associate with "parsley, sage, rosemary, and thyme"?
2. What kinds of demands does the speaker make on his former lover? What do these demands have in common?
3. What is the tone of this ballad?
4. Choose a contemporary song that you especially like and examine the lyrics. Write an essay explaining whether or not you consider the lyrics poetic.

Of course, reading "Scarborough Fair" is not the same as hearing it. Like the lyrics of a song, many poems must be heard — or at least read with listening eyes — before they can be fully understood and enjoyed. The sounds of words are a universal source of music for human beings. This has been so from ancient tribes to bards to the two-year-old child in a bakery gleefully chanting "Cuppitycake, cuppitycake!"

Listen to the sound of this poem as you read it aloud. How do the words provide, in a sense, their own musical accompaniment?

JOHN UPDIKE (b. 1932)
Player Piano

1958

My stick fingers click with a snicker
And, chuckling, they knuckle the keys;
Light-footed, my steel feelers flicker
And pluck from these keys melodies.

My paper can caper; abandon   5
Is broadcast by dint of my din,
And no man or band has a hand in
The tones I turn on from within.

At times I'm a jumble of rumbles,
At others I'm light like the moon,   10
But never my numb plunker fumbles,
Misstrums me, or tries a new tune.

The speaker in this poem is a piano that can play automatically by means of a mechanism that depresses keys in response to signals on a perforated roll. Notice how the speaker's voice approximates the sounds of a piano. In each stanza a predominant sound emerges from the carefully chosen words. How is the sound of each stanza tuned to its sense?

Like Updike's "Player Piano," this next poem is also primarily about sounds.

MAY SWENSON (b. 1919)
A Nosty Fright

1984

The roldengod and the soneyhuckle,
the sack eyed blusan and the wistle theed
are all tangled with the oison pivy,
the fallen nine peedles and the wumbleteed.

A mipchunk caught in a wobceb tried   5
to hip and skide in a dandy sune
but a stobler put up a EEP KOFF sign.
Then the unfucky lellow met a phytoon

and was sept out to swea. He difted for drays
till a hassgropper flying happened to spot   10
the boolish feast all debraggled and wet,
covered with snears and tot.

Loonmight shone through the winey poods
where rushmooms grew among risted twoots.
Back blats flew betreen the twees   15
and orned howls hounded their soots.

A kumkpin stood with tooked creeth
on the sindow will of a house
where a icked wold itch lived all alone
except for her stoombrick, a mitten and a kouse.   20

"Here we part," said hassgropper.
"Pere we hart," said mipchunk, too.
They purried away on opposite haths,
both scared of some "Bat!" or "Scoo!"

October was ending on a nosty fright   25
with scroans and greeches and chanking clains,
with oblins and gelfs, coaths and urses,
skinning grulls and stoodblains.

Will it ever be morning, Nofember virst,
skue bly and the sappy hun, our friend?   30
With light breaves of wall by the fayside?
I sope ho, so that this oem can pend.

At just the right moments Swenson transposes letters to create amusing sound
effects and wild wordplays. Although there is a story lurking in "A Nosty
Fright," any serious attempt to interpret its meaning is confronted with "a EEP
KOFF sign." Instead, we are invited to enjoy the delicious sounds the poet has
cooked up.

Few poems revel in sound so completely. More typically, the sounds of
a poem contribute to its meaning rather than become its meaning. Consider
how sound is used in the next poem.

EMILY DICKINSON (1830–1886)
A Bird came down the Walk —   c. 1862

A Bird came down the Walk —
He did not know I saw —
He bit an Angleworm in halves
And ate the fellow, raw,

And then he drank a Dew   5
From a convenient Grass —
And then hopped sidewise to the Wall
To let a Beetle pass —

He glanced with rapid eyes
That hurried all around —   10
They looked like frightened Beads, I thought —
He stirred his Velvet Head

Like one in danger, Cautious,
I offered him a Crumb
And he unrolled his feathers   15
And rowed him softer home —

Than Oars divide the Ocean,
Too silver for a seam —
Or Butterflies, off Banks of Noon
Leap, plashless as they swim.   20

This description of a bird offers a close look at how differently a bird
moves when it hops on the ground than when it flies in the air. On the
ground the bird moves quickly, awkwardly, and irregularly as it plucks up a
worm, washes it down with dew, and then hops aside to avoid a passing
beetle. The speaker recounts the bird's rapid, abrupt actions from a somewhat
superior, amused perspective. By describing the bird in human terms (as if,
for example, it chose to eat the worm "raw"), the speaker is almost condescending. But when the attempt to offer a crumb fails and the frightened bird
flies off, the speaker is left looking up instead of down at the bird.

With that shift in perspective the tone shifts from amusement to awe in
response to the bird's graceful flight. The jerky movements of lines 1–13 give
way to the smooth motion of lines 15–20. The pace of the first three stanzas
is fast and discontinuous. We tend to pause at the end of each line, and this
reinforces a sense of disconnected movements. In contrast, the final six lines
are to be read as a single sentence in one flowing movement, lubricated by
various sounds.

Read again the description of the bird flying away. Several o-sounds contribute to the image of the serene, expansive, confident flight, just as the
s-sounds serve as smooth transitions from one line to the next. Notice how
these sounds are grouped in the following vertical columns:

unrolled	softer	too	his	Ocean	Banks
rowed	Oars	Noon	feathers	silver	plashless
home ·	Or		softer	seam	as
Ocean	off		Oars	Butterflies	swim

This blending of sounds (notice how "Leap, plashless" brings together the
p- and l-sounds without a ripple) helps convey the bird's smooth grace in the
air. Like a feathered oar, the bird moves seamlessly in its element.

The repetition of sounds in poetry is similar to the function of the tones
and melodies that are repeated, with variations, in music. Just as the patterned
sounds in music unify a work, so do the words in poems, which have been
carefully chosen for the combinations of sounds they create. These sounds
are produced in a number of ways.

The most direct way in which the sound of a word suggests its meaning
is through *onomatopoeia,* which is the use of a word that resembles the
sound it denotes: *quack, buzz, rattle, bang, squeak, bowwow, burp, choo-
choo, ding-a-ling, sizzle.* The sound and sense of these words are closely

related, but they represent a very small percentage of the words available to us. Poets usually employ more subtle means for echoing meanings.

Onomatopoeia can consist of more than just single words. In its broadest meaning the term refers to lines or passages in which sounds help to convey meanings, as in these lines from Updike's "Player Piano."

> My stick fingers click with a snicker
> And, chuckling, they knuckle the keys.

The sharp, crisp sounds of these two lines approximate the sounds of a piano; the syllables seem to "click" against one another. Contrast Updike's rendition with the following lines:

> My long fingers play with abandon
> And, laughing, they cover the keys.

The original version is more interesting and alive, because the sounds of the words are pleasurable and they reinforce the meaning through a careful blending of consonants and vowels.

Alliteration is the repetition of the same consonant sounds at the beginnings of nearby words: "*d*escending *d*ewdrops"; "*l*uscious *l*emons." Sometimes the term is also used to describe the consonant sounds within words: "tres*p*asser's re*p*roach"; "we*dd*ed la*d*y." Alliteration is based on sound rather than spelling. "*K*een" and "*c*ar" alliterate, but "*c*ar" does not alliterate with "*c*ite." Rarely is heavy-handed alliteration effective. Used too self-consciously, it can be distracting instead of strengthening meaning or emphasizing a relation between words. Consider the relentless *h*'s in this line: "Horrendous horrors haunted Helen's happiness." Those *h*'s certainly suggest that Helen is being pursued, but they have a more comic than serious effect because they are overdone.

Assonance is the repetition of the same vowel sound in nearby words: "asl*ee*p under a tr*ee*"; "t*i*me and t*i*de"; "h*au*nt" and "*aw*esome"; "*ea*ch *e*vening." Both alliteration and assonance help to establish relations among words in a line or a series of lines. Whether the effect is *euphony* (lines that are musically pleasant to the ear and smooth, like the final lines of Dickinson's "A Bird came down the Walk — ") or the effect is *cacophony* (lines that are discordant and difficult to pronounce, like the claim that "never my numb plunker fumbles" in Updike's "Player Piano"), the sounds of words in poetry can be as significant as the words' denotative or connotative meanings.

This next poem provides a feast of sounds. Read the poem aloud and try to determine the effects of its sounds.

GALWAY KINNELL (b. 1927)
Blackberry Eating   1980

I love to go out in late September
among the fat, overripe, icy, black blackberries
to eat blackberries for breakfast,
the stalks very prickly, a penalty

they earn for knowing the black art   5
of blackberry-making; and as I stand among them
lifting the stalks to my mouth, the ripest berries
fall almost unbidden to my tongue,
as words sometimes do, certain peculiar words
like *strengths* or *squinched*,   10
many-lettered, one-syllabled lumps,
which I squeeze, squinch open, and splurge well
in the silent, startled, icy, black language
of blackberry-eating in late September.

Considerations for Critical Thinking and Writing

1. Underline the alliteration and circle the assonance throughout this poem. What is the effect of these sounds?
2. How do lines 4–6 fit into the poem? What does this prickly image add to the poem?
3. Explain what you think the poem's theme is.
4. Write an essay that considers the speaker's love of blackberry eating along with the speaker's appetite for words. How are the two blended in the poem?

RHYME

Like alliteration and assonance, ***rhyme*** is a way of creating sound patterns. Rhyme, broadly defined, consists of two or more words or phrases that repeat the same sounds: *happy* and *snappy*. Rhyme words often have similar spellings, but that is not a requirement of rhyme; what matters is that the words sound alike: *vain* rhymes with *reign* as well as *rain*. Moreover, words may look alike but not rhyme at all. In ***eye rhyme*** the spellings are similar, but the pronunciations are not, as with *bough* and *cough*, or *brow* and *blow*.

Not all poems employ rhyme. Many great poems have no rhymes, and many weak verses use rhyme as a substitute for poetry. These are especially apparent in commercial messages and greeting-card lines. At its worst, rhyme is merely a distracting decoration that can lead to dullness and predictability. But used skillfully, rhyme creates lines that are memorable and musical.

Following is a poem using rhyme that you might remember the next time you are in a restaurant.

RICHARD ARMOUR (1906–1989)
Going to Extremes   1954

Shake and shake
  The catsup bottle
None'll come —
  And then a lot'll.

whatever.

The experience recounted in Armour's poem is common enough, but the rhyme's humor is special. The final line clicks the poem shut, an effect that is often achieved by the use of rhyme. That click provides a sense of a satisfying and fulfilled form. Rhymes have a number of uses: they can emphasize words, direct a reader's attention to relations between words, and provide an overall structure for a poem.

Rhyme is used in the following poem to imitate the sound of cascading water.

ROBERT SOUTHEY (1774–1843)
From *The Cataract of Lodore*   1820

> "How does the water
> Come down at Lodore?"
> . . . .
> From its sources which well
> In the tarn on the fell;
> From its fountains   5
> In the mountains,
> Its rills and its gills;
> Through moss and through brake,
> It runs and it creeps
> For awhile, till it sleeps   10
> In its own little lake.
> And thence at departing,
> Awakening and starting,
> It runs through the reeds
> And away it proceeds,   15
> Through meadow and glade,
> In sun and in shade,
> And through the wood-shelter,
> Among crags in its flurry,
> Helter-skelter,   20
> Hurry-scurry.
> Here it comes sparkling,
> And there it lies darkling;
> Now smoking and frothing
> Its tumult and wrath in,   25
> Till in this rapid race
> On which it is bent,
> It reaches the place
> Of its steep descent.
>
> The cataract strong   30
> Then plunges along,
> Striking and raging
> As if a war waging

Its caverns and rocks among:
   Rising and leaping,   35
  Sinking and creeping,
  Swelling and sweeping,
Showering and springing,
    Flying and flinging,
   Writhing and ringing,   40
Eddying and whisking,
Spouting and frisking,
Turning and twisting,
   Around and around
  With endless rebound!   45
  Smiting and fighting,
   A sight to delight in;
  Confounding, astounding,
Dizzying and deafening the ear with its sound.

. . . .

Dividing and gliding and sliding,   50
And falling and brawling and spawling,
And driving and riving and striving,
And sprinkling and twinkling and wrinkling,
And sounding and bounding and rounding,
And bubbling and troubling and doubling,   55
And grumbling and rumbling and tumbling,
And clattering and battering and shattering;
Retreating and beating and meeting and sheeting,
Delaying and straying and playing and spraying,
Advancing and prancing and glancing and dancing,   60
Recoiling, turmoiling and toiling and boiling,
And gleaming and streaming and steaming and beaming,
And rushing and flushing and brushing and gushing,
And flapping and rapping and clapping and slapping,
And curling and whirling and purling and twirling,   65
And thumping and plumping and bumping and jumping,
And dashing and flashing and splashing and clashing;
And so never ending, but always descending,
Sounds and motions forever and ever are blending,
All at once and all o'er, with a mighty uproar;   70
And this way the water comes down at Lodore.

This deluge of rhymes consists of "Sounds and motions forever and ever . . . blending" (line 69). The pace quickens as the water creeps from its mountain source and then descends in rushing cataracts. As the speed of the water increases, so do the number of rhymes, until they run in fours: "dashing and flashing and splashing and clashing." Most rhymes meander through poems instead of flooding them; nevertheless, Southey's use of rhyme suggests how sounds can flow with meanings. "The Cataract of Lodore" has been criticized, however, for overusing onomatopoeia. Some readers find the poem silly; others regard it as a brilliant example of sound effects. What do you think?

A variety of types of rhyme is available to poets. The most common form, *__end rhyme,__* comes at the ends of lines.

> It runs through the reeds
>> And away it proceeds,
> Through meadow and glade,
>> In sun and in shade.

Internal rhyme places at least one of the rhymed words within the line, as in "Dividing and gliding and sliding" or, more subtly, in the fourth and final words of "In mist or cloud, on mast or shroud."

The rhyming of single-syllable words such as *grade* and *shade* is known as *__masculine rhyme.__*

> Loveliest of trees, the cherry now
> Is hung with bloom along the bough.
>> —A. E. Housman

Rhymes using words of more than one syllable are also called masculine when the same sound occurs in a final stressed syllable, as in *defend, contend; betray, away*. A *__feminine rhyme__* consists of a rhymed stressed syllable followed by one or more rhymed unstressed syllables, as in *butter, clutter; gratitude, attitude; quivering, shivering*.

> Lord confound this surly sister,
> Blight her brow and blotch and blister.
>> —John Millington Synge

All the examples so far have been *__exact rhymes,__* because they share the same stressed vowel sounds as well as any sounds that follow the vowel. In *near rhyme* (also called *off rhyme, slant rhyme,* and *approximate rhyme*), the sounds are almost but not exactly alike. There are several kinds of near rhyme. One of the most common is *__consonance,__* an identical consonant sound preceded by a different vowel sound: *home, same; worth, breath; trophy, daffy.* Near rhyme can also be achieved by using different vowel sounds with identical consonant sounds: *sound, sand; kind, conned; fellow, fallow*. The dissonance of *blade* and *blood* in the following lines helps to reinforce their grim tone.

> Let the boy try along this bayonet-blade
> How cold steel is, and keen with hunger of blood.
>> — Wilfred Owen

Near rhymes greatly broaden the possibility for musical effects in English, a language that, compared with Spanish or Italian, contains few exact rhymes. Do not assume, however, that a near rhyme represents a failed attempt at exact rhyme. Near rhymes allow a musical subtlety and variety, and can avoid the sometimes overpowering jingling effects that exact rhymes may create.

These basic terms hardly exhaust the ways in which the sounds in poems can be labeled and discussed, but the terms can help you to describe how poets manipulate sounds for effect. Read "God's Grandeur" (below) aloud and try to determine how the sounds of the lines contribute to their sense.

PERSPECTIVE

DAVID LENSON (b. 1945)
On the Contemporary Use of Rhyme

1988

One impediment to a respectable return to rhyme is the popular survival of "functional" verse: greeting cards, pedagogical and mnemonic devices ("Thirty days hath September"), nursery rhymes, advertising jingles, and of course song lyrics. Pentameters, irregular rhymes, and free verse aren't much use in songwriting, where the meter has to be governed by the time signature of the music.

Far from universities, there has been a revival of rhymed couplets in rap music, in which, to the accompaniment of synthesizers, vocalists deliver lengthy first-person narratives in tetrameter. While most writing teachers would dismiss such lyrics as doggerel, the aim of the songs is really not so far from that of Alexander Pope: to use rhyme to sharpen social insight, in the hope that the world may be reordered.

From *The Chronicle of Higher Education,* February 24, 1988

Considerations for Critical Thinking and Writing

1. Read some contemporary song lyrics from a wide range of groups or vocalists. Is Lenson correct in his assessment that irregular rhyme is not much use in song-writing?

2. Examine the rhymed couplets of some rap music. Discuss whether they are used "to sharpen social insight." What is the effect of using rhymes in rap music?

3. What is your own response to rhymed poetry? Do you like yours with or without? What do you think informs your preference?

SOUND AND MEANING

GERARD MANLEY HOPKINS (1844–1889)
God's Grandeur

1877

The world is charged with the grandeur of God
  It will flame out, like shining from shook foil;°   *shaken gold foil*
  It gathers to a greatness, like the ooze of oil
Crushed.° Why do men then now not reck his rod?°
Generations have trod, have trod, have trod;   5
  And all is seared with trade; bleared, smeared with toil;
  And wears man's smudge and shares man's smell: the soil
Is bare now, nor can foot feel, being shod.

4 *Crushed:* Olives crushed in their oil; *reck his rod:* Obey God.

And for all this, nature is never spent;
   There lives the dearest freshness deep down things;
And though the last lights off the black West went
   Oh, morning, at the brown brink eastward, springs —
Because the Holy Ghost over the bent
   World broods with warm breast and with ah! bright wings.

    The subject of this poem is announced in the title and the first line: "The world is charged with the grandeur of God." The poem is a celebration of the power and greatness of God's presence in the world, but the speaker is also perplexed and dismayed by people who refuse to recognize God's authority and grandeur as they are manifested in the creation. Instead of glorifying God, "men" have degraded the earth through meaningless toil and cut themselves off from the spiritual renewal inherent in the beauty of nature. The relentless demands of commerce and industry have blinded people to the earth's natural and spiritual resources. In spite of this abuse and insensitivity to God's grandeur, however, "nature is never spent"; the morning light that "springs" in the east redeems the "black West" of the night and is a sign that the spirit of the Holy Ghost is ever present in the world. This summary of the poem sketches some of the thematic significance of the lines, but it does not do justice to how they are organized around the use of sound. Hopkins's poem, unlike Southey's "The Cataract of Lodore," employs sounds in a subtle and complex way.

    In the opening line Hopkins uses alliteration — a device apparent in almost every line of the poem — to connect "God" to the "world," which is "charged" with his "grandeur." These consonants unify the line as well. The alliteration in lines 2–3 suggests a harmony in the creation: the f's in "flame" and "foil," the sh's in "shining" and "shook," the g's in "gathers" and "greatness," and the visual (not alliterative) similarities of "ooze of oil" emphasize a world that is held together by God's will.

    That harmony is abruptly interrupted by the speaker's angry question in line 4: "Why do men then now not reck his rod?" The question is as painful to the speaker as it is difficult to pronounce. The arrangement of the alliteration ("now," "not"; "reck," "rod"), the assonance ("not," "rod"; "men," "then," "reck"), and the internal rhyme ("men," "then") contribute to the difficulty in saying the line, a difficulty associated with human behavior. That behavior is introduced in line 5 by the repetition of "have trod" to emphasize the repeated mistakes — sins — committed by human beings. The tone is dirge-like because humanity persists in its mistaken path rather than progressing. The speaker's horror at humanity is evident in the cacophonous sounds of lines 6–8. Here the alliteration of "smeared," "smudge," and "smell" along with the internal rhymes of "seared," "bleared," and "smeared" echo the disgust with which the speaker views humanity's "toil" with the "soil," an end rhyme that calls attention to our mistaken equation of nature with production rather than with spirituality.

    In contrast to this cacophony, the final six lines build toward the joyful recognition of the new possibilities that accompany the rising sun. This recognition leads to the euphonic description of the "Holy Ghost over" (notice the reassuring consistency of the assonance) the world. Traditionally represented as a dove, the Holy Ghost brings love and peace to the "*w*orld," and "*br*oods *w*ith *w*arm *br*east and *w*ith ah! *br*ight *w*ings." The effect of this alliteration is mellifluous: the sound bespeaks the harmony that prevails at the end of the poem resulting from the speaker's recognition that nature can "never [be] spent" because God loves and protects the world.

The sounds of "God's Grandeur" enhance the poem's theme; more can be said about its sounds, but it is enough to point out here that for this poem the sound strongly echoes the theme in nearly every line. Here are some more poems in which sound plays a significant role.

POEMS FOR FURTHER STUDY

EDGAR ALLAN POE (1809-1849)
The Bells   1849

I

Hear the sledges with the bells —
    Silver bells!
What a world of merriment their melody foretells!
How they tinkle, tinkle, tinkle,
   In the icy air of night!   5
While the stars that oversprinkle
All the heavens, seem to twinkle
    With a crystalline delight;
     Keeping time, time, time,
    In a sort of Runic rhyme,   10
To the tintinnabulation that so musically wells
    From the bells, bells, bells, bells,
      Bells, bells, bells —
From the jingling and the tinkling of the bells

II

Hear the mellow wedding bells —   15
    Golden bells!
What a world of happiness their harmony foretells!
   Through the balmy air of night
   How they ring out their delight! —
    From the molten-golden notes,   20
     And all in tune,
    What a liquid ditty floats
To the turtle-dove that listens, while she gloats
     On the moon!
     Oh, from out the sounding cells,   25
What a gush of euphony voluminously wells!
    How it swells!
    How it dwells
    On the Future! — how it tells

Of the rapture that impels
To the swinging and the ringing
Of the bells, bells, bells —
Of the bells, bells, bells, bells,
Bells, bells, bells —
To the rhyming and the chiming of the bells!

III

Hear the loud alarum bells —
Brazen bells!
What a tale of terror, now, their turbulency tells!
In the startled ear of night
How they scream out their affright!
Too much horrified to speak,
They can only shriek, shriek,
Out of tune,
In a clamorous appealing to the mercy of the fire,
In a mad expostulation with the deaf and frantic fire,
Leaping higher, higher, higher,
With a desperate desire,
And a resolute endeavor
Now — now to sit, or never,
By the side of the pale-faced moon.
Oh, the bells, bells, bells!
What a tale their terror tells
Of Despair!
How they clang, and clash, and roar!
What a horror they outpour
On the bosom of the palpitating air!
Yet the ear, it fully knows,
By the twanging
And the clanging,
How the danger ebbs and flows;
Yet the ear distinctly tells,
In the jangling
And the wrangling,
How the danger sinks and swells,
By the sinking or the swelling in the anger of the bells —
Of the bells, —
Of the bells, bells, bells, bells,
Bells, bells, bells —
In the clamor and the clangor of the bells!

IV

Hear the tolling of the bells —
Iron bells!
What a world of solemn thought their monody compels!
In the silence of the night,
How we shiver with affright
At the melancholy menace of their tone!
For every sound that floats
From the rust within their throats

            Is a groan.
         And the people — ah, the people —
         They that dwell up in the steeple,
                  All alone,
         And who tolling, tolling, tolling,
            In that muffled monotone,
         Feel a glory in so rolling
               On the human heart a stone —
         They are neither man nor woman —
         They are neither brute nor human —
                  They are Ghouls: —
            And their king it is who tolls: —
            And he rolls, rolls, rolls,
                  Rolls
                  A pæan from the bells!
         And his merry bosom swells
               With the pæan of the bells!
            And he dances, and he yells;
         Keeping time, time, time,
         In a sort of Runic rhyme,
               To the pæan of the bells —
                  Of the bells:
         Keeping time, time, time,
         In a sort of Runic rhyme,
               To the throbbing of the bells —
            Of the bells, bells, bells —
               To the sobbing of the bells;
         Keeping time, time, time,
            As he knells, knells, knells.
         In a happy Runic rhyme,
            To the rolling of the bells —
         Of the bells, bells, bells: —
            To the tolling of the bells —
         Of the bells, bells, bells, bells,
               Bells, bells, bells —
   To the moaning and the groaning of the bells.

80

85

90

95

100

105

110

Considerations for Critical Thinking and Writing

1. What kinds of bells are described in each of the poem's four sections?
2. How is onomatopoeia used in each section to echo meanings?
3. What is the effect of the many repetitions of the word *bells*?
4. How do the length of the lines in the poem create musical rhythms?
5. What kinds of rhymes are used to achieve sound effects?
6. What do you think is the theme of "The Bells"?

Connection to Another Selection

1. Compare Poe's sound effects with Southey's in "The Cataract of Lodore" (p. 163). Which poem do you find more effective in its use of sound? Explain why.

LEWIS CARROLL
[CHARLES LUTWIDGE DODGSON] (1832–1898)
Jabberwocky was George Lucas a fan?   1871

'Twas brillig, and the slithy toves
  Did gyre and gimble in the wabe:
All mimsy were the borogoves,
  And the mome raths outgrabe.

"Beware the Jabberwock, my son!   5
  The jaws that bite, the claws that catch!
Beware the Jubjub bird, and shun
  The frumious Bandersnatch!"

He took his vorpal sword in hand;
  Long time the manxome foe he sought —   10
So rested he by the Tumtum tree,
  And stood awhile in thought.

And, as in uffish thought he stood,
  The Jabberwock, with eyes of flame,
Came whiffling through the tulgey wood,   15
  And burbled as it came!

One, two! One, two! And through and through
  The vorpal blade went snicker-snack!
He left it dead, and with its head
  He went galumphing back.   20

"And hast thou slain the Jabberwock?
  Come to my arms, my beamish boy!
O frabjous day! Callooh, Callay!"
  He chortled in his joy.

'Twas brillig, and the slithy toves   25
  Did gyre and gimble in the wabe:
All mimsy were the borogoves,
  And the mome raths outgrabe.

Considerations for Critical Thinking and Writing

1. What happens in this poem? Does it have any meaning?

2. Not all the words used in this poem appear in dictionaries. In *Through the Looking Glass*, Humpty Dumpty explains to Alice that " 'slithy' means 'lithe and slimy.' 'Lithe' is the same as 'active.' You see it's like a portmanteau — there are two meanings packed up into one word." Are there any other portmanteau words in the poem?

3. Which words in the poem sound especially meaningful, even if they are devoid of any denotative meanings?

Connection to Another Selection

1. Compare Carroll's strategies for creating sound and meaning with those used by Swenson in "A Nosty Fright" (p. 158).

SYLVIA PLATH (1932–1963)

Mushrooms   1960

Overnight, very
Whitely, discreetly,
Very quietly

Our toes, our noses
Take hold on the loam,   5
Acquire the air.

Nobody sees us,
Stops us, betrays us;
The small grains make room.

Soft fists insist on   10
Heaving the needles,
The leafy bedding,

Even the paving.
Our hammers, our rams,
Earless and eyeless,   15

Perfectly voiceless,
Widen the crannies,
Shoulder through holes. We

Diet on water,
On crumbs of shadow,   20
Bland-mannered, asking

Little or nothing.
So many of us!
So many of us!

We are shelves, we are   25
Tables, we are meek,
We are edible,

Nudgers and shovers
In spite of ourselves.
Our kind multiplies: 30

We shall by morning
Inherit the earth.
Our foot's in the door.

Considerations for Critical Thinking and Writing

1. Locate the use of alliteration and assonance in the poem. What effects do they
   have on your reading of the poem's tone? Is the tone serious or comic?
2. How important is the title?
3. Discuss what you take to be the poem's theme.

WILLIAM HEYEN (b. 1940)

The Trains

1984

Signed by Franz Paul Stangl, Commandant,
there is in Berlin a document,
an order of transmittal from Treblinka:

248 freight cars of clothing,
400,000 gold watches,   5
25 freight cars of women's hair.

Some clothing was kept, some pulped for paper.
The finest watches were never melted down.
All the women's hair was used for mattresses, or dolls.

Would these words like to use some of that same paper?   10
One of those watches may pulse in your own wrist.
Does someone you know collect dolls, or sleep on human hair?

He is dead at last, Commandant Stangl of Treblinka,
but the camp's three syllables still sound like freight cars
straining around a curve, Treblinka,   15

Treblinka. Clothing, time in gold watches,
women's hair for mattresses and dolls' heads.
Treblinka. The trains from Treblinka.

Considerations for Critical Thinking and Writing

1. Why does the place name of Treblinka continue to resonate over time? If you don't know why Treblinka is infamous, use the library to find out.
2. Why do you suppose Heyen uses the word *in* instead of *on* in line 11?
3. Why is sound so important for establishing the tone of this poem? In what sense do the "camp's three syllables still sound like freight cars" (line 14)?
4. How does this poem make you feel? Why?

Connection to Another Selection

1. Write an essay that considers the use of the past in "The Trains" and in Sadoff's "Nazis" (p. 73). Point to evidence in each poem that suggests it is haunted by the past.

JEAN TOOMER (1894–1967) *from: Kane*

Reapers

1923

Black reapers with the sound of steel on stones
Are sharpening scythes. I see them place the hones
In their hip-pockets as a thing that's done,
And start their silent swinging, one by one.
Black horses drive a mower through the weeds,

And there, a field rat, startled, squealing bleeds,
His belly close to ground. I see the blade,
Blood-stained, continue cutting weeds and shade.

Considerations for Critical Thinking and Writing

1. Is this poem primarily about harvesting or does it suggest something else? Are there any symbols?
2. What is the poem's tone?
3. The reapers' work is described alliteratively as "silent swinging." How are the alliteration and assonance of lines 1–2 and 6 related to their meaning?
4. Why is Toomer's version of line 6 more effective than this one: "And there a startled, squealing field rat bleeds"?

JOHN DONNE (1572–1631)
Song   1633

Go and catch a falling star
   Get with child a mandrake root,°
Tell me where all past years are,
   Or who cleft the Devil's foot,
Teach me to hear mermaids singing,   5
   Or to keep off envy's stinging,
      And find
      What wind
Serves to advance an honest mind.

If thou be'st borne to strange sights,   10
   Things invisible to see,
Ride ten thousand days and nights,
   Till age snow white hairs on thee,
Thou, when thou return'st, wilt tell me
   All strange wonders that befell thee,   15
      And swear
      Nowhere
Lives a woman true, and fair.

If thou findst one, let me know,
   Such a pilgrimage were sweet —   20
Yet do not, I would not go,
   Though at next door we might meet;
Though she were true, when you met her,
   And last, till you write your letter,
      Yet she   25
      Will be
False, ere I come, to two or three.

2 *mandrake root:* This V-shaped root resembles the lower half of the human body.

Considerations for Critical Thinking and Writing

1. What is the speaker's tone in this poem? What is his view of a woman's love? What does the speaker's use of hyperbole reveal about his emotional state?
2. Do you think Donne wants the speaker's argument to be taken seriously? Is there any humor in the poem?
3. Most of these lines end with masculine rhymes. What other kinds of rhymes are used for end rhymes?

JOSEPH BRODSKY (1940-1996)
Love Song

1996

If you were drowning, I'd come to the rescue,
    wrap you in my blanket and pour hot tea.
If I were a sheriff, I'd arrest you
    and keep you in the cell under lock and key.

If you were a bird, I'd cut a record   5
    and listen all night long to your high-pitched trill.
If I were a sergeant, you'd be my recruit,
    and boy I can assure you you'd love the drill.

If you were Chinese, I'd learn the language,
    burn a lot of incense, wear funny clothes.   10
If you were a mirror, I'd storm the Ladies,
    give you my red lipstick and puff your nose.

If you loved volcanoes, I'd be lava
    relentlessly erupting from my hidden source.
And if you were my wife, I'd be your lover   15
    because the church is firmly against divorce.

Considerations for Critical Thinking and Writing

1. Describe the poem's tone. Is it consistent throughout?
2. How do the rhymes contribute to the tone?
3. What is this poem finally about? How do you interpret the last line?

THOMAS HARDY (1840-1928)
The Oxen

1915

Christmas Eve, and twelve of the clock.
    "Now they are all on their knees,"
An elder said as we sat in a flock
    By the embers in hearthside ease.

We pictured the meek mild creatures where   5
    They dwelt in their strawy pen,

Nor did it occur to one of us there
    To doubt they were kneeling then.

So fair a fancy few would weave
    In these years! Yet, I feel,   10
If someone said on Christmas Eve,
    "Come; see the oxen kneel

"In the lonely barton° by yonder coomb°   *farmyard; ravine*
    Our childhood used to know,"
I should go with him in the gloom,   15
    Hoping it might be so.

Considerations for Critical Thinking and Writing

1. Traditionally, European peasants believed that animals worship God on Christmas Eve. How does the speaker feel about this belief? What is the difference
   between the speaker's attitude as a child and, "In these years," as an adult?
2. The speaker seems to feel nostalgic about his lost childhood. Does he feel the
   loss of anything more than that?
3. How do the sounds in the final stanza reinforce the tone and theme of the poem?

ALEXANDER POPE (1688–1774)

From *An Essay on Criticism*   1711

    But most by numbers° judge a poet's song;   *versification*
And smooth or rough, with them, is right or wrong;
In the bright muse though thousand charms conspire,
Her voice is all these tuneful fools admire;
Who haunt Parnassus° but to please their ear,   5
Not mend their minds; as some to church repair,
Not for the doctrine, but the music there.
These equal syllables alone require,
Though oft the ear the open vowels tire;
While expletives° their feeble aid do join;   10
And ten low words oft creep in one dull line;
While they ring round the same unvaried chimes,
With sure returns of still expected rhymes;
Where'er you find "the cooling western breeze,"
In the next line, it "whispers through the trees":   15
If crystal streams "with pleasing murmurs creep,"
The reader's threatened (not in vain) with "sleep":
Then, at the last and only couplet fraught
With some unmeaning thing they call a thought,
A needless Alexandrine° ends the song,   20
That, like a wounded snake, drags its slow length along.
Leave such to tune their own dull rhymes, and know

5 *Parnassus:* A Greek mountain sacred to the Muses.   10 *expletives:* Unnecessary words used to
fill a line, as the *do* in this line.   20 *Alexandrine:* A twelve-syllable line, as line 21.

What's roundly smooth, or languishingly slow;
And praise the easy vigor of a line,
Where Denham's strength, and Waller's° sweetness join.   25
True ease in writing comes from art, not chance,
As those move easiest who have learned to dance.
'Tis not enough no harshness gives offense,
The sound must seem an echo to the sense:
Soft is the strain when Zephyr° gently blows,   *the west wind* 30
And the smooth stream in smoother numbers flows;
But when loud surges lash the sounding shore,
The hoarse, rough verse should like the torrent roar:
When Ajax° strives some rock's vast weight to throw,
The line too labors, and the words move slow;   35
Not so, when swift Camilla° scours the plain,
Flies o'er th' unbending corn, and skims along the main.

25 *Denham's, Waller's:* Sir John Denham (1615–1669), Edmund Waller (1606–1687) were poets who used
heroic couplets.   34 *Ajax:* A Greek warrior famous for his strength in the Trojan War.   36 *Camilla:*
A goddess famous for her delicate speed.

Considerations for Critical Thinking and Writing

1. These lines make a case for sound as an important element in poetry. In them
   Pope describes some faults he finds in poems and illustrates those faults within
   the lines that describe them. How do lines 4, 9, 10, 11, and 21 illustrate what they
   describe?
2. What is the objection to the "expected rhymes" in lines 12–17? How do they differ from Pope's end rhymes?
3. Some lines discuss how to write successful poetry. How do lines 23, 24, 32–33,
   35, and 36–37 illustrate what they describe?
4. Do you agree that in a good poem "the sound must [always] seem an echo to the
   sense"?

MARILYN HACKER (b. 1942)
Groves of Academe   1984

The hour dragged on, and I was badly needing
coffee; that encouraged my perversity.
I asked the students of Poetry Writing,
"Tell me about the poetry you're reading."
There was some hair chewing and some nail biting.   5
Snowdrifts piled up around the university.
"I've really gotten into science fiction."
"I don't read much — it breaks my concentration.
I wouldn't want to influence my style."
"We taped some Sound Poems for the college station."   10
"When *I* give readings, should I work on diction?"
"Is it true that no really worthwhile
contemporary poets write in rhyme?"

"Do you think it would be a waste of time
to send my poems to *Vanity Fair*?
I mean — could they relate to my work there?"

15

Considerations for Critical Thinking and Writing

1. Characterize the speaker. Do you find any humor in line 6?
2. What do the student's comments and questions in response to their teacher's question (line 4) reveal about themselves?
3. How does the speaker implicitly answer the question about poetic rhyme in lines 12–13?

Connection to Another Selection

1. Write an essay that compares the teachers in "Groves of Academe" and in Mark Halliday's "Graded Paper" (p. 496). Which teacher would you rather have for a course? Explain why.

MAXINE HONG KINGSTON (b. 1940)
Restaurant

What's quality? & a rest.?

1981

for Lilah Kan

The main cook lies sick on a banquette, and his assistant
has cut his thumb. So the quiche cook takes
their places at the eight-burner range, and you and I
get to roll out twenty-three rounds of pie
dough and break a hundred eggs, four at a crack,   5
and sift out shell with a China cap, pack
spinach in the steel sink, squish and squeeze
the water out, and grate a full moon of cheese.
Pam, the pastry chef, who is baking Choco-
late Globs (once called Mulattos) complains about the disco,   10
which Lewis, the salad man, turns up louder out of spite.
"Black so-called musician," "Broads. Whites."
The porters, who speak French, from the Ivory Coast,
sweep up droppings and wash the pans without soap.
We won't be out of here until three A.M. In this basement,   15
I lose my size. I am a bent-over
child, Gretel or Jill, and I can
lift a pot as big as a tub with both hands.
Using a pitchfork, you stoke the broccoli and bacon.
Then I find you in the freezer, taking   20
a nibble of a slab of chocolate as big as a table.
We put the quiches in the oven, then we are able
to stick our heads up out of the sidewalk into the night
and wonder at the clean diners behind glass in candlelight.

Considerations for Critical Thinking and Writing

1. How do the sounds of this poem contribute to the descriptions of what goes on in the restaurant kitchen?
2. In what sense does the speaker "lose [her] size" (line 16) in the kitchen? How would you describe her?
3. Examine the poem's rhymes. What effect do they have on your reading?
4. Describe the tone of the final line. How does it differ from the rest of the poem?

Connections to Other Selections

1. Write an essay analyzing how the kitchen activities described in "Restaurant," Kizer's "Food for Love" (p. 101), and Magarrell's "The Joy of Cooking" (p. 123) are used to convey the themes of these poems.

PAUL HUMPHREY (b. 1915)
Blow

1983

Her skirt was lofted by the gale;
When I, with gesture deft,
Essayed to stay her frisky sail
She luffed, and laughed, and left.

Considerations for Critical Thinking and Writing

1. Point out instances of alliteration and assonance in this poem, and explain how they contribute to its euphonic effects.
2. What is the poem's controlling metaphor? Why is it especially appropriate?
3. Explain the ambiguity of the title.

ROBERT FRANCIS (1901–1987)
The Pitcher

1953

His art is eccentricity, his aim
How not to hit the mark he seems to aim at,

His passion how to avoid the obvious,
His technique how to vary the avoidance.

The others throw to be comprehended. He   5
Throws to be a moment misunderstood.

Yet not too much. Not errant, arrant, wild,
But every seeming aberration willed.

Not to, yet still, still to communicate
Making the batter understand too late.   10

Considerations for Critical Thinking and Writing

1. Explain how each pair of lines in this poem describes the pitcher's art.
2. Consider how the poem itself works the way a good pitcher does. Which lines illustrate what they describe?
3. Comment on the effects of the poem's rhymes. How are the final two lines different in their rhyme from the previous lines? How does sound echo sense in lines 9–10?
4. Write an essay that considers "The Pitcher" as an extended metaphor for talking about poetry. How well does the poem characterize strategies for writing poetry as well as pitching?
5. Write an essay that develops an extended comparison between writing or reading poetry and playing or watching another sport.

Connections to Other Selections

1. Compare this poem with Robert Wallace's "The Double-Play" (p. 461), another poem that explores the relation of baseball to poetry.
2. Write an essay comparing "The Pitcher" with Francis's "Catch" (p. 14). One poem defines poetry implicitly, the other defines it explicitly. Which poem do you prefer? Why?

HELEN CHASIN (b. 1938)
The Word Plum

1968

The word *plum* is delicious

pout and push, luxury of
self-love, and savoring murmur
full in the mouth and falling
like fruit   5

taut skin
pierced, bitten, provoked into
juice, and tart flesh

question
and reply, lip and tongue   10
of pleasure.

Considerations for Critical Thinking and Writing

1. Underline the alliteration and circle the assonance throughout the poem. What is the effect of these repetitions?
2. Which sounds in the poem are like the sounds one makes while eating a plum?
3. Discuss the title. Explain whether you think this poem is more about the word *plum* or about the plum itself. Consider whether the two can be separated in the poem.

Connection to Another Selection

1. How is Kinnell's "Blackberry Eating" (p. 161) similar in technique to Chasin's poem? Try writing such a poem yourself: choose a food to describe that allows you to evoke its sensuousness in sounds.

JOHN KEATS (1795–1821)
Ode to a Nightingale

1819

I

My heart aches, and a drowsy numbness pains
  My sense, as though of hemlock° I had drunk,   *a poison*
Or emptied some dull opiate to the drains
  One minute past, and Lethe-wards° had sunk:
'Tis not through envy of thy happy lot,   5
  But being too happy in thine happiness —
    That thou, light-wingèd Dryad° of the trees,   *wood nymph*
      In some melodious plot
  Of beechen green, and shadows numberless,
    Singest of summer in full-throated ease.   10

II

O, for a draught of vintage! that hath been
  Cooled a long age in the deep-delved earth,
Tasting of Flora° and the country green,   *goddess of flowers*
  Dance, and Provençal song,° and sunburnt mirth!
O for a beaker full of the warm South,   15
  Full of the true, the blushful Hippocrene,°
    With beaded bubbles winking at the brim,
      And purple-stainèd mouth;
  That I might drink, and leave the world unseen,
    And with thee fade away into the forest dim.   20

III

Fade far away, dissolve, and quite forget
  What thou among the leaves hast never known,
The weariness, the fever, and the fret
  Here, where men sit and hear each other groan;
Where palsy shakes a few, sad, last gray hairs,   25
  Where youth grows pale, and specter-thin, and dies,
    Where but to think is to be full of sorrow
      And leaden-eyed despairs,
  Where Beauty cannot keep her lustrous eyes;
    Or new Love pine at them beyond tomorrow.   30

---

4 *Lethe-wards:* Toward Lethe, the river of forgetfulness in the Hades of Greek mythology.
14 *Provençal song:* The medieval troubadours of Provence, France, were known for their singing.
16 *Hippocrene:* The fountain of the Muses in Greek mythology.

IV

Away! away! for I will fly to thee,
   Not charioted by Bacchus and his pards,°
But on the viewless wings of Poesy,
   Though the dull brain perplexes and retards:
Already with thee! tender is the night,   35
    And haply the Queen-Moon is on her throne,
      Clustered around by all her starry Fays;
        But here there is no light,
    Save what from heaven is with the breezes blown
        Through verdurous glooms and winding mossy ways.   40

V

I cannot see what flowers are at my feet,
   Nor what soft incense hangs upon the boughs,
But, in embalmèd° darkness, guess each sweet   *perfumed*
   Wherewith the seasonable month endows
The grass, the thicket, and the fruit-tree wild;   45
    What hawthorn, and the pastoral eglantine;
      Fast fading violets covered up in leaves;
        And mid-May's eldest child,
    The coming musk-rose, full of dewy wine,
        The murmurous haunt of flies on summer eves.   50

VI

Darkling° I listen; and for many a time   *in the dark*
   I have been half in love with easeful Death,
Called him soft names in many a musèd rhyme,
   To take into the air my quiet breath;
Now more than ever seems it rich to die,   55
   To cease upon the midnight with no pain,
     While thou art pouring forth thy soul abroad
       In such an ecstasy!
   Still wouldst thou sing, and I have ears in vain —
    To thy high requiem become a sod.   60

VII

Thou wast not born for death, immortal Bird!
   No hungry generations tread thee down;
The voice I hear this passing night was heard
   In ancient days by emperor and clown:
Perhaps the selfsame song that found a path   65
   Through the sad heart of Ruth,° when, sick for home,
     She stood in tears amid the alien corn:
       The same that oft-times hath
   Charmed magic casements, opening on the foam
    Of perilous seas, in faery lands forlorn.   70

---

32 *Bacchus and his pards:* The Greek god of wine traveled in a chariot drawn by leopards.
66 *Ruth:* A young widow in the Bible (see the Book of Ruth).

VIII

Forlorn! the very word is like a bell
 To toll me back from thee to my sole self!
Adieu! the fancy cannot cheat so well
 As she is famed to do, deceiving elf.
Adieu! adieu! thy plaintive anthem fades   75
 Past the near meadows, over the still stream,
  Up the hill side; and now 'tis buried deep
   In the next valley-glades:
 Was it a vision, or a waking dream?
  Fled is that music: — Do I wake or sleep?   80

Considerations for Critical Thinking and Writing

1. Why does the speaker in this ode want to leave his world for the nightingale's? What does the nightingale symbolize?
2. How does the speaker attempt to escape his world? Is he successful?
3. What changes the speaker's view of death at the end of stanza VI?
4. What does the allusion to Ruth (line 66) contribute to the ode's meaning?
5. In which lines is the imagery especially sensuous? How does this effect add to the conflict presented?
6. What calls the speaker back to himself at the end of stanza VII and the beginning of stanza VIII?
7. Choose a stanza and explain how sound is related to its meaning.
8. How regular is the stanza form of this ode?

7. Patterns of Rhythm

The rhythms of everyday life surround us in regularly recurring movements and sounds. As you read these words, your heart pulsates while somewhere else a clock ticks, a cradle rocks, a drum beats, a dancer sways, a foghorn blasts, a wave recedes, or a child skips. We may tend to overlook rhythm since it is so tightly woven into the fabric of our experience, but it is there nonetheless, one of the conditions of life. Rhythm is also one of the conditions of speech, because the voice alternately rises and falls as words are stressed or unstressed and as the pace quickens or slackens. In poetry *rhythm* refers to the recurrence of stressed and unstressed sounds. Depending on how the sounds are arranged, this can result in a pace that is fast or slow, choppy or smooth.

SOME PRINCIPLES OF METER

Poets use rhythm to create pleasurable sound patterns and to reinforce meanings. "Rhythm," Edith Sitwell once observed, "might be described as, to the world of sound, what light is to the world of sight. It shapes and gives new meaning." Prose can use rhythm effectively too, but prose that does so tends to be an exception. The following exceptional lines are from a speech by Winston Churchill to the House of Commons after Allied forces lost a great battle to German forces at Dunkirk during World War II.

> We shall not flag or fail. We shall go on to the end. We shall fight in France, we shall fight on the seas and oceans, we shall fight with growing confidence and growing strength in the air, we shall defend our island, whatever the cost may be, we shall fight on the beaches, we shall fight on the landing grounds, we shall fight in the fields and in the streets, we shall fight in the hills; we shall never surrender.

The stressed repetition of "we shall" bespeaks the resolute singleness of purpose that Churchill had to convey to the British people if they were to win the war. Repetition is also one of the devices used in poetry to create rhythmic effects. In the following excerpt from "Song of the Open Road," Walt Whitman urges the pleasures of limitless freedom upon his reader.

Allons!° the road is before us!   *Let's go!*
It is safe — I have tried it — my own feet have tried it well —
    be not detain'd!
Let the paper remain on the desk unwritten, and the book
    on the shelf unopen'd!
Let the tools remain in the workshop! Let the money remain
    unearn'd!
Let the school stand! mind not the cry of the teacher!   5
Let the preacher preach in his pulpit! Let the lawyer plead
    in the court, and the judge expound the law.

Camerado,° I give you my hand!   *friend*
I give you my love more precious than money,
I give you myself before preaching or law;
Will you give me yourself? will you come travel with me?   10
Shall we stick by each other as long as we live?

These rhythmic lines quickly move away from conventional values to the
open road of shared experiences. Their recurring sounds are not created by
rhyme or alliteration and assonance (see Chapter 6) but by the repetition of
words and phrases.

Although the repetition of words and phrases can be an effective means
of creating rhythm in poetry, the more typical method consists of patterns of
accented or unaccented syllables. Words contain syllables that are either
stressed or unstressed. A **stress** (or ***accent***) places more emphasis on one syllable than on another. We say "*syl*lable" not "syl*la*ble," "*em*phasis" not
"em*pha*sis." We routinely stress syllables when we speak: "*Is* she con*tent* with
the *con*tents of the *yel*low *pack*age?" To distinguish between two people we
might say "Is *she* con*tent*. . . ." In this way stress can be used to emphasize a
particular word in a sentence. Poets often arrange words so that the desired
meaning is suggested by the rhythm; hence, emphasis is controlled by the
poet rather than left entirely to the reader.

When a rhythmic pattern of stresses recurs in a poem, the result is ***meter.***
Scansion consists of measuring the stresses in a line to determine its metrical
pattern. Several methods can be used to mark lines. One widely used system
employs ´ for a stressed syllable and ˘ for an unstressed syllable. In a sense,
the stress mark represents the equivalent of tapping one's foot to a beat.

    Híckŏrў, díckŏrў, dóck,

    The móuse răn úp thĕ clóck.

    The clóck strŭck óne,

    Ănd dówn hĕ rún,

    Híckŏrў, díckŏrў, dóck.

In the first two lines and the final line of this familiar nursery rhyme we hear
three stressed syllables. In lines 3 and 4, where the meter changes for variety,
we hear just two stressed syllables. The combination of stresses provides the
pleasure of the rhythm we hear.

To hear the rhythms of "Hickory, dickory, dock" does not require a formal study of meter. Nevertheless, an awareness of the basic kinds of meter that appear in English poetry can enhance your understanding of how a poem achieves its effects. Understanding the sound effects of a poem and having a vocabulary with which to discuss those effects can intensify your pleasure in poetry. Although the study of meter can be extremely technical, the terms used to describe the basic meters of English poetry are relatively easy to comprehend.

The _foot_ is the metrical unit by which a line of poetry is measured. A foot usually consists of one stressed and one or two unstressed syllables. A vertical line is used to separate the feet: "The clŏck | strŭck óne" consists of two feet. A foot of poetry can be arranged in a variety of patterns; here are five of the chief ones.

Foot	Pattern	Example
iamb	˘ ´	ăwáy
trochee	´ ˘	lóvelĕ
anapest	˘ ˘ ´	ŭndĕrstánd
dactyl	´ ˘ ˘	déspĕrătĕ
spondee	´ ´	déad sét

The most common lines in English poetry contain meters based on iambic feet. However, even lines that are predominantly iambic will often include variations to create particular effects. Other important patterns include trochaic, anapestic, and dactylic feet. The spondee is not a sustained meter but occurs for variety or emphasis.

Rising **Iambic**

What kĕpt | hĭs eyés | frŏm gív | ĭng báck | thĕ gáze

Falling **Trochaic**

Hé wăs | loúdĕr | thán thĕ | préachĕr

R **Anapestic**

Ĭ ăm cálled | tŏ thĕ frónt | ŏf thĕ roóm

F **Dactylic**

Síng ĭt ăll | mérrĭlĕ

These meters have different rhythms and can create different effects. Iambic and anapestic are known as _**rising meters**_ because they move from unstressed to stressed sounds, while trochaic and dactylic are known as _**falling meters**_. Anapests and dactyls tend to move more lightly and rapidly than iambs or trochees. Although no single kind of meter can be considered always better than another for a given subject, it is possible to determine whether the meter of a specific poem is appropriate for its subject. A serious poem about a tragic death would most likely not be well served by lilting rhythms. Keep in mind too that though one or another of these four basic meters might constitute the predominant rhythm of a poem, variations can occur within lines to change the pace or call attention to a particular word.

A _line_ is measured by the number of feet it contains. Here, for example, is an iambic line with three feet: "If shĕ | shŏuld wrĭte | ă nŏte." These are the names for line lengths.

monometer: one foot pentameter: five feet

dimeter: two feet hexameter: six feet

trimeter: three feet heptameter: seven feet

tetrameter: four feet octameter: eight feet

By combining the name of a line length with the name of a foot, we can describe the metrical qualities of a line concisely. Consider, for example, the pattern of feet and length of this line.

I didn't want the boy to hit the dog.

The iambic rhythm of this line falls into five feet; hence it is called *iambic pentameter.* Iambic is the most common pattern in English poetry because its rhythm appears so naturally in English speech and writing. Unrhymed iambic pentameter is called *blank verse;* Shakespeare's plays are built upon such lines.

Less common than the iamb, trochee, anapest, or dactyl is the *spondee,* a two-syllable foot in which both syllables are stressed (´ ´). Note the effect of the spondaic foot at the beginning of this line.

Déad sét | ăgaiȟst | thĕ plăn | hĕ wĕnt | ăwáy.

Spondees can slow a rhythm and provide variety and emphasis, particularly in iambic and trochaic lines. A line that ends with a stressed syllable is said to have a *masculine ending,* whereas a line that ends with an extra unstressed syllable is said to have a *feminine ending.* Consider, for example, these two lines from Timothy Steel's "Waiting for the Storm" (the entire poem appears on p. 189):

feminine: Thĕ sánd | ăt my féet | grŏw cóld | eȟ,

masculine: Thĕ damp | air chíll | and spréad.

The effects of English meters are easily seen in the following lines by Samuel Taylor Coleridge, in which the rhythm of each line illustrates the meter described in it.

Trochee trips from long to short;
From long to long in solemn sort
Slow Spondee stalks; strong foot yet ill able
Ever to come up with Dactylic trisyllable.
Iambics march from short to long —
With a leap and a bound the swift Anapests throng.

The speed of a line is also affected by the number of pauses in it. A pause within a line is called a *caesura* and is indicated by a double vertical line (‖). A caesura can occur anywhere within a line and need not be indicated by punctuation.

Camerado, ‖ I give you my hand!
I give you my love ‖ more precious than money.

A slight pause occurs within each of these lines and at its end. Both kinds of pauses contribute to the lines' rhythm.

When a line has a pause at its end, it is called an ***end-stopped line***. Such pauses reflect normal speech patterns and are often marked by punctuation. A line that ends without a pause and continues into the next line for its meaning is called a ***run-on line***. Running over from one line to another is also called ***enjambment***. The first and eighth lines of the following poem are run-on lines; the rest are end-stopped.

WILLIAM WORDSWORTH (1770–1850)
My Heart Leaps Up   1807

My heart leaps up when I behold
  A rainbow in the sky:
So was it when my life began;
So is it now I am a man;
So be it when I shall grow old,
  Or let me die!
The child is father of the Man;
And I could wish my days to be
Bound each to each by natural piety.

Run-on lines have a different rhythm from end-stopped lines. Lines 3–4 and 8–9 are both iambic, but the effect of their rhythms is very different when we read these lines aloud. The enjambment of lines 8 and 9 reinforces their meaning; just as the "days" are bound together, so are the lines.

The rhythm of a poem can be affected by several devices: the kind and number of stresses within lines, the length of lines, and the kinds of pauses that appear within lines or at their ends. In addition, as we saw in Chapter 6, the sound of a poem is affected by alliteration, assonance, rhyme, and consonance. These sounds help to create rhythms by controlling our pronunciations, as in the following lines by Alexander Pope.

> Soft is the strain when Zephyr gently blows,
> And the smooth stream in smoother numbers flows;
> But when loud surges lash the sounding shore,
> The hoarse, rough verse should like the torrent roar.

These lines are effective because their rhythm and sound work with their meaning.

SUGGESTIONS FOR SCANNING A POEM

These suggestions should help you in talking about a poem's meter.

1. After reading the poem through, read it aloud and mark the stressed syllables in each line. Then mark the unstressed syllables.
2. From your markings, identify what kind of foot is dominant (iambic,

trochaic, dactylic, or anapestic) and divide the lines into feet, keeping in mind that the vertical line marking a foot may come in the middle of a word as well as at its beginning or end.

3. Determine the number of feet in each line. Remember that there may be variations; some lines may be shorter or longer than the predominant meter. What is important is the overall pattern. Do not assume that variations represent the poet's inability to fulfill the overall pattern. Notice the effects of variations and whether they emphasize words and phrases or disrupt your expectation for some other purpose.

4. Listen for pauses within lines and mark the caesuras; many times there will be no punctuation to indicate them.

5. Recognize that scansion does not always yield a definitive measurement of a line. Even experienced readers may differ over the scansion of a given line. What is important is not a precise description of the line but an awareness of how a poem's rhythms contribute to its effects.

The following poem demonstrates how you can use an understanding of meter and rhythm to gain a greater appreciation for what a poem is saying.

TIMOTHY STEELE (b. 1948)
Waiting for the Storm   1986

Bréeze sént | ă wrínk | lĭng dárk | nĕss
Ácróss | thĕ báy. ‖ Ĭ knélt
Bĕnéath | ăn úp | turnĕd bóat,
Ănd, mó | mĕnt bў mó | mĕnt, félt

Thĕ sánd | ăt mў féet | grŏw cóld | ér,
Thĕ dámp | áir chíll | ănd spréad.
Thĕn thĕ | first ráin | dróps sóund | ĕd
Ŏn thĕ húll | ăbóve | mў héad.

The predominant meter of this poem is iambic trimeter, but there is plenty of variation as the storm rapidly approaches and finally begins to pelt the sheltered speaker. The emphatic spondee ("Breeze sent") pushes the darkness quickly across the bay while the caesura at the end of the sentence in line 2 creates a pause that sets up a feeling of suspense and expectation that is measured in the ticking rhythm of line 4, a run-on line that brings us into the chilly sand and air of the second stanza. Perhaps the most impressive sound effect used in the poem appears in the second syllable of "sounded" in line 7. That "*ed* " precedes the sound of the poem's final word "head" just as if it were the first drop of rain hitting the hull above the speaker. The visual, tactile, and auditory images make "Waiting for the Storm" an intense sensory experience.

This next poem also reinforces meanings through its use of meter and rhythm.

WILLIAM BUTLER YEATS (1865-1939)
That the Night Come 1912

She lĭved | ĭn stórm | ănd strífe,
Hĕr soúl | hăd súch | ă̆ desiré
Fŏr whát | proŭd déath | mă̆y bríng
Thă̆t ĭt | coŭld nót | ĕndure
Thĕ cóm | mŏn goód | ŏf lífe,
Bŭt lívĕd | aš 'twére | ă̆ kíng
Thă̆t pácked | hĭs már | riă̆ge dáy
Wĭth bán | nĕrét | ănd pén | nŏn,
Trúmpĕt | ănd két | tlĕdrum,
Ănd thĕ | oŭtrág | eoŭs cán | nŏn,
Tŏ bun | dlĕ tíme | ă̆wáy
Thă̆t thĕ | níght cóme.

Scansion reveals that the predominant meter here is iambic trimeter. Each line contains three stressed and unstressed syllables that form a regular, predictable rhythm through line 7. That rhythm is disrupted, however, when the speaker compares the woman's longing for what death brings to a king's eager anticipation of his wedding night. The king packs the day with noisy fanfares and celebrations to fill up time and distract himself. Unable to accept "the common good of life," the woman fills her days with "storm and strife." In a determined effort to "bundle time away," she, like the king, impatiently awaits the night.

Lines 8–10 break the regular pattern established in the first seven lines. The extra unstressed syllable in lines 8 and 10 along with the trochaic feet in lines 9 (*trúmpĕt*) and 10 (*Ănd thĕ*) interrupt the basic iambic trimeter and parallel the woman's and the king's frenetic activity. These lines thus echo the inability of the woman and king to "endure" regular or normal time. The last line is the most irregular in the poem. The final two accented syllables sound like the deep resonant beats of a kettledrum or a cannon firing. The words "night come" dramatically remind us that what the woman anticipates is not a lover but the mysterious finality of death. The meter serves, then, in both its regularity and variations to reinforce the poem's meaning and tone.

The following poems are especially rich in their rhythms and sounds. As you read and study them, notice how patterns of rhythm and the sounds of words reinforce meanings and contribute to the poems' effects. And, perhaps most important, read the poems aloud so that you can hear them.

POEMS FOR FURTHER STUDY

ALICE JONES (b. 1949)
The Foot   1993

Our improbable support, erected
on the osseous architecture
of the calcaneus, talus, cuboid,
navicular, cuneiforms, metatarsals,
phalanges, a plethora of hinges,   5

all strung together by gliding
tendons, covered by the pearly
plantar fascia, then fat-padded
to form the sole, humble surface
of our contact with earth.   10

Here the body's broadest tendon
anchors the heel's fleshy base,
the finely wrinkled skin stretches
forward across the capillaried arch,
to the ball, a balance point.   15

A wide web of flexor tendons
and branched veins maps the dorsum,
fades into the stub-laden bone
splay, the stuffed sausage sacks
of toes, each with a tuft   20

of proximal hairs to introduce
the distal nail, whose useless
curve remembers an ancestor,
the vanished creature's wild
and necessary claw.   25

Considerations for Critical Thinking and Writing

1. Alice Jones has described the form of "The Foot" as "five stubby stanzas." Explain why the lines of this poem may or may not warrant this description of the stanzas.
2. What is the effect of the diction? What sort of tone is established by the use of anatomical terms?
3. Describe the effect of the final stanza. How would your reading be affected if the poem ended after the comma in the middle of line 22?

A. E. HOUSMAN (1859–1936)
When I was one-and-twenty   1896

When I was one-and-twenty
    I heard a wise man say,
"Give crowns and pounds and guineas
    But not your heart away;

Give pearls away and rubies   5
    But keep your fancy free."
But I was one-and-twenty,
    No use to talk to me.

When I was one-and-twenty
    I heard him say again,   10
"The heart out of the bosom
    Was never given in vain;
'Tis paid with sighs a plenty
    And sold for endless rue."
And I am two-and-twenty,   15
    And oh, 'tis true, 'tis true.

Considerations for Critical Thinking and Writing

1. Scan this poem. What is the basic metrical pattern?
2. How do lines 1–8 parallel lines 9–16 in their use of rhyme and metaphor? Are there any significant differences between the stanzas?
2. What do you think has happened to change the speaker's attitude toward love?
3. Explain why you agree or disagree with the advice given by the "wise man."
4. What is the effect of the repetition in line 16?

RACHEL HADAS (b. 1948)
The Red Hat   1995

It started before Christmas. Now our son
officially walks to school alone.
Semi-alone, it's accurate to say:
I or his father track him on the way.
He walks up on the east side of West End,   5
we on the west side. Glances can extend
(and do) across the street; not eye contact.
Already ties are feeling and not fact.
Straus Park is where these parallel paths part;
he goes alone from there. The watcher's heart   10
stretches, elastic in its love and fear,
toward him as we see him disappear,
striding briskly. Where two weeks ago,
holding a hand, he'd dawdle, dreamy, slow,
he now is hustled forward by the pull   15
of something far more powerful than school.

The mornings we turn back to are no more
than forty minutes longer than before,
but they feel vastly different — flimsy, strange,
wavering in the eddies of this change,   20
empty, unanchored, perilously light
since the red hat vanished from our sight.

Considerations for Critical Thinking and Writing

1. What prevents the rhymed couplets in this poem from sounding sing-songy? What is the predominant meter?
2. What is it that "pull[s]" the boy along in lines 15–16?
3. What emotions do the parents experience in lines 17–22? How do you think the boy feels?
4. Why do you think Hadas titled the poem "The Red Hat" rather than, for example, "Paths Part" (line 9)?

Connection to Another Selection

1. In an essay discuss the themes of "The Red Hat" and Bly's "Sitting Down to Dinner" (p. 154). Pay particular attention to the way parents are presented in each poem.

ROBERT HERRICK (1591-1674)
Delight in Disorder   1648

A sweet disorder in the dress
Kindles in clothes a wantonness.
A lawn° about the shoulders thrown   *linen scarf*
Into a fine distraction;
An erring lace, which here and there   5
Enthralls the crimson stomacher,
A cuff neglectful, and thereby
Ribbons to flow confusedly;
A winning wave, deserving note,
In the tempestuous petticoat;   10
A careless shoestring, in whose tie
I see a wild civility;
Do more bewitch me than when art
Is too precise in every part.

Considerations for Critical Thinking and Writing

1. Why does the speaker in this poem value "disorder" so highly?
2. What is the principal rhythmic order of the poem? Is it "precise in every part"? How does the poem's organization relate to its theme?
3. Which words in the poem indicate disorder? Which words indicate the speaker's response to that disorder? What are the connotative meanings of each set of words? Why are they appropriate? What do they suggest about the woman and the speaker?
4. Write a short essay in which you agree or disagree with the speaker's views on dress.

BEN JONSON (1573-1637)
Still to Be Neat

1609

Still° to be neat, still to be dressed,   *continually*
As you were going to a feast;
Still to be powdered, still perfumed;
Lady, it is to be presumed,
Though art's hid causes are not found,   5
All is not sweet, all is not sound.

Give me a look, give me a face
That makes simplicity a grace;
Robes loosely flowing, hair as free;
Such sweet neglect more taketh me   10
Then all th' adulteries of art.
They strike mine eyes, but not my heart.

Considerations for Critical Thinking and Writing

1. What are the speaker's reservations about the lady in the first stanza? What do you think "sweet" means in line 6?
2. What does the speaker want from the lady in the second stanza? How has the meaning of "sweet" shifted from line 6 to line 10? What other words in the poem are especially charged with connotative meanings?
3. How do the rhythms of Jonson's lines help to reinforce meanings? Pay particular attention to lines 6 and 12.

Connections to Another Selection

1. Write an essay comparing the themes of "Still to Be Neat" and Herrick's preceding poem, "Delight in Disorder." How do the speakers make similar points but from different perspectives?
2. How does the rhythm of "Still to Be Neat" compare with that of "Delight in Disorder"? Which do you find more effective? Explain why.

CHARLES MARTIN (b. 1942)
Victoria's Secret

1994

Victorian mothers instructed their daughters, ahem,
That whenever their husbands were getting it on them,
The only thing for it was just to lie perfectly flat
And try to imagine themselves out buying a new hat;
So, night after night, expeditions grimly set off   5
Each leaving a corpse in its wake to service the toff°   *dandy*
With the whiskers and whiskey, the lecherous ogre bent
Over her, thrashing and thrusting until he was spent.
Or so we imagine, persuaded that our ancestors

Couldn't have been as free from repression as we are,   10
As our descendants will no doubt mock any passion
They think we were prone to, if thinking comes back into fashion.
And here is *Victoria's Secret,* which fondly supposes
That the young women depicted in various poses
Of complaisant negligence somehow or other reveal   15
More than we see of them: we're intended to feel
That this isn't simply a matter of sheer lingerie,
But rather the baring of something long hidden away
Behind an outmoded conception of rectitude:
Liberation appears to us, not entirely nude,   20
In the form of a fullbreasted nymph, impeccably slim,
Airbrushed at each conjunction of torso and limb,
Who looks up from the page with large and curious eyes
That never close: and in their depths lie frozen
The wordless dreams shared by all merchandise,   25
Even the hats that wait in the dark to be chosen.

Considerations for Critical Thinking and Writing

1. Describe the speaker. What reflections does he (and is it a he?) have about past and future generations?
2. Does the speaker's description of *Victoria's Secret* models ring true to you? Explain why or why not.
3. What is the effect of the changed rhyme scheme in lines 23–26?
4. Comment on the title. How is it related to the poem's theme?

Connection to Another Selection

1. Write an essay on the social criticism aimed at advertising in this poem and in Fearing's "AD" (p. 134).

WILLIAM BLAKE (1757–1827)
The Lamb   1789

    Little Lamb, who made thee?
    Dost thou know who made thee?
Gave thee life, and bid thee feed
By the stream and o'er the mead;
Gave thee clothing of delight,   5
Softest clothing, wooly, bright;
Gave thee such a tender voice,
Making all the vales rejoice?
    Little Lamb, who made thee?
    Dost thou know who made thee?   10

    Little Lamb, I'll tell thee,
    Little Lamb, I'll tell thee:

He is callèd by thy name,
For he calls himself a Lamb.
He is meek, and he is mild;   15
He became a little child.
I a child, and thou a lamb,
We are callèd by his name.
    Little Lamb, God bless thee!
    Little Lamb, God bless thee!   20

Considerations for Critical Thinking and Writing

1. This poem is from Blake's *Songs of Innocence*. Describe its tone. How do the
   meter, rhyme, and repetition help to characterize the speaker's voice?
2. Why is it significant that the animal addressed by the speaker is a lamb? What
   symbolic value would be lost if the animal were, for example, a doe?
3. How does the second stanza answer the question raised in the first? What is the
   speaker's view of the creation?

WILLIAM BLAKE (1757–1827)
The Tyger   1794

Tyger! Tyger! burning bright
In the forests of the night,
What immortal hand or eye
Could frame thy fearful symmetry?

In what distant deeps or skies   5
Burnt the fire of thine eyes?
On what wings dare he aspire?
What the hand dare seize the fire?

And what shoulder, and what art,
Could twist the sinews of thy heart?   10
And when thy heart began to beat,
What dread hand? and what dread feet?

What the hammer? what the chain?
In what furnace was thy brain?
What the anvil? what dread grasp   15
Dare its deadly terrors clasp?

When the stars threw down their spears,
And watered heaven with their tears,
Did he smile his work to see?
Did he who made the Lamb make thee?   20

Tyger! Tyger! burning bright
In the forests of the night,
What immortal hand or eye
Dare frame thy fearful symmetry?

Considerations for Critical Thinking and Writing

1. This poem from Blake's *Songs of Experience* is often paired with "The Lamb." Describe the poem's tone. Is the speaker's voice the same here as in "The Lamb"? Which words are repeated, and how do they contribute to the tone?
2. What is revealed about the nature of the tiger by the words used to describe its creation? What do you think the tiger symbolizes?
3. Unlike in "The Lamb," more than one question is raised in "The Tyger." What are these questions? Are they answered?
4. Compare the rhythms in "The Lamb" and "The Tyger." Each basically uses a seven-syllable line, but the effects are very different. Why?
5. Using these two poems as the basis of your discussion, describe what distinguishes innocence from experience.

DOROTHY PARKER (1893–1967)
One Perfect Rose   1926

A single flow'r he sent me, since we met.
   All tenderly his messenger he chose;
Deep-hearted, pure, with scented dew still wet —
   One perfect rose.

I knew the language of the floweret;   5
   "My fragile leaves," it said, "his heart enclose."
Love long has taken for his amulet
   One perfect rose.

Why is it no one ever sent me yet
   One perfect limousine, do you suppose?   10
Ah no, it's always just my luck to get
   One perfect rose.

Considerations for Critical Thinking and Writing

1. Describe the tone of the first two stanzas. How do rhyme and meter help to establish the tone?
2. How does the meaning of "One perfect rose" in line 12 compare with the way you read it in lines 4 and 8?
3. Describe the speaker. What sort of woman is she? How do you respond to her?

ALFRED, LORD TENNYSON (1809–1892)
The Charge of the Light Brigade   1855

1

Half a league, half a league,
  Half a league onward,
All in the valley of Death
  Rode the six hundred.

"Forward, the Light Brigade!   5
Charge for the guns!" he said:
Into the valley of Death
    Rode the six hundred.

                    2
"Forward, the Light Brigade!"
Was there a man dismayed?   10
Not though the soldier knew
    Some one had blundered:
Their's not to make reply,
Their's not to reason why,
Their's but to do and die: 15
Into the valley of Death
    Rode the six hundred.

                    3
Cannon to right of them,
Cannon to left of them,
Cannon in front of them   20
    Volleyed and thundered;
Stormed at with shot and shell,
Boldly they rode and well,
Into the jaws of Death,
Into the mouth of Hell   25
    Rode the six hundred.

                    4
Flashed all their sabers bare,
Flashed as they turned in air
Sabring the gunners there,
Charging an army, while   30
    All the world wondered:
Plunged in the battery-smoke
Right through the line they broke;
Cossack and Russian
Reeled from the saber-stroke   35
    Shattered and sundered.
Then they rode back, but not
    Not the six hundred.

                    5
Cannon to right of them,
Cannon to left of them,   40
Cannon behind them
    Volleyed and thundered;
Stormed at with shot and shell,
While horse and hero fell,
They that had fought so well   45
Came through the jaws of Death,
Back from the mouth of Hell,
All that was left of them,
    Left of six hundred.

6

When can their glory fade? 50
O the wild charge they made!
  All the world wondered.
Honor the charge they made!
Honor the Light Brigade,
  Noble six hundred! 55

Considerations for Critical Thinking and Writing

1. How do the meter and rhyme contribute to the meaning of its lines?
2. What is the speaker's attitude toward war?
3. Describe the tone, paying particular attention to stanza 2.

Connection to Another Selection

1. Compare the theme of "The Charge of the Light Brigade" with Owen's *"Dulce et Decorum Est"* (p. 93).

THEODORE ROETHKE (1908–1963)
My Papa's Waltz 1948

trimeter

The whiskey on your breath
Could make a small boy dizzy;
But I hung on like death:
Such waltzing was not easy.

fear?

We romped until the pans 5
Slid from the kitchen shelf;
My mother's countenance
Could not unfrown itself.

The hand that held my wrist
Was battered on one knuckle; 10
At every step you missed
My right ear scraped a buckle.

You beat time on my head
With a palm caked hard by dirt,
Then waltzed me off to bed 15
Still clinging to your shirt.

Considerations for Critical Thinking and Writing

1. What details characterize the father in this poem? How does the speaker's choice of words reveal his feeling about his father? Is the remembering speaker still a boy?
2. Characterize the rhythm of the poem. Does it move "like death," or is it more like a waltz? Is the rhythm regular throughout the poem? What is its effect?
3. Comment on the appropriateness of the title. Why do you suppose Roethke didn't use "My Father's Waltz"?

ARON KEESBURY (b. 1971)
Song to a Waitress

1997

Yes. I want a big fat cup of coffee and
I want it hot. I want a big hot cup
of coffee in a big fat mug. And bring
it here and put it down and get the hell

away from me. And I want sugar in 5
a jar. A glass jar. Big, fat, glass jar with
a metal top and none of them pink, pansy
sugar packets in dainty little cups.

And come back every now and then and fill
my big fat mug and keep it hot and full. 10
And I don't want to hear your waitress talk
and I don't want to see you smile. So fill

my big fat mug and get the hell away.
I don't want to see your face today.

Considerations for Critical Thinking and Writing

1. What is the predominant metrical pattern in the poem? Where does the poem deviate from that pattern? How do these deviations affect the speaker's tone?
2. What does this speaker want?
3. In what ways does this poem resemble a sonnet? How does it differ? (See page 207 for a description of a sonnet.) What do the similarities and differences to the form add to your understanding of the speaker's intent?
4. What is the effect of the repetition of "big," "fat," and "mug" throughout the poem? What other patterns of repetition can you find? Why does the speaker repeat those specific words when he does?

Connection to Another Selection

1. Write a reply to the speaker in "Song to a Waitress" from the point of view of the waitress. You might begin by writing a prose paragraph and then try organizing it into lines of poetry. Read Machan's "Hazel Tells LaVerne" (p. 53) for a source of inspiration.

EDWARD HIRSCH (b. 1950)
Fast Break

1985

(In Memory of Dennis Turner, 1946–1984)

A hook shot kisses the rim and
hangs there, helplessly, but doesn't drop

and for once our gangly starting center
boxes out his man and times his jump

perfectly, gathering the orange leather   5
from the air like a cherished possession

and spinning around to throw a strike
to the outlet who is already shoveling

an underhand pass toward the other guard
scissoring past a flat-footed defender   10

who looks stunned and nailed to the floor
in the wrong direction, turning to catch sight

of a high, gliding dribble and a man
letting the play develop in front of him

in slow motion, almost exactly   15
like a coach's drawing on the blackboard,

both forwards racing down the court
the way that forwards should, fanning out

and filling the lanes in tandem, moving
together as brothers passing the ball   20

between them without a dribble, without
a single bounce hitting the hardwood

until the guard finally lunges out
and commits to the wrong man

while the power-forward explodes past them   25
in a fury, taking the ball into the air

by himself now and laying it gently
against the glass for a layup,

but losing his balance in the process,
inexplicably falling, hitting the floor   30

with a wild, headlong motion
for the game he loved like a country

and swiveling back to see an orange blur
floating perfectly through the net.

Considerations for Critical Thinking and Writing

1. Why are run-on lines especially appropriate for this poem? How do they affect its sound and sense? What is the effect of the poem being one long sentence? Do the lines have a regular meter?
2. In addition to describing accurately a fast break, this poem is a tribute to a dead friend. How are the two purposes related in the poem?
3. How might this poem — to borrow a phrase from Robert Frost — represent a "momentary stay against confusion"?

GREG WILLIAMSON (b. 1964)
Waterfall   1995

In still transparency, the water pools
  High in a mountain stream, then spills
Over the lip and in a sheet cascades
Across the shoal, obeying hidden rules,
    So that the pleats and braids,   5
The feather-stitched white water, little rills
  And divots seem to ride in place
  Above the crevices and sills,
Although the water runs along the race.

What makes these rapids, this little waterfall,   10
  Cascading like a chandelier
Of frosted glass or like a willow tree,
Is not the water only nor the fall
    But some complicity
Of both, so that these similes appear   15
  Inaccurate and limited,
  Neglecting that the bed will steer
The water as the water steers the bed.

So too with language, so even with this verse.
  From a pool of syllables, words hover   20
With rich potential, then spill across the lip
And riffle down the page, for better or worse,
    Making their chancy trip,
Becoming sentences as they discover
  (Now flowing, now seeming to stammer)   25
  Their English channels, trickling over
The periodic pauses of its grammar.

Considerations for Critical Thinking and Writing

1. Is this poem primarily about a waterfall or writing poetry — or both? Explain your answer.
2. In what ways can stanza 2 be considered a transitional device between stanzas 1 and 3?
3. Comment on the rhythm of the lines. How do the varying meters flow with the movements described?
4. How well does stanza 3 explain how poetry is created?

LOUISE BOGAN (1897–1970)
On Formal Poetry 1953

What is formal poetry? It is poetry written in form. And what is *form?* The elements of form, so far as poetry is concerned, are meter and rhyme. Are these elements merely mold and ornaments that have been impressed upon poetry from without? Are they indeed restrictions which bind and fetter language and the thought and emotion behind, under, within language in a repressive way? Are they arbitrary rules which have lost all validity since they have been broken to good purpose by "experimental poets," ancient and modern? Does the breaking up of form, or its total elimination, always result in an increase of power and of effect; and is any return to form a sort of relinquishment of freedom, or retreat to old fogeyism?

From *A Poet's Alphabet*

Considerations for Critical Thinking and Writing

1. Choose one of the questions Bogan raises and write an essay in response to it using two or three poems from this chapter to illustrate your answer.
2. Try writing a poem in meter and rhyme. Does the experience make your writing feel limited or not?

8. Poetic Forms

Poems come in a variety of shapes. Although the best poems always have their own unique qualities, many of them also conform to traditional patterns. Frequently the *form* of a poem — its overall structure or shape — follows an already established design. A poem that can be categorized by the patterns of its lines, meter, rhymes, and stanzas is considered a *fixed form*, because it follows a prescribed model such as a sonnet. However, poems written in a fixed form do not always fit models precisely; writers sometimes work variations on traditional forms to create innovative effects.

Not all poets are content with variations on traditional forms. Some prefer to create their own structures and shapes. Poems that do not conform to established patterns of meter, rhyme, and stanza are called *free verse* or *open form* poetry. (See Chapter 9 for further discussion of open forms.) This kind of poetry creates its own ordering principles through the careful arrangement of words and phrases in line lengths that embody rhythms appropriate to the meaning. Modern and contemporary poets in particular have learned to use the blank space on the page as a significant functional element (for a striking example, see Cummings's "l(a," p. 25). Good poetry of this kind is structured in ways that can be as demanding, interesting, and satisfying as fixed forms. Open and fixed forms represent different poetic styles, but they are identical in the sense that both use language in concentrated ways to convey meanings, experiences, emotions, and effects.

SOME COMMON POETIC FORMS

A familiarity with some of the most frequently used fixed forms of poetry is useful, because it allows for a better understanding of how a poem works. Classifying patterns allows us to talk about the effects of established rhythm and rhyme and recognize how significant variations from them affect the pace and meaning of the lines. An awareness of form also allows us to anticipate how a poem is likely to proceed. As we shall see, a sonnet creates a different set of expectations in a reader from those of, say, a limerick. A reader isn't likely to find in limericks the kind of serious themes that often make their way into sonnets. The discussion that follows identifies some of the important poetic forms frequently encountered in English poetry.

The shape of a fixed form poem is often determined by the way in which the lines are organized into stanzas. A *stanza* consists of a grouping of lines, set off by a space, that usually has a set pattern of meter and rhyme. This pattern is ordinarily repeated in other stanzas throughout the poem. What is usual is not obligatory, however; some poems may use a different pattern for each stanza, somewhat like paragraphs in prose.

Traditionally, though, stanzas do share a common **rhyme scheme,** the pattern of end rhymes. We can map out rhyme schemes by noting patterns of rhyme with lowercase letters: the first rhyme sound is designated *a,* the second becomes *b,* the third *c,* and so on. Using this system, we can describe the rhyme scheme in the following poem this way: *aabb, ccdd, eeff.*

A. E. HOUSMAN (1859–1936)
Loveliest of trees, the cherry now

1896

Loveliest of trees, the cherry now	*a*
Is hung with bloom along the bough,	*a*
And stands about the woodland ride	*b*
Wearing white for Eastertide.	*b*
Now, of my threescore years and ten,	*c*
Twenty will not come again,	*c*
And take from seventy springs a score,	*d*
It only leaves me fifty more.	*d*
And since to look at things in bloom	*e*
Fifty springs are little room,	*e*
About the woodlands I will go	*f*
To see the cherry hung with snow.	*f*

5

10

Considerations for Critical Thinking and Writing

1. What is the speaker's attitude in this poem toward time and life?
2. Why is spring an appropriate season for the setting rather than, say, winter?
3. Paraphrase each stanza. How do the images in each reinforce the poem's themes?
4. Lines 1 and 12 are not intended to rhyme, but they are close. What is the effect of the near rhyme of "now" and "snow"? How does the rhyme enhance the theme?

Poets often create their own stanzaic patterns; hence there is an infinite number of kinds of stanzas. One way of talking about stanzaic forms is to describe a given stanza by how many lines it contains.

A *couplet* consists of two lines that usually rhyme and have the same meter; couplets are frequently not separated from each other by space on the page. A **heroic couplet** consists of rhymed iambic pentameter. Here is an example from Pope's "An Essay on Criticism."

One science only will one genius fit;   *a*
So vast is art, so narrow human wit: *a*
Not only bounded to peculiar arts,   *b*
But oft in those confined to single parts.   *b*

A *tercet* is a three-line stanza. When all three lines rhyme they are called a *triplet*. Two triplets make up this captivating poem.

ROBERT HERRICK (1591–1674)
Upon Julia's Clothes

1648

Whenas in silks my Julia goes,   *a*
Then, then, methinks, how sweetly flows   *a*
That liquefaction of her clothes.   *a*

Next, when I cast mine eyes, and see   *b*
That brave vibration, each way free,   *b*
O, how that glittering taketh me!   *b*

Considerations for Critical Thinking and Writing

1. Underline the alliteration in this poem. What purpose does it serve?
2. Comment on the effect of the meter. How is it related to the speaker's description of Julia's clothes?
3. Look up the word *brave* in the *Oxford English Dictionary*. Which of its meanings is appropriate to describe Julia's movement? Some readers interpret lines 4–6 to mean that Julia has no clothes on. What do you think?

Connection to Another Selection

1. Compare the tone of this poem with that of Humphrey's "Blow" (p. 179). Are the situations and speakers similar? Is there any difference in tone between these two poems?

Terza rima consists of an interlocking three-line rhyme scheme: *aba, bcb, cdc, ded,* and so on. Dante's *The Divine Comedy* uses this pattern, as does Frost's "Acquainted with the Night" (p. 129) and Percy Bysshe Shelley's "Ode to the West Wind" (p. 222).

A *quatrain*, or four-line stanza, is the most common stanzaic form in the English language and can have various meters and rhyme schemes (if any). The most common rhyme schemes are *aabb, abba, aaba,* and *abcb*. This last pattern is especially characteristic of the popular *ballad stanza,* which consists of alternating eight- and six-syllable lines. Samuel Taylor Coleridge adopted this pattern in "The Rime of the Ancient Mariner"; here is one representative stanza.

All in a hot and copper sky   a
The bloody Sun, at noon,   b
Right up above the mast did stand,   c
No bigger than the Moon.   b

There are a number of longer stanzaic forms and the list of types of stanzas could be extended considerably, but knowing these three most basic patterns should prove helpful to you in talking about the form of a great many poems. In addition to stanzaic forms, there are fixed forms that characterize entire poems. Lyric poems can be, for example, sonnets, villanelles, sestinas, or epigrams.

Sonnet

The *sonnet* has been a popular literary form in English since the sixteenth century, when it was adopted from the Italian *sonnetto,* meaning "little song." A sonnet consists of fourteen lines, usually written in iambic pentameter. Because the sonnet has been such a favorite form, writers have experimented with many variations on its essential structure. Nevertheless, there are two basic types of sonnets: the Italian and the English.

The *Italian sonnet* (also known as the **Petrarchan sonnet,** from the fourteenth-century Italian poet Petrarch) divides into two parts. The first eight lines (the *octave*) typically rhyme *abbaabba*. The final six lines (the *sestet*) may vary; common patterns are *cdecde, cdcdcd,* and *cdccdc.* Very often the octave presents a situation, attitude, or problem that the sestet comments upon or resolves, as in John Keats's "On First Looking into Chapman's Homer."

JOHN KEATS (1795-1821)
On First Looking into Chapman's Homer°   1816

Much have I traveled in the realms of gold,
    And many goodly states and kingdoms seen;
    Round many western islands have I been
Which bards in fealty to Apollo° hold.
Oft of one wide expanse had I been told   5
    That deep-browed Homer ruled as his demesne;
    Yet did I never breathe its pure serene°   *atmosphere*
Till I heard Chapman speak out loud and bold:
Then felt I like some watcher of the skies
    When a new planet swims into his ken;   10
Or like stout Cortez° when with eagle eyes
    He stared at the Pacific — and all his men
Looked at each other with a wild surmise —
    Silent, upon a peak in Darien.

Chapman's Homer: Before reading George Chapman's (c. 1560–1634) poetic Elizabethan translations of Homer's *Iliad* and *Odyssey,* Keats had known only stilted and pedestrian eighteenth-century translations.   4 *Apollo:* Greek god of poetry.   11 *Cortez:* Vasco Núñez de Balboa, not Hernando Cortés, was the first European to sight the Pacific from Darien, a peak in Panama.

Considerations for Critical Thinking and Writing

1. What is the controlling metaphor of this poem?
2. What is it that the speaker discovers?

3. How do the images shift from the octave to the sestet? How does the tone change?

4. How does the rhythm of the lines change between the octave and the sestet? How does that change reflect the tones of both the octave and the sestet?

5. Does Keats's mistake concerning Cortés and Balboa affect your reading of the poem? Explain why or why not.

The Italian sonnet pattern is also used in the next sonnet, but notice that the thematic break between octave and sestet comes within line 9 rather than between lines 8 and 9. This unconventional break helps to reinforce the speaker's impatience with the conventional attitudes he describes.

WILLIAM WORDSWORTH (1770–1850)
The World Is Too Much with Us

1807

The world is too much with us; late and soon, *a*
Getting and spending, we lay waste our powers; *b*
Little we see in Nature that is ours; *b*
We have given our hearts away, a sordid boon! *a*
This Sea that bares her bosom to the moon; *a*   5
The winds that will be howling at all hours, *b*
And are up-gathered now like sleeping flowers; *b*
For this, for everything, we are out of tune; *a*
It moves us not. — Great God! I'd rather be *c*
A Pagan suckled in a creed outworn; *d*   10
So might I, standing on this pleasant lea, *c*
Have glimpses that would make me less forlorn; *d*
Have sight of Proteus rising from the sea; *c*
Or hear old Triton blow his wreathèd horn. *d*

Considerations for Critical Thinking and Writing

1. What is the speaker's complaint in this sonnet? How do the conditions described affect him?

2. Look up "Proteus" and "Triton." What do these mythological allusions contribute to the sonnet's tone?

3. What is the effect of the personification of the sea and wind in the octave?

Connection to Another Selection

1. Compare the theme of this sonnet with that of Hopkins's "God's Grandeur" (p. 166).

The *English sonnet,* more commonly known as the *Shakespearean sonnet,* is organized into three quatrains and a couplet, which typically rhyme *abab cdcd efef gg.* This rhyme scheme is more suited to English poetry because English has fewer rhyming words than Italian. English sonnets, because of their four-part organization, also have more flexibility about where thematic breaks can occur. Frequently, however, the most pronounced break or turn comes with the concluding couplet.

In the following Shakespearean sonnet, the three quatrains compa[re] speaker's loved one to a summer's day and explain why the loved one i[s] more lovely. The couplet bestows eternal beauty and love upon both t[he] loved one and the sonnet.

WILLIAM SHAKESPEARE (1564–1616)

Shall I compare thee to a summer's day?

1609

Shall I compare thee to a summer's day?
Thou art more lovely and more temperate:
Rough winds do shake the darling buds of May,
And summer's lease hath all too short a date.
Sometime too hot the eye of heaven shines,   5
And often is his gold complexion dimmed;
And every fair from fair sometime declines,
By chance, or nature's changing course, untrimmed.
But thy eternal summer shall not fade,
Nor lose possession of that fair thou ow'st°   *possess* 10
Nor shall death brag thou wand'rest in his shade,
When in eternal lines to time thou grow'st.
    So long as men can breathe or eyes can see,
    So long lives this, and this gives life to thee.

Considerations for Critical Thinking and Writing

1. Why is the speaker's loved one more lovely than a summer's day? What qualities does he admire in the loved one?
2. Describe the shift in tone and subject matter that begins in line 9.
3. What does the couplet say about the relation between art and love?
4. Which syllables are stressed in the final line? How do these syllables relate to the meaning of the line?

Sonnets have been the vehicles for all kinds of subjects, including love, death, politics, and cosmic questions. Although most sonnets tend to treat their subjects seriously, this fixed form does not mean a fixed expression; humor is also possible in it. Compare this next Shakespearean sonnet with "Shall I compare thee to a summer's day?" They are, finally, both love poems, but their tones are markedly different.

WILLIAM SHAKESPEARE (1564–1616)

My mistress' eyes are nothing like the sun

1609

My mistress' eyes are nothing like the sun;
Coral is far more red than her lips' red;
If snow be white, why then her breasts are dun;
If hairs be wires, black wires grow on her head.

I have seen roses damasked red and white,   5
But no such roses see I in her cheeks;
And in some perfumes is there more delight
Than in the breath that from my mistress reeks.
I love to hear her speak, yet well I know
That music hath a far more pleasing sound;   10
I grant I never saw a goddess go:
My mistress, when she walks, treads on the ground.
    And yet, by heaven, I think my love as rare
    As any she,° belied with false compare.   *lady*

Considerations for Critical Thinking and Writing

1. What does "mistress" mean in this sonnet?
2. Write a description of the mistress based on the images used in the sonnet.
3. What sort of person is the speaker? Does he truly love the woman he describes?
4. In what sense are this sonnet and "Shall I compare thee" about poetry as well as love?

EDNA ST. VINCENT MILLAY (1892–1950)
I will put Chaos into fourteen lines   1954

I will put Chaos into fourteen lines
And keep him there; and let him thence escape
If he be lucky; let him twist, and ape
Flood, fire, and demon — his adroit designs
Will strain to nothing in the strict confines   5
Of this sweet Order, where, in pious rape,
I hold his essence and amorphous shape,
Till he with Order mingles and combines.
Past are the hours, the years, of our duress,
His arrogance, our awful servitude: 10
I have him. He is nothing more nor less
Than something simple not yet understood;
I shall not even force him to confess;
Or answer. I will only make him good.

Considerations for Critical Thinking and Writing

1. What properties of a sonnet does this poem possess? How does the poem contain "Chaos"?
2. What do you think is meant by the phrase "pious rape" in line 6?
3. What is the effect of the personification in the poem?

Connection to Another Selection

1. Compare the theme of this poem with that of Robert Frost's "Design" (p. 318).

MOLLY PEACOCK (b. 1947)
Desire

1984

It doesn't speak and it isn't schooled,
like a small foetal animal with wettened fur.
It is the blind instinct for life unruled,
visceral frankincense and animal myrrh.
It is what babies bring to kings,   5
an eyes-shut, ears-shut medicine of the heart
that smells and touches endings and beginnings
without the details of time's experienced *part-*
fit-into-part-fit-into-part. Like a paw,
it is blunt; like a pet who knows you   10
and nudges your knee with its snout — but more raw
and blinder and younger and more divine, too,
than the tamed wild — it's the drive for what is real,
deeper than the brain's detail: the drive to feel.

Considerations for Critical Thinking and Writing

1. Make a list of all the metaphors that appear in this poem. Taken together, what do they reveal about the speaker's conception of desire?
2. What is the "it" being described in lines 3–5? How do the allusions to the three wise men relate to the other metaphors used to define desire?
3. How is this English sonnet structured? What is the effect of its irregular meter?

Connection to Another Selection

1. Compare the treatment of desire in this poem with that of Ackerman's "A Fine, a Private Place" (p. 61). In an essay, identify the theme of each poem and compare their conceptions of desire. How alike are these two poems?

MARK JARMAN (b. 1952)
Unholy Sonnet

1993

After the praying, after the hymn-singing,
After the sermon's trenchant commentary
On the world's ills, which make ours secondary,
After communion, after the hand-wringing,
And after peace descends upon us, bringing   5
Our eyes up to regard the sanctuary
And how the light swords through it, and how, scary
In their sheer numbers, motes of dust ride, clinging —
There is, as doctors say about some pain,
Discomfort knowing that despite your prayers,   10
Your listening and rejoicing, your small part
In this communal stab at coming clean,

There is one stubborn remnant of your cares
Intact. There is still murder in your heart.

Considerations for Critical Thinking and Writing

1. Describe the rhyme scheme and structure of this sonnet. Explain why it is an English or Italian sonnet.
2. What are the effects of the use of the word *after* in lines 1, 2, 4, and 5 and the word *there* in lines 9, 13, and 14?
3. In what sense might this poem be summed up as a "communal stab" (line 12)? Discuss the accuracy of this assessment.
4. Try writing a reply to the theme of Jarman's poem using the same sonnet form that he uses.

Connections to Other Selections

1. Jarman has said that his "Unholy Sonnets" (there are about twenty of them) are modeled after John Donne's *Holy Sonnets,* but that he does not share the same Christian assumptions about faith and mercy that inform Donne's sonnets. Instead, Jarman says, he "work[s] against any assumption or shared expression of faith, to write a devotional poetry against the grain." Keeping this statement in mind, write an essay comparing and contrasting the tone and theme of Jarman's sonnet with John Donne's "Batter My Heart" (p. 409) or "Death Be Not Proud" (p. 409).

Villanelle

The *villanelle* is a fixed form consisting of nineteen lines of any length divided into six stanzas: five tercets and a concluding quatrain. The first and third lines of the initial tercet rhyme; these rhymes are repeated in each subsequent tercet *(aba)* and in the final two lines of the quatrain *(abaa).* Moreover, line 1 appears in its entirety as lines 6, 12, and 18, while line 3 appears as lines 9, 15, and 19. This form may seem to risk monotony, but in competent hands a villanelle can create haunting echoes, as in Dylan Thomas's "Do not go gentle into that good night."

DYLAN THOMAS (1914–1953)
Do not go gentle into that good night

1952

Do not go gentle into that good night,
Old age should burn and rave at close of day;
Rage, rage against the dying of the light.

Though wise men at their end know dark is right,
Because their words had forked no lightning they
Do not go gentle into that good night.

5

Good men, the last wave by, crying how bright
Their frail deeds might have danced in a green bay,
Rage, rage against the dying of the light.

Wild men who caught and sang the sun in flight,
And learn, too late, they grieved it on its way,
Do not go gentle into that good night.

Grave men, near death, who see with blinding sight
Blind eyes could blaze like meteors and be gay,
Rage, rage against the dying of the light.

And you, my father, there on the sad height,
Curse, bless, me now with your fierce tears, I pray.
Do not go gentle into that good night.
Rage, rage against the dying of the light.

Considerations for Critical Thinking and Writing

1. Thomas's father was close to death when this poem was written. How does the tone contribute to the poem's theme?
2. How is "good" used in line 1?
3. Characterize the men who are "wise" (line 4), "Good" (7), "Wild" (10), and "Grave" (13).
4. What do figures of speech contribute to this poem?
5. Discuss this villanelle's sound effects.

Connection to Another Selection

1. In Thomas's poem we experience "rage against the dying of the light." Contrast this with the rage you find in Sylvia Plath's "Daddy" (p. 442). What produces the emotion in Plath's poem?

JULIA ALVAREZ (b. 1950)
Woman's Work

1996

Who says a woman's work isn't high art?
She'd challenge as she scubbed the bathroom tiles.
Keep house as if the address were your heart.

We'd clean the whole upstairs before we'd start
downstairs. I'd sigh, hearing my friends outside.
Doing her woman's work was a hard art

to practice when the summer sun would bar
the floor I swept till she was satisfied.
She kept me prisoner in her housebound heart.

She'd shine the tines of forks, the wheels of carts,
cut lacy lattices for all her pies.
Her woman's work was nothing less than art.

And, I, her masterpiece since I was smart,
was primed, praised, polished, scolded and advised
to keep a house much better than my heart.

I did not want to be her counterpart!
I struck out . . . but became my mother's child:
a woman working at home on her art,
housekeeping paper as if it were her heart.

Considerations for Critical Thinking and Writing

1. How is the structure of this poem different from a conventional villanelle? How do these differences contribute to the speaker's description of "woman's work"?
2. Characterize the mother and daughter. How are they similar to one another?
3. How does the concluding quatrain make an important distinction between the mother and daughter while redefining "woman's work"?

Connection to Another Selection

1. Compare and contrast the themes and tone of "Woman's Work" and Thomas's "Do not go gentle into that good night." Will the speaker in Alvarez's poem "go gentle into that good night"? Would the speaker in Thomas's call woman's work, as described above, "high art"?

Sestina

Although the **sestina** usually does not rhyme, it is perhaps an even more demanding fixed form than the villanelle. A sestina consists of thirty-nine lines of any length divided into six six-line stanzas and a three-line concluding stanza called an **envoy.** The difficulty is in repeating the six words at the ends of the first stanza's lines at the ends of the lines in the other five six-line stanzas as well. Those words must also appear in the final three lines, where they often resonate important themes. The sestina originated in the Middle Ages, but contemporary poets continue to find it a fascinating and challenging form.

ELIZABETH BISHOP (1911-1979)
Sestina

1965

September rain falls on the house.
In the failing light, the old grandmother
sits in the kitchen with the child
beside the Little Marvel Stove,
reading the jokes from the almanac,   5
laughing and talking to hide her tears.

She thinks that her equinoctial tears
and the rain that beats on the roof of the house
were both foretold by the almanac,
but only known to a grandmother.
The iron kettle sings on the stove.   10
She cuts some bread and says to the child,

It's time for tea now; but the child
is watching the teakettle's small hard tears
dance like mad on the hot black stove,
the way the rain must dance on the house.
Tidying up, the old grandmother
hangs up the clever almanac

on its string. Birdlike, the almanac
hovers half open above the child,
hovers above the old grandmother
and her teacup full of dark brown tears.
She shivers and says she thinks the house
feels chilly, and puts more wood in the stove.

It was to be, says the Marvel Stove.
I know what I know, says the almanac.
With crayons the child draws a rigid house
and a winding pathway. Then the child
puts in a man with buttons like tears
and shows it proudly to the grandmother.

But secretly, while the grandmother
busies herself about the stove,
the little moons fall down like tears
from between the pages of the almanac
into the flower bed the child
has carefully placed in the front of the house.

Time to plant tears, says the almanac.
The grandmother sings to the marvelous stove
and the child draws another inscrutable house.

Considerations for Critical Thinking and Writing

1. Number the end words of the first stanza 1, 2, 3, 4, 5, and 6, and then use those numbers for the corresponding end words in the remaining five stanzas to see how the pattern of the line-end words is worked out in this sestina. Also locate the six end words in the envoy.

2. What happens in this sestina? Why is the grandmother "laughing and talking to hide her tears" (line 6)?

3. Underline the images that seem especially vivid to you. What effects do they create? What is the tone of the sestina?

4. How are the six end words — "house," "grandmother," "child," "stove," "almanac," and "tears" — central to the sestina's meaning?

5. How is the almanac used symbolically? Does Bishop use any other symbols to convey meanings?

6. Write a brief essay explaining why you think a poet might derive pleasure from writing in a fixed form such as a villanelle or sestina. Can you think of similar activities outside the field of writing in which discipline and restraint give pleasure?

FLORENCE CASSEN MAYERS (b. 1940)
All-American Sestina   1996

One nation, indivisible
two-car garage
three strikes you're out
four-minute mile
five-cent cigar   5
six-string guitar

six-pack Bud
one-day sale
five-year warranty
two-way street   10
fourscore and seven years ago
three cheers

three-star restaurant
sixty-
four-dollar question   15
one-night stand
two-pound lobster
five-star general

five-course meal
three sheets to the wind
two bits   20
six-shooter
one-armed bandit
four-poster

four-wheel drive   25
five-and-dime
hole in one
three-alarm fire
sweet sixteen
two-wheeler   30

two-tone Chevy
four rms, hi flr, w/vu
six-footer
high five
three-ring circus   35
one-room schoolhouse

two thumbs up, five-karat diamond
Fourth of July, three-piece suit
six feet under, one-horse town

Considerations for Critical Thinking and Writing

1. How is the structure of this poem different from a conventional sestina? (What structural requirement does Mayers add for this sestina?)
2. Discuss the significance of the title; what is "All-American"?

3. Do you think important themes are raised by this poem, as is traditional for a sestina? If so, what are they? If not, what is being played with by using this convention?

Connection to Another Selection

1. Describe and compare the strategy used to create meaning in "All-American Sestina" with that used by Cummings in "next to of course god america i" (p. 136).

Epigram

An *epigram* is a brief, pointed, and witty poem. Although most rhyme and often are written in couplets, epigrams take no prescribed form. Instead, they are typically polished bits of compressed irony, satire, or paradox. Here is an epigram that defines itself.

SAMUEL TAYLOR COLERIDGE (1772-1834)
What Is an Epigram?   1802

What is an epigram? A dwarfish whole;
Its body brevity, and wit its soul.

These additional examples by A. R. Ammons, David McCord, and Paul Laurence Dunbar satisfy Coleridge's definition.

A. R. AMMONS (b. 1926)
Coward   1975

Bravery runs in my family.

DAVID McCORD (1897-1997)
Epitaph on a Waiter   1954

By and by
God caught his eye.

PAUL LAURENCE DUNBAR (1872-1906)
Theology   1896

There is a heaven, for ever, day by day,
The upward longing of my soul doth tell me so.
There is a hell, I'm quite as sure; for pray,
If there were not, where would my neighbors go?

Considerations for Critical Thinking and Writing

1. In what sense is each of these epigrams, as Coleridge puts it, a "dwarfish whole"?
2. Explain which of these epigrams, in addition to being witty, makes a serious point.
3. Try writing a few epigrams that say something memorable about whatever you choose to focus upon.

Limerick

The *limerick* is always light and humorous. Its usual form consists of five predominantly anapestic lines rhyming *aabba*; lines 1, 2, and 5 contain three feet, while lines 3 and 4 contain two. Limericks have delighted everyone from schoolchildren to sophisticated adults, and they range in subject matter from the simply innocent and silly to the satiric or obscene. The sexual humor helps to explain why so many limericks are written anonymously. Here is one that is anonymous but more concerned with physics than physiology.

> There was a young lady named Bright,
> Who traveled much faster than light,
>   She started one day
>   In a relative way,
> And returned on the previous night.

This next one is a particularly clever definition of a limerick.

LAURENCE PERRINE (b. 1915)
The limerick's never averse   1982

> The limerick's never averse
> To expressing itself in a terse
>   Economical style,
>   And yet, all the while,
> The limerick's *always* a verse.

Considerations for Critical Thinking and Writing

1. Scan Perrine's limerick. How do the lines measure up to the traditional fixed metrical pattern?
2. Try writing a limerick. Use the following basic pattern.

```
 ˘  ˘  ´     ˘  ˘  ´     ˘  ˘  ´
 ˘  ˘  ´     ˘  ˘  ´     ˘  ˘  ´
             ˘  ˘  ´     ˘  ˘  ´
             ˘  ˘  ´     ˘  ˘  ´
 ˘  ˘  ´     ˘  ˘  ´     ˘  ˘  ´
```

You might begin with a friend's name or the name of your school or town. Your instructor is, of course, fair game, too, provided your tact matches your wit.

Haiku

Another brief fixed poetic form, borrowed from the Japanese, is the *haiku*. A haiku is usually described as consisting of seventeen syllables organized into three unrhymed lines of five, seven, and five syllables. Owing to language difference, however, English translations of haiku are often only approximated, because a Japanese haiku exists in time (Japanese syllables have duration). The number of syllables in our sense is not as significant as the duration. These poems typically present an intense emotion or vivid image of nature, which, in the Japanese, are also designed to lead to a spiritual insight.

MATSUO BASHŌ (1644–1694)
Under cherry trees   date unknown

Under cherry trees
Soup, the salad, fish and all . . .
Seasoned with petals.

ETHERIDGE KNIGHT (b. 1931)
Eastern Guard Tower   1968

Eastern guard tower
glints in sunset; convicts rest
like lizards on rocks.

Considerations for Critical Thinking and Writing

1. What different emotions do these two haiku evoke?
2. What differences and similarities are there between the effects of a haiku and those of an epigram?
3. Compose a haiku; try to make it as allusive and suggestive as possible.

Elegy

An elegy in classical Greek and Roman literature was written in alternating hexameter and pentameter lines. Since the seventeenth century, however, the term *elegy* has been used to describe a lyric poem written to commemorate someone who is dead. The word is also used to refer to a serious meditative poem produced to express the speaker's melancholy thoughts. Elegies no longer conform to a fixed pattern of lines and stanzas, but their characteristic subject is related to death and their tone is mournfully contemplative.

SEAMUS HEANEY (b. 1939)

Mid-term Break

1966

I sat all morning in the college sick bay
Counting bells knelling classes to a close.
At two o'clock our neighbors drove me home.

In the porch I met my father crying —
He had always taken funerals in his stride —   5
And Big Jim Evans saying it was a hard blow.

The baby cooed and laughed and rocked the pram
When I came in, and I was embarrassed
By old men standing up to shake my hand

And tell me they were "sorry for my trouble,"   10
Whispers informed strangers I was the eldest,
Away at school, as my mother held my hand

In hers and coughed out angry tearless sighs.
At ten o'clock the ambulance arrived
With the corpse, stanched and bandaged by the nurses.   15

Next morning I went up into the room. Snowdrops
And candles soothed the bedside; I saw him
For the first time in six weeks. Paler now,

Wearing a poppy bruise on his left temple,
He lay in the four foot box as in his cot.   20
No gaudy scars, the bumper knocked him clear.

A four foot box, a foot for every year.

Considerations for Critical Thinking and Writing

1. How do simple details contribute to the effects of this elegy?
2. Does this elegy use any kind of formal pattern for its structure? What is the effect of the last line standing by itself?
3. Another spelling for *stanched* (line 15) is *staunched*. Usage is about evenly divided between the two in the United States. What is the effect of Heaney's choosing the former spelling rather than the latter?
4. Comment on the elegy's title.

Connections to Other Selections

1. Compare Heaney's elegy with A. E. Housman's "To an Athlete Dying Young" (p. 423). Which do you find more moving? Explain why.
2. Write an essay comparing this story of a boy's death with Updike's "Dog's Death" (p. 11). Do you think either of the poems is sentimental? Explain why or why not.

ANDREW HUDGINS (b. 1951)
Elegy for My Father, Who Is Not Dead (1991)

One day I'll lift the telephone
and be told my father's dead. He's ready.
In the sureness of his faith, he talks
about the world beyond this world
as though his reservations have 5
been made. I think he wants to go,
a little bit — a new desire
to travel building up, an itch
to see fresh worlds. Or older ones.
He thinks that when I follow him 10
he'll wrap me in his arms and laugh,
the way he did when I arrived
on earth. I do not think he's right.
He's ready. I am not. I can't
just say good-bye as cheerfully 15
as if he were embarking on a trip
to make my later trip go well.
I see myself on deck, convinced
his ship's gone down, while he's convinced
I'll see him standing on the dock 20
and waving, shouting, Welcome back.

Considerations for Critical Thinking and Writing

1. How does the speaker's view of immortality differ from his father's?
2. Explain why you think this is an optimistic or pessimistic poem — or explain why these two categories fail to describe the poem.
3. In what sense can this poem be regarded as an elegy?

Connection to Another Selection

1. Write an essay comparing attitudes toward death in this poem and in Thomas's "Do not go gentle into that good night" (p. 212). Both speakers invoke their fathers, nearer to death than they are; what impact does this have?

Ode

An *ode* is characterized by a serious topic and formal tone, but no prescribed formal pattern describes all odes. In some odes the pattern of each stanza is repeated throughout, while in others each stanza introduces a new pattern. Odes are lengthy lyrics that often include lofty emotions conveyed by a dignified style. Typical topics include truth, art, freedom, justice, and the meaning of life. Frequently such lyrics tend to be more public than private, and their speakers often employ apostrophe.

PERCY BYSSHE SHELLEY (1792–1822)

Ode to the West Wind

1820

I

O wild West Wind, thou breath of Autumn's being,
Thou, from whose unseen presence the leaves dead
Are driven, like ghosts from an enchanter fleeing,

Yellow, and black, and pale, and hectic red,
Pestilence-stricken multitudes: O thou,   5
Who chariotest to their dark wintry bed

The wingèd seeds, where they lie cold and low,
Each like a corpse within its grave, until
Thine azure sister of the Spring shall blow

Her clarion o'er the dreaming earth, and fill   10
(Driving sweet buds like flocks to feed in air)
With living hues and odors plain and hill:

Wild Spirit, which art moving everywhere;
Destroyer and preserver; hear, oh, hear!

II

Thou on whose stream, mid the steep sky's commotion,   15
Loose clouds like earth's decaying leaves are shed,
Shook from the tangled boughs of Heaven and Ocean,

Angels° of rain and lightning: there are spread   *messengers*
On the blue surface of thine airy surge,
Like the bright hair uplifted from the head   20

Of some fierce Maenad,° even from the dim verge
Of the horizon to the zenith's height,
The locks of the approaching storm. Thou dirge

Of the dying year, to which this closing night
Will be the dome of a vast sepulcher,   25
Vaulted with all thy congregated might

Of vapors, from whose solid atmosphere
Black rain, and fire, and hail will burst: oh, hear!

III

Thou who didst waken from his summer dreams
The blue Mediterranean, where he lay,   30
Lulled by the coil of his crystálline streams,

Beside a pumice isle in Baiae's bay,°
And saw in sleep old palaces and towers
Quivering within the wave's intenser day,

All overgrown with azure moss and flowers   35
So sweet, the sense faints picturing them! Thou
For whose path the Atlantic's level powers

---

21 *Maenad:* In Greek mythology a frenzied worshiper of Dionysus, god of wine and fertility.
32 *Baiae's bay:* A bay in the Mediterranean Sea.

Cleave themselves into chasms, while far below
The sea-blooms and the oozy woods which wear
The sapless foliage of the ocean, know   40

Thy voice, and suddenly grow gray with fear,
And tremble and despoil themselves: oh, hear!

IV
If I were a dead leaf thou mightest bear;
If I were a swift cloud to fly with thee;
A wave to pant beneath thy power, and share   45

The impulse of thy strength, only less free
Than thou, O uncontrollable! If even
I were as in my boyhood, and could be

The comrade by thy wanderings over Heaven,
As then, when to outstrip thy skyey speed   50
Scarce seemed a vision; I would ne'er have striven

As thus with thee in prayer in my sore need.
Oh, lift me as a wave, a leaf, a cloud!
I fall upon the thorns of life! I bleed!

A heavy weight of hours has chained and bowed   55
One too like thee: tameless, and swift, and proud.

V
Make me thy lyre,° even as the forest is:
What if my leaves are falling like its own!
The tumult of thy mighty harmonies

Will take from both a deep, autumnal tone,   60
Sweet though in sadness. Be thou, Spirit fierce,
My spirit! Be thou me, impetuous one!

Drive my dead thoughts over the universe
Like withered leaves to quicken a new birth!
And, by the incantation of this verse,   65

Scatter, as from an unextinguished hearth
Ashes and sparks, my words among mankind!
Be through my lips to unawakened earth

The trumpet of a prophecy! O Wind,
If Winter comes, can Spring be far behind?   70

57 *Make me thy lyre:* Sound is produced on an Aeolian lyre, or wind harp, by wind blowing across its strings.

Considerations for Critical Thinking and Writing

1. Write a summary of each of this ode's five sections.
2. What is the speaker's situation? What is his "sore need"? What does the speaker ask of the wind in lines 57–70?
3. What does the wind signify in this ode? How is it used symbolically?
4. Determine the meter and rhyme of the first five stanzas. How do these elements contribute to the ode's movement? Is this pattern continued in the other four sections?

Picture Poem

By arranging lines into particular shapes, poets can sometimes organize typography into *picture poems* of what they describe. Words have been arranged into all kinds of shapes, from apples to light bulbs. Notice how the shape of this next poem embodies its meaning.

MICHAEL McFEE (b. 1954)
In Medias Res°   1985

His waist
like the plot
thickens, wedding
pants now breathtaking,
belt no longer the cinch   5
it once was, belly's cambium
expanding to match each birthday,
his body a wad of anonymous tissue
swung in the same centrifuge of years
that separates a house from its foundation,   10
undermining sidewalks grim with joggers
and loose-filled graves and families
and stars collapsing on themselves,
no preservation society capable
of plugging entropy's dike,   15
under his zipper's sneer
a belly hibernation-
soft, ready for
the kill.

In Medias Res: A Latin term for a story that begins "in the middle of things."

Considerations for Critical Thinking and Writing

1. Explain how the title is related to this poem's shape.
2. Identify the puns. How do they work in the poem?
3. What is "cambium"? Why is the phrase "belly's cambium" especially appropriate?
4. What is the tone of this poem? Is it consistent throughout?

Parody

A *parody* is a humorous imitation of another, usually serious, work. It can take any fixed or open form because parodists imitate the tone, language, and shape of the original. While a parody may be teasingly close to a work's style, it typically deflates the subject matter to make the original seem absurd. Parody can be used as a kind of literary criticism to expose the defects in a work, but it is also very often an affectionate acknowledgment that a well-known work has become both institutionalized in our culture and fair game for some fun. Read Marvell's "To His Coy Mistress" (p. 57) and then study this parody.

PETER DE VRIES (b. 1910)
To His Importunate Mistress 1986

Andrew Marvell Updated

Had we but world enough, and time,
My coyness, lady, were a crime,
But at my back I always hear
Time's wingèd chariot, striking fear
The hour is nigh when creditors   5
Will prove to be my predators.
As wages of our picaresque,
Bag lunches bolted at my desk
Must stand as fealty to you
For each expensive rendezvous.   10
Obeisance at your marble feet
Deserves the best-appointed suite,
And would have, lacked I not the pelf
To pleasure also thus myself;
But aptly sumptuous amorous scenes   15
Rule out the rake of modest means.

Since mistress presupposes wife,
It means a doubly costly life;
For fools by second passion fired
A second income is required,   20
The earning which consumes the hours
They'd hoped to spend in rented bowers.
To hostelries the worst of fates
That weekly raise their daily rates!
I gather, lady, from your scoffing   25
A bloke more solvent in the offing.
So revels thus to rivals go
For want of monetary flow.
How vexing that inconstant cash
The constant suitor must abash,   30
Who with excuses vainly pled
Must rue the undisheveled bed,
And that for paltry reasons given
His conscience may remain unriven.

Considerations for Critical Thinking and Writing

1. How is De Vries's use of the term *mistress* different from Marvell's (p. 57)? How
   does the speaker's complaint in this poem differ from that in "To His Coy Mistress"?

2. Explain how "picaresque" is used in line 7.

3. To what extent does this poem duplicate Marvell's style?

4. Choose a poet whose work you know reasonably well or would like to know better and determine what is characteristic about his or her style. Then choose a poem to parody. It's probably best to attempt a short poem or a section of a long work. If you have difficulty selecting an author, you might consider Herrick, Blake, Keats, Dickinson, Whitman, or Frost, since a number of their works are included in this book.

Connection to Another Selection

1. Read Anthony Hecht's "The Dover Bitch" (p. 417), a parody of Arnold's "Dover Beach" (p. 88). Write an essay comparing the effectiveness of Hecht's parody with that of De Vries's "To His Importunate Mistress." Which parody do you prefer? Explain why.

Here's a parody for all seasons — not just Christmas — that brings together two popular icons of our culture.

X. J. KENNEDY (b. 1929)
A Visit from St. Sigmund   1993

> *Freud is just an old Santa Claus.*
> —Margaret Mead°

'Twas the night before Christmas, when all through each kid
Not an Ego was stirring, not even an Id.
The hangups were hung by the chimney with care
In hopes that St. Sigmund Freud soon would be there.
The children in scream class had knocked off their screams,   5
Letting Jungian archetypes dance through their dreams,
And Mamma with her bra off and I on her lap
Had just snuggled down when a vast thunderclap
Boomed and from my unconscious arose such a chatter
As Baptist John's teeth made on Salome's platter.   10
Away from my darling I flew like a flash,
Tore straight to the bathroom and threw up, and — *smash!*
Through the windowpane hurtled and bounced on the floor
A big brick — holy smoke, it was hard to ignore.
As I heard further thunderclaps — lo and behold —   15
Came a little psychiatrist eighty years old.
He drove a wheeled couch pulled by five fat psychoses
And the gleam in his eye might induce a hypnosis.
Like subliminal meanings his coursers they came
And, consulting his notebook, he called them by name: 20
"Now Schizo, now Fetish, now Fear of Castration!
On Paranoia! on Penis-fixation!

Margaret Mead (1901–1978): Noted American anthropologist.

Ach, yes, that big brick through your glass I should mention:
Just a simple device to compel your attention.
You need, boy, to be in an analyst's power: 25
You talk, I take notes — fifty schillings an hour."
A bag full of symbols he'd slung on his back;
He looked smug as a junk-peddler laden with smack
Or a shrewd politician soliciting votes
And his chinbeard was stiff as a starched billygoat's.   30
Then laying one finger aside of his nose,
He chortled, "What means this? Mein Gott, I suppose
There's a meaning in fingers, in candles und wicks,
In mouseholes und doughnut holes, steeples und sticks.
You see, it's the imminent prospect of sex   35
That makes all us humans run round till we're wrecks,
Und each innocent infant since people began
Wants to bed with his momma und kill his old man;
So never you fear that you're sick as a swine —
Your hangups are every sane person's und mine.   40
Even Hamlet was hot for his mom — there's the rub;
Even Oedipus Clubfoot was one of the club.
Hmmm, that's humor unconscious." He gave me rib-pokes
And for almost two hours explained phallic jokes.
Then he sprang to his couch, to his crew gave a nod,   45
And away they all flew like the concept of God.
In the worst of my dreams I can hear him shout still,
"Merry Christmas to all! In the mail comes my bill."

Considerations for Critical Thinking and Writing

1. What is the tone of this parody? How does the quotation from Margaret Mead help to establish the poem's tone?
2. What makes Freud a particularly appropriate substitute for Santa Claus? Comment on the humor in the poem.
3. What do you think is the poet's attitude toward Freud? Cite specific lines to support your point.
4. Is the focus of this parody the Christmas story or Freud? Explain your response.

PERSPECTIVE

ROBERT MORGAN (b. 1944)
On the Shape of a Poem   1983

In the body of the poem, lineation is part flesh and part skeleton, as form is the towpath along which the burden of content, floating on the formless, is pulled. All language is both mental and sacramental, is not "real" but is the working of lip and tongue to subvert the "real." Poems empearl irritating facts until they become opalescent spheres of moment, not so much résumés of history as of human faculties working with pain. Every poem is necessarily a fragment empowered by its implicitness. We sing to charm the snake in our spines,

to make it sway with the pulse of the world, balancing the weight of consciousness on the topmost vertebra.

From Epoch, Fall–Winter 1983

Considerations for Critical Thinking and Writing

1. Explain Morgan's metaphors for describing lineation and form in a poem. Why are these metaphors useful?
2. Choose one of the poems in this chapter that makes use of a particular form and explain how it is "a fragment empowered by its implicitness."

PERSPECTIVE

ELAINE MITCHELL (b. 1924)
Form 1994

Is it a corset
or primal wave?
Don't try to force it.

Even endorse it
to shape and deceive.   5
Ouch, too tight a corset.

Take it off. No remorse. It
's an ace up your sleeve.
No need to force it.

Can you make a horse knit?   10
Who would believe?
Consider. Of course, it

might be a resource. Wit,
your grateful slave.
Form. Sometimes you force it,   15

sometimes divorce it
to make it behave.
So don't try to force it.
Respect a good corset.

Considerations for Critical Thinking and Writing

1. What is the speaker's attitude toward form?
2. Explain why you think the form of this poem does or does not conform to the advice of the speaker.
3. Why is the metaphor of a corset a particularly apt image for this poem?

9. Open Form

Many poems, especially those written in the twentieth century, are composed of lines that cannot be scanned for a fixed or predominant meter. Moreover, very often these poems do not rhyme. Known as *free verse* (from the French, *vers libre*), such lines can derive their rhythmic qualities from the repetition of words, phrases, or grammatical structures; the arrangement of words on the printed page; or some other means. In recent years the term *open form* has been used in place of *free verse* to avoid the erroneous suggestion that this kind of poetry lacks all discipline and shape.

Although the following two poems do not use measurable meters, they do have rhythm.

E. E. CUMMINGS (1894–1962)
in Just-   1923

in Just-
spring   when the world is mud-
luscious the little
lame balloonman

whistles   far   and wee   5

and eddieandbill come
running from marbles and
piracies and it's
spring

when the world is puddle-wonderful   10

the queer
old balloonman whistles
far   and   wee
and bettyandisbel come dancing
from hop-scotch and jump-rope and   15

it's
spring

and

    the

        goat-footed   20

balloonMan   whistles
far
and
wee

Considerations for Critical Thinking and Writing

1. What is the effect of this poem's arrangement of words and use of space on the page?
2. What is the effect of Cummings's combining the names "eddieandbill" and "bettyandisbel"?
3. The allusion in line 20 refers to Pan, a Greek god associated with nature. How does this allusion add to the meaning of the poem?

WALT WHITMAN (1819–1892)
From *I Sing the Body Electric*   1855

O my body! I dare not desert the likes of you in other men and women, nor the
    likes of the parts of you,
I believe the likes of you are to stand or fall with the likes of the soul, (and that
    they are the soul,)
I believe the likes of you shall stand or fall with my poems, and that they are
    my poems.
Man's, woman's, child's, youth's, wife's, husband's, mother's, father's, young
    man's, young woman's poems.
Head, neck, hair, ears, drop and tympan of the ears.   5
Eyes, eye-fringes, iris of the eye, eyebrows, and the waking or sleeping of the
    lids,
Mouth, tongue, lips, teeth, roof of the mouth, jaws, and the jaw-hinges,
Nose, nostrils of the nose, and the partition,
Cheeks, temples, forehead, chin, throat, back of the neck, neck-slue,
Strong shoulders, manly beard, scapula, hind-shoulders, and the ample side-
    round of the chest,   10
Upper-arm, armpit, elbow-socket, lower-arm, arm-sinews, arm-bones,
Wrist and wrist-joints, hand, palm, knuckles, thumb, forefinger, finger-joints,
    finger-nails,
Broad breast-front, curling hair of the breast, breast-bone, breast-side,
Ribs, belly, backbone, joints of the backbone,
Hips, hip-sockets, hip-strength, inward and outward round, man-balls, man-
    root,   15
Strong set of thighs, well carrying the trunk above,
Leg-fibers, knee, knee-pan, upper-leg, under-leg,
Ankles, instep, foot-ball, toes, toe-joints, the heel;

All attitudes, all the shapeliness, all the belongings of my or your body or of any
    one's body, male or female,
The lung-sponges, the stomach-sac, the bowels sweet and clean,   20
The brain in its folds inside the skull-frame,
Sympathies, heart-valves, palate-valves, sexuality, maternity,
Womanhood, and all that is a woman, and the man that comes from woman,
The womb, the teats, nipples, breast-milk, tears, laughter, weeping, love-looks,
    love-perturbations and risings,
The voice, articulation, language, whispering, shouting aloud,   25
Food, drink, pulse, digestion, sweat, sleep, walking, swimming,
Poise on the hips, leaping, reclining, embracing, arm-curving and tightening,
The continual changes of the flex of the mouth, and around the eyes,
The skin, the sunburnt shade, freckles, hair,
The curious sympathy one feels when feeling with the hand the naked meat of
    the body,   30
The circling rivers the breath, and breathing it in and out,
The beauty of the waist, and thence of the hips, and thence downward toward
    the knees,
The thin red jellies within you or within me, the bones and the marrow in the
    bones,
The exquisite realization of health;
O I say these are not the parts and poems of the body only, but of the soul, 35
O I say now these are the soul!

Considerations for Critical Thinking and Writing

1. What informs the speaker's attitude toward the human body in this poem?
2. Read the poem aloud. Is it simply a tedious enumeration of body parts, or do the
   lines achieve some kind of rhythmic cadence?

PERSPECTIVE

WALT WHITMAN (1819–1892)
On Rhyme and Meter   1855

    The poetic quality is not marshaled in rhyme or uniformity or abstract
addresses to things nor in melancholy complaints or good precepts, but is the
life of these and much else and is in the soul. The profit of rhyme is that it drops
seeds of a sweeter and more luxuriant rhyme, and of uniformity that it conveys
itself into its own roots in the ground out of sight. The rhyme and uniformity of
perfect poems show the free growth of metrical laws and bud from them as
unerringly and loosely as lilacs or roses on a bush, and take shapes as compact
as the shapes of chestnuts and oranges and melons and pears, and shed the perfume impalpable to form. The fluency and ornaments of the finest poems or
music or orations or recitations are not independent but dependent. All beauty
comes from beautiful blood and a beautiful brain. If the greatnesses are in conjunction in a man or woman it is enough . . . the fact will prevail through the
universe . . . but the gaggery and gilt of a million years will not prevail. Who
troubles himself about his ornaments or fluency is lost.

        From the preface to the 1855 edition of *Leaves of Grass*

Considerations for Critical Thinking and Writing

1. According to Whitman, what determines the shape of a poem?
2. Why does Whitman prefer open forms over fixed forms such as the sonnet?
3. Is Whitman's poetry devoid of any structure or shape? Choose one of his poems (listed in the index) to illustrate your answer.

Open form poetry is sometimes regarded as formless because it is unlike the strict fixed forms of a sonnet, villanelle, or sestina. But even though open form poems may not employ traditional meters and rhymes, they still rely on an intense use of language to establish rhythms and relations between meaning and form. Open form poems use the arrangement of words and phrases on the printed page, pauses, line lengths, and other means to create unique forms that express their particular meaning and tone.

Cummings's "in Just-" and the excerpt from Whitman's "I Sing the Body Electric" demonstrate how the white space on a page and rhythmic cadences can be aligned with meaning, but there is one kind of open form poetry that doesn't even look like poetry on a page. A *prose poem* is printed as prose and represents, perhaps, the most clear opposite of fixed forms. Here is a brief example.

GALWAY KINNELL (b. 1927)
After Making Love We Hear Footsteps   1980

For I can snore like a bullhorn
or play loud music
or sit up talking with any reasonably sober Irishman
and Fergus will only sink deeper
into his dreamless sleep, which goes by all in one flash,   5
but let there be that heavy breathing
or a stifled come-cry anywhere in the house
and he will wrench himself awake
and make for it on the run — as now, we lie together,
after making love, quiet, touching along the length of our bodies,   10
familiar touch of the long-married,
and he appears — in his baseball pajamas, it happens,
the neck opening so small
he has to screw them on, which one day may make him wonder
about the mental capacity of baseball players —   15
and says, "Are you loving and snuggling? May I join?"
He flops down between us and hugs us and snuggles himself to sleep,
his face gleaming with satisfaction at being this very child.

In the half darkness we look at each other
and smile   20
and touch arms across his little, startlingly muscled body —
this one whom habit of memory propels to the ground of his making,
sleeper only the mortal sounds can sing awake,
this blessing love gives again into our arms.

Considerations for Critical Thinking and Writing

1. How does the speaker's language reveal his character?
2. Describe the shift in tone between lines 18 and 19 with the shift in focus from child to adult. How does the use of space here emphasize this shift?
3. Do you think this poem is sentimental? Explain why or why not.

Connections to Other Selections

1. Discuss how this poem helps to bring into focus the sense of loss Robert Frost evokes in "Home Burial" (p. 306).
2. Write an essay comparing the tone and theme of this poem with those of Donald Hall's "My Son, My Executioner" (p. 413), paying particular attention to the treatment of the child in each poem.

WILLIAM CARLOS WILLIAMS (1883–1963)
The Red Wheelbarrow   1923

so much depends
upon

a red wheel
barrow

glazed with rain
water

beside the white
chickens.

Considerations for Critical Thinking and Writing

1. What is the effect of these images? Do they have a particular meaning? What "depends upon" the things mentioned in the poem?
2. Do these lines have any kind of rhythm?
3. How does this poem resemble a haiku? How is it different?

DENISE LEVERTOV (b. 1923)
Gathered at the River   1983

For Beatrice Hawley and John Jagel

As if the trees were not indifferent . . .

A breeze flutters the candles but the trees give off
a sense of listening, of hush.

The dust of August on their leaves.
But it grows dark. Their dark green   5
is something known about, not seen.

But summer twilight takes away
only color, not form. The tree-forms,
massive trunks and the great domed heads,
leaning in towards us, are visible,   10

a half-circle of attention.

They listen because the war
we speak of, the human war with ourselves,

the war against earth,
against nature,   15
is a war against them.

The words are spoken
of those who survived a while,
living shadowgraphs, eyes fixed forever
on witnessed horror,   20
who survived to give
testimony, that no-one
may plead ignorance.
Contra naturam.° The trees,   *Against nature (Latin)*
the trees are not indifferent.   25

We intone together, *Never again,*

we stand in a circle,
singing, speaking, making vows,

remembering the dead
of Hiroshima,   30
of Nagasaki.

We are holding candles: we kneel to set them
afloat on the dark river
as they do
there in Hiroshima. We are invoking   35

saints and prophets,
heroes and heroines of justice and peace,
to be with us, to help us
stop the torment of our evil dreams . . .

Windthreatened flames bob on the current . . .   40

They don't get far from shore. But none capsizes
even in the swell of a boat's wake.

The waxy paper cups sheltering them
catch fire. But still the candles
sail their gold downstream.   45

And still the trees ponder our strange doings, as if
well aware that if we fail,
we fail for them:
if our resolves and prayers are weak and fail

there will be nothing left of their slow and innocent wisdom,   50

no roots,
no bole nor branch,

no memory
of shade,
of leaf,   55

no pollen.

Considerations for Critical Thinking and Writing

1. The first line is a fragment that is initially puzzling. Why is it nonetheless an appropriate beginning to this poem?
2. Why do you think the speaker focuses more on the trees than the human victims of the atomic bombings?
3. Discuss the symbolic significance of the trees, paying particular attention to lines 51–56.

Connections to Other Selections

1. In her comments on "Gathered at the River," Levertov affirms her "underlying belief in a great design, a potential harmony which can be violated or be sustained." How does Robert Frost's "Design" (p. 318) comment on Levertov's beliefs? Explain whether you agree with Levertov or not.
2. Levertov also expresses a concern in her essay for the necessity of having "a sense of the sacredness of the earthly creation" and mentions that Gerard Manley Hopkins has always been one of her favorite poets. Write an essay comparing "Gathered at the River" with Hopkins's "God's Grandeur" (p. 166) or "Pied Beauty" (p. 421). What significant similarities do you find?

MARILYN NELSON WANIEK (b. 1946)
Emily Dickinson's Defunct   1978

She used to
pack poems
in her hip pocket.
Under all the
gray old lady   5
clothes she was
dressed for action.
She had hair,
imagine,
in certain places, and   10
believe me
she smelled human
on a hot summer day.
Stalking snakes
or counting   15
the thousand motes
in sunlight
she walked just
like an Indian.

She was New England's 20
favorite daughter,
she could pray
like the devil.
She was a
two-fisted woman, 25
this babe.
All the flies
just stood around
and buzzed
when she died. 30

Considerations for Critical Thinking and Writing

1. How does the speaker characterize Dickinson? Explain why this characterization is different from the popular view of Dickinson.
2. How does the diction of the poem serve to characterize the speaker?
3. Discuss the function of the poem's title.

Connections to Other Selections

1. Waniek alludes to at least two other poems in "Emily Dickinson's Defunct." The title refers to E. E. Cummings's "Buffalo Bill 's" (p. 407), and the final lines (27–30) refer to Dickinson's "I heard a Fly buzz — when I died — " (p. 274). Read those poems and write an essay discussing how they affect your reading of Waniek's poem.

JIM DANIELS (b. 1956)
Short-order Cook

1985

An average joe comes in
and orders thirty cheeseburgers and thirty fries.

I wait for him to pay before I start cooking.
He pays.
He ain't no average joe. 5

The grill is just big enough for ten rows of three.
I slap the burgers down
throw two buckets of fries in the deep frier
and they pop pop spit spit . . .
psss . . . 10
The counter girls laugh.
I concentrate.
It is the crucial point —
they are ready for the cheese:
my fingers shake as I tear off slices 15
toss them on the burgers/fries done/dump/

refill buckets/burgers ready/flip into buns/
beat that melting cheese/wrap burgers in plastic/
into paper bags/fries done/dump/fill thirty bags/
bring them to the counter/wipe sweat on sleeve   20
and smile at the counter girls.
I puff my chest out and bellow:
"Thirty cheeseburgers, thirty fries!"
They look at me funny.
I grab a handful of ice, toss it in my mouth   25
do a little dance and walk back to the grill.
Pressure, responsibility, success,
thirty cheeseburgers, thirty fries.

Considerations for Critical Thinking and Writing

1. What function do the three stanzas serve?
2. How do the varying line lengths contribute to the poem's meaning?
3. What is the effect of the slashes in lines 16–20?
4. What role do the counter girls play in the poem?

Connection to Another Selection

1. Write a narrative poem or prose poem in which you imagine an encounter
   between this short-order cook and the speaker of Keesbury's "Song to a Waitress"
   (p. 200).

CAROLYN FORCHÉ (b. 1950)
The Colonel   May 1978

What you have heard is true. I was in his house. His wife carried a
tray of coffee and sugar. His daughter filed her nails, his son went
out for the night. There were daily papers, pet dogs, a pistol on the
cushion beside him. The moon swung bare on its black cord over
the house. On the television was a cop show. It was in English.   5
Broken bottles were embedded in the walls around the house to
scoop the kneecaps from a man's legs or cut his hands to lace. On
the windows there were gratings like those in liquor stores. We had
dinner, rack of lamb, good wine, a gold bell was on the table for
calling the maid. The maid brought green mangoes, salt, a type of   10
bread. I was asked how I enjoyed the country. There was a brief
commercial in Spanish. His wife took everything away. There was
some talk then of how difficult it had become to govern. The parrot
said hello on the terrace. The colonel told it to shut up, and pushed
himself from the table. My friend said to me with his eyes: say noth-   15
ing. The colonel returned with a sack used to bring groceries home.
He spilled many human ears on the table. They were like dried
peach halves. There is no other way to say this. He took one of
them in his hands, shook it in our faces, dropped it into a water

glass. It came alive there. I am tired of fooling around he said. As   20
for the rights of anyone, tell your people they can go fuck themselves. He swept the ears to the floor with his arm and held the last
of his wine in the air. Something for your poetry, no? he said. Some
of the ears on the floor caught this scrap of his voice. Some of the
ears on the floor were pressed to the ground.   25

Considerations for Critical Thinking and Writing

1. What kind of horror is described in this prose poem? Characterize the colonel.
2. What makes this prose poem not a typical prose passage? How is it organized differently?
3. What poetic elements can you find in it?
4. What is the tone of the final two sentences?

SHARON OLDS (b. 1942)
Rite of Passage

1983

As the guests arrive at my son's party
they gather in the living room —
short men, men in first grade
with smooth jaws and chins.
Hands in pockets, they stand around   5
jostling, jockeying for place, small fights
breaking out and calming. One says to another
How old are you? Six. I'm seven. So?
They eye each other, seeing themselves
tiny in the other's pupils. They clear their   10
throats a lot, a room of small bankers,
they fold their arms and frown. *I could beat you
up,* a seven says to a six,
the dark cake, round and heavy as a
turret, behind them on the table. My son,   15
freckles like specks of nutmeg on his cheeks,
chest narrow as the balsa keel of a
model boat, long hands
cool and thin as the day they guided him
out of me, speaks up as a host   20
for the sake of the group.
We could easily kill a two-year-old,
he says in his clear voice. The other
men agree, they clear their throats
like Generals, they relax and get down to   25
playing war, celebrating my son's life.

Considerations for Critical Thinking and Writing

1. In what sense is this birthday party a "rite of passage"?

2. How does the speaker transform these six- and seven-year-old boys into men? What is the point of doing so?

3. Comment on the appropriateness of the image of the cake in lines 14–15.

4. Why does the son's claim that "We could easily kill a two-year-old" come as such a shock at that point in the poem?

Connections to Other Selections

1. In an essay discuss the treatment of violence in "Rite of Passage" and Forché's "The Colonel" (p. 237). To what extent might the colonel be regarded as an adult version of the generals in Olds's poem?

2. Discuss the use of irony in "Rite of Passage" and Owen's "Dulce et Decorum Est" (p. 93). Which do you think is a more effective antiwar poem? Explain why.

CAROLYNN HOY (b. 1947)
In the Summer Kitchen   1993

We speared long wooden spoons
into steaming galvanized tubs
churning and scooping the checked cotton
to feed back and forth
through a wringer   5
from her hand to mine.

And there, on that Monday,
she mentioned Harry, her first born,
my uncle, who died at three months.
That was all,   10
a slip of the tongue
as she hastily turned away.

On the stoop by the clothesline
beyond the screen door,
she snapped our flattened   15
shirts to attention,
shoulders as straight and squared
as her chiselled headstone
I now visit.

That silence.   20

The dignity of it all.

Considerations for Critical Thinking and Writing

1. Explain how the details about doing the wash take on more than a literal significance.

2. How do the grouping of stanzas and the spacing of lines affect your reading?

3. How do you think the speaker feels about her grandmother?

4. How might the poem be regarded as a kind of elegy for the grandmother?

Connection to Another Selection

1. Compare the tone of this poem with that of Emily Dickinson's "The Bustle in a House" (p. 277).

ALLEN GINSBERG (1926–1997)
First Party at Ken Kesey's with Hell's Angels

1965

Cool black night thru the redwoods
cars parked outside in shade
behind the gate, stars dim above
the ravine, a fire burning by the side
porch and a few tired souls hunched over   5
in black leather jackets. In the huge
wooden house, a yellow chandelier
at 3 A.M. the blast of loudspeakers
hi-fi Rolling Stones Ray Charles Beatles
Jumping Joe Jackson and twenty youths   10
dancing to the vibration thru the floor,
a little weed in the bathroom, girls in scarlet
tights, one muscular smooth skinned man
sweating dancing for hours, beer cans
bent littering the yard, a hanged man   15
sculpture dangling from a high creek branch,
children sleeping softly in their bedroom bunks.
And 4 police cars parked outside the painted
gate, red lights revolving in the leaves.

Considerations for Critical Thinking and Writing

1. Who is Ken Kesey? Use the library to find out the kinds of books he writes. How does his name help to establish the poem's setting?
2. How does the absence of commas in lines 8–10 indicate how to read these lines aloud?
3. What is the effect of the poem's last two lines (18–19) on its overall tone?

Connection to Another Selection

1. Write an essay that compares the impact of this poem's ending with that of Hathaway's "Oh, Oh" (p. 13).

ANONYMOUS
The Frog

date unknown

What a wonderful bird the frog are!
When he stand he sit almost;
When he hop he fly almost.

He ain't got no sense hardly;
He ain't got no tail hardly either.
When he sit, he sit on what he ain't got almost.

Considerations for Critical Thinking and Writing

1. Though this poem is ungrammatical, it does have a patterned structure. How does the pattern of sentences create a formal structure?
2. How is the poem a description of the speaker as well as of a frog?

TATO LAVIERA (b. 1951)
AmeRícan

1985

we gave birth to a new generation,
AmeRícan, broader than lost gold
never touched, hidden inside the
puerto rican mountains.

we gave birth to a new generation,   5
AmeRícan, it includes everything
imaginable you-name-it-we-got-it
society.

we gave birth to a new generation,
AmeRícan salutes all folklores,   10
european, indian, black, spanish,
and anything else compatible:

AmeRícan,   singing to composer pedro flores'° palm
             trees high up in the universal sky!

AmeRícan,   sweet soft spanish danzas gypsies   15
             moving lyrics la *española*° cascabelling   *Spanish*
             presence always singing at our side!

AmeRícan,   beating jíbaro° modern troubadours
             crying guitars romantic continental
             bolero love songs!   20

AmeRícan,   across forth and across back
             back across and forth back
             forth across and back and forth
             our trips are walking bridges!

             it all dissolved into itself, the attempt   25
             was truly made, the attempt was truly
             absorbed, digested, we spit out
             the poison, we spit out the malice,
             we stand, affirmative in action,

13 *Pedro Flores:* Puerto Rican composer of popular romantic songs.   18 *jíbaro:* A particular style
of music played by Puerto Rican mountain farmers.

| | to reproduce a broader answer to the | 30 |
| | marginality that gobbled us up abruptly! | |

AmeRícan,   walking plena- rhythms° in new york,
            strutting beautifully alert, alive,
            many turning eyes wondering,
            admiring!   35

AmeRícan,   defining myself my own way any way many
            ways Am e Rícan, with the big R and the
            accent on the í!

AmeRícan,   like the soul gliding talk of gospel
            boogie music!   40

AmeRícan,   speaking new words in spanglish tenements,
            fast tongue moving street corner "*que*
            corta"° talk being invented at the insistence   *that cuts*
            of a smile!

AmeRícan,   abounding inside so many ethnic english   45
            people, and out of humanity, we blend
            and mix all that is good!

AmeRícan,   integrating in new york and defining our
            own *destino,*° our own way of life,   *destiny*

AmeRícan,   defining the new america, humane america,   50
            admired america, loved america, harmonious
            america, the world in peace, our energies
            collectively invested to find other civili-
            zations, to touch God, further and further,
            to dwell in the spirit of divinity!   55

AmeRícan,   yes, for now, for i love this, my second
            land, and i dream to take the accent from
            the altercation, and be proud to call
            myself american, in the u.s. sense of the
            word, AmeRícan, America!   60

32 *plena- rhythms:* African–Puerto Rican folklore, music, and dance.

Considerations for Critical Thinking and Writing

1. How does the arrangement of lines communicate a sense of energy and vitality?
2. How does the speaker portray Puerto Ricans living in the United States?
3. How does the poet describe the United States?

Connection to Another Selection

1. In an essay consider the themes, styles, and tones of "AmeRícan" and Divakaruni's "Indian Movie, New Jersey" (p. 149).

THOM WARD (b. 1963)
Vasectomy

1996

    for Adam Smith°

No one's notified the workers
special dividends have been issued,
the factory sold. Frames
are still being welded, transmissions
bolted to engines, acetylene torches lit   5
gold like the light from miners' helmets
on groaning timber. Coal
is still chiseled and dust
spun into lungs. No one's posted signs:
Road Out. Bridge Out. Danger Ahead.   10
Fingers black with dye, young girls
disappear in looms. Women
boil metal, pour it steaming into molds.
Day fused to night, millions of laborers,
backs crooked and hands cracked,   15
manufacture bottles, canisters and cogs,
replicating product
that will never reach foreign markets.
Soldiers turn semis back at the border.
Executives charter planes,   20
shift funds into Swiss accounts.
How long before word of this
hits the factories, the mines, the wicked
textile mills? What good, what possible good,
is supply without demand?   25

Adam Smith (1723–1790): Scottish political economist and philosopher.

Considerations for Critical Thinking and Writing

1. What is this poem about? What is its tone?
2. How does the title reveal the poem's meaning? What has been removed?
3. Why is the dedication of the poem relevant to its theme?

Connection to Another Selection

1. Compare the themes of "Vasectomy" and Langston Hughes's "Let America Be America Again" (p. 349), paying special attention to the role of the laborer in these poems.

JOSEPH BRUCHAC (b. 1942)
Ellis Island

1979

Beyond the red brick of Ellis Island
where the two Slovak children
who became my grandparents
waited the long days of quarantine,
after leaving the sickness,   5
the old Empires of Europe,
a Circle Line° ship slips easily   *a tour boat*
on its way to the island
of the tall woman,° green   *Statue of Liberty*
as dreams of forests and meadows   10
waiting for those who'd worked
a thousand years
yet never owned their own.

Like millions of others,
I too come to this island,   15
nine decades the answerer
of dreams.

Yet only one part of my blood loves that memory.
Another voice speaks
of native lands   20
within this nation.
Lands invaded
when the earth became owned.
Lands of those who followed
the changing Moon,   25
knowledge of the seasons
in their veins.

Considerations for Critical Thinking and Writing

1. Joseph Bruchac is part Slovakian and part Native American (Abenaki) in heritage. How does this information affect your reading of the poem? Do you think the speaker values one part of his heritage more than another? Why or why not?
2. Discuss the rhythm of lines 1–13 and 18–27. How does the rhythm of the lines reinforce their meaning?
3. How do you regard your own relationship to America? How does it compare with the speaker's in "Ellis Island"?

Connection to Another Selection

1. Write an essay that discusses the speakers' attitudes toward immigration in "Ellis Island" and in Laviera's "AmeRícan."

PETER MEINKE (b. 1932)

The ABC of Aerobics

1983

Air seeps through alleys and our diaphragms
balloon blackly with this mix of
carbon monoxide and the thousand corrosives a city
doles out free to its constituents;
everyone's jogging through Edgemont Park,   5
frightened by death and fatty tissue,
gasping at the maximal heart rate,
hoping to outlive all the others streaming
in the lanes like lemmings lurching toward their last
jump. I join in despair   10
knowing my arteries jammed with
lint and tobacco, lard and bourbon — my
medical history a noxious marsh:
newts and moles slink through the sodden veins,
owls hoot in the lungs' dark branches;   15
probably I shall keel off the john like
queer Uncle George and lie on the bathroom floor
raging about Shirley Clark, my true love in
seventh grade, God bless her wherever she lives
tied to that turkey who hugely   20
undervalues the beauty of her tiny earlobes, one
view of which (either one: they are both perfect)
would add years to my life and I could skip these
x-rays, turn in my insurance card, and trade
yoga and treadmills and jogging and zen and   25
zucchini for drinking and dreaming of her, breathing hard.

Considerations for Critical Thinking and Writing

1. How does the speaker feel about exercise? How do his descriptions of his physical condition serve to characterize him?

2. A primer is a book that teaches children to read or introduces them, in an elementary way, to the basics of a subject. The title "The ABC of Aerobics" indicates that this poem is meant to be a primer. What is it trying to teach us? Is its final lesson serious or ironic?

3. Discuss Meinke's use of humor. Is it effective?

Connections to Other Selections

1. Write an essay comparing the way Olds connects sex and exercise in "Sex without Love" (p. 68) with Meinke's treatment here.

2. Compare the voice in this poem with that in Kinnell's "After Making Love We Hear Footsteps" (p. 232). Which do you find more appealing? Why?

GARY SOTO (b. 1952)
Mexicans Begin Jogging

1995

At the factory I worked
In the fleck of rubber, under the press
Of an oven yellow with flame,
Until the border patrol opened
Their vans and my boss waved for us to run.   5
"Over the fence, Soto," he shouted,
And I shouted that I was American.
"No time for lies," he said, and pressed
A dollar in my palm, hurrying me
Through the back door.   10

Since I was on his time, I ran
And became the wag to a short tail of Mexicans —
Ran past the amazed crowds that lined
The street and blurred like photographs, in rain.
I ran from that industrial road to the soft   15
Houses where people paled at the turn of an autumn sky.
What could I do but yell *vivas*
To baseball, milkshakes, and those sociologists
Who would clock me
As I jog into the next century   20
On the power of a great, silly grin.

Considerations for Critical Thinking and Writing

1. Soto was born and raised in Fresno, California. How does this fact affect your reading of the first stanza?
2. In what different ways does the speaker become "the wag" (line 12) in this poem? (You may want to look up the word to consider all possible meanings.)
3. Explain lines 17–21. What serious point is being made in these humorous lines?

Connection to Another Selection

1. Compare the speakers' ironic attitudes toward exercise in this poem and in Meinke's "The ABC of Aerobics."

Found Poem

This next poem is a *found poem,* an unintentional poem discovered in a nonpoetic context, such as a conversation, news story, or an advertisement. Found poems are playful reminders that the words in poems are very often the language we use every day. Whether such found language should be regarded as a poem is an issue left for you to consider.

DONALD JUSTICE (b. 1925)
Order in the Streets   1969

(From instructions printed on a child's toy, Christmas 1968, as reported in the New York
Times)

1. 2. 3.
Switch on.

Jeep rushes
to the scene
of riot   5

Jeep goes
in all directions
by mystery action.

Jeep stops periodically
to turn hood over   10

machine gun appears
with realistic
shooting noise.

After putting down riot,
jeep goes   15
back to the headquarters.

Considerations for Critical Thinking and Writing

1. What is the effect of arranging these instructions in lines? How are the language
   and meaning enhanced by this arrangement?
2. Look for phrases or sentences in ads, textbooks, labels, or directions — in anything that might inadvertently contain provocative material that would be
   revealed by arranging the words in lines. You may even discover some patterns
   of rhyme and rhythm. After arranging the lines, explain why you organized them
   as you did.

10. Writing about Poetry

QUESTIONS FOR RESPONSIVE READING AND WRITING

The following questions can help you respond to important elements that reveal a poem's effects and meanings. The questions are general, so not all of them will necessarily be relevant to a particular poem. Many, however, should prove useful for thinking, talking, and writing about each poem in this collection. If you are uncertain about the meaning of a term used in a question, consult the Glossary of Literary Terms beginning on p. 625.

Before addressing these questions, read the poem you are studying in its entirety. Don't worry about interpretation on a first reading; allow yourself the pleasure of enjoying whatever makes itself apparent to you. Then on subsequent readings, use the questions to understand and appreciate how the poem works.

1. Who is the speaker? Is it possible to determine the speaker's age, sex, sensibilities, level of awareness, and values?
2. Is the speaker addressing anyone in particular?
3. How do you respond to the speaker? favorably? negatively? What is the situation? Are there any special circumstances that inform what the speaker says?
4. Is there a specific setting of time and place?
5. Does reading the poem aloud help you to understand it?
6. Does a paraphrase reveal the basic purpose of the poem?
7. What does the title emphasize?
8. Is the theme presented directly or indirectly?
9. Do any allusions enrich the poem's meaning?
10. How does the diction reveal meaning? Are any words repeated? Do any carry evocative connotative meanings? Are there any puns or other forms of verbal wit?
11. Are figures of speech used? How does the figurative language contribute to the poem's vividness and meaning?
12. Do any objects, persons, places, events, or actions have allegorical or symbolic meanings? What other details in the poem support your interpretation?

13. Is irony used? Are there any examples of situational irony, verbal irony, or dramatic irony? Is understatement or paradox used?
14. What is the tone of the poem? Is the tone consistent?
15. Does the poem use onomatopoeia, assonance, consonance, or alliteration? How do these sounds affect you?
16. What sounds are repeated? If there are rhymes, what is their effect? Do they seem forced or natural? Is there a rhyme scheme? Do the rhymes contribute to the poem's meaning?
17. Do the lines have a regular meter? What is the predominant meter? Are there significant variations? Does the rhythm seem appropriate for the tone of the poem?
18. Does the poem's form — its overall structure — follow an established pattern? Do you think the form is a suitable vehicle for the poem's meaning and effects?
19. Is the language of the poem intense and concentrated? Do you think it warrants more than one or two close readings?
20. Did you enjoy the poem? What, specifically, pleased or displeased you about what was expressed and how it was expressed?
21. Is there a particular critical approach that seems especially appropriate for this poem? (See the discussion of "Critical Strategies for Reading" beginning on p. 525.)
22. How might biographical information about the author help to determine the central concerns of the poem?
23. How might historical information about the poem provide a useful context for interpretation?
24. To what extent do your own experiences, values, beliefs, and assumptions inform your interpretation?
25. What kinds of evidence from the poem are you focusing on to support your interpretation? Does your interpretation leave out any important elements that might undercut or qualify your interpretation?
26. Given that there are a variety of ways to interpret the poem, which one seems the most useful to you?

A SAMPLE PAPER: MEMORY IN ELIZABETH BISHOP'S "MANNERS"

The following sample paper on Elizabeth Bishop's "Manners" was written in response to an assignment that called for a 750-word discussion of the ways in which at least five of the following elements work to develop and reinforce the poem's themes.

diction and tone	irony	form
images	sound and rhyme	speaker
figures of speech	rhythm and meter	setting and situation
symbols		

In her paper, Debra Epstein discusses the ways in which a number of these elements contribute to what she sees as a central theme of "Manners": the loss of a way of life that Bishop associates with the end of World War I. Not all of the elements of poetry are covered equally in Epstein's paper, because some, such as the speaker and setting, are more important to her argument than others. Notice how rather than merely listing each of the elements, Epstein mentions them in her discussion as she needs to in order to develop the thesis that she clearly and succinctly expresses in her opening paragraph.

ELIZABETH BISHOP (1911–1979)
Manners   1965

for a Child of 1918

My grandfather said to me
as we sat on the wagon seat,
"Be sure to remember to always
speak to everyone you meet."

We met a stranger on foot.   5
My grandfather's whip tapped his hat.
"Good day, sir. Good day. A fine day."
And I said it and bowed where I sat.

Then we overtook a boy we knew
with his big pet crow on his shoulder.   10
"Always offer everyone a ride;
don't forget that when you get older,"

my grandfather said. So Willy
climbed up with us, but the crow
gave a "Caw!" and flew off. I was worried.   15
How would he know where to go?

But he flew a little way at a time
from fence post to fence post, ahead;
and when Willy whistled he answered.
"A fine bird," my grandfather said,   20

"and he's well brought up. See, he answers
nicely when he's spoken to.
Man or beast, that's good manners.
Be sure that you both always do."

When automobiles went by,   25
the dust hid the people's faces,
but we shouted "Good day! Good day!
Fine day!" at the top of our voices.

When we came to Hustler Hill,
he said that the mare was tired,   30
so we all got down and walked,
as our good manners required.

Debra Epstein
Professor Brown
English 210
May 1, 19--

Memory in Elizabeth Bishop's "Manners"

The subject of Elizabeth Bishop's "Manners" has to do
with behaving well, but the theme of the poem has more to
do with a way of life than with etiquette. The poem suggests that modern society has lost something important--a
friendly openness, a generosity of spirit, a sense of
decency and consideration--in its race toward progress.
Although the narrative is simply told, Bishop enriches
this poem about manners by developing an implicit theme
through her subtle use of such elements of poetry as
speaker, setting, rhyme, meter, symbol, and images.

The dedication suggests that the speaker is "a Child
of 1918" who accompanies his or her grandfather on a wagon
ride and who is urged to practice good manners by greeting
people, offering everyone a ride, and speaking when spoken
to by anyone. During the ride they say hello to a
stranger, give a ride to a boy with a pet crow, shout
greetings to a passing automobile, and get down from the
wagon when they reach a hill because the horse is tired.
They walk because "good manners required" (line 32) such
consideration, even for a horse. This summary indicates
what goes on in the poem but not its significance. That
requires a closer look at some of the poem's elements.

Given the speaker's simple language (there are no
metaphors or similes and only a few words out of thirty-
two lines are more than two syllables), it seems likely
that he or she is a fairly young child, rather than an
adult reminiscing. (It is interesting to note that Bishop

herself, though not identical with the speaker, would have been seven in 1918.) Because the speaker is a young child who uses simple diction, Bishop has to show us the ride's significance indirectly rather than having the speaker explicitly state it.

The setting for the speaker's narrative is important, because 1918 was the year World War I ended, and it marked the beginning of a new era of technology that was the result of rapid industrialization during the war. Horses and wagons would soon be put out to pasture. The grandfather's manners emphasize a time gone by; the child must be told to "remember" what the grandfather says, because he or she will take that advice into a new and very different world.

The grandfather's world of the horse and wagon is uncomplicated, and this is reflected in both the simple quatrains that move predictably along in an <u>abcb</u> rhyme scheme and the frequent anapestic meter (ăs wĕ sát ŏn thĕ wágŏn [2]) that pulls the lines rapidly and lightly. The one moment Bishop breaks the set rhyme scheme is in the seventh stanza when the automobile (the single four-syllable word in the poem) rushes by in a cloud of dust so that people cannot see or hear each other. The only off rhymes in the poem--"faces" (26) and "voices" (28)--are also in this stanza, which suggests that the automobile and the people in it are somehow off or out of sync with what goes on in the other stanzas. The automobile is a symbol of a way of life in which people--their faces hidden--and manners take a back seat to speed and noise. The people in the car don't wave, don't offer a ride, and don't speak when spoken to.

Maybe the image of the crow's noisy cawing and flying

from post to post is a foreshadowing that should prepare readers for the automobile. The speaker feels "worried" about the crow's apparent directionlessness: "How would he know where to go?" (16). However, neither the child nor the grandfather (nor the reader on a first reading) clearly sees the two worlds that Bishop contrasts in the final stanza.

"Hustler Hill" is the perfect name for what finally tires out the mare. There is no hurry for the grandfather and child, but there is for those people in the car and the postwar hustle and bustle they represent. The fast-paced future overtakes the tired symbol of the past in the poem. The pace slows as the wagon passengers get down to walk, but the reader recognizes that the grandfather's way has been lost to a world in which good manners are not required.

11. A Study of Three Poets: Emily Dickinson, Robert Frost, and Langston Hughes

This chapter includes poems by Emily Dickinson, Robert Frost, and Langston Hughes in order to provide an opportunity to study three major poets in some depth. None of the collections is wholly representative of the poet's work, but each offers enough poems to suggest some of the techniques and concerns that characterize the poet's writings. The poems within each group speak not only to readers but also to one another. That's natural enough: the more familiar you are with a writer's work, the easier it is to perceive and enjoy the strategies and themes he or she employs. If you are asked to write about these authors, you may find useful the Questions for Writing About an Author in Depth (p. 292) and the sample paper on Emily Dickinson's attitudes toward religious faith in four of her poems (pp. 294–295).

EMILY DICKINSON (1830-1886)

Emily Dickinson grew up in a prominent and prosperous household in Amherst, Massachusetts. Along with her younger sister Lavinia and older brother Austin, she experienced a quiet and reserved family life headed by her father, Edward Dickinson. In a letter to Austin at law school, she once described the atmosphere in her father's house as "pretty much all sobriety." Her mother, Emily Norcross Dickinson, was not as powerful a presence in her life; she seems not to have been as emotionally accessible as Dickinson would have liked. Her daughter is said to have characterized her as not the sort of mother "to whom you hurry when you are troubled." Both parents raised Dickinson to be a cultured Christian woman who would one day be responsible for a family of her own. Her father attempted to protect her from reading books that might "joggle" her mind, particularly her religious faith, but Dickinson's individualistic instincts and irreverent sensibilities created conflicts that did not allow her to fall into step with the conventional piety, domesticity, and social duty prescribed by her father and the orthodox Congregationalism of Amherst.

The Dickinsons were well known in Massachusetts. Her father was a lawyer and served as the treasurer of Amherst College (a position Austin eventually took up as well), and her grandfather was one of the college's founders. Although nineteenth-century politics, economics, and social issues do not appear in the foreground of her poetry, Dickinson lived in a family environment that was steeped in them: her father was an active town official and served in the General Court of Massachusetts, the State Senate, and the United States House of Representatives.

Dickinson, however, withdrew not only from her father's public world but also from almost all social life in Amherst. She refused to see most people, and aside from a single year at South Hadley Female Seminary (now Mount Holyoke College), one excursion to Philadelphia and Washington, and several brief trips to Boston to see a doctor about eye problems, she lived all her life in her father's house. She dressed only in white and developed a reputation as a reclusive eccentric. Dickinson selected her own society carefully and frugally. Like her poetry, her relationship to the world was intensely reticent. Indeed, during the last twenty years of her life she rarely left the house.

Though Dickinson never married, she had significant relationships with several men who were friends, confidantes, and mentors. She also enjoyed an intimate relationship with her friend Susan Huntington Gilbert, who became her sister-in-law by marrying Austin. Susan and her husband lived next door and were extremely close with Dickinson. Biographers have attempted to find in a number of her relationships the source for the passion of some of her love poems and letters. Several possibilities have been put forward as the person she addressed in three letters as "Dear Master": Benjamin Newton, a clerk in her father's office who talked about books with her; Samuel Bowles, editor of the *Springfield Republican* and friend of the family; the Reverend Charles Wadsworth, a Presbyterian preacher with a reputation for powerful sermons; and an old friend and widower, Judge Otis P. Lord. Despite these speculations, no biographer has been able to identify definitively the object of Dickinson's love. What matters, of course, is not with whom she was in love — if, in fact, there was any single person — but that she wrote about such passions so intensely and convincingly in her poetry.

Choosing to live life internally within the confines of her home, Dickinson brought her life into sharp focus. For she also chose to live within the limitless expanses of her imagination, a choice she was keenly aware of and which she described in one of her poems this way: "I dwell in Possibility — " (p. 270). Her small circle of domestic life did not impinge upon her creative sensibilities. Like Henry David Thoreau, she simplified her life so that doing without was a means of being within. In a sense she redefined the meaning of deprivation because being denied something — whether it was faith, love, literary recognition, or some other desire — provided a sharper, more intense understanding than she would have experienced had she achieved what she wanted: "'Heaven,'" she wrote, "is what I cannot reach!" This poem (p. 264), along with many others, such as "Water, is taught by thirst" (p. 261) and "Success is counted sweetest / By those who ne'er succeed" (p. 260), suggest just how persistently she saw deprivation as a way of sensitizing herself to the value of what she was missing. For Dickinson hopeful expectation was always more satisfying than achieving a golden moment. Perhaps that's one reason she was so attracted to John Keats's poetry (see, for example, his "Ode on a Grecian Urn," p. 69).

Dickinson enjoyed reading Keats as well as Emily and Charlotte Brontë; Robert and Elizabeth Barrett Browning; Alfred, Lord Tennyson; and George Eliot. Even so, these writers had little or no effect upon the style of her writing. In her own work she was original and innovative, but she did draw upon her knowledge of the Bible, classical myths, and Shakespeare for allusions and references in her poetry. She also used contemporary popular church hymns, transforming their standard rhythms into free-form hymn meters. Among American writers she appreciated Ralph Waldo Emerson and Thoreau, but she apparently felt Walt Whitman was better left unread. She once mentioned to Thomas Wentworth Higginson, a leading critic with whom she corresponded about her poetry, that as for Whitman "I never read his Book — but was told that he was disgraceful" (for the kind of Whitman poetry she had been warned against see his "I Sing the Body Electric," p. 230). Nathaniel Hawthorne, however, intrigued her with his faith in the imagination and his dark themes: "Hawthorne appals — entices," a remark that might be used to describe her own themes and techniques.

Today, Dickinson is regarded as one of America's greatest poets, but when she died at the age of fifty-six after devoting most of her life to writing poetry, her nearly two thousand poems — only a dozen of which were published, anonymously, during her lifetime — were unknown except to a small number of friends and relatives. Dickinson was not recognized as a major poet until the twentieth century, when modern readers ranked her as a major new voice whose literary innovations were unmatched by any other nineteenth-century poet in the United States.

Dickinson neither completed many poems nor prepared them for publication. She wrote her drafts on scraps of paper, grocery lists, and the backs of recipes and used envelopes. Early editors of her poems took the liberty of making them more accessible to nineteenth-century readers when several volumes of selected poems were published in the 1890s. The poems were made to appear like traditional nineteenth-century verse by assigning them titles, rearranging their syntax, normalizing their grammar, and regularizing their capitalizations. Instead of dashes editors used standard punctuation; instead of the highly elliptical telegraphic lines so characteristic of her poems editors added articles, conjunctions, and prepositions to make them more readable and in line with conventional expectations. In addition, the poems were made more predictable by organizing them into categories such as friendship, nature, love, and death. Not until 1955, when Thomas Johnson published Dickinson's complete works in a form that attempted to be true to her manuscript versions, did readers have the opportunity to see the full range of her style and themes.

Like that of Robert Frost, Dickinson's popular reputation has sometimes relegated her to the role of a New England regionalist who writes quaint uplifting verses that touch the heart. In 1971 that image was mailed first class all over the country by the United States Postal Service. In addition to issuing a commemorative stamp featuring a portrait of Dickinson, the Postal Service affixed the stamp to a first-day-of-issue envelope that included an engraved rose and one of her poems. Here's the poem chosen from among the nearly 2,000 she wrote:

If I can stop one Heart from breaking

c. 1864

If I can stop one Heart from breaking
I shall not live in vain
If I can ease one Life the Aching
or cool one Pain

Or help one fainting Robin
Unto his Nest again
I shall not live in Vain.

This is typical not only of many nineteenth-century popular poems, but of the kind of verse that can be found in contemporary greeting cards. The speaker tells us what we imagine we should think about and makes the point simply with a sentimental image of a "fainting Robin." To point out that robins don't faint or that altruism isn't necessarily the only rule of conduct by which one should live one's life is to make trouble for this poem. Moreover, its use of language is unexceptional; the metaphors used, like that Robin, are a bit weary. If this poem were characteristic of Dickinson's poetry, the Postal Service probably would not have been urged to issue a stamp in her honor, nor would you be reading her poems in this anthology or many others. Here's a poem by Dickinson that is more typical of her writing:

If I shouldn't be alive

c. 1860

If I shouldn't be alive
When the Robins come,
Give the one in Red Cravat,
A Memorial crumb.

If I couldn't thank you,
Being fast asleep,
You will know I'm trying
With my Granite lip!

This poem is more representative of Dickinson's sensibilities and techniques. Although the first stanza sets up a rather mild concern that the speaker might not survive the winter (a not uncommon fear for those who fell prey to pneumonia, for example, during Dickinson's time), the concern can't be taken too seriously — a gentle humor lightens the poem when we realize that all robins have red cravats and are therefore the speaker's favorite. Furthermore, the euphemism that describes the speaker "Being fast asleep" in line 6 makes death seem not so threatening after all. But the sentimental expectations of the first six lines — lines that could have been written by any number of popular nineteenth-century writers — are dashed by the penultimate word of the last line. "Granite" is the perfect word here because it forces us to reread the poem and to recognize that it's not about feeding robins or offering a cosmetic treatment of death; rather, it's a bone-chilling description of a corpse's lip that evokes the cold, hard texture and grayish color of tombstones. These lips will never say "Thank you" or anything else.

Instead of the predictable rhymes and sentiments of "If I can stop one Heart from breaking," this poem is unnervingly precise in its use of language and tidily points out how much emphasis Dickinson places on an individual word. Her use of near rhyme with "asleep" and "lip" brilliantly mocks a euphemistic approach to death by its jarring dissonance. This is a better poem, not because it's grim or about death, but because it demonstrates Dickinson's skillful use of language to produce a shocking irony.

Dickinson found irony, ambiguity, and paradox lurking in the simplest and commonest experiences. The materials and subject matter of her poetry are quite conventional. Her poems are filled with robins, bees, winter light, household items, and domestic duties. These materials represent the range of what she experienced in and around her father's house. She used them because they constituted so much of her life and, more important, because she found meanings latent in them. Though her world was simple, it was also complex in its beauties and its terrors. Her lyric poems capture impressions of particular moments, scenes, or moods, and she characteristically focuses upon topics such as nature, love, immortality, death, faith, doubt, pain, and the self.

Though her materials were conventional, her treatment of them was innovative, because she was willing to break whatever poetic conventions stood in the way of the intensity of her thought and images. Her conciseness, brevity, and wit are tightly packed. Typically she offers her observations via one or two images that reveal her thought in a powerful manner. She once characterized her literary art by writing "My business is circumference." Her method is to reveal the inadequacy of declarative statements by evoking qualifications and questions with images that complicate firm assertions and affirmations. In one of her poems she describes her strategies this way: "Tell all the Truth but tell it slant — / Success in Circuit lies." This might well stand as a working definition of Dickinson's aesthetics and is embodied in the following poem:

The Thought beneath so slight a film —   c. 1860

The Thought beneath so slight a film —
Is more distinctly seen —
As laces just reveal the surge —
Or Mists — the Apennine°   *Italian mountain range*

Paradoxically, "thought" is more clearly understood precisely because a slight "film" — in this case language — covers it. Language, like lace, enhances what it covers and reveals it all the more — just as a mountain range is more engaging to the imagination if it is covered in mists rather than starkly presenting itself. Poetry for Dickinson intensifies, clarifies, and organizes experience.

Dickinson's poetry is challenging because it is radical and original in its rejection of most traditional nineteenth-century themes and techniques. Her poems require active engagement from the reader, because she seems to leave out so much with her elliptical style and remarkable contracting metaphors. But these apparent gaps are filled with meaning if we are sensitive to her use of devices such as personification, allusion, symbolism, and startling syntax and grammar. Since her use of dashes is sometimes puzzling, it helps to read her poems aloud to hear how carefully the words are arranged. What might initially seem intimidating on a silent page can surprise the reader with meaning when heard. It's also worth keeping in mind that Dickinson was not always consistent in her views and that they can change from poem to poem, depending on how she felt at a given moment. For example, her definition of religious belief in "'Faith' is a fine invention" (p. 294) reflects an ironically detached wariness in contrast to the faith embraced in "I never saw a Moor —" (p. 294). Dickinson was less interested in absolute answers to questions than she was in examining and exploring their "circumference."

Because Dickinson's poems are all relatively brief (none is longer than fifty lines), they invite browsing and sampling, but perhaps a useful way into their highly metaphoric and witty world is this "how to" poem that reads almost like a recipe:

To make a prairie
it takes a clover and one bee   date unknown

To make a prairie it takes a clover and one bee,
One clover, and a bee,
And revery.
The revery alone will do,
If bees are few.

This quiet but infinite claim for a writer's imagination brings together the range of ingredients in Dickinson's world of domestic and ordinary natural details. Not surprisingly, she deletes rather than adds to the recipe, because the one essential ingredient is the writer's creative imagination. *Bon appétit.*

Chronology

1830   Born December 10 in Amherst, Massachusetts.

1840   Starts her first year at Amherst Academy.

1847–48	Graduates from Amherst Academy and enters South Hadley Female Seminary (now Mount Holyoke College).
1855	Visits Philadelphia and Washington, D.C.
1857	Emerson lectures in Amherst.
1862	Starts corresponding with Thomas Wentworth Higginson, asking for advice about her poems.
1864	Visits Boston for eye treatments.
1870	Higginson visits her in Amherst.
1873	Higginson visits her for a second and final time.
1874	Her father dies in Boston.
1875	Her mother suffers from paralysis.
1882	Her mother dies.
1886	Dies on May 15 in Amherst, Massachusetts.
1890	First edition of her poetry, edited by Mabel Loomis Todd and Thomas Wentworth Higginson, is published.
1955	Thomas H. Johnson publishes *The Poems of Emily Dickinson* in three volumes, thereby making available her poetry known to that date.

Success is counted sweetest
c. 1859

Success is counted sweetest
By those who ne'er succeed.
To comprehend a nectar
Requires sorest need.

Not one of all the purple Host   5
Who took the Flag today
Can tell the definition
So clear of Victory

As he defeated — dying —
On whose forbidden ear   10
The distant strains of triumph
Burst agonized and clear!

Considerations for Critical Thinking and Writing

1. How is success defined in this poem? To what extent does that definition agree with your own understanding of the word?
2. What do you think is meant by the use of "comprehend" in line 3? How can a nectar be comprehended?

3. Why do the defeated understand victory better than the victorious?
4. Discuss the effect of the poem's final line.

Connection to Another Selection

1. In an essay compare the themes of this poem with those of John Keats's "Ode on a Grecian Urn" (p. 69).

Water, is taught by thirst

c. 1859

Water, is taught by thirst.
Land — by the Oceans passed.
Transport — by throe —
Peace — by its battles told —
Love, by Memorial Mold —
Birds, by the Snow.

Considerations for Critical Thinking and Writing

1. How is the paradox of each line of the poem resolved? How is the first word of each line "taught" by the phrase that follows it?
2. Which image do you find most powerful? Explain why.
3. Try your hand at writing similar lines in which something is "taught."

Connections to Other Selections

1. What does this poem have in common with the preceding poem, "Success is counted sweetest"? Which poem do you think is more effective? Explain why.
2. How is the crucial point of this poem related to "I like a look of Agony," (p. 266)?

Safe in their Alabaster Chambers —

1859 version

Safe in their Alabaster Chambers —
Untouched by Morning
And untouched by Noon —
Sleep the meek members of the Resurrection —
Rafter of satin,   5
And Roof of stone.

Light laughs the breeze
In her Castle above them —
Babbles the Bee in a stolid Ear,
Pipe the Sweet Birds in ignorant cadence —   10
Ah, what sagacity perished here!

Safe in their Alabaster Chambers —

1861 version

Safe in their Alabaster Chambers —
Untouched by Morning —
And untouched by Noon —
Lie the meek members of the Resurrection —
Rafter of Satin — and Roof of Stone!   5

Grand go the Years — in the Crescent — above them —
Worlds scoop their arcs —
And Firmaments — row —
Diadems — drop — and Doges° — surrender —
Soundless as dots — on a Disc of Snow —   10

9 *Doges:* Chief magistrates of Venice from the twelfth to the sixteenth centuries.

Considerations for Critical Thinking and Writing

1. Dickinson permitted the 1859 version of this poem, entitled "The Sleeping," to be printed in the *Springfield Republican*. The second version she sent privately to Thomas W. Higginson. Why do you suppose she would agree to publish the first but not the second version?
2. Are there any significant changes in the first stanzas of the two versions? If you answered yes, explain the significance of the changes.
3. Describe the different kinds of images used in the two second stanzas. How do those images affect the tones and meanings of those stanzas?
4. Discuss why you prefer one version of the poem to the other.

Connections to Other Selections

1. Compare the theme in the 1861 version with the theme of Robert Frost's "Design" (p. 318).
2. In an essay discuss the attitude toward death in the 1859 version and in "Apparently with no surprise" (p. 295).

Portraits are to daily faces

c. 1860

Portraits are to daily faces
As an Evening West,
To a fine, pedantic sunshine —
In a satin Vest!

Considerations for Critical Thinking and Writing

1. How is the basic strategy of this poem similar to the following statement: "Doorknob is to door as button is to sweater"?

2. Identify the four metonymies in the poem. Pay close attention to their connotative meanings.

3. If you don't know the meaning of *pedantic*, look it up in a dictionary. How does its meaning affect your reading of the word *fine*?

4. Dickinson once described her literary art this way: "My business is circumference." Discuss how this poem explains and expresses this characterization of her poetry.

Connections to Other Selections

1. Compare Dickinson's view of poetry in this poem with Francis's perspective in "Catch" (p. 14). What important similarities and differences do you find?

2. Write an essay describing Robert Frost's strategy in "Mending Wall" (p. 304) or "Birches" (p. 311) as the business of circumference.

3. How is the theme of this poem related to the central idea in "The Thought beneath so slight a film — " (p. 258)?

4. Compare the use of the word *fine* here with its use in " 'Faith' is a fine invention" (p. 294).

Some keep the Sabbath going to Church —   c. 1860

Some keep the Sabbath going to Church —
I keep it, staying at Home —
With a Bobolink for a Chorister —
And an Orchard, for a Dome —

Some keep the Sabbath in Surplice°   *holy robes*   5
I just wear my Wings —
And instead of tolling the Bell, for Church,
Our little Sexton — sings.

God preaches, a noted Clergyman —
And the sermon is never long,   10
So instead of getting to Heaven, at last —
I'm going, all along.

Considerations for Critical Thinking and Writing

1. What is the effect of referring to "Some" people?

2. Characterize the speaker's tone.

3. How does the speaker distinguish himself or herself from those who go to church?

4. How might "Surplice" be read as a pun?

5. According to the speaker, how should the Sabbath be observed?

Connection to Another Selection

1. Write an essay that discusses nature in this poem and in Walt Whitman's "When I Heard the Learned Astronomer" (p. 507).

I taste a liquor never brewed —   1861

I taste a liquor never brewed —
From Tankards scooped in Pearl —
Not all the Vats upon the Rhine
Yield such an Alcohol!

Inebriate of Air — am I —   5
And Debauchee of Dew —
Reeling — thro endless summer days —
From inns of Molten Blue —

When "Landlords" turn the drunken Bee
Out of the Foxglove's door —   10
When Butterflies — renounce their "drams" —
I shall but drink the more!

Till Seraphs° swing their snowy Hats —   *angels*
And Saints — to windows run —
To see the little Tippler   15
Leaning against the — Sun —

Considerations for Critical Thinking and Writing

1. What is the poem's central metaphor? How is it developed in each stanza?
2. Which images suggest the causes of the speaker's intoxication?
3. Characterize the speaker's relationship to nature.

Connections to Other Selections

1. In an essay compare this speaker's relationship with nature to that in "A narrow Fellow in the Grass" (p. 2).
2. Discuss the tone created by the images in this poem and in Kinnell's "Blackberry Eating" (p. 161).

"Heaven" — is what I cannot reach!   c. 1861

"Heaven" — is what I cannot reach!
The Apple on the Tree —
Provided it do hopeless — hang —
That — "Heaven" is — to Me!

The Color, on the Cruising Cloud —   5
The interdicted Land —
Behind the Hill — the House behind —
There — Paradise — is found!

Her teasing Purples — Afternoons —
The credulous — decoy —   10
Enamored — of the Conjuror —
That spurned us — Yesterday!

Considerations for Critical Thinking and Writing

1. Look up the myth of Tantalus and explain the allusion in line 3.
2. How does the speaker define heaven? How does that definition compare with conventional views of heaven?
3. Given the speaker's definition of heaven, how do you think the speaker would describe hell?

Connections to Other Selections

1. Write an essay that discusses desire in this poem and in "Water, is taught by thirst" (p. 261).
2. Discuss the speakers' attitudes toward pleasure in this poem and in Ackerman's "A Fine, a Private Place" (p. 61).

Of Bronze — and Blaze —   c. 1861

Of Bronze — and Blaze —
The North — Tonight —
So adequate — it forms —
So preconcerted with itself —
So distant — to alarms —   5
An Unconcern so sovereign
To Universe, or me —
Infects my simple spirit
With Taints of Majesty —
Till I take vaster attitudes —   10
And strut upon my stem —
Disdaining Men, and Oxygen,
For Arrogance of them —

My Splendors, are Menagerie —
But their Competeless Show   15
Will entertain the Centuries
When I, am long ago,
An Island in dishonored Grass —
Whom none but Beetles — know.

Considerations for Critical Thinking and Writing

1. What is the tone of this description of northern lights in the sky?
2. How does the rhythm of lines 1–5 help to convey their meaning?
3. How does the speaker feel about ordinary life as a result of viewing the sky (lines 6–13)?
4. What comparison is made between human life and the "Competeless Show" (line 15) in the sky?

Connections to Other Selections

1. Compare the theme of this poem with that of Crane's "A Man Said to the Universe" (p. 136).

2. In an essay compare the sense of wonder expressed in "Of Bronze — and Blaze — " and in Keats's "On First Looking into Chapman's Homer" (p. 207).

I like a look of Agony, {c. 1861}

I like a look of Agony,
Because I know it's true —
Men do not sham Convulsion,
Nor simulate, a Throe —

The Eyes glaze once — and that is Death —
Impossible to feign
The Beads upon the Forehead
By homely Anguish strung.

Considerations for Critical Thinking and Writing

1. Why does the speaker "like a look of Agony"?
2. Discuss the image of "The Eyes glaze once — ." Why is that a particularly effective metaphor for death?
3. Characterize the speaker. One critic once described the voice in this poem as "almost a hysterical shriek." Explain why you agree or disagree.

Connection to Another Selection

1. Write an essay on Dickinson's attitudes toward pain and deprivation, using this poem, " 'Heaven' — is what I cannot reach!" (p. 264), and "Success is counted sweetest" (p. 260) as the basis for your discussion.

I'm Nobody! Who are you? {c. 1861}

I'm Nobody! Who are you?
Are you — Nobody — too?
Then there's a pair of us!
Don't tell! they'd advertise — you know!

How dreary — to be — Somebody!
How public — like a Frog —
To tell your name — the livelong June —
To an admiring Bog!

Considerations for Critical Thinking and Writing

1. What does the speaker wish to have in common with the reader? Explain whether you feel it is better to be "Nobody" or "Somebody."
2. Explain why it is "dreary — to be — Somebody!"

3. Discuss the simile in line 6. Why does it work so well?
4. What does the speaker think of most people?

Connection to Another Selection

1. Contrast the sense of self in this poem and Walt Whitman's "One's-Self I Sing" (p. 463).

Wild Nights — Wild Nights! c. 1861

Wild Nights — Wild Nights!
Were I with thee
Wild Nights should be
Our luxury!

Futile — the Winds —   5
To a Heart in port —
Done with the Compass —
Done with the Chart!

Rowing in Eden —
Ah, the Sea!   10
Might I but moor — Tonight —
In Thee!

Considerations for Critical Thinking and Writing

1. Look up the meaning of "luxury" in a dictionary. Why does this word work especially well here?
2. Given the imagery of the final stanza, do you think the speaker is a man or woman? Explain why.
3. T. W. Higginson, Dickinson's mentor, once said he was afraid that some "malignant" readers might "read into [a poem like this] more than that virgin recluse ever dreamed of putting there." What do you think?

Connection to Another Selection

1. Write an essay that compares the voice, figures of speech, and theme of this poem with those of Atwood's "you fit into me" (p. 109).

I cannot dance upon my Toes — c. 1862

I cannot dance upon my Toes —
No Man instructed me —
But oftentimes, among my mind,
A Glee possesseth me,

That had I Ballet knowledge —   5
Would put itself abroad

In Pirouette to blanch a Troupe —
Or lay a Prima, mad,

And though I had no Gown of Gauze —
No Ringlet, to my Hair,   10
Nor hopped to Audiences — like Birds,
One Claw upon the Air,

Nor tossed my shape in Eider Balls,
Nor rolled on wheels of snow
Till I was out of sight, in sound,   15
The House encore me so —

Nor any know I know the Art
I mention — easy — Here —
Nor any Placard boast me —
It's full as Opera —   20

Considerations for Critical Thinking and Writing

1. Why is the speaker possessed by "Glee" (line 4)?
2. Discuss the images of dancing in lines 6–15 and explain their effects. What is the speaker's attitude toward dance, do you think?
3. Paraphrase the final stanza and explain how it relates to the poem's theme.

Connection to Another Selection

1. Consider the power of "mind" in this poem and in "To make a prairie it takes a clover and one bee" (p. 259).

What Soft — Cherubic Creatures —   1862

What Soft — Cherubic Creatures —
These Gentlewomen are —
One would as soon assault a Plush —
Or violate a Star —

Such Dimity° Convictions —   *sheer cotton fabric*   5
A Horror so refined
Of freckled Human Nature —
Of Deity — ashamed —

It's such a common — Glory —
A Fisherman's — Degree —   10
Redemption — Brittle Lady —
Be so — ashamed of Thee —

Considerations for Critical Thinking and Writing

1. Characterize the "Gentlewomen" in this poem.
2. How do the sounds produced in the first line help to reinforce their meaning?
3. What are "Dimity Convictions," and what do they make of "freckled Human Nature"?
4. Discuss the irony in the final stanza.

Connection to Another Selection

1. How are the "Gentlewomen" in this poem similar to the "Gentlemen" in "'Faith' is a fine invention" (p. 294)?

The Soul selects her own Society —

c. 1862

The Soul selects her own Society —
Then — shuts the Door —
To her divine Majority —
Present no more —

Unmoved — she notes the Chariots — pausing —   5
At her low Gate —
Unmoved — an Emperor be kneeling
Upon her Mat —

I've known her — from an ample nation —
Choose One —   10
Then — close the Valves of her attention —
Like Stone —

Considerations for Critical Thinking and Writing

1. What images reveal the speaker to be self-reliant and self-sufficient?
2. Why do you suppose the "Soul" in this poem is female? Would it make any difference if it were male?
3. Discuss the effect of the images in the final two lines. Pay particular attention to the meanings of "Valves" in line 11.

This is my letter to the World

c. 1862

This is my letter to the World
That never wrote to Me —
The simple News that Nature told —
With tender Majesty

Her Message is committed
To Hands I cannot see —
For love of Her — Sweet — countrymen —
Judge tenderly — of Me

Considerations for Critical Thinking and Writing

1. In what sense did the world not write to the speaker?
2. Read the section on biographical criticism in Chapter 15, "Critical Strategies for Reading" (p. 525). Why and how is biographical criticism especially useful for interpreting this poem?

Connections to Other Selections

1. In an essay compare the tone of this poem with that of "The Soul selects her own Society — ."
2. Consider in an essay how "This is my letter to the World" might be explained using the themes in " 'Heaven' — is what I cannot reach!" (p. 264).

Much Madness is divinest Sense —

c. 1862

Much Madness is divinest Sense —
To a discerning Eye —
Much Sense — the starkest Madness —
'Tis the Majority
In this, as All, prevail —
Assent — and you are sane —
Demur — you're straightway dangerous —
And handled with a Chain —

Considerations for Critical Thinking and Writing

1. Discuss the conflict between the individual and society in this poem. Which images are used to describe each? How do these images affect your attitudes about them?
2. Comment on the effectiveness of the poem's final line.
3. T. W. Higginson's wife once referred to Dickinson as the "partially cracked poetess of Amherst." Assuming that Dickinson had some idea of how she was regarded by the "Majority," how might this poem be seen as an insight into her life?

Connection to Another Selection

1. Discuss the theme of self-reliance in this poem and in "The Soul selects her own Society — ."

I dwell in Possibility —

c. 1862

I dwell in Possibility —
A fairer House than Prose —
More numerous of Windows —
Superior — for Doors —

Of Chambers as the Cedars —   5
Impregnable of Eye —
And for an Everlasting Roof
The Gambrels° of the Sky —   *angled roofs*

Of Visitors — the fairest —
For Occupation — This —   10
The spreading wide my narrow Hands
To gather Paradise —

Considerations for Critical Thinking and Writing

1. What distinction is made between poetry and prose in this poem? Explain why you agree or disagree with the speaker's distinctions.
2. What is the poem's central metaphor in the second and third stanzas?
3. How does the use of metaphor in this poem become a means for the speaker to envision and create a world beyond the circumstances of the speaker's actual life?

Connections to Other Selections

1. Compare what this poem says about poetry and prose with Hulme's comments in the perspective "On the Differences between Poetry and Prose" (p. 105).
2. How can the speaker's sense of expansiveness in this poem be reconciled with the speaker's insistence upon contraction in "The Soul selects her own Society — " (p. 269)? Are these poems contradictory? Explain why or why not.

This was a Poet — It is That   c. 1862

This was a Poet — It is That
Distills amazing sense
From ordinary Meanings —
And Attar so immense

From the familiar species   5
That perished by the Door —
We wonder it was not Ourselves
Arrested it — before —

Of Pictures, the Discloser —
The Poet — it is He —   10
Entitles Us — by Contrast —
To ceaseless Poverty —

Of Portion — so unconscious —
The Robbing — could not harm —
Himself — to Him — a Fortune —   15
Exterior — to Time —

Considerations for Critical Thinking and Writing

1. According to the speaker, what powers does a poet have? Why are these powers important?
2. Explain the metaphors of "Poverty" (line 12) and "Fortune" (line 15) and how they contribute to the poem's theme.

Connections to Other Selections

1. Write an essay about a life lived in imagination as depicted in this poem and in "I dwell in Possibility — ."
2. Discuss "A Bird came down the Walk" (p. 159) as an example of a poem that "Distills amazing sense / From ordinary Meanings — " (lines 2–3).

I read my sentence — steadily —

c. 1862

I read my sentence — steadily —
Reviewed it with my eyes,
To see that I made no mistake
In its extremest clause —
The Date, and manner, of the shame —   5
And then the Pious Form
That "God have mercy" on the Soul
The Jury voted Him —
I made my soul familiar — with her extremity —
That at the last, it should not be a novel Agony —   10
But she, and Death, acquainted —
Meet tranquilly, as friends —
Salute, and pass, without a Hint —
And there, the Matter ends —

Considerations for Critical Thinking and Writing

1. What is the speaker's "sentence?"
2. What is the central metaphor? Why is it appropriate for this poem's subject matter?
3. How does the speaker regard death in lines 9–14?

Connections to Other Selections

1. Compare the treatment of death in this poem and in "Because I could not stop for Death — " (p. 275).
2. In an essay discuss the "Agony" in this poem and "I like a look of Agony," (p. 266).

The Grass so little has to do —

c. 1862

The Grass so little has to do —
A Sphere of simple Green —
With only Butterflies to brood
And Bees to entertain —

And stir all day to pretty Tunes   5
The Breezes fetch along —
And hold the Sunshine in its lap
And bow to everything —

And thread the Dews, all night, like Pearls —
And make itself so fine   10
A Duchess were too common
For such a noticing —

And even when it dies — to pass
In Odors so divine —

Like Lowly spices, lain to sleep —
Or Spikenards, perishing —

And then, in Sovereign Barns to dwell —
And dream the Days away,
The Grass so little has to do
I wish I were a Hay —

Considerations for Critical Thinking and Writing

1. What is the effect of the repeated use of "And"?
2. How is the grass described? Which images seem especially effective to you?
3. Do you think this is a sentimental poem? Explain your response.

Connections to Other Selections

1. Discuss the tone of this poem and "Presentiment — is that long Shadow — on the lawn —."
2. In an essay compare the speaker's contemplation of death in this poem and in Robert Frost's "Stopping by Woods on a Snowy Evening" (p. 314).

After great pain, a formal feeling comes —　　　　　c. 1862

After great pain, a formal feeling comes —
The Nerves sit ceremonious, like Tombs —
The stiff Heart questions was it He, that bore,
And Yesterday, or Centuries before?

The Feet, mechanical, go round —　　　　　　　　　　　5
Of Ground, or Air, or Ought —
A Wooden way
Regardless grown,
A Quartz contentment, like a stone —

This is the Hour of Lead —　　　　　　　　　　　　　10
Remembered, if outlived,
As Freezing persons, recollect the Snow —
First — Chill — then Stupor — then the letting go —

Considerations for Critical Thinking and Writing

1. What is the cause of the speaker's pain?
2. How does the rhythm of the lines create a slow, somber pace?
3. Discuss why "the Hour of Lead" (line 10) could serve as a useful title for this poem.

Connections to Other Selections

1. How might this poem be read as a kind of sequel to "The Bustle in a House" (p. 277).
2. Write an essay that discusses this poem in relation to Robert Frost's "Home Burial" (p. 306).

I heard a Fly buzz — when I died —

c. 1862

I heard a Fly buzz — when I died —
The Stillness in the Room
Was like the Stillness in the Air —
Between the Heaves of Storm —

The Eyes around — had wrung them dry —   5
And Breaths were gathering firm
For that last Onset — when the King
Be witnessed — in the Room —

I willed my Keepsakes — Signed away
What portion of me be   10
Assignable — and then it was
There interposed a Fly —

With Blue — uncertain stumbling Buzz —
Between the light — and me —
And then the Windows failed — and then   15
I could not see to see —

Considerations for Critical Thinking and Writing

1. What was expected to happen "when the King" was "witnessed"? What happened instead?
2. Why do you think Dickinson chooses a fly rather than perhaps a bee or gnat?
3. What is the effect of the last line? Why not end the poem with "I could not see" instead of the additional "to see"?
4. Discuss the sounds in the poem. Are there any instances of onomatopoeia?

Connections to Other Selections

1. Contrast the symbolic significance of the fly with the spider in Whitman's "A Noiseless Patient Spider" (p. 120).
2. Consider the meaning of "light" in this poem and in "There's a certain Slant of light" (p. 584).

One need not be a Chamber — to be Haunted —

c. 1863

One need not be a Chamber — to be Haunted —
One need not be a House —
The Brain has Corridors — surpassing
Material Place —

Far safer, of a Midnight Meeting   5
External Ghost
Than its interior Confronting —
That Cooler Host.

Far safer, through an Abbey gallop,
The Stones a'chase —   10

Than Unarmed, one's a'self encounter —
In lonesome Place —

Ourself behind ourself, concealed —
Should startle most —
Assassin hid in our Apartment   15
Be Horror's least.

The Body — borrows a Revolver —
He bolts the Door —
O'erlooking a superior spectre —
Or More —   20

Considerations for Critical Thinking and Writing

1. Paraphrase the poem. Which stanza is most difficult to paraphrase? Why?
2. What is the controlling metaphor? Explain why you think it is effective or not.
3. What is the "superior spectre" in line 19?

Connections to Other Selections

1. Compare and contrast this poem with Poe's "The Haunted Palace" (p. 131) and Stevens's "Schizophrenia" (p. 119). In an essay explain which poem you find the most frightening.

Because I could not stop for Death —   c. 1863

Because I could not stop for Death —
He kindly stopped for me —
The Carriage held but just Ourselves —
And Immortality.

We slowly drove — He knew no haste   5
And I had put away
My labor and my leisure too,
For His Civility —

We passed the School, where Children strove
At Recess — in the Ring —   10
We passed the Fields of Gazing Grain —
We passed the Setting Sun —

Or rather — He passed Us —
The Dews drew quivering and chill —
For only Gossamer, my Gown —   15
My Tippet° — only Tulle —   *shawl*

We paused before a House that seemed
A Swelling of the Ground —
The Roof was scarcely visible —
The Cornice — in the Ground —   20

Since then — 'tis Centuries — and yet
Feels shorter than the Day

I first surmised the Horses' Heads
Were toward Eternity —

Considerations for Critical Thinking and Writing

1. Why couldn't the speaker stop for Death?
2. How is Death personified in this poem? How does the speaker respond to him? Why are they accompanied by Immortality?
3. What is the significance of the things they "passed" in the third stanza?
4. What is the "House" in lines 17–20?
5. Discuss the rhythm of the lines. How, for example, is the rhythm of line 14 related to its meaning?

Connections to Other Selections

1. Compare the tone of this poem with that of Dickinson's "Apparently with no surprise" (p. 295).
2. Write an essay comparing Dickinson's view of death in this poem and in "If I shouldn't be alive" (p. 257). Which poem is more powerful for you? Explain why.

A Light exists in Spring

c. 1864

A Light exists in Spring
Not present on the Year
At any other period —
When March is scarcely here

A Color stands abroad   5
On Solitary Fields
That Science cannot overtake
But Human Nature feels.

It waits upon the Lawn,
It shows the furthest Tree
Upon the furthest Slope you know   10
It almost speaks to you.

Then as Horizons step
Or Noons report away
Without the Formula of sound   15
It passes and we stay —

A quality of loss
Affecting our Content
As Trade had suddenly encroached
Upon a Sacrament.   20

Considerations for Critical Thinking and Writing

1. What does the speaker associate with the spring light of March? Paraphrase each stanza; which one reveals most clearly the nature of this light for you?
2. Discuss the meaning of the speaker's use of "Trade" (line 19).

3. Describe the poem's tone. Explain whether you think the tone changes from the beginning to the end.

Connections to Other Selections

1. Discuss the treatment of spring in this poem and in cummings's "in Just — " (p. 229).
2. In an essay compare Dickinson's use of "light" in this poem, in "I heard a Fly buzz — when I died — " (p. 274), and in "There's a certain Slant of light" (p. 584).

I felt a Cleaving in my Mind —   c. 1864

I felt a Cleaving in my Mind —
As if my Brain had split —
I tried to match it — Seam by Seam —
But could not make them fit.

The thought behind, I strove to join
Unto the thought before —
But Sequence ravelled out of Sound
Like Balls — upon a Floor.

Considerations for Critical Thinking and Writing

1. What is going on in the speaker's mind?
2. What is the poem's controlling metaphor? Describe the simile in lines 7 and 8. How does it clarify further the first stanza?
3. Discuss the rhymes. How do they reinforce meaning?

Connection to Another Selection

1. Compare the power of the speaker's mind described here with the power of imagination described in "To make a prairie it takes a clover and one bee" (p. 259).

The Bustle in a House   c. 1866

The Bustle in a House
The Morning after Death
Is solemnest of industries
Enacted upon Earth —

The Sweeping up the Heart
And putting Love away
We shall not want to use again
Until Eternity.

Considerations for Critical Thinking and Writing

1. What is the relationship between love and death in this poem?
2. Why do you think mourning (notice the pun in line 2) is described as an industry?

3. Discuss the tone of the ending of the poem. Consider whether you think it is hopeful, sad, resigned, or some other mood.

Connections to Other Selections

1. Compare this poem with "After great pain, a formal feeling comes — " (p. 273). Which poem is, for you, a more powerful treatment of mourning?
2. How does this poem qualify "I like a look of Agony," (p. 266)? Does it contradict the latter poem? Explain why or why not.

Tell all the Truth but tell it slant —   c. 1868

Tell all the Truth but tell it slant —
Success in Circuit lies
Too bright for our infirm Delight
The Truth's superb surprise

As Lightning to the Children eased
With explanation kind
The Truth must dazzle gradually
Or every man be blind —

Considerations for Critical Thinking and Writing

1. Why should truth be told "slant" and circuitously?
2. How does the second stanza explain the first?
3. How is this poem an example of its own theme?

Connections to Other Selections

1. How does the first stanza of "I know that He exists" (p. 294) suggest an idea similar to this poem's? Why do you think the last eight lines of the former aren't similar in theme to this poem?
2. Write an essay on Dickinson's attitudes about the purpose and strategies of poetry by considering this poem as well as "The Thought beneath so slight a film — " (p. 258) and "Portraits are to daily faces" (p. 262).

From all the Jails the Boys and Girls   c. 1881

From all the Jails the Boys and Girls
Ecstatically leap —
Beloved only Afternoon
That Prison doesn't keep

They storm the Earth and stun the Air,
A Mob of solid Bliss —
Alas — that Frowns should lie in wait
For such a Foe as this —

Considerations for Critical Thinking and Writing

1. What are the "jails"?
2. Comment on the effectiveness of the description in lines 5 and 6.
3. How might "Frowns" be read symbolically?

Connections to Other Selections

1. Compare the theme of this poem with that of William Blake's "The Garden of Love" (p. 393).
2. In an essay discuss the treatment of childhood in this poem and in Robert Frost's "Out, Out — " (p. 313).

The Lightning is a yellow Fork

c. 1870

The Lightning is a yellow Fork
From Tables in the sky
By inadvertent fingers dropt
The awful Cutlery

Of mansions never quite disclosed
And never quite concealed
The Apparatus of the Dark
To ignorance revealed.

Considerations for Critical Thinking and Writing

1. What is the controlling metaphor in the first stanza?
2. Describe the tone. Does the tone change in any way from the first to the second stanza?
3. Write a paraphrase of this poem. Why is it difficult to do so?

Connection to Another Selection

1. Compare the controlling metaphors in "The Lightning is a yellow Fork" and "I know that He exists" (p. 294).

PERSPECTIVES ON DICKINSON

Dickinson's Description of Herself

1862

Mr Higginson,
Your kindness claimed earlier gratitude — but I was ill — and write today, from my pillow.
Thank you for the surgery — it was not so painful as I supposed. I bring you others° — as you ask — though they might not differ —

---

others: Dickinson had sent poems to Higginson for his opinions and enclosed more with this letter.

While my thought is undressed — I can make the distinction, but when I put them in the Gown — they look alike, and numb.

You asked how old I was? I made no verse — but one or two° — until this winter — Sir —

I had a terror — since September — I could tell to none — and so I sing, as the Boy does by the Burying Ground — because I am afraid — You inquire my Books — For Poets — I have Keats — and Mr and Mrs Browning. For Prose — Mr Ruskin — Sir Thomas Browne — and the Revelations. I went to school — but in your manner of the phrase — had no education. When a little Girl, I had a friend, who taught me Immortality — but venturing too near, him-self — he never returned — Soon after, my Tutor, died — and for several years, my Lexicon — was my only companion — Then I found one more — but he was not contented I be his scholar — so he left the Land.

You ask of my Companions Hills — Sir — and the Sundown — and a Dog — large as myself, that my Father bought me — They are better than Beings — because they know — but do not tell — and the noise in the Pool, at Noon — excels my Piano. I have a Brother and Sister — My Mother does not care for thought — and Father, too busy with his Briefs — to notice what we do — He buys me many Books — but begs me not to read them — because he fears they joggle the Mind. They are religious — except me — and address an Eclipse, every morning — whom they call their "Father." But I fear my story fatigues you — I would like to learn — Could you tell me how to grow — or is it unconveyed — like Melody — or Witchcraft?

From a letter to Thomas Wentworth Higginson, April 25, 1862

one or two: Actually she had written almost 300 poems.

Considerations for Critical Thinking and Writing

1. What impression does this letter give you of Dickinson?
2. What kinds of thoughts are there in the foreground of her thinking?
3. To what extent is the style of her letter writing like that of her poetry?

THOMAS WENTWORTH HIGGINSON (1823–1911)
On Meeting Dickinson for the First Time   1870

A large county lawyer's house, brown brick, with great trees & a garden — I sent up my card. A parlor dark & cool & stiffish, a few books & engravings & an open piano. . . .

A step like a pattering child's in entry & in glided a little plain woman with two smooth bands of reddish hair & a face a little like Belle Dove's; not plainer — with no good feature — in a very plain & exquisitely clean white pique & a blue net worsted shawl. She came to me with two day lilies which she put in a sort of childlike way into my hand & said "These are my introduc-tion" in a soft frightened breathless childlike voice — & added under her breath Forgive me if I am frightened; I never see strangers & hardly know what I say — but she talked soon & thenceforward continuously — & deferentially — sometimes stopping to ask me to talk instead of her — but readily recommencing . . . thoroughly ingenuous & simple . . . & saying many things which you would have thought foolish & I wise — & some things you wd. hv. liked. I add a few over the page. . . .

"Women talk; men are silent; that is why I dread women."

"My father only reads on Sunday — he reads *lonely* & *rigorous* books."

"If I read a book [and] it makes my whole body so cold no fire ever can warm me I know *that* is poetry. If I feel physically as if the top of my head were taken off, I know *that* is poetry. These are the only ways I know it. Is there any other way."

"How do most people live without any thoughts. There are many people in the world (you must have noticed them in the street) How do they live. How do they get strength to put on their clothes in the morning"

"When I lost the use of my Eyes it was a comfort to think there were so few real *books* that I could easily find some one to read me all of them"

"Truth is such a *rare* thing it is delightful to tell it."

"I find ecstasy in living — the mere sense of living is joy enough"

I asked if she never felt want of employment, never going off the place & never seeing any visitor "I never thought of conceiving that I could ever have the slightest approach to such a want in all future time" (& added) "I feel that I have not expressed myself strongly enough."

From a letter to his wife, August 16, 1870

Considerations for Critical Thinking and Writing

1. How old is Dickinson when Higginson meets her? Does this description seem commensurate with her age? Explain why or why not.

2. Choose one of the quotations from Dickinson that Higginson includes and write an essay about what it reveals about her.

MABEL LOOMIS TODD (1856–1932)
The Character *of Amherst*   1881

I must tell you about the *character* of Amherst. It is a lady whom the people call the *Myth*. She is a sister of Mr. Dickinson, & seems to be the climax of all the family oddity. She has not been outside of her own house in fifteen years, except once to see a new church, when she crept out at night, & viewed it by moonlight. No one who calls upon her mother & sister ever see her, but she allows little children once in a great while, & one at a time, to come in, when she gives them cake or candy, or some nicety, for she is very fond of little ones. But more often she lets down the sweetmeat by a string, out of a window, to them. She dresses wholly in white, & her mind is said to be perfectly wonderful. She writes finely, but no one *ever* sees her. Her sister, who was at Mrs. Dickinson's party, invited me to come & sing to her mother sometime. . . . People tell me the *myth* will hear every note — she will be near, but unseen. . . . Isn't that like a book? So interesting.

From a letter to her parents, November 6, 1881

Considerations for Critical Thinking and Writing

1. Todd, who in the 1890s would edit Dickinson's poems and letters, had known her for only two months when she wrote this letter. How does Todd characterize Dickinson?

2. Does this description seem positive or negative to you? Explain your answer.

3. A few of Dickinson's poems, such as "Much Madness is divinest Sense — ," suggest that she was aware of this perception of her. Refer to her poems in discussing Dickinson's response to this perception.

RICHARD WILBUR (b. 1921)
On Dickinson's Sense of Privation   1960

What did Emily Dickinson do, as a poet, with her sense of privation? One thing she quite often did was to pose as the laureate and attorney of the empty-handed, and question God about the economy of His creation. Why, she asked, is a fatherly God so sparing of His presence? Why is there never a sign that prayers are heard? Why does Nature tell us no comforting news of its Maker? Why do some receive a whole loaf, while others must starve on a crumb? Where is the benevolence in shipwreck and earthquake? By asking such questions as these, she turned complaint into critique, and used her own sufferings as experiential evidence about the nature of the deity. The God who emerges from these poems is a God who does not answer, an unrevealed God whom one cannot confidently approach through Nature or through doctrine.

But there was another way in which Emily Dickinson dealt with her sentiment of lack — another emotional strategy which was both more frequent and more fruitful. I refer to her repeated assertion of the paradox that privation is more plentiful than plenty; that to renounce is to possess the more; that "The Banquet of abstemiousness / Defaces that of wine." We all know how the poet illustrated this ascetic paradox in her behavior — how in her latter years she chose to live in relative retirement, keeping the world, even in its dearest aspects, at a physical remove. She would write her friends, telling them how she missed them, then flee upstairs when they came to see her; afterward, she might send a note of apology, offering the odd explanation that "We shun because we prize." Any reader of Dickinson biographies can furnish other examples, dramatic or homely, of this prizing and shunning, this yearning and renouncing: in my own mind's eye is a picture of Emily Dickinson watching a gay circus caravan from the distance of her chamber window.

From "Sumptuous Destination" in *Emily Dickinson: Three Views,*
by Richard Wilbur, Louise Bogan, and Archibald MacLeish

Considerations for Critical Thinking and Writing

1. Which poems by Dickinson reprinted in this anthology suggest that she was "the laureate and attorney of the empty-handed"?

2. Which poems suggest that "privation is more plentiful"?

3. Of these two types of poems, which do you prefer? Write an essay that explains your preference.

SANDRA M. GILBERT (b. 1936) AND
SUSAN GUBAR (b. 1944)
On Dickinson's White Dress   1979

Today a dress that the Amherst Historical Society assures us is *the* white dress Dickinson wore — or at least one of her "Uniforms of Snow" — hangs in a drycleaner's plastic bag in the closet of the Dickinson homestead. Perfectly preserved, beautifully flounced and tucked, it is larger than most readers would have expected this self-consciously small poet's dress to be, and thus reminds visiting scholars of the enduring enigma of Dickinson's central metaphor, even while it draws gasps from more practical visitors, who reflect with awe upon the difficulties of maintaining such a costume. But what exactly did the literal and figurative whiteness of this costume represent? What rewards did it offer that would cause an intelligent woman to overlook those practical difficulties? Comparing Dickinson's obsession with whiteness to Melville's, William R. Sherwood suggests that "it reflected in her case the Christian mystery and not a Christian enigma . . . a decision to announce . . . the assumption of a worldly death that paradoxically involved regeneration." This, he adds, her gown — "a typically slant demonstration of truth" — should have revealed "to anyone with the wit to catch on."[1]

We might reasonably wonder, however, if Dickinson herself consciously intended her wardrobe to convey any one message. The range of associations her white poems imply suggests, on the contrary, that for her, as for Melville, white is the ultimate symbol of enigma, paradox, and irony, "not so much a color as the visible absence of color, and at the same time the concrete of all colors." Melville's question [in *Moby-Dick*] might, therefore, also be hers: "is it for these reasons that there is such a dumb blankness, full of meaning, in a wide landscape of snows — a colorless, all-color of atheism from which we shrink?" And his concluding speculation might be hers too, his remark "that the mystical cosmetic which produces every one of [Nature's] hues, the great principle of light, for ever remains white or colorless in itself, and if operating without medium upon matter, would touch all objects . . . with its own blank tinge." For white, in Dickinson's poetry, frequently represents both the energy (the white heat) of Romantic creativity, and the loneliness (the polar cold) of the renunciation or tribulation Romantic creativity may demand, both the white radiance of eternity — or Revelation — and the white terror of a shroud.

> From *The Madwoman in the Attic: The Woman Writer*
> *and the Nineteenth-Century Literary Imagination*

[1] *Circumference and Circumstance: Stages in the Mind and Art of Emily Dickinson* (New York: Columbia UP, 1968) 152, 231.

Considerations for Critical Thinking and Writing

1. What meanings do Gilbert and Gubar attribute to Dickinson's white dress?

2. Discuss the meaning of the implicit whiteness in "Safe in their Alabaster Chambers — " (pp. 261–262) and "After great pain, a formal feeling comes — " (p. 273). To what extent do these poems incorporate the meanings of whiteness that Gilbert and Gubar suggest?

3. What other possible reasons can you think of that would account for Dickinson's wearing only white?

KARL KELLER (b. 1933)
Robert Frost on Dickinson   1979

Frost lived in Amherst for quite a number of years — 1917–20, 1923–25, 1926–38, and then intermittently in the late 1940s and throughout the 1950s when he taught regularly at Amherst College. He often recited her poems from memory, and he conversed with students, friends, and townspeople about her poetry; his concern was almost always over her ability to contain/limit an open-ended universe. He felt this was "what Emily Dickinson surely intends," as he put it, "when she contends: 'In insecurity to lie / Is Joy's insuring quality.' "

It appears that Frost had a one-track mind about Emily Dickinson — her doggedness. For him she was an example of the poet "whose 'state,' " as he put it himself, "never gets sidetracked."

> Since she wrote without thought of publication and was not under the neces-sity of revamping and polishing, it was easy for her to go right to the point and say precisely what she thought and felt. Her technical irregularities give her poems strength as if she were saying, "Look out, Rhyme and Meter, here I come."

Frost apparently liked this willfulness, the unmanageability of the thought by the poetic form, and yet he thought she arrived at it a little too easily and that it was therefore sometimes indistinguishable from carelessness. He felt she had given up the technical struggle too easily. For Frost, to use a general statement of his about poetic rhythm, she was a little too "easy in [her] harness."[1]

Emily Dickinson succeeded, Frost was forced to admit, by flouting poetic systems, by playing freely with the form.

> I try to make good sentences fit the meter. That is important. Good grammar. I don't like to twist the order around in order to fit a form. I try to keep to regular structure and good rhymes. Though I admit that Emily Dickinson, for one, didn't do this always. When she started a poem, it was "Here I come!" and she came plunging through. The meter and rhyme often had to take care of itself.[2]

Though envious of this carefree energy, Frost was also critical of her when she did not achieve regular forms.

> Emily Dickinson didn't study technique. But she should have been more careful. She was more interested in getting the poem down and writing a new one. I feel that she left some to be revised later, and she never revised them. And those two ladies at Amherst printed a lot of her slipshod work which she might not have liked to see printed. She has all kinds of off rhymes. Some that do not rhyme. Her meter does not always go together.[3]

She was therefore substantially different from him; her ability to be conscious of poetic conventions and yet to rise above them surprised him. He generously yielded her his highest admiration for the heresy.

> One of the great things in life is being true within the conventions. I deny in a good poem or a good life that there is compromise. When there is, it is an attempt to so flex the lines that no suspicion can be cast upon what the poet does. Emily Dickinson's poems are examples of this. When the rhyme begins

[1]Robert Francis, *Frost: A Time to Talk* (Amherst, 1972) 53–54.
[2]Daniel Smythe, *Robert Frost Speaks* (New York, np, 1964) 140.
[3]Smythe, 140.

to bother, she says, "Here I come with my truth. Let the rhyme take care of itself." This makes me feel her strength.[4]

For him the large strain of poetry was "a little shifted from the straight-out, a little curved from the straight." Emily Dickinson's poems were, for him, the best examples of this liberty, this flawing. "Can you imagine some people taking that? Can't you imagine some people not accepting that kind of play at all?"[5]

It was this factor of play in Emily Dickinson's poetry that consistently attracted Frost. "Rime reminds you that poetry is play," he said on one occasion, after reciting a Dickinson poem ("The Mountains — grow unnoticed") and calling it "particularly fine," "and that is one of its chief importances. You shouldn't be too sincere to play or you'll be a fraud."[6] Her mischief with poetic form was an indication to him that she was serious about what she was saying and would bend conventions to get it said, and also that she was having a good time trying to say it, but more important than that, that with her poetry (and her ideas) she was *at play*. He appears to have marveled at that in her. "Poetry," Frost used to exclaim to his friends, "is fooling."[7]

From *The Only Kangaroo Among the Beauty: Emily Dickinson in America*

[4]Reginald Lansing Cook, *The Dimensions of Robert Frost* (New York: Barnes and Noble, 1968) 57–58.
[5]Cook, 99.
[6]Cook, 180.
[7]Cook, 181.

Considerations for Critical Thinking and Writing

1. According to Keller, how did Frost respond to Dickinson's "poetic systems" of rhyme and meter?
2. Explain why you agree or disagree with Frost's assessment of Dickinson's poetry as being "slipshod."
3. Choose a poem from each poet and demonstrate how both are versions of "play."

CYNTHIA GRIFFIN WOLFF (b. 1935)
On the Many Voices in Dickinson's Poetry   1986

There were many "Voices." This fact has sometimes puzzled Dickinson's readers. One poem may be delivered in a child's Voice; another in the Voice of a young woman scrutinizing nature and the society in which she makes her place. Sometimes the Voice is that of a woman self-confidently addressing her lover in a language of passion and sexual desire. At still other times, the Voice of the verse seems so precariously balanced at the edge of hysteria that even its calmest observations grate like the shriek of dementia. There is the Voice of the housewife and the Voice that has recourse to the occasionally agonizing, occasionally regal language of the conversion experience of latter-day New England Puritanism. In some poems the Voice is distinctive principally because it speaks in the aftermath of wounding and can comprehend extremities of pain. Moreover, these Voices are not always entirely distinct from one another: the child's Voice that opens a poem may yield to the Voice of a young woman speaking the idiom of ardent love; in a different poem, the speaker may fall into a mood of almost religious contemplation in an attempt to analyze or define such abstract entities as loneliness or madness or eternity; the diction of the housewife may be conflated with the sovereign language of the New Jerusalem, and taken together, they may render some aspect of the wordsmith's labor. No manageable set of discrete categories suffices to capture the diversity of discourse, and any attempt to simplify Dickinson's methods does violence to the verse.

Yet there is a paradox here. This is, by no stretch of the imagination, a body of poetry that might be construed as a series of lyrics spoken by many different people. Disparate as these many Voices are, somehow they all appear to issue from the same "self." . . . It is the enigmatic "Emily Dickinson" readers suppose themselves to have found in this poetry, even in the extreme case when Dickinson's supposed speaker is male. One explanation for this sense of intrinsic unity in the midst of diversity is the persistence with which Dickinson addresses the same set of problems, using a remarkably durable repertoire of linguistic modes. Evocations of injury and wounding — threats to the coherence of the self — appear in the earliest poems and continue until the end; ways of rendering face-to-face encounters change, but this preoccupation with "interview" is sustained by metaphors of "confrontation" that weave throughout. The summoning of one or another Voice in a given poem, then, is not an unselfconscious emotive reflection of Emily Dickinson's mood at the moment of creation. Rather, each different Voice is a calculated tactic, an attempt to touch her readers and engage them intimately with the poetry. Each Voice had its unique advantages; each its limitations. A poet self-conscious in her craft, she calculated this element as carefully as every other.

From *Emily Dickinson*

Considerations for Critical Thinking and Writing

1. From the poems in this anthology, try adding to the list of voices Wolff cites.
2. Despite the many voices in Dickinson's poetry, why, according to Wolff, is there still a "sense of intrinsic unity" in her poetry?
3. Choose a Dickinson poem and describe how the choice of voice is a "calculated tactic."

PAULA BENNETT (b. 1936)
On "I heard a Fly buzz — when I died — "   1990

Dickinson's rage against death, a rage that led her at times to hate both life and death, might have been alleviated, had she been able to gather hard evidence about an afterlife. But, of course, she could not. "The *Bareheaded life —* under the grass — ," she wrote to Samuel Bowles in c. 1860, "worries one like a Wasp." If death was the gate to a better life in "the childhood of the kingdom of Heaven," as the sentimentalists — and Christ — claimed, then, perhaps, there was compensation and healing for life's woes. . . . But how do we know? What can we know? In "I heard a Fly buzz — when I died," Dickinson concludes that we do not know much. . . .

Like many people in her period, Dickinson was fascinated by death-bed scenes. How, she asked various correspondents, did this or that person die? In particular, she wanted to know if their deaths revealed any information about the nature of the afterlife. In this poem, however, she imagines her own death-bed scene, and the answer she provides is grim, as grim (and, at the same time, as ironically mocking), as anything she ever wrote.

In the narrowing focus of death, the fly's insignificant buzz, magnified ten-fold by the stillness in the room, is all that the speaker hears. This kind of dis-tortion in scale is common. It is one of the "illusions" of perception. But here it is horrifying because it defeats every expectation we have. Death is supposed to be an experience of awe. It is the moment when the soul, departing the body, is taken up by God. Hence the watchers at the bedside wait for the moment when the "King" (whether God or death) "be witnessed" in the room. And hence the speaker assigns away everything but that which she expects God (her soul) or death (her body) to take.

What arrives instead, however, is neither God nor death but a fly, "[w]ith Blue — uncertain — stumbling Buzz," a fly, that is, no more secure, no more sure, than we are. Dickinson had associated flies with death once before in the exquisite lament, "How many times these low feet / staggered." In this poem, they buzz "on the / chamber window," and speckle it with dirt, reminding us that the housewife, who once protected us from such intrusions, will protect us no longer. Their presence is threatening but only in a minor way, "dull" like themselves. They are a background noise we do not have to deal with yet.

In "I heard a Fly buzz," on the other hand, there is only one fly and its buzz is not only foregrounded. Before the poem is over, the buzz takes up the entire field of perception, coming between the speaker and the "light" (of day, of life, of knowledge). It is then that the "Windows" (the eyes that are the windows of the soul as well as, metonymically, the light that passes through the panes of glass) "fail" and the speaker is left in darkness — in death, in ignorance. She cannot "see" to "see" (understand).

Given that the only sure thing we know about "life after death" is that flies — in their adult form and more particularly, as maggots — devour us, the poem is at the very least a grim joke. In projecting her death-bed scene, Dick-inson confronts her ignorance and gives back the only answer human knowl-edge can with any certainty give. While we may hope for an afterlife, no one, not even the dying, can prove it exists.

From Emily Dickinson: Woman Poet

Considerations for Critical Thinking and Writing

1. According to Bennett, what is the symbolic value of the fly?
2. Does Bennett leave out any significant elements of the poem in her analysis? Explain why you think she did or did not.
3. Choose a Dickinson poem and write a detailed analysis that attempts to account for all its major elements.

JOAN KIRKBY
On the Fragility of Language in Dickinson's Poetry   1991

The abyss between one meaning and another — when the mind experi-ences the world bereft of articulation — was for Dickinson an exhilarating if dangerous moment of expanse. In [a] prose fragment this experience becomes her definition of life: "Emerging from an Abyss and entering it again — that is Life, is it not?" It is an experience that she courted daily in the poetry, referring in Poem 1323, to "the Daily mind . . . tilling its abyss." She found power and expanse in the moment of transition between an old meaning and a new one.

If language is the tool of thought and gives access to power in the world, it is also a flawed instrument and much of Dickinson's effort is to make us aware of the way language structures and familiarizes the world and makes us blind to it in the process. There are a number of abyss poems which suggest the precarious nature of language performing its trapeze acts over the void. The difficulty of the poems, their frequent resistance to interpretation, is a function of the poet's determination to problematize the fitting of language to experience. The fractures of syntax and diction call attention to the very processes of signification by which we structure the world and challenge familiar and comfortable assumptions. By altering the grammar she alters perception.

The method varies; sometimes she takes a familiar word and shows just how frightening its meaning might be; sometimes she takes an experience and shows up the inadequacy of any word to contain it. In a letter written to Thomas Higginson shortly after he had enlisted in the Civil War, Dickinson wrote: "I should have liked to see you, before you became improbable." "Improbable" used in this context has the impact of a rifle shot. The friend is turned into a statistic, something not likely to be true or to happen; authenticity and agency are despatched in a word. . . .

Dickinson's poems constantly remind us of the fragility of our worded world. Daily life rests upon the articulation of a significant and coherent world, but Dickinson reminds us that this articulation is but a plank over the abyss.

From *Emily Dickinson*

Considerations for Critical Thinking and Writing

1. How does Kirkby define the "abyss" in Dickinson's poetry?
2. The brief discussion following Dickinson's "Presentiment — is that long Shadow — on the lawn — " in this textbook (p. 109) uses that poem to suggest how Dickinson, to quote Kirkby, takes "a familiar word and show[s] just how frightening its meaning might be." First read this discussion and then write about either "Success is counted sweetest" (p. 260) or " 'Heaven' — is what I cannot reach!" (p. 264) as yet another example that illustrates Kirkby's point.
3. In an essay discuss several Dickinson poems from this anthology that can be used to illustrate Kirkby's observation that "fractures of syntax and diction call attention to the very processes of signification by which we structure the world and challenge familiar and comfortable assumptions" (para. 2).

GALWAY KINNELL (b. 1927)
The Deconstruction of Emily Dickinson   1994

The lecture had ended when I came in,
and the professor was answering questions.
I do not know what he had been doing with her
poetry, but now he was speaking of her
as a victim of reluctant male publishers.   5

When the questions dwindled, I put up my hand.
I said the ignorant meddling of the Springfield *Daily Republican*
and the hidebound response of literary men,
and the gulf between the poetic wishfulness
then admired and her own harsh knowledge,   10
had let her see that her poems
would not be understood in her time;
and therefore, passionate to publish,
she vowed not to publish again. I said
I would recite a version of her vow,   15

       Publication — is the Auction
       Of the mind of Man —

But before I could, the professor broke in.
"Yes," he said, " 'the Auction' — 'auction,' from *augere, auctum,* to
    augment, to author . . ."
"Let's hear the poem!" "The poem!" several women,   20
who at such a moment are more outspoken than men, shouted,
but I kept still and he kept going.
"In *auctum* the economy of the signifier is split, revealing an uncon-
    scious collusion in the bourgeois commodification of con-
    sciousness. While our author says 'no,' the unreified text says
    'yes,' yes?"
He kissed his lips together and turned to me
saying, "Now, may we hear the poem?"   25
I waited a moment for full effect.
Without rising to my feet, I said,
"Professor, to understand Dickinson
it may not always be necessary to uproot her words.
Why not, first, try *listening* to her?   30
Loyalty forbids me to recite her poem now."
No, I didn't say that — I realized
she would want me to finish him off with one wallop.
So I said, "Professor, I thought you
would welcome the words of your author.   35
I see you prefer to hear yourself speak."
No, I held back — for I could hear her
urging me to put outrage into my voice
and substance into my argument.
I stood up so that everyone might see   40
the derision in my smile. "Professor," I said,
"you live in Amherst at the end of the twentieth century.
For you 'auction' means a quaint event
where somebody coaxes out the bids
on butter churns on a summer Saturday.   45
Forget etymology, this is history.
In Amherst in 1860 'auction' meant
the slave auction, you dope!"
Well, I didn't say that either,
although I have said them all,   50
many times, in the middle of the night.

In reality, I stood up and recited
like a schoolboy called upon in class.
My voice gradually weakened, and the women
who had called out for the poem   55
now looked as though they were thinking
of errands to be done on the way home.
When I finished, the professor smiled.
"Thank you. So, what at first some of us may have taken as
        a simple outcry, we all now see is an ambivalent, self-
        subversive text."
As people got up to go, I moved   60
into that sanctum within me where Emily
sometimes speaks a verse, and listened
for a sign of how she felt, such as,
"Thanks — Sweet — countryman —
for wanting — to Sing out — of Me —   65
after all that Humbug." But she was silent.

Considerations for Critical Thinking and Writing

1. Describe the professor's critical approach to Dickinson's poetry (for information
   about deconstructionist criticism, see p. 543). How does it compare to the speaker's
   approach? What does he value in Dickinson's poetry?
2. Discuss the use of irony in the poem.
3. Do you think it inevitable that a poet's response to poetry will be different from
   a critic's? Explain your answer.

TWO COMPLEMENTARY CRITICAL READINGS

CHARLES R. ANDERSON (b. 1902)
Eroticism in "Wild Nights — Wild Nights!"   1960

The frank eroticism of this poem might puzzle the biographer of a spinster,
but the critic can only be concerned with its effectiveness as a poem. Unless
one insists on taking the "I" to mean Emily Dickinson, there is not even any
reversal of the lovers' roles (which has been charged, curiously enough, as a
fault in this poem). The opening declaration — "Wild Nights should be / Our
luxury!" — sets the key of her song, for *luxuria* included the meaning of lust as
well as lavishness of sensuous enjoyment, as she was Latinist enough to know.
This is echoed at the end in "Eden," her recurring image, in letters and poems,
for the paradise of earthly love. The theme here is that of sexual passion which
is lawless, outside the rule of "Chart" and "Compass." But it lives by a law of its
own, the law of Eden, which protects it from mundane wind and wave.

This is what gives the magic to her climactic vision, "Rowing in Eden,"
sheltered luxuriously in those paradisiac waters while the wild storms of this
world break about them. Such love was only possible before the Fall. Since then
the bower of bliss is frugal of her leases, limiting each occupant to "an instant"
she says in another poem, for "Adam taught her Thrift / Bankrupt once through

his excesses." In the present poem she limits her yearning to the mortal term, just "Tonight." But this echoes the surge of ecstasy that initiated her song and gives the reiterated "Wild Nights!" a double reference, to the passionate experience in Eden as well as to the tumult of the world shut out by it. So she avoids the chief pitfall of the love lyric, the tendency to exploit emotion for its own sake. Instead she generates out of the conflicting aspects of love, its ecstasy and its brevity, the symbol that contains the poem's meaning.

From *Emily Dickinson's Poetry: Stairway of Surprise*

Considerations for Critical Thinking and Writing

1. According to Anderson what is the theme of "Wild Nights — Wild Nights!"?
2. How does Anderson discuss the "frank eroticism" of the poem? How detailed is his discussion?
3. If there is a "reversal of the lovers' roles" in this poem, do you think it represents, as some critics have charged, "a fault in this poem"? Explain why or why not.
4. Compare Anderson's treatment of this poem with David S. Reynolds's reading that follows. Discuss which one you find more useful and explain why.

DAVID S. REYNOLDS (b. 1949)
Popular Literature and "Wild Nights — Wild Nights!"   1988

It is not known whether Dickinson had read any of the erotic literature of the day or if she knew of the stereotype of the sensual woman. Given her fascination with sensational journalism and with popular literature in general, it is hard to believe she would not have had at least some exposure to erotic literature. At any rate, her treatment of the daring theme of woman's sexual fantasy in this deservedly famous poem bears comparison with erotic themes as they appeared in popular sensational writings. The first stanza of the poem provides an uplifting or purification of sexual fantasy not distant from the effect of Whitman's cleansing rhetoric, which, as we have seen, was consciously designed to counteract the prurience of the popular "love plot." Dickinson's repeated phrase "Wild Nights" is a simple but dazzling metaphor that communicates wild passion — even lust — but simultaneously lifts sexual desire out of the scabrous by fusing it with the natural image of the night. The second verse introduces a second nature image, the turbulent sea and the contrasting quiet port, which at once universalizes the passion and purifies it further by distancing it through a more abstract metaphor. Also, the second verse makes clear that this is not a poem of sexual consummation but rather of pure fantasy and sexual impossibility. Unlike popular erotic literature, the poem portrays neither a consummated seduction nor the heartless deception that it involves. There is instead a pure, fervent fantasy whose frustration is figured forth in the contrasting images of the ocean (the longed-for-but-never-achieved consummation) and the port (the reality of the poet's isolation). The third verse begins with an image, "Rowing in Eden," that further uplifts sexual passion by yoking it with a religious archetype. Here as elsewhere, Dickinson capitalizes nicely on the new religious style, which made possible such fusions of the divine and the earthly. The persona's concluding wish to "moor" in the sea expresses the sustained intense sexual longing and the simultaneous frustration of that longing. In the course of the poem, Dickinson has communicated great erotic passion, and yet, by effectively projecting this passion through unusual nature and religious images, has rid it of even the tiniest residue of sensationalism.

From *Beneath the American Renaissance: The Subversive Imagination in the Age of Emerson and Melville*

Considerations for Critical Thinking and Writing

1. According to Reynolds, how do Dickinson's images provide a "cleansing effect" in the poem?
2. Explain whether you agree that the poem portrays a "pure, fervent fantasy" or something else.
3. Does Reynolds's reading of the poem compete with Anderson's or complement it? Explain your answer.
4. Given the types of critical strategies described in Chapter 15, how would you characterize Anderson's and Reynolds's approaches?

QUESTIONS FOR WRITING ABOUT AN AUTHOR IN DEPTH

This section includes four poems by Emily Dickinson as the subject of a sample in-depth study of her poetry. The following questions can help you to respond to multiple works by the same author. You're likely to be struck by the similarities and differences in works by the same author. Previous knowledge of a writer's work can set up useful expectations in a reader. By being familiar with a number of works by the same writer you can begin to discern particular kinds of concerns and techniques that characterize and help to shed light on a writer's work.

As you read multiple works by the same author you'll begin to recognize situations, events, characters, issues, perspectives, styles, and strategies — even recurring words or phrases — that provide a kind of signature, making the poem in some way identifiable with that particular writer. In the case of the four Dickinson poems included in this section, religion emerges as a central topic linked to a number of issues including faith, immortality, skepticism, and the nature of God. The student selected these poems because he noticed Dickinson's intense interest in religious faith owing to the many poems that explore a variety of religious attitudes in her work. He chose these four because they were closely related, but he also might have found equally useful clusters of poems about love, nature, domestic life, or writing as well as other topics. What especially intrigued him was some of the information he read about Dickinson's sternly religious father and the orthodox nature of the religious values of her hometown of Amherst, Massachusetts. Since this paper was not a research paper, he did not pursue these issues beyond the level of the general remarks provided in an introduction to her poetry (though he might have). He did, however, use this biographical and historical information as a means of framing his search for poems that were related to one another. In doing so he discovered consistent concerns along with contradictory themes that became the basis of his paper.

The questions provided below should help you to listen to how a writer's works can speak to each other and to you. Additional useful questions will be found in other chapters of this book. See Writing About Poetry (p. 248) and Arguing About Literature (p. 573).

1. What topics reappear in the writer's work? What seem to be the major concerns of the author?
2. Does the author have a definable world view that can be discerned from work to work? Is, for example, the writer liberal, conservative, apolitical, or religious?
3. What social values come through in the author's work? Does he or she seem to identify with a particular group or social class?
4. Is there a consistent voice or point of view from work to work? Is it a persona or the author's actual self?
5. How much of the author's own life experiences and historical moment make their way into the works?
6. Does the author experiment with style from work to work, or are the works mostly consistent with one another?
7. Can the author's work be identified with a literary tradition, such as *carpe diem* poetry, that aligns his or her work with that of other writers?
8. What is distinctive about the author's writing? Is the language innovative? Are the themes challenging? Are the voices conventional? Is the tone characteristic?
9. Could you identify another work by the same author without a name being attached to it? What are the distinctive features that allow you to do so?
10. Do any of the writer's works seem *not* to be by that writer? Why?
11. What other writers are most like this author in style and content? Why?
12. Has the writer's work evolved over time? Are there significant changes or developments? Are these new ideas and styles, or do the works remain largely the same?
13. How would you characterize the writing habits of the writer? Is it possible to anticipate what goes on in different works or are you surprised by their content or style?
14. Can difficult or ambiguous passages in a work be resolved by referring to a similar passage in another work?
15. What does the writer say about his or her own work? Do you trust the teller or the tale? Which do you think is more reliable?

A SAMPLE IN-DEPTH STUDY: RELIGIOUS FAITH
IN FOUR POEMS BY EMILY DICKINSON

The following paper was written for an assignment that called for an analysis (about 750 words) on any topic that could be traced in three or four poems by Dickinson. The student chose " 'Faith' is a fine invention," "I know that He exists," "I never saw a Moor — ," and "Apparently with no surprise."

"Faith" is a fine invention   c. 1860

"Faith" is a fine invention
When Gentlemen can *see* —
But *Microscopes* are prudent
In an Emergency.

I know that He exists   c. 1862

I know that He exists.
Somewhere — in Silence —
He has hid his rare life
From our gross eyes.

'Tis an instant's play.   5
'Tis a fond Ambush —
Just to make Bliss
Earn her own surprise!

But — should the play
Prove piercing earnest —   10
Should the glee-glaze —
In Death's — stiff — stare —

Would not the fun
Look too expensive!
Would not the jest —   15
Have crawled too far!

I never saw a Moor —   c. 1865

I never saw a Moor —
I never saw the Sea —
Yet know I how the Heather looks
And what a Billow be.

I never spoke with God
Nor visited in Heaven —
Yet certain am I of the spot
As if the Checks were given —

Apparently with no surprise c. 1884

Apparently with no surprise
To any happy Flower
The Frost beheads it at its play —
In accidental power —
The blond Assassin passes on —
The Sun proceeds unmoved
To measure off another Day
For an Approving God.

Michael Weitz

Professor Pearl

English 270

May 5, 19--

Religious Faith in Four Poems by Emily Dickinson

Throughout much of her poetry, Emily Dickinson wrestles with complex notions of God, faith, and religious devotion. She adheres to no consistent view of religion: rather, her poetry reveals a vision of God and faith that is constantly evolving. Dickinson's gods range from the strict and powerful Old Testament father to a loving spiritual guide to an irrational and ridiculous imaginary figure. Through these varying images of God, Dickinson portrays contrasting images of the meaning and validity of religious faith. Her work reveals competing attitudes toward religious devotion as conventional religious piety struggles with a more cynical perception of God and religious worship.

Dickinson's "I never saw a Moor--" reveals a vision of traditional religious sensibilities. Although the speaker readily admits that "I never spoke with God / Nor visited in Heaven," her devout faith in a supreme being does not waver. The poem appears to be a straightforward profession of true faith stemming from the argument that

the proof of God's existence is the universe's existence.
Dickinson's imagery therefore evolves from the natural to
the supernatural, first establishing her convictions that
Moors and Seas exist, in spite of her lack of personal
contact with either. This leads to the foundation of her
religious faith, again based not on physical experience
but on intellectual convictions. The speaker professes
that she believes in the existence of Heaven even without
conclusive evidence: "Yet certain am I of the spot / As
if the Checks were given--." But the appearance of such
idealistic views of God and faith in "I never saw a
Moor--" are transformed in Dickinson's other poems into a
much more skeptical vision of the validity of religious
piety.

While faith is portrayed as an authentic and deeply
important quality in "I Never Saw a Moor--," Dickinson's
" 'Faith' is a fine invention" portrays faith as much
less essential. Faith is defined in the poem as "a fine
invention," suggesting that it is created by man for man
and therefore is not a crucial aspect of the natural universe. Thus the strong idealistic faith of "I never saw
a Moor--" becomes discredited in the face of scientific
rationalism. The speaker compares religious faith with
actual microscopes, both of which are meant to enhance
one's vision in some way. But "Faith" is only useful
"When Gentlemen can see--" already; in an "Emergency,"
when one ostensibly cannot see, "Microscopes are prudent." Dickinson pits religion against science, suggesting that science, with its tangible evidence and rational
attitude, is a more reliable lens through which to view
the world. Faith is irreverently reduced to a mere
invention, and one that is ultimately less useful than
microscopes or other scientific instruments.

Rational, scientific observations are not the only contributing factor to the portrayal of religious skepticism in Dickinson's poems; nature itself is seen to be incompatible in some ways with conventional religious ideology. In "Apparently with no surprise," the speaker recognizes the inexorable cycle of natural life and death as a morning frost kills a flower. But the tension in this poem stems not from the "happy Flower" struck down by the frost's "accidental power," but from the apparent indifference of the "Approving God" who condones this seemingly cruel and unnecessary death. God is seen as remote and uncompromising, and it is this perceived distance between the speaker and God that reveals the increasing absurdity of traditional religious faith. The speaker understands that praying to God or believing in religion cannot change the course of nature, and as a result feels so helplessly distanced from God that religious faith becomes virtually meaningless.

Dickinson's religious skepticism becomes even more explicit in "I know that He exists," in which the speaker attempts to understand the connection between seeing God and facing death. In this poem Dickinson characterizes God as a remote and mysterious figure; the speaker mockingly asserts, "I know that He exists," even though "He has hid his rare life / From our gross eyes." The skepticism toward religious faith revealed in this poem stems from the speaker's recognition of the paradoxical quest that people undertake to know and to see God. A successful attempt to see God, to win the game of hide-and-seek that He apparently is orchestrating, results inevitably in death. With this recognition the speaker comes to view religion as an absurd and reckless game in which the prize may be "Bliss" but more likely is "Death's--stiff--

stare--." For to see God and to meet one's death as a result certainly suggests that the game of trying to see God (the so-called "fun") is much "too expensive" and that religion itself is a "jest" that, like the serpent in Genesis, has "crawled too far."

Ultimately, the vision of religious faith that Dickinson describes in her poems is one of suspicion and cynicism. She cannot reconcile the physical world to the spiritual existence that Christian doctrine teaches, and as a result the traditional perception of God becomes ludicrous. "I never saw a Moor--" does attempt to sustain a conventional vision of religious devotion, but Dickinson's poems overall are far more likely to suggest that God is elusive, indifferent, and often cruel, thus undermining the traditional vision of God as a loving father worthy of devout worship. Thus, not only religious faith but also those who are religiously faithful become targets for Dickinson's irreverent criticism of conventional belief.

ROBERT FROST (1874-1963)

Few poets have enjoyed the popular success that Robert Frost achieved during his lifetime, and no twentieth-century American poet has had his or her work as widely read and honored. Frost is as much associated with New England as the stone walls that help define its landscape; his reputation, however, transcends regional boundaries. Although he was named poet laureate of Vermont only two years before his death, he was for many years the nation's unofficial poet laureate. Frost collected honors the way some people pick up burrs on country walks. Among his awards were four Pulitzer Prizes, the Bollingen Prize, a Congressional Medal, and dozens of honorary degrees. Perhaps his most moving appearance was his recitation of "The Gift Outright" for millions of Americans at the inauguration of John F. Kennedy in 1961.

Frost's recognition as a poet is especially remarkable because his career as a writer did not attract any significant attention until he was nearly forty years old. He taught himself to write while he labored at odd jobs, taught school, or farmed.

Frost's early identity seems very remote from the New England soil. Although his parents were descended from generations of New Englanders, he was born in San Francisco and was named Robert Lee Frost after the Confederate general. After his father died in 1885, his mother moved the family back to Massachusetts to live with relatives. Frost graduated from high school sharing valedictorian honors with the classmate who would become his wife three years later. Between high school and marriage, he attended Dartmouth College for a few months and then taught. His teaching prompted him to enroll in Harvard in 1897, but after less than two years he withdrew without a degree (though Harvard would eventually award him an honorary doctorate in 1937, four years after Dartmouth conferred its honorary degree upon him). For the next decade, Frost read and wrote poems when he was not chicken farming or teaching. In 1912, he sold his farm and moved his family to England, where he hoped to find the audience that his poetry did not have in America.

Three years in England made it possible for Frost to return home as a poet. His first two volumes of poetry, *A Boy's Will* (1913) and *North of Boston* (1914), were published in England. During the next twenty years, honors and awards were conferred on collections such as *Mountain Interval* (1916), *New Hampshire* (1923), *West-Running Brook* (1928), and *A Further Range* (1936). These are the volumes on which most of Frost's popular and critical reputation rests. Later collections include *A Witness Tree* (1942), *A Masque of Reason* (1945), *Steeple Bush* (1947), *A Masque of Mercy* (1947), *Complete Poems* (1949), and *In the Clearing* (1962). In addition to publishing his works, Frost endeared himself to audiences throughout the country by presenting his poetry almost as conversations. He also taught at a number of schools, including Amherst College, the University of Michigan, Harvard University, Dartmouth College, and Middlebury College.

Frost's countless poetry readings generated wide audiences eager to claim him as their poet. The image he cultivated resembled closely what the public likes to think a poet should be. Frost was seen as a lovable, wise old man; his simple wisdom and cracker-barrel sayings appeared comforting and homey. From this Yankee rustic, audiences learned that "There's a lot yet that isn't understood" or "We love the things we love for what they are" or "Good fences make good neighbors."

In a sense, Frost packaged himself for public consumption. "I am . . . my own salesman," he said. When asked direct questions about the meanings of his poems, he often winked or scratched his head to give the impression that the customer was always right. To be sure, there is a simplicity in Frost's language, but that simplicity does not fully reflect the depth of the man, the complexity of his themes, or the richness of his art.

The folksy optimist behind the public lectern did not reveal his private troubles to his audiences, although he did address those problems at his writing desk. Frost suffered from professional jealousies, anger, and depression. His family life was especially painful. Three of his four children died: a son at the age of four, a daughter in her late twenties from tuberculosis, and another son who was a suicide. His marriage was filled with tension. Although Frost's work is landscaped with sunlight, snow, birches, birds, blueberries, and squirrels, it is important to recognize that he was also intimately "acquainted with the night," a phrase that serves as the haunting title of one of his poems (see p. 129).

As a corrective to Frost's popular reputation, one critic, Lionel Trilling, described the world Frost creates in his poems as a "terrifying universe," characterized by loneliness, anguish, frustration, doubts, disappointment, and despair (see p. 327 for an excerpt from this essay). To point this out is not to annihilate the pleasantness and even good-natured cheerfulness that can be enjoyed in Frost's poetry, but it is to say that Frost is not so one-dimensional as he is sometimes assumed to be. Frost's poetry requires readers who are alert and willing to penetrate the simplicity of its language to see the elusive and ambiguous meanings that lie below the surface.

Frost's treatment of nature helps to explain the various levels of meaning in his poetry. The familiar natural world his poems evoke is sharply detailed. We hear icy branches clicking against themselves, we see the snow-white trunks of birches, we feel the smarting pain of a twig lashing across a face. The aspects of the natural world Frost describes are designated to give pleasure, but they are also frequently calculated to provoke thought. His use of nature tends to be symbolic. Complex meanings are derived from simple facts, such as a spider killing a moth or the difference between fire and ice (see "Design," p. 318, and "Fire and Ice," p. 314). Although Frost's strategy is to talk about particular events and individual experiences, his poems evoke universal issues.

Frost's poetry has strong regional roots and is "versed in country things," but it flourishes in any receptive imagination because, in the final analysis, it is concerned with human beings. Frost's New England landscapes are the occasion rather than the ultimate focus of his poems. Like the rural voices he creates in his poems, Frost typically approaches his themes indirectly. He explained the reason for this in a talk titled "Education by Poetry."

> Poetry provides the one permissible way of saying one thing and
> meaning another. People say, "why don't you say what you mean?" We
> never do that, do we, being all of us too much poets. We like to talk in
> parables and in hints and in indirections — whether from diffidence or
> some other instinct.

The result is that the settings, characters, and situations that make up the subject matter of Frost's poems are vehicles for his perceptions about life.

In "Stopping by Woods on a Snowy Evening" (p. 328), for example, Frost uses the kind of familiar New England details that constitute his poetry for more than descriptive purposes. He shapes them into a meditation on the tension we sometimes feel between life's responsibilities and the "lovely, dark, and deep" attraction that death offers. When the speaker's horse "gives his harness bells a shake," we are reminded that we are confronting a universal theme as well as a quiet moment of natural beauty.

Among the major concerns that appear in Frost's poetry are the fragility of life, the consequences of rejecting or accepting the conditions of one's life, the passion of inconsolable grief, the difficulty of sustaining intimacy, the fear of loneliness and isolation, the inevitability of change, the tensions between the individual and society, and the place of tradition and custom.

Whatever theme is encountered in a poem by Frost, a reader is likely to agree with him that "the initial delight is in the surprise of remembering something I didn't know." To achieve that fresh sense of discovery, Frost allowed himself to follow his instincts; his poetry

> inclines to the impulse, it assumes direction with the first line laid down, it runs a course of lucky events, and ends in a clarification of life — not necessarily a great clarification, such as sects and cults are founded on, but in a momentary stay against confusion.

This description from "The Figure a Poem Makes" (see p. 324 for the complete essay), Frost's brief introduction to *Complete Poems,* may sound as if his poetry is formless and merely "lucky," but his poems tend to be more conventional than experimental: "The artist in me," as he put the matter in one of his poems, "cries out for design."

From Frost's perspective, "free verse is like playing tennis with the net down." He exercised his own freedom in meeting the challenges of rhyme and meter. His use of fixed forms such as couplets, tercets, quatrains, blank verse, and sonnets was not slavish, because he enjoyed working them into the natural English speech patterns — especially the rhythms, idioms, and tones of speakers living north of Boston — that give voice to his themes. Frost often liked to use "Stopping by Woods on a Snowy Evening" as an example of his graceful way of making conventions appear natural and inevitable. He explored "the old ways to be new."

Frost's eye for strong, telling details was matched by his ear for natural speech rhythms. His flexible use of what he called "iambic and loose iambic" enabled him to create moving lyric poems that reveal the personal thoughts of a speaker and dramatic poems that convincingly characterize people caught in intense emotional situations. The language in his poems appears to be little more than a transcription of casual and even rambling speech, but it is in actuality Frost's poetic creation, carefully crafted to reveal the joys and sorrows that are woven into people's daily lives. What is missing from Frost's poems is artificiality, not art. Consider this poem.

The Road Not Taken 1916

Two roads diverged in a yellow wood,
And sorry I could not travel both
And be one traveler, long I stood
And looked down one as far as I could
To where it bent in the undergrowth; 5

Then took the other, as just as fair,
And having perhaps the better claim,
Because it was grassy and wanted wear;

Though as for that the passing there
Had worn them really about the same,   10

And both that morning equally lay
In leaves no step had trodden black.
Oh, I kept the first for another day!
Yet knowing how way leads on to way,
I doubted if I should ever come back.   15

I shall be telling this with a sigh
Somewhere ages and ages hence:
Two roads diverged in a wood, and I —
I took the one less traveled by,
And that has made all the difference.   20

This poem intrigues readers because it is at once so simple and so deeply resonant. Recalling a walk in the woods, the speaker describes how he came upon a fork in the road, which forced him to choose one path over another. Though "sorry" that he "could not travel both," he made a choice after carefully weighing his two options. This, essentially, is what happens in the poem; there is no other action. However, the incident is charged with symbolic significance by the speaker's reflections on the necessity and consequences of his decision.

The final stanza indicates that the choice concerns more than simply walking down a road, for the speaker says that his chosen path has affected his entire life — "that [it] has made all the difference." Frost draws on a familiar enough metaphor when he compares life to a journey, but he is also calling attention to a less commonly noted problem: despite our expectations, aspirations, appetites, hopes, and desires, we can't have it all. Making one choice precludes another. It is impossible to determine what particular decision the speaker refers to: perhaps he had to choose a college, a career, a spouse; perhaps he was confronted with mutually exclusive ideas, beliefs, or values. There is no way to know, because Frost wisely creates a symbolic choice and implicitly invites us to supply our own circumstances.

The speaker's reflections about his choice are as central to an understanding of the poem as the choice itself; indeed, they may be more central. He describes the road taken as "having perhaps the better claim, / Because it was grassy and wanted wear"; he prefers the "less traveled" path. This seems to be an expression of individualism, which would account for "the difference" his choice made in his life. But Frost complicates matters by having the speaker also acknowledge that there was no significant difference between the two roads; one was "just as fair" as the other; each was "worn . . . really about the same"; and "both that morning equally lay / In leaves no step had trodden black."

The speaker imagines that in the future, "ages and ages hence," he will recount his choice with "a sigh" that will satisfactorily explain the course of his life, but Frost seems to be having a little fun here by showing us how the speaker will embellish his past decision to make it appear more dramatic. What we hear is someone trying to convince himself that the choice he made significantly changed his life. When he recalls what happened in the "yellow wood," a color that gives a glow to that irretrievable moment when his life seemed to be on verge of a momentous change, he appears more concerned with the path he did not choose than with the one he took. Frost shrewdly titles the poem to suggest the speaker's sense of loss at not being able to "travel both" roads. When the speaker's reflections about his choice are examined, the poem reveals his nostalgia instead of affirming his decision to travel a self-reliant path in life.

The rhymed stanzas of "The Road Not Taken" follow a pattern established in the first five lines (*abaab*). This rhyme scheme reflects, perhaps, the speaker's efforts to shape his life into a pleasing and coherent form. The natural speech rhythms Frost uses allow him to integrate the rhymes unobtrusively, but there is a slight shift in lines 19–20, when the speaker asserts self-consciously that the "less traveled" road — which we already know to be basically the same as the other road — "made all the difference." Unlike all the other rhymes in the poem, "difference" does not rhyme precisely with "hence." The emphasis that must be placed on "differ*ence*" to make it rhyme perfectly with "hence" may suggest that the speaker is trying just a little too hard to pattern his life on his earlier choice in the woods.

Perhaps the best way to begin reading Frost's poetry is to accept the invitation he placed at the beginning of many volumes of his poems. "The Pasture" means what it says of course; it is about taking care of some farm chores, but it is also a means of "saying one thing in terms of another."

The Pasture   1913

I'm going out to clean the pasture spring;
I'll only stop to rake the leaves away
(And wait to watch the water clear, I may):
I shan't be gone long. — You come too.

I'm going out to fetch the little calf
That's standing by the mother. It's so young
It totters when she licks it with her tongue.
I shan't be gone long. — You come too.

"The Pasture" is a simple but irresistible songlike invitation to the pleasure of looking at the world through the eyes of a poet.

Chronology

1874	Born on March 26 in San Francisco, California.
1885	Father dies and family moves to Lawrence, Massachusetts.
1892	Graduates from Lawrence High School.
1893–94	Studies at Dartmouth College.
1895	Marries his high school sweetheart, Elinor White.

1897–99	Studies at Harvard College.
1900	Moves to a farm in West Derry, New Hampshire.
1912	Moves to England, where he farms and writes.
1913	*A Boy's Will* is published in London.
1914	*North of Boston* is published in London.
1915	Moves to a farm near Franconia, New Hampshire.
1916	Elected to National Institute of Letters.
1917–20	Teaches at Amherst College.
1919	Moves to South Shaftsbury, Vermont.
1921–23	Teaches at the University of Michigan.
1923	*Selected Poems* and *New Hampshire* are published; the latter is awarded a Pulitzer Prize.
1928	*West-Running Brook* is published.
1930	*Collected Poems* is published.
1936	*A Further Range* is published; teaches at Harvard.
1938	Wife dies.
1939–42	Teaches at Harvard.
1942	*A Witness Tree* is published, which is awarded a Pulitzer Prize.
1943–49	Teaches at Dartmouth.
1945	*A Masque of Reason* is published.
1947	*Steeple Bush* and *A Masque of Mercy* are published.
1949	*Complete Poems* (enlarged) is published.
1961	Reads "The Gift Outright" at President John F. Kennedy's inauguration.
1963	Dies on January 29 in Boston.

Mending Wall   1914

Something there is that doesn't love a wall,
That sends the frozen-ground-swell under it,
And spills the upper boulders in the sun;
And makes gaps even two can pass abreast.
The work of hunters is another thing: 5
I have come after them and made repair
Where they have left not one stone on a stone,

But they would have the rabbit out of hiding,
To please the yelping dogs. The gaps I mean,
No one has seen them made or heard them made,   10
But at spring mending-time we find them there.
I let my neighbor know beyond the hill;
And on a day we meet to walk the line
And set the wall between us once again.
We keep the wall between us as we go.   15
To each the boulders that have fallen to each.
And some are loaves and some so nearly balls
We have to use a spell to make them balance:
"Stay where you are until our backs are turned!"
We wear our fingers rough with handling them.   20
Oh, just another kind of outdoor game,
One on a side. It comes to little more:
There where it is we do not need the wall:
He is all pine and I am apple orchard.
My apple trees will never get across   25
And eat the cones under his pines, I tell him.
He only says, "Good fences make good neighbors."
Spring is the mischief in me, and I wonder
If I could put a notion in his head:
"*Why* do they make good neighbors? Isn't it   30
Where there are cows? But here there are no cows.
Before I built a wall I'd ask to know
What I was walling in or walling out,
And to whom I was like to give offense.
Something there is that doesn't love a wall,   35
That wants it down." I could say "Elves" to him,
But it's not elves exactly, and I'd rather
He said it for himself. I see him there
Bringing a stone grasped firmly by the top
In each hand, like an old-stone savage armed.   40
He moves in darkness as it seems to me,
Not of woods only and the shade of trees.
He will not go behind his father's saying,
And he likes having thought of it so well
He says again, "Good fences make good neighbors."   45

Considerations for Critical Thinking and Writing

1. How do the speaker and his neighbor in this poem differ in sensibilities? What is suggested about the neighbor in lines 41–42?
2. What might the "Something" be that "doesn't love a wall"? Why does the speaker remind his neighbor each spring that the wall needs to be repaired? Is it ironic that the *speaker* initiates the mending? Is there anything good about the wall?
3. The neighbor likes the saying "Good fences make good neighbors" so well that he repeats it. Does the speaker also say something twice? What else suggests that the speaker's attitude toward the wall is not necessarily Frost's?
4. Although the speaker's language is colloquial, what is poetic about the sounds and rhythms he uses?

5. This poem was first published in 1914; Frost read it to an audience when he visited Russia in 1962. What do these facts suggest about the symbolic value of "Mending Wall"?

Connections to Other Selections

1. How do you think the neighbor in this poem would respond to Dickinson's idea of imagination in "To make a prairie it takes a clover and one bee" (p. 259)?
2. What similarities and differences does the neighbor have with the people Frost describes in "Neither Out Far nor In Deep" (p. 319)?

Home Burial   1914

He saw her from the bottom of the stairs
Before she saw him. She was starting down,
Looking back over her shoulder at some fear.
She took a doubtful step and then undid it
To raise herself and look again. He spoke   5
Advancing toward her: "What is it you see
From up there always — for I want to know."
She turned and sank upon her skirts at that,
And her face changed from terrified to dull.
He said to gain time: "What is it you see,"   10
Mounting until she cowered under him.
"I will find out now — you must tell me, dear."
She, in her place, refused him any help
With the least stiffening of her neck and silence.
She let him look, sure that he wouldn't see,   15
Blind creature; and awhile he didn't see.
But at last he murmured, "Oh," and again, "Oh."

"What is it — what?" she said.

                          "Just that I see."

"You don't," she challenged. "Tell me what it is."   20

"The wonder is I didn't see at once.
I never noticed it from here before.
I must be wonted to it — that's the reason.
The little graveyard where my people are!
So small the window frames the whole of it.   25
Not so much larger than a bedroom, is it?
There are three stones of slate and one of marble,
Broad-shouldered little slabs there in the sunlight
On the sidehill. We haven't to mind *those*.
But I understand: it is not the stones,   30
But the child's mound — "

               "Don't, don't, don't, don't," she cried.

She withdrew, shrinking from beneath his arm
That rested on the banister, and slid downstairs;

And turned on him with such a daunting look,   35
He said twice over before he knew himself:
"Can't a man speak of his own child he's lost?"

"Not you! — Oh, where's my hat? Oh, I don't need it!
I must get out of here. I must get air.
I don't know rightly whether any man can."   40

"Amy! Don't go to someone else this time.
Listen to me. I won't come down the stairs."
He sat and fixed his chin between his fists.
"There's something I should like to ask you, dear."

"You don't know how to ask it."   45

                  "Help me, then."
Her fingers moved the latch for all reply.

"My words are nearly always an offense.
I don't know how to speak of anything
So as to please you. But I might be taught,   50
I should suppose. I can't say I see how.
A man must partly give up being a man
With women-folk. We could have some arrangement
By which I'd bind myself to keep hands off
Anything special you're a-mind to name.   55
Though I don't like such things 'twixt those that love.
Two that don't love can't live together without them.
But two that do can't live together with them."
She moved the latch a little. "Don't — don't go.
Don't carry it to someone else this time.   60
Tell me about it if it's something human.
Let me into your grief. I'm not so much
Unlike other folks as your standing there
Apart would make me out. Give me my chance.
I do think, though, you overdo it a little.   65
What was it brought you up to think it the thing
To take your mother-loss of a first child
So inconsolably — in the face of love.
You'd think his memory might be satisfied — "

"There you go sneering now!"   70

                  "I'm not, I'm not!
You make me angry. I'll come down to you.
God, what a woman! And it's come to this,
A man can't speak of his own child that's dead."

"You can't because you don't know how to speak.   75
If you had any feelings, you that dug
With your own hand — how could you? — his little grave;
I saw you from that very window there,
Making the gravel leap and leap in air,
Leap up, like that, like that, and land so lightly   80
And roll back down the mound beside the hole.

I thought, Who is that man? I didn't know you.
And I crept down the stairs and up the stairs
To look again, and still your spade kept lifting.
Then you came in. I heard your rumbling voice 85
Out in the kitchen, and I don't know why,
But I went near to see with my own eyes.
You could sit there with the stains on your shoes
Of the fresh earth from your own baby's grave
And talk about your everyday concerns. 90
You had stood the spade up against the wall
Outside there in the entry, for I saw it."

"I shall laugh the worst laugh I ever laughed.
I'm cursed. God, if I don't believe I'm cursed."

"I can repeat the very words you were saying. 95
'Three foggy mornings and one rainy day
Will rot the best birch fence a man can build.'
Think of it, talk like that at such a time!
What had how long it takes a birch to rot
To do with what was in the darkened parlor 100
You *couldn't* care! The nearest friends can go
With anyone to death, comes so far short
They might as well not try to go at all.
No, from the time when one is sick to death,
One is alone, and he dies more alone. 105
Friends make pretense of following to the grave.
But before one is in it, their minds are turned
And making the best of their way back to life
And living people, and things they understand.
But the world's evil. I won't have grief so 110
If I can change it. Oh, I won't, I won't!"

"There, you have said it all and you feel better.
You won't go now. You're crying. Close the door.
The heart's gone out of it: why keep it up.
Amy! There's someone coming down the road!" 115

"*You* — oh, you think the talk is all. I must go —
Somewhere out of this house. How can I make you — "

"If — you — do!" She was opening the door wider.
"Where do you mean to go? First tell me that.
I'll follow and bring you back by force. I *will!* — " 120

Considerations for Critical Thinking and Writing

1. How has the burial of the child within sight of the stairway window affected the relationship of the couple in this poem? Is the child's grave a symptom or a cause of the conflict between them?

2. Is the husband insensitive and indifferent to his wife's grief? Characterize the wife. Has Frost invited us to sympathize with one character more than with the other?

3. What is the effect of splitting the iambic pentameter pattern in lines 18–19, 31–32, 45–46, and 70–71?
4. Is the conflict resolved at the conclusion of the poem? Do you think the husband and wife will overcome their differences?

After Apple-Picking

1914

My long two-pointed ladder's sticking through a tree
Toward heaven still,
And there's a barrel that I didn't fill
Beside it, and there may be two or three
Apples I didn't pick upon some bough.   5
But I am done with apple-picking now.
Essence of winter sleep is on the night,
The scent of apples: I am drowsing off.
I cannot rub the strangeness from my sight
I got from looking through a pane of glass   10
I skimmed this morning from the drinking trough
And held against the world of hoary grass.
It melted, and I let it fall and break.
But I was well
Upon my way to sleep before it fell,   15
And I could tell
What form my dreaming was about to take.
Magnified apples appear and disappear,
Stem end and blossom end,
And every fleck of russet showing clear.   20
My instep arch not only keeps the ache,
It keeps the pressure of a ladder-round.
I feel the ladder sway as the boughs bend.
And I keep hearing from the cellar bin
The rumbling sound   25
Of load on load of apples coming in.
For I have had too much
Of apple-picking: I am overtired
Of the great harvest I myself desired.
There were ten thousand thousand fruit to touch,   30
Cherish in hand, lift down, and not let fall.
For all
That struck the earth,
No matter if not bruised or spiked with stubble,
Went surely to the cider-apple heap   35
As of no worth.
One can see what will trouble
This sleep of mine, whatever sleep it is.
Were he not gone,
The woodchuck could say whether it's like his   40
Long sleep, as I describe its coming on,
Or just some human sleep.

Considerations for Critical Thinking and Writing

1. How does this poem illustrate Frost's view that "Poetry provides the one permissible way of saying one thing and meaning another"? When do you first sense that the detailed description of apple picking is being used that way?

2. What comes after apple picking? What does the speaker worry about in the dream beginning in line 18?

3. Why do you suppose Frost uses apples rather than, say, pears or squash?

The Wood-Pile

1914

Out walking in the frozen swamp one gray day,
I paused and said, "I will turn back from here.
No, I will go on farther — and we shall see."
The hard snow held me, save where now and then
One foot went through. The view was all in lines   5
Straight up and down of tall slim trees
Too much alike to mark or name a place by
So as to say for certain I was here
Or somewhere else: I was just far from home.
A small bird flew before me. He was careful   10
To put a tree between us when he lighted,
And say no word to tell me who he was
Who was so foolish as to think what *he* thought.
He thought that I was after him for a feather —
The white one in his tail; like one who takes   15
Everything said as personal to himself.
One flight out sideways would have undeceived him.
And then there was a pile of wood for which
I forgot him and let his little fear
Carry him off the way I might have gone,   20
Without so much as wishing him good-night.
He went behind it to make his last stand.
It was a cord of maple, cut and split
And piled — and measured, four by four by eight.
And not another like it could I see.   25
No runner tracks in this year's snow looped near it.
And it was older sure than this year's cutting,
Or even last year's or the year's before.
The wood was gray and the bark warping off it
And the pile somewhat sunken. Clematis   30
Had wound strings round and round it like a bundle.
What held it though on one side was a tree
Still growing, and on one a stake and prop,
These latter about to fall. I thought that only
Someone who lived in turning to fresh tasks   35
Could so forget his handiwork on which
He spent himself, the labor of his ax,
And leave it there far from a useful fireplace

To warm the frozen swamp as best it could
With the slow smokeless burning of decay.   40

Considerations for Critical Thinking and Writing

1. Write a paraphrase of the poem.
2. How does the "small bird" figure in the poem? Why do you think it's there? How is it related to the woodpile?
3. What symbolic value can you find in the speaker's account of his discovery of the woodpile?
4. Characterize the speaker's tone. How does the rhythm of the poem's lines help to create the tone?

Connections to Other Selections

1. Write an essay comparing the speaker in this poem to the speaker in "Stopping by Woods on a Snowy Evening" (p. 314) How, in each poem, do simple activities reveal something important about the speaker?
2. Discuss the speaker's sense of time in "The Wood-Pile" and in "Nothing Gold Can Stay" (p. 315).

Birches   1916

When I see birches bend to left and right
Across the lines of straighter darker trees,
I like to think some boy's been swinging them.
But swinging doesn't bend them down to stay
As ice-storms do. Often you must have seen them   5
Loaded with ice a sunny winter morning
After a rain. They click upon themselves
As the breeze rises, and turn many-colored
As the stir cracks and crazes their enamel.
Soon the sun's warmth makes them shed crystal shells   10
Shattering and avalanching on the snow-crust —
Such heaps of broken glass to sweep away
You'd think the inner dome of heaven had fallen.
They are dragged to the withered bracken by the load,
And they seem not to break; though once they are bowed   15
So low for long, they never right themselves:
You may see their trunks arching in the woods
Years afterwards, trailing their leaves on the ground
Like girls on hands and knees that throw their hair
Before them over their heads to dry in the sun.   20
But I was going to say when Truth broke in
With all her matter-of-fact about the ice-storm,
I should prefer to have some boy bend them
As he went out and in to fetch the cows —
Some boy too far from town to learn baseball,   25
Whose only play was what he found himself,

Summer or winter, and could play alone.
One by one he subdued his father's trees
By riding them down over and over again
Until he took the stiffness out of them,   30
And not one but hung limp, not one was left
For him to conquer. He learned all there was
To learn about not launching out too soon
And so not carrying the tree away
Clear to the ground. He always kept his poise   35
To the top branches, climbing carefully
With the same pains you use to fill a cup
Up to the brim, and even above the brim.
Then he flung outward, feet first, with a swish,
Kicking his way down through the air to the ground.   40
So was I once myself a swinger of birches.
And so I dream of going back to be.
It's when I'm weary of considerations,
And life is too much like a pathless wood
Where your face burns and tickles with the cobwebs   45
Broken across it, and one eye is weeping
From a twig's having lashed across it open.
I'd like to get away from earth awhile
And then come back to it and begin over.
May no fate willfully misunderstand me   50
And half grant what I wish and snatch me away
Not to return. Earth's the right place for love:
I don't know where it's likely to go better.
I'd like to go by climbing a birch tree,
And climb black branches up a snow-white trunk,   55
Toward heaven, till the tree could bear no more,
But dipped its top and set me down again.
That would be good both going and coming back.
One could do worse than be a swinger of birches.

Considerations for Critical Thinking and Writing

1. Why does the speaker in this poem prefer the birches to have been bent by boys instead of ice storms?
2. What does the swinging of birches symbolize?
3. How is "earth" described in the poem? Why does the speaker choose it over "heaven"?
4. How might the effect of this poem be changed if it were written in heroic couplets instead of blank verse?

"Out, Out — "°

The buzz-saw snarled and rattled in the yard
And made dust and dropped stove-length sticks of wood,
Sweet-scented stuff when the breeze drew across it.
And from there those that lifted eyes could count
Five mountain ranges one behind the other   5
Under the sunset far into Vermont.
And the saw snarled and rattled, snarled and rattled,
As it ran light, or had to bear a load.
And nothing happened: day was all but done.
Call it a day, I wish they might have said   10
To please the boy by giving him the half hour
That a boy counts so much when saved from work.
His sister stood beside them in her apron
To tell them "Supper." At the word, the saw,
As if to prove saws knew what supper meant,   15
Leaped out at the boy's hand, or seemed to leap —
He must have given the hand. However it was,
Neither refused the meeting. But the hand!
The boy's first outcry was a rueful laugh,
As he swung toward them holding up the hand   20
Half in appeal, but half as if to keep
The life from spilling. Then the boy saw all —
Since he was old enough to know, big boy
Doing a man's work, though a child at heart —
He saw all spoiled. "Don't let him cut my hand off —   25
The doctor, when he comes. Don't let him, sister!"
So. But the hand was gone already.
The doctor put him in the dark of ether.
He lay and puffed his lips out with his breath.
And then — the watcher at his pulse took fright.   30
No one believed. They listened at his heart.
Little — less — nothing! — and that ended it.
No more to build on there. And they, since they
Were not the one dead, turned to their affairs.

"Out, Out — ": From Act V, Scene v, of Shakespeare's *Macbeth*. The passage appears on page 108.

Considerations for Critical Thinking and Writing

1. How does Frost's allusion to *Macbeth* contribute to the meaning of this poem? Does the speaker seem to agree with the view of life expressed in Macbeth's lines?

2. This narrative poem is about the accidental death of a Vermont boy. What is the purpose of the story? Some readers have argued that the final lines reveal the speaker's callousness and indifference. What do you think?

Connections to Other Selections

1. What are the similarities and differences in theme between this poem and Frost's "Nothing Gold Can Stay" (p. 315)?

2. Write an essay comparing how grief is handled by the boy's family in this poem and the couple in "Home Burial" (p. 306).
3. Compare the tone and theme of "'Out, Out —'" and those of Crane's "A Man Said to the Universe" (p. 136).

Fire and Ice   1923

Some say the world will end in fire,
Some say in ice.
From what I've tasted of desire
I hold with those who favor fire.
But if it had to perish twice,
I think I know enough of hate
To say that for destruction ice
Is also great
And would suffice.

Considerations for Critical Thinking and Writing

1. What theories about the end of the world are alluded to in lines 1 and 2?
2. What characteristics of human behavior does the speaker associate with fire and ice?
3. How does the speaker's use of understatement and rhyme affect the tone of this poem?

Stopping by Woods on a Snowy Evening   1923

Whose woods these are I think I know.
His house is in the village, though;
He will not see me stopping here
To watch his woods fill up with snow.

My little horse must think it queer   5
To stop without a farmhouse near
Between the woods and frozen lake
The darkest evening of the year.

He gives his harness bells a shake
To ask if there is some mistake.   10
The only other sound's the sweep
Of easy wind and downy flake.

The woods are lovely, dark and deep,
But I have promises to keep,
And miles to go before I sleep,   15
And miles to go before I sleep.

Considerations for Critical Thinking and Writing

1. What is the significance of the setting in this poem? How is tone conveyed by the images?
2. What does the speaker find appealing about the woods? What is the purpose of the horse in the poem?
3. Although the last two lines are identical, they are not read at the same speed. Why the difference? What is achieved by the repetition?
4. What is the rhyme scheme of this poem? What is the effect of the rhyme in the final stanza?

Nothing Gold Can Stay

1923

Nature's first green is gold,
Her hardest hue to hold.
Her early leaf's a flower;
But only so an hour.
The leaf subsides to leaf.
So Eden sank to grief.
So dawn goes down to day.
Nothing gold can stay.

Considerations for Critical Thinking and Writing

1. What is meant by "gold" in the poem? Why can't it "stay"?
2. What do the leaf, humanity, and a day have in common?

Connection to Another Selection

1. Write an essay comparing the tone and theme of "Nothing Gold Can Stay" with Herrick's "To the Virgins, to Make Much of Time" (p. 56).

Once by the Pacific

1928

The shattered water made a misty din.
Great waves looked over others coming in,
And thought of doing something to the shore
That water never did to land before.
The clouds were low and hairy in the skies,   5
Like locks blown forward in the gleam of eyes.
You could not tell, and yet it looked as if
The shore was lucky in being backed by cliff,
The cliff in being backed by continent;
It looked as if a night of dark intent   10
Was coming, and not only a night, an age.
Someone had better be prepared for rage.
There would be more than ocean-water broken
Before God's last *Put out the Light* was spoken.

Considerations for Critical Thinking and Writing

1. How is nature presented in the poem? How do you know this is about more than just an approaching storm?
2. What kind of sonnet is this poem? Does its form seem suited to the subject matter? Why or why not?
3. Comment on the title. What purpose does it serve?
4. Write an alternative line for line 14 and explain how your line changes the poem's effect and meaning.

Connection to Another Selection

1. Write an essay that discusses Frost's use of the ocean in "Once by the Pacific" and in "Neither Out Far nor In Deep" (p. 319).

Two Tramps in Mud Time 1936

Out of the mud two strangers came
And caught me splitting wood in the yard.
And one of them put me off my aim
By hailing cheerily 'Hit them hard!'
I knew pretty well why he dropped behind   5
And let the other go on a way.
I knew pretty well what he had in mind:
He wanted to take my job for pay.

Good blocks of oak it was I split,
As large around as the chopping block;   10
And every piece I squarely hit
Fell splinterless as a cloven rock.
The blows that a life of self-control
Spares to strike for the common good
That day, giving a loose to my soul,   15
I spent on the unimportant wood.

The sun was warm but the wind was chill.
You know how it is with an April day
When the sun is out and the wind is still,
You're one month on in the middle of May.   20
But if you so much as dare to speak,
A cloud comes over the sunlit arch,
A wind comes off a frozen peak,
And you're two months back in the middle of March.

A bluebird comes tenderly up to alight   25
And turns to the wind to unruffle a plume
His song so pitched as not to excite
A single flower as yet to bloom.
It is snowing a flake: and he half knew
Winter was only playing possum.   30

Except in color he isn't blue,
But he wouldn't advise a thing to blossom.

The water for which we may have to look
In summertime with a witching-wand,
In every wheelrut's now a brook,   35
In every print of a hoof a pond.
Be glad of water, but don't forget
The lurking frost in the earth beneath
That will steal forth after the sun is set
And show on the water its crystal teeth.   40

The time when most I loved my task
These two must make me love it more
By coming with what they came to ask.
You'd think I never had felt before
The weight of an ax-head poised aloft,   45
The grip on earth of outspread feet.
The life of muscles rocking soft
And smooth and moist in vernal heat.

Out of the woods two hulking tramps
(From sleeping God knows where last night,   50
But not long since in the lumber camps).
They thought all chopping was theirs of right
Men of the woods and lumberjacks,
They judged me by their appropriate tool.
Except as a fellow handled an ax,   55
They had no way of knowing a fool.

Nothing on either side was said.
They knew they had but to stay their stay
And all their logic would fill my head:
As that I had no right to play   60
With what was another man's work for gain.
My right might be love but theirs was need.
And where the two exist in twain
Theirs was the better right — agreed.

But yield who will to their separation,   65
My object in living is to unite
My avocation and my vocation
As my two eyes make one in sight.
Only where love and need are one,
And the work is play for mortal stakes,   70
Is the deed ever really done
For Heaven and the future's sakes.

Considerations for Critical Thinking and Writing

1. Explain lines 13–16. How do they serve to characterize the speaker?
2. Make a list of all the images related to nature and the changing seasons. How would you characterize "mud time"? Is there a relationship between this time between seasons and the speaker's "object in living" (lines 65–72)?

3. Describe the poem's rhythm and rhyme. How do they contribute to its meaning?
4. Does the speaker offer to pay the tramp to chop his wood? Explain.

Connection to Another Selection

1. In an essay discuss attitudes toward work in this poem and in "After Apple-Picking" (p. 309).

Design   1936

I found a dimpled spider, fat and white,
On a white heal-all,° holding up a moth
Like a white piece of rigid satin cloth —
Assorted characters of death and blight
Mixed ready to begin the morning right,   5
Like the ingredients of a witches' broth —
A snow-drop spider, a flower like a froth,
And dead wings carried like a paper kite.

What had the flower to do with being white,
The wayside blue and innocent heal-all?   10
What brought the kindred spider to that height,
Then steered the white moth thither in the night?
What but design of darkness to appall? —
If design govern in a thing so small.

2 *heal-all:* A common flower, usually blue, once used for medicinal purposes.

Considerations for Critical Thinking and Writing

1. How does the division of the octave and sestet in this sonnet serve to organize the speaker's thoughts and feelings? What is the predominant rhyme? How does that rhyme relate to the poem's meaning?
2. Which words seem especially rich in connotative meanings? Explain how they function in the sonnet.
3. What kinds of speculations are raised in the final two lines? Consider the meaning of the title. Is there more than one way to read it?

Connections to Other Selections

1. Compare the ironic tone of "Design" with the tone of Hathaway's "Oh, Oh" (p. 13). What would you have to change in Hathaway's poem to make it more like Frost's?
2. In an essay discuss Frost's view of God in this poem and Dickinson's perspective in "I know that He exists" (p. 294).
3. Compare "Design" with "In White," Frost's early version of it (p. 322).

Neither Out Far nor In Deep

1936

The people along the sand
All turn and look one way.
They turn their back on the land.
They look at the sea all day.

As long as it takes to pass   5
A ship keeps raising its hull;
The wetter ground like glass
Reflects a standing gull.

The land may vary more;
But wherever the truth may be —   10
The water comes ashore,
And the people look at the sea.

They cannot look out far.
They cannot look in deep.
But when was that ever a bar   15
To any watch they keep?

Considerations for Critical Thinking and Writing

1. Frost built this poem around a simple observation that raises some questions. Why do people at the beach almost always face the ocean? What feelings and thoughts are evoked by looking at the ocean?
2. Notice how the verb *look* takes on added meaning as the poem progresses. What are the people looking for?
3. How does the final stanza extend the poem's significance?
4. Does the speaker identify with the people described, or does he ironically distance himself from them?

Come In

1942

As I came to the edge of the woods,
Thrush music — hark!
Now if it was dusk outside,
Inside it was dark.

Too dark in the woods for a bird   5
By sleight of wing
To better its perch for the night,
Though it still could sing.

The last of the light of the sun
That had died in the west   10
Still lived for one song more
In a thrush's breast.

Far in the pillared dark
Thrush music went —

Almost like a call to come in   15
To the dark and lament.

But no, I was out for stars:
I would not come in.
I meant not even if asked,
And I hadn't been.   20

Considerations for Critical Thinking and Writing

1. Discuss the meanings of "dark" in this poem. Can it be read as more than simply literal darkness?
2. How does the bird's song affect the poem's tone?
3. In what sense is the speaker "out for stars"? Why won't the speaker "come in"?

Connection to Another Selection

1. Write an essay comparing the themes of "Come In" with those of "The Pasture" (p. 303). How might each poem be regarded as a kind of invitation?

The Silken Tent   1942

She is as in a field a silken tent
At midday when a sunny summer breeze
Has dried the dew and all its ropes relent,
So that in guys° it gently sways at ease,   *ropes that steady a tent*
And its supporting central cedar pole,   5
That is its pinnacle to heavenward
And signifies the sureness of the soul,
Seems to owe naught to any single cord,
But strictly held by none, is loosely bound
By countless silken ties of love and thought   10
To everything on earth the compass round,
And only by one's going slightly taut
In the capriciousness of summer air
Is of the slightest bondage made aware.

Considerations for Critical Thinking and Writing

1. What is being compared in this sonnet? How does the detail accurately describe both elements of the comparison?
2. How does the form of this one-sentence sonnet help to express its theme? Pay particular attention to the final three lines.
3. How do the sonnet's sounds contribute to its meaning?

The Most of It   1942

He thought he kept the universe alone;
For all the voice in answer he could wake
Was but the mocking echo of his own
From some tree-hidden cliff across the lake.
Some morning from the boulder-broken beach   5
He would cry out on life, that what it wants
Is not its own love back in copy speech,
But counter-love, original response.
And nothing ever came of what he cried
Unless it was the embodiment that crashed   10
In the cliff's talus on the other side,
And then in the far distant water splashed.
But after a time allowed for it to swim,
Instead of proving human when it neared
And someone else additional to him,   15
As a great buck it powerfully appeared,
Pushing the crumpled water up ahead,
And landed pouring like a waterfall,
And stumbled through the rocks with horny tread,
And forced the underbrush — and that was all.   20

Considerations for Critical Thinking and Writing

1. What does the voice cry out for (line 6)? What does he want?
2. Comment on the effects of the sounds in this poem.
3. Does the description of the buck have any symbolic meaning? Explain, paying special attention to the language describing it.
4. Discuss the meaning of the title, "The Most of It." What is the "It," do you think?

Connections to Other Selections

1. Write an essay that compares the images of nature in "The Most of It" with those in "Two Tramps in Mud Time" (p. 316). Is nature presented the same way by the two poems? What ideas about nature are expressed by their imagery?
2. Compare and contrast ideas about solitude in this poem and in Emily Dickinson's "The Soul selects her own Society — " (p. 269).

Away!   1962

Now I out walking
The world desert,
And my shoe and my stocking
Do me no hurt.

I leave behind   5
Good friends in town.
Let them get well-wined
And go lie down.

Don't think I leave
For the outer dark   10
Like Adam and Eve
Put out of the Park.

Forget the myth.
There is no one I
Am put out with   15
Or put out by.

Unless I'm wrong
I but obey
The urge of a song:
I'm — bound — away!   20

And I may return
If dissatisfied
With what I learn
From having died.

Considerations for Critical Thinking and Writing

1. What "myth" is referred to in line 13?
2. Discuss the speaker's tone. (Pay attention to the poem's date and Frost's age when he wrote this.)
3. Characterize the humor in this poem.

Connection to Another Selection

1. In an essay compare what the speaker expects to learn in "Away!" and what "the people" hope to learn in "Neither Out Far nor In Deep" (p. 319).

PERSPECTIVES ON FROST

"In White": Frost's Early Version of "Design"   1912

A dented spider like a snow drop white
On a white Heal-all, holding up a moth
Like a white piece of lifeless satin cloth —
Saw ever curious eye so strange a sight? —
Portent in little, assorted death and blight   5
Like the ingredients of a witches' broth? —
The beady spider, the flower like a froth,
And the moth carried like a paper kite.

What had that flower to do with being white,
The blue prunella every child's delight.   10
What brought the kindred spider to that height?
(Make we no thesis of the miller's° plight.)   *miller moth*
What but design of darkness and of night?
Design, design! Do I use the word aright?

Considerations for Critical Thinking and Writing

1. Read "In White" and "Design" (p. 318) aloud. Which version sounds better to you? Why?
2. Compare these versions line for line, paying particular attention to word choice. List the differences, and try to explain why you think Frost revised the lines.
3. How does the change in titles reflect a shift in emphasis in the poem?

Frost on the Living Part of a Poem   1914

The living part of a poem is the intonation entangled somehow in the syntax, idiom, and meaning of a sentence. It is only there for those who have heard it previously in conversation. . . . It is the most volatile and at the same time important part of poetry. It goes and the language becomes dead language, the poetry dead poetry. With it go the accents, the stresses, the delays that are not the property of vowels and syllables but that are shifted at will with the sense. Vowels have length there is no denying. But the accent of sense supersedes all other accent, overrides it and sweeps it away. I will find you the word *come* variously used in various passages, a whole, half, third, fourth, fifth, and sixth note. It is as long as the sense makes it. When men no longer know the intonations on which we string our words they will fall back on what I may call the absolute length of our syllables, which is the length we would give them in passages that meant nothing. . . . I say you can't read a single good sentence with the salt in it unless you have previously heard it spoken. Neither can you with the help of all the characters and diacritical marks pronounce a single word unless you have previously heard it actually pronounced. Words exist in the mouth not books.

From a letter to Sidney Cox in *A Swinger of Birches: A Portrait of Robert Frost*

Considerations for Critical Thinking and Writing

1. Why does Frost place so much emphasis on hearing poetry spoken?
2. Choose a passage from "Home Burial" (p. 306) or "After Apple-Picking" (p. 309) and read it aloud. How does Frost's description of his emphasis on intonation help explain the effects he achieves in the passage you have selected?
3. Do you think it is true that all poetry must be heard? Do "Words exist in the mouth not books"?

AMY LOWELL (1874–1925)
On Frost's Realistic Technique   1915

I have said that Mr. Frost's work is almost photographic. The qualification was unnecessary, it is photographic. The pictures, the characters, are reproduced directly from life, they are burnt into his mind as though it were a sensitive plate. He gives out what has been put in unchanged by any personal mental process. His imagination is bounded by what he has seen, he is confined within the limits of his experience (or at least what might have been his experience) and bent all one way like the windblown trees of New England hillsides.

From a review of *North of Boston, The New Republic*, February 20, 1915

Considerations for Critical Thinking and Writing

1. Consider the "photographic" qualities of Frost's poetry by discussing particular passages that strike you as having been "reproduced directly from life."
2. Write an essay that supports or refutes Lowell's assertion that "He gives out what has been put in unchanged by any personal mental process."

Frost on the Figure a Poem Makes   1939

Abstraction is an old story with the philosophers, but it has been like a new toy in the hands of the artists of our day. Why can't we have any one quality of poetry we choose by itself? We can have in thought. Then it will go hard if we can't in practice. Our lives for it.

Granted no one but a humanist much cares how sound a poem is if it is only *a* sound. The sound is the gold in the ore. Then we will have the sound out alone and dispense with the inessential. We do till we make the discovery that the object in writing poetry is to make all poems sound as different as possible from each other, and the resources for that of vowels, consonants, punctuation, syntax, words, sentences, meter are not enough. We need the help of context — meaning — subject matter. That is the greatest help towards variety. All that can be done with words is soon told. So also with meters — particularly in our language where there are virtually but two, strict iambic and loose iambic. The ancients with many were still poor if they depended on meters for all tune. It is painful to watch our sprung-rhythmists straining at the point of omitting one short from a foot for relief from monotony. The possibilities for tune from the dramatic tones of meaning struck across the rigidity of a limited meter are endless. And we are back in poetry as merely one more art of having something to say, sound or unsound. Probably better if sound, because deeper and from wider experience.

Then there is this wildness whereof it is spoken. Granted again that it has an equal claim with sound to being a poem's better half. If it is a wild tune, it is a poem. Our problem then is, as modern abstractionists, to have the wildness pure; to be wild with nothing to be wild about. We bring up as aberrationists, giving way to undirected associations and kicking ourselves from one chance suggestion to another in all directions as of a hot afternoon in the life of a grasshopper. Theme alone can steady us down. Just as the first mystery was how a poem could have a tune in such a straightness as meter, so the second mystery is how a poem can have wildness and at the same time a subject that shall be fulfilled.

It should be of the pleasure of a poem itself to tell how it can. The figure a poem makes. It begins in delight and ends in wisdom. The figure is the same as for love. No one can really hold that the ecstasy should be static and stand still in one place. It begins in delight, it inclines to the impulse, it assumes direction with the first line laid down, it runs a course of lucky events, and ends in a clarification of life — not necessarily a great clarification, such as sects and cults are founded on, but in a momentary stay against confusion. It has denouement. It has an outcome that though unforeseen was predestined from the first image of the original mood — and indeed from the very mood. It is but a trick poem and no poem at all if the best of it was thought of first and saved for the last. It finds its own name as it goes and discovers the best waiting for it in some final phrase at once wise and sad — the happy-sad blend of the drinking song.

No tears in the writer, no tears in the reader. No surprise for the writer, no surprise for the reader. For me the initial delight is in the surprise of remembering something I didn't know I knew. I am in a place, in a situation, as if I had materialized from cloud or risen out of the ground. There is a glad recognition of the long lost and the rest follows. Step by step the wonder of unexpected supply keeps going. The impressions most useful to my purpose seem always those I was unaware of and so made no note of at the time when taken, and the conclusion is come to that like giants we are always hurling experience ahead of us to pave the future with against the day when we may want to strike a line of purpose across it for somewhere. The line will have the more charm for not being mechanically straight. We enjoy the straight crookedness of a good walking stick. Modern instruments of precision are being used to make things crooked as if by eye and hand in the old days.

I tell how there may be a better wildness of logic than of inconsequence. But the logic is backward, in retrospect, after the act. It must be more felt than seen ahead like prophecy. It must be a revelation, or a series of revelations, as much for the poet as for the reader. For it to be that there must have been the greatest freedom of the material to move about in it and to establish relations in it regardless of time and space, previous relation, and everything but affinity. We prate of freedom. We call our schools free because we are not free to stay away from them till we are sixteen years of age. I have given up my democratic prejudices and now willingly set the lower classes free to be completely taken care of by the upper classes. Political freedom is nothing to me. I bestow it right and left. All I would keep for myself is the freedom of my material — the condition of body and mind now and then to summons aptly from the vast chaos of all I have lived through.

Scholars and artists thrown together are often annoyed at the puzzle of where they differ. Both work for knowledge; but I suspect they differ most importantly in the way their knowledge is come by. Scholars get theirs with conscientious thoroughness along projected lines of logic; poets theirs cavalierly and as it happens in and out of books. They stick to nothing deliberately, but let what will stick to them like burrs where they walk in the fields. No acquirement is on assignment, or even self-assignment. Knowledge of the second kind is much more available in the wild free ways of wit and art. A school boy may be defined as one who can tell you what he knows in the order in which he learned it. The artist must value himself as he snatches a thing from some previous order in time and space into a new order with not so much as a ligature clinging to it of the old place where it was organic.

More than once I should have lost my soul to radicalism if it had been the originality it was mistaken for by its young converts. Originality and initiative are what I ask for my country. For myself the originality need be no more than the freshness of a poem run in the way I have described: from delight to wisdom. The figure is the same as for love. Like a piece of ice on a hot stove the poem must ride on its own melting. A poem may be worked over once it is in being, but may not be worried into being. Its most precious quality will remain its having run itself and carried away the poet with it. Read it a hundred times: it will forever keep its freshness as a metal keeps its fragrance. It can never lose its sense of a meaning that once unfolded by surprise as it went.

From *Complete Poems of Robert Frost*

Considerations for Critical Thinking and Writing

1. Frost places a high premium on sound in his poetry, because it "is the gold in the ore." Choose one of Frost's poems in this book and explain the effects of its sounds and how they contribute to its meaning.

2. Discuss Frost's explanation of how his poems are written. In what sense is the process both spontaneous and "predestined"?

3. What do you think Frost means when he says he's given up his "democratic prejudices"? Why is "political freedom" nothing to him?

4. Write an essay that examines in more detail the ways scholars and artists "come by" knowledge.

5. Explain what you think Frost means when he writes that "Like a piece of ice on a hot stove the poem must ride on its own melting."

Frost on the Way to Read a Poem   1951

The way to read a poem in prose or verse is in the light of all the other poems ever written. We may begin anywhere. We *duff* into our first. We read that imperfectly (thoroughness with it would be fatal), but the better to read the second. We read the second the better to read the third, the third the better to read the fourth, the fourth better to read the fifth, the fifth the better to read the first again, or the second if it so happens. For poems are not meant to be read in course any more than they are to be made a study of. I once made a resolve never to put any book to any use it wasn't intended for by its author. Improvement will not be a progression but a widening circulation. Our instinct is to settle down like a revolving dog and make ourselves at home among the poems, completely at our ease as to how they should be taken. The same people will be apt to take poems right as know how to take a hint when there is one and not to take a hint when none is intended. Theirs is the ultimate refinement.

From "Poetry and School," *Atlantic Monthly,* June 1951

Considerations for Critical Thinking and Writing

1. Given your own experience, how good is Frost's advice about reading in general and his poems in particular?

2. In what sense is a good reader like a "revolving dog" and a person who knows "how to take a hint"?

3. Frost elsewhere in this piece writes, "One of the dangers of college to anyone who wants to stay a human reader (that is to say a humanist) is that he will become a specialist and lose his sensitive fear of landing on the lovely too hard. (With beak and talon.)" Write an essay in response to this concern. Do you agree with Frost's distinction between a "human reader" and a "specialist"?

LIONEL TRILLING (1905-1975)
On Frost as a Terrifying Poet

1959

I have to say that my Frost — *my Frost:* what airs we give ourselves when once we believe that we have come into possession of a poet! — I have to say that my Frost is not the Frost I seem to perceive existing in the minds of so many of his admirers. He is not the Frost who confounds the characteristically modern practice of poetry by his notable democratic simplicity of utterance: on the contrary. He is not the Frost who controverts the bitter modern astonishment at the nature of human life: the opposite is so. He is not the Frost who reassures us by his affirmation of old virtues, simplicities, pieties, and ways of feeling: anything but. I will not go so far as to say that my Frost is not essentially an American poet at all: I believe that he is quite as American as everyone thinks he is, but not in the way that everyone thinks he is.

In the matter of the Americanism of American literature one of my chief guides is that very remarkable critic, D. H. Lawrence. Here are the opening sentences of Lawrence's great outrageous book about classic American literature. "We like to think of the old fashioned American classics as children's books. Just childishness on our part. The old American art speech contains an alien quality which belongs to the American continent and to nowhere else." And this unique alien quality, Lawrence goes on to say, the world has missed. "It is hard to hear a new voice," he says, "as hard as to listen to an unknown language. . . . Why? Out of fear. The world fears a new experience more than it fears anything. It can pigeonhole any idea. But it can't pigeonhole a real new experience. It can only dodge. The world is a great dodger, and the Americans the greatest. Because they dodge their own very selves." I should like to pick up a few more of Lawrence's sentences, feeling the freer to do so because they have an affinity to Mr. Frost's prose manner and substance: "An artist is usually a damned liar, but his art, if it be art, will tell you the truth of his day. And that is all that matters. Away with eternal truth. Truth lives from day to day. . . . The old American artists were hopeless liars. . . . Never trust the artist. Trust the tale. The proper function of the critic is to save the tale from the artist who created it. . . . Now listen to me, don't listen to him. He'll tell you the lie you expect, which is partly your fault for expecting it."

Now in point of fact Robert Frost is *not* a liar. I would not hesitate to say that he was if I thought he was. But no, he is not. In certain of his poems — I shall mention one or two in a moment — he makes it perfectly plain what he is doing; and if we are not aware of what he is doing in other of his poems, where he is not quite so plain, that is not his fault but our own. It is not from him that the tale needs to be saved.

I conceive that Robert Frost is doing in his poems what Lawrence says the great writers of the classic American tradition did. That enterprise of theirs was of an ultimate radicalism. It consisted, Lawrence says, of two things: a disintegration and sloughing off of the old consciousness, by which Lawrence means the old European consciousness, and the forming of a new consciousness underneath.

So radical a work, I need scarcely say, is not carried out by reassurance, nor by the affirmation of old virtues and pieties. It is carried out by the representation of the terrible actualities of life in a new way. I think of Robert Frost as a terrifying poet. Call him, if it makes things any easier, a tragic poet, but it might be useful every now and then to come out from under the shelter of that literary word. The universe that he conceives is a terrifying universe. Read the poem called "Design" and see if you sleep the better for it. Read "Neither Out Far nor In Deep," which often seems to me the most perfect poem of our time, and see if you are warmed by anything in it except the energy with which emptiness is perceived.

But the *people,* it will be objected, the *people* who inhabit this possibly terrifying universe! About them there is nothing that can terrify; surely the people in Mr. Frost's poems can only reassure us by their integrity and solidity. Perhaps so. But I cannot make the disjunction. It may well be that ultimately they reassure us in some sense, but first they terrify us, or should. We must not be misled about them by the curious tenderness with which they are represented, a tenderness which extends to a recognition of the tenderness which they themselves can often give. But when ever have people been so isolated, so lightning-blasted, so tried down and calcined by life, so reduced, each in his own way, to some last irreducible core of being. Talk of the disintegration and sloughing off of the old consciousness! The people of Robert Frost's poems have done that with a vengeance. Lawrence says that what the Americans refused to accept was "the post-Renaissance humanism of Europe," "the old European spontaneity," "the flowing easy humor of Europe" and that seems to me a good way to describe the people who inhabit Robert Frost's America. In the interests of what great other thing these people have made this rejection we cannot know for certain. But we can guess that it was in the interest of truth, of some truth of the self. This is what they all affirm by their humor (which is so *not* "the easy flowing humor of Europe"), by their irony, by their separateness and isolateness. They affirm *this* of themselves: that they are what they are, that this is their truth, and that if the truth be bare, as the truth often is, it is far better than a lie. For me the process by which they arrive at that truth is always terrifying. The manifest America of Mr. Frost's poems may be pastoral; the actual America is tragic.

From "A Speech on Robert Frost: A Cultural Episode,"
Partisan Review, Summer 1959

Considerations for Critical Thinking and Writing

1. How does Trilling distinguish *"my Frost"* from other readers'?
2. Read the section on biographical criticism in Chapter 15 (p. 531) and familiarize yourself with Frost's life. How does a knowledge of Frost's biography influence your reading of his poems?
3. Write an essay indicating whether you agree or disagree with Trilling's assessment of Frost "as a terrifying poet." Use evidence from the poems to support your view.

HERBERT R. COURSEN JR. (b. 1932)
A Parodic Interpretation of "Stopping by Woods on a Snowy Evening" 1962

Much ink has spilled on many pages in exegesis of this little poem. Actually, critical jottings have only obscured what has lain beneath critical noses all these years. To say that the poem means merely that a man stops one night to observe a snowfall, or that the poem contrasts the mundane desire for creature comfort with the sweep of aesthetic appreciation, or that it renders worldly responsibilities paramount, or that it reveals the speaker's latent death-wish is to miss the point rather badly. Lacking has been that mind simple enough to see what is *really* there. . . .

The "darkest evening of the year" in New England is December 21st, a date near that on which the western world celebrates Christmas. It may be that December 21st *is* the date of the poem, or (and with poets this seems more likely) that this is the closest the poet can come to Christmas without giving it all away. Who has "promises to keep" at or near this date, and who must traverse much territory to fulfill these promises? Yes, and who but St. Nick would know the location of *each* home? Only he would know who had "just settled down for a long winter's nap" (the poem's third line — "He will not see me stopping here" — is clearly a veiled allusion) and would not be out inspecting his acreage this night. The unusual phrase "fill up with snow," in the poem's fourth line, is a transfer of Santa's occupational preoccupation to the countryside; he is mulling the filling of countless stockings hung above countless fireplaces by countless careful children. "Harness bells," of course, allude to "Sleighing Song," a popular Christmas tune of the time the poem was written in which the refrain "Jingle Bells! Jingle Bells!" appears; thus again are we put on the Christmas track. The "little horse," like the date, is another attempt at poetic obfuscation. Although the "rein-reindeer" ambiguity has been eliminated from the poem's final version,[1] probably because too obvious, we may speculate that the animal is really a reindeer disguised as a horse by the poet's desire for obscurity, a desire which we must concede has been fulfilled up to now.

The animal is clearly concerned, like the faithful Rudolph — another possible allusion (post facto, hence unconscious) — lest his master fail to complete his mission. Seeing no farmhouse in the second quatrain, but pulling a load of presents, no wonder the little beast wonders! It takes him a full two quatrains to rouse his driver to remember all the empty stockings which hang ahead. And Santa does so reluctantly at that, poor soul, as he ponders the myriad farmhouses and villages which spread between him and his own "winter's nap." The modern St. Nick, lonely and overworked, tosses no "Happy Christmas to all and to all a good night!" into the precipitation. He merely shrugs his shoulders and resignedly plods away.

> From "The Ghost of Christmas Past: 'Stopping by Woods
> on a Snowy Evening,' " *College English,* December 1962

[1]The original draft contained the following line: "That bid me give the reins a shake" (Stageberg-Anderson, *Poetry as Experience* [New York, 1952], p. 457). [Coursen's note]

Considerations for Critical Thinking and Writing

1. Is this critical spoof at all credible? Does the interpretation hold any water? Is the evidence reasonable? Why or why not? Which of the poem's details are accounted for and which are ignored?

2. Choose a Frost poem and try writing a parodic interpretation of it.

3. What criteria do you use to distinguish between a sensible interpretation of a poem and an absurd one? In an essay compare and contrast your criteria with the criteria suggested by Stanley Fish in his perspective "On What Makes an Interpretation Acceptable" (p. 549).

DONALD J. GREINER (b. 1940)
On What Comes "After Apple-Picking"

1982

"After Apple-Picking" was first published in *North of Boston* (1914), and it is my nomination for Frost's greatest poem. In the letter to John Cournos (27 July 1914), Frost explains that "After Apple-Picking" is the only poem in his second book that "will intone." Although he does not elaborate, he means that the rest of the poems sound like human speech whereas "After Apple-Picking" is a lyrical meditation on the tension between a job well done and the uncertainties accompanying the end of something significant. Note that the first word in the title is "After." Frost's refusal to specify what has ended, other than apple picking, is one of the glories of the poem.

The other glories are the examples of technical brilliance. The rhymes alone are worth the reading. Every one of the forty-two lines is rhymed, but Frost eschews the tradition of rhyme scheme altogether. The result is a beautiful, even haunting, rendering of the natural progression of a person's meditation as he uneasily ponders the ambiguities which suddenly well up before him now that his job is done. Similarly, the brilliant use of irregular iambic pentameter . . . to suggest the uncertain balance between the poet figure's need to maintain form in the face of confusion and the threat to his effort cast in the form of truncated lines illustrates the union of technique and theme when Frost is at his best. Although the poem begins with its longest line, the iambic heptameter "My long two-pointed ladder's sticking through a tree," and includes a line as short as "For all," the meter invariably returns to the predominant rhythm of iambic pentameter as the meditator struggles to keep his balance in uncertainty as he has kept it on the ladder of his life.

Nuances of aspiration, satisfaction, completion, rest, and death echo throughout "After Apple-Picking" beginning with the title. Like the speaker, the reader never knows how far to pursue the mythical association between apples and man's expulsion from Eden. If such associations are to be dismissed, then the speaker has safely and satisfactorily completed his task — whatever it literally is — of harvesting the "ten thousand thousand fruit." The phrase "after apple-picking" thus suggests rest. But the genius of the poem is that the speaker is never sure. If the associations between apples and Eden are not to be dismissed, then the poet figure has finished his life's work only to be confronted with an overwhelming uncertainty about what awaits him now. "After Apple-Picking" thus suggests death.

The imagery of hazy speculation is precise. The phrase "toward heaven" indicates the speaker's ultimate aspiration, and the line "Essence of winter sleep is on the night" reverberates with suggestions of termination and the question of rebirth. The point is that the poet figure needs answers to questions he will not pose, and he can only see as through a glass darkly:

I cannot rub the strangeness from my sight
I got from looking through a pane of glass
I skimmed this morning from the drinking trough. . . .

The woodchuck, so unthinkingly confident of rebirth from its winter hibernation, cannot help him. "After Apple-Picking" is a poem of encroaching fear because it is a poem of uncertainty. Although the religious connotations are never obtrusive, this great poem is another of Frost's explorations of what he considered to be man's greatest terror: that our best may not be good enough in Heaven's sight.

From "The Indispensable Robert Frost," in *Critical Essays on Robert Frost,* edited by Philip L. Gerber

Considerations for Critical Thinking and Writing

1. How far do you think "the mythical associations between apples and man's expulsion from Eden" should be pursued by readers of this poem?
2. Greiner cites several examples of the poem's "technical brilliance." What other examples can you find?
3. Write an essay that explores as the theme of the poem Greiner's idea that "our best may not be good enough in Heaven's sight."

BLANCHE FARLEY (b. 1937)
The Lover Not Taken　　　　　　　　　　　　　　　　　1984

Committed to one, she wanted both
And, mulling it over, long she stood,
Alone on the road, loath
To leave, wanting to hide in the undergrowth.
This new guy, smooth as a yellow wood　　　　　　　　　　5

Really turned her on. She liked his hair,
His smile. But the other, Jack, had a claim
On her already and she had to admit, he did wear
Well. In fact, to be perfectly fair,
He understood her. His long, lithe frame　　　　　　　　　10

Beside hers in the evening tenderly lay.
Still, if this blond guy dropped by someday,
Couldn't way just lead on to way?
No. For if way led on and Jack
Found out, she doubted if he would ever come back.　　　15

Oh, she turned with a sigh.
Somewhere ages and ages hence,
She might be telling this. "And I — "
She would say, "stood faithfully by."
But by then who would know the difference?　　　　　　　20

With that in mind, she took the fast way home,
The road by the pond, and phoned the blond.

Considerations for Critical Thinking and Writing

1. Which Frost poem is the object of this parody?
2. Describe how the stylistic elements mirror Frost's poem.
3. Does this parody seem successful to you? Explain what makes a successful parody.
4. Choose a Frost poem — or a portion of one if it is long — and try writing a parody of it.

DEREK WALCOTT (b. 1930)
The Road Taken 1996

Robert Frost: the icon of Yankee values, the smell of wood smoke, the sparkle of dew, the reality of farmhouse dung, the jocular honesty of an uncle.

Why is the favorite figure of American patriotism not paternal but avuncular? Because uncles are wiser than fathers. They have humor, they keep their distance, they are bachelors, they can't be fooled by rhetoric. Frost loved playing the uncle, relishing the dry enchantment of his own voice, the homely gravel in the throat, the keep-your-distance pseudo-rusticity that suspected every stranger, meaning every reader. The voice is like its weather. It tells you to stay away until you are invited. Its first lines, in the epigraph to Frost's 1949 *Complete Poems,* are not so much invitations as warnings.

> I'm going out to clean the pasture spring;
> I'll only stop to rake the leaves away
> (And wait to watch the water clear, I may):
> I sha'n't be gone long. — You come too.

From the very epigraph, then, the surly ambiguities slide in. Why "I may"? Not for the rhyme, the desperation of doggerel, but because of this truth: that it would take too long to watch the agitated clouded water settle, that is, for as long as patience allows the poet to proceed to the next line. (Note that the parentheses function as a kind of container, or bank, or vessel, of the churned spring.) The refrain, "You come too." An invitation? An order? And how sincere is either? That is the point of Frost's tone, the authoritative but ambiguous distance of a master ironist.

Frost is an autocratic poet rather than a democratic poet. His invitations are close-lipped, wry, quiet; neither the voice nor the metrical line has the open-armed municipal mural expansion of the other democratic poet, Whitman. The people in Frost's dramas occupy a tight and taciturn locale. They are not part of Whitman's parade of blacksmiths, wheelwrights made communal by work. Besieged and threatened, their virtues are as cautious and measured as the scansion by which they are portrayed.

From Joseph Brodsky, Seamus Heaney, and Derek Walcott,
Homage to Robert Frost

Considerations for Critical Thinking and Writing

1. Why does Walcott characterize Frost as more an uncle than a father? Explain why you agree or disagree.

2. Choose one of Frost's poems in this anthology and use it to demonstrate that he is a "master ironist."

3. Write an essay that fleshes out Walcott's observation that the people in Frost's poems are "besieged and threatened, their virtues . . . as cautious and measured as the scansion by which they are portrayed."

RICHARD POIRIER (b. 1925)
On Emotional Suffocation in "Home Burial" 1977

Frost's poetry recurrently dramatizes the discovery that the sharing of a "home" can produce imaginations of uncontrollable threat inside or outside. "Home" can become the source of those fears from which it is supposed to protect us; it can become the habitation of that death whose anguish it is supposed to ameliorate. And this brings us to one of Frost's greatest poetic dramatizations of the theme, "Home Burial." [T]he pressure is shared by a husband and wife, but . . . the role of the husband is ambiguous. Though he does his best to comprehend the wife's difficulties, he is only partly able to do so. The very title of the poem means something about the couple as well as about the dead child buried in back of the house. It is as if "home" were a burial plot for all of them.

The opening lines of Frost's dramatic narratives are usually wonderfully deft in suggesting the metaphoric nature of "home," the human opportunities or imperatives which certain details represent for a husband or a wife. . . . [I]n "Home Burial," the couple are trapped inside the house, which is described as a kind of prison, or perhaps more aptly, a mental hospital. Even the wife's glance out the window can suggest to the husband the desperation she feels within the confines of what has always been his family's "home"; it looks directly on the family graveyard which now holds the body of their recently dead child: [lines 1–30 of "Home Burial" are quoted here].

The remarkable achievement here is that the husband and wife have become so nearly inarticulate in their animosities that the feelings have been transferred to a vision of household arrangements and to their own bodily movements. They and the house conspire together to create an aura of suffocation. . . . Frost's special genius is in the placement of words. The first line poses the husband as a kind of spy; the opening of the second line suggests a habituated wariness on her part, but from that point to line 5 we are shifted back to his glimpse of her as she moves obsessively again, as yet unaware of being watched, to the window. Suggestions of alienation, secretiveness, male intimidation ("advancing toward her") within a situation of mutual distrust, a miasmic fear inside as well as outside the house — we are made to sense this before anyone speaks. Initially the fault seems to lie mostly with the husband. But as soon as she catches him watching her, and as soon as he begins to talk, it is the grim mutuality of their dilemma and the shared responsibilities for it that sustain the dramatic intelligence and power of the poem.

From Robert Frost: The Work of Knowing

Considerations for Critical Thinking and Writing

1. According to Poirier, how can the couple's home be regarded as a kind of "mental hospital"? Compare Poirier's view with Kearns's description in the following perspective on the house as a "marital asylum."
2. Explain why you agree or disagree that the husband's behavior is a form of "male intimidation."
3. Write an essay that discusses the "grim mutuality" of the couple's "dilemma."

KATHERINE KEARNS (b. 1949)
On the Symbolic Setting of "Home Burial"

1987

"Home Burial" may be used to clarify Frost's intimate relationships between sex, death, and madness. The physical iconography is familiar — a stairwell, a window, a doorway, and a grave — elements which Frost reiterates throughout his poetry. The marriage in "Home Burial" has been destroyed by the death of a first and only son. The wife is in the process of leaving the house, crossing the threshold from marital asylum into freedom. The house is suffocating her. Her window view of the graveyard is not enough and is, in fact, a maddening reminder that she could not enter the earth with her son. With its transparent barrier, the window is a mockery of a widened vision throughout Frost's poetry and seems to incite escape rather than quelling it; in "Home Burial" the woman can "see" through the window and into the grave in a way her husband cannot, and the fear is driving her down the steps toward the door — "She was starting down — / Looking back over her shoulder at some fear" — even before she sees her husband. He threatens to follow his wife and bring her back by force, as if he is the cause of her leaving, but his gesture will be futile because it is based on the mistaken assumption that she is escaping him. Pathetically, he is merely an obstacle toward which she reacts at first dully and then with angry impatience. He is an inanimate part of the embattled household, her real impetus for movement comes from the grave.

The house itself, reduced symbolically and literally to a womblike passageway between the bedroom and the threshold, is a correlative for the sexual tension generated by the man's insistence on his marital rights. He offers to "give up being a man" by binding himself "to keep hands off," but their marriage is already sexually damaged and empty. The man and woman move in an intricate dance, she coming downward and then retracing a step, he "Mounting until she cower[s] under him," she "shrinking from beneath his arm" to slide downstairs. Randall Jarrell examines the image of the woman sinking into "a modest, compact, feminine bundle" upon her skirts;[1] it might be further observed that this childlike posture is also very much a gesture of sexual denial, body bent, knees drawn up protectively against the breasts, all encompassed by voluminous skirts. The two are in profound imbalance, and Frost makes the wife's speech and movements the poetic equivalent of stumbling and resistance; her lines are frequently eleven syllables, and often are punctuated by spondees whose forceful but awkward slowness embodies the woman's vacillations "from terrified to dull," and from frozen and silent immobility to anger. Her egress from the house will be symbolic verification of her husband's impotence, and if she leaves it and does not come back, the house will rot as the best birch fence will rot. Unfilled, without a woman with child, it will fall into itself, an image that recurs throughout Frost's poetry. Thus the child's grave predicts the dissolution of household, . . . almost a literal "home burial."

From " 'The Place Is the Asylum': Women and Nature in Robert Frost's Poetry,"

American Literature, May 1987

---

[1]"Robert Frost's 'Home Burial,' " in *The Moment of Poetry,* ed. Don Cameron Allen (Baltimore: Johns Hopkins UP, 1962), p. 104.

Considerations for Critical Thinking and Writing

1. How does Kearns's discussion of the stairwell, window, doorway, and grave shed light on your reading of "Home Burial"?
2. Discuss whether Kearns sympathizes more with the wife or the husband. Which character do you feel more sympathetic toward? Do you think Frost sides with one or the other? Explain your response.
3. Write an essay in which you agree or disagree with Kearns's assessment that the "wife is in the process of crossing the threshold from marital asylum into freedom."

LANGSTON HUGHES (1902–1967)

Even as a child, Langston Hughes was wrapped in an important African American legacy. He was raised by his maternal grandmother, who was the widow of Lewis Sheridan Leary, one of the band of men who participated in John Brown's raid on the federal arsenal at Harpers Ferry in 1859. The raid was a desperate attempt to ignite an insurrection that would ultimately liberate slaves in the South. It was a failure. Leary was killed, but the shawl he wore, which was returned to his wife bloodstained and riddled with bullet holes, was proudly worn by Hughes's grandmother fifty years after the raid, and she used it to cover her grandson at night when he was a young boy.

Throughout his long career as a professional writer, Hughes remained true to the African American heritage he celebrated in his writings, which were frankly "racial in theme and treatment, derived from the life I know." In an influential essay published in *The Nation,* "The Negro Artist and the Racial Mountain" (1926), he insisted on the need for black artists to draw on their heritage rather than "to run away spiritually from . . . race":

> We younger Negro artists who create now intend to express our individual dark-skinned selves without fear or shame. If white people are pleased we are glad. If they are not, it doesn't matter. We know we are beautiful. And ugly too. The tom-tom cries and the tom-tom laughs. If colored people are pleased we are glad. If they are not, their displeasure doesn't matter either. We build our temples for tomorrow, strong as we know how, and we stand on top of the mountain, free within ourselves.

That freedom was hard won for Hughes. His father, James Nathaniel Hughes, could not accommodate the racial prejudice and economic frustration that were the result of James's black and white racial ancestry. James abandoned his wife, Carrie Langston Hughes, only one year after their son was born in Joplin, Missouri, and went to find work in Mexico, where he hoped the color of his skin would be less of an issue than in the United States. During the periods when Hughes's mother shuttled from city to city in the Midwest looking for work, she sent her son to live with his grandmother.

Hughes's spotty relationship with his father — a connection he developed in his late teens and maintained only sporadically thereafter — consisted mostly of arguments about his becoming a writer rather than an engineer and businessman as his father wished. Hughes's father could not appreciate or even tolerate his son's ambition to write about the black experience, and Hughes (whose given name was also James but who refused to be identified by it) could not abide his father's contempt for blacks. Consequently, his determination, as he put it in "The Negro Artist," "to express our individual dark-skinned selves without fear or shame" was not only a profound response to African American culture but also an intensely personal commitment that made a relationship with his own father impossible. Though Hughes had been abandoned by his father, he nevertheless felt an early and deep connection to his ancestors, as he reveals in the following poem, written while crossing over the Mississippi River by train as he traveled to visit his father in Mexico, just a month after his high-school graduation.

The Negro Speaks of Rivers   1921

I've known rivers:
I've known rivers ancient as the world and older than the
    flow of human blood in human veins.

My soul has grown deep like the rivers.

I bathed in Euphrates when dawns were young.   5
I built my hut near the Congo and it lulled me to sleep.
I looked upon the Nile and raised the pyramids above it.
I heard the singing of the Mississippi when Abe Lincoln
    went down to New Orleans, and I've seen its muddy
    bosom turn all golden in the sunset.   10

I've known rivers:
Ancient, dusky rivers.

My soul has grown deep like the rivers.

This poem appeared in *The Crisis,* the official publication of the National Association for the Advancement of Colored People, which eventually published more of Hughes's poems than any other magazine or journal. This famous poem's simple and direct free verse makes clear that the "dusky [African] rivers" run concurrently with the poet's soul as he draws spiritual strength as well as individual identity from the collective experience of his ancestors. The themes of racial pride and personal dignity work their way through some forty books that Hughes wrote, edited, or compiled during his forty-five years of writing.

His works include volumes of poetry, novels, short stories, essays, plays, opera librettos, histories, documentaries, autobiographies, biographies, anthologies, children's books, and translations, as well as radio and television scripts. This impressive body of work makes him an important literary artist and a leading African American voice of the twentieth century. First and foremost, he considered himself a poet. He set out to be a poet who could address himself to the concerns of his people in poems that could be read with no formal training or extensive literary background. He wanted his poetry to be "direct, comprehensible and the epitome of simplicity."

His poetry echoes the voices of ordinary African Americans and the rhythms of their music. Hughes drew on an oral tradition of working-class folk poetry that embraced black vernacular language at a time when some middle-class blacks of the 1920s felt that the use of the vernacular was an embarrassing handicap and an impediment to social progress. Hughes's response to such concerns was unequivocal; at his readings, some of which were accompanied by jazz musicians or singers, his innovative voice found an appreciative audience. As Hughes very well knew, much of the pleasure associated with his poetry comes from reading it aloud; his many recorded readings give testimony to that pleasure.

The blues can be heard moving through Hughes's poetry as well as in the works of many of his contemporaries associated with the Harlem Renaissance, a movement of African American artists — writers, painters, sculptors, actors, and musicians — who were active in New York City's Harlem of the 1920s. Hughes's introduction to the "laughter and pain, hunger and heartache" of blues music began the year he spent at Columbia University. He dropped out after only two semesters because he preferred the night life and culture of Harlem to academic life. The sweet, sad blues songs captured for Hughes the intense pain and yearning that he saw around him and that he incorporated into poems such as "The Weary Blues" (p. 344). He also reveled in the jazz music of Harlem and discovered in its open forms and improvisations an energy and freedom that significantly influenced the style of his poetry.

Hughes's life, like the jazz music that influenced his work, was characterized by improvisation and openness. After leaving Columbia, he worked a series of odd jobs and then traveled as a merchant seaman to Africa and Europe in 1923–24. He jumped ship to work for several months in the kitchen of a Paris nightclub. As he broadened his experience through travel, he continued to write poetry. After his return to the United States in 1925 he published poems in two black magazines, *The Crisis* and *Opportunity,* and met the critic Carl Van Vechten, who sent his poems to the publisher Alfred A. Knopf. He also — as a busboy in a Washington, D.C., hotel — met the poet Vachel Lindsay, who was instrumental in advancing Hughes's reputation as a poet. In 1926 Hughes published his first volume of poems, *The Weary Blues,* and enrolled in Lincoln University in Pennsylvania, his education funded by a generous patron. His second volume of verse, *Fine Clothes to the Jew,* appeared in 1927, and by the time he graduated from Lincoln in 1929 he was on a book tour of the South giving poetry readings. Hughes ended the decade as more than a promising poet; as Countee Cullen pronounced in a mixed review of *The Weary Blues* (mixed because Cullen believed that black poets should embrace universal themes rather than racial themes), Hughes had "arrived."

Hughes wrote more prose than poetry during the 1930s, publishing his first novel, *Not Without Laughter* (1930), and a collection of stories, *The Ways of White Folks* (1934). In addition to writing a variety of magazine articles, he also worked on a number of plays and screenplays. Many of his poems from this period, such as "Let America Be America Again" (p. 349), reflect proletarian issues. During this decade Hughes's travels took him to all points of the compass — Cuba, Haiti, the Soviet Union, China, Japan, Mexico, France, and Spain — but his general intellectual movement was decidedly toward the left. Hughes was attracted to the American Communist Party, owing to its insistence on equality for all working-class people regardless of race. Like many other Americans of the thirties, he turned his attention away from the exotic twenties and focused on the economic and political issues attending the Great Depression that challenged the freedom and dignity of common humanity.

During World War II, Hughes helped the war effort by writing jingles and catchy verses to sell war bonds and to bolster morale. His protest poems of the thirties were largely replaced by poems that returned to earlier themes centered on the everyday lives of African Americans. In 1942 Hughes described his new collection of poems, *Shakespeare in Harlem,* as "light verse. Afro-American in the blues mood . . . to be read aloud, crooned, shouted, recited, and sung. Some with gestures, some not — as you like." Soon after this collection appeared, the character of Jesse B. Simple emerged from Hughes's 1943 newspaper column for the Chicago *Defender.* Hughes developed this popular urban African American character in five humorous books published over a fifteen-year period: *Simple Speaks His Mind* (1950), *Simple Takes a Wife* (1953), *Simple Stakes a Claim* (1957), *The Best of Simple* (1961), and *Simple's Uncle Sam* (1965). Two more poetry collections appeared in the forties: *Fields of Wonder* (1947) and *One-Way Ticket* (1949).

In the 1950s and 1960s Hughes's poetry again revealed the strong influence of black music, especially in the rhythms of *Montage of a Dream Deferred* (1951) and *Ask Your Mama: 12 Moods for Jazz* (1961). From the poem "Harlem" (p. 356) in *Montage of a Dream Deferred,* Lorraine Hansberry derived the title of her 1959 play *A Raisin in the Sun.* This is only a small measure of Hughes's influence on his fellow African American writers, but it is suggestive nonetheless. For some in the 1950s, however, Hughes and his influence occasioned suspicion. He was watched closely by the FBI and the Special Committee on Un-American Activities of the House of Representatives because of his alleged communist activities in the 1930s. Hughes denied that he was ever a member of the Communist Party, but he and others, including Albert Einstein and Paul Robeson, were characterized as "dupes and fellow travelers" by *Life* magazine in 1949. Hughes was subpoenaed to appear before Senator Joseph McCarthy's subcommittee on subversive activities in 1953, and listed by the FBI as a security risk until 1959. His anger and indignation over these attacks from the right can be seen in his poem "Un-American Investigators" (p. 357), published posthumously in *The Panther and the Lash* (1967).

Despite the tremendous amount that Hughes published, including two autobiographies, *The Big Sea* (1940) and *I Wonder as I Wander* (1956), he remains somewhat elusive. He never married or had friends who can lay claim to truly knowing him beyond what he wanted them to know (even though there are several biographies). And yet Hughes is well known — not for his personal life but for his treatment of the possibilities of African American experiences and identities. Like Walt Whitman, one of his favorite writers, Hughes created a persona that spoke for more than himself. Consider Hughes's voice in the following poem:

I, Too

I, too, sing America.

I am the darker brother.
They send me to eat in the kitchen
When company comes,
But I laugh,   5
And eat well,
And grow strong.

Tomorrow,
I'll be at the table
When company comes.   10
Nobody'll dare
Say to me,
"Eat in the kitchen,"
Then.

Besides,   15
They'll see how beautiful I am
And be ashamed —

I, too, am America.

The "darker brother" who celebrates America is certain of a better future
when he will no longer be shunted aside by "company." The poem is characteristic of Hughes's faith in the racial consciousness of African Americans, a
consciousness that reflects their integrity and beauty while simultaneously
demanding respect and acceptance from others: "Nobody'll dare / Say to me,
/ 'Eat in the kitchen,' / Then."

Hughes's poetry reveals his hearty appetite for all humanity, his insistence on justice for all, and his faith in the transcendent possibilities of joy and
hope that make room for everyone at America's table.

Chronology

1902   Born on February 1, in Joplin, Missouri.

1903–14 Lives primarily with his grandmother in Lawrence, Kansas.

1920   Graduates from high school in Cleveland, Ohio.

1921–22 Attends Columbia University for one year, but then drops out to
             work odd jobs and discover Harlem.

1923–24 Travels to Africa and Europe while working on a merchant ship.

1926   Publishes his first collection of poems, *The Weary Blues,* and
             enters Lincoln University in Pennsylvania.

1929   Graduates from Lincoln University.

1930   Publishes his first novel, *Not without Laughter.*

1932	Travels to the Soviet Union.
1934	Publishes his first collection of short stories, *The Ways of White Folks.*
1935	His play *Mulatto* is produced on Broadway.
1937	Covers the Spanish Civil War for the Baltimore *Afro-American.*
1938–39	Founds African American theaters in Harlem and Los Angeles.
1940	Publishes his first autobiography, *The Big Sea.*
1943	Creates the character of Simple in columns for the Chicago *Defender.*
1947	Is poet-in-residence at Atlanta University.
1949	Teaches at University of Chicago's Laboratory School.
1950	Publishes his first volume of Simple sketches, *Simple Speaks His Mind.*
1951	Publishes a translation of Federico García Lorca's *Gypsy Ballads.*
1953	Is subpoenaed to appear before Senator Joseph McCarthy's subcommittee on subversive activities in Washington, D.C.
1954–55	Publishes a number of books for young readers including *The First Book of Jazz* and *Famous American Negroes.*
1956	Publishes his second autobiography, *I Wonder as I Wander.*
1958	Publishes *The Langston Hughes Reader.*
1960	Publishes *An African Treasury: Articles, Essays, Stories, Poems by Black Africans.*
1961	Is inducted into the National Institute of Arts and Letters.
1962	Publishes *Fight for Freedom: The Story of the NAACP.*
1963	Publishes *Five Plays by Langston Hughes.*
1964	Publishes *New Negro Poets: U.S.A.*
1965	Defends Martin Luther King, Jr., from attacks by militant blacks.
1966	Is appointed by President Johnson to lead the American delegation to the First World Festival of Negro Arts in Dakar.
1967	Dies on May 22 in New York City; his last volume of poems, *The Panther and the Lash,* is published posthumously.
1994	*The Collected Poems of Langston Hughes,* edited by Arnold Rampersad and David Roessel, published posthumously.

Negro

1922

I am a Negro:
    Black as the night is black,
    Black like the depths of my Africa.

I've been a slave:
    Caesar told me to keep his door-steps clean.   5
    I brushed the boots of Washington.

I've been a worker:
    Under my hand the pyramids arose.
    I made mortar for the Woolworth Building.

I've been a singer: 10
    All the way from Africa to Georgia
    I carried my sorrow songs.
    I made ragtime.

I've been a victim:
    The Belgians cut off my hands in the Congo.   15
    They lynch me still in Mississippi.

I am a Negro:
    Black as the night is black,
    Black like the depths of my Africa.

Considerations for Critical Thinking and Writing

1. What is the effect of the repetition of the first and last stanzas?
2. What kind of history of black people does the speaker describe?
3. What sort of identity does the speaker claim for the Negro?

Connections to Other Selections

1. How does Hughes's use of night and blackness in "Negro" help to explain their meaning in the poem, "Dream Variations" (p. 343)?
2. Write an essay comparing the treatment of oppression in "Negro" with that in Blake's "The Chimney Sweeper" (p. 152).

Danse Africaine

1922

The low beating of the tom-toms,
The slow beating of the tom-toms,
    Low . . . slow
    Slow . . . low —
    Stirs your blood.   5
      Dance!
A night-veiled girl
    Whirls softly into a
    Circle of light.

Whirls softly . . . slowly,   10
Like a wisp of smoke around the fire —
    And the tom-toms beat,
    And the tom-toms beat,
And the low beating of the tom-toms
    Stirs your blood.   15

Considerations for Critical Thinking and Writing

1. Why are the sounds of this poem crucial to its meaning? (What is its meaning?)
2. What effect do the repeated rhythms have? You may need to read the poem aloud to answer.

Connection to Another Selection

1. Try rewriting this poem based on the prescription for poetry in "Formula" (p. 345).

Jazzonia   1923

Oh, silver tree!
Oh, shining rivers of the soul!

In a Harlem cabaret
Six long-headed jazzers play.
A dancing girl whose eyes are bold
Lifts high a dress of silken gold.   5

Oh, singing tree!
Oh, shining rivers of the soul!

Were Eve's eyes
In the first garden
Just a bit too bold?   10
Was Cleopatra gorgeous
In a gown of gold?

Oh, shining tree!
Oh, silver rivers of the soul!   15

In a whirling cabaret
Six long-headed jazzers play.

Considerations for Critical Thinking and Writing

1. Discuss the importance of the setting being a Harlem cabaret.
2. What is the effect of the variations in lines 1–2, 7–8, and 14–15?
3. What do the allusions to Eve and Cleopatra add to the poem's meaning? Are the questions raised about them answered?

Connection to Another Selection

1. Compare in an essay the rhythms of "Jazzonia" and "Danse Africaine."

Dream Variations

To fling my arms wide
In some place of the sun,
To whirl and to dance
Till the white day is done.
Then rest at cool evening   5
Beneath a tall tree
While night comes on gently,
         Dark like me —
That is my dream!

To fling my arms wide   10
In the face of the sun,
Dance! Whirl! Whirl!
Till the quick day is done.
Rest at pale evening . . .
A tall, slim tree . . .   15
Night coming tenderly
         Black like me.

Considerations for Critical Thinking and Writing

1. Describe the speaker's "dream." How might the dream be understood metaphorically?
2. What distinctions are made in the poem between night and day?
3. How do the rhythms of the lines contribute to the effects of the poem?

Connections to Other Selections

1. In an essay compare and contrast the meanings of darkness and the night in this poem and in Stafford's "Traveling through the Dark" (p. 141).
2. Discuss the significance of the dream in this poem and in "Dream Boogie" (p. 355).

Johannesburg Mines

1925

In the Johannesburg mines
There are 240,000
Native Africans working.
What kind of poem
Would you
Make out of that?
240,000 natives
Working in the
Johannesburg mines.

Considerations for Critical Thinking and Writing

1. What "kind of poem" does the speaker make out of the fact that 240,000 natives work in the mines of Johannesburg, South Africa?

2. Describe the poem's tone.

3. What do you think is the poem's theme?

Connection to Another Selection

1. Read the perspective by Hulme, "On the Differences between Poetry and Prose" (p. 105), and write an essay on why you think "Johannesburg Mines" is best described as poetry or prose.

The Weary Blues   1925

Droning a drowsy syncopated tune,
Rocking back and forth to a mellow croon,
   I heard a Negro play.
Down on Lenox Avenue° the other night   *street in Harlem*
By the pale dull pallor of an old gas light   5
   He did a lazy sway. . . .
   He did a lazy sway. . . .
To the tune o' those Weary Blues.
With his ebony hands on each ivory key
He made that poor piano moan with melody.   10
   O Blues!
Swaying to and fro on his rickety stool
He played that sad raggy tune like a musical fool.
   Sweet Blues!
Coming from a black man's soul.   15
   O Blues!
In a deep song voice with a melancholy tone
I heard that Negro sing, that old piano moan —
   "Ain't got nobody in all this world,
     Ain't got nobody but ma self.   20
     I's gwine to quit ma frownin'
     And put ma troubles on the shelf."

Thump, thump, thump, went his foot on the floor.
He played a few chords then he sang some more —
   "I got the Weary Blues   25
     And I can't be satisfied.
     Got the Weary Blues
     And can't be satisfied —
     I ain't happy no mo'
     And I wish that I had died."   30
And far into the night he crooned that tune.
The stars went out and so did the moon.
The singer stopped playing and went to bed
While the Weary Blues echoed through his head.
He slept like a rock or a man that's dead.   35

Considerations for Critical Thinking and Writing

1. How does the rhythm of the lines reflect their meaning?
2. Write a one-paragraph description of the blues based on how the poem presents blues music.
3. How does the speaker's voice compare with the singer's?
4. Comment on the effects of the rhymes.

Connection to Another Selection

1. Discuss "The Weary Blues" and "Lenox Avenue: Midnight" (p. 346) as vignettes of urban life in America. Do you think that, though written more than seventy years ago, they are still credible descriptions of city life? Explain why or why not.

Cross   1925

My old man's a white old man
And my old mother's black.
If ever I cursed my white old man
I take my curses back.

If ever I cursed my black old mother   5
And wished she were in hell,
I'm sorry for that evil wish
And now I wish her well.

My old man died in a fine big house.
My ma died in a shack.   10
I wonder where I'm gonna die,
Being neither white nor black?

Considerations for Critical Thinking and Writing

1. Discuss the possible meaning of the title.
2. Why do you think the speaker regrets having "cursed" his or her father and mother? Is it possible to determine if the speaker is male or female? Why or why not?
3. What informs the speaker's attitude toward life?

Connection to Another Selection

1. Read the perspective by Francis, "On 'Hard' Poetry" (p. 35), and write an essay explaining why you would characterize "Cross" as "hard" or "soft" poetry.

Formula   1926

Poetry should treat
    Of lofty things
Soaring thoughts
    And birds with wings.

The Muse of Poetry   5
    Should not know

That roses
        In manure grow.

The Muse of Poetry
        Should not care   10
That earthly pain
        Is everywhere.

Poetry!
        Treats of lofty things:
Soaring thoughts   15
        And birds with wings.

Considerations for Critical Thinking and Writing

1. What makes this poem a parody? What assumptions about poetry are being made
   fun of in the poem?
2. How does "Formula" fit the prescriptions offered in the advice to greeting-card
   free-lancers (p. 30)?

Connections to Other Selections

1. Choose any two poems by Hughes in this collection and explain why they do not
   fit the "Formula."
2. Write an essay that explains how Farries's "Magic of Love" (p. 30) conforms to the
   ideas about poetry presented in "Formula."

Lenox Avenue: Midnight   1926

The rhythm of life
Is a jazz rhythm,
Honey.
The gods are laughing at us.

The broken heart of love,   5
The weary, weary heart of pain, —
        Overtones,
        Undertones,
To the rumble of street cars,
To the swish of rain.   10

Lenox Avenue,
Honey.
Midnight,
And the gods are laughing at us.

Considerations for Critical Thinking and Writing

1. What, in your own experience, is the equivalent of Lenox Avenue?
2. For so brief a poem there are many sounds in these fourteen lines. What are they?
   How do they reinforce the poem's meanings?
3. What do you think is the poem's theme?

Connections to Other Selections

1. In an essay compare the theme of this poem with that of Emily Dickinson's "I know that He exists" (p. 294).
2. Compare and contrast the speaker's tone in this poem with the tone of the speaker in Thomas Hardy's "Hap" (p. 414).

Red Silk Stockings   1927

Put on yo' red silk stockings,
Black gal.
Go out an' let de white boys
Look at yo' legs.

Ain't nothin' to do for you, nohow,   5
Round this town, —
You's too pretty.
Put on yo' red silk stockings, gal,
An' tomorrow's chile'll
Be a high yaller.   10

Go out an' let de white boys
Look at yo' legs.

Considerations for Critical Thinking and Writing

1. Discuss the racial dimensions of this poem.
2. Who do you think is speaking? Describe his or her tone.
3. Write a response from the girl — does she put on the red silk stockings? Explain why you imagine her reacting in a certain way.

Connection to Another Selection

1. Write an essay that compares relations between whites and blacks in this poem and in "Dinner Guest: Me" (p. 359).

Rent-Party° Shout: For a Lady Dancer   1930

Whip it to a jelly!
Too bad Jim!
Mamie's got ma man —
An' I can't find him.
Shake that thing! O!   5
Shake it slow!
That man I love is
Mean an' low.

Rent-Party: In Harlem during the 1920s, parties were given that charged admission to raise money for rent.

Pistol an' razor!
Razor an' gun!   10
If I sees ma man he'd
Better run —
For I'll shoot him in de shoulder,
Else I'll cut him down,
Cause I knows I can find him   15
When he's in de ground —
Then can't no other women
Have him layin' round.
So play it, Mr. Nappy!
Yo' music's fine!   20
I'm gonna kill that
Man o' mine!

Considerations for Critical Thinking and Writing

1. In what sense is this poem a kind of "shout"?
2. How is the speaker's personality characterized by her use of language?
3. Describe the type of music you think might be played at this party.
4. How does Hughes's use of short lines affect your reading of the poem?

Connection to Another Selection

1. Write an essay comparing the tone and theme of this poem with that of the anonymous "Frankie and Johnny" (p. 388).

The English   1930

In ships all over the world
The English comb their hair for dinner,
Stand watch on the bridge,
Guide by strange stars,
Take on passengers,   5
Slip up hot rivers,
Nose across lagoons,
Bargain for trade,
Buy, sell or rob,
Load oil, load fruit,   10
Load cocoa beans, load gold
In ships all over the world,
Comb their hair for dinner.

Considerations for Critical Thinking and Writing

1. How does combing one's hair take on symbolic significance in the poem?
2. What is the speaker's attitude toward the English?
3. Which words reveal the speaker's attitudes?

Connection to Another Selection

1. Write an essay that discusses hair combing as symbolic action in this poem and in Ho's "A Beautiful Girl Combs Her Hair" (p. 42).

Let America Be America Again   1936

Let America be America again.
Let it be the dream it used to be.
Let it be the pioneer on the plain
Seeking a home where he himself is free.

(America never was America to me.)   5

Let America be the dream the dreamers dreamed —
Let it be that great strong land of love
Where never kings connive nor tyrants scheme
That any man be crushed by one above.

(It never was America to me.)   10

O, let my land be a land where Liberty
Is crowned with no false patriotic wreath,
But opportunity is real, and life is free,
Equality is in the air we breathe.

(There's never been equality for me,   15
Nor freedom in this "homeland of the free.")

Say, who are you that mumbles in the dark?
And who are you that draws your veil across the stars?

I am the poor white, fooled and pushed apart,
I am the Negro bearing slavery's scars.   20
I am the red man driven from the land,
I am the immigrant clutching the hope I seek —
And finding only the same old stupid plan
Of dog eat dog, of mighty crush the weak.

I am the young man, full of strength and hope,   25
Tangled in that ancient endless chain
Of profit, power, gain, of grab the land!
Of grab the gold! Of grab the ways of satisfying need!
Of work the men! Of take the pay!
Of owning everything for one's own greed!   30

I am the farmer, bondsman to the soil.
I am the worker sold to the machine.
I am the Negro, servant to you all.
I am the people, humble, hungry, mean —
Hungry yet today despite the dream.   35
Beaten yet today — O, Pioneers!

I am the man who never got ahead,
The poorest worker bartered through the years.

Yet I'm the one who dreamt our basic dream
In that Old World while still a serf of kings,   40
Who dreamt a dream so strong, so brave, so true,
That even yet its mighty daring sings
In every brick and stone, in every furrow turned
That's made America the land it has become.
O, I'm the man who sailed those early seas   45
In search of what I meant to be my home —
For I'm the one who left dark Ireland's shore,
And Poland's plain, and England's grassy lea,
And torn from Black Africa's strand I came
To build a "homeland of the free."   50

The free?

Who said the free? Not me?
Surely not me? The millions on relief today?
The millions shot down when we strike?
The millions who have nothing for our pay?   55
For all the dreams we've dreamed
And all the songs we've sung
And all the hopes we've held
And all the flags we've hung,
The millions who have nothing for our pay —   60
Except the dream that's almost dead today.

O, let America be America again —
The land that never has been yet —
And yet must be — the land where *every* man is free.
The land that's mine — the poor man's, Indian's, Negro's, ME —   65
Who made America,
Whose sweat and blood, whose faith and pain,
Whose hand at the foundry, whose plow in the rain,
Must bring back our mighty dream again.

Sure, call me any ugly name you choose —   70
The steel of freedom does not stain.
From those who live like leeches on the people's lives,
We must take back our land again,
America!

O, yes,   75
I say it plain,
America never was America to me,
And yet I swear this oath —
America will be!

Out of the rack and ruin of our gangster death,   80
The rape and rot of graft, and stealth, and lies,
We, the people, must redeem
The land, the mines, the plants, the rivers.
The mountains and the endless plain —

All, all the stretch of these great green states —   85
And make America again!

Considerations for Critical Thinking and Writing

1. How does the speaker describe the meaning of the American "dream"? Why has
   it failed? How might the "dream" be redeemed, according to the speaker?
2. Notice that the stanzaic patterns begin to change at line 19 as the quatrains give
   way to freer forms. Why do you think that happens?
3. Comment on Hughes's use of alliteration to drive home his points. Cite several
   examples and explain their effects.
4. What kinds of rhymes are used in the poem? How do these sounds reinforce
   meanings?
5. What common phrases — even clichés — can be found in the poem? Explain
   whether or not you think the poet's use of them makes them fresh again.

Connections to Other Selections

1. This poem was first published in *Esquire* in July 1936, during the Great Depression. Read the section in "Critical Strategies for Reading" on historical approaches
   to literature (pp. 535–537) and write an essay on this poem using a New Historicist approach.
2. Compare and contrast the views about the United States expressed in this poem
   with those expressed in Laviera's "AmeRícan" (p. 241).
3. Read the selections by Walt Whitman in this anthology (see the Index of Authors
   and Titles) and write an essay comparing Hughes's style with Whitman's.

Note on Commercial Theatre   1940

You've taken my blues and gone —
You sing 'em on Broadway
And you sing 'em in Hollywood Bowl,
And you mixed 'em up with symphonies
And you fixed 'em   5
So they don't sound like me.
Yep, you done taken my blues and gone.

You also took my spirituals and gone.
You put me in *Macbeth* and *Carmen Jones*
And all kinds of *Swing Mikados*   10
And in everything but what's about me —
But someday somebody'll
Stand up and talk about me,
And write about me —
Black and beautiful —   15
And sing about me,
And put on plays about me!
I reckon it'll be
Me myself!

Yes, it'll be me.   20

Considerations for Critical Thinking and Writing

1. What is the speaker's complaint? Does it remain valid today?
2. Compare the tone of the title with that of the poem. Are they consistent?
3. Do you think the speaker is male or female? Explain your response.

Connection to Another Selection

1. Compare in an essay the tone and theme of this poem and "Frederick Douglass: 1817–1895" (p. 360).

Ballad of the Landlord   1940

Landlord, landlord,
My roof has sprung a leak.
Don't you 'member I told you about it
Way last week?

Landlord, landlord,   5
These steps is broken down.
When you come up yourself
It's a wonder you don't fall down.

Ten Bucks you say I owe you?
Ten Bucks you say is due?   10
Well, that's Ten Bucks more'n I'll pay you
Till you fix this house up new.

What? You gonna get eviction orders?
You gonna cut off my heat?
You gonna take my furniture and   15
Throw it in the street?

Um-huh! You talking high and mighty.
Talk on — till you get through.
You ain't gonna be able to say a word
If I land my fist on you.   20

Police! Police!
Come and get this man!
He's trying to ruin the government
And overturn the land!

Copper's whistle!   25
Patrol bell!
Arrest.

Precinct Station.
Iron cell.
Headlines in press: 30

MAN THREATENS LANDLORD
TENANT HELD NO BAIL
JUDGE GIVES NEGRO 90 DAYS IN COUNTY JAIL

Considerations for Critical Thinking and Writing

1. Why is the literary ballad an especially appropriate form for the content of this poem?
2. How does the speaker's language simultaneously characterize him and the landlord?
3. How does the poem manage to incorporate both humor and serious social commentary? Which do you think is dominant? Explain.

Connection to Another Selection

1. Write an essay on landlords based on this poem and Soyinka's "Telephone Conversation" (p. 19).

Midnight Raffle 1949

I put my nickel
In the raffle of the night.
Somehow that raffle
Didn't turn out right.

I lost my nickel. 5
I lost my time.
I got back home
Without a dime.

When I dropped that nickel
In the subway slot, 10
I wouldn't have dropped it,
Knowing what I got.

I could just as well've
Stayed home inside:
My bread wasn't buttered 15
On neither side.

Considerations for Critical Thinking and Writing

1. How is the phrase "raffle of the night" different from "Midnight Raffle"? Which seems more suggestive to you? Explain why.
2. Discuss the meaning and tone of the last stanza.

Connection to Another Selection

1. Compare in an essay the meaning of home in "Midnight Raffle" and "doorknobs" (p. 358).

The instructor said,

> *Go home and write*
> *a page tonight.*
> *And let that page come out of you —*
> *Then, it will be true.* 5

I wonder if it's that simple?
I am twenty-two, colored, born in Winston-Salem.
I went to school there, then Durham, then here
to this college on the hill above Harlem.
I am the only colored student in my class. 10
The steps from the hill lead down into Harlem,
through a park, then I cross St. Nicholas,
Eighth Avenue, Seventh, and I come to the Y,
the Harlem Branch Y, where I take the elevator
up to my room, sit down, and write this page: 15

It's not easy to know what is true for you or me
at twenty-two, my age. But I guess I'm what
I feel and see and hear, Harlem, I hear you:
hear you, hear me — we two — you, me, talk on this page.
(I hear New York, too.) Me — who? 20
Well, I like to eat, sleep, drink, and be in love.
I like to work, read, learn, and understand life.
I like a pipe for a Christmas present,
or records — Bessie,° bop, or Bach.
I guess being colored doesn't make me *not* like 25
the same things other folks like who are other races.
So will my page be colored that I write?
Being me, it will not be white.
But it will be
a part of you, instructor. 30
You are white —
yet a part of me, as I am part of you.
That's American.
Sometimes perhaps you don't want to be a part of me.
Nor do I often want to be a part of you. 35
But we are, that's true!
As I learn from you,
I guess you learn from me —
although you're older — and white —
and somewhat more free. 40

This is my page for English B.

24 *Bessie:* Bessie Smith (1898?–1937), a famous blues singer.

Considerations for Critical Thinking and Writing

1. What complicates the writing assignment for the speaker? Does he fulfill the assignment? Explain why or why not.

2. What are the circumstances of the speaker's life? How does the speaker respond to the question "So will my page be colored that I write?" (line 27). Discuss the tone of lines 27–40.

3. Write a one-paragraph response to this poem as you think the speaker's instructor would in grading it.

Connections to Other Selections

1. Use your imagination and write about an encounter between the student-speaker in this poem and the instructor-speaker of Mark Halliday's "Graded Paper" (p. 496). Choose a form (such as an essay, a dialogue, or a short story) that will allow you to explore their responses to one another.

2. Discuss the attitudes expressed toward the United States in this poem and in Divakaruni's "Indian Movie, New Jersey" (p. 149).

Juke Box Love Song   1950

I could take the Harlem night
and wrap around you,
Take the neon lights and make a crown,
Take the Lenox Avenue busses,
Taxis, subways,   5
And for your love song tone their rumble down.
Take Harlem's heartbeat,
Make a drumbeat,
Put it on a record, let it whirl,
And while we listen to it play,   10
Dance with you till day —
Dance with you, my sweet brown Harlem girl.

Considerations for Critical Thinking and Writing

1. What kinds of songs do you associate with juke boxes? What kind of song do you think this poem would be?

2. Discuss the images in the poem. Are they effective? What makes them work or fail?

Connection to Another Selection

1. Compare the tone of this poem with "Red Silk Stockings" (p. 347). Which poem do you prefer? Explain why.

Dream Boogie   1951

Good morning, daddy!
Ain't you heard
The boogie-woogie rumble
Of a dream deferred?

Listen closely: 5
You'll hear their feet
Beating out and beating out a —

    You think
    It's a happy beat?

Listen to it closely: 10
Ain't you heard
something underneath
like a —

    What did I say?

Sure,   15
I'm happy!
Take it away!

    Hey, pop!
    Re-bop!
    Mop!   20

    Y-e-a-h!

Considerations for Critical Thinking and Writing

1. Discuss the poem's musical qualities. Which lines are most musical?
2. Answer the question, *"You think / It's a happy beat?"*
3. Describe the competing tones in the poem. Which do you think is predominant?

Connections to Other Selections

1. In an essay compare and contrast the thematic tensions in this poem and in "Harlem" (below).
2. How are the "dreams" different in "Dream Boogie" and "Dream Variations" (p. 343)?

Harlem   1951

What happens to a dream deferred?

    Does it dry up
    like a raisin in the sun?
    Or fester like a sore —
    And then run?   5
    Does it stink like rotten meat?
    Or crust and sugar over —
    like a syrupy sweet?

    Maybe it just sags
    like a heavy load.   10

    Or does it explode?

Considerations for Critical Thinking and Writing

1. How might the question asked in this poem be raised by any individual or group whose dreams and aspirations are thwarted?
2. In some editions of Hughes's poetry the title of this poem is "Dream Deferred." What would the effect of this change be on your reading of the poem's symbolic significance?
3. How might the final line be completed as a simile? What is the effect of the speaker not completing the simile? Why is this an especially useful strategy?

Connection to Another Selection

1. Write an essay on the themes of "Harlem" and Merrill's "Casual Wear" (p. 147).

Un-American Investigators   1953

The committee's fat,
Smug, almost secure
Co-religionists
Shiver with delight
In warm manure   5
As those investigated —
Too brave to name a name —
Have pseudonyms revealed
In Gentile game
    Of who,   10
    Born Jew,
    Is who?
Is not your name Lipshitz?
    Yes.
Did you not change it   15
For subversive purposes?
    No.
For nefarious gain?
    Not so.
Are you sure?   20
The committee shivers
With delight in
Its manure.

Considerations for Critical Thinking and Writing

1. Research in the library the hearings and investigations of the House of Representatives' Special Committee on Un-American Activities. How is this background information relevant to an understanding of this poem?
2. How does the speaker characterize the investigators?
3. Given the images in the poem, what might serve as a substitute for its ironic title?

Connection to Another Selection

1. Write an essay that connects the committee described in this poem with the speaker in E. E. Cummings's "next to of course god america i" (p. 136). What do they have in common?

Old Walt   1954

Old Walt Whitman
Went finding and seeking,
Finding less than sought
Seeking more than found,
Every detail minding   5
Of the seeking or the finding.

Pleasured equally
In seeking as in finding,
Each detail minding,
Old Walt went seeking   10
And finding.

Considerations for Critical Thinking and Writing

1. Write an explication of "Old Walt." (For a discussion of how to explicate a poem, see the sample explication on p. 585.)
2. What is the effect of the poem's repeated sounds?
3. To what extent do you think lines 3 and 4 could be used to describe Hughes's poetry as well as Whitman's?

Connection to Another Selection

1. How does Hughes's tribute to Whitman compare with his tribute to Frederick Douglass (p. 360)?

doorknobs   1961

The simple silly terror
of a doorknob on a door
that turns to let in life
on two feet standing,
walking, talking,   5
wearing dress or trousers,
maybe drunk or maybe sober,
maybe smiling, laughing, happy,
maybe tangled in the terror
of a yesterday past grandpa   10
when the door from out there opened
into here where I, antenna,

recipient of your coming,
received the talking image
of the simple silly terror   15
of a door that opens
at the turning of a knob
to let in life
walking, talking, standing
wearing dress or trousers,   20
drunk or maybe sober,
smiling, laughing, happy,
or tangled in the terror
of a yesterday past grandpa
not of our own doing.   25

Considerations for Critical Thinking and Writing

1. How do the style and content of this poem differ from those of the other poems by Hughes in this anthology?
2. Why is the doorknob associated with "terror"?
3. The final eight lines repeat much of the first part of the poem. What is repeated and what is changed? What is the effect of this repetition?
4. Does the doorknob have any symbolic value or should it be read literally?

Connection to Another Selection

1. Write an essay comparing the theme of this poem with that of Stevens's "Schizophrenia" (p. 119).

Dinner Guest: Me   1965

I know I am
The Negro Problem
Being wined and dined,
Answering the usual questions
That come to white mind   5
Which seeks demurely
To probe in polite way
The why and wherewithal
Of darkness U.S.A. —
Wondering how things got this way   10
In current democratic night,
Murmuring gently
Over *fraises du bois,*
"I'm so ashamed of being white."

The lobster is delicious,   15
The wine divine,
And center of attention
At the damask table, mine.

To be a Problem on
Park Avenue at eight   20
Is not so bad.
Solutions to the Problem,
Of course, wait.

Considerations for Critical Thinking and Writing

1. What does the speaker satirize in this description of a dinner party?
2. Why is line 9, "Of darkness U.S.A. — ," especially resonant?
3. What effects are created by the speaker's diction?
4. Discuss the effects of the rhymes in lines 15–23.

Connection to Another Selection

1. Write an essay on the speaker's treatment of the diners in this poem and in
   Kingston's "Restaurant" (p. 178).

Frederick Douglass: 1817–1895°   1966

Douglass was someone who,
Had he walked with wary foot
And frightened tread,
From very indecision
Might be dead,   5
Might have lost his soul,
But instead decided to be bold
And capture every street
On which he set his feet,
To route each path   10
Toward freedom's goal,
To make each highway
Choose *his* compass' choice,
To all the world cried,
Hear my voice! . . .   15
Oh, to be a beast, a bird,
Anything but a slave! he said.

Who would be free
Themselves must strike
The first blow, he said.   20

     He died in 1895.
     He is not dead.

1817–1895: Douglass was actually born in 1818; as a slave, he did not know his actual birth date.

Considerations for Critical Thinking and Writing

1. What does Hughes celebrate about the life of Douglass, author of *Narrative of the
   Life of Frederick Douglass, an American Slave, Written by Himself* (1845)?

2. This poem was published when the civil rights movement was very active in America. How does that information affect your reading of it?

Connection to Another Selection

1. How is the speaker's attitude toward violence in this poem similar to that of the speaker in "Harlem" (p. 356)?

PERSPECTIVES ON HUGHES

Hughes on Racial Shame and Pride   1926

[J]azz to me is one of the inherent expressions of Negro life in America: the eternal tom-tom beating in the Negro soul — the tom-tom of revolt against weariness in a white world, a world of subway trains, and work, work, work; the tom-tom of joy and laughter, and pain swallowed in a smile. Yet the Philadelphia clubwoman is ashamed to say that her race created it and she does not like me to write about it. The old subconscious "white is best" runs through her mind. Years of study under white teachers, a lifetime of white books, pictures, and papers, and white manners, morals, and Puritan standards made her dislike the spirituals. And now she turns up her nose at jazz and all its manifestations — likewise almost everything else distinctly racial. She doesn't care for the Winold Reiss° portraits of Negroes because they are "too Negro." She does not want a true picture of herself from anybody. She wants the artist to flatter her, to make the white world believe that all Negroes are as smug and as near white in soul as she wants to be. But, to my mind, it is the duty of the younger Negro artist, if he accepts any duties at all from outsiders, to change through the force of his art that old whispering "I want to be white," hidden in the aspirations of his people, to "Why should I want to be white? I am a Negro — and beautiful!"

From "The Negro Artist and the Racial Mountain," *The Nation,* June 23, 1926

Winold Reiss (1887–1953): A white painter whose work emphasized the individuality of blacks.

Considerations for Critical Thinking and Writing

1. Why does the Philadelphia clubwoman refuse to accept jazz as part of her heritage?
2. Compare and contrast Hughes's description of the Philadelphia clubwoman with M. Carl Holman's "Mr. Z" (p. 419). In what sense are these two characters made for each other?

Hughes on Harlem Rent Parties   1940

Then [in the late twenties and early thirties] it was that house-rent parties began to flourish — and not always to raise the rent either. But, as often as not, to have a get-together of one's own, where you could do the black-bottom with no stranger behind you trying to do it, too. Non-theatrical, non-intellectual Harlem was an unwilling victim of its own vogue. It didn't like to be stared at by white folks. But perhaps the downtowners never knew this — for the cabaret owners, the entertainers, and the speakeasy proprietors treated them fine — as long as they paid.

The Saturday night rent parties that I attended were often more amusing than any night club, in small apartments where God knows who lived — because the guests seldom did — but where the piano would often be augmented by a guitar, or an odd cornet, or somebody with a pair of drums walking in off the street. And where awful bootleg whiskey and good fried fish or steaming chitterling were sold at very low prices. And the dancing and singing and impromptu entertaining went on until dawn came in at the windows.

These parties, often termed whist parties or dances, were usually announced by brightly colored cards stuck in the grille of apartment house elevators. Some of the cards were highly entertaining in themselves:

We got yellow girls, we've got black and tan
Will you have a good time? - YEAH MAN !

A Social Whist Party
—GIVEN BY—
MARY WINSTON
147 West 145th Street   Apt. 5

SATURDAY EVE., MARCH 19th, 1932

GOOD MUSIC   **REFRESHMENTS**

Almost every Saturday night when I was in Harlem I went to a house-rent party. I wrote lots of poems about house-rent parties, and ate thereat many a fried fish and pig's foot — with liquid refreshments on the side. I met ladies' maids and truck drivers, laundry workers and shoe shine boys, seamstresses and porters. I can still hear their laughter in my ears, hear the soft slow music, and feel the floor shaking as the dancers danced.

From "When the Negro Was in Vogue," in *The Big Sea*

Considerations for Critical Thinking and Writing

1. What, according to Hughes, was the appeal of the rent parties in contrast to the nightclubs?
2. Describe the tone in which Hughes recounts his memory of these parties.

DONALD B. GIBSON (b. 1933)
The Essential Optimism of Hughes and Whitman 1971

As optimists generally do, Langston Hughes and Walt Whitman lacked a sense of evil. This (and all it implies) puts Hughes in a tradition with other American writers. He stands with Whitman, Emerson, Thoreau, and later Sandburg, Lindsay, and Steinbeck, as opposed to Hawthorne, Poe, Melville, James, Faulkner, and Eliot. This is not to say that he did not recognize the existence of evil, but, as Yeats says of Emerson and Whitman, he lacked the "Vision of Evil." He did not see evil as inherent in the character of nature and man, hence he felt that the evil (small *e*) about which he wrote so frequently in his poems (lynchings, segregation, discrimination of all kinds) would be eradicated with the passage of time. Of course the Hughes of *The Panther and the Lash* (1967) is not as easily optimistic as the poet was twenty or twenty-five years before. Hughes could not have written "I, Too," or even "The Negro Speaks of Rivers" in the sixties. But the evidence as I see it has it that though he does not speak so readily about the fulfillment of the American ideal for black people, and though something of the spirit of having waited too long prevails, still the optimism remains. . . .

Montage of a Dream Deferred (1951), included in *Selected Poems,* describes the dream as deferred, not dead nor incapable of fulfillment. There is a certain grimness in the poem, for example in its most famous section, "Harlem," which begins, "What happens to a dream deferred? / Does it dry up / like a raisin in the sun?" but the grimness is by no means unrelieved. There is, as a matter of fact, a lightness of tone throughout the poem which could not exist did the poet see the ravages of racial discrimination as manifestations of Evil. . . . The whole tone of *Montage of a Dream Deferred* is characterized by the well-known "Ballad of the Landlord." There the bitter-sweet quality of Hughes's attitude toward his subject is clear.

From "The Good Black Poet and the Good Grey Poet: The Poetry of
Hughes and Whitman," in *Langston Hughes: Black Genius: A Critical
Evaluation,* edited by Therman B. O'Daniel

Considerations for Critical Thinking and Writing

1. What distinction does Gibson make between "Evil" and "evil"?
2. Discuss whether you agree or disagree that Hughes lacked a "Vision of Evil."
3. Why do you think Gibson writes that Hughes couldn't have written "The Negro Speaks of Rivers" (p. 336) or "I, Too" (p. 339) in the 1960s?
4. What aspects of Whitman does Hughes seem to admire in "Old Walt" (p. 358)?

JAMES A. EMANUEL (b. 1921)
Hughes's Attitudes toward Religion 1973

Religion, because of its historical importance during and after slavery, is an undeniably useful theme in the work of any major Black writer. In a writer whose special province for almost forty-five years was more recent Black experience, the theme is doubly vital. Hughes's personal religious orientation is pertinent. Asked about it by the Reverend Dana F. Kennedy of the "Viewpoint" radio and television show (on December 10, 1960), the poet responded:

> I grew up in a not very religious family, but I had a foster aunt who saw that I went to church and Sunday school . . . and I was very much moved, always, by the, shall I say, the rhythms of the Negro church . . . of the spirituals, . . . of those wonderful old-time sermons. . . . There's great beauty in the mysticism of much religious writing, and great help there — but I also think that we live in a world . . . of solid earth and vegetables and a need for jobs and a need for housing. . . .

Two years earlier, the poet had told John Kirkwood of British Columbia's *Vancouver Sun* (December 3, 1958): "I'm not anti-Christian. I'm not against anyone's religion. Religion is one of the innate needs of mankind. What I am against is the misuse of religion. But I won't ridicule it. . . . Whatever part of God is in anybody is not to be played with, and everybody has got a part of God in them."

These typical public protestations by Hughes boil down to his insistence that religion is naturally sacred and beautiful, and that its needed sustenance must not be exploited.

From "Christ in Alabama: Religion in the Poetry of Langston Hughes,"
in Modern Black Poets, edited by Donald B. Gibson

Considerations for Critical Thinking and Writing

1. Why do you think Emanuel asserts that, owing to slavery, religion "is an undeniably useful theme in the work of any major Black writer"?

2. How does Hughes's concern for the "solid earth and vegetables and a need for jobs and a need for housing" qualify his attitudes toward religion?

RICHARD K. BARKSDALE (b. 1915)
On Censoring "Ballad of the Landlord"   1977

In 1940, ["Ballad of the Landlord"] was a rather innocuous rendering of an imaginary dialogue between a disgruntled tenant and a tight-fisted landlord. In creating a poem about two such social archetypes, the poet was by no means taking any new steps in dramatic poetry. The literature of most capitalist and noncapitalist societies often pits the haves against the have-nots, and not infrequently the haves are wealthy men of property who "lord" it over improvident men who own nothing. So the confrontation between tenant and landlord was in 1940 just another instance of the social malevolence of a system that punished the powerless and excused the powerful. In fact, Hughes's tone of dry irony throughout the poem leads one to suspect that the poet deliberately overstated a situation and that some sardonic humor was supposed to be squeezed out of the incident. . . .

Ironically, this poem, which in 1940 depicted a highly probable incident in American urban life and was certainly not written to incite an economic revolt or promote social unrest, became, by the mid-1960s, a verboten assignment in a literature class in a Boston high school. In his Langston Hughes headnote in *Black Voices* (1967), Abraham Chapman reported that a Boston high school English teacher named Jonathan Kozol was fired for assigning it to his students. By the mid-sixties, Boston and many other American cities had become riot-torn, racial tinderboxes, and their ghettos seethed with tenant anger and discontent. So the poem gathered new meanings reflecting the times, and the word of its tenant persona bespoke the collective anger of thousands of black have-nots.

From *Langston Hughes: The Poet and His Critics*

Considerations for Critical Thinking and Writing

1. Why do you think the Boston School Committee believed the "Ballad of the Landlord" (p. 352) should be censored?
2. Do you agree with Barksdale that the poem is a "rather innocuous rendering" of economic and social issues? Explain your answer.
3. How did the poem acquire "new meanings reflecting the times" between the 1940s and 1960s? What new meanings might it have for readers today?

STEVEN C. TRACY (b. 1954)
A Reading of "The Weary Blues"   1988

Clearly in this poem the blues unite the speaker and the performer in some way. There is an immediate implied relationship between the two because of the ambiguous syntax. The "droning" and "rocking" can refer either to the "I" or to the "Negro," immediately suggesting that the music invites, even requires, the participation of the speaker. Further, the words suggest that the speaker's poem is a "drowsy syncopated tune" as well, connecting speaker and performer even further by having them working in the same tradition. The performer remains anonymous . . . because he is not a famous, celebrated performer; he is one of the main practitioners living the unglamorous life that is far more common than the kinds of lives the most successful blues stars lived. His "drowsy syncopated tune," which at once implies both rest and activity (a tune with shifting accents), signals the tension between the romantic image and the reality, and very likely influences the speaker to explore the source of the tension between the singer's stoicism and his resignation to his fate as expressed in his blues lyrics. Significantly, the eight-bar blues stanza, the one with no repeat line, is his hopeful stanza. Its presence as an eight-bar stanza works by passing more quickly, reinforcing both his loneliness *and* the fleeting nature of the kind of hope expressed. This is especially true since the singer's next stanza, a twelve-bar blues, uses the repeat line to emphasize his weariness and lack of satisfaction, and his wish to die.

All the singer seems to have is his moaning blues, the revelation of "a black man's soul," and those blues are what helps keep him alive. Part of that ability to sustain is apparently the way the blues help him keep his identity. Even in singing the blues, he is singing about his life, about the way that he and other blacks have to deal with white society. As his black hands touch the white keys, the accepted Western sound of the piano and the form of Western music are changed. The piano itself comes to life as an extension of the singer, and moans, transformed by the black tradition to a mirror of black sorrow that also reflects the transforming power and beauty of the black tradition. Finally, it is that tradition that helps keep the singer alive and gives him his identity, since when he is done and goes to bed he sleeps like an inanimate or de-animated object, with the blues echoing beyond his playing, beyond the daily cycles, and through both conscious and unconscious states.

Another source of the melancholy aura of the poem is the lack of an actual connection between the performer and the speaker. They do not strike up a conversation, share a drink, or anything else. The speaker observes, helpless to do anything about the performer and his weariness save to write the poem and try to understand the performer's experiences and how they relate to his own. Ultimately he finds the man and his songs wistfully compelling; and he hears in his song the collective weary blues of blacks in America and tries to reconcile the sadness with the sweetness of the form and expression.

From *Langston Hughes and the Blues*

Considerations for Critical Thinking and Writing

1. How does Tracy use the blues form to inform his reading of "The Weary Blues" (p. 344)?
2. What is the relationship between the speaker and the performer, according to Tracy?
3. How is the performer's playing of the piano different from "the accepted Western sound . . . and the form of Western music"?

DAVID CHINITZ (b. 1962)
The Romanticization of Africa in the 1920s   1997

In Europe black culture was an exotic import; in America it was domestic and increasingly mass-produced. If postwar [World War I] disillusionment judged the majority culture mannered, neurotic, and repressive, Americans had an easily accessible alternative. The need for such an Other produced a discourse in which black Americans figured as barely civilized exiles from the jungle, with — so the clichés ran — tom-toms beating in their blood and dark laughter in their souls. The African American became a model of "natural" human behavior to contrast with the falsified, constrained and impotent modes of the "civilized."

Far from being immune to the lure of this discourse, for the better part of the 1920s Hughes asserted an open pride in the supposed primitive qualities of his race, the atavistic legacy of the African motherland. Unlike most of those who romanticized Africa, Hughes had at least some firsthand experience of the continent; yet he processed what he saw there in images conditioned by European primitivism, rendering "[the land] wild and lovely, the people dark and beautiful, the palm trees tall, the sun bright, and the rivers deep."[1] His short story "Luani of the Jungle," in attempting to glorify aboriginal African vigor as against European anemia, shows how predictable and unextraordinary even Hughes's primitivism could be. To discover in the descendents of idealized Africans the same qualities of innate health, spontaneity, and naturalness

[1]*The Big Sea.* 1940. N.Y.: Thunder's Mouth, 1986, 11.

requires no great leap; one has only to identify the African American as a displaced primitive, as Hughes does repeatedly in his first book, *The Weary Blues:*

> They drove me out of the forest.
> They took me away from the jungles.
> I lost my trees.
> I lost my silver moons.
>
> Now they've caged me
> In the circus of civilization.[2]

Hughes depicts black atavism vividly and often gracefully, yet in a way that is entirely consistent with the popular iconography of the time. His African Americans retain "among the skyscrapers" the primal fears and instincts of their ancestors "among the palms in Africa."[3] The scion of Africa is still more than half primitive: "All the tom-toms of the jungles beat in my blood, / And all the wild hot moons of the jungles shine in my soul."[4]

From "Rejuvenation through Joy: Langston Hughes, Primitivism and Jazz," in *American Literary History,* Spring 1997

[2] *The Weary Blues.* N.Y.: Knopf, 1926, 100.
[3] *Ibid.* 101.
[4] *Ibid.* 102.

Considerations for Critical Thinking and Writing

1. According to Chinitz, why did Europeans and Americans romanticize African culture?
2. Consider the poems published by Hughes in the 1920s reprinted in this anthology. Explain whether you find any "primitivism" in these poems.
3. Later in this essay, Chinitz points out that Hughes eventually rejected the "reductive mischaracterizations of black culture, the commercialism, the sham sociology, and the downright silliness of the primitivist fad." Choose and discuss a poem from this anthology that you think reflects Hughes's later views of primitivism.

TWO COMPLEMENTARY CRITICAL READINGS

COUNTEE CULLEN (1903–1946)
On Racial Poetry   1926

Here is a poet with whom to reckon, to experience, and here and there, with that apologetic feeling of presumption that should companion all criticism, to quarrel.

What has always struck me most forcibly in reading Mr. Hughes' poems has been their utter spontaneity and expression of a unique personality. . . . This poet represents a transcendently emancipated spirit among a class of young writers whose particular battle-cry is freedom. With the enthusiasm of a zealot, he pursues his way, scornful, in subject matter, in photography, and rhythmical treatment, of whatever obstructions time and tradition have placed before him. To him it is essential that he be himself. Essential and commendable surely; yet the thought persists that some of these poems would have been better had Mr. Hughes held himself a bit in check. . . .

If I have the least powers of prediction, the first section of this book, *The Weary Blues,* will be most admired, even if less from intrinsic poetical worth than because of its dissociation from the traditionally poetic. Never having been one to think all subjects and forms proper for poetic consideration, I regard these jazz poems as interlopers in the company of the truly beautiful poems in other sections of the book. They move along with the frenzy and electric heat of a Methodist or Baptist revival meeting, and affect me in much the same manner. The revival meeting excites me, cooling and flushing me with alternate chills and fevers of emotion; so do these poems. But when the storm is over, I wonder if the quiet way of communing is not more spiritual for the God-seeking heart; and in the light of reflection I wonder if jazz poems really belong to that dignified company, that select and austere circle of high literary expression which we call poetry. . . .

Taken as a group the selections in this book seem one-sided to me. They tend to hurl this poet into the gaping pit that lies before all Negro writers, in the confines of which they become racial artists instead of artists pure and simple. There is too much emphasis here on strictly Negro themes; and this is probably an added reason for my coldness toward the jazz poems — they seem to set a too definite limit upon an already limited field.

From *Opportunity: A Journal of Negro Life*

Considerations for Critical Thinking and Writing

1. In Cullen's review of *The Weary Blues,* what is his "quarrel" with Hughes?
2. Given the tenor of Hughes's comments on racial pride in the excerpt from "The Negro Artist and the Racial Mountain" (p. 361), what do you think his response to Cullen would be?
3. Explain why you agree or disagree with Cullen's view that Hughes's poems are "one-sided."
4. Do you think his argument is dated, or is it relevant to today's social climate?

ONWUCHEKWA JEMIE (b. 1940)
On Universal Poetry   1976

Hughes entertained no doubts as to the sufficiency and greatness of the molds provided by black music, nor of black life as subject matter. On the question of whether such black matter and manner could attain "universality," Hughes in his Spingarn Speech issued a definitive answer:

> There is so much richness in Negro humor, so much beauty in black dreams, so much dignity in our struggle, and so much universality in our problems, in us — in each living human being of color — that I do not understand the tendency today that some American Negro artists have of seeking to run away from themselves, of running away from us, of being afraid to sing our own songs, paint our own pictures, write about ourselves — when it is our music that has given America its greatest music, our humor that has enriched its entertainment media, our rhythm that has guided its dancing feet from plantation days to the Charleston, the Lindy Hop, and currently the Madison. . . .
>
> Could you possibly be afraid that the rest of the world will not accept it?

Our spirituals are sung and loved in the great concert halls of the whole world. Our blues are played from Topeka to Tokyo. Harlem's jive talk delights Hong Kong. Those of our writers who have concerned themselves with our very special problems are translated and read around the world. The local, the regional can — and does — become universal. Sean O'Casey's Irishmen are an example. So I would say to young Negro writers, do not be afraid of yourselves. You are the world.[1]

Hughes's confidence in blackness is a major part of his legacy, for the questions he had to answer have had to be answered over again by subsequent generations of black artists. Black culture is still embattled; and Hughes provides a model for answering the questions and making the choices. Whether they say so or not, those who, like Cullen, . . . plead the need to be "universal" as an excuse for avoiding racial material, or for treating such material from perspectives rooted in alien sensibilities, invariably equate "white" or "Western" with "universal," and "black" or "non-Western" with its opposite, forgetting that the truly universal — that is, the foundation elements of human experience, the circumstances attending birth, growth, decline, and death, the emotions of joy and grief, love and hate, fear and guilt, anger and pain — are common to all humanity. The multiplicity of nations and cultures in the world makes it inevitable that the details and particulars of human experience will vary according to time, place, and circumstance, and it follows that the majority of writers will dramatize and interpret human life according to the usages of their particular nation and epoch. Indeed, the question whether a writer's work is universal or not rarely arises when that writer is European or white American. It arises so frequently in discussions of black writers for no other reason than that the long-standing myth of white superiority and black inferiority has led so many to believe that in literature, and in other areas of life as well, the black particular of universal human experience is less appropriate than the white particular.

From *Langston Hughes: An Introduction to Poetry*

Considerations for Critical Thinking and Writing

1. How does Jemie go beyond Hughes's own argument to make a case for the universality of poetry about black experience?
2. How might Jemie's argument be extended to other minority groups or to women?
3. Do you think that Jemie's or Cullen's argument is more persuasive? Explain.

[1]See Hughes, Letter to the Editor, *The Crisis,* 35:9 (September 1928), 302.

12. Critical Case Study: T. S. Eliot's "The Love Song of J. Alfred Prufrock"

This chapter provides several critical approaches to a challenging but highly rewarding poem by T. S. Eliot. After studying this poem, you're likely to find yourself quoting bits of its striking imagery. At the very least, you'll recognize the lines when you hear other people fold them into their own conversations. There have been numerous critical approaches to this poem because it raises so many issues relating to matters such as history and biography as well as imagery, symbolism, irony, and myth. The following critical excerpts offer a small and partial sample of the possible formalist, biographical, historical, mythological, psychological, sociological, and other perspectives that have attempted to shed light on the poem (see Chapter 15, "Critical Strategies for Reading," for a discussion of a variety of critical methods). They should help you to enjoy the poem more by raising questions, providing insights, and inviting you further into the text.

T. S. ELIOT (1888–1965)

Born into a prominent New England family that had moved to St. Louis, Missouri, Thomas Stearns Eliot was a major in English literature between the two world wars. He studied literature and philosophy at Harvard and on the Continent, subsequently choosing to live in England for most of his life and becoming a citizen of that country in 1927. His allusive and challenging poetry had a powerful influence on other writers, particularly his treatment of postwar life in *The Waste Land* (1922) and his exploration of religious questions in *The Four Quartets* (1943). In addition, he wrote plays, including *Murder in the Cathedral* (1935) and *The Cocktail Party* (1950). He was awarded the Nobel Prize for literature in 1948. In "The Love Song of J. Alfred Prufrock," Eliot presents a comic but serious figure who expresses through a series of fragmented images the futility, boredom, and meaninglessness associated with much of modern life.

The Love Song of J. Alfred Prufrock   1917

S'io credesse che mia risposta fosse
A persona che mai tornasse al mondo,
Questa fiamma staria senza più scosse.
Ma perciocchè giammai di questo fondo
Non tornò vivo alcun, s'i'odo il vero,
Senza tema d'infamia ti rispondo.°

Let us go then, you and I,
When the evening is spread out against the sky
Like a patient etherized upon a table;
Let us go, through certain half-deserted streets,
The muttering retreats   5
Of restless nights in one-night cheap hotels
And sawdust restaurants with oyster-shells:
Streets that follow like a tedious argument
Of insidious intent
To lead you to an overwhelming question . . .   10

Oh, do not ask, "What is it?"
Let us go and make our visit.

In the room the women come and go
Talking of Michelangelo.

The yellow fog that rubs its back upon the window panes, 15
The yellow smoke that rubs its muzzle on the window panes
Licked its tongue into the corners of the evening,
Lingered upon the pools that stand in drains,
Let fall upon its back the soot that falls from chimneys,
Slipped by the terrace, made a sudden leap,   20
And seeing that it was a soft October night,
Curled once about the house, and fell asleep.

And indeed there will be time°
For the yellow smoke that slides along the street,
Rubbing its back upon the window panes;   25
There will be time, there will be time·
To prepare a face to meet the faces that you meet;
There will be time to murder and create,
And time for all the works and days° of hands
That lift and drop a question on your plate: 30
Time for you and time for me,

Epigraph: *S'io credesse . . . rispondo:* Dante's *Inferno*, XXVII, 58–63. In the Eighth Chasm of the Inferno, Dante and Virgil meet Guido da Montefeltro, one of the False Counselors, who is punished by being enveloped in an eternal flame. When Dante asks Guido to tell his life story, the spirit replies: "If I thought that my answer were to one who might ever return to the world, this flame would shake no more; but since from this depth none ever returned alive, if what I hear is true, I answer you without fear of infamy." 23 *there will be time:* An allusion to Ecclesiastes 3:1–8: "To everything there is a season, and a time to every purpose under heaven. . . ." 29 *works and days:* Hesiod's eighth century B.C. poem *Works and Days* gave practical advice on how to conduct one's life in accordance with the seasons.

And time yet for a hundred indecisions,
And for a hundred visions and revisions,
Before the taking of a toast and tea.

In the room the women come and go   35
Talking of Michelangelo.

   And indeed there will be time
To wonder, "Do I dare?" and, "Do I dare?" —
Time to turn back and descend the stair,
With a bald spot in the middle of my hair —   40
(They will say: "How his hair is growing thin!")
My morning coat, my collar mounting firmly to the chin,
My necktie rich and modest, but asserted by a simple pin —
(They will say: "But how his arms and legs are thin!")
Do I dare   45
Disturb the universe?
In a minute there is time
For decisions and revisions which a minute will reverse.

   For I have known them all already, known them all:
Have known the evenings, mornings, afternoons,   50
I have measured out my life with coffee spoons;
I know the voices dying with a dying fall
Beneath the music from a farther room.
   So how should I presume?

   And I have known the eyes already, known them all —   55
The eyes that fix you in a formulated phrase.
And when I am formulated, sprawling on a pin,
When I am pinned and wriggling on the wall,
Then how should I begin
To spit out all the butt-ends of my days and ways?   60
   And how should I presume?

   And I have known the arms already, known them all —
Arms that are braceleted and white and bare
(But in the lamplight, downed with light brown hair!)
   Is it perfume from a dress   65
   That makes me so digress?
Arms that lie along a table, or wrap about a shawl.
   And should I then presume?
   And how should I begin?

                    . . . . .

   Shall I say, I have gone at dusk through narrow streets,   70
And watched the smoke that rises from the pipes
Of lonely men in shirtsleeves, leaning out of windows? . . .

I should have been a pair of ragged claws
Scuttling across the floors of silent seas.

                    . . . . .

   And the afternoon, the evening, sleeps so peacefully!   75
Smoothed by long fingers,
Asleep . . . tired . . . or it malingers,

Stretched on the floor, here beside you and me.
Should I, after tea and cakes and ices,
Have the strength to force the moment to its crisis? 80
But though I have wept and fasted, wept and prayed,
Though I have seen my head (grown slightly bald) brought in upon a platter,°
I am no prophet — and here's no great matter;
I have seen the moment of my greatness flicker,
And I have seen the eternal Footman hold my coat, and snicker, 85
    And in short, I was afraid.

  And would it have been worth it, after all,
After the cups, the marmalade, the tea,
Among the porcelain, among some talk of you and me,
Would it have been worth while 90
To have bitten off the matter with a smile,
To have squeezed the universe into a ball°
To roll it toward some overwhelming question,
To say: "I am Lazarus,° come from the dead,
Come back to tell you all, I shall tell you all" — 95
If one, settling a pillow by her head,
    Should say: "That is not what I meant at all;
      That is not it, at all."

  And would it have been worth it, after all,
Would it have been worth while, 100
After the sunsets and the dooryards and the sprinkled streets,
After the novels, after the teacups, after the skirts that trail along the floor —
And this, and so much more? —
It is impossible to say just what I mean!
But as if a magic lantern threw the nerves in patterns on a screen: 105
Would it have been worth while
If one, settling a pillow or throwing off a shawl,
And turning toward the window, should say:
    "That is not it at all,
    That is not what I meant, at all." 110

     . . . . .

No! I am not Prince Hamlet, nor was meant to be;
Am an attendant lord,° one that will do
To swell a progress,° start a scene or two   *state procession*
Advise the prince: withal, an easy tool,
Deferential, glad to be of use, 115
Politic, cautious, and meticulous;
Full of high sentence, but a bit obtuse;
At times, indeed, almost ridiculous —
Almost, at times, the Fool.

---

82 *head . . . upon a platter:* At Salome's request, Herod had John the Baptist decapitated and had the severed head delivered to her on a platter (see Matt. 14:1–12 and Mark 6:17–29).   92 *squeezed the universe into a ball:* See Marvell's "To His Coy Mistress" (p. 57), lines 41–42: "Let us roll all our strength and all / Our sweetness up into one ball."   94 *Lazarus:* The brother of Mary and Martha who was raised from the dead by Jesus (John 11:1–44). In Luke 16:19–31, a rich man asks that another Lazarus return from the dead to warn the living about their treatment of the poor 112 *attendant lord:* Like Polonius in Shakespeare's *Hamlet.*

I grow old . . . I grow old . . .   120
I shall wear the bottoms of my trowsers rolled.

   Shall I part my hair behind? Do I dare to eat a peach?
I shall wear white flannel trowsers, and walk upon the beach.
I have heard the mermaids singing, each to each.

I do not think that they will sing to me.   125

I have seen them riding seaward on the waves,
Combing the white hair of the waves blown back
When the wind blows the water white and black.

We have lingered in the chambers of the sea
By seagirls wreathed with seaweed red and brown,   130
Till human voices wake us, and we drown.

Considerations for Critical Thinking and Writing

1. What does J. Alfred Prufrock's name connote? How would you characterize him?
2. What do you think is the purpose of the epigraph from Dante's *Inferno?*
3. What is it that Prufrock wants to do? How does he behave? What does he think of himself? Which parts of the poem answer these questions?
4. Who is the "you" of line 1 and the "we" in the final lines?
5. Discuss the imagery in the poem. How does the imagery reveal Prufrock's character? Which images seem especially striking to you?

Connections to Other Selections

1. Write an essay comparing Prufrock's sense of himself as an individual with that of Walt Whitman's speaker in "One's-Self I Sing" (p. 463).
2. Discuss in an essay the tone of "The Love Song of J. Alfred Prufrock" and Frost's "Acquainted with the Night" (p. 129).

ELISABETH SCHNEIDER (1897–1984)

Schneider uses a biographical approach to the poem to suggest that part of what went into the characterization of Prufrock were some of Eliot's own sensibilities.

Hints of Eliot in Prufrock   1952

   Perhaps never again did Eliot find an epigraph quite so happily suited to his use as the passage from the *Inferno* which sets the underlying serious tone for *Prufrock* and conveys more than one level of its meaning: "S'io credesse che mia risposta . . . ," lines in which Guido da Montefeltro consents to tell his story to Dante only because he believes that none ever returns to the world of the living from his depth. One in Hell can bear to expose his shame only to another of the damned; Prufrock speaks to, will be understood only by, other Prufrocks (the "you and I" of the opening, perhaps), and, I imagine the epigraph also hints, Eliot himself is speaking to those who know this kind of hell. The poem, I need hardly say, is not in a literal sense autobiographical: for one thing, though it is clear that Prufrock will never marry, the poem was published in the year of Eliot's own first marriage. Nevertheless, friends who knew the young Eliot almost all describe him, retrospectively but convincingly, in Prufrockian terms; and Eliot himself once said of dramatic monologue in general that what we normally hear in it "is the voice of the poet, who has put on the costume and make-up either of some historical character, or of one out of fiction." . . . I suppose it to be one of the many indirect clues to his own poetry planted with evident deliberation throughout his prose. "What every poet starts from," he also once said, "is his own emotions," and, writing of Dante, he asserted that the *Vita nuova* "could only have been written around a personal experience," a statement that, under the circumstances, must be equally applicable to Prufrock; Prufrock was Eliot, though Eliot was much more than Prufrock. We miss the whole tone of the poem, however, if we read it as social satire only. Eliot was not either the dedicated apostle in theory, or the great exemplar in practice, of complete "depersonalization" in poetry that one influential early essay of his for a time led readers to suppose.

From "Prufrock and After: The Theme of Change," *PMLA,* October 1952

Considerations for Critical Thinking and Writing

1. Though Schneider concedes that the poem is not literally autobiographical, she does assert that "Prufrock was Eliot." How does she argue this point? Explain why you find her argument convincing or unconvincing.

2. Find information in the library about Eliot's early career when he was writing this poem. To what extent does the poem reveal his circumstances and concerns at that point in his life?

BARBARA EVERETT

Everett's discussion of tone is used to make a distinction between Eliot and his characterization of Prufrock.

The Problem of Tone in Prufrock   1974

Eliot's poetry presents a peculiar problem as far as tone is concerned. *Tone* really means the way the attitude of a speaker is manifested by the inflections of his speaking voice. Many critics have already recognized that for a mixture of reasons it is difficult, sometimes almost impossible, to ascertain Eliot's tone in this way. It is not that the poetry lacks "voice," for in fact Eliot has an extraordinarily recognizable poetic voice, often imitated and justifying his own comment in the . . . *Paris Review* that "in a poem you're writing for your own voice, which is very important. You're thinking in terms of your own voice." It is this authoritative, idiosyncratic, and exact voice that holds our complete attention in poem after poem, however uninterested we are in what opinions it may seem or happen to be expressing. But Eliot too seems uninterested in what opinions it may happen to be expressing, for he invariably dissociates himself from his poems before they are even finished — before they are hardly begun — by balancing a derisory name or title against an "I," by reminding us that there is always going to be a moment at which detachment will take place or has taken place, a retrospective angle from which, far in the future, critical judgment alters the scene, and the speaking voice of the past has fallen silent. "I have known them all already, known them all." Thus whatever started to take place in the beginning of a poem by Eliot cannot truly be said to be Eliot's opinion because at some extremely early stage he began that process of dissociation to be loosely called "dramatization," a process reflected in the peculiar distances of the tone, as though everything spoken was in inverted commas.

From "In Search of Prufrock," *Critical Quarterly*, Summer 1974

Considerations for Critical Thinking and Writing

1. According to Everett, why is it difficult to describe Eliot's tone in his poetry?
2. How does Eliot's tone make it difficult to make an autobiographical connection between Prufrock and Eliot?
3. How does Everett's reading of the relationship between Prufrock and Eliot differ from Schneider's in the preceding perspective?

MICHAEL L. BAUMANN (b. 1926)

Baumann takes a close look at the poem's images in his formalist efforts to make a point about Prufrock's character.

The "Overwhelming Question" for Prufrock   1981

Most critics . . . have seen the overwhelming question related to sex. . . . They have implicitly assumed — and given their readers to understand — that Prufrock's is the male's basic question: Can I?

Delmore Schwartz once said that "J. Alfred Prufrock is unable to make love to women of his own class and kind because of shyness, self-consciousness, and fear of rejection."[1] This is undoubtedly true, but Prufrock's inability to *feel* love has something to do with his inability to *make* love, too. . . . A simple desire, lust, is more than honest Prufrock can cope with as he mounts the stairs.

But Prufrock is coping with another, less simple desire as well. . . . If birth, copulation, and death is all there is, then, once we are born, once we have copulated, only death remains (for the male of the species, at least). Prufrock, having "known them all already, known them all," having "known the evenings, mornings, afternoons," having "measured out" his life "with coffee spoons," desires death. The "overwhelming question" that assails him would no longer

---

[1] "T. S. Eliot as the International Hero," *Partisan Review*, 12 (1945), 202; rpt in *T. S. Eliot: A Selected Critique*, ed. Leonard Unger (New York: Rinehart & Company, Inc., 1948), 46.

be the romantic rhetorical "Is life worth living?" (to which the answer is obviously No), but the more immediate shocker: "Should one commit suicide?" which is to say: "Should I?" . . .

. . . The poem makes clear that Prufrock wants more than the "entire destruction of consciousness as we understand it," a notion Prufrock expresses by wishing he were "a pair of ragged claws, / Scuttling across the floors of silent seas." Prufrock wants death itself, physical death, and the poem, I believe, is explicit about this desire.

Not only does Prufrock seem to be tired of time — "time yet for a hundred indecisions" — a tiredness that goes far beyond the acedia Prufrock is generally credited with feeling, if only because "there will be time to murder and create," time, in other words (in one sense at least) to copulate, but Prufrock is also tired of his own endless vanities, from feeling he must "prepare a face to meet the faces that you meet," to having to summon up those ironies with which to contemplate his own thin arms and legs, and, indeed, to asking if, in the rather tedious enterprise of preparing for copulation, the moment is worth "forcing to its crisis." No wonder Prufrock compares himself to John the Baptist and, in conjuring up this first concrete image of his own death, sees his head brought in upon a platter. That would be the easy way out. He had, after all, "wept and fasted, wept and prayed," but he realizes he is no prophet — and no Salome will burst into passion, will ignite for him. When the eternal Footman, Death, who holds his coat, snickers, he does so because Prufrock has let "the moment" of his "greatness" flicker, because Prufrock was unable to comply with the one imperative greatness would have thrust upon him: to kill himself. Prufrock explains: "I was afraid." Yet the achievement of his vision at the end of the poem, his being able to linger "in the chambers of the sea / By sea-girls wreathed with seaweed red and brown," is an act of the imagination that only physical death can complete, unless Prufrock wants human voices to wake him, and drown him. His romantic vision demands the voluntary act: suicide. It is to be expected that he will fail in this too, as he has failed in everything else.

From "Let Us Ask 'What Is It,'" Arizona Quarterly, Spring 1981

Considerations for Critical Thinking and Writing

1. Describe the evidence used by Baumann to argue that Prufrock contemplates suicide.
2. Explain in an essay why you do or do not find Baumann's argument convincing.
3. Later in his essay Baumann connects Prufrock's insistence that "No, I am not Prince Hamlet" with Hamlet's "To be or not to be" speech. How do you think this reference might be used to support Baumann's argument?

FREDERIK L. RUSCH (b. 1938)

Rusch makes use of the insights developed by Erich Fromm, a social psychologist who believed "psychic forces [are] a process of constant interaction between man's needs and the social and historical reality in which he participates."

Society and Character in
"The Love Song of J. Alfred Prufrock"

1984

In looking at fiction, drama, and poetry from the Frommian point of view, the critic understands literature to be social portrayal as well as character portrayal or personal statement. Society and character are inextricably joined. The Frommian approach opens up the study of literary work, giving a social context to its characters, which suggests why those characters behave as they do. The Frommian approach recognizes human beings for what they are — basically gregarious individuals who are interdependent upon each other, in need of each other, and thus, to a certain degree, products of their social environments, although those environments may be inimical to their mental well-being. That is, as stated earlier, the individual's needs and drives have a social component and are not purely biological. The Frommian approach to literature assumes that a writer is — at least by implication — analyzing society and its setting as well as character. . . .

In T. S. Eliot's "The Love Song of J. Alfred Prufrock," Prufrock is talking to himself, expressing a fantasy or daydream. In his monologue, Prufrock, as noted by Grover Smith, "is addressing, as if looking into a mirror, his whole public personality."[1] Throughout the poem, Prufrock is extremely self-conscious, believing that the people in his imaginary drawing room will examine him as a specimen insect, "sprawling on a pin, / . . . pinned and wriggling on the wall. . . ." Of course, self-consciousness — being conscious of one's self — is not necessarily neurotic. Indeed, it is part of being a human being. It is only when self-consciousness, which has always led man to feel a separation from nature, becomes obsessive that we have a problem. Prufrock is certainly obsessed with his self-consciousness, convinced that everyone notices his balding head, his clothes (his prudent frocks), his thin arms and legs.

On one level, however, Prufrock is merely expressing the pain that all human beings must feel. Although his problem is extreme, he is quite representative of the human race:

> Self-awareness, reason, and imagination have disrupted the "harmony" that characterizes animal existence. Their emergence has made man into an anomaly, the freak of the universe. He is part of nature, subject to her physical laws and unable to change them, yet he transcends nature. He is set apart while being a part; he is homeless, yet chained to the home he shares with all creatures. . . . Being aware of himself, he realizes his powerlessness and the limitations of his existence. He is never free from the dichotomy of his existence: he cannot rid himself of his mind, even if he would want to; he cannot rid himself of his body as long as he is alive — and his body makes him want to be alive.[2]

This is the predicament of the human being. His self-awareness has made him feel separate from nature. This causes pain and sorrow. What, then, is the solution to the predicament? Fromm believed that mankind filled the void of alienation from nature with the creation of a culture, a society: "Man's existential, and hence unavoidable disequilibrium can be relatively stable when he has found, with the support of his culture, a more or less adequate way of coping

[1] Grover Smith, *T. S. Eliot's Poetry and Plays: A Study in Sources and Meaning* (Chicago: U of Chicago P, 1962), 16.

[2] Erich Fromm, *The Anatomy of Human Destructiveness* (New York: Holt, Rinehart & Winston, 1973), 225.

with his existential problems" (*Destructiveness* 225). But, unfortunately for Prufrock, his culture and society do not allow him to overcome his existential predicament. The fact is, he is bored by his modern, urban society.

In image after image, Prufrock's mind projects boredom:

> For I have known them all already, known them all:
> Have known the evenings, mornings, afternoons,
> I have measured out my life with coffee spoons. . . .
> . . . .
>
> And I have known the eyes already, known them all —
> . . . .
>
> Then how should I begin
> To spit out all the butt-ends of my days and ways?
> . . . .
>
> And I have known the arms already, known them all — . . . .

Prufrock is completely unstimulated by his social environment, to the point of near death. The evening in which he proposes to himself to make a social visit is "etherized upon a table." The fog, as a cat, falls asleep; it is "tired . . . or it malingers, / Stretched on the floor. . . ."

Prufrock, living in a city of "half-deserted streets, / . . . one-night cheap hotels/ And sawdust restaurants with oyster-shells," gets no comfort, no nurturing from his environment. He is, in the words of Erich Fromm, a "modern mass man . . . isolated and lonely" (*Destructiveness* 107). He lives in a destructive environment. Instead of providing communion with fellow human beings, it alienates him through boredom. Such boredom leads to "a state of chronic depression" that can cause the pathology of "insufficient inner productivity" in the individual (*Destructiveness* 243). Such a lack of productivity is voiced by Prufrock when he confesses that he is neither Hamlet nor John the Baptist.

An interesting tension in "The Love Song of J. Alfred Prufrock" is caused by the reader's knowledge that Prufrock understands his own predicament quite well. Although he calls himself a fool, he has wisdom about himself and his predicament. This, however, only reinforces his depression and frustration. In his daydream, he is able to reveal truths about himself that, while they lead to self-understanding, apparently cannot alleviate his problems in his waking life. The poem suggests no positive movement out of the predicament. Prufrock is like a patient cited by Fromm, who under hypnosis envisioned "a black barren place with many masks," and when asked what the vision meant said "that everything was dull, dull, dull; that the masks represent the different roles he takes to fool people into thinking he is feeling well" (*Destructiveness* 246). Likewise, Prufrock understands that "There will be time, there will be time / To prepare a face to meet the faces that you meet. . . ." But despite his understanding of the nature of his existence, he cannot attain a more productive life.

It was Fromm's belief that with boredom "the decisive conditions are to be found in the overall environmental situation. . . . It is highly probable that even cases of severe depression-boredom would be less frequent and less intense . . . in a society where a mood of hope and love of life predominated. But in recent decades the opposite is increasingly the case, and thus a fertile soil for the development of individual depressive states is provided" (*Destructiveness* 251). There is no "mood of hope and love of life" in Prufrock's society. Prufrock is a lonely man, as lonely as "the lonely men in shirt-sleeves, leaning out of windows" of his fantasy. His only solution is to return to the animal state that his race was in before evolving into human beings.

Animals are one with nature, not alienated from their environments. They *are* nature, unselfconscious. Prufrock would return to a preconscious existence in the extreme: "I should have been a pair of ragged claws / Scuttling across the floors of silent seas." Claws *without a head* surely would not be alienated, bored, or depressed. They would seek and would need no psychological nurturing from their environment. And in the end Prufrock's fantasy of becoming claws is definitely more positive for him than his life as a human being. He completes his monologue with depressing irony, to say the least: it is with human voices waking us, bringing us back to human society, that we drown.

From "Approaching Literature through the Social Psychology of Erich Fromm,"
in *Psychological Perspectives on Literature: Freudian Dissidents
and Non-Freudians,* edited by Joseph Natoli

Considerations for Critical Thinking and Writing

1. According to Rusch, why is Fromm's approach useful for understanding Prufrock's character as well as his social context?
2. In what ways is Prufrock "representative of the human race"? Is he like any other characters you have read about in this anthology? Explain your response.
3. In an essay consider how Rusch's analysis of Prufrock might be used to support Baumann's argument that Prufrock's "overwhelming question" is whether or not he should kill himself (p. 376).

ROBERT SWARD (b. 1933)

Sward, a poet, provides a detailed explication, framed by his own personal experiences during the war in Korea.

A Personal Analysis of "The Love Song of J. Alfred Prufrock"   1996

In 1952, sailing to Korea as a U.S. Navy librarian for Landing Ship Tank 914, I read T. S. Eliot's *The Love Song of J. Alfred Prufrock*. Ill-educated, a product of Chicago's public-school system, I was nineteen-years-old and, awakened by Whitman, Eliot, and Williams, had just begun writing poetry. I was also reading all the books I could get my hands on.

Eliot had won the Nobel Prize in 1948 and, curious, I was trying to make sense of poems like *Prufrock* and *The Waste Land*.

"What do you know about T. S. Eliot?" I asked a young officer who'd been to college and studied English literature. I knew from earlier conversations that we shared an interest in what he called "modern poetry." A yeoman third class, two weeks at sea and bored, I longed for someone to talk to. "T. S. Eliot was born in St. Louis, Missouri, but he lives now in England and is studying to become an Englishman," the officer said, tapping tobacco into his pipe. "The 'T. S.' stands for 'tough shit.' You read Eliot's *Love Song of J. Alfred Prufrock*, what one English prof called 'the first poem of the modern movement,' and if you don't understand it, 'tough shit.' All I can say is that's some love song."

An anthology of poetry open before us, we were sitting in the ship's all-metal, eight by eight-foot library eating bologna sandwiches and drinking coffee. Fortunately, the captain kept out of sight and life on the slow-moving (eight to ten knots), flat-bottomed amphibious ship was unhurried and anything but formal.

"Then why does Eliot bother calling it a love song?" I asked, as the ship rolled and the coffee sloshed onto a steel table. The tight metal room smelled like a cross between a diesel engine and a New York deli.

"Eliot's being ironic, sailor. *Prufrock* is the love song of a sexually repressed and horny man who has no one but himself to sing to." Drawing on his pipe, the officer scratched his head. "Like you and I, Mr. Prufrock is a lonely man on his way to a war zone. We're sailing to Korea and we know the truth, don't we? We may never make it back. Prufrock marches like a brave soldier to a British drawing room that, he tells us, may be the death of him. He's a mock heroic figure who sings of mermaids and peaches and drowning."

Pointing to lines 129–31, the officer read aloud:

We have lingered in the chambers of the sea
By sea-girls wreathed with seaweed red and brown
Till human voices wake us and we drown.

"Prufrock is also singing because he's a poet. Prufrock *is* T. S. Eliot and, the truth is, Eliot is so much like Prufrock that he has to distance himself from his creation. That's why he gives the man that pompous name. Did you know 'Tough Shit,' as a young man, sometimes signed himself 'T. Stearns Eliot?' You have to see the humor — the irony — in *Prufrock* to understand the poem."

"I read it, I hear it in my head, but I still don't get it," I confessed. "What is *Prufrock* about?"

" 'Birth, death and copulation, that's all there is.' That's what Eliot himself says. Of course the poem also touches on aging, social status, and fashion."

"Aging and fashion?" I asked.

The officer threw back his head and recited:

(They will say: "How his hair is growing thin!")
My morning coat, my collar mounting firmly to the chin,
My necktie rich and modest, but asserted by a simple pin.

He paused, then went on:

I grow old . . . I grow old . . .
I shall wear the bottoms of my trousers rolled.

"At the time the poem was written it was fashionable for young men to roll their trousers. In lines 120–21, Thomas Stearns Prufrock is laughing at himself for being middle-aged and vain.

"Anyway, *The Love Song of J. Alfred Prufrock* is an interior monologue," said the officer, finishing his bologna sandwich and washing it down with dark rum. Wiping mustard from his mouth, he continued. "The whole thing takes place in J. Alfred Prufrock's head. That's clear, isn't it?"

I had read Browning's *My Last Duchess* and understood about interior monologues.

"Listen, sailor: Prufrock thinks about drawing rooms, but he never actually sets foot in one. Am I right?"

"Yeah," I said after rereading the first ten lines. "I think so."

"The poem is about what goes through Prufrock's mind on his way to some upper-class drawing room. It's a foggy evening in October, and what Mr. Prufrock really needs is a drink. He's a tightass Victorian, a lonely teetotaling intellectual. Anyone else would forget the toast and marmalade and step into a pub and ask for a pint of beer."

Setting down his pipe, the naval officer opened the flask and refilled our coffee mugs.

"Every time I think I know what *Prufrock* means it turns out to mean something else," I said. "Eliot uses too many symbols. Why doesn't he just say what he means?"

"The city — 'the lonely men in shirt-sleeves' and the 'one-night cheap hotels' — are masculine," said the officer. "That's what cities are like, aren't they: ugly and oppressive. What's symbolic — or should I say, what's obscure — about that?"

"Nothing," I said. "That's the easy part — Prufrock walking along like that."

"Okay," said the officer. "And in contrast to city streets, you've got the oppressive drawing room that, in Prufrock's mind, is feminine — 'Arms that are braceleted and white and bare' and 'the marmalade, the tea, / Among the porcelain, among some talk of you and me.'" Using a pencil, the officer underlined those images in the paperback anthology.

"You ever been to a tea party, Sward?"

"No, sir, I haven't. Not like Prufrock's."

"Well," said the officer, "I have and I have a theory about that 'overwhelming question' Prufrock wants to ask in line 10 — and again in line 93. Twice in the poem we hear about an 'overwhelming question.' sailor?"

"Prufrock wants to ask the women what they're doing with their lives, but he's afraid they'll laugh at him," I said.

"Guess again, Sward," he said leaning back in his chair, stretching his arms.

"What's your theory, sir?"

"Sex," said the officer. "On the one hand, it's true, he wants to fit in and play the game because, after all, he's privileged. He belongs in the drawing room with the clever Englishwomen. At the same time he fantasizes. If he could, I think he'd like to shock them. Prufrock longs to put down his dainty porcelain teacup and shout, 'I am Lazarus, come from the dead, / Come back to tell you all, I shall tell you all.'"

"Why doesn't he do it?" I asked.

"Because Prufrock is convinced no matter what he says he won't reach them. He feels the English gentlewomen he's dealing with are unreachable. He believes his situation is as hopeless as theirs. He's dead and they're dead, too. That's why the poem begins with an image of sickness, 'a patient etherized upon a table,' and ends with people drowning. Prufrock is tough shit, man."

"You said you think there's a connection between Eliot the poet and J. Alfred Prufrock," I said.

"Of course there's a connection. Tommy Eliot from St. Louis, Missouri," said the officer. "Try as he will, he doesn't fit in. His English friends call him 'The American' and laugh. Tom Eliot the outsider with his rolled umbrella. T. S. Eliot is a self-conscious, make-believe Englishman and you have to understand that to understand *Prufrock*.

"The poem is dark and funny at the same time. It's filled with humor and Prufrock is capable of laughing at himself. Just read those lines, 'Is it perfume from a dress / That makes me so digress?' "

"You were talking about Prufrock being sexually attracted to the women. How could that be if he is, as you say, 'dead.' " I asked.

"By 'dead' I mean desolate, inwardly barren, godforsaken. Inwardly, spiritually, Prufrock is a desolate creature. He's a moral man, he's a civilized man, but he's also hollow. But there's hope for him. In spite of himself, Prufrock is drawn to women.

"Look at line 64. He's attracted and repelled. Prufrock attends these teas, notices the women's arms 'downed with light brown hair!' and it scares the hell out of him because what he longs to do is to get them onto a drawing-room floor or a beach somewhere and bury his face in that same wonderfully tantalizing 'light brown hair.' What do you think of that, sailor?"

"I think you're right, sir."

"Then tell me this, Mr. Sward: Why doesn't he ask the overwhelming question? Hell, man, maybe it's not sexual. Maybe I'm wrong. Maybe what he wants to do is to ask some question like what you yourself suggested: 'What's the point in going on living when, in some sense, we're all already dead?' "

"I think he doesn't ask the question because he's so repressed, sir. He longs for physical contact, like you say, but he also wants another kind of intimacy, and he's afraid to ask for it and it's making him crazy."

"That's right, sailor. He's afraid. Eliot wrote the poem in 1911 when women were beginning to break free."

"Break free of what?" I asked.

"Of the prim and proper Victorian ideal. Suffragettes, feminists they called themselves. At the time Eliot wrote *Prufrock,* women in England and America were catching on to the fact that they were disfranchised and had begun fighting for the right to vote, among other things, and for liberation, equality with men.

"Of course Prufrock is more prim and proper than the bored, overcivilized women in the poem. And it's ironic, isn't it, that he doesn't understand that the women are one step ahead of him. What you have in Prufrock is a man who tries to reconcile the image of real women with 'light brown hair' on their arms with some ideal, women who are a cross between the goddess Juno and a sweet Victorian maiden."

"Prufrock seems to know pretty well what he's feeling," I said. "He's not a liar and he's not a coward. To be honest, sir, I identify with Prufrock. He may try on one mask or another, but he ends up removing the mask and exposing himself."

"Now, about interior monologues: to understand *Prufrock* you have to understand that most poems have one or more speakers and an audience, implied or otherwise. Let's go back to line 1. Who is this "you and I" Eliot writes about?"

"Prufrock is talking to both his inner self and the reader," I said.

"How do you interpret the first ten lines?" the officer asked, pointing with his pencil.

" 'Let us go then, you and I,' he's saying, let us stroll, somnolent and numb as a sedated patient, through these seedy 'half-deserted streets, / The muttering retreats / Of restless nights in one-night cheap hotels.' "

"That's it, sailor. And while one might argue that Prufrock 'wakes' at the end of the poem, he is for the most part a ghostly inhabitant of a world that is, for him, a sort of hell. He is like the speaker in the Italian epigraph from Dante's *Inferno,* who says, essentially, 'Like you, reader, I'm in purgatory and there is no way out. Nobody ever escapes from this pit and, for that reason, I can speak the truth without fear of ill fame.'

"Despairing and sick of heart, Prufrock is a prisoner. Trapped in himself and trapped in society, he attends another and another in an endless series of effete, decorous teas.

> In the room the women come and go
> Talking of Michelangelo.

"Do you get it now? Do you see what I mean when I say 'tough shit'?" said the officer.

"Yeah, I'm beginning to," I said.

"T. S. Eliot's *Prufrock* has become so much a part of the English language that people who have never read the poem are familiar with phrases like "I have measured out my life with coffee spoons' and 'I grow old . . . I grow old . . . / I shall wear the bottoms of my trousers rolled' and 'Do I dare to eat a peach?' and 'In the room the women come and go.'

"Do you get it now? Eliot's irregularly rhymed, 131-line interior monologue has become part of the monologue all of us carry on in our heads. We are all of us, whether we know it or not, love-hungry, sex-crazed soldiers and sailors, brave, bored and lonely. At some level in our hearts, we are all J. Alfred Prufrock, every one of us, and we are all sailing into a war zone from which, as the last line of the poem implies, we may never return."

From "T. S. Eliot's 'Love Song of J. Alfred Prufrock' " in *Touchstones: American Poets on a Favorite Poem,* edited by Robert Pack and Jay Parini

Considerations for Critical Thinking and Writing

1. How satisfactory is this reading of the poem? Are any significant portions of the poem left out of this reading?

2. Compare the tone of this critical approach to any other in this chapter. Explain why you prefer one over another.

3. Using Sward's personal approach, write an analysis of a poem of your choice in this anthology.

13. A Collection of Poems

MAYA ANGELOU (b. 1924)

Africa

Thus she had lain
sugar cane sweet
deserts her hair
golden her feet
mountains her breasts 5
two Niles her tears
Thus she has lain
Black through the years.

Over the white seas
rime white and cold 10
brigands ungentled
icicle bold
took her young daughters
sold her strong sons
churched her with Jesus 15
bled her with guns.
Thus she has lain.

Now she is rising
remember her pain
remember the losses 20
her screams loud and vain
remember her riches
her history slain
now she is striding
although she had lain. 25

ANONYMOUS (traditional Scottish ballad)
Bonny Barbara Allan

date unknown

It was in and about the Martinmas° time,
    When the green leaves were afalling,
That Sir John Graeme, in the West Country,
    Fell in love with Barbara Allan.

He sent his men down through the town,   5
    To the place where she was dwelling:
"Oh haste and come to my master dear,
    Gin° ye be Barbara Allan."   *if*

O hooly,° hooly rose she up,   *slowly*
    To the place where he was lying,   10
And when she drew the curtain by:
    "Young man, I think you're dying."

"O it's I'm sick, and very, very sick,
    And 'tis a' for Barbara Allan." —
"O the better for me ye's never be,   15
    Tho your heart's blood were aspilling."

"O dinna ye mind,° young man," she said,   *don't you remember*
    "When ye was in the tavern adrinking,
That ye made the health° gae round and round,   *toasts*
    And slighted Barbara Allan?"   20

He turned his face unto the wall,
    And death was with him dealing:
"Adieu, adieu, my dear friends all,
    And be kind to Barbara Allan."

And slowly, slowly raise her up,   25
    And slowly, slowly left him,
And sighing said she could not stay,
    Since death of life had reft him.

She had not gane a mile but twa,
    When she heard the dead-bell ringing,   30
And every jow° that the dead-bell geid,   *stroke*
    It cried, "Woe to Barbara Allan!"

"O mother, mother, make my bed!
    O make it saft and narrow!
Since my love died for me today,   35
    I'll die for him tomorrow."

---

1 *Martinmas:* St. Martin's Day, November 11.

ANONYMOUS

Lord Randal

1500s

"Oh, where have you been, Lord Randal, my son?
Oh, where have you been, my handsome young man?"
"Oh, I've been to the wildwood; mother, make my bed soon,
I'm weary of hunting and I fain° would lie down."   *gladly*

"And whom did you meet there, Lord Randal, my son?   5
And whom did you meet there, my handsome young man?"
"Oh, I met with my true love; mother, make my bed soon,
I'm weary of hunting and I fain would lie down."

"What got you for supper, Lord Randal, my son?
What got you for supper, my handsome young man?"   10
"I got eels boiled in broth; mother, make my bed soon,
I'm weary of hunting and I fain would lie down."

"And who got your leavings, Lord Randal, my son?
And who got your leavings, my handsome young man?"
"I gave them to my dogs; mother, make my bed soon,   15
I'm weary of hunting and I fain would lie down."

"And what did your dogs do, Lord Randal, my son?
And what did your dogs do, my handsome young man?"
"Oh, they stretched out and died; mother, make my bed soon,
I'm weary of hunting and I fain would lie down."   20

"Oh, I fear you are poisoned, Lord Randal, my son,
Oh, I fear you are poisoned, my handsome young man."
"Oh, yes, I am poisoned; mother, make my bed soon,
For I'm sick at my heart and I fain would lie down."

"What will you leave your mother, Lord Randal, my son?   25
What will you leave your mother, my handsome young man?"
"My house and my lands; mother, make my bed soon,
For I'm sick at my heart and I fain would lie down."

"What will you leave your sister, Lord Randal, my son?
What will you leave your sister, my handsome young man?"   30
"My gold and my silver; mother, make my bed soon,
For I'm sick at my heart and I fain would lie down."

"What will you leave your brother, Lord Randal, my son?
What will you leave your brother, my handsome young man?"
"My horse and my saddle; mother, make my bed soon,   35
For I'm sick at my heart and I fain would lie down."

"What will you leave your true-love, Lord Randal, my son?
What will you leave your true-love, my handsome young man?"
"A halter to hang her; mother, make my bed soon,
For I'm sick at my heart and I want to lie down."   40

ANONYMOUS
Frankie and Johnny   date unknown

Frankie and Johnny were lovers,
  Lordy, how they could love,
Swore to be true to each other,
  True as the stars up above,
    He was her man, but he done her wrong.   5

Frankie went down to the corner,
  To buy her a bucket of beer,
Frankie says "Mister Bartender,
  Has my lovin' Johnny been here?
    He is my man, but he's doing me wrong."   10

"I don't want to cause you no trouble
  Don't want to tell you no lie,
I saw your Johnny half-an-hour ago
  Making love to Nelly Bly.
    He is your man, but he's doing you wrong."   15

Frankie went down to the hotel
  Looked over the transom so high,
There she saw her lovin' Johnny
  Making love to Nelly Bly.
    He was her man; he was doing her wrong.   20

Frankie threw back her kimono
  Pulled out her big forty-four;
Rooty-toot-toot: three times she shot
  Right through that hotel door,
    She shot her man, who was doing her wrong.   25

"Roll me over gently,
  Roll me over slow,
Roll me over on my right side,
  'Cause these bullets hurt me so,
    I was your man, but I done you wrong."   30

Bring all your rubber-tired hearses
  Bring all your rubber-tired hacks,
They're carrying poor Johnny to the burying ground
  And they ain't gonna bring him back,
    He was her man, but he done her wrong.   35

Frankie says to the sheriff,
  "What are they going to do?"
The sheriff he said to Frankie,
  "It's the 'lectric chair for you.
    He was your man, and he done you wrong."   40

"Put me in that dungeon,
  Put me in that cell,
Put me where the northeast wind
  Blows from the southeast corner of hell,
    I shot my man, 'cause he done me wrong."   45

ANONYMOUS
Scottsboro°

Paper come out — done strewed de news
Seven po' chillun moan deat' house blues,
Seven po' chillun moanin' deat' house blues.
Seven nappy heads wit' big shiny eye
All boun' in jail and framed to die,   5
All boun' in jail and framed to die.

Messin' white woman — snake lyin' tale
Hang and burn and jail wit' no bail.
Dat hang and burn and jail wit' no bail.
Worse ol' crime in white folks' lan'   10
Black skin coverin' po' workin' man,
Black skin coverin' po' workin' man.

Judge and jury — all in de stan'
Lawd, biggety name for same lynchin' ban'
Lawd, biggety name for same lynchin' ban'.   15
White folks and nigger in great co't house
Like cat down cellar wit' nohole mouse.
Like cat down cellar wit' nohole mouse.

Scottsboro: This blues song refers to the 1931 arrest of nine black youths in Scottsboro, Alabama, who were charged with raping two white women. All nine were acquitted after several trials, but a few of them had already been sentenced to death when this song was written.

ANONYMOUS (traditional Scottish ballad)
The Twa Corbies°

As I was walking all alane,
I heard twa corbies making a mane;°   *lament*
The tane° unto the t' other say,   *one*
"Where sall we gang° and dine to-day?"   *shall we go*

"In behint yon auld fail dyke,°   *old turf wall* 5
I wot° there lies a new-slain knight;   *know*
And naebody kens that he lies there,
But his hawk, his hound, and lady fair.

"His hound is to the hunting gane,
His hawk, to fetch the wild-fowl hame,   10
His lady's ta'en another mate,
So we may mak our dinner sweet.

"Ye'll sit on his white hause-bane,°   *neck bone*
And I'll pike out his bonny blue een.°   *eyes*

The Twa Corbies: The two ravens.

Wi' ae° lock o' his gowden° hair   *with one; golden*   15
We'll theek° our nest when it grows bare.   *thatch*

"Mony a one for him makes mane,
But nane sall ken whare he is gane;
O'er his white banes, when they are bare,
The wind sall blaw for evermair."   20

JOHN ASHBERY (b. 1927)
Paradoxes and Oxymorons   1981

This poem is concerned with language on a very plain level.
Look at it talking to you. You look out a window
Or pretend to fidget. You have it but you don't have it.
You miss it, it misses you. You miss each other.

The poem is sad because it wants to be yours, and cannot.   5
What's a plain level? It is that and other things,
Bringing a system of them into play. Play?
Well, actually, yes, but I consider play to be

A deeper outside thing, a dreamed role-pattern,
As in the division of grace these long August days   10
Without proof. Open-ended. And before you know
It gets lost in the steam and chatter of typewriters.

It has been played once more. I think you exist only
To tease me into doing it, on your level, and then you aren't there
Or have adopted a different attitude. And the poem   15
Has set me softly down beside you. The poem is you.

W. H. AUDEN (1907-1973)
Musée des Beaux Arts°   1938

About suffering they were never wrong,
The Old Masters: how well they understood
Its human position; how it takes place
While someone else is eating or opening a window or just walking dully along;
How, when the aged are reverently, passionately waiting   5
For the miraculous birth, there always must be
Children who did not specially want it to happen, skating
On a pond at the edge of the wood:
They never forgot
That even the dreadful martyrdom must run its course   10
Anyhow in a corner, some untidy spot
Where the dogs go on with their doggy life and the torturer's horse
Scratches its innocent behind on a tree.

Musée des Beaux Arts: Museum of Fine Arts, in Brussels.

In Brueghel's *Icarus,*° for instance: how everything turns away
Quite leisurely from the disaster; the plowman may   15
Have heard the splash, the forsaken cry,
But for him it was not an important failure; the sun shown
As it had to on the white legs disappearing into the green
Water; and the expensive delicate ship that must have seen
Something amazing, a boy falling out of the sky,   20
Had somewhere to get to and sailed calmly on.

14 *Brueghel's* Icarus: *Landscape with the Fall of Icarus,* painting by Pieter Brueghel the Elder
(c. 1525–1569), in the Brussels museum.

W. H. AUDEN (1907–1973)
The Unknown Citizen   1940

(To JS/07/M/378
This Marble Monument
Is Erected by the State)

He was found by the Bureau of Statistics to be
One against whom there was no official complaint,
And all the reports on his conduct agree
That, in the modern sense of an old-fashioned word, he was a saint,
For in everything he did he served the Greater Community.   5
Except for the War till the day he retired
He worked in a factory and never got fired,
But satisfied his employers, Fudge Motors Inc.
Yet he wasn't a scab or odd in his views,
For his Union reports that he paid his dues,   10
(Our report on his Union shows it was sound)
And our Social Psychology workers found
That he was popular with his mates and liked a drink.
The Press are convinced that he bought a paper every day
And that his reactions to advertisements were normal in every way.   15
Policies taken out in his name prove that he was fully insured,
And his Health-card shows he was once in hospital but left it cured.
Both Producers Research and High-Grade Living declare
He was fully sensible to the advantages of the Installment Plan
And had everything necessary to the Modern Man,   20
A phonograph, radio, car and a frigidaire.
Our researchers into Public Opinion are content
That he held the proper opinions for the time of year;
When there was peace, he was for peace; when there was war, he went.
He was married and added five children to the population,   25
Which our Eugenist says was the right number for a parent of his generation,
And our teachers report that he never interfered with their education.
Was he free? Was he happy? The question is absurd:
Had anything been wrong, we should certainly have heard.

AMIRI BARAKA (b. 1934)
SOS

1969

Calling black people
Calling all black people, man woman child
Wherever you are, calling you, urgent, come in
Black People, come in, wherever you are, urgent, calling
you, calling all black people
calling all black people, come in, black people, come
on in.

APHRA BEHN (1640-1689)
Love Armed

1665

Love in Fantastic Triumph sat,
Whilst Bleeding Hearts around him flowed,
For whom Fresh pains he did Create,
And strange Tyrannic power he showed;
From thy Bright Eyes he took his fire,   5
Which round about, in sport he hurled;
But 'twas from mine he took desire,
Enough to undo the Amorous World

From me he took his sighs and tears,
From thee his Pride and Cruelty;   10
From me his Languishments and Fears,
And every Killing Dart from thee;
Thus thou and I, the God° have armed,   *Cupid, god of love*
And set him up a Deity;
But my poor Heart alone is harmed,   15
Whilst thine the Victor is, and free.

JOHN BERRYMAN (1914-1972)
Dream Song 14

1964

Life, friends, is boring. We must not say so.
After all, the sky flashes, the great sea yearns,
we ourselves flash and yearn,
and moreover my mother told me as a boy
(repeatedly) "Ever to confess you're bored   5
means you have no

Inner Resources." I conclude now I have no
inner resources, because I am heavy bored.

Peoples bore me,
literature bores me, especially great literature,
Henry bores me, with his plights & gripes
as bad as achilles,°

Who loves people and valiant art, which bores me.
And the tranquil hills, & gin, look like a drag
and somehow a dog   15
has taken itself & its tail considerably away
into mountains or sea or sky, leaving
behind: me, wag.

12 *Achilles:* Greek hero who fought in the Trojan War.

WILLIAM BLAKE (1757–1827)
The Garden of Love   1794

I went to the Garden of Love,
And saw what I never had seen:
A Chapel was built in the midst,
Where I used to play on the green.

And the gates of this Chapel were shut,   5
And "Thou shalt not" writ over the door;
So I turned to the Garden of Love
That so many sweet flowers bore;

And I saw it was filled with graves,
And tomb-stones where flowers should be;   10
And Priests in black gowns were walking their rounds,
And binding with briars my joys and desires.

WILLIAM BLAKE (1757–1827)
Ah Sun-flower   1794

Ah Sun-flower, weary of time,
Who countest the steps of the Sun,
Seeking after that sweet golden clime
Where the traveller's journey is done:

Where the Youth pined away with desire,
And the pale Virgin shrouded in snow
Arise from their graves and aspire
Where my Sun-flower wishes to go.

WILLIAM BLAKE (1757–1827)
The Little Black Boy   1789

Illuminated printing: Blake etched his poems and designs in relief, with acid on copper. Each printed page was then colored by hand. The design and the text work together to express Blake's vision.

ROBERT BLY (b. 1926)
Snowfall in the Afternoon   1962

1
The grass is half-covered with snow.
It was the sort of snowfall that starts in late afternoon.
And now the little houses of the grass are growing dark.

2
If I reached my hands down, near the earth,
I could take handfuls of darkness!
A darkness was always there, which we never noticed.   5

3
As the snow grows heavier, the cornstalks fade farther away,
And the barn moves nearer to the house.
The barn moves all alone in the growing storm.

4
The barn is full of corn, and moving toward us now,   10
Like a hulk blown toward us in a storm at sea;
All the sailors on deck have been blind for many years.

ROBERT BLY (b. 1926)
Waking from Sleep   1962

Inside the veins there are navies setting forth,
Tiny explosions at the water lines,
And seagulls weaving in the wind of the salty blood.

It is the morning. The country has slept the whole winter.
Window seats were covered with fur skins, the yard was full   5
Of stiff dogs, and hands that clumsily held heavy books.

Now we wake, and rise from bed, and eat breakfast! —
Shouts rise from the harbor of the blood,
Mist, and masts rising, the knock of wooden tackle in the sunlight.

Now we sing, and do tiny dances on the kitchen floor.   10
Our whole body is like a harbor at dawn;
We know that our master has left us for the day.

ANNE BRADSTREET (c. 1612–1672)
Before the Birth of One of Her Children   1678

All things within this fading world hath end,
Adversity doth still our joys attend;
No ties so strong, no friends so dear and sweet,
But with death's parting blow is sure to meet.
The sentence past is most irrevocable,   5
A common thing, yet oh, inevitable.
How soon, my Dear, death may my steps attend,
How soon't may be thy lot to lose thy friend,
We both are ignorant, yet love bids me
These farewell lines to recommend to thee,   10
That when that knot's untied that made us one,
I may seem thine, who is effect am none.
And if I see not half my days that's due,
What nature would, God grant to yours and you;
The many faults that well you know I have   15
Let be interred in my oblivious grave;
If any worth or virtue were in me,
Let that live freshly in thy memory
And when thou feel'st no grief, as I no harms,
Yet love thy dead, who long lay in thine arms,   20
And when thy loss shall be repaid with gains
Look to my little babes, my dear remains.

And if thou love thyself, or loved'st me,
These O protect from stepdame's° injury.   *stepmother's*
And if chance to thine eyes shall bring this verse,   25
With some sad sighs honor my absent hearse;
And kiss this paper for thy love's dear sake,
Who with salt tears this last farewell did take.

ANNE BRADSTREET (c. 1612–1672)
To My Dear and Loving Husband   1678

If ever two were one, then surely we.
If ever man were loved by wife, then thee;
If ever wife was happy in a man,
Compare with me, ye women, if you can.
I prize thy love more than whole mines of gold   5
Or all the riches that the East doth hold.
My love is such that rivers cannot quench,
Nor ought but love from thee, give recompense.
Thy love is such I can no way repay,
The heavens reward thee manifold, I pray.   10
Then while we live, in love let's so persevere
That when we live no more, we may live ever.

GWENDOLYN BROOKS (b. 1917)
The Bean Eaters   1959

They eat beans mostly, this old yellow pair.
Dinner is a casual affair.
Plain chipware on a plain and creaking wood,
Tin flatware.

Two who are Mostly Good.   5
Two who have lived their day,
But keep on putting on their clothes
And putting things away.

And remembering . . .
Remembering, with twinklings and twinges,
As they lean over the beans in their rented back room   10
        that is full of beads and receipts and dolls and cloths,
        tobacco crumbs, vases and fringes.

GWENDOLYN BROOKS (b. 1917)
The Mother   1945

Abortions will not let you forget.
You remember the children you got that you did not get,
The damp small pulps with a little or with no hair,

The singers and workers that never handled the air.
You will never neglect or beat   5
Them, or silence or buy with a sweet.
You will never wind up the sucking-thumb
Or scuttle off ghosts that come.
You will never leave them, controlling your luscious sigh,
Return for a snack of them, with gobbling mother-eye.   10

I have heard in the voices of the wind the voices of my dim
    killed children
I have contracted. I have eased
My dim dears at the breasts they could never suck.
I have said, Sweets, if I sinned, if I seized
Your luck   15
And your lives from your unfinished reach,
If I stole your births and your names,
Your straight baby tears and your games,
Your stilted or lovely loves, your tumults, your marriages, aches,
    and your deaths,
If I poisoned the beginnings of your breaths,   20
Believe that even in my deliberateness I was not deliberate.
Though why should I whine,
Whine that the crime was other than mine? —
Since anyhow you are dead.
Or rather, or instead,   25
You were never made.

But that too, I am afraid,
Is faulty: oh, what shall I say, how is the truth to be said?
You were born, you had body, you died.
It is just that you never giggled or planned or cried.   30

Believe me, I loved you all.
Believe me, I knew you, though faintly, and I loved, I loved you
All.

ROBERT BROWNING (1812–1889)
Meeting at Night   1845

The gray sea and the long black land;
And the yellow half-moon large and low;
And the startled little waves that leap
In firey ringlets from their sleep,
As I gain the cove with pushing prow,   5
And quench its speed i' the slushy sand.

Then a mile of warm sea-scented beach;
Three fields to cross till a farm appears;
A tap at the pane, the quick sharp scratch
And blue spurt of a lighted match,   10
And a voice less loud, through its joys and fears,
Than the two hearts beating each to each!

ROBERT BROWNING (1812-1889)
Parting at Morning

1845

Round the cape of a sudden came the sea,
And the sun looked over the mountain's rim:
And straight was a path of gold for him,
And the need of a world of men for me.

ROBERT BURNS (1759-1796)
To a Mouse

1786

ON TURNING HER UP IN HER NEST WITH
THE PLOW, NOVEMBER, 1785

Wee, sleekit,° cow'rin', tim'rous beastie,	*sleek*
O, what a panic's in thy breastie!	
Thou need na start awa sae hasty,	
Wi' bickering brattle!	
I wad be laith° to rin an' chase thee	*loath* 5
Wi' murd'ring pattle!°	*plowstaff*

I'm truly sorry man's dominion
Has broken Nature's social union,
An' justifies that ill opinion
      Which makes thee startle   10
At me, thy poor, earth-born companion,
      An' fellow mortal!

I doubt na, whiles,° but thou may thieve;	*sometimes*
What then? poor beastie, thou maun° live!	*must*
A daimen-icker in a thrave°	*occasional corn-ear in a sheaf* 15
'S a sma' request:	
I'll get a blessin' wi' the lave,°	*remainder*
And never miss 't!	

Thy wee-bit housie, too, in ruin!	
Its silly° wa's the win's are strewin'!	*frail* 20
An' naething, now, to big° a new ane,	*build*
O' foggage° green!	*moss*
An' bleak December's winds ensuin',	
Baith snell° an' keen!	*bitter*

Thou saw the fields laid bare and waste,	25
An' weary winter comin' fast,	
An' cozie here, beneath the blast,	
Thou thought to dwell,	
Till crash! the cruel coulter° passed	*cutter-blade*
Out-through thy cell.	30

That wee-bit heap o' leaves an' stibble
Has cost thee mony a weary nibble!

Now thou's turned out, for a' thy trouble,
    But° house or hald,°   *without; land*
To thole° the winter's sleety dribble,   *endure* 35
    An' cranreuch° cauld!   *frost*

But Mousie, thou art no thy lane,°   *not alone*
In proving foresight may be vain:
The best-laid schemes o' mice an' men
    Gang aft a-gley,°   *often go awry* 40
An' lea'e us nought but grief an' pain,
    For promised joy.

Still thou art blest compared wi' me!
The present only toucheth thee:
But och! I backward cast my e'e   45
    On prospects drear!
An' forward though I canna see,
    I guess an' fear!

GEORGE GORDON, LORD BYRON (1788-1824)
She Walks in Beauty   1814

FROM HEBREW MELODIES

I

She walks in Beauty, like the night
    Of cloudless climes and starry skies;
And all that's best of dark and bright
    Meet in her aspect and her eyes:
Thus mellowed to that tender light   5
    Which Heaven to gaudy day denies.

II

One shade the more, one ray the less,
    Had half impaired the nameless grace
Which waves in every raven tress,
    Or softly lightens o'er her face;   10
Where thoughts serenely sweet express,
    How pure, how dear their dwelling-place.

III

And on that cheek, and o'er that brow,
    So soft, so calm, yet eloquent,
The smiles that win, the tints that glow,   15
    But tell of days in goodness spent,
A mind at peace with all below,
    A heart whose love is innocent!

THOMAS CAMPION (1567–1620)
There is a garden in her face   1617

    There is a garden in her face
Where roses and white lilies grow;
    A heav'nly paradise is that place
Wherein all pleasant fruits do flow.
      There cherries grow which none may buy   5
      Till "Cherry-ripe"° themselves do cry.

    Those cherries fairly do enclose
Of orient pearl a double row,
    Which when her lovely laughter shows,
They look like rose-buds filled with snow;   10
      Yet them nor° peer nor prince can buy,   *neither*
      Till "Cherry-ripe" themselves do cry.

    Her eyes like angels watch them still;
Her brows like bended bows do stand,
    Threat'ning with piercing frowns to kill   15
All that attempt, with eye or hand
      Those sacred cherries to come nigh
      Till "Cherry-ripe" themselves do cry.

6 *"Cherry-ripe":* Street cry of London fruit peddlers.

AMY CLAMPITT (1920–1994)
Dancers Exercising   1983

Frame within frame, the evolving conversation
is dancelike, as though two could play
at improvising snowflakes'
six-feather-vaned evanescence,
no two ever alike. All process   5
and no arrival: the happier we are,
the less there is for memory to take hold of,
or — memory being so largely a predilection
for the exceptional — come to a halt
in front of. But finding, one evening   10
on a street not quite familiar,
inside a gated
November-sodden garden, a building
of uncertain provenance,
peering into whose vestibule we were   15
arrested — a frame within a frame,
a lozenge of impeccable clarity —
by the reflection, no, not
of our two selves, but of
dancers exercising in a mirror   20
at the center

of that clarity, what we saw
was not stillness
but movement: the perfection
of memory consisting, it would seem,   25
in the never-to-be-completed.
We saw them mirroring themselves,
never guessing the vestibule
that defined them, frame within frame,
contained two other mirrors.   30

LUCILLE CLIFTON (b. 1936)
for deLawd   1969

people say they have a hard time
understanding how I
go on about my business
playing my Ray Charles
hollering at the kids —   5
seem like my Afro
cut off in some old image
would show I got a long memory
and I come from a line
of black and going on women   10
who got used to making it through murdered sons
and who grief kept on pushing
who fried chicken
ironed
swept off the back steps   15
who grief kept
for their still alive sons
for their sons coming
for their sons gone
just pushing   20

SAMUEL TAYLOR COLERIDGE (1772–1834)
Kubla Khan: or, a Vision in a Dream°   1798

In Xanadu did Kubla Khan°
    A stately pleasure-dome decree:
Where Alph, the sacred river, ran
Through caverns measureless to man
    Down to a sunless sea.   5

Vision in a Dream: This poem came to Coleridge in an opium-induced dream, but he was interrupted by a visitor while writing it down. He was later unable to remember the rest of the poem.   1 *Kubla Khan:* The historical Kublai Khan (1216–1294, grandson of Genghis Khan) was the founder of the Mongol dynasty in China.

So twice five miles of fertile ground
With walls and towers were girdled round:
And here were gardens bright with sinuous rills
Where blossomed many an incense-bearing tree;
And there were forests ancient as the hills, 10
Enfolding sunny spots of greenery.

But oh! that deep romantic chasm which slanted
Down the green hill athwart a cedarn cover!°
A savage place! as holy and enchanted
As e'er beneath a waning moon was haunted 15
By woman wailing for her demon-lover!
And from this chasm, with ceaseless turmoil seething,
As if this earth in fast thick pants were breathing,
A mighty fountain momently was forced,
Amid whose swift half-intermitted burst 20
Huge fragments vaulted like rebounding hail,
Of chaffy grain beneath the thresher's flail:
And 'mid these dancing rocks at once and ever
It flung up momently the sacred river.
Five miles meandering with a mazy motion 25
Through wood and dale the sacred river ran,
Then reached the caverns measureless to man,
And sank in tumult to a lifeless ocean:
And 'mid this tumult Kubla heard from far
Ancestral voices prophesying war! 30
  The shadow of the dome of pleasure
  Floated midway on the waves;
  Where was heard the mingled measure
  From the fountain and the caves.
It was a miracle of rare device, 35
A sunny pleasure-dome with caves of ice!

  A damsel with a dulcimer
  In a vision once I saw:
  It was an Abyssinian maid,
  And on her dulcimer she played, 40
  Singing of Mount Abora.
  Could I revive within me
  Her symphony and song,
  To such a deep delight 'twould win me,
That with music loud and long, 45
I would build that dome in air,
That sunny dome! those caves of ice!
And all who heard should see them there,
And all should cry, Beware! Beware!
His flashing eyes, his floating hair! 50
Weave a circle round him thrice,
And close your eyes with holy dread,
For he on honey-dew hath fed,
And drunk the milk of Paradise.

13 *athwart . . . cover:* Spanning a grove of cedar trees.

WENDY COPE (b. 1945)
Lonely Hearts   1986

Can someone make my simple wish come true?
Male biker seeks female for touring fun.
Do you live in North London? Is it you?

Gay vegetarian whose friends are few,
I'm into music, Shakespeare and the sun,   5
Can someone make my simple wish come true?

Executive in search of something new —
Perhaps bisexual woman, arty, young.
Do you live in North London? Is it you?

Successful, straight and solvent? I am too —   10
Attractive Jewish lady with a son.
Can someone make my simple wish come true?

I'm Libran, inexperienced and blue —
Need slim non-smoker, under twenty-one.
Do you live in North London? Is it you?   15

Please write (with photo) to Box 152.
Who knows where it may lead once we've begun?
Can someone make my simple wish come true?
Do you live in North London? Is it you?

WILLIAM COWPER (1731–1800)
Epitaph on a Hare   1784

Here lies, whom hound did ne'er pursue,
     Nor swifter greyhound follow,
Whose foot ne'er tainted° morning dew,   *left a scent on*
     Nor ear heard huntsman's hallo',

Old Tiney, surliest of his kind,   5
     Who, nursed with tender care,
And to domestic bounds confined,
     Was still a wild jack-hare.

Though duly from my hand he took
     His pittance every night,   10
He did it with a jealous look,
     And, when he could, would bite.

His diet was of wheaten bread,
     And milk, and oats, and straw,
Thistles, or lettuces instead,   15
     With sand to scour his maw.

On twigs of hawthorn he regaled,°   *feasted*
     On pippins'° russet peel;   *apples'*

And, when his juicy salads failed,
　　Sliced carrot pleased him well.

A Turkey carpet was his lawn,
　　Whereon he loved to bound,
To skip and gambol like a fawn,
　　And swing his rump around.

His frisking was at evening hours,
　　For then he lost his fear;
But most before approaching showers,
　　Or when a storm drew near.

Eight years and five round-rolling moons
　　He thus saw steal away,
Dozing out all his idle noons,
　　And every night at play.

I kept him for his humor's sake,
　　For he would oft beguile
My heart of thoughts that made it ache,
　　And force me to a smile.

But now, beneath this walnut-shade
　　He finds his long, last home,
And waits in snug concealment laid,
　　Till gentler Puss shall come.

He, still more agèd, feels the shocks
　　From which no care can save,
And, partner once of Tiney's box,
　　Must soon partake his grave.

20

25

30

35

40

VICTOR HERNÁNDEZ CRUZ (b. 1949)
Anonymous

1982

And if I lived in those olden times
With a funny name like Choicer or
Henry Howard, Earl of Surrey, what chimes!
I would spend my time in search of rhymes
Make sure the measurement termination surprise
In the court of kings snapping till woo sunrise
Plus always be using the words *alas* and *hath*
And not even knowing that that was my path
Just think on the Lower East Side of Manhattan
It would have been like living in satin
Alas! The projects hath not covered the river
Thou see-est vision to make thee quiver
Hath I been delivered to that "wildernesse"
So past
I would have been the last one in the

5

10

15

Dance to go
Taking note the minuet so slow
All admire my taste
Within thou *mambo* of much more haste.

COUNTEE CULLEN (1903–1946)
Saturday's Child°

1925

Some are teethed on a silver spoon,
With the stars strung for a rattle;
I cut my teeth as the black raccoon —
For implements of battle.

Some are swaddled in silk and down,   5
And heralded by a star;
They swathed my limbs in a sackcloth gown
On a night that was black as tar.

For some, godfather and goddame
The opulent fairies be;   10
Dame Poverty gave me my name,
And Pain godfathered me.

For I was born on Saturday —
"Bad time for planting a seed,"
Was all my father had to say,   15
And, "One mouth more to feed."

Death cut the strings that gave me life,
And handed me to Sorrow,
The only kind of middle wife
My folks could beg or borrow.   20

Saturday's Child: Reference to the nursery rhyme: Monday's child is fair of face . . . / Saturday's child
must work hard for a living. . . .

COUNTEE CULLEN (1903–1946)
Yet Do I Marvel

1925

I doubt not God is good, well-meaning, kind,
And did He stoop to quibble could tell why
The little buried mole continues blind,
Why flesh that mirrors Him must some day die,
Make plain the reason tortured Tantalus   5
Is baited by the fickle fruit, declare
If merely brute caprice dooms Sisyphus
To struggle up a never-ending stair.
Inscrutable His ways are, and immune
To catechism by a mind too strewn   10

With petty cares to slightly understand
What awful brain compels His awful hand.
Yet do I marvel at this curious thing:
To make a poet black, and bid him sing!

E. E. CUMMINGS (1894–1962)
anyone lived in a pretty how town

1940

anyone lived in a pretty how town
(with up so floating many bells down)
spring summer autumn winter
he sang his didn't he danced his did.

Women and men (both little and small)   5
cared for anyone not at all
they sowed their isn't they reaped their same
sun moon stars rain

children guessed (but only a few
and down they forgot as up they grew   10
autumn winter spring summer)
that noone loved him more by more

when by now and tree by leaf
she laughed his joy she cried his grief
bird by snow and stir by still   15
anyone's any was all to her

someones married their everyones
laughed their cryings and did their dance
(sleep wake hope and then) they
said their nevers they slept their dream   20

stars rain sun moon
(and only the snow can begin to explain
how children are apt to forget to remember
with up so floating many bells down)

one day anyone died i guess   25
(and noone stooped to kiss his face)
busy folk buried them side by side
little by little and was by was

all by all and deep by deep
and more by more they dream their sleep   30
noone and anyone earth by april
wish by spirit and if by yes.

Women and men (both dong and ding)
summer autumn winter spring
reaped their sowing and went their came   35
sun moon stars rain

E. E. CUMMINGS (1894-1962)
Buffalo Bill 's°   1923

Buffalo Bill 's
defunct
            who used to
            ride a watersmooth-silver
                                    stallion   5

and break onetwothreefourfive pigeonsjustlikethat
                                    Jesus
he was a handsome man
                    and what i want to know is
how do you like your blueeyed boy   10
Mister Death

Buffalo Bill: William Frederick Cody (1846–1917). An American frontier scout and Indian killer turned international circus showman with his Wild West show, which employed Sitting Bull and Annie Oakley.

E. E. CUMMINGS (1894-1962)
since feeling is first   1926

since feeling is first
who pays any attention
to the syntax of things
will never wholly kiss you;

wholly to be a fool   5
while Spring is in the world

my blood approves,
and kisses are a better fate
than wisdom
lady i swear by all flowers. Don't cry   10
— the best gesture of my brain is less than
your eyelids' flutter which says

we are for each other: then
laugh, leaning back in my arms
for life's not a paragraph   15

And death i think is no parenthesis

GREGORY DJANIKIAN (b. 1949)
When I First Saw Snow

1989

TARRYTOWN, N.Y.

Bing Crosby was singing "White Christmas"
    on the radio, we were staying at my aunt's house
    waiting for papers, my father was looking for a job.
We had trimmed the tree the night before,
    sap had run on my fingers and for the first time   5
    I was smelling pine wherever I went.
Anais, my cousin, was upstairs in her room
    listening to Danny and the Juniors.
Haigo was playing Monopoly with Lucy, his sister,
    Buzzy, the boy next door, had eyes for her   10
    and there was a rattle of dice, a shuffling
    of Boardwalk, Park Place, Marvin Gardens.
There were red bows on the Christmas tree.
It had snowed all night.
My boot buckles were clinking like small bells   15
    as I thumped to the door and out
    onto the gray planks of the porch dusted with snow.
The world was immaculate, new,
    even the trees had changed color,
    and when I touched the snow on the railing   20
    I didn't know what I had touched, ice or fire.
I heard, "I'm dreaming . . ."
I heard, "At the hop, hop, hop . . . oh, baby."
I heard "B & O" and the train in my imagination
    was whistling through the great plains.   25
And I was stepping off,
I was falling deeply into America.

JOHN DONNE (1572–1631)
The Apparition

c. 1600

When by thy scorn, O murderess, I am dead,
    And that thou thinkst thee free
From all solicitation from me,
Then shall my ghost come to thy bed,
And thee, feigned vestal, in worse arms shall see;   5
Then thy sick taper° will begin to wink,   *candle*
And he, whose thou art then, being tired before,
Will, if thou stir, or pinch to wake him, think
    Thou call'st for more,
And in false sleep will from thee shrink.   10

And then, poor aspen wretch, neglected, thou,
Bathed in a cold quicksilver sweat, wilt lie
      A verier° ghost than I.   *truer*
What I will say, I will not tell thee now,
Lest that preserve thee; and since my love is spent,   15
I had rather thou shouldst painfully repent,
Than by my threatenings rest still innocent.

JOHN DONNE (1572-1631)
Batter My Heart   1610

Batter my heart, three-personed God; for You
As yet but knock, breathe, shine, and seek to mend;
That I may rise and stand, o'erthrow me, and bend
Your force, to break, blow, burn, and make me new.
I, like an usurped town, to another due,   5
Labor to admit You, but Oh, to no end!
Reason, Your viceroy in me, me should defend,
But is captived, and proves weak or untrue.
Yet dearly I love You, and would be loved fain.
But am betrothed unto Your enemy: 10
Divorce me, untie, or break that knot again,
Take me to You, imprison me, for I,
Except You enthrall me, never shall be free,
Nor ever chaste, except You ravish me.

JOHN DONNE (1572-1631)
Death Be Not Proud   1611

Death be not proud, though some have callèd thee
Mighty and dreadful, for thou art not so;
For those whom thou think'st thou dost overthrow
Die not, poor Death, nor yet canst thou kill me.
From rest and sleep, which but thy pictures° be,   *images* 5
Much pleasure; then from thee much more must flow,
And soonest our best men with thee do go,
Rest of their bones, and soul's delivery.°   *deliverance*
Thou art slave to Fate, Chance, kings, and desperate men,
And dost with Poison, War, and Sickness dwell;   10
And poppy or charms can make us sleep as well,
And better than thy stroke; why swell'st° thou then?   *swell with pride*
One short sleep past, we wake eternally
And death shall be no more; Death, thou shalt die.

JOHN DONNE (1572–1631)
The Flea   1633

Mark but this flea, and mark in this°
How little that which thou deny'st me is;
It sucked me first, and now sucks thee,
And in this flea our two bloods mingled be;
Thou know'st that this cannot be said   5
A sin, nor shame, nor loss of maidenhead,
    Yet this enjoys before it woo,
      And pampered swells with one blood made of two,
      And this, alas, is more than we would do.°

Oh stay, three lives in one flea spare,   10
Where we almost, yea more than, married are.
This flea is you and I, and this
Our marriage bed, and marriage temple is;
Though parents grudge, and you, we're met
And cloistered in these living walls of jet.   15
    Though use° make you apt to kill me,   *habit*
      Let not to that, self-murder added be,
      And sacrilege, three sins in killing three.

Cruel and sudden, hast thou since
Purpled thy nail in blood of innocence?   20
Wherein could this flea guilty be,
Except in that drop which it sucked from thee?
Yet thou triumph'st, and say'st that thou
Find'st not thyself, nor me, the weaker now;
    'Tis true; then learn how false, fears be;   25
      Just so much honor, when thou yield'st to me,
      Will waste, as this flea's death took life from thee.

1 *mark in this:* Take note of the moral lesson in this object.   9 *more than we would do:* I.e., if we
do not join our blood in conceiving a child.

JOHN DONNE (1572–1631)
Hymn to God, My God, in My Sickness   1635

Since I am coming to that holy room
    Where, with thy choir of saints for evermore,
I shall be made thy music, as I come
    I tune the instrument here at the door,
    And what I must do then, think now before.   5

Whilst my physicians by their love are grown
    Cosmographers, and I their map, who lie
Flat on this bed, that by them may be shown

That this is my southwest discovery,
    Per fretum febris,° by these straits to die,   *through the strait of fever*   10

I joy that in these straits I see my west;
    For though those currents yield return to none,
What shall my west hurt me? As west and east
    In all flat maps (and I am one) are one,
    So death doth touch the resurrectiön.   15

Is the Pacific Sea my home? Or are
    The eastern riches? Is Jerusalem?
Anyan° and Magellan and Gibraltar,   *Bering Strait*
    All straits, and none but straits, are ways to them,
    Whether where Japhet dwelt, or Cham, or Shem.°   20

We think that Paradise and Calvary,
    Christ's cross and Adam's tree, stood in one place;
Look, Lord, and find both Adams met in me;
    As the first Adam's sweat surrounds my face,
    May the last Adam's blood my soul embrace.   25

So, in his purple wrapped receive me, Lord;
    By these his thorns give me his other crown;
And as to others' souls I preached thy word,
    Be this my text, my sermon to mine own:
    Therefore that he may raise, the Lord throws down.   30

20 *Japhet . . . Cham . . . Shem:* The three sons of Noah, who after the flood became the progenitors
of the northern, southern, and Semitic peoples, respectively (see Gen. 9:18–27).

GEORGE ELIOT
[MARY ANN EVANS] (1819–1880)
In a London Drawingroom   1865

The sky is cloudy, yellowed by the smoke.
For view there are the houses opposite,
Cutting the sky with one long line of wall
Like solid fog: far as the eye can stretch
Monotony of surface and of form   5
Without a break to hang a guess upon.
No bird can make a shadow as it flies,
For all its shadow, as in ways o'erhung
By thickest canvas, where the golden rays
Are clothed in hemp. No figure lingering   10
Pauses to feed the hunger of the eye
Or rest a little on the lap of life.
All hurry on and look upon the ground
Or glance unmarking at the passersby.
The wheels are hurrying, too, cabs, carriages   15
All closed, in multiplied identity.
The world seems one huge prison-house and court

Where men are punished at the slightest cost,
With lowest rate of color, warmth, and joy.

LOUISE ERDRICH (b. 1954)
Windigo   1984

> *The Windigo is a flesh-eating, wintry demon with a man buried deep inside of it. In
> some Chippewa stories, a young girl vanquishes this monster by forcing boiling lard
> down its throat, thereby releasing the human at the core of ice.*

You knew I was coming for you, little one,
when the kettle jumped into the fire.
Towels flapped on the hooks,
and the dog crept off, groaning,
to the deepest part of the woods.   5
In the hackles of dry brush a thin laughter started up.
Mother scolded the food warm and smooth in the pot
and called you to eat.
But I spoke in the cold trees:
New one, I have come for you, child hide and lie still.   10

The sumac pushed sour red cones through the air.
Copper burned in the raw wood.
You saw me drag toward you.
Oh touch me. I murmured, and licked the soles of your feet.
You dug your hands into my pale, melting fur.   15

I stole you off, a huge thing in my bristling armor.
Steam rolled from my wintry arms, each leaf shivered
from the bushes we passed
until they stood, naked, spread like the cleaned spines of fish.

Then your warm hands hummed over and shoveled themselves full   20
of the ice and the snow. I would darken and spill
all night running, until at last morning broke the cold earth
and I carried you home,
a river shaking in the sun.

LOUISE GLÜCK (b. 1943)
The School Children   1975

The children go forward with their little satchels.
And all morning the mothers have labored
to gather the late apples, red and gold,
like words of another language.

And on the other shore   5
are those who wait behind great desks
to receive these offerings.

How orderly they are — the nails
on which the children hang
their overcoats of blue or yellow wool.   10

And the teachers shall instruct them in silence
and the mothers shall scour the orchards for a way out,
drawing to themselves the gray limbs of the fruit trees
bearing so little ammunition.

DONALD HALL (b. 1928)
Scenic View   1981

Every year the mountains
get paler and more distant —
trees less green, rock piles
disappearing — as emulsion
from a billion Kodaks   5
sucks color out.
In fifteen years
Monadnock and Kearsarge,
the Green Mountains
and the White, will turn   10
invisible, all
tint removed
atom by atom to albums
in Medford and Greenwich,
while over the valleys   15
the still intractable granite
rears with unseeable peaks
fatal to airplanes.

DONALD HALL (b. 1928)
My Son, My Executioner   1955

My son, my executioner,
    I take you in my arms,
Quiet and small and just astir,
    And whom my body warms.

Sweet death, small son, our instrument   5
    Of immortality,
Your cries and hungers document
    Our bodily decay.

We twenty-five and twenty-two,
    Who seemed to live forever,   10
Observe enduring life in you
    And start to die together.

THOMAS HARDY (1840-1928)
Hap

1866

If but some vengeful god would call to me
From up the sky, and laugh: "Thou suffering thing,
Know that thy sorrow is my ecstasy,
That thy love's loss is my hate's profiting!"

Then would I bear it, clench myself, and die,   5
Steeled by the sense of ire unmerited;
Half-eased in that a Powerfuller than I
Had willed and meted me the tears I shed.

But not so. How arrives it joy lies slain,
And why unblooms the best hope ever sown?   10
— Crass Casualty obstructs the sun and rain,
And dicing Time for gladness casts a moan. . . .
These purblind Doomsters had as readily strown
Blisses about my pilgrimage as pain.

THOMAS HARDY (1840-1928)
The Ruined Maid

1902

"O'Melia, my dear, this does everything crown!
Who could have supposed I should meet you in Town?
And whence such fair garments, such prosperi-ty?"
"O didn't you know I'd been ruined?" said she.

"You left us in tatters, without shoes or socks,   5
Tired of digging potatoes, and spudding up docks;
And now you've gay bracelets and bright feathers three!"
"Yes: that's how we dress when we're ruined," said she.

"At home in the barton° you said 'thee' and 'thou,'   *farm*
And 'thik oon,' and 'theäs oon,' and 't'other'; but now   10
Your talking quite fits 'ee for high compa-ny!"
"Some polish is gained with one's ruin," said she.

Your hands were like paws then, your face blue and bleak
But now I'm bewitched by your delicate cheek,
And your little gloves fit as on any la-dy!"   15
"We never do work when we're ruined," said she.

"You used to call home-life a hag-ridden dream,
And you'd sigh, and you'd sock; but at present you seem
To know not of megrims° or melancho-ly!"   *depressions*
"True. One's pretty lively when ruined," said she.   20

"I wish I had feathers, a fine sweeping gown,
And a delicate face, and could strut about Town!"
"My dear — a raw country girl, such as you be,
Cannot quite expect that. You ain't ruined," said she.

JOY HARJO (b. 1951)
Fishing   1991

This is the longest day of the year, on the Illinois River or a similar river in
the same place. Cicadas are part of the song as they praise their invisible
ancestors while fish blinking back the relentless sun in Oklahoma circle in
the muggy river of life. They dare the fisher to come and get them. Fish too
anticipate the game of fishing. Their ancestors perfected the moves, sent   5
down stories that appear as electrical impulse when sunlight hits water.
The hook carries great symbology in the coming of age, and is crucial to
the making of warriors. The greatest warriors are those who dangle a
human for hours on a string, break sacred water for the profanity of air
then snap fiercely back into pearly molecules that describe fishness. They   10
smell me as I walk the banks with fishing pole, nightcrawlers and a
promise I made to that old friend Louis to fish with him this summer. This
is the only place I can keep that promise, inside a poem as familiar to him
as the banks of his favorite fishing place. I try not to let the fish see me see
them as they look for his tracks on the soft earth made of fossils and ashes.   15
I hear the burble of fish talk: When is that old Creek coming back? He
was the one we loved to tease most, we liked his songs and once in awhile
he gave us a good run. Last night I dreamed I tried to die, I was going to
look for Louis. It was rather comical. I worked hard to muster my last
breath, then lay down in the summer, along the banks of the last mythic   20
river, my pole and tackle box next to me. What I thought was my last
breath floated off as a cloud making an umbrella of grief over my relatives.
How embarrassing when the next breath came, and then the next. I reeled
in one after another, as if I'd caught a bucket of suckers instead of bass. I
guess it wasn't my time, I explained, and went fishing anyway as a liar   25
and I know most fishers to be liars most of the time. Even Louis when it
came to fishing, or even dying. The leap between the sacred and profane is
as thin as a fishing line, and is part of the mystery on this river of life, as is
the way our people continue to make warriors in the strangest of times. I
save this part of the poem for the fish camp next to the oldest spirits whose 30
dogs bark to greet visitors. It's near Louis's favorite spot where the wisest
and fattest fish laze. I'll meet him there.

MICHAEL S. HARPER (b. 1938)
Grandfather   1975

In 1915 my grandfather's
neighbors surrounded his house
near the dayline he ran
on the Hudson
in Catskill, NY   5
and thought they'd burn
his family out
in a movie they'd just seen

and be rid of his kind:
the death of a lone black   10
family is *the Birth*
of a Nation,°
or so they thought.
His 5'4" waiter gait
quenched the white jacket smile   15
he'd brought back from watered
polish of my father
on the turning seats,
and he asked his neighbors
up on his thatched porch   20
for the first blossom of fire
that would burn him down.

They went away, his nation,
spittooning their torched necks
in the shadows of the riverboat   25
they'd seen, posse decomposing;
and I see him on Sutter
with white bag from your
restaurant, challenged by his first
grandson to a foot-race   30
he will win in white clothes.

I see him as he buys galoshes
for his railed yard near Mineo's
metal shop, where roses jump
as the el circles his house   35
toward Brooklyn, where his rain fell;
and I see cigar smoke in his eyes,
chocolate Madison Square Garden chews
he breaks on his set teeth,
stitched up after cancer,   40
the great white nation immovable
as his weight wilts
and he is on a porch
that won't hold my arms,
or the legs of the race run   45
forwards, or the film
played backwards on his grandson's eyes.

11–12 *Birth of a Nation:* A 1915 film directed by D. W. Griffith that praises the rise of the Ku Klux
Klan in the South during Reconstruction.

ANTHONY HECHT (b. 1923)
The Dover Bitch°

A Criticism of Life

So there stood Matthew Arnold and this girl
With the cliffs of England crumbling away behind them,
And he said to her, "Try to be true to me,
And I'll do the same for you, for things are bad
All over, etc., etc."   5
Well now, I knew this girl. It's true she had read
Sophocles in a fairly good translation
And caught that bitter allusion to the sea,°
But all the time he was talking she had in mind
The notion of what his whiskers would feel like   10
On the back of her neck. She told me later on
That after a while she got to looking out
At the lights across the channel, and really felt sad,
Thinking of all the wine and enormous beds
And blandishments in French and the perfumes.   15
And then she got really angry. To have been brought
All the way down from London, and then be addressed
As a sort of mournful cosmic last resort
Is really tough on a girl, and she was pretty.
Anyway, she watched him pace the room   20
And finger his watch-chain and seem to sweat a bit,
And then she said one or two unprintable things.
But you mustn't judge her by that. What I mean to say is,
She's really all right. I still see her once in a while
And she always treats me right. We have a drink   25
And I give her a good time, and perhaps it's a year
Before I see her again, but there she is,
Running to fat, but dependable as they come.
And sometimes I bring her a bottle of *Nuit d'Amour.*

The Dover Bitch: A parody of Arnold's poem "Dover Beach" (see p. 88).   8 *Allusion to the sea:*
Lines 9–18 in "Dover Beach" refer to Sophocles' *Antigone,* lines 583–591.

GEORGE HERBERT (1593–1633)
The Collar

I struck the board° and cried, "No more;   *table*
       I will abroad!
What? shall I ever sigh and pine?
My lines and life are free, free as the road,
       Loose as the wind, as large as store.°   5

5 *store:* A storehouse or warehouse.

A Collection of Poems **417**

Shall I be still in suit?°   *serving another*
Have I no harvest but a thorn
To let me blood, and not restore
What I have lost with cordial° fruit?   *restorative*
    Sure there was wine   10
Before my sighs did dry it; there was corn
    Before my tears did drown it.
Is the year only lost to me?
    Have I no bays° to crown it,   *triumphal wreaths*
No flowers, no garlands gay? All blasted?   15
    All wasted?
Not so, my heart; but there is fruit,
    And thou hast hands.
Recover all thy sigh-blown age
On double pleasures: leave thy cold dispute   20
Of what is fit, and not. Forsake thy cage,
    Thy rope of sands,
Which petty thoughts have made, and made to thee
    Good cable, to enforce and draw,
      And be thy law,   25
While thou didst wink and wouldst not see.
    Away! take heed;
    I will abroad.
Call in thy death's-head° there; tie up thy fears.
    He that forbears   30
    To suit and serve his need,
      Deserves his load."
But as I raved and grew more fierce and wild
    At every word,
Methought I heard one calling, *Child!*   35
    And I replied, *My Lord.*

29 *death's-head:* A skull, reminder of mortality.

LINDA HOGAN (b. 1947)
Song for My Name   1979

Before sunrise
think of brushing out an old woman's
dark braids.
Think of your hands,
fingertips on the soft hair.   5

If you have this name,
your grandfather's dark hands
lead horses toward the wagon
and a cloud of dust follows,
ghost of silence.   10

That name is full of women
with black hair
and men with eyes like night.
It means no money
tomorrow.   15

Such a name my mother loves
while she works gently
in the small house.
She is a white dove
and in her own land   20
the mornings are pale,
birds sing into the white curtains
and show off their soft breasts.

If you have a name like this,
there's never enough water.   25
There is too much heat.
When lightning strikes, rain
refuses to follow.
It's my name,
that of a woman living   30
between the white moon
and the red sun, waiting to leave.
It's the name that goes with me
back to earth
no one else can touch.   35

M. CARL HOLMAN (1919–1988)
Mr. Z   1967

Taught early that his mother's skin was the sign of error,
He dressed and spoke the perfect part of honor;
Won scholarships, attended the best schools,
Disclaimed kinship with jazz and spirituals;
Chose prudent, raceless views for each situation,   5
Or when he could not cleanly skirt dissension,
Faced up to the dilemma, firmly seized
Whatever ground was Anglo-Saxonized.

In diet, too, his practice was exemplary:
Of pork in its profane forms he was wary;   10
Expert in vintage wines, sauces and salads,
His palate shrank from cornbread, yams and collards.

He was as careful whom he chose to kiss:
His bride had somewhere lost her Jewishness,
But kept her blue eyes; an Episcopalian   15
Prelate proclaimed them matched chameleon.
Choosing the right addresses, here, abroad,

They shunned those places where they might be barred;
Even less anxious to be asked to dine
Where hosts catered to kosher accent or exotic skin.   20

And so he climbed, unclogged by ethnic weights,
An airborne plant, flourishing without roots.
Not one false note was struck — until he died:
His subtly grieving widow could have flayed
The obit writers, ringing crude changes on a clumsy phrase: 25
"One of the most distinguished members of his race."

GARRETT KAORU HONGO (b. 1951)
The Cadence of Silk 1988

When I lived in Seattle, I loved watching
the Sonics play basketball; something
about that array of trained and energetic
bodies set in motion to attack a more
sluggish, less physically intelligent opponent   5
appealed to me, taught me about cadence
and play, the offguard breaking free
before the rebound, "releasing," as is said
in the parlance of the game, getting to
the center's downcourt pass and streaking   10
to the basket for a scoopshot layup
off the glass, all in rhythm, all in
perfect declensions of action, smooth
and strenuous as Gorgiasian° rhetoric.
I was hooked on the undulant ballet   15
of the pattern offense, on the set play
back-door under the basket, and, at times,
even on the auctioneer's pace and elocution
of the play-by-play man. Now I watch
the Lakers, having returned to Los Angeles   20
some years ago, love them even more than
the Seattle team, long since broken up and aging.
The Lakers are incomparable, numerous
options for any situation, their players
the league's quickest, most intelligent,   25
and, it is my opinion, frankly, the most *cool.*
Few bruisers, they are sleek as arctic seals,
especially the small forward
as he dodges through the key, away from
the ball, rubbing off his man on the screen,   30
setting for his shot. Then, slick as spit,
comes the ball from the point guard,
and my man goes up, cradling the ball

14 *Gorgiasian:* Gorgias (c. 485–c. 378 B.C.), Greek philosopher.

in his right hand like a waiter balancing
a tray piled with champagne in stemmed glasses,   35
cocking his arm and bringing the ball
back behind his ear, pumping, letting fly then
as he jumps, popcorn-like, in the corner,
while the ball, launched, slung dextrously
with a slight backspin, slashes through   40
the basket's silk net with a small,
sonorous splash of completion.

GERARD MANLEY HOPKINS (1844–1889)
Pied Beauty   1877

Glory be to God for dappled things —
    For skies of couple-color as a brinded cow;
        For rose-moles all in stipple upon trout that swim;
Fresh-firecoal chestnut-falls;° finches' wings;   *fallen chestnut*
        Landscape plotted and pieced — fold, fallow, and plow;   5
          And all trades, their gear and tackle and trim.

All things counter, original, spare, strange;
        Whatever is fickle, freckled (who knows how?)
          With swift, slow; sweet, sour; adazzle, dim;
He fathers-forth whose beauty is past change: 10
            Praise him.

GERARD MANLEY HOPKINS (1844–1889)
Spring and Fall   1880

To a Young Child

Márgarét áre you gríeving
Over Goldengrove unleaving?
Leáves, like the things of man, you
With your fresh thoughts care for, can you?
Áh! ás the heart grows older   5
It will come to such sights colder
By and by, nor spare a sigh
Though worlds of wanwood° leafmeal° lie;
And yet you wíll weep and know why.
Now no matter, child, the name: 10

Sórrow's spríngs áre the same.
Nor mouth had, no nor mind, expressed

---

8 *wanwood:* Gloomy woods; *leafmeal:* Leaves broken up piecemeal.

What heart heard of, ghost° guessed: *soul*
It ís the blight man was born for,
It is Margaret you mourn for.   15

GERARD MANLEY HOPKINS (1844–1889)
The Windhover°   1877

To Christ Our Lord

I caught this morning morning's minion,° king-   *favorite*
    dom of daylight's dauphin, dapple-dawn-drawn Falcon, in his riding
    Of the rolling level underneath him steady air, and striding
High there, how he rung upon the rein of a wimpling wing
In his ecstasy! then off, off forth on swing,   5
    As a skate's heel sweeps smooth on a bow-bend: the hurl and gliding
    Rebuffed the big wind. My heart in hiding
Stirred for a bird, — the achieve of, the mastery of the thing!

Brute beauty and valour and act, oh, air, pride, plume, here
    Buckle!° AND the fire that breaks from thee then, a billion   10
Times told lovelier, more dangerous, O my chevalier!

    No wonder of it: shéer plód makes plough down sillion°   *furrow*
Shine, and blue-bleak embers, ah my dear,
    Fall, gall themselves, and gash gold-vermilion.

The Windhover: "A name for the kestrel [a kind of small hawk], from its habit of hovering or hanging with its head to the wind" [*OED*].   10 *Buckle:* To join, to equip for battle, to crumple.

A. E. HOUSMAN (1859–1936)
Is my team ploughing   1896

"Is my team ploughing,
    That I was used to drive
And hear the harness jingle
    When I was man alive?"

Ay, the horses trample,   5
    The harness jingles now;
No change though you lie under
    The land you used to plough.

"Is football playing
    Along the river shore,   10
With lads to chase the leather,
    Now I stand up no more?"

Ay, the ball is flying,
    The lads play heart and soul;

The goal stands up, the keeper   15
    Stands up to keep the goal.

"Is my girl happy,
    That I thought hard to leave,
And has she tired of weeping
    As she lies down at eve?"   20

Ay, she lies down lightly,
    She lies not down to weep:
Your girl is well contented.
    Be still, my lad, and sleep.

"Is my friend hearty,   25
    Now I am thin and pine,
And has he found to sleep in
    A better bed than mine?"

Yes, lad, I lie easy,
    I lie as lads would choose;   30
I cheer a dead man's sweetheart,
    Never ask me whose.

A. E. HOUSMAN (1859–1936)
To an Athlete Dying Young   1896

The time you won your town the race
We chaired° you through the marketplace;
Man and boy stood cheering by,
And home we brought you shoulder-high.

Today, the road all runners come,   5
Shoulder-high we bring you home,
And set you at your threshold down,
Townsman of a stiller town.

Smart lad, to slip betimes away
From fields where glory does not stay,   10
And early though the laurel° grows
It withers quicker than the rose.

Eyes the shady night has shut
Cannot see the record cut,
And silence sounds no worse than cheers   15
After earth has stopped the ears:

Now you will not swell the rout
Of lads that wore their honors out,
Runners whom renown outran
And the name died before the man.   20

2 *chaired:* Carried on the shoulders in triumphal parade.   11 *laurel:* Flowering shrub traditionally
used to fashion wreaths of honor.

To set, before its echoes fade,
The fleet foot on the sill of shade,
And hold to the low lintel up
The still-defended challenge-cup.

And round that early-laureled head   25
Will flock to gaze the strengthless dead,
And find unwithered on its curls
The garland briefer than a girl's.

TED HUGHES (b. 1930)
Thistles   1961

Against the rubber tongues of cows and the hoeing hands of men
Thistles spike the summer air
Or crackle open under a blue-black pressure.

Every one a revengeful burst
Of resurrection, a grasped fistful   5
Of splintered weapons and Icelandic frost thrust up

From the underground stain of a decayed Viking.
They are like pale hair and the gutturals of dialects.
Every one manages a plume of blood.

Then they grow grey, like men.   10
Mown down, it is a feud. Their sons appear,
Stiff with weapons, fighting back over the same ground.

RANDALL JARRELL (1914–1965)
Next Day   1965

Moving from Cheer to Joy, from Joy to All,
I take a box
And add it to my wild rice, my Cornish game hens.
The slacked or shorted, basketed, identical
Food-gathering flocks   5
Are selves I overlook. Wisdom, said William James,°

Is learning what to overlook. And I am wise
If that is wisdom
Yet somehow, as I buy All from these shelves
And the boy takes it to my station wagon,   10
What I've become
Troubles me even if I shut my eyes.

6 *William James* (1842–1910): A psychologist and philosopher, author of *Principles of Psychology*
(1890).

When I was young and miserable and pretty
And poor, I'd wish
What all girls wish: to have a husband,   15
A house and children. Now that I'm old, my wish
Is womanish:
That the boy putting groceries in my car

See me. It bewilders me he doesn't see me.
For so many years   20
I was good enough to eat: the world looked at me
And its mouth watered. How often they have undressed me,
The eyes of strangers!
And, holding their flesh within my flesh, their vile

Imaginings within my imagining,   25
I too have taken
The chance of life. Now the boy pats my dog
And we start home. Now I am good.
The last mistaken,
Ecstatic, accidental bliss, the blind   30

Happiness that, bursting, leaves upon the palm
Some soap and water —
It was so long ago, back in some Gay
Twenties, Nineties, I don't know . . . Today I miss
My lovely daughter   35
Away at school, my sons away at school,

My husband away at work — I wish for them.
The dog, the maid,
And I go through the sure unvarying days
At home in them. As I look at my life,   40
I am afraid
Only that it will change, as I am changing:

I am afraid, this morning, of my face.
It looks at me
From the rear-view mirror, with the eyes I hate,   45
The smile I hate. Its plain, lined look
Of gray discovery
Repeats to me: "You're old." That's all, I'm old.

And yet I'm afraid, as I was at the funeral
I went to yesterday.   50
My friend's cold made-up face, granite among its flowers,
Her undressed, operated-on, dressed body
Were my face and body.
As I think of her I hear her telling me

How young I seem: I *am* exceptional;   55
I think of all I have.
But really no one is exceptional,
No one has anything, I'm anybody,
I stand beside my grave
Confused with my life, that is commonplace and solitary.   60

BEN JONSON (1573-1637)
On My First Son

1603

Farewell, thou child of my right hand,° and joy.
My sin was too much hope of thee, loved boy;
Seven years thou wert lent to me, and I thee pay,
Exacted by thy fate, on the just day.°
Oh, could I lose all father° now. For why
Will man lament the state he should envỳ? —
To have so soon 'scaped world's and flesh's rage,
And, if no other misery, yet age.
Rest in soft peace, and asked, say, "Here doth lie
Ben Jonson his best piece of poetry,"
For whose sake henceforth all his vows be such
As what he loves may never like too much.

his birthday
fatherhood 5

10

1 *child of my right hand:* This phrase translates the Hebrew name "Benjamin," Jonson's son.

BEN JONSON (1573-1637)
To Celia

1616

Drink to me only with thine eyes,
    And I will pledge with mine;
Or leave a kiss but in the cup,
    And I'll not ask for wine.
The thirst that from the soul doth rise
    Doth ask a drink divine;
But might I of Jove's nectar sup,
    I would not change for thine.

5

I sent thee late a rosy wreath,
    Not so much honoring thee
As giving it a hope that there
    It could not withered be.
But thou thereon didst only breathe,
    And sent'st it back to me;
Since when it grows, and smells, I swear,
    Not of itself but thee.

10

15

JOHN KEATS (1795-1821)
When I have fears that I may cease to be

1818

When I have fears that I may cease to be
    Before my pen has gleaned my teeming brain,
Before high-piled books, in charactery,°
    Hold like rich garners the full ripened grain;

print

When I behold, upon the night's starred face,   5
    Huge cloudy symbols of a high romance,
And think that I may never live to trace
    Their shadows, with the magic hand of chance;
And when I feel, fair creature of an hour,
    That I shall never look upon thee more,   10
Never have relish in the faery° power   *magic*
    Of unreflecting love; — then on the shore
Of the wide world I stand alone, and think
Till love and fame to nothingness do sink.

JOHN KEATS (1795–1821)
Bright star! would I were steadfast as thou art —   1819

Bright star, would I were steadfast as thou art —
    Not in lone splendor hung aloft the night
And watching, with eternal lids apart,
    Like nature's patient, sleepless Eremite,
The moving waters at their priestlike task   5
    Of pure ablution round earth's human shores,
Or gazing on the new soft fallen mask
    Of snow upon the mountains and the moors —
No — yet still steadfast, still unchangeable,
    Pillowed upon my fair love's ripening breast,   10
To feel forever its soft fall and swell,
    Awake forever in a sweet unrest,
Still, still to hear her tender-taken breath,
And so live ever — or else swoon to death.

JOHN KEATS (1795–1821)
La Belle Dame sans Merci°   1819

O what can ail thee, knight-at-arms,
    Alone and palely loitering?
The sedge has withered from the lake,
    And no birds sing.

O what can ail thee, knight-at-arms,   5
    So haggard and so woe-begone?
The squirrel's granary is full,
    And the harvest's done.

I see a lily on thy brow,
    With anguish moist and fever dew,   10

La Belle Dame sans Merci: This title is borrowed from a medieval poem and means "The Beautiful Lady without Mercy."

And on thy cheeks a fading rose
    Fast withereth too.

I met a lady in the meads,
    Full beautiful — a faery's child,
Her hair was long, her foot was light,   15
    And her eyes were wild.

I made a garland for her head,
    And bracelets too, and fragrant zone;°   *belt*
She looked at me as she did love,
    And made sweet moan.   20

I set her on my pacing steed,
    And nothing else saw all day long,
For sidelong would she bend, and sing
    A faery's song.

She found me roots of relish sweet,   25
    And honey wild, and manna dew,
And sure in language strange she said,
    "I love thee true."

She took me to her elfin grot,
    And there she wept, and sighed full sore,   30
And there I shut her wild wild eyes
    With kisses four.

And there she lullèd me asleep,
    And there I dreamed — Ah! woe betide!
The latest° dream I ever dreamed   *last*   35
    On the cold hill side.

I saw pale kings and princes too,
    Pale warriors, death-pale were they all;
They cried — "La Belle Dame sans Merci
    Hath thee in thrall!"   40

I saw their starved lips in the gloam,
    With horrid warning gapèd wide,
And I awoke and found me here,
    On the cold hill's side.

And this is why I sojourn here,   45
    Alone and palely loitering,
Though the sedge has withered from the lake,
    And no birds sing.

ETHERIDGE KNIGHT (b. 1931)
A Watts Mother Mourns While Boiling Beans   1973

The blooming flower of my life is roaming
in the night, and I think surely
that never since he was born

have I been free from fright.
My boy is bold, and his blood   5
grows quickly hot/ even now
he could be crawling in the street
bleeding out his life, likely as not.
Come home, my bold and restless son. — Stop
my heart's yearning! But I must quit   10
this thinking — my husband is coming
and the beans are burning.

TED KOOSER (b. 1939)
The Urine Specimen   1985

In the clinic, a sun-bleached shell of stone
on the shore of the city, you enter
the last small chamber, a little closet
chastened with pearl, cool, white, and glistening,
and over the chilly well of the toilet   5
you trickle your precious sum in a cup.
It's as simple as that. But the heat
of this gold your body's melted and poured out
into a form begins to enthrall you,
warming your hand with your flesh's fevers   10
in a terrible way. It's like holding
an organ — spleen or fatty pancreas,
a lobe from your foamy brain still steaming
with worry. You know that just outside
a nurse is waiting to cool it into a gel   15
and slice it onto a microscope slide
for the doctor, who in it will read your future,
wringing his hands. You lift the chalice and toast
the long life of your friend there in the mirror,
who wanly smiles, but does not drink to you.   20

PHILIP LARKIN (1922-1985)
This Be The Verse   1974

They fuck you up, your mum and dad.
    They may not mean to, but they do.
They fill you with the faults they had
    And add some extras, just for you.

But they were fucked up in their turn   5
    By fools in old-style hats and coats,
Who half the time were soppy-stern
    And half at one another's throats.

Man hands on misery to man.
    It deepens like a coastal shelf.
Get out as early as you can,
    And don't have any kids yourself.

10

LI-YOUNG LEE (b. 1957)
Eating Together

1986

In the steamer is the trout
seasoned with slivers of ginger,
two sprigs of green onion, and sesame oil.
We shall eat it with rice for lunch,
brothers, sister, my mother who will
taste the sweetest meat of the head,
holding it between her fingers
deftly, the way my father did
weeks ago. Then he lay down
to sleep like a snow-covered road
winding through pines older than him,
without any travelers, and lonely for no one.

5

10

DENISE LEVERTOV (b. 1923)
News Items

1975

i   America the Bountiful

After the welfare hotel
crumbled suddenly (after repeated warnings)
into the street,

Seventh Day Adventists brought supplies
of clothing to the survivors.
" 'Look at this,' exclaimed
Loretta Rollock, 48 years old,
as she held up a green dress
and lingerie. 'I've never worn
such nice clothes. I feel like
when I was a kid and my mom
brought me something.' Then
she began to cry."

5

10

ii   In the Rubble

For some the hotel's collapse meant
life would have to be started
all over again.

Sixty-year-old Charles, on welfare
like so many of the others, who said,

15

"We are the rootless people," and
"I have no home, no place that I can say I
really live in," and,
"I had become used to it here,"
also said:
"I lost
all I ever had,
in the rubble.
I lost my clothes,
I lost the picture of my parents
and I lost my television."

20

25

PHILIP LEVINE (b. 1928)
The Simple Truth

1995

I bought a dollar and a half's worth of small red potatoes,
took them home, boiled them in their jackets
and ate them for dinner with a little butter and salt.
Then I walked through the dried fields
on the edge of town. In middle June the light
hung on in the dark furrows at my feet,
and in the mountain oaks overhead the birds
were gathering for the night, the jays and mockers
squawking back and forth, the finches still darting
into the dusty light. The woman who sold me
the potatoes was from Poland; she was someone
out of my childhood in a pink spangled sweater and sunglasses
praising the perfection of all her fruits and vegetables
at the road-side stand and urging me to taste
even the pale, raw sweet corn trucked all the way,
she swore, from New Jersey. "Eat, eat," she said,
"Even if you don't I'll say you did."
                              Some things
you know all your life. They are so simple and true
they must be said without elegance, meter and rhyme,
they must be laid on the table beside the salt shaker,
the glass of water, the absence of light gathering
in the shadows of picture frames, they must be
naked and alone, they must stand for themselves.
My friend Henri and I arrived at this together in 1965
before I went away, before he began to kill himself,
and the two of us to betray our love. Can you taste
what I'm saying? It is onions or potatoes, a pinch
of simple salt, the wealth of melting butter, it is obvious,
it stays in the back of your throat like a truth
you never uttered because the time was always wrong,
it stays there for the rest of your life, unspoken,
made of that dirt we call earth, the metal we call salt,
in a form we have no words for, and you live on it.

5

10

15

20

25

30

HENRY WADSWORTH LONGFELLOW (1807–1882)
Snow-Flakes

1863

Out of the bosom of the Air,
   Out of the cloud-folds of her garments shaken,
Over the woodlands brown and bare
   Over the harvest-fields forsaken,
     Silent, and soft, and slow
     Descends the snow.   5

Even as our cloudy fancies take
   Suddenly shape in some divine expression,
Even as the troubled heart doth make
In the white countenance confession,   10
     The troubled sky reveals
     The grief it feels.

This is the poem of the air,
   Slowly in silent syllables recorded;
This is the secret of despair,
   Long in its cloudy bosom hoarded,   15
     Now whispered and revealed
     To wood and field.

AUDRE LORDE (1934–1992)
Hanging Fire

1978

I am fourteen
and my skin has betrayed me
the boy I cannot live without
still sucks his thumb
in secret
how come my knees are   5
always so ashy
what if I die
before morning
and mamma's in the bedroom
with the door closed.   10

I have to learn how to dance
in time for the next party
my room is too small for me
suppose I die before graduation
they will sing sad melodies   15
but finally
tell the truth about me
There is nothing I want to do
and too much
that has to be done   20

and momma's in the bedroom
with the door closed.

Nobody even stops to think
about my side of it
I should have been on Math Team
my marks were better than his
why do I have to be
the one
wearing braces
I have nothing to wear tomorrow
will I live long enough
to grow up
and momma's in the bedroom
with the door closed.

CHRISTOPHER MARLOWE (1564–1593)
The Passionate Shepherd to His Love   1599

Come live with me and be my love,
And we will all the pleasure prove
That valleys, groves, hills, and fields,
Woods, or steepy mountain yields.

And we will sit upon the rocks,   5
Seeing the shepherds feed their flocks,
By shallow rivers to whose falls
Melodious birds sing madrigals.

And I will make thee beds of roses
And a thousand fragrant posies,   10
A cap of flowers, and a kirtle
Embroidered all with leaves of myrtle;

A gown made of the finest wool
Which from our pretty lambs we pull;
Fair lined slippers for the cold,   15
With buckles of the purest gold;

A belt of straw and ivy buds,
With coral clasps and amber studs:
And if these pleasures may thee move,
Come live with me, and be my love.   20

The shepherd swains shall dance and sing
For thy delight each May morning:
If these delights thy mind may move,
Then live with me and be my love.

ANDREW MARVELL (1621–1678)
The Garden

1681

How vainly men themselves amaze°   *become frenzied*
To win the palm, the oak, or bays;°   *awards*
And their incessant labors see
Crowned from some single herb, or tree,
Whose short and narrow-vergèd° shade
Does prudently their toils upbraid;   *trimmed*   5
While all flowers and all trees do close
To weave the garlands of repose!

Fair Quiet, have I found thee here,
And Innocence, thy sister dear!   10
Mistaken long, I sought you then
In busy companies of men.
Your sacred plants, if here below,
Only among the plants will grow;
Society is all but rude
To this delicious solitude.   15

No white nor red was ever seen
So amorous as this lovely green.
Fond lovers, cruel as their flame,
Cut in these trees their mistress' name: 20
Little, alas! they know or heed
How far these beauties hers exceed!
Fair trees! wheres'e'er your barks I wound
No name shall but your own be found.

When we have run our passion's heat,   25
Love hither makes his best retreat.
The gods, that mortal beauty chase,
Still in a tree did end their race;
Apollo hunted Daphne so,
Only that she might laurel grow;   30
And Pan did after Syrinx speed,
Not as a nymph, but for a reed.°

What wondrous life is this I lead!
Ripe apples drop about my head;
The luscious clusters of the vine
Upon my mouth do crush their wine;   35
The nectarine, and curious° peach,   *exquisite*
Into my hands themselves do reach;
Stumbling on melons, as I pass,
Ensnar'd with flowers, I fall on grass.   40

Meanwhile, the mind, from pleasure less,
Withdraws into its happiness:
The mind, that ocean where each kind

29–32 *Apollo . . . reed:* In Ovid's *Metamorphoses,* Apollo chases Daphne, who is turned into a laurel, and Pan chases Syrinx, who is turned into a reed.

Does straight its own resemblance find;
Yet it creates, transcending these,   45
Far other worlds, and other seas;
Annihilating all that's made
To a green thought in a green shade.

Here at the fountain's sliding foot,
Or at some fruit-tree's mossy root,   50
Casting the body's vest aside,
My soul into the boughs does glide:
There like a bird it sits, and sings,
Then whets° and combs its silver wings;   *grooms*
And, till prepared for longer flight,   55
Waves in its plumes the various light.

Such was that happy garden-state,
While man there walked without a mate:
After a place so pure and sweet,
What other help could yet be meet?°   *appropriate*   60
But 'twas beyond a mortal's share
To wander solitary there:
Two paradises 'twere in one,
To live in paradise alone.

How well the skillful gardener drew   65
Of flowers, and herbs, this dial new;
Where, from above, the milder sun
Does through a fragrant zodiac run;
And, as it works, the industrious bee
Computes its time as well as we.   70
How could such sweet and wholesome hours
Be reckoned but with herbs and flowers!

HERMAN MELVILLE (1819–1891)
The Maldive Shark   1888

About the Shark, phlegmatical one,
Pale sot of the Maldive sea,
The sleek little pilot-fish, azure and slim,
How alert in attendance be.
From his saw-pit of mouth, from his charnel of maw   5
They have nothing of harm to dread,
But liquidly glide on his ghastly flank
Or before his Gorgonian head;
Or lurk in the port of serrated teeth
In white triple tiers of glittering gates,   10
And there find a haven when peril's abroad,
An asylum in jaws of the Fates!

They are friends; and friendly they guide him to prey,
Yet never partake of the treat —

Eyes and brains to the dotard lethargic and dull,   15
Pale ravener of horrible meat.

EDNA ST. VINCENT MILLAY (1892–1950)
What Lips My Lips Have Kissed   1923

What lips my lips have kissed, and where, and why,
I have forgotten, and what arms have lain
Under my head till morning; but the rain
Is full of ghosts tonight, that tap and sigh
Upon the glass and listen for reply,   5
And in my heart there stirs a quiet pain
For unremembered lads that not again
Will turn to me at midnight with a cry.
Thus in the winter stands the lonely tree,
Nor knows what birds have vanished one by one,   10
Yet knows its boughs more silent than before:
I cannot say what loves have come and gone,
I only know that summer sang in me
A little while, that in me sings no more.

JOHN MILTON (1608–1674)
On the Late Massacre in Piedmont°   1655

Avenge, O Lord, thy slaughtered saints, whose bones
   Lie scattered on the Alpine mountains cold;
   Even them who kept thy truth so pure of old,
When all our fathers worshiped stocks and stones,°
Forget not: in thy book record their groans   5
   Who were thy sheep, and in their ancient fold
   Slain by the bloody Piedmontese, that rolled
Mother with infant down the rocks.° Their moans
The vales redoubled to the hills, and they
   To heaven. Their martyred blood and ashes sow   10
O'er all the Italian fields, where still doth sway
   The triple Tyrant;° that from these may grow
   A hundredfold, who, having learnt thy way,
Early may fly the Babylonian woe.°

On the Late Massacre . . . .: Milton's protest against the treatment of the Waldenses, members of a Puritan sect living in Piedmont, was not limited to this sonnet. It is thought that he wrote Cromwell's appeals to the duke of Savoy and to others to end the persecution.   4 *When . . . stones:* In Milton's Protestant view, English Catholics had worshiped their stone and wooden statues in the twelfth century, when the Waldensian sect was formed.   5–8 *in thy book . . . rocks:* On Easter Day, 1655, 1,700 members of the Waldensian sect were massacred in Piedmont by the duke of Savoy's forces.   12 *triple Tyrant:* The Pope, with his three-crowned tiara, has authority on earth and in Heaven and Hell. 14 *Babylonian woe:* The destruction of Babylon, symbol of vice and corruption, at the end of the world (see Rev. 17–18). Protestants interpreted the "Whore of Babylon" as the Roman Catholic Church.

JOHN MILTON (1608–1674)
When I consider how my light is spent

c. 1655

When I consider how my light is spent,°
    Ere half my days in this dark world and wide,
    And that one talent° which is death to hide
Lodged with me useless, though my soul more bent
To serve therewith my Maker, and present   5
    My true account, lest He returning chide;
    "Doth God exact day-labor, light denied?"
I fondly° ask. But Patience, to prevent   *foolishly*
That murmur, soon replies, "God doth not need
    Either man's work or His own gifts. Who best   10
    Bear His mild yoke, they serve Him best. His state
Is kingly: thousands at His bidding speed,
    And post o'er land and ocean without rest;
    They also serve who only stand and wait."

1 *how my light is spent:* Milton had been totally blind since 1651.   3 *that one talent:* Refers to Jesus' parable of the talents (units of money), in which a servant entrusted with a talent buries it rather than invests it, and is punished upon his master's return (Matt. 25:14–30).

N. SCOTT MOMADAY (b. 1934)
The Bear

1992

    What ruse of vision,
escarping the wall of leaves,
    rending incision
into countless surfaces,

    would cull and color   5
his somnolence, whose old age
    has outworn valor,
all but the fact of courage?

    Seen, he does not come,
move, but seems forever there,   10
    dimensionless, dumb,
in the windless noon's hot glare.

    More scarred than others
these years since the trap maimed him,
    pain slants his withers,   15
drawing up the crooked limb.

    Then he is gone, whole,
without urgency, from sight,
    as buzzards control,
imperceptibly, their flight.   20

MARIANNE MOORE (1887-1972)
Poetry

1921

I, too, dislike it: there are things that are important beyond all this fiddle.
    Reading it, however, with a perfect contempt for it, one discovers in it
    after all, a place for the genuine.
        Hands that can grasp, eyes
        that can dilate, hair that can rise
            if it must, these things are important not because a   5

high-sounding interpretation can be put upon them but because they are
    useful. When they become so derivative as to become unintelligible,
    the same thing may be said for all of us, that we
        do not admire what
        we cannot understand: the bat   10
            holding on upside down or in quest of something to

eat, elephants pushing, a wild horse taking a roll, a tireless wolf under
    a tree, the immovable critic twitching his skin like a horse that feels a
        flea, the base-
    ball fan, the statistician —   15
        nor is it valid
            to discriminate against "business documents and

school-books"; all these phenomena are important. One must make a distinction
    however: when dragged into prominence by half poets, the result is
    not poetry,
    nor till the poets among us can be   20
        "literalists of
        the imagination" — above
            insolence and triviality and can present

for inspection, "imaginary gardens with real toads in them," shall we have
    it. In the meantime, if you demand on the one hand,   25
    the raw material of poetry in
        all its rawness and
        that which is on the other hand
            genuine, you are interested in poetry.

JON MUKAND (b. 1959)
Lullaby

1987

Each morning I finish my coffee,
And climb the stairs to the charts,
Hoping yours will be filed away.
But you can't hear me,
You can't see yourself clamped   5
Between this hard plastic binder:

Lab reports and nurses' notes, a sample
In a test tube. I keep reading
These terse comments: stable as before,
Urine output still poor, respiration normal. 10
And you keep on poisoning
Yourself, your kidneys more useless
Than seawings drenched in an oil spill.
I find my way to your room
And lean over the bedrails 15
As though I can understand
Your wheezed-out fragments.
What can I do but check
Your tubes, feel your pulse, listen
To your heartbeat insistent 20
As a spoiled child who goes on begging?

Old man, listen to me:
Let me take you in a wheelchair
To the back room of the records office,
Let me lift you in my arms 25
And lay you down in the cradle
Of a clean manila folder.

SUSAN MUSGRAVE (b. 1951)
Right through the Heart 1982

and out the other side,
pumping like a bitch in heat,
beast with two backs, the
left and right ventricles.

It has to be love 5
when it goes straight through;
no bone can stop it,
no barb impede its journey.

When it happens you have to bleed,
you want to kiss and hold on 10

despite all the messy blood
you want to embrace it.

You want it to last forever,
you want to own it.
You want to take love's tiny life 15
in your hands

and crush it to death before it dies.

FRANK O'HARA (1926–1966)
Autobiographia Literaria

When I was a child
I played by myself in a
corner of the schoolyard
all alone.

I hated dolls and I   5
hated games, animals were
not friendly and birds
flew away.

If anyone was looking
for me I hid behind a
tree and cried out "I am   10
an orphan."

And here I am, the
center of all beauty!
writing these poems!
Imagine!   15

MARY OLIVER (b. 1935)
The Black Snake

1979

When the black snake
flashed onto the morning road,
and the truck could not swerve —
death, that is how it happens.

Now he lies looped and useless   5
as an old bicycle tire.
I stop the car
and carry him into the bushes.

He is as cool and gleaming
as a braided whip, he is as beautiful and quiet   10
as a dead brother.
I leave him under the leaves

and drive on, thinking,
about *death:* its suddenness,
its terrible weight,   15
its certain coming. Yet under

reason burns a brighter fire, which the bones
have always preferred.
It is the story of endless good fortune.
It says to oblivion: not me!   20

It is the light at the center of every cell.
It is what sent the snake coiling and flowing forward

440 A Collection of Poems

happily all spring through the green leaves before
he came to the road.

WILFRED OWEN (1893–1918)
Arms and The Boy°   1917

Let the boy try along this bayonet-blade
How cold steel is, and keen with hunger of blood;
Blue with all malice, like a madman's flash;
And thinly drawn with famishing for flesh.

Lend him to stroke these blind, blunt bullet-leads,   5
Which long to nuzzle in the hearts of lads,
Or give him cartridges whose fine zinc teeth
Are sharp with sharpness of grief and death.

For his teeth seem for laughing round an apple.
There lurk no claws behind his fingers supple;   10
And God will grow no talons at his heels,
Nor antlers through the thickness of his curls.

Arms and The Boy: A variation on Virgil's the *Aeneid:* "Of arms and the man I sing."

LINDA PASTAN (b. 1932)
after minor surgery   1982

this is the dress rehearsal
when the body
like a constant lover
flirts for the first time
with faithlessness   5

when the body
like a passenger on a long journey
hears the conductor call out
the name
of the first stop   10

when the body
in all its fear and cunning
makes promises to me
it knows
it cannot keep   15

MARGE PIERCY (b. 1936)
Barbie Doll

1969

This girlchild was born as usual
and presented dolls that did pee-pee
and miniature GE stoves and irons
and wee lipsticks the color of cherry candy.
Then in the magic of puberty, a classmate said: 5
You have a great big nose and fat legs.

She was healthy, tested intelligent,
possessed strong arms and back,
abundant sexual drive and manual dexterity.
She went to and fro apologizing.   10
Everyone saw a fat nose on thick legs.

She was advised to play coy,
exhorted to come on hearty,
exercise, diet, smile and wheedle.
Her good nature wore out   15
like a fan belt.

So she cut off her nose and her legs
and offered them up.
In the casket displayed on satin she lay
with the undertaker's cosmetics painted on,   20
a turned-up putty nose,
dressed in a pink and white nightie.
Doesn't she look pretty? everyone said.
Consummation at last.
To every woman a happy ending.   25

SYLVIA PLATH (1932–1963)
Daddy

1962

You do not do, you do not do
Any more, black shoe
In which I have lived like a foot
For thirty years, poor and white,
Barely daring to breathe or Achoo.   5

Daddy, I have had to kill you.
You died before I had time —
Marble-heavy, a bag full of God,
Ghastly statue with one gray toe
Big as a Frisco seal   10

And a head in the freakish Atlantic
Where it pours bean green over blue
In the waters off beautiful Nauset.°   *Cape Cod inlet*

I used to pray to recover you.
Ach, du.°   *Oh, you*   15

In the German tongue, in the Polish Town°
Scraped flat by the roller
Of wars, wars, wars.
But the name of the town is common.
My Polack friend   20

Says there are a dozen or two.
So I never could tell where you
Put your foot, your root,
I never could talk to you.
The tongue stuck in my jaw.   25

It stuck in a barb wire snare.
Ich, ich, ich, ich,°   *I, I, I, I,*
I could hardly speak.
I thought every German was you.
And the language obscene   30

An engine, an engine
Chuffing me off like a Jew.
A Jew to Dachau, Auschwitz, Belsen.°
I began to talk like a Jew.
I think I may well be a Jew.   35

The snows of the Tyrol, the clear beer of Vienna
Are not very pure or true.
With my gypsy-ancestress and my weird luck
And my Taroc° pack and my Taroc pack
I may be a bit of a Jew.   40

I have always been scared of *you,*
With your Luftwaffe,° your gobbledygoo.
And your neat mustache
And your Aryan eye, bright blue.
Panzer-man, panzer-man,° O You —   45

Not God but a swastika
So black no sky could squeak through.
Every woman adores a Fascist,
The boot in the face, the brute
Brute heart of a brute like you.   50

You stand at the blackboard, daddy,
In the picture I have of you,
A cleft in your chin instead of your foot

---

16 *Polish Town:* Refers to Otto Plath's birthplace, Granbow.   33 *Dachau . . . Belsen:* Nazi death camps in World War II.   39 *Taroc:* Or *Tarot,* a pack of cards used to tell fortunes. It is said to have originated among the early Jewish Cabalists, and to have been transmitted to European Gypsies during the Middle Ages.   42 *Luftwaffe:* World War II German air force.   45 *panzer-man:* A member of the panzer division of the German army in World War II, which used armored vehicles and was organized for rapid attack.

But no less a devil for that, no not
Any less the black man who 55

Bit my pretty red heart in two.
I was ten when they buried you.
At twenty I tried to die
And get back, back, back to you.
I thought even the bones would do 60

But they pulled me out of the sack,
And they stuck me together with glue.
And then I knew what to do.
I made a model of you,
A man in black with a Meinkampf° look 65

And a love of the rack and the screw.
And I said I do, I do.
So daddy, I'm finally through.
The black telephone's off at the root,
The voices just can't worm through. 70

If I've killed one man, I've killed two —
The vampire who said he was you
And drank my blood for a year,
Seven years, if you want to know.
Daddy, you can lie back now. 75

There's a stake in your fat black heart
And the villagers never liked you.
They are dancing and stamping on you.
They always *knew* it was you.
Daddy, daddy, you bastard, I'm through. 80

65 *Meinkampf:* An allusion to Hitler's autobiography (*My Struggle*).

SYLVIA PLATH (1932–1963)
Metaphors 1960

I'm a riddle in nine syllables,
An elephant, a ponderous house,
A melon strolling on two tendrils.
O red fruit, ivory, fine timbers!
This loaf's big with its yeasty rising.
Money's new-minted in this fat purse.
I'm a means, a stage, a cow in calf.
I've eaten a bag of green apples,
Boarded the train there's no getting off.

EDGAR ALLAN POE (1809-1849)
Alone 1875

From childhood's hour I have not been
As others were — I have not seen
As others saw — I could not bring
My passions from a common spring —
From the same source I have not taken 5
My sorrow — I could not awaken
My heart to joy at the same tone —
And all I lov'd — *I* lov'd alone —
Then — in my childhood — in the dawn
Of a most stormy life — was drawn 10
From ev'ry depth of good and ill
The mystery which binds me still —
From the torrent, or the fountain —
From the red cliff of the mountain —
From the sun that round me roll'd 15
In its autumn tint of gold —
From the lightning in the sky
As it pass'd me flying by —
From the thunder, and the storm —
And the cloud that took the form 20
(When the rest of Heaven was blue)
Of a demon in my view —

EZRA POUND (1885-1972)
The River-Merchant's Wife: A Letter° 1915

While my hair was still cut straight across my forehead
I played about the front gate, pulling flowers.
You came by on bamboo stilts, playing horse,
You walked about my seat, playing with blue plums.
And we went on living in the village of Chokan: 5
Two small people, without dislike or suspicion.
At fourteen I married My Lord you.
I never laughed, being bashful.
Lowering my head, I looked at the wall.
Called to, a thousand times, I never looked back. 10

At fifteen I stopped scowling,
I desired my dust to be mingled with yours
Forever and forever and forever.
Why should I climb the lookout?

At sixteen you departed, 15
You went into far Ku-to-yen, by the river of swirling eddies,

The River-Merchant's Wife: A Letter: A free translation of a poem by Li Po (Chinese, 701–762).

And you have been gone five months.
The monkeys make sorrowful noise overhead.

You dragged your feet when you went out.
By the gate now, the moss is grown, the different mosses,   20
Too deep to clear them away!
The leaves fall early this autumn, in wind.
The paired butterflies are already yellow with August
Over the grass in the West garden;
They hurt me. I grow older.   25
If you are coming down through the narrows of the river Kiang,
Please let me know before hand,
And I will come out to meet you
     As far as Cho-fu-sa.

ADRIENNE RICH (b. 1929)

Living in Sin   1955

She had thought the studio would keep itself,
no dust upon the furniture of love.
Half heresy, to wish the taps less vocal,
the panes relieved of grime. A plate of pears,
a piano with a Persian shawl, a cat   5
stalking the picturesque amusing mouse
had risen at his urging.
Not that at five each separate stair would writhe
under the milkman's tramp; that morning light
so coldly would delineate the scraps   10
of last night's cheese and three sepulchral bottles;
that on the kitchen shelf among the saucers
a pair of beetle-eyes would fix her own —
envoy from some black village in the mouldings . . .
Meanwhile, he, with a yawn,   15
sounded a dozen notes upon the keyboard,
declared it out of tune, shrugged at the mirror,
rubbed at his beard, went out for cigarettes;
while she, jeered by the minor demons,
pulled back the sheets and made the bed and found   20
a towel to dust the table-top,
and let the coffee-pot boil over on the stove.
By evening she was back in love again,
though not so wholly but throughout the night
she woke sometimes to feel the daylight coming   25
like a relentless milkman up the stairs.

EDWIN ARLINGTON ROBINSON (1869–1935)

Mr. Flood's Party

1921

Old Eben Flood, climbing alone one night
Over the hill between the town below
And the forsaken upland hermitage
That held as much as he should ever know
On earth again of home, paused warily.   5
The road was his and not a native near;
And Eben, having leisure, said aloud,
For man else in Tilbury Town to hear:

"Well, Mr. Flood, we have the harvest moon
Again, and we may not have many more;   10
The bird is on the wing, the poet says,°
And you and I have said it here before.
Drink to the bird." He raised up to the light
The jug that he had gone so far to fill,
And answered huskily: "Well, Mr. Flood,   15
Since you propose it, I believe I will."

Alone, as if enduring to the end
A valiant armor of scarred hopes outworn,
He stood there in the middle of the road
Like Roland's ghost winding a silent horn.°   20
Below him, in the town among the trees,
Where friends of other days had honored him,
A phantom salutation of the dead
Rang thinly till old Eben's eyes were dim.

Then, as a mother lays her sleeping child   25
Down tenderly, fearing it may awake,
He set the jug down slowly at his feet
With trembling care, knowing that most things break;
And only when assured that on firm earth
It stood, as the uncertain lives of men   30
Assuredly did not, he paced away,
And with his hand extended paused again:

"Well, Mr. Flood, we have not met like this
In a long time; and many a change has come
To both of us, I fear, since last it was   35
We had a drop together. Welcome home!"
Convivially returning with himself,
Again he raised the jug up to the light;
And with an acquiescent quaver said:
"Well, Mr. Flood, if you insist, I might.   40

"Only a very little, Mr. Flood —
For auld lang syne. No more, sir; that will do."

11 *The bird . . . says:* Edward Fitzgerald says this of the "Bird of Time" in "The Rubáiyát of Omar Khayyám."   20 *Like Roland's . . . horn:* Roland, hero of French romance, blew his ivory horn to warn his allies of impending attack.

So, for the time, apparently it did,
And Eben evidently thought so too;
For soon amid the silver loneliness   45
Of night he lifted up his voice and sang,
Secure, with only two moons listening,
Until the whole harmonious landscape rang —

"For auld lang syne." The weary throat gave out,
The last word wavered, and the song being done.   50
He raised again the jug regretfully
And shook his head, and was again alone.
There was not much that was ahead of him,
And there was nothing in the town below —
Where strangers would have shut the many doors   55
That many friends had opened long ago.

THEODORE ROETHKE (1908-1963)
I Knew a Woman   1958

I knew a woman, lovely in her bones,
When small birds sighed, she would sigh back at them;
Ah, when she moved, she moved more ways than one:
The shapes a bright container can contain!
Of her choice virtues only gods should speak,   5
Or English poets who grew up on Greek
(I'd have them sing in chorus, cheek to cheek).

How well her wishes went! She stroked my chin,
She taught me Turn, and Counter-turn, and Stand;°
She taught me Touch, that undulant white skin;   10
I nibbled meekly from her proffered hand;
She was the sickle; I, poor I, the rake,
Coming behind her for her pretty sake
(But what prodigious mowing we did make).

Love likes a gander, and adores a goose: 15
Her full lips pursed, the errant note to seize;
She played it quick, she played it light and loose;
My eyes, they dazzled at her flowing knees;
Her several parts could keep a pure repose,
Or one hip quiver with a mobile nose   20
(She moved in circles, and those circles moved).

Let seed be grass, and grass turn into hay:
I'm martyr to a motion not my own;
What's freedom for? To know eternity.
I swear she cast a shadow white as stone.   25
But who would count eternity in days?
These old bones live to learn her wanton ways:
(I measure time by how a body sways).

9 *Turn . . . Stand:* Parts of a Pindaric ode.

CHRISTINA GEORGINA ROSSETTI (1830–1894)
Some Ladies Dress in Muslin Full and White   c. 1848

    Some ladies dress in muslin full and white,
Some gentlemen in cloth succinct and black;
Some patronise a dog-cart, some a hack,
    Some think a painted clarence only right.
    Youth is not always such a pleasing sight: 5
Witness a man with tassels on his back;
Or woman in a great-coat like a sack,
    Towering above her sex with horrid height.
If all the world were water fit to drown,
    There are some whom you would not teach to swim,   10
    Rather enjoying if you saw them sink:
    Certain old ladies dressed in girlish pink,
With roses and geraniums on their gown.
    Go to the basin, poke them o'er the rim —

VERN RUTSALA (b. 1934)
Words   1981

We had more than
we could use.
They embarrassed us,
our talk fuller than our
rooms. They named   5
nothing we could see —
dining room, study,
mantel piece, lobster
thermidor. They named
things you only   10
saw in movies —
the thin flicker Friday
nights that made us
feel empty in the cold
as we walked home   15
through our only great
abundance, snow.
This is why we said "ain't"
and "he don't."
We wanted words to fit   20
our cold linoleum,
our oil lamps, our
outhouse. We knew
better but it was wrong
to use a language   25
that named ghosts,

nothing you could touch.
We left such words at school
locked in books
where they belonged. 30
It was the vocabulary
of our lives that was
so thin. We knew this
and grew to hate
all the words that named 35
the vacancy of our rooms —
looking here we said
studio couch and saw cot;
looking there we said
venetian blinds and saw only the yard; 40
brick meant tarpaper,
fireplace meant wood stove.
And this is why we came to love
the double negative.

ANNE SEXTON (1928-1974)
Lobster 1976

A shoe with legs,
a stone dropped from heaven,
he does his mournful work alone,
he is like the old prospector for gold,
with secret dreams of God-heads and fish heads. 5
Until suddenly a cradle fastens round him
and he is trapped as the U.S.A. sleeps.
Somewhere far off a woman lights a cigarette;
somewhere far off a car goes over a bridge;
somewhere far off a bank is held up. 10
This is the world the lobster knows not of.
He is the old hunting dog of the sea
who in the morning will rise from it
and be undrowned
and they will take his perfect green body 15
and paint it red.

WILLIAM SHAKESPEARE (1564-1616)
Not marble, nor the gilded monuments 1609

Not marble, nor the gilded monuments
Of princes, shall outlive this powerful rhyme;
But you shall shine more bright in these conténts

Than unswept stone, besmeared with sluttish time.
When wasteful war shall statues overturn,   5
And broils root out the work of masonry,
Nor Mars his° swords nor war's quick fire shall burn   *possessive of Mars*
The living record of your memory.
'Gainst death and all-oblivious enmity
Shall you pace forth; your praise shall still find room   10
Even in the eyes of all posterity
That wear this world out to the ending doom.
    So, till the judgment that yourself arise,
    You live in this, and dwell in lovers' eyes.

WILLIAM SHAKESPEARE (1564–1616)
Spring°   c. 1595

When daisies pied and violets blue
    And ladysmocks all silver-white
And cuckoobuds of yellow hue
    Do paint the meadows with delight,
The cuckoo then, on every tree,   5
Mocks married men;° for thus sings he,
      Cuckoo;
Cuckoo, cuckoo: Oh word of fear,
Unpleasing to a married ear!

When shepherds pipe on oaten straws,   10
    And merry larks are plowmen's clocks,
When turtles tread,° and rooks, and daws,
    And maidens bleach their summer smocks,
The cuckoo then, on every tree,
Mocks married men; for thus sings he,   15
      Cuckoo;
Cuckoo, cuckoo: Oh word of fear,
Unpleasing to a married ear!

Spring: Song from *Love's Labour's Lost,* V.ii.   6 *Mocks married men:* By singing "cuckoo," which sounds like "cuckold."   12 *turtles tread:* Turtledoves copulate.

WILLIAM SHAKESPEARE (1564–1616)
That time of year thou mayst in me behold   1609

That time of year thou mayst in me behold
When yellow leaves, or none, or few, do hang
Upon those boughs which shake against the cold,
Bare ruined choirs, where late the sweet birds sang.
In me thou see'st the twilight of such day   5

As after sunset fadeth in the west;
Which by and by black night doth take away,
Death's second self,° that seals up all in rest.   *sleep*
In me thou see'st the glowing of such fire,
That on the ashes of his youth doth lie,   10
As the deathbed whereon it must expire,
Consumed with that which it was nourished by.
    This thou perceiv'st, which makes thy love more strong,
    To love that well which thou must leave ere long.

WILLIAM SHAKESPEARE (1564–1616)
When forty winters shall besiege thy brow   1609

When forty winters shall besiege thy brow
And dig deep trenches in thy beauty's field,
Thy youth's proud livery, so gazed on now,
Will be a tattered weed,° of small worth held.   *garment*
Then being asked where all thy beauty lies,   5
Where all the treasure of thy lusty days,
To say within thine own deep-sunken eyes
Were an all-eating shame and thriftless praise.
How much more praise deserved thy beauty's use
If thou couldst answer, "This fair child of mine   10
Shall sum my count and make my old excuse,"
Proving his beauty by succession thine.
    This were to be new made when thou art old,
    And see thy blood warm when thou feel'st it cold.

WILLIAM SHAKESPEARE (1564–1616)
When, in disgrace with Fortune and men's eyes   1609

When, in disgrace with Fortune and men's eyes,
I all alone beweep my outcast state,
And trouble deaf heaven with my bootless cries,
And look upon myself and curse my fate,
Wishing me like to one more rich in hope,   5
Featured like him, like him with friends possessed,
Desiring this man's art, and that man's scope,
With what I most enjoy contented least,
Yet in these thoughts myself almost despising,
Haply I think on thee, and then my state,   10
Like to the lark at break of day arising
From sullen earth, sings hymns at heaven's gate;
    For thy sweet love remembered such wealth brings
    That then I scorn to change my state with kings.

WILLIAM SHAKESPEARE (1564–1616)
Winter°

c. 1595

When icicles hang by the wall
    And Dick the shepherd blows his nail,°
And Tom bears logs into the hall,
    And milk comes frozen home in pail.
When blood is nipped and ways be foul,   5
Then nightly sings the staring owl,
        Tu-who;
Tu-whit, tu-who: a merry note,
While greasy Joan doth keel the pot.°

When all aloud the wind doth blow,   10
    And coughing drowns the parson's saw,°   *maxim*
And birds sit brooding in the snow,
    And Marian's nose looks red and raw,
When roasted crabs° hiss in the bowl,   *crabapples*
Then nightly sings the staring owl,   15
        Tu-who;
Tu-whit, tu-who: a merry note
While greasy Joan doth keel the pot.

Winter: Song from *Love's Labour's Lost,* V.ii.   *2 blows his nail:* Blows on his hand for warmth.
9 keel the pot: Cool the contents of the pot by stirring.

PERCY BYSSHE SHELLEY (1792–1822)
Ozymandias°

1818

I met a traveler from an antique land
Who said: Two vast and trunkless legs of stone
Stand in the desert. . . . Near them, on the sand,
Half sunk, a shattered visage lies, whose frown,
And wrinkled lip, and sneer of cold command,   5
Tell that its sculptor well those passions read
Which yet survive, stamped on these lifeless things,
The hand that mocked them, and the heart that fed:
And on the pedestal these words appear:
"My name is Ozymandias, King of Kings: 10
Look on my works, ye Mighty, and despair!"
Nothing beside remains. Round the decay
Of that colossal wreck, boundless and bare
The lone and level sands stretch far away.

Ozymandias: Greek name for Ramses II, pharaoh of Egypt for sixty-seven years during the thirteenth century B.C. His colossal statue lies prostrate in the sands of Luxor. Napoleon's soldiers measured it (56 feet long, ear 3½ feet long, weight 1,000 tons). Its inscription, according to the Greek historian Diodorus Siculus, was "I am Ozymandias, King of Kings; if anyone wishes to know what I am and where I lie, let him surpass me in some of my exploits."

SIR PHILIP SIDNEY (1554–1586)

Loving in Truth, and Fain in Verse
My Love to Show   1591

Loving in truth, and fain in verse my love to show,
That she, dear she, might take some pleasure of my pain,
Pleasure might cause her read, reading might make her know,
Knowledge might pity win, and pity grace obtain,
I sought fit words to paint the blackest face of woe,   5
Studying inventions fine, her wits to entertain,
Oft turning others' leaves, to see if thence would flow
Some fresh and fruitful showers upon my sunburnt brain.
But words came halting forth, wanting Invention's stay;
Invention, Nature's child, fled step-dame° Study's blows;   *stepmother*   10
And others' feet still seemed but strangers in my way.
Thus great with child to speak, and helpless in my throes,
Biting my truant pen, beating myself for spite:
"Fool," said my Muse to me, "look in thy heart and write."

GARY SNYDER (b. 1930)

How Poetry Comes to Me   1992

It comes blundering over the
Boulders at night, it stays
Frightened outside the
Range of my campfire
I go to meet it at the
Edge of the light

GARY SOTO (b. 1952)

Black Hair   1985

At eight I was brilliant with my body.
In July, that ring of heat
We all jumped through, I sat in the bleachers
Of Romain Playground, in the lengthening
Shade that rose from our dirty feet.   5
The game before us was more than baseball.
It was a figure — Hector Moreno
Quick and hard with turned muscles,
His crouch the one I assumed before an altar
Of worn baseball cards, in my room.   10
I came here because I was Mexican, a stick

Of brown light in love with those
Who could do it — the triple and hard slide,
The gloves eating balls into double plays.
What could I do with 50 pounds, my shyness,   15
My black torch of hair, about to go out?
Father was dead, his face no longer
Hanging over the table or our sleep,
And mother was the terror of mouths
Twisting hurt by butter knives.   20

In the bleachers I was brilliant with my body,
Waving players in and stomping my feet,
Growing sweaty in the presence of white shirts.
I chewed sunflower seeds. I drank water
And bit my arm through the late innings.   25
When Hector lined balls into deep
Center, in my mind I rounded the bases
With him, my face flared, my hair lifting
Beautifully, because we were coming home
To the arms of brown people.   30

WALLACE STEVENS (1879–1955)
The Emperor of Ice-Cream   1923

Call the roller of big cigars,
The muscular one, and bid him whip
In kitchen cups concupiscent curds.°
Let the wenches dawdle in such dress
As they are used to wear, and let the boys   5
Bring flowers in last month's newspapers.
Let be be finale of seem.°
The only emperor is the emperor of ice-cream.

Take from the dresser of deal,
Lacking the three glass knobs, that sheet   10
On which she embroidered fantails once
And spread it so as to cover her face.
If her horny feet protrude, they come
To show how cold she is, and dumb.
Let the lamp affix its beam.   15
The only emperor is the emperor of ice-cream.

3 *concupiscent curds:* "The words 'concupiscent curds' have no genealogy; they are merely expressive: at least, I hope they are expressive. They express the concupiscence of life, but, by contrast with
the things in relation in the poem, they express or accentuate life's destitution, and it is this that gives
them something more than a cheap lustre" (Wallace Stevens, *Letters* [New York: Knopf, 1960], p. 500).
7 *Let . . . seem:* "The true sense of 'Let be be the finale of seem' is let being become the conclusion
or denouement of appearing to be: in short, ice cream is an absolute good. The poem is obviously
not about ice cream, but about being as distinguished from seeming to be" (*Letters*, p. 341).

MARK STRAND (b. 1934)
Sleeping with One Eye Open

1964

Unmoved by what the wind does,
The windows
Are not rattled, nor do the various
Areas
Of the house make their usual racket —   5
Creak at
The joints, trusses and studs.
Instead,
They are still. And the maples,
Able   10
At times to raise havoc,
Evoke
Not a sound from their branches'
Clutches.
It's my night to be rattled,   15
Saddled
With spooks. Even the half-moon
(Half man,
Half dark), on the horizon,
Lies on   20
Its side casting a fishy light
Which alights
On my floor, lavishly lording
Its morbid
Look over me. Oh, I feel dead,   25
Folded
Away in my blankets for good, and
Forgotten.
My room is clammy and cold,
Moonhandled   30
And weird. The shivers
Wash over
Me, shaking my bones, my loose ends
Loosen,
And I lie sleeping with one eye open,   35
Hoping
That nothing, nothing will happen.

ALFRED, LORD TENNYSON (1809–1892)
Crossing the Bar

1889

Sunset and evening star,
        And one clear call for me!
And may there be no moaning of the bar
        When I put out to sea.

But such a tide as moving seems asleep, 5
    Too full for sound and foam,
When that which drew from out the boundless deep
    Turns again home.

Twilight and evening bell,
    And after that the dark! 10
And may there be no sadness of farewell
    When I embark;

For though from out our bourne of Time and Place
    The flood may bear me far,
I hope to see my Pilot face to face 15
    When I have crossed the bar.

ALFRED, LORD TENNYSON (1809–1892)

Ulysses° 1833

    It little profits that an idle king,
By this still hearth, among these barren crags,
Matched with an agèd wife,° I mete and dole   *Penelope*
Unequal laws unto a savage race,
That hoard, and sleep, and feed, and know not me. 5
    I cannot rest from travel; I will drink
Life to the lees. All times I have enjoyed
Greatly, have suffered greatly, both with those
That loved me, and alone; on shore, and when
Through scudding drifts the rainy Hyades° 10
Vexed the dim sea. I am become a name;
For always roaming with a hungry heart
Much have I seen and known — cities of men
And manners, climates, councils, governments,
Myself not least, but honored of them all — 15
And drunk delight of battle with my peers,
Far on the ringing plains of windy Troy.
I am a part of all that I have met;
Yet all experience is an arch wherethrough
Gleams that untraveled world, whose margin fades 20
For ever and for ever when I move.
How dull it is to pause, to make an end,
To rust unburnished, not to shine in use!
As though to breathe were life. Life piled on life
Were all too little, and of one to me 25
Little remains; but every hour is saved
From that eternal silence, something more,
A bringer of new things; and vile it were

<hr>

Ulysses: Ulysses, the hero of Homer's epic poem the *Odyssey,* is presented by Dante in *The Inferno,*
XXVI, as restless after his return to Ithaca, and eager for new adventures.   10 *Hyades:* Five stars in
the constellation Taurus, supposed by the ancients to predict rain when they rose with the sun.

For some three suns to store and hoard myself,
And this gray spirit yearning in desire
To follow knowledge like a sinking star,
Beyond the utmost bound of human thought.

    This is my son, mine own Telemachus,
To whom I leave the scepter and the isle —
Well-loved of me, discerning to fulfill
This labor, by slow prudence to make mild
A rugged people, and through soft degrees
Subdue them to the useful and the good.
Most blameless is he, centered in the sphere
Of common duties, decent not to fail
In offices of tenderness, and pay
Meet adoration to my household gods,
When I am gone. He works his work, I mine.

    There lies the port; the vessel puffs her sail:
There gloom the dark, broad seas. My mariners,
Souls that have toiled, and wrought, and thought with me —
That ever with a frolic welcome took
The thunder and the sunshine, and opposed
Free hearts, free foreheads — you and I are old;
Old age hath yet his honor and his toil.
Death closes all; but something ere the end,
Some work of noble note, may yet be done,
Not unbecoming men that strove with Gods.
The lights begin to twinkle from the rocks;
The long day wanes; the slow moon climbs; the deep
Moans round with many voices. Come, my friends.
'Tis not too late to seek a newer world.
Push off, and sitting well in order smite
The sounding furrows; for my purpose holds
To sail beyond the sunset, and the baths
Of all the western stars, until I die.
It may be that the gulfs will wash us down;
It may be we shall touch the Happy Isles,°
And see the great Achilles,° whom we knew.
Though much is taken, much abides; and though
We are not now that strength which in old days
Moved earth and heaven, that which we are, we are:
One equal temper of heroic hearts,
Made weak by time and fate, but strong in will
To strive, to seek, to find, and not to yield.

63 *Happy Isles:* Elysium, the home after death of heroes and others favored by the gods. It was thought by the ancients to lie beyond the sunset in the uncharted Atlantic.   64 *Achilles:* The hero of Homer's *Iliad.*

DYLAN THOMAS (1914-1953)
Fern Hill   1946

Now as I was young and easy under the apple boughs
About the lilting house and happy as the grass was green,
   The night above the dingle starry,
    Time let me hail and climb
   Golden in the heydays of his eyes,   5
And honored among wagons I was prince of the apple towns
And once below a time I lordly had the trees and leaves
    Trail with daisies and barley
   Down the rivers of the windfall light.

And as I was green and carefree, famous among the barns   10
About the happy yard and singing as the farm was home,
   In the sun that is young once only,
    Time let me play and be
   Golden in the mercy of his means,
And green and golden I was huntsman and herdsman, the calves   15
Sang to my horn, the foxes on the hills barked clear and cold,
    And the sabbath rang slowly
   In the pebbles of the holy streams.

All the sun long it was running, it was lovely, the hay
Fields high as the house, the tunes from the chimneys, it was air   20
   And playing, lovely and watery
    And fire green as grass.
   And nightly under the simple stars
As I rode to sleep the owls were bearing the farm away,
All the moon long I heard, blessed among stables, the nightjars   25
   Flying with the ricks, and the horses
    Flashing into the dark.

And then to awake, and the farm, like a wanderer white
With the dew, come back, the cock on his shoulder; it was all
   Shining, it was Adam and maiden,   30
    The sky gathered again
   And the sun grew round that very day.
So it must have been after the birth of the simple light
In the first, spinning place, the spellbound horses walking warm
   Out of the whinnying green stable   35
    On to the fields of praise.

And honored among foxes and pheasants by the gay house
Under the new made clouds and happy as the heart was long,
   In the sun born over and over,
    I ran my heedless ways,   40
   My wishes raced through the house-high hay
And nothing I cared, at my sky-blue trades, that time allows
In all his tuneful turning so few and such morning songs
   Before the children green and golden
    Follow him out of grace,   45

Nothing I cared, in the lamb white days, that time would take me
Up to the swallow-thronged loft by the shadow of my hand,
   In the moon that is always rising,
     Nor that riding to sleep
   I should hear him fly with the high fields
And wake to the farm forever fled from the childless land.   50
Oh as I was young and easy in the mercy of his means,
    Time held me green and dying
   Though I sang in my chains like the sea.

DIANE WAKOSKI (b. 1937)
Belly Dancer   1966

Can these movements which move themselves
be the substance of my attraction?
Where does this thin green silk come from that covers my body?
Surely any woman wearing such fabrics
would move her body just to feel them touching every part of her.   5

Yet most of the women frown, or look away, or laugh stiffly.
They are afraid of these materials and these movements in some way.
The psychologists would say they are afraid of themselves, somehow.
Perhaps awakening too much desire —
that their men could never satisfy?   10

So they keep themselves laced and buttoned and made up
in hopes that the framework will keep them stiff enough not to feel
the whole register.
In hopes that they will not have to experience that unquenchable desire
for rhythm and contact.   15

If a snake glided across this floor
most of them would faint or shrink away.
Yet that movement could be their own.
That smooth movement frightens them —
awakening ancestors and relatives to the tips of the arms and toes.   20

So my bare feet
and my thin green silks
my bells and finger cymbals
offend them — frighten their old-young bodies.
While the men simper and leer —   25
glad for the vicarious experience and exercise.
They do not realize how I scorn them:
or how I dance for their frightened,
unawakened, sweet
women.   30

ROBERT WALLACE (b. 1932)
The Double-Play

1961

In his sea lit
distance, the pitcher winding
like a clock about to chime comes down with

the ball, hit
sharply, under the artificial
banks of arc-lights, bounds like a vanishing string

over the green
to the shortstop magically
scoops to his right whirling above his invisible

shadows
in the dust redirects
its flight to the running poised second baseman

pirouettes
leaping, above the slide, to throw
from mid-air, across the colored tightened interval,

to the leaning-
out first baseman ends the dance
drawing it disappearing into his long brown glove

stretches. What
is too swift for deception
is final, lost, among the loosened figures

jogging off the field
(the pitcher walks), casual
in the space where the poem has happened.

5

10

15

20

EDMUND WALLER (1606–1687)
Go, Lovely Rose

1645

   Go, lovely rose,
Tell her that wastes her time and me
   That now she knows,
When I resemble° her to thee,
How sweet and fair she seems to be.

compare

5

   Tell her that's young
And shuns to have her graces spied,
   That hadst thou sprung
In deserts where no men abide,
Thou must have uncommended died.

10

   Small is the worth
Of beauty from the light retired:

Bid her come forth,
Suffer herself to be desired,
And not blush so to be admired.   15

Then die, that she
The common fate of all things rare
    May read in thee,
How small a part of time they share
That are so wondrous sweet and fair.   20

WALT WHITMAN (1819–1892)
The Dalliance of the Eagles   1880

Skirting the river road, (my forenoon walk, my rest,)
Skyward in air a sudden muffled sound, the dalliance of the eagles,
The rushing amorous contact high in space together,
The clinching interlocking claws, a living, fierce, gyrating wheel,
Four beating wings, two beaks, a swirling mass tight grappling,   5
In tumbling turning clustering loops, straight downward falling,
Till o'er the river poised, the twain yet one, a moment's lull,
A motionless still balance in the air, then parting, talons loosing,
Upward again on slow-firm pinions slanting, their separate diverse flight,
She hers, he his, pursuing.   10

WALT WHITMAN (1819–1892)
One Hour to Madness and Joy   1860

One hour to madness and joy! O furious! O confine me not!
(What is this that frees me so in storms?
What do my shouts amid lightnings and raging winds mean?)

O to drink the mystic deliria deeper than any other man!
O savage and tender achings! (I bequeath them to you my children,   5
I tell them to you, for reasons, O bridegroom and bride.)
O to be yielded to you whoever you are, and you to be yielded to me in
    defiance of the world!
O to return to Paradise! O bashful and feminine!
O to draw you to me, to plant on you for the first time the lips of a determin'd
    man.

O the puzzle, the thrice-tied knot, the deep and dark pool, all untied and   10
    illumin'd!
O to speed where there is space enough and air enough at last!
To be absolv'd from previous ties and conventions, I from mine and you from
    yours!

To find a new unthought-of nonchalance with the best of Nature!
To have the gag remov'd from one's mouth!
To have the feeling to-day or any day I am sufficient as I am. 15

O something unprov'd! something in a trance!
To escape utterly from others' anchors and holds!
To drive free! to love free! to dash reckless and dangerous!
To court destruction with taunts, with invitations!
To ascend, to leap to the heavens of the love indicated to me! 20
To rise thither with my inebriate soul!
To be lost if it must be so!
To feed the remainder of life with one hour of fulness and freedom!
With one brief hour of madness and joy.

WALT WHITMAN (1819–1892)
One's-Self I Sing   1867

One's-Self I sing, a simple separate person,
Yet utter the word Democratic, the word En-Masse.

Of physiology from top to toe I sing,
Not physiognomy alone nor brain alone is worthy for the Muse, I say the Form
    complete is worthier far,
The Female equally with the Male I sing.

Of Life immense in passion, pulse, and power,
Cheerful, for freest action formed under the laws divine,
The Modern Man I sing.

WALT WHITMAN (1819–1892)
There Was a Child Went Forth   1855

There was a child went forth every day,
And the first object he looked upon, that object he became,
And that object became part of him for the day or a certain part of the day,
Or for many years or stretching cycles of years.

The early lilacs became part of this child,   5
And grass and white and red morning-glories, and white and red clover, and the
    song of the phoebe-bird,
And the Third-month° lambs and the sow's pink-faint litter, and the mare's foal
    and the cow's calf,
And the noisy brood of the barnyard or by the mire of the pond-side,

---

7 *Third-month:* Quaker term for March.

And the fish suspending themselves so curiously below there, and the beautiful
    curious liquid,
And the water-plants with their graceful flat heads, all became part of him.   10

The field-sprouts of Fourth-month and Fifth-month became part of him,
Winter-grain sprouts and those of the light-yellow corn, and the esculent roots
    of the garden,
And the apple-trees covered with blossoms and the fruit afterward, and wood-
    berries, and the commonest weeds by the road,
And the old drunkard staggering home from the outhouse of the tavern whence
    he had lately risen,
And the schoolmistress that passed on her way to the school,   15
And the friendly boys that passed, and the quarrelsome boys,
And the tidy and fresh-cheeked girls, and the barefoot negro boy and girl,
And all the changes of city and country wherever he went.

His own parents, he that had fathered him and she that had conceived him in
    her womb and birthed him,
They gave this child more of themselves than that,   20
They gave him afterward every day, they became part of him.

The mother at home quietly placing the dishes on the supper-table,
The mother with mild words, clean her cap and gown, a wholesome odor
    falling off her person and clothes as she walks by,
The father, strong, self-sufficient, manly, mean, angered, unjust,
The blow, the quick loud word, the tight bargain, the crafty lure,   25
The family usages, the language, the company, the furniture, the yearning and
    swelling heart,
Affection that will not be gainsayed, the sense of what is real, the thought if
    after all it should prove unreal,
The doubts of day-time and the doubts of night-time, the curious whether and
    how,
Whether that which appears so is so, or is it all flashes and specks?
Men and women crowding fast in the streets, if they are not flashes and specks
    what are they?   30
The streets themselves and the facades of houses, and goods in the windows,
Vehicles, teams, the heavy-planked wharves, the huge crossing at the ferries,
The village on the highland seen from afar at sunset, the river between,
Shadows, aureola and mist, the light falling on roofs and gables of white or
    brown two miles off,
The schooner near by sleepily dropping down the tide, the little boat
    slack-towed astern,   35
The hurrying tumbling waves, quick-broken crests, slapping,
The strata of colored clouds, the long bar of maroon-tint away solitary by itself,
    the spread of purity it lies motionless in,
The horizon's edge, the flying sea-crow, the fragrance of salt marsh and shore
    mud,
These became part of that child who went forth every day, and who now goes,
    and will always go forth every day.

RICHARD WILBUR (b. 1921)

Love Calls Us to the Things of This World°   1956

    The eyes open to a cry of pulleys,°
And spirited from sleep, the astounded soul
Hangs for a moment bodiless and simple
As false dawn.
                Outside the open window   5
The morning air is all awash with angels.
Some are in bed-sheets, some are in blouses,
Some are in smocks: but truly there they are.
Now they are rising together in calm swells
Of halcyon feeling, filling whatever they wear   10
With the deep joy of their impersonal breathing;
Now they are flying in place, conveying
The terrible speed of their omnipresence, moving
And staying like white water; and now of a sudden
They swoon down into so rapt a quiet   15
That nobody seems to be there.
                      The soul shrinks

                 From all that it is about to remember,
From the punctual rape of every blessèd day,
And cries,   20
          "Oh, let there be nothing on earth but laundry,
Nothing but rosy hands in the rising steam
And clear dances done in the sight of heaven."

Yet, as the sun acknowledges
With a warm look the world's hunks and colors,   25
The soul descends once more in bitter love
To accept the waking body, saying now
In a changed voice as the man yawns and rises,

"Bring them down from their ruddy gallows;
Let there be clean linen for the backs of thieves;   30
Let lovers go fresh and sweet to be undone,
And the heaviest nuns walk in a pure floating
Of dark habits,
            keeping their difficult balance."

Loves Calls Us . . . : From St. Augustine's *Commentary on the Psalms.*   1 *pulleys:* Grooved wheels at
each end of a laundry line; clothes are hung on the line and advance as the line is moved.

MILLER WILLIAMS (b. 1930)

Thinking about Bill, Dead of AIDS   1989

We did not know the first thing about
how blood surrenders to even the smallest threat
when old allergies turn inside out,

the body rescinding all its normal orders
to all defenders of flesh, betraying the head,   5
pulling its guards back from all its borders.

Thinking of friends afraid to shake your hand,
we think of your hand shaking, your mouth set,
your eyes drained of any reprimand.

Loving, we kissed you, partly to persuade   10
both you and us, seeing what eyes had said,
that we were loving and we were not afraid.

If we had had more, we would have given more.
As it was we stood next to your bed,
stopping, though, to set our smiles at the door.   15

Not because we were less sure at the last.
Only because, not knowing anything yet,
we didn't know what look would hurt you least.

WILLIAM CARLOS WILLIAMS (1883-1963)
Spring and All   1923

By the road to the contagious hospital
under the surge of the blue
mottled clouds driven from the
northeast — a cold wind. Beyond, the
waste of broad, muddy fields   5
brown with dried weeds, standing and fallen

patches of standing water
and scattering of tall trees

All along the road the reddish
purplish, forked, upstanding, twiggy
stuff of bushes and small trees   10
with dead, brown leaves under them
leafless vines —

Lifeless in appearance, sluggish
dazed spring approaches —   15

They enter the new world naked,
cold, uncertain of all
save that they enter. All about them
the cold, familiar wind —

Now the grass, tomorrow   20
the stiff curl of wildcarrot leaf
One by one objects are defined —
It quickens: clarity, outline of leaf

But now the stark dignity of
entrance — Still, the profound change   25

has come upon them: rooted, they
grip down and begin to awaken

WILLIAM CARLOS WILLIAMS (1883–1963)
This Is Just to Say   1934

I have eaten
the plums
that were in
the icebox

and which   5
you were probably
saving
for breakfast

Forgive me
they were delicious   10
so sweet
and so cold

WILLIAM WORDSWORTH (1770–1850)
I Wandered Lonely as a Cloud   1807

I wandered lonely as a cloud
That floats on high o'er vales and hills,
When all at once I saw a crowd,
A host, of golden daffodils,
Beside the lake, beneath the trees,   5
Fluttering and dancing in the breeze.

Continuous as the stars that shine
And twinkle on the milky way,
They stretched in never-ending line
Along the margin of a bay;   10
Ten thousand saw I at a glance,
Tossing their heads in sprightly dance.

The waves beside them danced, but they
Outdid the sparkling waves in glee;
A poet could not but be gay,   15
In such a jocund company;
I gazed — and gazed — but little thought
What wealth the show to me had brought:

For oft, when on my couch I lie
In vacant or in pensive mood,   20
They flash upon that inward eye

Which is the bliss of solitude;
And then my heart with pleasure fills,
And dances with the daffodils.

WILLIAM WORDSWORTH (1770–1850)
A Slumber Did My Spirit Seal
1800

A slumber did my spirit seal;
  I had no human fears —
She seemed a thing that could not feel
  The touch of earthly years.

No motion has she now, no force;
  She neither hears nor sees;
Rolled round in earth's diurnal course,
  With rocks, and stones, and trees.

WILLIAM WORDSWORTH (1770–1850)
The Solitary Reaper°
1807

Behold her, single in the field,
Yon solitary Highland lass!
Reaping and singing by herself;
Stop here, or gently pass!
Alone she cuts and binds the grain,   5
And sings a melancholy strain;
O listen! for the vale profound
Is overflowing with the sound.

No nightingale did ever chaunt
More welcome notes to weary bands   10
Of travelers in some shady haunt
Among Arabian sands.
A voice so thrilling ne'er was heard
In springtime from the cuckoo-bird,
Breaking the silence of the seas   15
Among the farthest Hebrides.

Will no one tell me what she sings? —
Perhaps the plaintive numbers flow
For old, unhappy, far-off things,
And battles long ago.   20
Or is it some more humble lay,
Familiar matter of today?

The Solitary Reaper: Dorothy Wordsworth (William's sister) writes that the poem was suggested by this sentence in Thomas Wilkinson's *Tour of Scotland:* "Passed a female who was reaping alone; she sung in Erse, as she bended over her sickle; the sweetest human voice I ever heard; her strains were tenderly melancholy, and felt delicious, long after they were heard no more."

Some natural sorrow, loss, or pain,
That has been, and may be again?

Whate'er the theme, the maiden sang   25
As if her song could have no ending;
I saw her singing at her work,
And o'er the sickle bending —
I listened, motionless and still;
And, as I mounted up the hill,   30
The music in my heart I bore
Long after it was heard no more.

JAMES WRIGHT (1927–1980)
A Blessing   1961

Just off the highway to Rochester, Minnesota,
Twilight bounds softly forth on the grass.
And the eyes of those two Indian ponies
Darken with kindness.
They have come gladly out of the willows   5
To welcome my friend and me.
We step over the barbed wire into the pasture
Where they have been grazing all day, alone.
They ripple tensely, they can hardly contain their happiness
That we have come.   10
They bow shyly as wet swans. They love each other.
There is no loneliness like theirs.
At home once more,
They begin munching the young tufts of spring in the darkness.
I would like to hold the slenderer one in my arms,   15
For she has walked over to me
And nuzzled my left hand.
She is black and white,
Her mane falls wild on her forehead,
And the light breeze moves me to caress her long ear 20
That is delicate as the skin over a girl's wrist.
Suddenly I realize
That if I stepped out of my body I would break
Into blossom.

SIR THOMAS WYATT (1503–1542)
They Flee from Me   1557

They flee from me that sometime did me seek
With naked foot stalking in my chamber.
I have seen them gentle, tame, and meek
That now are wild and do not remember

That sometime they put themselves in danger 5
To take bread at my hand; and now they range
Busily seeking with a continual change.

Thankèd be Fortune, it hath been otherwise
Twenty times better; but once in special,
In thin array after a pleasant guise, 10
When her loose gown from her shoulders did fall,
And she me caught in her arms long and small;° *narrow*
And therewithall sweetly did me kiss,
And softly said, "Dear heart, how like you this?"

It was no dream; I lay broad waking. 15
But all is turned thorough° my gentleness *through*
Into a strange fashion of forsaking;
And I have leave to go of her goodness,
And she also to use newfangleness.
But since that I so kindely° am served, *kindly (ironic)* 20
I fain would know what she hath deserved.

MITSUYE YAMADA (b. 1923)

A Bedtime Story 1976

Once upon a time,
an old Japanese legend
goes as told
by Papa,
an old woman traveled through 5
many small villages
seeking refuge
for the night.
Each door opened
a sliver 10
in answer to her knock
then closed.
Unable to walk
any further
she wearily climbed a hill 15
found a clearing
and there lay down to rest
a few moments to catch
her breath.

The village town below 20
lay asleep except
for a few starlike lights.
Suddenly the clouds opened
and a full moon came into view
over the town. 25

The old woman sat up
turned toward

the village town
and in supplication
called out   30
Thank you people
of the village,
If it had not been for your
kindness
in refusing me a bed   35
for the night
these humble eyes would never
have seen this
memorable sight.

Papa paused, I waited.   40
In the comfort of our
hilltop home in Seattle
overlooking the valley,
I shouted
"That's the *end?*"   45

WILLIAM BUTLER YEATS (1865-1939)

Adam's Curse°   1903

We sat together at one summer's end,
That beautiful mild woman, your close friend,
And you and I, and talked of poetry.
I said, "A line will take us hours maybe;
Yet if it does not seem a moment's thought,   5
Our stitching and unstitching has been naught.
Better go down upon your marrow-bones
And scrub a kitchen pavement, or break stones
Like an old pauper, in all kinds of weather;
For to articulate sweet sounds together   10
Is to work harder than all these, and yet
Be thought an idler by the noisy set
Of banker, schoolmasters, and clergymen
The martyrs call the world!"
                              And thereupon   15
That beautiful mild woman for whose sake
There's many a one shall find out all heartache
On finding that her voice is sweet and low
Replied, "To be born woman is to know —
Although they do not talk of it at school —   20
That we must labor to be beautiful."

I said, "It's certain there is no fine thing
Since Adam's fall but needs much laboring.
There have been lovers who thought love should be

Adam's Curse: After his fall from grace and eviction from Eden, Adam was cursed with hard work,
pain, and death.

So much compounded of high courtesy 25
That they would sigh and quote with learned looks
Precedents out of beautiful old books;
Yet now it seems an idle trade enough."

We sat grown quiet at the name of love;
We saw the last embers of daylight die, 30
And in the trembling blue-green of the sky
A moon, worn as if it had been a shell
Washed by time's waters as they rose and fell
About the stars and broke in days and years.

I had a thought for no one's but your ears: 35
That you were beautiful, and that I strove
To love you in the old high way of love;
That it had all seemed happy; and yet we'd grown
As weary-hearted as that hollow moon.

WILLIAM BUTLER YEATS (1865–1939)
Crazy Jane Talks with the Bishop 1933

I met the Bishop on the road
And much said he and I.
"Those breasts are flat and fallen now,
Those veins must soon be dry;
Live in a heavenly mansion,
Not in some foul sty." 5

"Fair and foul are near of kin,
And fair needs foul," I cried.
"My friends are gone, but that's a truth
Nor grave nor bed denied, 10
Learned in bodily lowliness
And in the heart's pride.

"A woman can be proud and stiff
When on love intent;
But Love has pitched his mansion in 15
The place of excrement;
For nothing can be sole or whole
That has not been rent."

WILLIAM BUTLER YEATS (1865–1939)
The Lake Isle of Innisfree° 1892

I will arise and go now, and go to Innisfree,
And a small cabin build there, of clay and wattles made:

The Lake Isle of Innisfree: An island in Lough (or Lake) Gill, in western Ireland.

Nine bean-rows will I have there, a hive for the honey-bee,
And live alone in the bee-loud glade.

And I shall have some peace there, for peace comes dropping slow,   5
Dropping from the veils of the morning to where the cricket sings;
There midnight's all a glimmer, and noon a purple glow,
And evening full of the linnet's wings.

I will arise and go now, for always night and day
I hear lake water lapping with low sounds by the shore: 10
While I stand on the roadway, or on the pavements grey,
I hear it in the deep heart's core.

WILLIAM BUTLER YEATS (1865–1939)
Leda and the Swan°   1924

A sudden blow: the great wings beating still
Above the staggering girl, her thighs caressed
By the dark webs, her nape caught in his bill,
He holds her helpless breast upon his breast.

How can those terrified vague fingers push   5
The feathered glory from her loosening thighs?
And how can body, laid in that white rush,
But feel the strange heart beating where it lies?

A shudder in the loins engenders there
The broken wall, the burning roof and tower   10
And Agamemnon dead.
                              Being so caught up,
So mastered by the brute blood of the air,
Did she put on his knowledge with his power
Before the indifferent beak could let her drop?   15

Leda and the Swan: In Greek myth, Zeus in the form of a swan seduced Leda and fathered Helen of Troy (whose abduction started the Trojan War) and Clytemnestra, Agamemnon's wife and murderer. Yeats thought of Zeus's appearance to Leda as a type of annunciation, like the angel appearing to Mary.

WILLIAM BUTLER YEATS (1865–1939)
Sailing to Byzantium°   1927

I
That is no country for old men.° The young
In one another's arms, birds in the trees

Byzantium: Old name for the modern city of Istanbul, capital of the Eastern Roman Empire, ancient artistic and intellectual center. Yeats uses Byzantium as a symbol for "artificial" (and therefore, death-less) art and beauty, as opposed to the beauty of the natural world, which is bound to time and death.   1 *That . . . men:* Ireland, part of the time-bound world.

— Those dying generations — at their song,
The salmon-falls, the mackerel-crowded seas
Fish, flesh, or fowl, commend all summer long   5
Whatever is begotten, born and dies.
Caught in that sensual music all neglect
Monuments of unaging intellect.

II
An aged man is but a paltry thing,
A tattered coat upon a stick, unless   10
Soul clap its hands and sing, and louder sing
For every tatter in its mortal dress,
Nor is there singing school but studying
Monuments of its own magnificence;
And therefore I have sailed the seas and come   15
To the holy city of Byzantium.

III
O sages standing in God's holy fire
As in the gold mosaic of a wall,
Come from the holy fire, perne in a gyre,°
And be the singing-masters of my soul.   20
Consume my heart away; sick with desire
And fastened to a dying animal
It knows not what it is; and gather me
Into the artifice of eternity.

IV
Once out of nature I shall never take   25
My bodily form from any natural thing,
But such a form as Grecian goldsmiths make
Of hammered gold and gold enameling
To keep a drowsy Emperor awake;°
Or set upon a golden bough° to sing   30
To lords and ladies of Byzantium
Of what is past, or passing, or to come.

19 *perne in a gyre:* Bobbin making a spiral pattern.   27–29 *such . . . awake:* "I have read somewhere that in the Emperor's palace at Byzantium was a tree made of gold and silver, and artificial
birds that sang." [Yeats's note.]   30 *golden bough:* In Greek legend, Aeneas had to pluck a golden
bough from a tree in order to descend into Hades. As soon as the bough was plucked, another grew
in its place.

WILLIAM BUTLER YEATS (1865–1939)
The Second Coming°   1921

Turning and turning in the widening gyre°
The falcon cannot hear the falconer;

The Second Coming: According to Matthew 24:29–44, Christ will return to earth after a time of
tribulation to reward the righteous and establish the Millennium of Heaven on earth. Yeats saw his
troubled time as the end of the Christian era, and feared the portents of the new cycle.   1 *gyre:*
Widening spiral of a falcon's flight, used by Yeats to describe the cycling of history.

Things fall apart; the center cannot hold;
Mere anarchy is loosed upon the world,
The blood-dimmed tide is loosed, and everywhere   5
The ceremony of innocence is drowned;
The best lack all conviction, while the worst
Are full of passionate intensity.

Surely some revelation is at hand;
Surely the Second Coming is at hand.   10
The Second Coming! Hardly are those words out
When a vast image out of *Spiritus Mundi*°   Soul of the world
Troubles my sight: somewhere in sands of the desert
A shape with lion body and the head of a man,
A gaze blank and pitiless as the sun,   15
Is moving its slow thighs, while all about it
Reel shadows of the indignant desert birds.
The darkness drops again; but now I know
That twenty centuries of stony sleep
Were vexed to nightmare by a rocking cradle,   20
And what rough beast, its hour come round at last,
Slouches towards Bethlehem to be born?

AN ALBUM OF WORLD LITERATURE

ANNA AKHMATOVA (Russian / 1888–1966)

Born in Russia, Anna Akhmatova was a poet and translator who was regarded as a major modern poet in Russia. Although she was expelled from the
Union of Soviet Writers during Stalin's rule, she was reclaimed by her country
in the 1960s. Her poetry is characterized by its clarity, precision, and simplicity. Her work is translated in *Complete Poems of Anna Akhmatova* (1990).

Dedication   1940

TRANSLATED BY RICHARD MCKANE

Such grief might make the mountains stoop,
reverse the waters where they flow,
but cannot burst these ponderous bolts
that block us from the prison cells
crowded with mortal woe. . . .   5
For some the wind can freshly blow,
for some the sunlight fade at ease,
but we, made partners in our dread,
hear but the grating of the keys,
and heavy-booted soldiers' tread.   10
As if for early mass, we rose
and each day walked the wilderness,

trudging through silent street and square,
to congregate, less live than dead.
The sun declined, the Neva blurred,   15
and hope sang always from afar.
Whose sentence is decreed? . . . That moan,
that sudden spurt of woman's tears,
shows one distinguished from the rest,
as if they'd knocked her to the ground   20
and wrenched the heart out of her breast,
then let her go, reeling, alone.
Where are they now, my nameless friends
from those two years I spent in hell?
What specters mock them now, amid   25
the fury of Siberian snows,
or in the blighted circle of the moon?
To them I cry, Hail and Farewell!

Connections to Other Selections

1. Compare the metaphors of imprisonment in "Dedication" and Faiz Ahmed Faiz's "If You Look at the City from Here" (p. 479).
2. Write an essay on the "sentence" decreed in this poem and in Dickinson's "I read my sentence — steadily —" (p. 272).

CLARIBEL ALEGRÍA (Salvadoran / b. 1924)

Born in Estelí, Nicaragua, Claribel Alegría moved with her family to El Salvador within a year of her birth. A 1948 graduate of George Washington University, she considers herself a Salvadoran, and much of her writing reflects the political upheaval of recent Latin American history. In 1978 she was awarded the Casa de las Americas Prize for her book *I Survive*. A bilingual edition of her major works, *Flowers from the Volcano*, was published in 1982.

I Am Mirror   1978

TRANSLATED BY ELECTA ARENAL AND MARSHA GABRIELA DREYER

Water sparkles
on my skin
and I don't feel it
water streams
down my back   5
I don't feel it
I rub myself with a towel
I pinch myself in the arm

I don't feel
frightened I look at myself in the mirror 10
she also pricks herself
I begin to get dressed
stumbling
from the corners
shouts like lightning bolts 15
tortured eyes
scurrying rats
and teeth shoot forth
although I feel nothing
I wander through the streets: 20
children with dirty faces
ask me for charity
child prostitutes
who are not yet fifteen
the streets are paved with pain 25
tanks that approach
raised bayonets
bodies that fall
weeping
finally I feel my arm 30
I am no longer a phantom
I hurt
therefore I exist
I return to watch the scene:
children who run 35
bleeding
women with panic
in their faces
this time it hurts me less
I pinch myself again 40
and already I feel nothing
I simply reflect
what happens at my side
the tanks
are not tanks 45
nor are the shouts
shouts
I am a blank mirror
that nothing penetrates
my surface 50
is hard
is brilliant
is polished
I became a mirror
and I am fleshless 55
scarcely preserving
a vague memory
of pain.

Connections to Other Selections

1. Compare the ways Alegría uses mirror images to reflect life in El Salvador with Plath's concerns in "Mirror" (p. 118).
2. Write an essay comparing the speaker's voice in this poem and that in Blake's "London" (p. 93). How do the speakers evoke emotional responses to what they describe?

KATERINA ANGHELÁKI-ROOKE (Greek / b. 1939)

Born in Athens, Katerina Angheláki-Rooke graduated from the University of Geneva in 1962. She has been awarded Ford Foundation and Fulbright grants and has taught at the universities of Iowa and Utah as well as San Francisco State University and Harvard University. Her works include *Wolves and Clouds* (1963); *Magdalene the Vast Mammal* (1974); *Counter Love* (1982), which was reprinted as *Being and Things on Their Own;* and *Wind Dialogue* (1990).

Jealousy   1990
TRANSLATED BY RAE DALVEN

On Sundays he goes out with that woman
together they enjoy the rural
landscapes in ruins.
Here they are now, passing in front of the farms;
two dead pigs against the fence   5
stretch their hoofs in the afternoon;
light frost covers the mud
the snows have melted
but the earth is still mute
and alone before it becomes a butterfly.   10
Is their love peace,
is it tyranny?
The sun is a lemon color.
Who is she?
What is her face like?   15
Her breast?
The countryside gluts itself slowly with night
this geography has nothing
exotic; and he
holds the woman with so much passion   20
and they slip as one body into the room.
He removes his shirt
his tormented breast
smells of sweat and fresh air
little by little the dry branches retreat   25

in memory
and the landscape starts anew within them
in full spring.

Connections to Other Selections

1. Compare the speaker's attitude toward desire in "Jealousy" with that of the speaker in Dickinson's "'Heaven' — is what I cannot reach!" (p. 264)
2. In an essay discuss the treatment of love in "Jealousy" and in Olds's "Sex without Love" (p. 68).

FAIZ AHMED FAIZ (Pakistani / 1911-1984)

Born in Pakistan, Faiz Ahmed Faiz served in the British Indian Army during World War II. After the war he became a spokesman for Pakistani and Indian rights by editing the *Pakistani Times* and writing poetry in Urdu. Faiz served several jail sentences for his political activism, spending a considerable amount of time in solitary confinement. His poetry is widely known in India and the subcontinent; a translation of some is available as *Poems by Faiz* (1971).

If You Look at the City from Here   1971
TRANSLATED BY NAOMI LAZARD

If you look at the city from here
you see it is laid out in concentric circles,
each circle surrounded by a wall
          exactly like a prison.
Each street is a dog-run for prisoners,   5
no milestones, no destinations, no way out.

If anyone moves too quickly you wonder
why he hasn't been stopped by a shout.
If someone raises his arm
you expect to hear the jangling of chains.   10

If you look at the city from here
there is no one with dignity,
no one fully in control of his senses.
Every young man bears the brand of a criminal,
every young woman the emblem of a slave.   15

You cannot tell whether you see
          a group of revelers or mourners
in the shadows dancing around the distant lamps,
and from here you cannot tell
whether the color streaming down the walls   20
is that of blood or roses.

Connections to Other Selections

1. Compare the treatment of the city in this poem and in Blake's "London" (p. 93).
2. Write an essay on the meaning of confinement in Faiz's poem and in Rilke's "The Panther" (p. 99).

XU GANG (Chinese / b. 1945)

Born in Shanghai, China, Xu Gang served in the army after being drafted in 1962 and began writing poetry in support of the Cultural Revolution. However, after graduating from Beijing University in 1974, he questioned the principles and brutally disruptive consequences of the Cultural Revolution, a disillusionment suggested by "Red Azalea on the Cliff." His collections of poems include *The Flower of Rain, Songs for the Far Away*, and *One Hundred Lyrics*.

Red Azalea on the Cliff 1982

TRANSLATED BY FANG DAI, DENNIS DING, AND EDWARD MORIN

Red azalea, smiling
From the cliffside at me,
You make my heart shudder with fear!
A body could smash and bones splinter in the canyon —
Beauty, always looking on at disaster. 5

But red azalea on the cliff,
That you comb your twigs even in a mountain gale
Calms me down a bit.
Of course you're not wilfully courting danger,
Nor are you at ease with whatever happens to you. 10
You're merely telling me: beauty is nature.

Would anyone like to pick a flower
To give to his love
Or pin to his own lapel?
On the cliff there is no road 15
And no azalea grows where there is a road.
If someone actually reached that azalea,
Then an azalea would surely bloom in his heart.

Red azalea on the cliff,
You smile like the Yellow Mountains, 20
Whose sweetness encloses slyness,
Whose intimacy embraces distance.
You remind us all of our first love.

Sometimes the past years look
Just like the azalea on the cliff.   25

MAY 1982
Yellow Mountain
Revised at Hangzhou

Connections to Other Selections

1. Compare the significance of the flower in "Red Azalea on the Cliff" with that of
   the flower in Blake's "The Sick Rose" (p. 138).
2. In an essay explain how beauty is associated with danger in Xu Gang's poem and
   in Keats's "La Belle Dame sans Merci" (p. 427).

PABLO NERUDA (Chilean / 1904–1973)

Born in Chile, Pablo Neruda insisted all his life on the connection
between poetry and politics. He was an activist and a Chilean diplomat in a
number of countries during the 1920s and 1930s and remained politically
active until his death. Neruda was regarded as a great and influential poet (he
was awarded the Nobel Prize in 1971) whose poetry ranged from specific
political issues to the yearnings of romantic love. Among his many works are
Twenty Love Poems and a Song of Despair (1924), *Residence on Earth* (three
series, 1925–45), *Spain in the Heart* (1937), *The Captain's Verses* (1952), and
Memorial of Isla Negra (1964).

Sweetness, Always   1958

TRANSLATED BY ALASTAIR REID

Why such harsh machinery?
Why, to write down the stuff
and people of every day,
must poems be dressed up in gold,
in old and fearful stone?   5
I want verses of felt or feather
which scarcely weigh, mild verses
with the intimacy of beds
where people have loved and dreamed.
I want poems stained   10
by hands and everydayness.

Verses of pastry which melt
into milk and sugar in the mouth,
air and water to drink,
the bites and kisses of love.   15
I long for eatable sonnets,
poems of honey and flour.

Vanity keeps prodding us
to lift ourselves skyward
or to make deep and useless   20
tunnels underground.
So we forget the joyous
love-needs of our bodies.
We forget about pastries.
We are not feeding the world.   25

In Madras a long time since,
I saw a sugary pyramid,
a tower of confectionery —
one level after another,
and in the construction, rubies,   30
and other blushing delights,
medieval and yellow.

Someone dirtied his hands
to cook up so much sweetness.

Brother poets from here   35
and there, from earth and sky,
from Medellín, from Veracruz,
Abyssinia, Antofagasta,
do you know the recipe for honeycombs?

Let's forget all about that stone.   40

Let your poetry fill up
the equinoctial pastry shop
our mouths long to devour —
all the children's mouths
and the poor adults' also.   45
Don't go on without seeing,
relishing, understanding
all these hearts of sugar.

Don't be afraid of sweetness.

With us or without us,   50
sweetness will go on living
and is infinitely alive,
forever being revived,
for it's in a man's mouth,
whether he's eating or singing,   55
that sweetness has its place.

Connections to Other Selections

1. Compare the view of life offered in this poem with that in Frost's "Birches"
   (p. 311).
2. Write an essay that discusses Kinnell's "Blackberry Eating" (p. 161) and Chasin's
   "The Word *Plum*" (p. 180) as the sort of "eatable" poetry the speaker calls for in
   this poem.

OCTAVIO PAZ (Mexican / b. 1914)

Born in Mexico City, Octavio Paz studied at the National Autonomous University and in 1943 helped found one of Mexico's most important literary reviews, *The Prodigal Son*. He served in the Mexican diplomatic corps in Paris, New Delhi, and New York. Much of Paz's poetry reflects Hispanic traditions and European modernism as well as Buddhism. In 1990 he received the Nobel Prize for literature. Paz's major works include *Sun Stone* (1958), *The Violent Season* (1958), *Salamander* (1962), *Blanco* (1966), *Eastern Rampart* (1968), *Renga* (1971), and *Collected Poems, 1957–1987* (1987).

The Street   1963

A long silent street.
I walk in blackness and I stumble and fall
and rise, and I walk blind, my feet
stepping on silent stones and dry leaves.
Someone behind me also stepping on stones, leaves: 5
if I slow down, he slows;
if I run, he runs. I turn: nobody.
Everything dark and doorless.
Turning and turning among these corners
which lead forever to the street   10
where nobody waits for, nobody follows me,
where I pursue a man who stumbles
and rises and says when he sees me: nobody.

Connections to Other Selections

1. How does the speaker's anxiety in this poem compare with that in Frost's "Acquainted with the Night" (p. 129)?
2. Write an essay comparing the tone of this poem and that of Hughes's "Lenox Avenue: Midnight" (p. 346).

INDIRA SANT (Indian / b. 1914)

Born in Pune in the state of Maharashtra, India, Indira Sant began her career as a teacher and a writer of children's fiction. In the 1950s she focused her talent on writing feminist poetry that sympathetically described the hardships endured by Indian mothers, wives, and daughters. Her work has not been widely translated, but the following poem appeared in the journal *Daedalus*.

Household Fires   1989

TRANSLATED BY VINAY DHARWADKER

The daughter's job: without a murmur
to do the chores piling up around the house
until she leaves for work,
to pay her younger brother's fees,
to buy her sister ribbons,   5
to get her father's spectacles changed.
To take the others to the movies on holidays,
to keep back a little and hand over the rest
on payday.

The son's job: fresh savory snacks   10
for the whole household to eat:
to bring back the clothes from the washerman,
to clean and put away the bicycle,
to sing out of key while packing his father's lunch
at the stroke of the hour,   15
to open the door sulkily
whenever someone comes home from the movies,
to wrinkle his brow
when he puts out his hand for money
and is asked instead, "How much? For what?"   20

The younger daughter's job:
to savor the joys of shyness,
to shrink back minute by minute.
The younger son's job:
to choke all the while, grow up slowly   25
in states of wet and dry.

Four children learning in her fold,
her body drained by hardship,
what's left of her? A mass of tatters,
five tongues of flame   30
licking and licking at her on every side,
fanning and fanning the fire in her eyes
till her mind boils over,
gets burned.

Connections to Other Selections

1. Implicit in this poem is the father's presence. Compare the treatment of the father in "Household Fires" and Plath's "Daddy" (p. 442).

2. Write an essay that compares the life described in this poem with Divakaruni's "Indian Movie, New Jersey" (p. 149).

WOLE SOYINKA (Nigerian / b. 1934)

Born Oluwole Akinwande Soyinka, in the western Nigerian town of Akinwande, Wole Soyinka has embodied in his life and art the contradictions and tensions that can often seem inevitable for the European-educated, English-speaking African writers. Although he has written and published novels and poetry (the following poem is from *A Shuttle in the Crypt* [1972]), Soyinka is most renowned as a playwright whose work embodies his concerns as a political reformer and social critic. His many plays include *The Lion and the Jewel* (1959), *The Strong Bond* (1963), and *Death of the King's Horseman* (1976). His autobiography *The Man Died* (1973) records his experiences as a political prisoner in Nigeria. In 1986 he was awarded the Nobel Prize for Literature.

Future Plans   1972

The meeting is called
To odium: Forgers, framers
Fabricators Inter-
national. Chairman,
A dark horse, a circus nag turned blinkered sprinter   5

Mach Three°
We rate him — one for the Knife°
Two for 'iavelli,° Three —
Breaking speed
Of the truth barrier by a swooping detention decree   10
Projects in view:
Mao Tse Tung° in league
With Chiang Kai. Nkrumah°
Makes a secret
Pact with Verwood, sworn by Hastings Banda.°   15
Proven: Arafat°
In flagrante cum
Golda Meir. Castro° drunk
With Richard Nixon°
Contraceptives stacked beneath the papal bunk . . .   20
         . . . and more to come

6 *Mach Three:* An air speed of three times the speed of sound.   7 *Knife:* Mack the Knife, an unsavory character from *The Threepenny Opera* (1933), by Bertolt Brecht and Kurt Weill.   8 *'iavelli:* Niccolò Machiavelli (1469–1527), an Italian political theorist who described ruthless strategies for gaining power in *The Prince* (1532).   12 *Mao Tse Tung:* Mao Tse-tung (1893–1975), Chinese Communist leader.   13 *Chiang Kai, Nkrumah:* Chiang Kai-shek (1887–1975), Chinese Nationalist leader exiled in Taiwan by Mao Tse-tung; Kwame Nkrumah (1909–1972), first president of Ghana.   15 *Verwood, Hastings Banda:* Hendrick Verwoerd (1901–1966), former prime minister of South Africa, assassinated in 1966; Hastings Banda (b. 1905), African political leader and first president of Malawi.   16 *Arafat:* Yasir Arafat (b. 1929), Palestinian leader.   18 *Golda Meir, Castro:* Golda Meir (1898–1978), former prime minister of Israel; Fidel Castro (b. 1927), Cuban premier since 1959.   19 *Richard Nixon* (1913–1994): Former U.S. president forced to resign in 1974 due to political scandal.

Connections to Other Selections

1. Discuss the political satire in "Future Plans" and in Fearing's "AD" (p. 134).
2. Write an essay on whether the leaders alluded to in "Future Plans" are manifestations of the type of leader described in Thomas's "The Hand That Signed the Paper" (p. 113).

WISLAWA SZYMBORSKA   (Polish / b. 1923)

Born in Poland, Wislawa Szymborska has lived in Cracow since the age of eight. She steadfastly refuses to reveal biographical details of her life, insisting that her poems should speak for themselves. With the exception of *Sounds, Feelings, Thoughts: Seventy Poems by Wislawa Szymborska* (1981), translated and introduced by Magnus J. Krynski and Robert A. Maguire, and *View with a Grain of Sand: Selected Poems* (1995), translated by Stanislaw Barańczak and Clare Cavanagh, only some of Szymborska's poems have been translated into English. Three of her later poetry collections — as yet untranslated — are *There But for the Grace* (1972), *A Great Number* (1976), and *The People of the Bridge* (1986). She was awarded the Nobel Prize in Literature in 1996.

Hatred   1993

TRANSLATED BY STANISLAW BARAŃCZAK AND CLARE CAVANAGH

See how efficient it still is,
how it keeps itself in shape —
our century's hatred.
How easily it vaults the tallest obstacles.
How rapidly it pounces, tracks us down.   5

It's not like other feelings.
At once both older and younger.
It gives birth itself to the reasons
that give it life.
When it sleeps, it's never eternal rest.   10
And sleeplessness won't sap its strength; it feeds it.

One religion or another —
whatever gets it ready, in position.
One fatherland or another —
whatever helps it get a running start.   15
Justice also works well at the outset
until hate gets its own momentum going.
Hatred. Hatred.
Its face twisted in a grimace
of erotic ecstasy.   20

Oh these other feelings,
listless weaklings.

Since when does brotherhood
draw crowds?
Has compassion   25
ever finished first?
Does doubt ever really rouse the rabble?
Only hatred has just what it takes.

Gifted, diligent, hard-working.
Need we mention all the songs it has composed?   30
All the pages it has added to our history books?
All the human carpets it has spread
over countless city squares and football fields?

Let's face it:
it knows how to make beauty.   35
The splendid fire-glow in midnight skies.
Magnificent bursting bombs in rosy dawns.
You can't deny the inspiring pathos of ruins
and a certain bawdy humor to be found
in the sturdy column jutting from their midst.   40

Hatred is a master of contrast —
between explosions and dead quiet,
red blood and white snow.
Above all, it never tires
of its leitmotif — the impeccable executioner   45
towering over its soiled victim.

It's always ready for new challenges.
If it has to wait awhile, it will.
They say it's blind. Blind?
It has a sniper's keen sight   50
and gazes unflinchingly at the future
as only it can.

Connections to Other Selections

1. Discuss the speaker's tone in "Hatred" and in Neruda's "Sweetness, Always"
   (p. 481).
2. Write an essay comparing and contrasting the themes in "Hatred" and Szymborska's "End and Beginning" (p. 94). Explain why you prefer one poem over
   another.

TOMAS TRANSTROMER (Swedish / b. 1931)

Born in Stockholm, Sweden, Tomas Transtromer's work is translated
more than any other contemporary Scandinavian poet's. He has worked as a
psychologist with juvenile offenders and handicapped persons. His collections of poetry include *Night Vision* (1971), *Windows and Stones: Selected*

Poems (1972), *Truth Barriers* (1978), and *Selected Poems* (1981). Among his awards are the Petrarch Prize (1981) and a lifetime subsidy from the government of Sweden.

April and Silence   1991
TRANSLATED BY ROBIN FULTON

Spring lies desolate.
The velvet-dark ditch
crawls by my side
without reflections.

The only thing that shines   5
is yellow flowers.

I am carried in my shadow
like a violin
in its black box.

The only thing I want to say   10
glitters out of reach
like the silver
in a pawnbroker's.

Connections to Other Selections

1. Discuss the description of spring in this poem and in Williams's "Spring and All" (p. 466).
2. In an essay explain how the dictions used in "April and Silence" and Espada's "Late Night at the Pawnshop" (p. 54) contribute to the poems' meanings and tone.

AN ALBUM OF CONTEMPORARY POEMS

ELIZABETH ALEXANDER (b. 1962)

Born in New York City, Elizabeth Alexander has taught at the University of Chicago and Yale University. She has published two collections of poetry: *The Venus Hottentot* (1990) and *Body of Life* (1996).

Harlem Birthday Party   1996

When my grandfather turned ninety we had a party
in a restaurant in Harlem called Copeland's.
Harlem restaurants are always dim to dark and this
was no exception. Daddy would have gone downtown

but Baba, as we called him, wanted to stay 5
in the neighborhood, and this place was "swanky."
We picked him up in his house on Hamilton Terrace.
His wife, "poor Minnette," had Alzheimer's disease
and thought Hordgie, who was not dead, was dead. She kept
cluck-clucking, "Poor Hordgie," and filling with tears. 10
They had organized a block watch on Hamilton
Terrace, which I was glad of; I worried always
about old people getting mugged; I was afraid
of getting old myself and knocked down in the street;
I was afraid it would happen to my grandfather. 15

My father moves fast always but in Harlem
something clicks into his walk which I love watching.
We argued about taking a car, about parking;
in the end some walked, some drove, and the restaurant
parked the car for us. They treated my grandfather 20
like a Pope or like Duke Ellington. We ate salad,
fried chicken, mashed potatoes, broccoli, chocolate
cake, and Gustavo, who was then my boyfriend, cut Minnette's
meat for her and that became one of the things I would cite
forever when people asked me, How did you know 25
you wanted to marry him? I remember looking
at all the people at the party I had never seen,
and thinking, My grandfather has a whole life
we know nothing about, like at his funeral,
two years later, when a dreadlocked man about my age 30
went on and on about coming to Harlem
from Jamaica, they all said, talk to Mister Alexander, and they talked, and my grandfather scolded,
advised, and today the young brother owns a patty stand
in Brooklyn. Who ever knew this young man, or all the rest? 35

The star appearance at Copeland's, besides my father, was
my grandfather's wife's cousin, Jane Tillman Irving,
who broadcast on WCBS all-news radio.
What is a Harlem birthday party without a star?
What is a black family without someone 40
who's related to someone else who is a little
bit famous, if only to other black people?

And then goodbye, and then goodbye, and back
to New Haven, Washington, and Philadelphia,
where I lived with Gustavo. We walked downtown 45
after the party to Macy's to get feather pillows
on sale, and then we took Amtrak home. I cannot think
about this party without thinking how glad I am
we had it, that he lived long and healthy, that two years
later he was gone. He was born in Jamaica, 50
West Indies, and he died in Harlem, New York.

Connections to Other Selections

1. Compare the speaker's tone in this poem with that in Harper's "Grandfather" (p. 415).
2. Write an essay that compares the grandfather's identity in "Harlem Birthday Party" with the man described in Holman's "Mr. Z" (p. 419).

CORNELIUS EADY (b. 1954)

Cornelius Eady, born in Rochester, New York, has taught poetry at several colleges and universities; he is currently director of the Poetry Center at the State University of New York at Stony Brook. The recipient of many fellowships and awards, he has published five books of poetry including *Victims of the Latest Dance Craze* (1986) and *The Gathering of My Name* (1991).

The Supremes   1991

We were born to be gray. We went to school,
Sat in rows, ate white bread,
Looked at the floor a lot. In the back
Of our small heads

A long scream. We did what we could,   5
And all we could do was
Turn on each other. How the fat kids suffered!
Not even being jolly could save them.

And then there were the anal retentives,
The terrified brown-noses, the desperately   10
Athletic or popular. This, of course,
Was training. At home

Our parents shook their heads and waited.
We learned of the industrial revolution,
The sectioning of the clock into pie slices.   15
We drank cokes and twiddled our thumbs. In the
Back of our minds

A long scream. We snapped butts in the showers,
Froze out shy girls on the dance floor,
Pin-pointed flaws like radar.   20
Slowly we understood: this was to be the world.

We were born insurance salesmen and secretaries,
Housewives and short order cooks,
Stock room boys and repairmen,
And it wouldn't be a bad life, they promised,   25
In a tone of voice that would force some of us
To reach in self-defense for wigs,
Lipstick,

Sequins.

Connections to Other Selections

1. Discuss the speakers' memories of school in "The Supremes" and in Judy Page Heitzman's "The Schoolroom on the Second Floor of the Knitting Mill" (p. 498).
2. In an essay compare the themes of "The Supremes" and Dickinson's "From all the Jails the Boys and Girls" (p. 278).

MARTÍN ESPADA (b. 1957)

Martín Espada was born in Brooklyn, New York. He has worked as a tenant lawyer in Boston and now teaches in the English Department at the University of Massachusetts at Amherst. He has been awarded several fellowships including two from the National Endowment for the Arts. His books of poetry include *Rebellion Is the Circle of a Lover's Hand* (1990), *City of Coughing and Dead Radiators* (1993), and *Imagine the Angels of Bread* (1996).

Coca-Cola and Coco Frío   1993

On his first visit to Puerto Rico,
island of family folklore,
the fat boy wandered
from table to table
with his mouth open.   5
At every table, some great-aunt
would steer him with cool spotted hands
to a glass of Coca-Cola.
One even sang to him, in all the English
she could remember, a Coca-Cola jingle   10
from the forties. He drank obediently, though
he was bored with this potion, familiar
from soda fountains in Brooklyn.

Then, at a roadside stand off the beach, the fat boy
opened his mouth to coco frío, a coconut   15
chilled, then scalped by a machete
so that a straw could inhale the clear milk.
The boy tilted the green shell overhead
and drooled coconut milk down his chin;
suddenly, Puerto Rico was not Coca-Cola   20
or Brooklyn, and neither was he.

For years afterward, the boy marveled at an island
where the people drank Coca-Cola
and sang jingles from World War II
in a language they did not speak,   25
while so many coconuts in the trees
sagged heavy with milk, swollen
and unsuckled.

Connections to Other Selections

1. Compare what the boy in this poem discovers about Puerto Rico with what the speaker learns in Hughes's "Theme for English B" (p. 354).

2. Write an essay discussing the images used to describe Puerto Rico and the United States in this poem and in Laviera's "AmeRícan" (p. 241).

DEBORAH GARRISON (b. 1965)

Raised in Ann Arbor, Michigan, Deborah Garrison graduated from Brown University and currently lives in New York City, where she works on the editorial staff of *The New Yorker*. She has not published a collection of poems to date, but her poetry appears regularly in *The New Yorker*.

She Was Waiting to Be Told 1990

For you she learned to wear a short black slip
and red lipstick,
how to order a glass of red wine
and finish it. She learned to reach out
as if to touch your arm and then not   5
touch it, changing the subject
Didn't you think, she'd begin, or
Weren't you sorry. . . .

To call your best friends
by their schoolboy names   10
and give them kisses good-bye,
to turn her head away when they say
Your wife! So your confidence grows.
She doesn't ask what you want
because she knows.   15

Isn't that what you think?

When actually she was only waiting
to be told *Take off your dress —*
to be stunned, and then do this,
never rehearsed, but perfectly obvious: 20
in one motion up, over, and gone,
the X of her arms crossing and uncrossing,
her face flashing away from you in the fabric
so that you couldn't say if she was
appearing or disappearing.   25

Connections to Other Selections

1. Write an essay comparing the women in Garrison's "She Was Waiting to Be Told" and Keats's "La Belle Dame sans Merci" (p. 427).

2. Discuss the relationship between the man and woman in Garrison's poem and the lovers in Wilbur's "A Late Aubade" (p. 60).

DONALD HALL (b. 1928)

Born in New Haven, Connecticut, Donald Hall taught at the University of Michigan and for years has made his living in New Hampshire as a freelance writer of numerous books of poetry as well as literary criticism, essays, and children's books. His collections of poems include *The One Day* (1988), winner of the National Book Critics Award, and *The Museum of Clear Ideas* (1993).

Letter with No Address   1996

Your daffodils rose up
and collapsed in their yellow
bodies on the hillside
garden above the bricks
you laid out in sand, squatting   5
with pants pegged and face
masked like a beekeeper's
against the black flies.
Buttercups circle the planks
of the old wellhead   10
this May while your silken
gardener's body withers or moulds
in the Proctor graveyard.
I drive and talk to you crying
and come back to this house   15
to talk to your photographs.

There's news to tell you:
Maggie Fisher's pregnant.
I carried myself like an egg
at Abigail's birthday party   20
a week after you died,
as three-year-olds bounced
uproarious on a mattress.
Joyce and I met for lunch
at the mall and strolled weepily   25
through Sears and B. Dalton.

Today it's four weeks
since you lay on our painted bed
and I closed your eyes.
Yesterday I cut irises to set   30
in a pitcher on your grave;

today I brought a carafe
to fill it with fresh water.
I remember the bone-pain,
vomiting, and delirium. I remember   35
the pond afternoons.

               My routine
is established: coffee;
the *Globe;* breakfast;
writing you this letter   40
at my desk. When I go to bed
to sleep after baseball,
Gus follows me into the bedroom
as he used to follow us.
Most of the time he flops   45
down in the parlor
with his head on his paws.

Once a week I drive to Tilton
to see Dick and Nan.
Nan doesn't understand much   50
but she knows you're dead;
I feel her fretting. The tune
of Dick and me talking
seems to console her.

              You know now   55
whether the soul survives death.
Or you don't. When you were dying
you said you didn't fear
punishment. We never dared
to speak of Paradise.   60

At five a.m., when I walk outside,
mist lies thick on hayfields.
By eight, the air is clear,
cool, sunny with the pale yellow
light of mid-May. Kearsarge   65
rises huge and distinct,
each birch and balsam visible.
To the west the waters
of Eagle Pond waver
and flash through popples just   70
leafing out.

            Always the weather,
writing its book of the world,
returns you to me.
Ordinary days were best,
when we worked over poems   75
in our separate rooms.
I remember watching you gaze
out the January window
into the garden of snow   80

and ice, your face rapt
as you imagined burgundy lilies.

Your presence in this house
is almost as enormous
and painful as your absence.   85
Driving home from Tilton,
I remember how you cherished
that vista with its center
the red door of a farmhouse
against green fields.   90
Are you past pity?
If you have consciousness now,
if something I can call
"you" has something
like "consciousness," I doubt   95
you remember the last days.
I play them over and over:
I lift your wasted body
onto the commode, your arms
looped around my neck, aiming   100
your bony bottom so that
it will not bruise on a rail.
Faintly you repeat,
"Momma, Momma."

                              You lay   105
astonishing in the long box
while Alice Ling prayed
and sang "Amazing Grace"
a capella. Three times today
I drove to your grave.   110
Sometimes, coming back home
to our circular driveway,
I imagine you've returned
before me, bags of groceries upright
in the back of the Saab,   115
its trunklid delicately raised
as if proposing an encounter,
dog-fashion, with the Honda.

Connections to Other Selections

1. Compare how the speaker copes with grief in "Letter with No Address" with the speaker in Dickinson's "The Bustle in a House" (p. 277).
2. Write an essay on the tone of this poem and Frost's "Home Burial" (p. 306).

MARK HALLIDAY (b. 1949)

Born in Ann Arbor, Michigan, Mark Halliday earned a B.A. and an M.A. from Brown University and a Ph.D. from Brandeis University. A teacher at the University of Pennsylvania, his poems have appeared in a variety of periodicals, including *The Massachusetts Review, Michigan Quarterly Review,* and *The New Republic.* His collection of poems, *Little Star,* was selected by The National Poetry Series for publication in 1987. He has also written a critical study on poet Wallace Stevens titled *Stevens and the Interpersonal* (1991).

Graded Paper   1991

On the whole this is quite successful work:
your main argument about the poet's ambivalence —
how he loves the very things he attacks —
is mostly persuasive and always engaging.
At the same time,   5
          there are spots
where your thinking becomes, for me,
alarmingly opaque, and your syntax seems to jump
backwards through unnecessary hoops,
as on p. 2 where you speak of "precognitive awareness   10
not yet disestablished by the shell that encrusts
each thing that a person actually says"
or at the top of p. 5 where your discussion of
"subverbal undertow miming the subversion of self-belief
woven counter to desire's outreach"   15
leaves me groping for firmer footholds.
(I'd have said it differently,
or rather, said something else.)
And when you say that women "could not fulfill themselves" (p. 6)
"in that era" (only forty years ago, after all!)   20
are you so sure that the situation is so different today?
Also, how does Whitman bluff his way into
your penultimate paragraph? He is the *last* poet
I would have quoted in this context!
What plausible way of behaving   25
does the passage you quote represent? Don't you think
literature should ultimately reveal possibilities for *action?*

Please notice how I've repaired your use of semicolons.

And yet, despite what may seem my cranky response,
I do admire the freshness of   30
your thinking and your style; there is
a vitality here; your sentences thrust themselves forward
with a confidence as impressive as it is cheeky. . . .
You are not
         me, finally,   35

and though this is an awkward problem, involving
the inescapable fact that you are so young, so young
it is also a delightful provocation.

Connections to Other Selections

1. Compare the ways in which Halliday reveals the speaker's character in this poem
   with the strategies used by Browning in "My Last Duchess" (p. 150).
2. Write an essay on the teacher in this poem and the one in Judy Page Heitzman's
   "The Schoolroom on the Second Floor of the Knitting Mill" (p. 498). What are the
   significant similarities and differences between them?

ROBERT HASS (b. 1941)

Born and raised in San Francisco, Robert Hass was educated at St. Mary's
College and Stanford University. He has taught at the State University of New
York at Buffalo, St. Mary's College, and the University of California at Berkeley. His first collection of poems, *Field Guide* (1973), was awarded the Yale
Series of Younger Poets Award; this collection was followed by three more:
Praise (1978), *Human Wishes* (1989), and *Sun Under Wood* (1996). He has
also published a collection of essays, *Twentieth-Century Pleasures* (1984),
and been the recipient of the National Book Circle Critics Award for criticism
as well as the John D. and Catherine T. MacArthur Fellowship. In 1995 he was
named the nation's Poet Laureate to the Library of Congress.

A Story About the Body   1989

The young composer, working that summer at an artists' colony, had
watched her for a week. She was Japanese, a painter, almost sixty, and he
thought he was in love with her. He loved her work, and her work was like
the way she moved her body, used her hands, looked at him directly when
she made amused and considered answers to his questions. One night, walking back from a concert, they came to her door and she turned to him and
said, "I think you would like to have me. I would like that too, but I must tell
you that I have had a double mastectomy," and when he didn't understand,
"I've lost both my breasts." The radiance that he had carried around in his
belly and chest cavity — like music — withered very quickly, and he made
himself look at her when he said, "I'm sorry. I don't think I could." He walked
back to his own cabin through the pines, and in the morning he found a small
blue bowl on the porch outside his door. It looked to be full of rose petals,
but he found when he picked it up that the rose petals were on top; the rest
of the bowl — she must have swept them from the corners of her studio —
was full of dead bees.

Connections to Other Selections

1. Discuss the treatments of love in "A Story About the Body" and Nims's "Love Poem" (p. 31).

2. Read Hulme's remarks "On the Differences between Poetry and Prose" (p. 105) and write an essay on what you think Hulme would have to say about "A Story About the Body."

JUDY PAGE HEITZMAN (b. 1952)

Judy Page Heitzman lives in Marshfield, Massachusetts, and teaches English at Duxbury High School. She has not published a collection of poems to date, but her poetry has appeared in *The New Yorker, Yankee Magazine, Wind, Yarro,* and *Three Rivers Poetry Journal.*

The Schoolroom on the Second Floor of the Knitting Mill

1991

While most of us copied letters out of books,
Mrs. Lawrence carved and cleaned her nails.
Now the red and buff cardinals at my back-room window
make me miss her, her room, her hallway,
even the chimney outside   5
that broke up the sky.

In my memory it is afternoon.
Sun streams in through the door
next to the fire escape where we are lined up
getting our coats on to go out to the playground,   10
the tether ball, its towering height, the swings.
She tells me to make sure the line
does not move up over the threshold.
That would be dangerous.
So I stand guard at the door.   15
Somehow it happens
the way things seem to happen when we're not really looking,
or we are looking, just not the right way.
Kids crush up like cattle, pushing me over the line.

Judy is not a good leader is all Mrs. Lawrence says.   20
She says it quietly. Still, everybody hears.
Her arms hang down like sausages.
I hear her every time I fail.

Connections to Other Selections

1. Compare the representations and meanings of being a schoolchild in this poem with those in Dickinson's "From all the Jails the Boys and Girls" (p. 278).

2. Discuss how the past impinges on the present in Heitzman's poem and in Larkin's "This Be the Verse" (p. 429).

JANE HIRSHFIELD (b. 1953)

Born in New York City, Jane Hirshfield is the author of four books of poetry, most recently *The Lives of the Heart* (1997), and a collection of essays, *Nine Gates: Entering The Mind of Poetry* (1997). She has also edited and co-translated two collections of poetry by women from the past, *Women in Praise of the Sacred; 43 Centuries of Spiritual Poetry by Women* (1995) and *The Ink Dark Moon: Poems by Ono no Komachi and Izumi Shikibu, Women of the Ancient Court of Japan* (1990). Hirshfield's awards include The Poetry Center Book Award, the Bay Area Book Reviewers Award, Columbia University's Translation Center Award, and fellowships from the Guggenheim and Rockefeller Foundations.

The Lives of the Heart   1997

Are ligneous, muscular, chemical.
Wear birch-colored feathers,
green tunnels of horse-tail reed.
Wear calcified spirals, Fibonnacian spheres.
Are edible; are glassy; are clay; blue schist.   5
Can be burned as tallow, as coal,
can be skinned for garnets, for shoes.
Cast shadows or light;
shuffle; snort; cry out in passion.
Are salt, are bitter,   10
tear sweet grass with their teeth.
Step silently into blue needle-fall at dawn.
Thrash in the net until hit.
Rise up as cities, as serpentined magma, as maples,
hiss lava-red into the sea.   15
Leave the strange kiss of their bodies
in Burgess Shale. Can be found, can be lost,
can be carried, broken, sung.
Lie dormant until they are opened by ice,
by drought. Go blind in the service of lace.   20
Are starving, are sated, indifferent, curious, mad.
Are stamped out in plastic, in tin.
Are stubborn, are careful, are slipshod,
are strung on the blue backs of flies
on the black backs of cows.   25
Wander the vacant whale-roads, the white thickets
heavy with slaughter.
Wander the fragrant carpets of alpine flowers.

Not one is not held in the arms of the rest, to blossom.
Not one is not given to ecstasy's lions.   30
Not one does not grieve.
Each of them opens and closes, closes and opens
the heavy gate — violent, serene, consenting, suffering it all.

Connections to Other Selections

1. Discuss the use of personification in this poem and Steven's "Schizophrenia" (p. 119).
2. Write an essay that compares the diction and images of "The Lives of the Heart" and Alice Jones's "The Foot" (p. 191).

LINDA HOGAN (b. 1947)

   Born in Denver, Colorado, and raised in Oklahoma, Linda Hogan is a member of the Chickasaw tribe. She was educated at the University of Colorado, where she now teaches creative writing. She has been awarded fellowships from the Guggenheim Foundation and the National Endowment for the Arts and has received an American Book Award. In addition to publishing fiction — her novel *Mean Spirit* appeared in 1989 — she has published several volumes of poetry including *Eclipse* (1985), *Seeing through the Sun* (1985), *Savings* (1988), and *The Book of Medicines* (1993).

Hunger   1993

Hunger crosses oceans.
It loses its milk teeth.
It sits on the ship and cries.

Thin, afraid,
it fashioned hooks to catch   5
the passing songs of whales so large
the men grew small
as distant, shrinking lands.
They sat on the ship and cried.

Hunger was the fisherman   10
who said dolphins are like women,
we took them from the sea
and had our way
with them.

Hunger knows we have not yet reached   15
the black and raging depths of anything.

It is the old man
who comes in the night

to cast a line
and wait at the luminous shore.   20
He knows the sea is pregnant
with clear fish
and their shallow pools of eggs
and that the ocean has hidden
signs of its own hunger,   25
lost men and boats
and squid that flew
toward churning light.

Hunger lives in the town
whose walls are made of shells   30
white and shining in the moon,
where people live surrounded
by what they've eaten
to forget that hunger
sits on a ship and cries.   35

And it is a kind of hunger
that brings us to love,
to rocking currents of a secret wave
and the body that wants to live beyond itself
like the destitute men   40
who took the shining dolphins from the sea.
They were like women,
they said,
and had their way
with them,   45
wanting to be inside,
to drink
and be held in
the thin, clear milk of the gods.

Connections to Other Selections

1. Write an essay comparing Hogan's definition of hunger with Dickinson's definition of heaven in "'Heaven' — is what I cannot reach!" (p. 264). Which definition
   do you find more complete and satisfying? Explain why.
2. Discuss the relation between love and hunger in this poem and in Croft's "Home-
   Baked Bread" (p. 100).

YUSEF KOMUNYAKAA (b. 1947)

Yusef Komunyakaa, born in Bogalusa, Louisiana, a Vietnam veteran, earned
an M.F.A. from the University of California and now teaches creative writing and
African American studies at Indiana University. Among his awards is a National
Endowment for the Arts fellowship. His volumes of poetry include *Copacetic*
(1984), *I Apologize for the Eyes in My Head* (1986), *Dien Cai Dau* (1989), and
Magic City (1992). In 1994 *Neon Vernacular* was awarded a Pulitzer Prize.

Facing It

My black face fades,
hiding inside the black granite.
I said I wouldn't,
dammit: No tears.
I'm stone. I'm flesh.   5
My clouded reflection eyes me
like a bird of prey, the profile of night
slanted against morning. I turn
this way — the stone lets me go.
I turn that way — I'm inside   10
the Vietnam Veterans Memorial
again, depending on the light
to make a difference.
I go down the 58,022 names,
half-expecting to find   15
my own in letters like smoke.
I touch the name Andrew Johnson;
I see the booby trap's white flash.
Names shimmer on a woman's blouse
but when she walks away   20
the names stay on the wall.
Brushstrokes flash, a red bird's
wings cutting across my stare.
The sky. A plane in the sky.
A white vet's image floats   25
closer to me, then his pale eyes
look through mine. I'm a window.
He's lost his right arm
inside the stone. In the black mirror
a woman's trying to erase names: 30
No, she's brushing a boy's hair.

Connections to Other Selections

1. Discuss the speakers' attitudes toward war in "Facing It" and Cummings's "next to of course god america i" (p. 136).
2. In an essay compare the treatment of memory and sorrow in "Facing It" and Hall's "Letter with No Address" (p. 493).

JOAN MURRAY (b. 1945)

Born and raised in New York City, Joan Murray was educated at Hunter College and New York University. She has taught at Lehman College of the City University of New York. Among her awards for poetry are the National Endowment for the Arts and a Pushcart Prize. Her published volumes of poetry include *Egg Tooth* (1975) and *The Same Water* (1990).

Play-By-Play

Yaddo°

Would it surprise the young men
playing softball on the hill to hear the women
on the terrace admiring their bodies:
the slim waist of the pitcher, the strength
of the runner's legs, the torso of the catcher   5
rising off his knees to toss the ball back to the mound?
Would it embarrass them
to hear two women, sitting together after dinner,
praising even their futile motions:
the flex of a batter's hips   10
before his missed swing, the wide-spread stride
of a man picked off his base, the intensity
on the new man's face
as he waits on deck and fans the air?

Would it annoy them, the way some women   15
take offense when men caress them with their eyes?
And why should it surprise me that these women,
well past sixty, haven't put aside desire
but sit at ease and in pleasure,
watching the young men move above the rose garden   20
where the marble Naiads
pose and yawn in their fountain?
Who better than these women, with their sweaters
draped across their shoulders, their perspectives
honed from years of lovers, to recognize   25
the beauty that would otherwise
go unnoticed on this hill?
And will it compromise their pleasure
if I sit down at their table to listen
to the play-by-play and see it through their eyes?   30

Would it distract the young men if they realized
that three women laughing softly on the terrace
above closed books and half-filled wineglasses
are moving beside them on the field?
Would they want to know how they've been   35
held to the light till some motion or expression
showed the unsuspected loveliness
in a common shape or face?
Wouldn't they have liked to see how they looked
down there, as they stood for a moment at the plate,   40
bathed in the light of perfect expectation,
before their shadows lengthened, before they
walked together up the darkened hill,
so beautiful they would not have
recognized themselves?   45

Yaddo: a famous artist's colony.

1. Compare the voice of the speaker in "Play-By-Play" with that of Ackerman's "A Fine, a Private Place" (p. 61).
2. Write an essay on the speaker's gaze in this poem and Steele's "An Aubade" (p. 92).

RONALD WALLACE (b. 1945)

Born in Cedar Rapids, Iowa, Ronald Wallace earned a B.A. at The College of Wooster, and an M.A. and a Ph.D. at The University of Michigan. He has taught in the Department of English at The University of Wisconsin, Madison, since 1972. Among his awards are a Rackham Prize Fellowship and several American Council of Learned Society Fellowships. His collections of poems include *People and Dog in the Sun* (1987), *The Makings of Happiness* (1991), and *Time's Fancy* (1994).

Dogs

1997

When I was six years old I hit one with
a baseball bat. An accident, of course,
and broke his jaw. They put that dog to sleep,
a euphemism even then I knew
could not excuse me from the lasting wrath   5
of memory's flagellation. My remorse
could dog me as it would, it wouldn't keep
me from the life sentence that I drew:

For I've been barked at, bitten, nipped, knocked flat,
slobbered over, humped, sprayed, beshat,   10
by spaniel, terrier, retriever, bull, and Dane.
But through the years what's given me most pain
of all the dogs I've been the victim of
are those whose slow eyes gazed at me, in love.

Connections to Other Selections

1. Compare this poem's theme with Updike's "Dog's Death" (p. 11).
2. In an essay discuss the strategies used in this sonnet and Shakespeare's "My mistress' eyes are nothing like the sun" (p. 209) to create emotion in the reader.

14. Perspectives on Poetry

A variety of observations about poetry are presented in this chapter. The pieces offer a wide range of topics related to reading and writing poetry. The perspectives include William Wordsworth on the nature of poetry, Matthew Arnold on classic and popular literature, Ezra Pound on free verse, Dylan Thomas on the words used in poetry, and Denise Levertov on the background and form of one of her poems. In addition, there are poems about poetry by Walt Whitman and Archibald MacLeish. These relatively short pieces provide materials to explore some of the topics and issues that readers and writers of poetry have found perennially interesting and challenging.

WILLIAM WORDSWORTH (1770–1850)
On the Nature of Poets and Poetry   1802

Taking up the subject, then, upon general grounds, I ask what is meant by the word "poet"? What is a poet? To whom does he address himself? And what language is to be expected from him? He is a man speaking to men; a man, it is true, endued with more lively sensibility, more enthusiasm and tenderness, who has a greater knowledge of human nature, and a more comprehensive soul, than are supposed to be common among mankind; a man pleased with his own passions and volitions, and who rejoices more than other men in the spirit of life that is in him; delighting to contemplate similar volitions and passions as manifested in the goings-on of the universe, and habitually impelled to create them where he does not find them. To these qualities he has added a disposition to be affected more than other men by absent things as if they were present; an ability of conjuring up in himself passions, which are indeed far from being the same as those produced by real events, yet (especially in those parts of the general sympathy which are pleasing and delightful) do more nearly resemble the passions produced by real events, than anything which, from the motions of their own minds merely, other men are accustomed to feel in themselves; whence, and from practice, he has acquired a greater readiness and power in expressing what he thinks and feels, and especially those thoughts and feelings which, by his own choice, or from the structure of his own mind, arise in him without immediate external excitement. . . .

I have said that poetry is the spontaneous overflow of powerful feelings: it takes its origin from emotion recollected in tranquility: the emotion is contemplated till by a species of reaction the tranquility gradually disappears, and an emotion, kindred to that which was before the subject of contemplation, is gradually produced, and does itself actually exist in the mind. In this mood successful composition generally begins, and in a mood similar to this it is carried on; but the emotion, of whatever kind and in whatever degree, from various causes is qualified by various pleasures, so that in describing any passions whatsoever, which are voluntarily described, the mind will upon the whole be in a state of enjoyment. Now, if nature be thus cautious in preserving in a state of enjoyment a being thus employed, the poet ought to profit by the lesson thus held forth to him, and ought especially to take care, that whatever passions he communicates to his reader, those passions, if his reader's mind be sound and vigorous, should always be accompanied with an overbalance of pleasure. Now the music of harmonious metrical language, the sense of difficulty overcome, and the blind association of pleasure which has been previously received from works of rhyme or meter of the same or similar construction, an indistinct perception perpetually renewed of language closely resembling that of real life, and yet, in the circumstance of meter, differing from it so widely, all these imperceptibly make up a complex feeling of delight, which is of the most important use in tempering the painful feeling which will always be found intermingled with powerful descriptions of the deeper passions. This effect is always produced in pathetic and impassioned poetry; while, in lighter compositions, the ease and gracefulness with which the poet manages his numbers are themselves confessedly a principal source of the gratification of the reader. I might perhaps include all which it is *necessary* to say upon this subject by affirming, what few persons will deny, that, of two descriptions, either of passions, manners, or characters, each of them equally well executed, the one in prose and the other in verse, the verse will be read a hundred times where the prose is read once.

From *Preface to Lyrical Ballads, with Pastoral and Other Poems*

Considerations for Critical Thinking and Writing

1. Discuss Wordsworth's description of a poet's sensibility and "ability of conjuring up in himself passions." What characteristics do you associate with a poetic temperament?

2. Explain why you feel a writer's emotions are (or are not) more important in poetry than in prose.

3. Given that Wordsworth describes poetry as "the spontaneous overflow of powerful feelings," why can't his poems be characterized as formless bursts of raw emotion? Consider, for example, "London, 1802" (p. 119), "My Heart Leaps Up" (p. 188), or "The World Is Too Much with Us" (p. 208) to illustrate your response.

PERCY BYSSHE SHELLEY (1792–1822)
On Poets as "Unacknowledged Legislators"   1821

The most unfailing herald, companion, and follower of the awakening of a great people to work a beneficial change in opinion or institution, is poetry. At such periods there is an accumulation of the power of communicating and receiving intense and impassioned conceptions respecting man and nature. The persons in whom this power resides, may often, as far as regards many portions of their nature, have little apparent correspondence with that spirit of good of which they are the ministers. But even whilst they deny and abjure, they are yet compelled to serve, the power which is seated upon the throne of their own soul. It is impossible to read the compositions of the most celebrated writers of the present day without being startled with the electric life which burns within their words. They measure the circumference and sound the depths of human nature with a comprehensive and all-penetrating spirit, and they are themselves perhaps the most sincerely astonished at its manifestations, for it is less their spirit than the spirit of the age. Poets are the hierophants° of an unapprehended inspiration, the mirrors of the gigantic shadows which futurity casts upon the present, the words which express what they understand not; the trumpets which sing to battle, and feel not what they inspire: the influence which is moved not, but moves. Poets are the unacknowledged legislators of the world.

From *A Defense of Poetry*

hierophants: Interpreters of sacred mysteries.

Considerations for Critical Thinking and Writing

1. What kinds of powers does Shelley attribute to poets?
2. Compare Shelley's view of the poet with E. E. Cummings's (p. 510).

WALT WHITMAN (1819–1892)
When I Heard the Learn'd Astronomer   1865

When I heard the learn'd astronomer,
When the proofs, the figures, were ranged in columns before me,
When I was shown the charts and diagrams, to add, divide, and measure them,
When I sitting heard the astronomer where he lectured with much applause in
    the lecture-room,
How soon unaccountable I became tired and sick,
Till rising and gliding out I wandered off by myself,
In the mystical moist night-air, and from time to time,
Looked up in perfect silence at the stars.

Considerations for Critical Thinking and Writing

1. How does this poem illustrate the differences between poetry and science?
2. Many people today — rightly or wrongly — continue to regard science and poetry as antithetical. What do you think of their view? Write an essay about the methods and purposes of science and poetry in which you explore the differences and / or similarities between them. Use specific poems as evidence for your argument.

MATTHEW ARNOLD (1822-1888)
On Classic and Popular Literature 1888

The benefit of being able clearly to feel and deeply to enjoy the best, the truly classic, in poetry — is an end . . . of supreme importance. We are often told that an era is opening in which we are to see multitudes of a common sort of readers, and masses of a common sort of literature; that such readers do not want and could not relish anything better than such literature, and that to provide it is becoming a vast and profitable industry. Even if good literature entirely lost currency with the world, it would still be abundantly worth while to continue to enjoy it by oneself. But it never will lose currency with the world, in spite of momentary appearances; it never will lose supremacy. Currency and supremacy are insured to it, not indeed by the world's deliberate and conscious choice, but by something far deeper, — by the instinct of self-preservation in humanity.

From "The Study of Poetry"

Considerations for Critical Thinking and Writing

1. What, in your opinion, makes a work of literature "truly classic?"
2. What kinds of assumptions does Arnold implicitly make about readers of classics and the "multitudes of a common sort"? Do you agree with his categorizations and assessment of these two kinds of readers? Why or why not?
3. Take a stroll through your local bookstore to get a sense of the amount of space allocated to "classics," science fiction, romances, fantasy, mysteries, cookbooks, health books, and so on. Pay particular attention to the poetry section. Also, check to see what books are on the current best-seller lists (they're usually posted by the cash register). Then write a two-part report: in the first part write up your findings as you think Arnold would describe such a "vast and profitable industry"; in the second explain why you agree or disagree with Arnold's perspective.

EZRA POUND (1885-1972)
On Free Verse 1912

I think one should write vers libre [free verse] when one "must," that is to say, only when the "thing" builds up a rhythm more beautiful than that of set meters, or more real, more a part of the emotion of the "thing," more germane, intimate, interpretative than the measure of regular accentual verse; a rhythm which discontents one with set iambic or set anapestic.

From "Prolegomena," *Poetry Review*

Considerations for Critical Thinking and Writing

1. What implications are there in Pound's statement concerning the relation of a poem's form to its content?
2. Compare this view with Whitman's (p. 507).
3. Select a free verse poem from the text and apply Pound's criteria to it. How are the poem's lines arranged to be "a part of the emotion of the 'thing' "?

T. S. ELIOT (1888-1965)
On the Poet's Relation to Tradition 1920

If the only form of tradition, of handing down, consisted in following the ways of the immediate generation before us in a blind or timid adherence to its successes, "tradition" should positively be discouraged. We have seen many such simple currents soon lost in the sand; and novelty is better than repetition. Tradition is a matter of much wider significance. It cannot be inherited, and if you want it you must obtain it by great labour. It involves, in the first place, the historical sense, which we may call nearly indispensable to anyone who would continue to be a poet beyond his twenty-fifth year; and the historical sense involves a perception, not only of the pastness of the past, but of its presence; the historical sense compels a man to write not merely with his own generation in his bones, but with a feeling that the whole of the literature of Europe from Homer and within it the whole of the literature of his own country has a simultaneous existence and composes a simultaneous order. This historical sense, which is a sense of the timeless as well as of the temporal and of the timeless and of the temporal together, is what makes a writer traditional. And it is at the same time what makes a writer most acutely conscious of his place in time, of his own contemporaneity.

No poet, no artist of any art, has his complete meaning alone. His significance, his appreciation is the appreciation of his relation to the dead poets and artists. You cannot value him alone; you must set him, for contrast and comparison, among the dead. I mean this as a principle of aesthetic, not merely historical, criticism. The necessity that he shall conform, that he shall cohere, is not onesided; what happens when a new work of art is created is something that happens simultaneously to all the works of art which preceded it. The existing monuments form an ideal order among themselves, which is modified by the introduction of the new (the really new) work of art among them. The existing order is complete before the new work arrives; for order to persist after the supervention of novelty, the *whole* existing order must be, if ever so slightly, altered; and so the relations, proportions, values of each work of art toward the whole are readjusted; and this is conformity between the old and the new. Whoever has approved this idea of order, of the form of European, of English literature will not find it preposterous that the past should be altered by the present as much as the present is directed by the past. And the poet who is aware of this will be aware of great difficulties and responsibilities.

From "Tradition and the Individual Talent" in *The Sacred Wood*

Considerations for Critical Thinking and Writing

1. How does Eliot define tradition? Whom does his definition include and whom does it exclude?

2. How might Eliot's comments on tradition and the individual help to shed light on his poem "The Love Song of J. Alfred Prufrock" (p. 371)?

3. In an essay compare and contrast Eliot's view of the individual's relation to tradition with that of E. E. Cummings in "On the Artist's Responsibility" (p. 510).

ARCHIBALD MacLEISH (1892-1982)
Ars Poetica   1926

A poem should be palpable and mute
As a globed fruit,

Dumb
As old medallions to the thumb,

Silent as the sleeve-worn stone   5
Of casement ledges where the moss has grown —

A poem should be wordless
As the flight of birds.

A poem should be motionless in time
As the moon climbs,   10

Leaving, as the moon releases
Twig by twig the night-entangled trees,

Leaving, as the moon behind the winter leaves,
Memory by memory the mind —

A poem should be motionless in time   15
As the moon climbs.

A poem should be equal to:
Not true.

For all the history of grief
An empty doorway and a maple leaf.   20

For love
The leaning grasses and two lights above the sea —

A poem should not mean
But be.

Considerations for Critical Thinking and Writing

1. The Latin title of this poem is translated as "The Art of Poetry." What is MacLeish's view of good poetry? In what sense can a poem be "wordless"? How do lines 19–20 illustrate that idea?
2. Explain the final two lines. Does the poem contradict its own announced values?

E. E. CUMMINGS (1894-1962)
On the Artist's Responsibility   1953

So far as I am concerned, poetry and every other art was and is and forever will be strictly and distinctly a question of individuality . . . poetry is being, not doing. If you wish to follow, even at a distance, the poet's calling (and here, as always, I speak from my own totally biased and entirely personal point of view) you've got to come out of the measurable doing universe into the immeasurable house of being. . . . Nobody else can be alive for you; nor can you be alive for anybody else. Toms can be Dicks and Dicks can be Harrys, but none of them can ever be you. There's the artist's responsibility; and the most awful responsibility on earth. If you can take it, take it — and be. If you can't, cheer up and go about other people's business; and do (or undo) till you drop.

From i: Six Nonlectures

Considerations for Critical Thinking and Writing

1. What does Cummings mean when he says "poetry is being, not doing"? How does this compare with MacLeish's view in "Ars Poetica?"
2. How is Cummings's insistence upon individuality reflected in the style of "l(a" (p. 25) and the theme of "next to of course god america i" (p. 136)?

DYLAN THOMAS (1914-1953)
On the Words in Poetry 1961

You want to know why and how I just began to write poetry. . . .

To answer . . . this question, I should say I wanted to write poetry in the beginning because I had fallen in love with words. The first poems I knew were nursery rhymes, and before I could read them for myself I had come to love just the words of them, the words alone. What the words stood for, symbolized, or meant, was of very secondary importance. What mattered was the *sound* of them as I heard them for the first time on the lips of the remote and incomprehensible grown-ups who seemed, for some reason, to be living in my world. And these words were, to me, as the notes of bells, the sounds of musical instruments, the noises of wind, sea, and rain, the rattle of milkcarts, the clopping of hooves on cobbles, the fingering of branches on a window pane, might be to someone, deaf from birth, who has miraculously found his hearing. I did not care what the words said, overmuch, not what happened to Jack and Jill and the Mother Goose rest of them; I cared for the shapes of sound that their names, and the words describing their actions, made in my ears; I cared for the colors the words cast on my eyes. I realize that I may be, as I think back all that way, romanticizing my reactions to the simple and beautiful words of those pure poems; but that is all I can honestly remember, however much time might have falsified my memory. I fell in love — that is the only expression I can think of — at once, and am still at the mercy of words, though sometimes now, knowing a little of their behavior very well, I think I can influence them slightly and have even learned to beat them now and then, which they appear to enjoy. I tumbled for words at once. And, when I began to read the nursery rhymes for myself, and, later, to read other verses and ballads, I knew that I had discovered the most important things, to me, that could be ever. There they were, seemingly lifeless, made only of black and white, but out of them, out of their own being, came love and terror and pity and pain and wonder and all the other vague abstractions that make our ephemeral lives dangerous, great, and bearable. Out of them came the gusts and grunts and hiccups and heehaws of the common fun of the earth; and though what the words meant was, in its own way, often deliciously funny enough, so much funnier seemed to me, at that almost forgotten time, the shape and shade and size and noise of the words as they hummed, strummed, jugged, and galloped along. That was the time of

innocence; words burst upon me, unencumbered by trivial or portentous association; words were their springlike selves, fresh with Eden's dew, as they flew
out of the air. They made their own original associations as they sprang and
shone. The words "Ride a cock-horse to Banbury Cross" were as haunting to
me, who did not know then what a cock-horse was nor cared a damn where
Banbury Cross might be, as, much later, were such lines as John Donne's "Go
and catch a falling star, Get with child a mandrake root," which also I could not
understand when I first read them. And as I read more and more, and it was
not all verse, by any means, my love for the real life of words increased until I
knew that I must live *with* them and *in* them always. I knew, in fact, that I must
be a writer of words, and nothing else. The first thing was to feel and know
their sound and substance; what I was going to do with those words, what use
I was going to make of them, what I was going to *say* through them, would
come later. I knew I had to know them most intimately in all their forms and
moods, their ups and downs, their chops and changes, their needs and
demands. (Here, I am afraid, I am beginning to talk too vaguely. I do not like
writing *about* words, because then I often use bad and wrong and stale and
wooly words. What I like to do is treat words as a craftsman does his wood or
stone or what-have-you, to hew, carve, mold, coil, polish, and plane them into
patterns, sequences, sculptures, fugues of sound expressing some lyrical impulse, some spiritual doubt or conviction, some dimly-realized truth I must try
to reach and realize.)

From *Early Prose Writings*

Considerations for Critical Thinking and Writing

1. Why does Thomas value nursery rhymes so highly? What nursery rhyme was
   your favorite as a child? Why were you enchanted by it?
2. Explain what you think Thomas would have to say about Carroll's "Jabberwocky"
   (p. 171) or Swenson's "A Nosty Fright" (p. 158).
3. Consider Thomas's comparison at the end of this passage, in which he likens a
   poet's work to a craftsman's. In what sense is making poetry similar to sculpting,
   painting, or composing music? What are some of the significant differences?

AUDRE LORDE (1934–1992)
Poems Are Not Luxuries   1977

For each of us as women, there is a dark place within where hidden and
growing our true spirit rises, "Beautiful and tough as chestnut / Stanchions
against our nightmare of weakness" and of impotence. These places of possibility within ourselves are dark because they are ancient and hidden; they have
survived and grown strong through darkness. Within these deep places, each
one of us holds an incredible reserve of creativity and power, storehouse of
unexamined and unrecorded emotion and feeling. The woman's place of power
within each of us is neither white nor surface; it is dark, it is ancient, and it is
deep.

When we view living, in the european mode, only as a problem to be
solved, we rely solely upon our ideas to make us free, for these were what the
white fathers told us were precious. But as we become more in touch with our

own ancient, black, noneuropean view of living as a situation to be experienced and interacted with, we learn more and more to cherish our feelings, to respect those hidden sources of our power from where true knowledge and therefore lasting action comes. At this point in time, I believe that women carry within ourselves the possibility for fusion of these two approaches as a keystone for survival, and we come closest to this combination in our poetry. I speak here of poetry as the revelation or distillation of experience, not the sterile word play that, too often, the white fathers distorted the word *poetry* to mean — in order to cover their desperate wish for imagination without insight.

For women, then, poetry is not a luxury. It is a vital necessity of our existence. It forms the quality of the light within which we predicate our hopes and dreams toward survival and change, first made into language, then into idea, then into more tangible action. Poetry is the way we help give name to the nameless so it can be thought. The farthest external horizons of our hopes and fears are cobbled by our poems, carved from the rock experiences of our daily lives.

As they become known and accepted to ourselves, our feelings, and the honest exploration of them, become sanctuaries and fortresses and spawning grounds for the most radical and daring of ideas, the house of difference so necessary to change and the conceptualization of any meaningful action. Right now, I could name at least ten ideas I would once have found intolerable or incomprehensible and frightening, except as they came after dreams and poems. This is not idle fantasy, but the true meaning of "It feels right to me." We can train ourselves to respect our feelings and to discipline (transpose) them into a language that catches those feelings so they can be shared. And where that language does not yet exist, it is our poetry which helps to fashion it. Poetry is not only dream or vision, it is the skeleton architecture of our lives.

From "Poems Are Not Luxuries," in *Claims for Poetry,*
edited by Donald Hall

Considerations for Critical Thinking and Writing

1. What distinctions does Lorde make between black culture and "european" culture? How does she describe their different approaches to poetry? Do you agree or disagree with Lorde's assessment?
2. According to Lorde, why can't poetry be regarded as a luxury?
3. Read Lorde's poem "Hanging Fire" (p.432) and discuss whether you think it fulfills her description of what poetry can do.

DENISE LEVERTOV (b. 1923)
On "Gathered at the River" 1985

This is the prose of it: Each year on August 6 (and sometimes on August 9 as well) some kind of memorial observance of the bombing of Hiroshima and Nagasaki is held in the Boston/Cambridge area, as in so many other locations. Some years this has consisted of a silent vigil held near Faneuil Hall and other monuments of the American Revolution. Participants stand in a circle facing outward to display signs explaining the theme of the vigil, or pace slowly round, sometimes accompanied by the drums and chanting of attendant Buddhist monks. People stay for varying periods — there may be a constant presence for three days and nights. In 1982 the poet Suzanne Belote (of the Catholic radical peace group Ailanthus) and some others created a variation on this event. Participants (with the usual age range — babes in arms to white-haired old men and women) came to the Cambridge Friends' Meeting House for a brief preparatory assembly, then filed out to receive a candle apiece — thick Jahrzeit candles nailed to pieces of wood and shielded by paper cups — and proceeded to walk in a hushed column along Memorial Drive, beside the Charles River. The sun was low; a long summer day was ending. When we got to the wide grassy area near the Lars Anderson Bridge, where our ceremony was to take place, it was twilight. Shielding flickering flames from the evening breeze, we formed a large circle, into the center of which stepped successive readers of portions from the descriptions recorded (as in the book *Unforgettable Fire*) by survivors of the atomic bombings. A period of silence followed. And then "saints and prophets, heroes and heroines of justice and peace" — including Gandhi, Martin Luther King, A. J. Muste, Emma Goldman, Archbishop Romero, Eugene Debs, Pope John XXIII, Dorothy Day, Saint Francis of Assisi, Saint Thomas More, Prince Kropotkin, Ammon Hennacy, the Prophet Isaiah, and many others I can't remember — were invoked. A form of ritual — an ecumenical liturgy — had been devised for the occasion, and as each such name was uttered by some member of the circle, the rest responded with a phrase that said essentially, "Be with us, great spirits, in this time of great need." The persons conducting the continuum of the liturgy turned slowly as they read the survivors' testimony, or statements of dedication to the cause of peace, so that all could hear at least part of each passage: for we had no microphones, preferring to depend on the unaided human voice for an occasion which had a personal, intimate character for each participant rather than being a PR event. Some music was interspersed among the verbal antiphonies, and the human atmosphere was solemn, harmonious, truly dedicated: from within it I began to feel the strong presence of the trees which half encircled us. Cars passed along Memorial Drive — slowed as drivers craned to see what was happening — passed on. A few blinked their lights in a friendly way, guessing from the date, I suppose, why we were there.

While we earnestly committed — or recommitted — ourselves to do all in our power to prevent nuclear war from ever taking place, it was growing dark. In the soft summer darkness details stood out: hands cupping wicks, small children's gold-illumined faces gazing up in wonder at the crouch and leap of flames, adults' heads bent close to one another as they clustered in twos and threes to relight candles blown out. And now the first part of the ritual was over and it was time to set our candles afloat, as they are set on the river in Hiroshima each year, that river where many drowned in the vain attempt to escape the burning of their own flesh.

People scrambled and helped each other down the short slope of the riverbank to launch the little candle-boats. Oblivious, a motorboat or two sped upriver, and minutes after a big slow wave would reach the shore. The water was black; the candle-boats seemed so fragile, and so tenacious. And all the time the large plane trees (saved from a road-widening project years before, incidentally, by citizens who chained themselves to their trunks in protest), and the other trees and bushes near them, were intensely, watchfully present. I have been asked if I really believe trees can listen. I've always thought our scientific knowledge has made us very arrogant in our assumptions. Wiser and older individuals and cultures have believed other kinds of consciousness and feeling could and did exist alongside of ours; I see no reason to disagree. It is not that I don't know trees have no "gray matter." It is possible that there are other routes to sentience than those with which we consider ourselves familiar.

The form of the poem: The title came from the literal sense of our being gathered there on the shore of the Charles, and also with the cognizance of the Quaker sense of gathering — a *"gathered meeting"* being, to my understanding, one which has not merely acquired the full complement of those who are going to attend it but which has attained a certain level, or quality, of attunement. Then, too, I had a vague memory of the song or hymn from which James Wright took the title of one of his books, and which I presumed must refer to the river of Jordan — "one more river, one more river to cross," as another song says. And though the symbolism there is of heaven lying upon the far shore, yet there is also, in the implication of *lastness,* of a final ordeal, the clear sense of a cata-strophic alternative to attaining that shore. (No doubt *Pilgrim's Progress* was in the back of my mind too.) The analogy is obviously not a very close one, since survival of life on earth is a more modest goal than eternal bliss. Yet, relative to the hell proposed by our twentieth-century compound of the ancient vices of greed and love of power with nuclear and other "advanced" technology, mere survival would be a kind of heaven — especially since survival is not a static condition but offers the opportunity, and therefore the hope, of positive change. (For if one hopes for the survival of life on earth, one must logically hope and *intend* also the reshaping of those forces and factors which, unchanged, will only continue to threaten annihilation by one means or another.)

The structure of the poem stems as directly as the title from my experience of the event. The first line stands alone because that perception of the trees as animate and not uninterested presences — witnesses — was the discrete first in a series of heightened perceptions, most of which came in clusters. The follow-ing two-line stanza expands the first, more tentative observation, and places the trees' air of attention in the context of a breeze (which does not seem to distract them) and of the fluttering candles, which are thus introduced right at the start. Looking more closely at the trees, I see their late-summer color, but then recognize I am no longer seeing it, for dusk is falling — literally, but also metaphorically. The next stanza notes the largeness (and implied gravity, in both senses) of the trees, which it is not too dark to see, then again in a single line reasserts with more assurance the focus of my own attention: the trees' attentiveness. Following that comes the recognition of why, and for what, they are listening. The Latin words introduced here (echoing Pound's use of them) express the idea that "sin" occurs when humans violate the well-being of their own species and other living things, denying the natural law, the interdepen-dence of all. (That usury belongs in this category, as Pound reemphasized, is not irrelevant to the subject of this poem, recalling the economic underpinning of the arms race and of war itself.)

My underlying belief in a great design, a potential harmony which can be violated or be sustained, probably strikes some people as quaint; but I would be dishonest, as person and artist, if I disowned it. I don't at this stage of my life feel ready for a public discussion of my religious concepts: but I think it must be clear from my writings that I have never been an atheist, and that — given my background and the fact that all my life George Herbert, Henry Vaughan, Thomas Traherne, and Gerard Manley Hopkins have been on my "short list" of favorite poets — whatever degree of belief I might attain would have a Chris-tian context. This in turn implies a concern with the osmosis of "faith and works" and a sense of the sacredness of the earthly creation. That sense, not exclusive to Christianity, and deeply experienced and expressed by, for instance, Native Americans, is linked to Christians to the mystery of the Incarnation. To violate ourselves and our world is to violate the Divine.

The trees' concern, proposed with a tentative "as if" at the beginning, and then as an impression they "give off," is now asserted unequivocally. Once more comes a single line, "We intone together, *Never again,*" focused on the purpose of our gathering; and the words "never again" bring together the thought of the Nazi Holocaust with that of the crime committed by the U.S. against Japanese civilians, a crime advocates of the arms race prepare to commit again on a scale vaster than that of any massacre in all of history. This association might carry with it, I would hope, the sense that those who vow to work for prevention of war also are dedicated to political, economic, and racial justice, and understand something of the connections between long-standing oppression, major and "minor" massacres, and the giant shadow of global war and annihilation.

The narration continues, up to the launching of the candle-boats; pauses — a pause indicated by the asterisk — as we hold our breath to watch them go; and continues as they "bob on the current" and, though close to shore, begin to move downstream. Like ourselves, they are few and pitifully small. But at least they don't sink. Like all candles lit for the dead or in prayer, they combine remembrance with aspiration.

Finally the poem returns its regard to the trees, with the feeling that they know what we know — a knowledge those lines state and which it would be silly to paraphrase. The single lines again center on the primary realizations. Indeed, I see that a kind of précis of the entire poem could be extracted by reading the isolated lines alone:

> As if the trees were not indifferent . . .
> . . . .
> a half-circle of attention.
> . . . .
> We intone together, *Never again.*
> . . . .
> Windthreatened flames bob on the current . . .
> . . . .
> there will be nothing left of their slow and innocent wisdom,
> . . . .
> no pollen,

except that one absolutely essential bone would be missing from that skeleton: the "if" of "if we fail." The poem, like the ceremony it narrates, and which gives it its slow, serious *pace* and, I hope, tone, is about interconnection, about dread, and about hope; that word, *if,* is its core.

> " 'Gathered at the River': Background and Form" in *Singular Voices: American Poetry Today,* edited by Stephen Berg (Levertov's essay was written in response to a request from Berg)

Considerations for Critical Thinking and Writing

1. In this essay, Levertov describes why and how she wrote "Gathered at the River" (p. 233). Does her account of the memorial observance help you to appreciate the poem more? Why or why not? Is the background information to the poem ("the prose of it") essential for an understanding of it?

2. Why is the word *if* essential to the poem's meaning?

3. Does Levertov exhaust the possibilities for discussing the poem? What can you add to her comments?

4. Poets are usually extremely reluctant to comment on their own poetry. Why do you think they frequently refuse to talk about the background and form of their poems?

ALICE FULTON (b. 1952)
On the Validity of Free Verse 1987

Until recently, I believed that Pound (along with Blake and Whitman, among others) had managed to establish beyond all argument the value of *vers libre* as a poetic medium. I thought that questions concerning the validity of free verse could be filed along with such antique quarrels as "Is photography Art?" and "Is abstract art Art?" In the past few years, however, I've heard many people — professors, poets, readers — speak of free verse as a failed experiment. To these disgruntled souls, free verse apparently describes an amorphous prosaic spouting, distinguished chiefly by its neglect of meter or rhyme, pattern or plan. Perhaps the word *free* contributes to the misconception. It's easy to interpret *free* as "free from all constraints of form," which leads to "free-for-all." However, any poet struggling with the obdurate qualities of language can testify that the above connotations of "free" do not apply to verse.

Since it's impossible to write unaccented English, free verse has meter. Of course, rather than striving for regularity, the measure of free verse may change from line to line, just as the tempo of twentieth-century music may change from bar to bar. As for allegations about formlessness, it seems to me that only an irregular structure with no beginning or end could be described as formless. (If the structure were regular, we could deduce the whole from a part. If irregular and therefore unpredictable, we'd need to see the whole in order to grasp its shape.) By this definition, there are fairly few examples of formless phenomena: certain concepts of God or of the expanding universe come to mind. However, unlike the accidental forms of nature, free verse is characterized by the poet's conscious shaping of content and language: the poet's choices at each step of the creative process give rise to form. Rather than relying on regular meter or rhyme as a means of ordering, the structures of free verse may be based upon registers of diction, irregular meter, sound as analogue for content, syllabics, accentuals, the interplay of chance with chosen elements, theories of lineation, recurring words, or whatever design delights the imagination and intellect. I suspect that the relation between content and form can be important or arbitrary in both metered and free verse. In regard to conventional forms, it's often assumed that decisions concerning content follow decisions concerning form (the add-subject-and-stir approach). However, poets consciously choose different subjects for sonnets than for ballads, thus exemplifying the interdependency of content and form. The reverse assumption is made about free verse: that the subject supersedes or, at best, dictates the form. But this is not necessarily the case. The poet can decide to utilize a structural device, such as the ones suggested previously, and then proceed to devise the content.

When we read a sestina, the form is clearly discernible. This is partly because we've read so many sestinas (familiarity breeds recognition) and partly because it's easy to perceive a highly repetitive pattern. More complex designs, however, often appear to be random until scrutinized closely. Much of what we call free verse tries to create a structure suitable only to itself — a pattern that has never appeared before, perhaps. As in serious modern music or jazz, the repetitions, if they do exist, may be so widely spaced that it takes several readings to discern them. Or the poems' unifying elements may be new to the reader, who must become a creative and active participant in order to appreciate the overall scheme. This is not meant to be a dismissal of the time-honored poetic forms. I admire and enjoy poets who breathe new life into seemingly dead conventions or structures. And I'm intrigued by poetry that borrows its shape from the models around us: poems in the form of TV listings, letters, recipes, and so forth. But I also value the analysis required and the discovery inherent in reading work that invents a form peculiar to itself. I like the idea of varying the meter from line to line so that nuances of tone can find their rhythmic correlative (or antithesis).

From *Ecstatic Occasions, Expedient Forms,* edited by David Lehman

Considerations for Critical Thinking and Writing

1. How does Fulton defend free verse against "allegations about formlessness"?
2. Compare Fulton's comments on the relationship of a poem's form to its content with Whitman's views (p. 507).
3. Browse through Chapter 13 and choose a poem "that invents a form peculiar to itself." Now analyze that poem.

ROBERT J. FOGELIN (b. 1932)
A Case against Metaphors   1988

Recent writers on metaphor often insist, sometimes in extravagant terms, on the power of metaphors. They also complain about the prejudice against metaphor that springs, they suggest, from a narrow, literalist (positivist) conception of language. The fact of the matter is that the vast majority of metaphors are routine and uninteresting. Many metaphors are lame, misleading, overblown, inaccurate, et cetera. Metaphors, in indicating that one thing is like another, so far say very little. Their strength, which they share with comparisons in general, is that their near-emptiness makes them adaptable for use in a wide variety of contexts. On the reverse side, the near-emptiness of metaphors also makes them serviceable for those occasions when we want to avoid saying, and perhaps thinking, what we really mean. Euphemisms are typically couched in metaphors. Metaphors can be evasions — including poetic evasions.

From *Figuratively Speaking*

Considerations for Critical Thinking and Writing

1. Why does Fogelin object to many uses of metaphors? Explain why you agree or disagree with his assessment.
2. Choose a poem from this anthology and write an essay that either supports or refutes Fogelin's assertions.

DIANE ACKERMAN (b. 1948)
On What Poetry Is Not — and Is   1991

Poetry is not philosophy, not sociology, not psychology, not politics. One ought not to ask of it what's found to better advantage elsewhere. One should only ask poetry to do what it excels at: (1) reflect the working sensibility of its creator, ideally someone with a unique vision and a unique way of expressing it; (2) remind us of the truths about life and human nature that we knew all along, but forgot somehow because they weren't yet in memorable language; and (3) reveal to us many incidental things that a poem knows so well.

What does a poem know? For openers, it knows the vagaries of linguistic fashion, the arduous, ricochet, and sometimes fanciful evolution of society as reflected in its language. It knows quite a lot about social convention, mob psychology, and mores, as they surface in the euphemisms of twenty ages — words like "lynch," "bloomers," and "fornicate" — and then submerge into normal discourse. A poem knows about Creation, any creation, our creation. It takes a blank and makes something, adds *some thing* to the sum of existence. If a poet describes a panther's cage in a certain vivid way, that cage will be as real a fact as the sun. A poem knows more about human nature than its writer does, because a poem is often a camera, a logbook, an annal, not an interpreter. A poem says: These are the facts. And sometimes it goes on to say: And this is what I make of them. But the facts may be right, and the *what I make of them* hopelessly wrong, in what is nonetheless a meaningful and moving poem. A poem may know the subtlest elisions of feeling, the earliest signs of some pattern or discord. . . . A book of poems chronicles the poet's many selves, and as such knows more about the poet than the poet does at any given time, including the time when the book is finished and yet another self holds her book of previous selves in her hands. A poem knows a great deal about our mental habits, and about upheaval and discovery, loneliness and despair. And it knows the handrails a mind clings to in times of stress. . . .

From "White Lanterns" in *The Writer on Her Work,*
edited by Janet Sternburg

Considerations for Critical Thinking and Writing

1. Do you agree that poetry is *not* philosophy, sociology, psychology, or politics? Explain why or why not.
2. From your own perspective, discuss what you think is the most important thing that a poem can "know." You may expand upon one of Ackerman's ideas or suggest your own.

ROBERT BLY (b. 1926)
On "Snowbanks North of the House"   1996

William Stafford has spoken so beautifully about what an assertion means in a poem, and how early you can make one. In one of his books, maybe *Writing the Australian Crawl,* he says if you make strong assertions too early in the poem, you can lose the reader. The reader needs to receive a couple of assertions first that it can agree with, such as "It's summer," or "Animals own a fur world," or "Those lines on your palm, they can be read," or "There was a river under First and Main." The reader needs to experience rather mild assertions so that he or she can begin to trust your mind; then when you make a wilder assertion later, the reader is more likely to climb up with you into that intense place from which the assertion came. My first assertion is

Those great great sweeps of that stop suddenly six feet from the house.

Some snow blows all the way down from Canada and then stops six feet from the house. For people who've never lived on the prairie and have experienced only gently falling snow or snow interrupted by woods, my first line may seem a risky assertion. So my second line is mild.

Thoughts that go so far.

I want my poem to continue, but not to ascend, so I need an ordinary event, something we've all known a thousand times:

The boy gets out of high school and reads no more books.

I can stay with that ordinariness for a little while:

The son stops calling home.

I experienced that refusal to call home when I lived in New York during my late twenties. Certain ways of living come to an end:

The mother puts down her rolling pin and makes no more bread.

I was thinking of my grandmother making Norwegian flat bread; readers correctly told me that ordinary bread these days is not made with rolling pins. But the child in me wrote that line. The adult in me wrote the next line:

And the wife looks at her husband one night at a party, and loves him no more.

I'm not conscious that that line happened to me, but it's possible. I do recall seeing both halves of the line at one instant in the wife's glance. It's another sadness. It's just an ordinary sadness. It doesn't happen only to special people.

The energy leaves the wine, and the minister falls leaving the church.

My father always had a particular tenderness for the old Lutheran minister in our town, and made sure that he received game such as pheasants in the fall, and geese at Christmas; I had some sympathy for the way a minister has to hold himself up and perform his role no matter what is happening in his private life. He has to keep giving the Communion.

A month or two after I wrote the poem, I read it to a friend who was an Episcopal priest of great spirit; he told me that I had described exactly what had happened to him a month before. He couldn't say the Communion words whole-heartedly on that particular Sunday, and he fell on the steps outside. One could say that for many ordinary people — and I am one of those — a fine energy sometimes refuses to become friends with us, or perhaps we refuse to make the courtly gesture that would welcome that energy. When we fall, it's an ordinary sadness.

It will not come closer —
the one inside moves back, and the hands touch nothing, and are safe.

I think a lot of my childhood is alive in that last half-sentence. And I spent in my mid-twenties two years alone in New York, talking to people barely once a month. It was all right. I felt safe: "The hands touch nothing, and are safe."

I must have felt that grief during the poem. The poem is moving away from sadness now and toward grief. And I recalled a scene from Abraham Lincoln's life. He loved his son Tad so much, and when the boy was eight, he died of tuberculosis or some such thing. They put the coffin into a room by itself in that kind of home visitation that people did at that time. Lincoln went into the room and didn't come out. He stayed all afternoon, and then he stayed there all night, and then he stayed there the next day. Around noon people started pounding on the door and telling him to come out, but he paid no attention. There was something a little extraordinary in that, but the general situation is not unusual, it's something we've all noticed or heard about many times. Sometimes after the death of a child, the husband and wife never do come back to each other.

> The father grieves for his son, and will not leave the room where the coffin stands.
> He turns away from his wife, and she sleeps alone.

Now what to do? Now we've arrived at a really ordinary place, in which life and its motions go on, but the shocked man or woman doesn't pay much informed attention to those motions anymore. Donald Hall has written about this place in his poem called "Mr. Wakeville on Interstate 90":

> I will work forty hours a week clerking at the paintstore. . . .
> I will watch my neighbors' daughters grow up, marry,
> raise children. The joints of my fingers will stiffen.

The way such a life moves mechanically is a form of depression. At the beginning of *A Farewell to Arms,* Hemingway says, "That fall the war was still there, but we didn't go to it anymore."

> And the sea lifts and falls all night, the moon goes on through the unattached heavens alone.

I loved that word "unattached" when I saw it on the page. It brought together the son who stops calling home and the man who lives alone in New York for two years.

Then I saw the toe of a black shoe. It seemed like an ordinary shoe, not standing on marble or red carpet, but on ordinary dust. Some elegant movement as of a hinge suddenly arrived, breaking all these long forward motions:

> The toe of the shoe pivots
> in dust . . .
> and the man in the black coat turns, and goes back down the hill.

The first time I read the poem to an audience, there was some silence afterwards, and a woman asked, "Who is the man in the black coat?" I said, "I don't know." She said, "That's outrageous; you wrote the poem." I didn't answer. It was only when I got back to the farm that I thought of the proper answer: "If I had known who the man in the black coat was, I could have written an essay." I don't mean to demean essays with such a sentence, but it's good to think clearly in an essay, which can be a series of really clear and interlocking thoughts that are luminous. But sometimes a poem amounts to the creation of some sort of nourishing mud pond in which partly developed tadpoles can live for a while, and certain images can receive enough sustenance from the darkness around them to keep breathing without being forced into some early adulthood or job or retirement. It's possible the man in the black coat is Lincoln. He did turn and go back down the hill, and his face got sadder every year that the war went on. I also noticed in a family album a photograph of my father about 25 years old, standing by the windmill holding a baby rather awkwardly couched in his right arm; it's possible the baby was myself. He was wearing a large black coat. I don't know exactly why the last line closes the poem. I didn't intend it. It just came along. Perhaps it's the most ordinary thing of all. Our mother, or our grandmother, or grandfather, or our father, goes through incredible labors, keeping despite turbulent winds and strong blows the chosen direction forward, following some route. But why? What was the aim of Lincoln's life? What was the aim of my father's life? Or my life? We know a little bit of the story — what's the rest of the story? Why don't we know that?

> No one knows why he came, or why he turned away and did not climb the hill.

From a typed manuscript sent to Michael Meyer, 1997

Considerations for Critical Thinking and Writing

1. What do you think Bly means when he says he begins with "mild assertions" and "something ordinary" before "ascending" to "wilder assertion[s]"? How does "Snow-banks North of the House" (p. 139) proceed this way?

2. Why do you think the woman in the audience thinks it "outrageous" that the poet doesn't know the identity of "the man in the black coat"? Explain why you agree or disagree with her response.

3. Discuss Bly's idea that "sometimes a poem amounts to the creation of some sort of nourishing mud pond in which partly developed tadpoles can live for a while." What does this description (and the rest of the sentence in which it appears) suggest about the nature of meaning in this poem?

4. How does Bly's reading and explanation of the poem compare with your own experience of it? Do you think his essay limits or expands your interpretation of the poem? Explain your response.

CRITICAL THINKING
AND WRITING

15. Critical Strategies for Reading

CRITICAL THINKING

Maybe this has happened to you: the assignment is to write an analysis of some aspect of a work, let's say Nathaniel Hawthorne's *The Scarlet Letter,* that interests you, taking into account critical sources that comment on and interpret the work. You cheerfully begin research in the library but quickly find yourself bewildered by several seemingly unrelated articles. The first traces the thematic significance of images of light and darkness in the novel; the second makes a case for Hester Prynne as a liberated woman; the third argues that Arthur Dimmesdale's guilt is a projection of Hawthorne's own emotions; and the fourth analyzes the introduction, "The Custom House," as an attack on bourgeois values. These disparate treatments may seem random and capricious — a confirmation of your worst suspicions that interpretations of literature are hit-or-miss excursions into areas that you know little about or didn't know even existed. But if you understand that the articles are written from different perspectives — formalist, feminist, psychological, and Marxist — and that the purpose of each is to enhance your understanding of the work by discussing a particular element of it, then you can see that their varying strategies represent potentially interesting ways of opening up the text that might otherwise never have occurred to you. There are many ways to approach a text, and a useful first step is to develop a sense of direction, an understanding of how a perspective — your own or a critic's — shapes a discussion of a text.

This chapter offers an introduction to critical approaches to literature by outlining a variety of strategies for reading poetry, fiction, or drama. The emphasis is of course on poetry and to that end the approaches focus on Robert Frost's "Mending Wall" (p. 304); a rereading of that well-known poem will equip you for the discussions that follow. In addition to the emphasis on this poem to illustrate critical approaches, some fiction and drama examples are also included along the way to demonstrate how these critical approaches can be applied to any genre. These strategies include approaches that have long been practiced by readers who have used, for example, the insights gleaned from biography and history to illuminate literary works as well as more recent approaches, such as those used by feminist, reader-response, and deconstructionist critics. Each of these perspectives is sensitive to image, symbol, tone, irony, and other literary elements that you have been studying, but each also casts those elements in a special light. The formalist approach emphasizes how the elements within a work achieve their effects, whereas biographical and psychological approaches lead outward from the work to consider the author's life and other writings. Even broader approaches, such as historical and sociological perspectives, connect the work to historic, social, and economic forces. Mythological readings represent the broadest approach, because they discuss the cultural and universal responses readers have to a work.

Any given strategy raises its own types of questions and issues while seeking particular kinds of evidence to support itself. An awareness of the assumptions and methods that inform an approach can help you to understand better the validity and value of a given critic's strategy for making sense of a work. More important, such an understanding can widen and deepen the responses of your own reading.

The critical thinking that goes into understanding a professional critic's approach to a work is not foreign to you because you have already used essentially the same kind of thinking to understand the work itself. The skills you have developed to produce a literary *analysis* that, for example, describes how a character, symbol, or rhyme scheme supports a theme are also useful for reading literary criticism, because such skills allow you to keep track of how the parts of a critical approach create a particular reading of a literary work. When you analyze a poem, story, or play by closely examining how its various elements relate to the whole, your *interpretation* — your articulation of what the work means to you as supported by an analysis of its elements — necessarily involves choosing what you focus upon in the work. The same is true of professional critics.

Critical readings presuppose choices in the kinds of material that are discussed. An analysis of the setting of Robert Frost's "Home Burial" (p. 306) would probably bring into focus the oppressive environment of the couple's domestic life rather than, say, the economic history of New England farming. The economic history of New England farming might be useful to a Marxist critic concerned with how class is revealed in "Home Burial," but for a formalist critic interested in identifying the unifying structures of the poem such information would be irrelevant.

The Perspectives, Complementary Readings, and Critical Case Study in this anthology offer opportunities to read critics using a wide variety of approaches to analyze and interpret texts. In the Critical Case Study on T. S. Eliot's "The Love Song of J. Alfred Prufrock" (Chapter 12), for instance, Elisabeth Schneider offers a biographical interpretation of Prufrock by suggesting that Eliot shared some of his character's sensibilities. In contrast, Robert G. Cook argues that Prufrock's character can be explained by the historical influence of Ralph Waldo Emerson's 1841 essay "Self-Reliance." Each of these critics raises different questions, examines different evidence, and employs different assumptions to interpret Prufrock's character. Being aware of those differences — teasing them out so that you can see how they lead to competing conclusions — is a useful way to analyze the analysis itself. What is left out of an interpretation is sometimes as significant as what is included. As you read the critics, it's worth reminding yourself that your own critical thinking skills can help you to determine the usefulness of a particular approach.

The following overview is neither exhaustive in the types of critical approaches covered nor complete in its presentation of the complexities inherent in them, but it should help you to develop an appreciation of the intriguing possibilities that attend literary interpretation. The emphasis in this chapter is on ways of thinking about literature rather than on daunting lists of terms, names, and movements. Although a working knowledge of critical schools may be valuable and necessary for a fully informed use of a given critical approach, the aim here is more modest and practical. This chapter is no substitute for the shelves of literary criticism that can be found in your library, but it does suggest how readers using different perspectives organize their responses to texts.

The summaries of critical approaches that follow are descriptive, not evaluative. Each approach has its advantages and limitations, but those matters are best left to further study. Like literary artists, critics have their personal values, tastes, and styles. The appropriateness of a specific critical approach will depend, at least in part, on the nature of the literary work under discussion as well as on your own sensibilities and experience. However, any approach, if it is to enhance understanding, requires sensitivity, tact, and an awareness of the various literary elements of the text, including, of course, its use of language.

Successful critical approaches avoid eccentric decodings that reveal so-called hidden meanings, which are not only hidden but totally absent from the text. For a parody of this sort of critical excess, see "A Reading of 'Stopping by Woods on a Snowy Evening' " (p. 328), in which Herbert R. Coursen, Jr., has some fun with a Robert Frost poem and Santa Claus while making a serious point about the dangers of overly ingenious readings. Literary criticism attempts, like any valid hypothesis, to account for phenomena — the text — without distorting or misrepresenting what it describes.

THE LITERARY CANON: DIVERSITY AND CONTROVERSY

Before looking at the various critical approaches discussed in this chapter, it makes sense to consider first which literature has been traditionally considered worthy of such analysis. The discussion in the Introduction called The Changing Literary Canon (p. 5) may have already alerted you to the fact that in recent years many more works by women, minorities, and writers from around the world have been considered by scholars, critics, and teachers to merit serious study and inclusion in what is known as the literary canon. This increasing diversity has been celebrated by those who believe that multiculturalism taps new sources for the discovery of great literature while raising significant questions about language, culture, and society. At the same time, others have perceived this diversity as a threat to the established, traditional canon of Western culture.

The debates concerning whose work should be read, taught, and written about have sometimes been acrimonious as well as lively and challenging. Bitter arguments have been waged recently on campuses and in the press over what has come to be called "political correctness." Two camps — roughly — have formed around these debates: liberals and conservatives (the appropriateness of these terms is debatable but the oppositional positioning is unmistakable). The liberals are said to insist upon politically correct views from colleagues and students opening up the curriculum to multicultural texts from Asia, Africa, Latin America, and elsewhere, and to encourage more tolerant attitudes about race, class, gender, and sexual orientation. These revisionists, seeking a change in traditional attitudes, are sometimes accused of intimidating the opposition into silence and substituting ideological dogma for reason and truth. The conservatives are also portrayed as ideologues; in their efforts to preserve what they regard as the best from the past, they refuse to admit that Western classics, mostly written by white male Europeans, represent only a portion of human experience. These traditionalists are seen as advocating values that are neither universal nor eternal but merely privileged and entrenched. Conservatives are charged with refusing to acknowledge that their values also represent a political agenda, which is implicit in their preference for the works of canonical authors such as Homer, Virgil, Shakespeare, Milton, Tolstoy, and Faulkner. The reductive and contradictory nature of this national debate between liberals and conservatives has been neatly summed up by Katha Pollitt: "Read the conservatives' list and produce a nation of sexists and racists — or a nation of philosopher kings. Read the liberals' list and produce a nation of spiritual relativists — or a nation of open-minded world citizens" ("Canon to the Right of Me . . . ," *The Nation*, Sept. 23, 1991, p. 330).

These troubling and extreme alternatives can be avoided, of course, if the issues are not approached from such absolutist positions. Solutions to these issues cannot be suggested in this limited space, and, no doubt, solutions will evolve over time, but we can at least provide a perspective. Books — regardless of what list they are on — are not likely to unite a fragmented nation or to disunite a unified one. It is perhaps more useful and accurate to see issues of canonicity as reflecting political changes rather than being the primary causes of them. This is not to say that books don't have an impact on readers — that *Uncle Tom's Cabin,* for instance, did not galvanize antislavery sentiments in nineteenth-century America — but that book lists do not by themselves preserve or destroy the status quo.

It's worth noting that the curricula of American universities have always undergone significant and, some would say, wrenching changes. Only a little more than one hundred years ago there was strong opposition to teaching English, as well as other modern languages, alongside programs dominated by Greek and Latin. Only since the 1920s has American literature been made a part of the curriculum, and just five decades ago writers such as Emily Dickinson, Robert Frost, W. H. Auden, and Marianne Moore were regarded with the same raised eyebrows that today might be raised about contemporary writers such as Sharon Olds, Galway Kinnell, Rita Dove, or Robert Bly. New voices do not drown out the past; they build on it, and eventually become part of the past as newer writers take their place alongside them. Neither resistance to change nor a denial of the past will have its way with the canon. Though both impulses are widespread, neither is likely to dominate the other, because there are too many reasonable, practical readers and teachers who instead of replacing Shakespeare, Frost, and other canonical writers have supplemented them with neglected writers from Western and other cultures. These readers experience the current debates about the canon not as a binary opposition but as an opportunity to explore important questions about continuity and change in our literature, culture, and society.

FORMALIST STRATEGIES

Formalist critics focus on the formal elements of a work — its language, structure, and tone. A formalist reads literature as an independent work of art rather than as a reflection of the author's state of mind or as a representation of a moment in history. Historic influences on a work, an author's intentions, or anything else outside the work are generally not treated by formalists (this is particularly true of the most famous modern formalists, known as the *New Critics,* who dominated American criticism from the 1940s through the 1960s). Instead, formalists offer intense examinations of the relationship between form and meaning within a work, emphasizing the subtle complexity of how a work is arranged. This kind of close reading pays special attention to what are often described as *intrinsic* matters in a literary work, such as diction, irony, paradox, metaphor, and symbol, as well as larger elements, such as plot, characterization, and narrative technique. Formalists examine how these elements work together to give a coherent shape to a work while contributing to its meaning. The answers to the questions formalists raise about how the shape and effect of a work are related come from the work itself. Other kinds of information that go beyond the text — biography, history, politics, economics, and so on — are typically regarded by formalists as *extrinsic* matters, which are considerably less important than what goes on within the autonomous text.

Poetry especially lends itself to close readings, because a poem's relative brevity allows for detailed analyses of nearly all its words and how they achieve their effects. For a sample formalist reading of how a pervasive sense of death is worked into a poem, see "A Reading of Dickinson's 'There's a certain Slant of light' " (p. 584).

Formalist strategies are also useful for analyzing drama and fiction. In his well-known essay "The World of *Hamlet,*" Maynard Mack explores Hamlet's character and predicament by paying close attention to the words and images that Shakespeare uses to build a world in which appearances mask reality and mystery is embedded in scene after scene. Mack points to recurring terms, such as *apparition, seems, assume,* and *put on,* as well as repeated images of acting, clothing, disease, and painting, to indicate the treacherous surface world Hamlet must penetrate to get to the truth. This pattern of deception provides an organizing principle around which Mack offers a reading of the entire play:

> Hamlet's problem, in its crudest form, is simply the problem of the avenger: he must carry out the injunction of the ghost and kill the king. But this problem . . . is presented in terms of a certain kind of world. The ghost's injunction to act becomes so inextricably bound up for Hamlet with the character of the world in which the action must be taken — its mysteriousness, its baffling appearances, its deep consciousness of infection, frailty, and loss — that he cannot come to terms with either without coming to terms with both.

Although Mack places *Hamlet* in the tradition of revenge tragedy, his reading of the play emphasizes Shakespeare's arrangement of language rather than literary history as a means of providing an interpretation that accounts for various elements of the play. Mack's formalist strategy explores how diction reveals meaning and how repeated words and images evoke and reinforce important thematic significances.

A formalist reading of Robert Frost's "Mending Wall" leads to an examination of the tensions produced by the poem's diction, repetitions, and images that take us beyond a merely literal reading. The speaker describes how every spring he and his neighbor walk beside the stone wall bordering their respective farms to replace the stones that have fallen during winter. As they repair the wall, the speaker wonders what purpose the wall serves, given that "My apple trees will never get across / And eat the cones under his pines"; his neighbor, however, "only says, 'Good fences make good neighbors.' " The moment described in the poem is characteristic of the rural New England life that constitutes so much of Frost's poetry, but it is also typical of how he uses poetry as a means of "saying one thing in terms of another," as he once put it in an essay titled "Education by Poetry."

Just as the speaker teases his neighbor with the idea that the apple trees won't disturb the pines, so too does Frost tease the reader into looking at what it is "that doesn't love a wall." Frost's use of language in the poem does not simply consist of homespun casual phrases enlisted to characterize rural neighbors. From the opening lines, the "Something . . . that doesn't love a wall" and "That sends the frozen-ground swell under it" is, on the literal level, a frost heave that causes the stones to tumble from the wall. But after several close readings of the poem, we can see the implicit pun in these lines which suggest that it is *Frost* who objects to the wall, thus aligning the poet's perspective with the speaker's. A careful examination of some of the other formal elements in the poem supports this reading.

In contrast to the imaginative wit of the speaker who raises fundamental questions about the purpose of any wall, the images associated with his neighbor indicate that he is a traditionalist who "will not go behind his father's saying." Moreover, the neighbor moves "like an old-stone savage" in "darkness" that is attributed to his rigid, tradition-bound, walled-in sensibilities rather than to "the shade of trees." Whereas the speaker's wit and intelligence are manifested by his willingness to question the necessity or desirability of "walling in or walling out" anything, his benighted neighbor can only repeat again that "good fences make good neighbors." The stone-heavy darkness of the neighbor's mind is emphasized by the contrasting light wit and agility of the speaker, who speculates: "Before I built a wall I'd ask to know . . . to whom I was like to give offense." The pun on the final word of this line makes a subtle but important connection between giving "offense" and creating "a fence." Frost's careful use of diction, repetition, and images deftly reveals and reenforces thematic significances suggesting that the stone wall serves as a symbol of isolation, confinement, fear, and even savagery. The neighbor's conservative tradition-bound mindless support of the wall is a foil to the speaker's — read Frost's — poetic, liberal response, which imagines and encourages the possibilities of greater freedom and brotherhood.

Although this brief discussion of some of the formal elements of Frost's poem does not describe all there is to say about how they produce an effect and create meaning, it does suggest the kinds of questions, issues, and evidence that a formalist strategy might raise in providing a close reading of the text itself.

BIOGRAPHICAL STRATEGIES

A knowledge of an author's life can help readers understand his or her work more fully. Events in a work might follow actual events in a writer's life just as characters might be based on people known by the author. Ernest Hemingway's "Soldier's Home" is a story about the difficulties of a World War I veteran named Krebs returning to his small hometown in Oklahoma, where he cannot adjust to the pious assumptions of his family and neighbors. He refuses to accept their innocent blindness to the horrors he has witnessed during the war. They have no sense of the brutality of modern life; instead they insist he resume his life as if nothing has happened. There is plenty of biographical evidence to indicate that Krebs's unwillingness to lie about his war experiences reflects Hemingway's own responses upon his return to Oak Park, Illinois, in 1919. Krebs, like Hemingway, finds he has to leave the sentimentality, repressiveness, and smug complacency that threaten to render his experiences unreal: "the world they were in was not the world he was in."

An awareness of Hemingway's own war experiences and subsequent disillusionment with his hometown can be readily developed through available biographies, letters, and other works he wrote. Consider, for example, this passage from *By Force of Will: The Life and Art of Ernest Hemingway*, in which Scott Donaldson describes Hemingway's response to World War I:

> In poems, as in [*A Farewell to Arms*], Hemingway expressed his distaste for the first war. The men who had to fight the war did not die well:
>
> > Soldiers pitch and cough and twitch —
> > All the world roars red and black;

> Soldiers smother in a ditch,
>> Choking through the whole attack.

And what did they die for? They were "sucked in" by empty words and phrases —

> King and country,
> Christ Almighty,
> And the rest,
> Patriotism,
> Democracy,
> Honor —

which spelled death. The bitterness of these outbursts derived from the distinction Hemingway drew between the men on the line and those who started the wars that others had to fight.

This kind of information can help to deepen our understanding of just how empathetically Krebs is presented in the story. Relevant facts about Hemingway's life will not make "Soldier's Home" a better written story than it is, but such information can make clearer the source of Hemingway's convictions and how his own experiences inform his major concerns as a storyteller.

Some formalist critics — some New Critics, for example — argue that interpretation should be based exclusively on internal evidence rather than on any biographical information outside the work. They argue that it is not possible to determine an author's intention and that the work must stand by itself. Although this is a useful caveat for keeping the work in focus, a reader who finds biography relevant would argue that biography can at the very least serve as a control on interpretation. A reader who, for example, finds Krebs at fault for not subscribing to the values of his hometown would be misreading the story, given both its tone and the biographical information available about the author. Although the narrator never *tells* the reader that Krebs is right or wrong for leaving town, the story's tone sides with his view of things. If, however, someone were to argue otherwise, insisting that the tone is not decisive and that Krebs's position is problematic, a reader familiar with Hemingway's own reactions could refute that argument with a powerful confirmation of Krebs's instincts to withdraw. Hence, many readers find biography useful for interpretation.

However, it is also worth noting that biographical information can complicate a work. For example, readers who interpret "Mending Wall" as a celebration of an iconoclastic sensibility that seeks to break down the psychological barriers and physical walls that separate human beings may be surprised to learn that very few of Frost's other writings support this view. His life was filled with emotional turmoil, a life described by a number of biographers as egocentric and vindictive rather than generous and open to others. He once commented that "I always hold that we get forward as much by hating as by loving." Indeed, many facts about Frost's life — as well as many of the speakers in his poems — are typified by depression, alienation, tension, suspicion, jealous competitiveness, and suicidal tendencies. Instead of challenging wall-builders, Frost more characteristically built walls of distrust around himself among his family, friends, and colleagues. In this biographical context, it is especially worth noting that it is the speaker of "Mending Wall" who alone repairs the damage done to the walls by hunters, and it is he who initiates each spring the rebuilding of the wall. However much he may question its value, the speaker does, after all, rebuild the wall between himself and his neighbor. This biographical approach raises provocative questions about the text. Does the poem suggest that boundaries and walls are, in fact, necessary? Are walls a desirable foundation for relationships between people? Although these and other questions raised by a biographical approach cannot be answered here, this kind of biographical perspective certainly adds to the possibilities of interpretation.

Sometimes biographical information does not change our understanding so much as it enriches our appreciation of a work. It matters, for instance, that much of John Milton's poetry, so rich in visual imagery, was written after he became blind; and it is just as significant — to shift to a musical example — that a number of Ludwig van Beethoven's greatest works, including the Ninth Symphony, were composed after he succumbed to total deafness.

PSYCHOLOGICAL STRATEGIES

Given the enormous influence that Sigmund Freud's psychoanalytic theories have had on twentieth-century interpretations of human behavior, it is nearly inevitable that most people have some familiarity with his ideas concerning dreams, unconscious desires, and sexual repression, as well as his terms for different aspects of the psyche — the id, ego, and superego. Psychological approaches to literature draw upon Freud's theories and other psychoanalytic theories to understand more fully the text, the writer, and the reader. Critics use such approaches to explore the motivations of characters and the symbolic meanings of events, while biographers speculate about a writer's own motivations — conscious or unconscious — in a literary work. Psychological approaches are also used to describe and analyze the reader's personal responses to a text.

Although it is not feasible to explain psychoanalytic terms and concepts in so brief a space as this, it is possible to suggest the nature of a psychological approach. It is a strategy based heavily on the idea of the existence of a human unconscious — those impulses, desires, and feelings about which a person is unaware but which influence emotions and behavior.

Central to a number of psychoanalytic critical readings is Freud's concept of what he called the *Oedipus complex,* a term derived from Sophocles' tragedy *Oedipus the King.* This complex is predicated on a boy's unconscious rivalry with his father for his mother's love and his desire to eliminate his father in order to take his father's place with his mother. The female version of the psychological conflict is known as the *Electra complex,* a term used to describe a daughter's unconscious rivalry for her father. The name comes from a Greek legend about Electra, who avenged the death of her father,

Agamemnon, by killing her mother. In *The Interpretation of Dreams,* Freud explains why *Oedipus the King* "moves a modern audience no less than it did the contemporary Greek one." What unites their powerful attraction to the play is an unconscious response:

> There must be something which makes a voice within us ready to recognize the compelling force of destiny in the *Oedipus.* . . . His destiny moves us only because it might have been ours — because the oracle laid the same curse upon us before our birth as upon him. It is the fate of all of us, perhaps, to direct our first sexual impulse towards our mother and our first hatred and our first murderous wish against our father. Our dreams convince us that this is so. King Oedipus, who slew his father Laius and married his mother Jocasta, merely shows us the fulfillment of our own childhood wishes . . . and we shrink back from him with the whole force of the repression by which those wishes have since that time been held down within us.

In this passage Freud interprets the unconscious motives of Sophocles in writing the play, Oedipus in acting within it, and the audience in responding to it.

A further application of the Oedipus complex can be observed in a classic interpretation of *Hamlet* by Ernest Jones, who used this concept to explain why Hamlet delays in avenging his father's death. This reading has been tightly summarized by Norman Holland, a recent psychoanalytic critic, in *The Shakespearean Imagination.* Holland shapes the issues into four major components:

> One, people over the centuries have been unable to say why Hamlet delays in killing the man who murdered his father and married his mother. Two, psychoanalytic experience shows that every child wants to do just exactly that. Three, Hamlet delays because he cannot punish Claudius for doing what he himself wished to do as a child and, unconsciously, still wishes to do: he would be punishing himself. Four, the fact that this wish is unconscious explains why people could not explain Hamlet's delay.

Although the Oedipus complex is, of course, not relevant to all psychological interpretations of literature, interpretations involving this complex do offer a useful example of how psychoanalytic critics tend to approach a text.

The situation in Frost's "Mending Wall" is not directly related to an Oedipus complex, but the poem has been read as a conflict in which the "father's saying" represents the repressiveness of a patriarchal order that challenges the speaker's individual poetic consciousness. "Mending Wall" has also been read as another kind of struggle with repression. In "Up against the 'Mending Wall': The Psychoanalysis of a Poem by Frost" Edward Jayne offers a detailed reading of the poem as "the overriding struggle to suppress latent homosexual attraction between two men separated by a wall" (*College English* 1973). Jayne reads the poem as the working out of "unconscious homosexual inclinations largely repugnant to Frost and his need to divert and sublimate them." Regardless of whether or not a reader finds these arguments convincing, it is clear that the poem does have something to do with powerful forms of repression. And what about the reader's response? How might a psychological approach account for different responses from readers who argue that the poem calls for either a world that includes walls or one that dismantles them? One needn't be versed in psychoanalytic terms to entertain this question.

HISTORICAL STRATEGIES

Historians sometimes use literature as a window onto the past, because literature frequently provides the nuances of an historic period that cannot be readily perceived through other sources. The characters in Harriet Beecher Stowe's novel *Uncle Tom's Cabin* (1852) display, for example, a complex set of white attitudes toward blacks in mid-nineteenth-century America that is absent from more traditional historic documents such as census statistics or state laws. Another way of approaching the relationship between literature and history, however, is to use history as a means of understanding a literary work more clearly. The plot pattern of pursuit, escape, and capture in nineteenth-century slave narratives had a significant influence on Stowe's plotting of action in *Uncle Tom's Cabin.* This relationship demonstrates that the writing contemporary to an author is an important element of the history that helps to shape a work.

Literary historians shift the emphasis from the period to the work. Hence a literary historian might also examine mid-nineteenth-century abolitionist attitudes toward blacks to determine whether Stowe's novel is representative of those views or significantly to the right or left of them. Such a study might even indicate how closely the book reflects racial attitudes of twentieth-century readers. A work of literature may transcend time to the extent that it addresses the concerns of readers over a span of decades or centuries, but it remains for the literary historian a part of the past in which it was composed, a past that can reveal more fully a work's language, ideas, and purposes.

Literary historians move beyond both the facts of an author's personal life and the text itself to the social and intellectual currents in which the author composed the work. They place the work in the context of its time (as do many critical biographers who write "life and times" studies), and sometimes they make connections with other literary works that may have influenced the author. The basic strategy of literary historians is to illuminate the historic background in order to shed light on some aspect of the work itself.

In Hemingway's "Soldier's Home" we learn that Krebs had been at Belleau Wood, Soissons, the Champagne, St. Mihiel, and the Argonne. Although nothing is said of these battles in the story, they were among the most bloody battles of the war; the wholesale butchery and staggering casualties incurred by both sides make credible the way Krebs's unstated but lingering memories have turned him into a psychological prisoner of war. Knowing something about the ferocity of those battles helps us account for Krebs's response in the story. Moreover, we can more fully appreciate Hemingway's refusal to have Krebs lie about the realities of war for the folks back home if we are aware of the numerous poems, stories, and plays published during World War I that presented war as a glorious, manly, transcendent sacrifice for God and country. Juxtaposing those works with "Soldier's Home" brings the differences into sharp focus.

Similarly, a reading of Blake's poem "London" (p. 93) is less complete if we do not know of the horrific social conditions — the poverty, disease, exploitation, and hypocrisy — that characterized the city Blake laments in the late eighteenth century.

One last example: The potential historical meaning of the wall that is the subject of Frost's "Mending Wall" might be more distinctly seen if it is placed in the context of its publication date, 1914, when the world was on the verge of collapsing into the violent political landscape of World War I. The insistence that "Good fences make good neighbors" suggests a grim ironic tone in the context of European nationalist hostilities that seemed to be moving inexorably toward war. The larger historical context for the poem would have been more apparent to its readers contemporary with World War I, but a historical reconstruction of the horrific tensions produced by shifting national borders and shattered walls during the war can shed some light on the larger issues that may be at stake in the poem. Moreover, an examination of Frost's attitudes toward the war and America's potential involvement in it could help to produce a reading of the meaning and value of a world with or without walls.

Since the 1960s a development in historical approaches to literature known as *New Historicism* has emphasized the interaction between the historic context of a work and a modern reader's understanding and interpretation of the work. In contrast to many traditional literary historians, however, New Historicists attempt to describe the culture of a period by reading many different kinds of texts that traditional historians might have previously left for sociologists and anthropologists. New Historicists attempt to read a period in all its dimensions, including political, economic, social, and aesthetic concerns. These considerations could be used to explain something about the nature of rural New England life early in the twentieth century. The process of mending the stone wall authentically suggests how this tedious job simultaneously draws the two men together and keeps them apart. Pamphlets and other contemporary writings about farming and maintaining property lines could offer insight into either the necessity or the uselessness of the spring wall-mending rituals. A New Historicist might find useful how advice offered in texts about running a farm reflect or refute the speaker's or neighbor's competing points of view in the poem.

New Historicist criticism acknowledges more fully than traditional historical approaches the competing nature of readings of the past and thereby tends to offer new emphases and perspectives. New Historicism reminds us that there is not only one historic context for "Mending Wall." The year before Frost died, he visited Moscow as a cultural ambassador from the United States. During this 1962 visit — only one year after the Soviet Union's construction of the Berlin Wall — he read "Mending Wall" to his Russian audience. Like the speaker in that poem, Frost clearly enjoyed the "mischief" of that moment, and a New Historicist would clearly find intriguing the way the poem was both intended and received in so volatile a context. By emphasizing that historical perceptions are governed, at least in part, by our own concerns and preoccupations, New Historicists sensitize us to the fact that the history on which we choose to focus is colored by being reconstructed from our own present moment. This reconstructed history affects our reading of texts.

(See "A New Historical Approach to Keats's 'Ode on a Grecian Urn' " by Brook Thomas [p. 555] for an example of this type of criticism.)

SOCIOLOGICAL STRATEGIES, INCLUDING MARXIST AND FEMINIST STRATEGIES

Sociological approaches examine social groups, relationships, and values as they are manifested in literature. These approaches necessarily overlap historical analyses, but sociological approaches to a work emphasize more specifically the nature and effect of the social forces that shape power relationships among groups or classes of people. Such readings treat literature as either a document reflecting social conditions or a product of those conditions. The former view brings into focus the social milieu; the latter emphasizes the work. A sociological reading of Arthur Miller's drama *Death of a Salesman* might, for instance, discuss how the characters' efforts to succeed reflect an increasingly competitive twentieth-century urban sensibility in America. Or it might emphasize how the "American Dream" of success shapes Willy Loman's aspirations and behavior. Clearly, there are numerous ways to talk about the societal aspects of a work. Two sociological strategies that have been especially influential are Marxist and feminist approaches.

Marxist Criticism

Marxist readings developed from the heightened interest in radical reform during the 1930s, when many critics looked to literature as a means of furthering proletarian social and economic goals, based largely on the writings of Karl Marx. *Marxist critics* focus on the ideological content of a work — its explicit and implicit assumptions and values about matters such as culture, race, class, and power. Marxist studies typically aim at not only revealing and clarifying ideological issues but also correcting social injustices. Some Marxist critics have used literature to describe the competing socioeconomic interests that too often advance capitalist money and power rather than socialist morality and justice. They argue that criticism, like literature, is essentially political because it either challenges or supports economic oppression. Even if criticism attempts to ignore class conflicts, it is politicized, according to Marxists, because it supports the status quo.

It is not surprising that Marxist critics pay more attention to the content and themes of literature than to its form. A Marxist critic would more likely be concerned with the exploitive economic forces that cause Willy Loman to feel trapped in Miller's *Death of a Salesman* than with the playwright's use of non-realistic dramatic techniques to reveal Loman's inner thoughts. Similarly, a Marxist reading of Frost's "Mending Wall" might draw upon the poet's well-known conservative criticisms of President Franklin Delano Roosevelt's New Deal during the 1930s as a means of reading conservative ideology into the poem. Frost's deep suspicions of collective enterprise might suggest to a Marxist that the wall represents the status quo, that is, a capitalist construction that unnaturally divides individuals (in this case, the poem's speaker from his neighbor) and artificially defies nature. Complicit in their own oppression, both farmers, to a lesser and greater degree, accept the idea that "good fences make good neighbors," thereby maintaining and perpetuating an unnatural divisive order that oppresses and is mistakenly perceived as necessary and beneficial. A Marxist reading would see the speaker's and neighbor's conflicts as not only an individual issue but part of a larger class struggle.

Feminist Criticism

Feminist critics would also be interested in examining the status quo in "Mending Wall," because they seek to correct or supplement what they regard as a predominantly male-dominated critical perspective with a feminist consciousness. Like other forms of sociological criticism, feminist criticism places literature in a social context, and, like those of Marxist criticism, its analyses often have sociopolitical purposes, purposes that might explain, for example, how images of women in literature reflect the patriarchal social forces that have impeded women's efforts to achieve full equality with men.

Feminists have analyzed literature by both men and women in an effort to understand literary representations of women as well as the writers and cultures that create them. Related to concerns about how gender affects the way men and women write about each other is an interest in whether women use language differently from the way men do. Consequently, feminist critics' approach to literature is characterized by the use of a broad range of disciplines, including history, sociology, psychology, and linguistics, to provide a perspective sensitive to feminist issues.

A feminist approach to Frost's "Mending Wall" might initially appear to offer few possibilities given that no women appear in the poem and that no mention or allusion is made about women. And that is precisely the point: the landscape presented in the poem is devoid of women. Traditional gender roles are evident in the poem because it is men, not women, who work outdoors building walls and who discuss the significance of their work. For a feminist critic, the wall might be read as a symbol of patriarchal boundaries that are defined exclusively by men. If the wall can be seen as a manifestation of the status quo built upon the "father's saying[s]," then mending the wall each year and keeping everything essentially the same — with women securely out of the picture — essentially benefits the established patriarchy. The boundaries are reconstructed and rationalized in the absence of any woman's potential efforts to offer an alternative to the boundaries imposed by the men's rebuilding of the wall. Perhaps one way of considering the value of a feminist perspective on this work can be discerned if a reader imagines the speaker or the neighbor as a woman and how that change might extend the parameters of their conversation about the value of the wall.

MYTHOLOGICAL STRATEGIES

Mythological approaches to literature attempt to identify what in a work creates deep universal responses in readers. Whereas psychological critics interpret the symbolic meanings of characters and actions in order to understand more fully the unconscious dimensions of an author's mind, a character's motivation, or a reader's response, mythological critics (also frequently referred to as archetypal critics) interpret the hopes, fears, and expectations of entire cultures.

In this context myth is not to be understood simply as referring to stories about imaginary gods who perform astonishing feats in the causes of love, jealousy, or hatred. Nor are myths to be judged as merely erroneous, primitive accounts of how nature runs its course and humanity its affairs. Instead, literary critics use myths as a strategy for understanding how human beings try to account for their lives symbolically. Myths can be a window onto a culture's deepest perceptions about itself, because myths attempt to explain what otherwise seems unexplainable: a people's origin, purpose, and destiny.

All human beings have a need to make sense of their lives, whether they are concerned about their natural surroundings, the seasons, sexuality, birth, death, or the very meaning of existence. Myths help people organize their experiences; these systems of belief (less formally held than religious or political tenets but no less important) embody a culture's assumptions and values. What is important to the mythological critic is not the validity or truth of those assumptions and values; what matters is that they reveal common human concerns.

It is not surprising that although the details of mythic stories vary enormously, the essential patterns are often similar, because these myths attempt to explain universal experiences. There are, for example, numerous myths that redeem humanity from permanent death through a hero's resurrection and rebirth. For Christians the resurrection of Jesus symbolizes the ultimate defeat of death and coincides with the rebirth of nature's fertility in spring. Features of this rebirth parallel the Greek myths of Adonis and Hyacinth, who die but are subsequently transformed into living flowers; there are also similarities that connect these stories to the reincarnation of the Indian Buddha or the rebirth of the Egyptian Osiris. To be sure, important differences exist among these stories, but each reflects a basic human need to limit the power of death and to hope for eternal life.

Mythological critics look for underlying, recurrent patterns in literature that reveal universal meanings and basic human experiences for readers regardless of when or where they live. The characters, images, and themes that symbolically embody these meanings and experiences are called *archetypes.* This term designates universal symbols, which evoke deep and perhaps unconscious responses in a reader because archetypes bring with them the heft of our hopes and fears since the beginning of human time. Surely one of the most powerfully compelling archetypes is the death/rebirth theme that relates the human life cycle to the cycle of the seasons. Many others could be cited and would be exhausted only after all human concerns were catalogued, but a few examples can suggest some of the range of plots, images, and characters addressed.

Among the most common literary archetypes are stories of quests, initiations, scapegoats, meditative withdrawals, descents to the underworld, and heavenly ascents. These stories are often filled with archetypal images: bodies of water that may symbolize the unconscious or eternity or baptismal rebirth; rising suns, suggesting reawakening and enlightenment; setting suns, pointing toward death; colors such as green, evocative of growth and fertility, or black, indicating chaos, evil, and death. Along the way are earth mothers, fatal women, wise old men, desert places, and paradisal gardens. No doubt your own reading has introduced you to any number of archetypal plots, images, and characters.

Mythological critics attempt to explain how archetypes are embodied in literary works. Employing various disciplines, these critics articulate the power a literary work has over us. Some critics are deeply grounded in classical literature, whereas others are more conversant with philology, anthropology, psychology, or cultural history. Whatever their emphases, however, mythological critics examine the elements of a work in order to make larger connections that explain the work's lasting appeal.

A mythological reading of Sophocles' *Oedipus the King,* for example, might focus on the relationship between Oedipus's role as a scapegoat and the plague and drought that threaten to destroy Thebes. The city is saved and the fertility of its fields restored only after the corruption is located in Oedipus. His subsequent atonement symbolically provides a kind of rebirth for the city. Thus, the plot recapitulates ancient rites in which the well-being of a king was directly linked to the welfare of his people. If a leader were sick or corrupt, he had to be replaced in order to guarantee the health of the community.

A similar pattern can be seen in the rottenness that Shakespeare exposes in Hamlet's Denmark. *Hamlet* reveals an archetypal pattern similar to that of *Oedipus the King:* not until the hero sorts out the corruption in his world and in himself can vitality and health be restored in his world. Hamlet avenges his father's death and becomes a scapegoat in the process. When he fully accepts his responsibility to set things right, he is swept away along with the tide of intrigue and corruption that has polluted life in Denmark. The new order — established by Fortinbras at the play's end — is achieved precisely because Hamlet is willing and finally able to sacrifice himself in a necessary purgation of the diseased state.

These kinds of archetypal patterns exist potentially in any literary period. Frost's "Mending Wall," for example, is set in spring, an evocative season that marks the end of winter and earth's renewal. The action in the poem, however, does not lead to a celebration of new life and human community; instead there is for the poem's speaker and his neighbor an annual ritual to "set the wall between us as we go" that separates and divides human experience rather than unifying it. We can see that the rebuilding of the wall runs counter to nature itself because the stones are so round that "We have to use a spell to make them balance." The speaker also resists the wall and sets out to subvert it by toying with the idea of challenging his neighbor's assumption that "good fences make good neighbors," a seemingly ancient belief passed down through one "father's saying" to the next. The speaker, however, does not heroically overcome the neighbor's ritual; he merely points out that the wall is not needed where it is. The speaker's acquiescence results in the continuation of a ritual that confirms the old order rather than overthrowing the "old-stone savage," who demands the dark isolation and separateness associated with the "gaps" produced by winter's frost. The neighbor's old order prevails in spite of nature's and the speaker's protestations. From a mythological critic's perspective, the wall might itself be seen as a "gap," an unnatural disruption of nature and the human community.

READER-RESPONSE STRATEGIES

Reader-response criticism, as its name implies, focuses its attention on the reader rather than the work itself. This approach to literature describes what goes on in the reader's mind during the process of reading a text. In a sense, all critical approaches (especially psychological and mythological criticism) concern themselves with a reader's response to literature, but there is a stronger emphasis in reader-response criticism on the reader's active construction of the text. Although many critical theories inform reader-response criticism, all ***reader-response critics*** aim to describe the reader's experience of a work: in effect we get a reading of the reader, who comes to the work with certain expectations and assumptions, which are either met or not met. Hence the consciousness of the reader — produced by reading the work — is the subject matter of reader-response critics. Just as writing is a creative act, reading is, since it also produces a text.

Reader-response critics do not assume that a literary work is a finished product with fixed formal properties, as, for example, formalist critics do. Instead, the literary work is seen as an evolving creation of the reader's as he or she processes characters, plots, images, and other elements while reading. Some reader-response critics argue that this act of creative reading is, to a degree, controlled by the text, but it can produce many interpretations of the same text by different readers. There is no single definitive reading of a work, because the crucial assumption is that readers create rather than discover meanings in texts. Readers who have gone back to works they had read earlier in their lives often find that a later reading draws very different responses from them. What earlier seemed unimportant is now crucial; what at first seemed central is now barely worth noting. The reason, put simply, is that two different people have read the same text. Reader-response critics are not after the "correct" reading of the text or what the author presumably intended; instead they are interested in the reader's experience with the text.

These experiences change with readers; although the text remains the same, the readers do not. Social and cultural values influence readings, so that, for example, an avowed Marxist would be likely to come away from Miller's *Death of a Salesman* with a very different view of American capitalism than that of, say, a successful sales representative, who might attribute Willy Loman's fall more to his character than to the American economic system. Moreover, readers from different time periods respond differently to texts. An Elizabethan — concerned perhaps with the stability of monarchical rule — might respond differently to Hamlet's problems than would a twentieth-century reader well versed in psychology and concepts of what Freud called the Oedipus complex. This is not to say that anything goes, that Miller's play can be read as an amoral defense of cheating and rapacious business practices or that *Hamlet* is about the dangers of living away from home. The text does, after all, establish some limits that allow us to reject certain readings as erroneous. But reader-response critics do reject formalist approaches that describe a literary work as a self-contained object, the meaning of which can be determined without reference to any extrinsic matters, such as the social and cultural values assumed by either the author or the reader.

Reader-response criticism calls attention to how we read and what influences our readings. It does not attempt to define what a literary work means on the page but rather what it does to an informed reader, a reader who understands the language and conventions used in a given work. Reader-response criticism is not a rationale for mistaken or bizarre readings of works but an exploration of the possibilities for a plurality of readings shaped by the readers' experience with the text. This kind of strategy can help us understand how our responses are shaped by both the text and ourselves.

Frost's "Mending Wall" illustrates how reader-response critical strategies read the reader. Among the first readers of the poem in 1914, those who were eager to see the United States enter World War I might have been inclined to see the speaker as an imaginative thinker standing up for freedom rather than antiquated boundaries and sensibilities that don't know what they are "walling in or walling out." But for someone whose son could be sent to the trenches of France to fight the Germans, the phrase "Good fences make good neighbors" might sound less like an unthinking tradition and more like solid, prudent common sense. In each instance the reader's circumstances could have an effect upon his or her assessment of the value of walls and fences. Certainly the Russians who listened to Frost's reading of "Mending Wall" in 1962, only one year after the construction of the Berlin Wall, had a very different response from the Americans who heard about Frost's reading and who relished the discomfort they thought the reading had caused the Russians.

By imagining different readers we can imagine a variety of responses to the poem that are influenced by the readers' own impressions, memories, or experiences. Such imagining suggests the ways in which reader-response criticism opens up texts to a number of interpretations. As one final example, consider how readers' responses to "Mending Wall" would be affected if it were printed in two different magazines, read in the context of either *Farmer's Almanac* or *The New Yorker*. What assumptions and beliefs would each magazine's readership be likely to bring to the poem? How do you think the respective experiences and values of each magazine's readers would influence their readings?

DECONSTRUCTIONIST STRATEGIES

Deconstructionist critics insist that literary works do not yield fixed, single meanings. They argue that there can be no absolute knowledge about anything because language can never say what we intend it to mean. Anything we write conveys meanings we did not intend, so the deconstructionist argument goes. Language is not a precise instrument but a power whose meanings are caught in an endless web of possibilities that cannot be untangled. Accordingly, any idea or statement that insists on being understood separately can ultimately be "deconstructed" to reveal its relations and connections to contradictory and opposite meanings.

Unlike other forms of criticism, deconstructionism seeks to destabilize meanings instead of establishing them. In contrast to formalists such as the New Critics, who closely examine a work in order to call attention to how its various components interact to establish a unified whole, deconstructionists try to show how a close examination of the language in a text inevitably reveals conflicting, contradictory impulses that "deconstruct" or break down its apparent unity.

Although deconstructionists and New Critics both examine the language of a text closely, deconstructionists focus on the gaps and ambiguities that reveal a text's instability and indeterminacy, whereas New Critics look for patterns that explain how the text's fixed meaning is structured. Deconstructionists painstakingly examine the competing meanings within the text rather than attempting to resolve them into a unified whole.

The questions deconstructionists ask are aimed at discovering and describing how a variety of possible readings are generated by the elements of a text. In contrast to a New Critic's concerns about the ultimate meaning of a work, a deconstructionist's primary interest is in how the use of language — diction, tone, metaphor, symbol, and so on — yields only provisional, not definitive, meanings. Consider, for example, the following excerpt from an American Puritan poet, Anne Bradstreet. The excerpt is from "The Flesh and the Spirit" (1678), which consists of an allegorical debate between two sisters, the body and the soul. During the course of the debate, Flesh, a consummate materialist, insists that Spirit values ideas that do not exist and that her faith in idealism is both unwarranted and insubstantial in the face of the material values that earth has to offer — riches, fame, and physical pleasure. Spirit, however, rejects the materialistic worldly argument that the only ultimate reality is physical reality and pledges her faith in God:

> Mine eye doth pierce the heavens and see
> What is invisible to thee.
> My garments are not silk nor gold,
> Nor such like trash which earth doth hold,

But royal robes I shall have on,
More glorious than the glist'ring sun;
My crown not diamonds, pearls, and gold,
But such as angels' heads enfold
The city where I hope to dwell,
There's none on earth can parallel;
The stately walls both high and strong,
Are made of precious jasper stone;
The gates of pearl, both rich and clear,
And angels are for porters there;
The streets thereof transparent gold,
Such as no eye did e'er behold;
A crystal river there doth run,
Which doth proceed from the Lamb's throne.

A deconstructionist would point out that Spirit's language — her use of material images such as jasper stone, pearl, gold, and crystal — cancels the explicit meaning of the passage by offering a supermaterialistic reward to the spiritually faithful. Her language, in short, deconstructs her intended meaning by employing the same images that Flesh would use to describe the rewards of the physical world. A deconstructionist reading, then, reveals the impossibility of talking about the invisible and spiritual worlds without using materialistic (that is, metaphoric) language. Thus Spirit's very language demonstrates a contradiction and conflict in her conviction that the world of here and now must be rejected for the hereafter. Her language deconstructs her meaning.

Deconstructionists look for ways to question and extend the meanings of a text. In Frost's "Mending Wall," for example, the speaker presents himself as being on the side of the imaginative rather than hidebound, rigid responses to life. He seems to value freedom and openness rather than restrictions and narrowly defined limits. Yet his treatment of his Yankee farmer neighbor can be read as condescending and even smug in its superior attitude toward his neighbor's repeating his "father's saying," as if he were "an old-stone savage armed." The condescending attitude hardly suggests a robust sense of community and shared humanity. Moreover, for all the talk about unnecessary conventions and traditions, a deconstructionist would likely be quick to point out that Frost writes the poem in blank verse — unrhymed iambic pentameter — rather than free verse; hence the very regular rhythms of the narrator's speech may be seen to deconstruct its liberationist meaning.

As difficult as it is controversial, deconstructionism is not easily summarized or paraphrased. For an example of deconstructionism in practice and how it differs from New Criticism, see Andrew P. Debicki's "New Criticism and Deconstructionism: Two Attitudes in Teaching Poetry" in Perspectives (p. 552).

SELECTED BIBLIOGRAPHY

Given the enormous number of articles and books written about literary theory and criticism in recent years, the following bibliography is necessarily highly selective. Even so, it should prove useful as an introduction to many of the issues associated with the critical strategies discussed in this chapter. For a general encyclopedic reference book that describes important figures, schools, and movements, see *The Johns Hopkins Guide to Literary Theory & Criticism,* edited by Michael Grodin and Martin Kreiswirth (Baltimore: Johns Hopkins UP, 1994).

Canonical Issues

"The Changing Culture of the University." Special Issue. *Partisan Review* 58 (Spring 1991): 185–410.

Gates, Henry Louis, Jr. *The Signifying Monkey.* New York: Oxford UP, 1988.

Lauter, Paul. *Canons and Contexts.* New York: Oxford UP, 1991.

"The Politics of Liberal Education." Special Issue. *South Atlantic Quarterly* 89 (Winter 1990): 1–234.

Sykes, Charles J. *The Hollow Men: Politics and Corruption in Higher Education.* Washington, DC: Regnery Gateway, 1990.

Formalist Strategies

Brooks, Cleanth. *The Well Wrought Urn: Studies in the Structure of Poetry.* New York: Reynal and Hitchcock, 1947.

Crane, Ronald Salmon. *The Languages of Criticism and the Structure of Poetry.* Toronto: U of Toronto P, 1953.

Eliot, Thomas Stearns. *The Sacred Wood: Essays in Poetry and Criticism.* London: Methuen, 1920.

Fekete, John. *The Critical Twilight: Explorations in the Ideology of Anglo-American Literary Theory from Eliot to McLuhan.* London: Routledge, 1977.

Lemon, Lee T., and Marion J. Reis, eds. *Russian Formalist Criticism: Four Essays.* Lincoln: U of Nebraska P, 1965.

Ransom, John Crowe. *The New Criticism.* Norfolk, CT: New Directions, 1941.

Wellek, René, and Austin Warren. *Theory of Literature.* New York: Harcourt, Brace and World, 1949.

Biographical and Psychological Strategies

Bleich, David. *Subjective Criticism.* Baltimore: Johns Hopkins UP, 1978.

Bloom, Harold. *The Anxiety of Influence.* New York: Oxford UP, 1975.

Crews, Frederick. *Out of My System: Psychoanalysis, Ideology, and Critical Method.* New York: Oxford UP, 1975.

————. *The Sins of the Fathers: Hawthorne's Psychological Themes.* New York: Oxford UP, 1966.

Felman, Shoshana. *Writing and Madness (Literature/Philosophy/Psychoanalysis).* Ithaca: Cornell UP, 1985.

————, ed. *Literature and Psychoanalysis: The Question of Reading: Otherwise.* Baltimore: Johns Hopkins UP, 1981.

Freud, Sigmund. *The Standard Edition of the Complete Psychological Works*. 24 vols. 1940–1968. London: Hogarth Press and the Institute of Psychoanalysis, 1953.

Holland, Norman. *The Dynamics of Literary Response*. New York: Oxford UP, 1968.

Jones, Ernest. *Hamlet and Oedipus*. New York: Doubleday, 1949.

Lacan, Jacques. *Écrits: A Selection*. Trans. Alan Sheridan. New York: Norton, 1977.

—————. *The Four Fundamental Concepts of Psychoanalysis*. Trans. Alan Sheridan. London: Penguin, 1980.

Lesser, Simon O. *Fiction and the Unconscious*. Chicago: U of Chicago P, 1957.

Skura, Meredith Anne. *The Literary Use of the Psychoanalytic Process*. New Haven: Yale UP, 1981.

Weiss, Daniel. *The Critic Agonistes: Psychology, Myth, and the Art of Fiction*. Ed. Stephen Arkin and Eric Solomon. Seattle: U of Washington P, 1985.

Historical and New Historicist Strategies

Armstrong, Nancy. *Desire and Domestic Fiction*. New York: Oxford UP, 1987.

Dollimore, Jonathan. *Radical Tragedy: Religion, Ideology and Power in the Drama of Shakespeare and His Contemporaries*. Brighton, Eng.: Harvester, 1984.

Geertz, Clifford. *The Interpretation of Cultures: Selected Essays*. New York: Basic, 1973.

Greenblatt, Stephen. *Renaissance Self-Fashioning: From More to Shakespeare*. Chicago: U of Chicago P, 1980.

—————. *Shakespearean Negotiations: The Circulation of Social Energy in Renaissance England*. Berkeley: U of California P, 1985.

Lindenberger, Herbert. *Historical Drama: The Relation of Literature and Reality*. Chicago: U of Chicago P, 1975.

McGann, Jerome. *The Beauty of Inflections: Literary Investigations in Historical Method and Theory*. Oxford: Clarendon, 1985.

Tennenhouse, Leonard. *Power on Display: The Politics of Shakespeare's Genres*. New York: Methuen, 1986.

White, Hayden. *Tropics of Discourse: Essays in Cultural Criticism*. Baltimore: Johns Hopkins UP, 1978.

Sociological Strategies (Including Marxist and Feminist Strategies)

Adorno, Théodor. *Prisms: Cultural Criticism and Society*. 1955. London: Neville Spearman, 1967.

Beauvoir, Simone de. *The Second Sex*. Trans. H. M. Parshley. New York: Knopf, 1972. Trans. of *Le deuxième sexe*. Paris: Gallimard, 1949.

Benjamin, Walter. *Illuminations*. New York: Harcourt, Brace and World, 1968.

Benstock, Shari, ed. *Feminist Issues and Literary Scholarship*. Bloomington: Indiana UP, 1987.

Cixous, Hélène, and Catherine Clément. *The Newly Born Woman*. Trans. Betsy Wing. Minneapolis: U of Minnesota P, 1986.

Eagleton, Terry. *Criticism and Ideology: A Study in Marxist Literary Theory*. London: New Left, 1976.

Fetterley, Judith. *The Resisting Reader: A Feminist Approach to American Fiction*. Bloomington: Indiana UP, 1978.

Frow, John. *Marxist and Literary History*. Cambridge: Harvard UP, 1986.

Gilbert, Sandra M., and Susan Gubar. *The Madwoman in the Attic: The Woman Writer and the Nineteenth-Century Literary Imagination*. New Haven: Yale UP, 1979.

Irigaray, Luce. *This Sex Which Is Not One*. Trans. Catherine Porter. Ithaca: Cornell UP, 1985. Trans. of *Ce sexe qui n'en est pas un*. Paris: Éditions de Minuit, 1977.

Jameson, Fredric. *The Political Unconscious: Studies in the Ideology of Form*. Ithaca: Cornell UP, 1979.

Kolodny, Annette. "Some Notes on Defining a 'Feminist Literary Criticism.' " *Critical Inquiry* 2 (1975): 75–92.

Lukács, Georg. *Realism in Our Time: Literature and the Class Struggle*. 1957. New York: Harper and Row, 1964.

Marx, Karl, and Friedrich Engels. *Marx and Engels on Literature and Art*. St. Louis: Telos, 1973.

Millett, Kate. *Sexual Politics*. New York: Avon, 1970.

Showalter, Elaine. *A Literature of Their Own: British Women Novelists from Brontë to Lessing*. Princeton: Princeton UP, 1977.

Smith, Barbara. *Toward a Black Feminist Criticism*. New York: Out and Out, 1977.

Trotsky, Leon. *Literature and the Revolution*. 1924. Ann Arbor: U of Michigan P, 1960.

Williams, Raymond. *Marxism and Literature*. Oxford: Oxford UP, 1977.

Mythological Strategies

Bodkin, Maud. *Archetypal Patterns in Poetry*. London: Oxford UP, 1934.

Frye, Northrop. *Anatomy of Criticism: Four Essays*. Princeton: Princeton UP, 1957.

Jung, Carl Gustav. *Complete Works*. Ed. Herbert Read, Michael Fordham, and Gerhard Adler. 17 vols. New York: Pantheon, 1953– .

Reader-Response Strategies

Booth, Wayne, C. *The Rhetoric of Fiction*. 2nd ed. Chicago: U of Chicago P, 1983.

Eco, Umberto. *The Role of the Reader: Explorations in the Semiotics of Texts*. Bloomington: Indiana UP, 1979.

Escarpit, Robert. *Sociology of Literature*. Painesville, Ohio: Lake Erie College P, 1965.

Fish, Stanley. *Is There a Text in This Class? The Authority of Interpretive Communities.* Cambridge: Harvard UP, 1980.

Freund, Elizabeth. *The Return of the Reader: Reader-Response Criticism.* London: Methuen, 1987.

Holland, Norman N. *5 Readers Reading.* New Haven: Yale UP, 1975.

Iser, Wolfgang. *The Implied Reader: Patterns of Communication in Prose Fiction from Bunyan to Beckett.* Baltimore: Johns Hopkins UP, 1974.

Jauss, Hans Robert. "Literary History as a Challenge to Literary Theory." *Toward an Aesthetics of Reception.* Trans. Timothy Bahti. Minneapolis: U of Minnesota P, 1982. 3–46.

Rosenblatt, Louise. *Literature as Exploration.* 1938. New York: MLA, 1983.

Suleiman, Susan, and Inge Crosman, eds. *The Reader in the Text: Essays on Audience and Interpretation.* Princeton: Princeton UP, 1980.

Tompkins, Jane P., ed. *Reader-Response Criticism: From Formalism to Post-Structuralism.* Baltimore: Johns Hopkins UP, 1980.

Deconstructionist and Other Poststructuralist Strategies

Culler, Jonathan. *On Deconstruction: Theory and Criticism after Structuralism.* Ithaca: Cornell UP, 1982.

de Man, Paul. *Blindness and Insight.* New York: Oxford UP, 1971.

Derrida, Jacques. *Of Grammatology.* Trans. Gayatri C. Spivak. Baltimore: Johns Hopkins UP, 1976. Trans. of *De la Grammatologie.* 1967.

―――. *Writing and Difference.* 1967. Chicago: U of Chicago P, 1978.

Foucault, Michel. *Language, Counter-Memory, Practice.* Ithaca: Cornell UP, 1977.

―――. *The Order of Things: An Archaeology of the Human Sciences.* 1966. London: Tavistock, 1970.

Gasche, Rodolphe. "Deconstruction as Criticism." *Glyph* 6 (1979): 177–216.

Hartman, Geoffrey H. *Criticism in the Wilderness.* New Haven: Yale UP, 1980.

Johnson, Barbara. *The Critical Difference: Essays in the Contemporary Rhetoric of Reading.* Baltimore: Johns Hopkins UP, 1980.

Melville, Stephen W. *Philosophy Beside Itself: On Deconstruction and Modernism.* Theory and History of Literature 27. Minneapolis: U of Minnesota P, 1986.

Said, Edward W. *The World, the Text, and the Critic.* Cambridge: Harvard UP, 1983.

Smith, Barbara Herrnstein. *On the Margins of Discourse: The Relation of Literature to Language.* Chicago: U of Chicago P., 1979.

SUSAN SONTAG (b. 1933)
Against Interpretation 1964

Like the fumes of the automobile and of heavy industry which befoul the urban atmosphere, the effusion of interpretations of art today poisons our sensibilities. In a culture whose already classical dilemma is the hypertrophy of the intellect at the expense of energy and sensual capability, interpretation is the revenge of the intellect upon art.

Even more. It is the revenge of the intellect upon the world. To interpret is to impoverish, to deplete the world — in order to set up a shadow world of "meanings." It is to turn *the* world into *this* world. ("This world"! As if there were any other.)

The world, our world, is depleted, impoverished enough. Away with all duplicates of it, until we again experience more immediately what we have. . . .

In most modern instances, interpretation amounts to the philistine refusal to leave the work of art alone. Real art has the capacity to make us nervous. By reducing the work of art to its content and then interpreting *that,* one tames the work of art. Interpretation makes art manageable, conformable.

This philistinism of interpretation is more rife in literature than in any other art. For decades now, literary critics have understood it to be their task to translate the elements of the poem or play or novel or story into something else.

—From *Against Interpretation*

Considerations for Critical Thinking and Writing

1. What are Sontag's objections to "interpretation"? Explain whether you agree or disagree with them.
2. In what sense does interpretation make art "manageable" and "conformable"?
3. In an essay explore what you take to be both the dangers of interpretation and its contributions to your understanding of literature.

STANLEY FISH (b. 1938)
On What Makes an Interpretation Acceptable 1980

. . . After all, while "The Tyger" is obviously open to more than one interpretation, it is not open to an infinite number of interpretations. There may be disagreements as to whether the tiger is good or evil, or whether the speaker is Blake or a persona, and so on, but no one is suggesting that the poem is an allegory of the digestive processes or that it predicts the Second World War, and its limited plurality is simply a testimony to the capacity of a great work of art to generate multiple readings. The point is one that Wayne Booth makes when he asks, "Are we *right* to rule out at least some readings?" and then answers his own question with a resounding yes. It would be my answer too; but the real question is what gives us the right so to be right. A pluralist is committed to saying that there is something in the text which rules out some readings and allows others (even though no one reading can ever capture the text's "inexhaustible richness and complexity"). His best evidence is that in practice "we all in fact" do reject unacceptable readings and that more often than not we agree on the readings that are not rejected. . . . Booth concludes that there are justified limits to what we can legitimately do with a text, for "surely we could not go on disputing at all if a core of agreement did not exist." Again, I agree, but if, as I have argued, the text is always a function of interpretation, then the text cannot be the location of the core of agreement by means of which we reject interpretations. We seem to be at an impasse: on the one hand there would seem to be no basis for labeling an interpretation unacceptable, but on the other we do it all the time.

This, however, is an impasse only if one assumes that the activity of interpretation is itself unconstrained; but in fact the shape of that activity is determined by the literary institution which at any one time will authorize only a finite number of interpretative strategies. Thus, while there is no core of agreement *in* the text, there is a core of agreement (although one subject to change) concerning the ways of *producing* the text. Nowhere is this set of acceptable ways written down, but it is a part of everyone's knowledge of what it means to be operating within the literary institution as it is now constituted. A student of mine recently demonstrated this knowledge when, with an air of giving away a trade secret, she confided that she could go into any classroom, no matter what the subject of the course, and win approval for running one of a number of well-defined interpretive routines; she could view the assigned text as an instance of the tension between nature and culture; she could look in the text for evidence of large mythological oppositions; she could argue that the true subject of the text was its own composition, or that in the guise of fashioning a narrative the speaker was fragmenting and displacing his own anxieties and fears. She could not . . . argue that the text was a prophetic message inspired by the ghost of her Aunt Tilly.

My student's understanding of what she could and could not get away with, of the unwritten rules of the literary game, is shared by everyone who plays that game, by those who write and judge articles for publication in learned journals, by those who read and listen to papers at professional meetings, by those who seek and award tenure in innumerable departments of English and comparative literature, by the armies of graduate students for whom knowledge of the rules is the real mark of professional initiation. This does not mean that these rules and the practices they authorize are either monolithic or stable. Within the literary community there are subcommunities. . . . In a classroom whose authority figures include David Bleich and Norman Holland, a student might very well relate a text to her memories of a favorite aunt, while in other classrooms, dominated by the spirit of [Cleanth] Brooks and [Robert Penn] Warren, any such activity would immediately be dismissed as nonliterary, as something that isn't done.

The point is that while there is always a category of things that are not done (it is simply the reverse or flip side of the category of things that *are* done), the membership in that category is continually changing. It changes laterally as one moves from subcommunity to subcommunity, and it changes through time when once interdicted interpretive strategies are admitted into the ranks of the acceptable. Twenty years ago one of the things that literary critics didn't do was talk about the reader, at least in a way that made his experience the focus of the critical act. The prohibition on such talk was largely the result of [W. K.] Wimsatt's and [Monroe] Beardsley's famous essay "The Affective Fallacy," which argued that the variability of readers renders any investigation of their responses ad-hoc and relativistic: "The poem itself," the authors complained, "as an object of specifically critical judgment, tends to disappear." So influential was this essay that it was possible for a reviewer to dismiss a book merely by finding in it evidence that the affective fallacy had been committed. The use of a juridical terminology is not accidental; this was in a very real sense a *legal* finding of activity in violation of understood and institutionalized decorums. Today, however, the affective fallacy, no longer a fallacy but a methodology, is committed all the time, and its practitioners have behind them the full and authorizing weight of a fully articulated institutional apparatus. The "reader in literature" is regularly the subject of forums and workshops at the convention of the Modern Language Association; there is a reader newsletter which reports on the multitudinous labors of a reader industry; any list of currently active schools of literary criticism includes the school of "reader response," and two major university presses have published collections of essays designed both to display the variety of reader-centered criticism (the emergence of factions within a once interdicted activity is a sure sign of its having achieved the status of an orthodoxy) and to detail its history. None of this of course means that a reader-centered criticism is now invulnerable to challenge or attack, merely that it is now recognized as a competing literary strategy that cannot be dismissed simply by being named. It is acceptable not because everyone accepts it but because those who do not are now obliged to argue against it.

From *Is There a Text in This Class?*

Considerations for Critical Thinking and Writing

1. Why *can't* William Blake's "The Tyger" (see p. 196) be read as "an allegory of the digestive processes"? What principle does Fish use to rule out such a reading?
2. What kinds of strategies for reading have you encountered in your classroom experiences? Which have you found to be the most useful? Explain why.
3. Write an essay that describes what you "could and could not get away with" in the literature courses you have taken in high school and college.

ANNETTE KOLODNY (b. 1941)
On the Commitments of Feminist Criticism   1980

If feminist criticism calls anything into question, it must be that dog-eared myth of intellectual neutrality. For what I take to be the underlying spirit or message of any consciously ideologically premised criticism — that is, that ideas are important *because* they determine the ways we live, or want to live, in the world — is vitiated by confining those ideas to the study, the classroom, or the pages of our books. To write chapters decrying the sexual stereotyping of women in our literature, while closing our eyes to the sexual harassment of our women students and colleagues; to display Katharine Hepburn and Rosalind Russell in our courses on "The Image of the Independent Career Women in Film," while managing not to notice the paucity of female administrators on our own campus; to study the women who helped make universal enfranchisement a political reality, while keeping silent about our activist colleagues who are denied promotion or tenure; to include segments on "Women in the Labor Movement" in our American studies or women's studies courses, while remaining willfully ignorant of the department secretary fired for efforts to organize a clerical workers' union; to glory in the delusions of "merit," "privilege," and "status" which accompany campus life in order to insulate ourselves from the millions of women who labor in poverty — all this is not merely hypocritical; it destroys both the spirit and the meaning of what we are about.

From "Dancing through the Minefield: Some Observations on the Theory, Practice, and Politics of a Feminist Literary Criticism," *Feminist Studies,* 6, 1980

Considerations for Critical Thinking and Writing

1. Why does Kolodny reject "intellectual neutrality" as a "myth"? Explain whether you agree or disagree with her point of view.
2. Kolodny argues that feminist criticism can be used as an instrument for social reform. Discuss the possibility and desirability of her position. Do you think other kinds of criticism can and should be used to create social change?

ANDREW P. DEBICKI (b. 1934)
New Criticism and Deconstructionism: Two Attitudes in Teaching Poetry 1985

[Let's] look at the ways in which a New Critic and a deconstructivist might handle a poem. My first example, untitled, is a work by Pedro Salinas, which I first analyzed many years ago and which I have recently taught to a group of students influenced by deconstruction:

> Sand: sleeping on the beach today
> and tomorrow caressed
> in the bosom of the sea:
> the sun's today, water's prize tomorrow.
> Softly you yield
> to the hand that presses you
> and go away with the first
> courting wind that appears.
> Pure and fickle sand,
> changing and clear beloved,
> I wanted you for my own,
> and held you against my chest and soul.
> But you escaped with the waves, the wind, the sun,
> and I remained without a beloved,
> my face turned to the wind which robbed her,
> and my eyes to the far-off sea in which she had
> green loves in a green shelter.

My original study of this poem, written very much in the New Critical tradition, focused on the unusual personification of sand as beloved and on the metaphorical pattern that it engendered. In the first part of the work, the physical elusiveness of sand (which slips through one's hand, flies with the wind, moves from shore to sea) evokes a coquettish woman, yielding to her lover and then escaping, running off with a personified wind, moving from one being to another. Watching these images, the reader gradually forgets that the poem is metaphorically describing sand and becomes taken up by the unusual correspondences with the figure of a flirting woman. When in the last part of the poem the speaker laments his loss, the reader is drawn into his lament for a fickle lover who has abandoned him.

Continuing a traditional analysis of this poem, we would conclude that its unusual personification/metaphor takes us beyond a literal level and leads us to a wider vision. The true subject of this poem is not sand, nor is it a flirt who tricks a man. The comparison between sand and woman, however, has made us feel the elusiveness of both, as well as the effect that this elusiveness has had on the speaker, who is left sadly contemplating it at the end of the poem. The poem has used its main image to embody a general vision of fleetingness and its effects.

My analysis, as developed thus far, is representative of a New Critical study. It focuses on the text and its central image, it describes a tension produced within the text, and it suggests a way in which this tension is resolved so as to move the poem beyond its literal level. In keeping with the tenets of traditional analytic criticism, it shows how the poem conveys a meaning that is far richer than its plot or any possible conceptual message. But while it is careful not to reduce the poem to a simple idea or to an equivalent of its prose summary, it does attempt to work all of its elements into a single interpretation which would satisfy every reader . . . : it makes all of the poem's meanings reside in its verbal structures, and it suggests that those meanings can be discovered and combined into a single cohesive vision as we systematically analyze those structures.

By attempting to find a pattern that will incorporate and resolve the poem's tensions, however, this reading leaves some loose ends, which I noticed even in my New Critical perspective — and which I found difficult to explain. To see the poem as the discovery of the theme of fleetingness by an insightful speaker, we have to ignore the fanciful nature of the comparison, the whimsical attitude to reality that it suggests, and the excessively serious lament of the speaker, which is difficult to take at face value — he laments the loss of *sand* with the excessive emotion of a romantic lover! The last lines, with their evocation of the beloved/sand in an archetypal kingdom of the sea, ring a bit hollow. Once we notice all of this, we see the speaker as being somehow unreliable in his strong response to the situation. He tries too hard to equate the loss of sand with the loss of love, he paints himself as too much of a romantic, and he loses our assent when we realize that his rather cliché declarations are not very fitting. Once we become aware of the speaker's limitations, our perspective about the poem changes: we come to see its "meaning" as centered, not on the theme of fleetingness as such, but on a portrayal of the speaker's exaggerated efforts to embody this theme in the image of sand.

For the traditional New Critic, this would pose a dilemma. The reading of the poem as a serious embodiment of the theme of evanescence is undercut by an awareness of the speaker's unreliability. One can account for the conflict between readings, to some extent, by speaking of the poem's use of irony and by seeing a tension between the theme of evanescence and the speaker's excessive concern with an imaginary beloved (which blinds him to the larger issues presented by the poem). That still leaves unresolved, however, the poem's final meaning and effect. In class discussions, in fact, a debate between those students who asserted that the importance of the poem lay in its engendering the theme of fleetingness and those who noted the absurdity of the speaker often ended in an agreement that this was a "problem poem" which never resolved or integrated its "stresses" and its double vision. . . .

The deconstructive critic, however, would not be disturbed by a lack of resolution in the meanings of the poem and would use the conflict between interpretations as the starting point for further study. Noting that the view of evanescence produced by the poem's central metaphor is undercut by the speaker's unreliability, the deconstructive critic would explore the play of signification that the undercutting engenders. Calling into question the attempt to neatly define evanescence, on the one hand, and the speaker's excessive romanticism on the other, the poem would represent, for this critic, a creative confrontation of irresoluble visions. The image of the sand as woman, as well as the portrayal of the speaker, would represent a sort of "seam" in the text, an area of indeterminacy that would open the way to further readings. This image lets us see the speaker as a sentimental poet, attempting unsuccessfully to define evanescence by means of a novel metaphor but getting trapped in the theme of lost love, which he himself has engendered; it makes us think of the inadequacy of language, of the ways in which metaphorical expression and the clichés of a love lament can undercut each other.

Once we adopt such a deconstructivist perspective, we will find in the text details that will carry forward our reading. The speaker's statement that he held "her" against his "chest and his soul" underlines the conflict in his perspective: it juggles a literal perspective (he rubs sand against himself) and a metaphorical one (he reaches for his beloved), but it cannot fully combine them — "soul" is ludicrously inappropriate in reference to the former. The reader, noting the inappropriateness, has to pay attention to the inadequacy of language as used here. All in all, by engendering a conflict between various levels and perspectives, the poem makes us feel the incompleteness of any one reading, the way in which each one is a "misreading" (not because it is wrong, but because it is incomplete), and the creative lack of closure in the poem. By not being subject to closure, in fact, this text becomes all the more exciting: its view of the possibilities and limitations of metaphor, language, and perspective seems more valuable than any static portrayal of "evanescence."

The analyses I have offered of this poem exemplify the different classroom approaches that would be taken by a stereotypical New Critic, on the one hand, and a deconstructive critic on the other. Imbued with the desire to come to an overview of the literary work, the former will attempt to resolve its tensions (and probably remain unsatisfied with the poem). Skeptical of such a possibility and of the very existence of a definable "work," the latter will focus on the tensions that can be found in the text as vehicles for multiple readings. Given his or her attitude to the text, the deconstructive critic will not worry about going beyond its "limits" (which really do not exist). This will allow, of course, for more speculative readings; it will also lead to a discussion of ways in which the text can be extended and "cured" in successive readings, to the fact that it reflects on the process of its own creation, and to ways in which it will relate to other texts.

> From *Writing and Reading DIFFERENTLY: Deconstruction
> and the Teaching of Composition and Literature,*
> edited by G. Douglas Atkins and Michael L. Johnson

Considerations for Critical Thinking and Writing

1. Explain how the New Critical and deconstructionist approaches to the Salinas poem differ. What kinds of questions are raised by each? What elements of the poem are focused on in each approach?
2. Write an essay explaining which reading of the poem you find more interesting. In your opening paragraph define what you mean by "interesting."
3. Choose one of the critical strategies for reading discussed in this chapter and discuss Salinas's poem from that perspective.

BROOK THOMAS (b. 1947)

A New Historical Approach to Keats's "Ode on a Grecian Urn"   1987

The traditional reception of the poem invites a discussion of its implied aesthetic. The poem's aesthetic is, however, intricately linked to its attitude to the past. The urn is, after all, Keats's "sylvan historian." To ask what sort of history a piece of art presents to us is, of course, to raise one of the central questions of historical criticism. It also opens up a variety of directions to take in historicizing the teaching of literature. . . .

To ask what history the urn relates to the reader easily leads to a discussion of how much our sense of the past depends upon art and the consequences of that dependency. These are important questions, because even if our students have little knowledge of the past or even interest in it, they do have an attitude toward it. A poem like Keats's "Ode" can help them reflect upon what that attitude is and on how it has been produced.

Such a discussion also offers a way to raise what critics have traditionally seen as the poem's central conflict: that between the temporal world of man and the atemporal world of art. The urn records two different visions of the past, both at odds with what we normally associate with historical accounts. On the one hand, it preserves a beauty that resists the destructive force of time. On the other, it records a quotidian scene populated by nameless people rather than the account of "famous" personages and "important" events our students often associate with traditional histories. Art, Keats seems to suggest, both keeps alive a sense of beauty in a world of change *and* gives us a sense of the felt life of the past. But in its search for a realm in which truth and beauty co-exist, art risks freezing the "real" world and becoming a "cold pastoral," cut off from the very felt life it records. In dramatizing this conflict Keats's "Ode" allows students to see both art's power to keep the past alive and its tendency to distort it.

Chances are, however, that not all students share Keats's sense of the relationship between art and history. Rather than demonstrate their lack of "aesthetic appreciation," this difference can open up another direction to pursue in discussing the poem. To acknowledge a difference between our present attitude and the one embodied by Keats's poem is to call into question the conditions that have contributed to the changed attitude. Thus, if the first approach to the poem aims at having students reflect generally upon the influence art has on our attitude toward the past, this approach demands that we look at the specific historical conditions that help shape our general attitude toward both art and the past. In the case of the "Ode," this can lead to a discussion of the economic and political conditions of early nineteenth-century England that helped shape Keats's image of ancient Greece. On the one hand, there was England's self-image as the inheritor of ancient Greece's republican institutions and, on the other, a nostalgia for a harmonious pastoral world in contrast to the present state of industrialized, fragmented British society. Thus, the two versions of the past offered by Keats's sylvan historian — the aesthetic one in which harmony and beauty are preserved and the democratic one in which the life of everyday people is recorded — are related to specific historical conditions at the time Keats wrote. The challenge for our students — and for us — would be to speculate on how our attitudes towards art and history are shaped by our historical moment — how that moment is different from and similar to Keats's.

A third way to teach the poem historically is to concentrate on the urn itself as a historical as well as aesthetic object. "Where," we might ask our students, "would Keats have seen such an urn?" Most likely someone will respond, "A museum." If so, we are ready to discuss the phenomenon of the rise of the art museum in eighteenth- and nineteenth-century Europe, how cultural artifacts from the past were removed from their social setting and placed in museums to be contemplated as art. Seemingly taking us away from Keats's poem, such a discussion might be the best way to help our students understand Keats's aesthetic, for they will clearly see that in Keats's poem an urn that once had a practical social function now sparks aesthetic contemplation about the nature of truth, beauty, and the past. If we ask why the urn takes on this purely aesthetic function in a society that was increasingly practical, our students might start to glimpse how our modern notion of art has been defined in response to the social order.

To consider the urn a historical as well as an aesthetic object is also to raise political questions. For how, we might ask, did a Grecian urn (or the Elgin marbles, if we were to teach another Keats poem) end up in England in the first place? Such a question moves us from Keats's image of ancient Greece to a consideration of Greece in the early nineteenth century, and to how a number of Englishmen who sympathized with its struggle for liberation at the same time pillaged its cultural treasures and set them on display in London to advertise Britain's "advanced" cultural state. Thus, a very simple historical question about Keats's urn can force us to consider the political consequences of our cultural heritage. As Walter Benjamin warned, the cultural treasures that we so love have an origin we should not contemplate without horror: "They owe their existence not only to the efforts of the great minds and talents who have created them, but also to the anonymous toil of their contemporaries. There is no document of civilization which is not at the same time a document of barbarism" ("Theses on the Philosophy of History" in *Illuminations,* 256).

If we consider the task of historical scholarship to re-create the conditions of the past so that we can recover the author's original intention, the questions I have asked about Keats's "Ode" are not valid ones to ask. Clearly my questions are not primarily directed at recovering that intention. Instead, I am treating Keats's poem as social text, one that in telling us about the society that produced it also tells us about the society we inhabit today. This approach is not to say that we should completely abandon the effort to recover Keats's intention, but that, as in the case of formalist criticism, we need to go beyond the traditional historical scholar's efforts. We need to try both to reconstruct the author's intention — for instance, what Keats thought about art and history — and to read against the grain of his intention.

From "The Historical Necessities for — and Difficulties with — New Historical Analysis in Introductory Literature Courses," *College English,* September 1987

Considerations for Critical Thinking and Writing

1. Summarize the three historical approaches to "Ode on a Grecian Urn" (p. 69) Thomas describes. Which do you consider the most interesting? Explain why.
2. Write an essay that explores Thomas's claim that "a very simple historical question about the urn can force us to consider the political consequences of our cultural heritage."
3. Choose another poem from this anthology and treat it as a "social text." What kinds of questions can you ask about it that suggest the poem's historical significances?

PETER RABINOWITZ (b. 1944)
On Close Readings   1988

Belief in close reading may be the nearest thing literary scholars have to a shared critical principle. Academics who teach literature tend to accept as a matter of course that good reading is slow, attentive to linguistic nuance (especially figurative language), and suspicious of surface meanings.

Close reading is a fundamental link between the New Critics and the Yale deconstructionists. Indeed, deconstructionist J. Hillis Miller has gone so far as to characterize what he saw as an attack on close reading by Gerald Graff as "a major treason against our profession." Similarly, what Naomi Schor calls "clitoral" feminist criticism, and its "hermeneutics focused on the detail," is a variant of close reading. So is much reader-response criticism.

Despite its broad acceptance by scholars, however, close reading is not the natural, the only, or always the best way to approach a text. I'm not suggesting that it should never be taught or used. But I do want to argue that close reading rests on faulty assumptions about how literature is read, which can lead, especially in the classroom, to faulty prescriptions about how it *ought* to be read.

The fact is that there are a variety of ways to read, all of which engage the reader in substantially different kinds of activity. Which kind depends in part on the reader and his or her immediate purpose. Teasing out the implicit homoerotic tendencies in Turgenev's *Asya,* for instance, is a different activity from trying to determine its contribution to the development of first-person narrative techniques. In part, the way one reads also varies from text to text. Different authors, different genres, different periods, different cultures expect readers to approach texts in different ways.

The bias in academe toward close reading reduces that multiplicity. While all close readers obviously don't read in exactly the same way, the variations have a strong family resemblance. Their dominance in the aristocracy of critical activity — virtually undiminished by the critical revolutions of the last twenty years — can skew evaluation, distort interpretation, discourage breadth of vision, and separate scholars from students and other ordinary readers.

David Daiches was not being eccentric when he argued that literary value depends on the "degree to which the work lends itself" to the kind of reading demanded by New Critical theory. The schools in vogue may change, but we still assign value to what fits our prior conceptions of reading, and the academically sanctioned canon consequently consists largely of texts that respond well to close reading.

Once you give priority to close reading, you implicitly favor figurative writing over realistic writing, indirect expression over direct expression, deep meaning over surface meaning, form over content, and the elite over the popular. In the realm of poetry, that means giving preference to lyric over narrative poems, and in the realm of fiction, to symbolism and psychology over plot. Such preferences, in turn, devalue certain voices. A writer directly confronting brute oppression, for instance, is apt to be ranked below another who has the luxury minutely to explore the details of subtle middle-class crises. Thus, for a close reader, the unresonant prose of Harriet Wilson's *Our Nig* will automatically make the novel seem less "good" than Henry James's more intricate *What Maisie Knew,* although the racist brutality endured by Ms. Wilson's heroine is arguably more important for our culture — and thus more deserving of our consideration — than the affluent sexual merry-go-round that dizzies Maisie.

It would be bad enough if the preference for close reading simply meant that texts that didn't measure up were chucked onto a noncanonical pile — then, at least, the rebellious could rummage through the rejects. But close reading also has an insidious effect on interpretation. Not only do we reject many works that don't fit; more damaging, we also twist many others until they *do* fit.

Yet we fail to recognize the magnitude of this distortion. One of the major problems with much current critical practice is the tendency to underestimate the extent to which texts can serve as mirrors — not of the external world but of the reader, who is apt to find in a text not what is really there but what he expects or wants to find. . . .

When reading for class, many students read closely, but few continue the practice once they've left college. In fact, most people — including teachers — who really enjoy literature recognize that close reading is a special kind of interpretive practice. Literary scholars are apt to make a distinction between "real reading" and "reading for fun"; most nonacademic readers are likely to divide "real reading" from "reading for class." In either case, an artificial split is created between academe and "real life," which leads to theories that devalue the kinds of reading (and therefore the kinds of books) that engage most readers most of the time.

If I'm against close reading, then what am I for? The obvious alternative is pluralism.

We can legitimately show our students that different writers in different social, historical, and economic contexts write for different purposes and with different expectations. Likewise, we can teach our students that different readers (or the same reader under different circumstances) read for different reasons.

We must also give our students actual practice in various kinds of reading. For example, an introductory literature course should include many different sorts of texts: long novels as well as lyric poems; realistic (even didactic) works as well as symbolic ones; writing aimed at a broad audience as well as at a literate elite. The course should also include different kinds of tasks. Students should learn to approach a given text in several different ways, at least some of which arise out of their personal and cultural situations. Most important, we must help our students to be self-conscious about what they are doing, and to realize that every decision about how to read opens certain doors only by closing others.

It is not simply that learning new, less rigid ways of reading increases the number of works we can enjoy and learn from. More important, learning to read in different ways allows us to enjoy a wider range of texts and gain new perspectives on our cultural assumptions. Only such flexible reading leads to intellectual growth, for it is only that kind of reading that can enable us to be conscious of — and therefore able to deal effectively with — the narrowness of "standard" interpretive techniques.

From "Our Evaluation of Literature Has Been Distorted
by Academe's Bias toward Close Readings of Texts,"
Chronicle of Higher Education, April 6, 1988

Considerations for Critical Thinking and Writing

1. Why does Rabinowitz object to the bias toward close reading as the primary way to approach a literary work? Explain why you agree or disagree.
2. According to Rabinowitz, how does a critical emphasis on close reading affect the formation of the canon?
3. In an essay discuss Rabinowitz's observation that an emphasis on close reading "devalue[s] the kinds of reading (and therefore the kinds of books) that engage most readers most of the time."

HARRIET HAWKINS (b. 1939)
Should We Study King Kong *or* King Lear?   1988

> *There is nothing either good or bad, but thinking makes it so.*
> — *Hamlet*

> Troilus: *What's aught but as 'tis valued?*
> Hector: *But value dwells not in particular will:*
> *It holds its estimate and dignity*
> *As well wherein 'tis precious of itself*
> *As in the prizer.*
> — *Troilus and Cressida*

To what degree is great literature — or bad literature — an artificial category? Are there any good — or bad — reasons why most societies have given high status to certain works of art and not to others? Could Hamlet be right in concluding that there is *nothing* either good or bad but thinking — or critical or ideological discourse — makes it so? Or are certain works of art so precious, so magnificent — or so trashy — that they obviously ought to be included in the canon or expelled from the classroom? So far as I know, there is not now any sign of a critical consensus on the correct answer to these questions either in England or in the United States.

In England there are, on the one hand, eloquent cases for the defense of the value of traditional literary studies, like Dame Helen Gardner's last book, *In Defence of the Imagination*. On the other hand, there are critical arguments insisting that what really counts is not what you read, but the way that you read it. You might as well study *King Kong* as *King Lear,* because what matters is not the script involved, but the critical or ideological virtues manifested in your own "reading" of whatever it is that you are reading. Reviewing a controversial book entitled *Re-Reading English,* the poet Tom Paulin gives the following account of the issues involved in the debate:

> The contributors are collectively of the opinion that English literature is a dying subject and they argue that it can be revived by adopting a "socialist pedagogy" and introducing into the syllabus "other forms of writing and cultural production than the canon of literature" . . . it is now time to challenge "hierarchical" and "elitist" conceptions of literature and to demolish the bourgeois ideology which has been "naturalised" as literary value. . . . They wish to develop "a politics of reading" and to redefine the term "text" in order to admit newspaper reports, songs, and even mass demonstrations as subjects for tutorial discussion. Texts no longer have to be books: indeed, "it may be more democratic to study *Coronation Street* [England's most popular soap opera] than *Middlemarch*."

However one looks at these arguments, it seems indisputably true that the issues involved are of paramount critical, pedagogical, and social importance. There are, however, any number of different ways to look at the various arguments. So far as I am, professionally, concerned, they raise the central question, "Why should any of us still study, or teach, Shakespeare's plays (or *Paradise Lost* or *The Canterbury Tales*)?" After all, there are quite enough films, plays, novels, and poems being produced today (to say nothing of all those "other forms of writing," including literary criticism, that are clamoring for our attention) to satisfy anyone interested in high literature, or popular genres, or any form of "cultural production" whatsoever. They also raise the obviously reflexive question: "Assuming that all traditionally 'canonized' works were eliminated, overnight, from the syllabus of every English department in the world, would not comparable problems of priority, value, elitism, ideological pressure, authoritarianism, and arbitrariness almost(?) immediately arise with reference to *whatever* works — of whatsoever kind and nature — were substituted for them?"

If, say, the place on the syllabus currently assigned to *King Lear* were reassigned to *King Kong,* those of us currently debating the relative merits of the Quarto, the Folio, or a conflated version of *King Lear* would, *mutatis mutandis,*° have to decide whether to concentrate classroom attention on the "classic" version of *King Kong,* originally produced in 1933, or to focus on the 1974 remake (which by now has many ardent admirers of its own). Although classroom time might not allow the inclusion of both, a decision to exclude either version might well seem arbitrary or authoritarian and so give rise to grumbles about the "canon." Moreover, comparable questions of "canonization" might well arise with reference to other films excluded from a syllabus that included either version (or both versions) of *King Kong.* For example: why assign class time to *King Kong* and not to (say) *Slave Girls of the White Rhinoceros?* Who, if any, of us has the right to decide whether *King Lear* or *King Kong* or the *Slave*

---

mutatis mutandis: Substituting different terms (Latin).

Girls should, or should not, be included on, or excluded from, the syllabus? And can the decision to include, or exclude, any one of them be made, by any one of us, on any grounds whatsoever that do *not* have to do with comparative merit, or comparative value judgments, or with special interests — that is, with the aesthetic or ideological priorities, preferences, and prejudices of the assigners of positions on whatever syllabus there is? And insofar as most, if not all, of our judgments and preferences are comparative, are they not, inevitably, hierarchical?

Is there, in fact, any form of endeavor or accomplishment known to the human race — from sport to ballet to jazz to cooking — wherein comparative standards of excellence comparable to certain "hierarchical" and "elitist" conceptions of literature are nonexistent? Even bad-film buffs find certain bad films more gloriously bad than others. And, perhaps significantly given its comparatively short lifetime, the avant-garde cinema has, by now, produced snobs to rival the most elitist literary critic who ever lived, such as the one who thus puts down a friend who likes ordinary Hollywood films:

> Ah that's all right for you, I know the sort you are, but give me a private job that's shot on faded sepia sixteen millimetre stock with non-professional actors . . . no story and dialogue in French *any day of the week.*

What is striking about this snob's assumption is how characteristic it is of a long tradition of critical elitism that has consistently sneered at popular genres (e.g., romance fiction, soap operas, horror films, westerns, etc.) that are tainted by the profit motive and so tend to "give the public what it wants" in the way of sentimentality, sensationalism, sex, violence, romanticism, and the like.

From *"King Lear* to *King Kong* and Back: Shakespeare and Popular Modern Genres" in *"Bad" Shakespeare: Revaluations of the Shakespeare Canon,* edited by Maurice Charney

Considerations for Critical Thinking and Writing

1. Do you agree or disagree that "great literature — or bad literature — [is] an artificial category"? Explain why.

2. Why would problems of "priority, value, elitism, ideological pressure, authoritarianism, and arbitrariness" probably become issues for evaluating any new works that replaced canonized works?

3. Write an essay in which you argue for (or against) studying popular arts (for example, popular song lyrics) alongside the works of classic writers such as Shakespeare.

HENRY A. GIROUX (b. 1943)
The Canon and Liberal Arts Education   1990

In the current debate about the importance of constructing a particular canon, the notion of naming and transmitting from one generation to the next what can be defined as "cultural treasure" specifies what has become the central argument for reforming the liberal arts. For that reason, perhaps, it appears as though the debate were reducible to the question of the contents of course syllabi. The notion of critical pedagogy for which I am arguing provides a fundamental challenge to this position: it calls for an argument that transcends the limited focus on the canon, that recognizes the crisis in liberal arts education to be one of historical purpose and meaning, a crisis that challenges us to rethink in a critical fashion the relationship between the role of the university and the imperatives of a democracy in a mass society.

Historically, education in the liberal arts was conceived of as the essential preparation for governing, for ruling — more specifically, the preparation and outfitting of the governing *elite*. The liberal arts curriculum, composed of the "best" that had been said or written, was intended, as Elizabeth Fox-Genovese has observed, "to provide selected individuals with a collective history, culture, and epistemology so that they could run the world effectively."[1] In this context the canon was considered to be a possession of the dominant classes or groups. Indeed, the canon was fashioned as a safeguard to insure that the cultural property of such groups was passed on from generation to generation along with the family estates. Thus, in these terms it seems most appropriate that the literary canon should be subject to revision — as it has been before in the course of the expansion of democracy — such that it might also incorporate and reflect the experience and aspirations of the women, minorities, and children of the working class who have been entering the academy.

Conceived of in this way, a radical vision of liberal arts education is to be found within its elite social origins and purpose. But this does not suggest that the most important questions confronting liberal arts reform lie in merely establishing the content of the liberal arts canon on the model of the elite universities. Instead, the most important questions become [those] of reformulating the meaning and purpose of higher education in ways that contribute to the cultivation and regeneration of an informed citizenry capable of actively participating in the shaping and governing of a democratic society. Within this discourse, the pedagogical becomes political and the notion of a liberal arts canon commands a more historically grounded and critical reading. The pedagogical becomes more political in that it proposes that the way in which students engage and examine knowledge is just as important an issue as the choosing of texts to be used in a class or program. That is, a democratic notion of liberal education rejects those views of the humanities which would treat texts as sacred and instruction as merely transmission. This notion of the canon undermines the possibility for dialogue, argument, and critical thinking; it treats knowledge as a form of cultural inheritance that is beyond considerations regarding how it might be implicated in social practices that exploit, infantilize, and oppress. The canons we have inherited, in their varied forms, cannot be dismissed as simply part of the ideology of privilege and domination. Instead, the privileged texts of the dominant or official canons should be explored with respect to the important role they have played in shaping, for better or worse, the major events of our time. But there are also forms of knowledge that have been marginalized by the official canons. There are noble traditions, histories, and narratives that speak to important struggles by women, blacks, minorities, and other subordinate groups that need to be heard so that such groups can lay claim to their own voices as part of a process of both affirmation and inquiry. At issue here is a notion of pedagogy as a form of cultural politics that rejects a facile restoration of the past, that rejects history as a monologue. A critical ped-

---

[1] Elizabeth Fox-Genovese, "The Claims of a Common Culture: Gender, Race, Class and the Canon," *Salmagundi* 72 (Fall 1986): 133.

agogy recognizes that history is constituted in dialogue and that some of the voices that make up that dialogue have been eliminated. Such a pedagogy calls for a public debate regarding the dominant memories and repressed stories that constitute the historical narratives of a social order: in effect, canon formation becomes a matter of both rewriting and reinterpreting the past; canon formation embodies the ongoing "process of reconstructing the 'collective reflexivity' of lived cultural experience . . . which recognizes that the 'notions of the past and future are essentially notions of the present.' "[2] In this case, such notions are central to the politics of identity and power, and to the memories that structure how experience is individually and collectively authorized and experienced as a form of cultural identity. . . .

A critical pedagogy also rejects a discourse of value neutrality. Without subscribing to a language that polices behavior and desire, it aims at developing pedagogical practices informed by an ethical stance that contests racism, sexism, class exploitation, and other dehumanizing and exploitative social relations as ideologies and social practices that disrupt and devalue public life. This is a pedagogy that rejects detachment, though it does not silence in the name of its own ideological fervor or correctness. It acknowledges social injustices, but examines with care and in dialogue with itself and others how such injustices work through the discourses, experiences, and desires that constitute daily life and the subjectivities of the students who invest in them. It is a pedagogy guided by ethical principles that correspond to a radical practice rooted in historical experience. And it is a pedagogy that comprehends the historical consequences of what it means to take a moral and political position with respect to the horror and suffering of, for example, the Gulag, the Nazi Holocaust, or the Pol Pot regime. Such events not only summon up images of terror, domination, and resistance, but also provide a priori examples of what principles have to be both defended and fought against in the interest of freedom and life. Within this perspective, ethics becomes more than the discourse of moral relativism or a static transmission of reified history. Ethics becomes, instead, a continued engagement in which the social practices of everyday life are interrogated in relation to the principles of individual autonomy and democratic public life — not as a matter of received truth but as a constant engagement. This represents an ethical stance which provides the opportunity for individual capacities to be questioned and examined so that they can serve both to analyze and advance the possibilities inherent in all social forms. At issue is an ethical stance in which community, difference, remembrance, and historical consciousness become central categories as part of the language of public life.

From "Liberal Arts Education and the Struggle for Public Life: Dreaming about Democracy," *South Atlantic Quarterly* 89, 1990

[2]Gail Guthrie Valaskakis, "The Chippewa and the Other: Living the Heritage of Lac Du Flambeau," *Cultural Studies* 2 (October 1988): 268.

Considerations for Critical Thinking and Writing

1. Why does Giroux take debates about canonical issues beyond course reading lists? Upon what historical conditions does he base his argument?
2. What kind of teaching — "critical pedagogy" — does Giroux call for? Why?

3. According to Giroux, why should "value neutrality" be rejected by teachers and students?

4. Write an essay in which you agree or disagree that literature should be used to help create an "ethical stance" for its readers.

MORRIS DICKSTEIN (b. 1940)
On the Social Responsibility of the Critic   1993

. . . Many critics today, as if in violent reaction to the reading habits of the ordinary citizen, are haunted by the fear of becoming the passive consumer of ideological subtexts or messages. As the country grew more conservative in the eighties, many academic critics turned more radical, and this led to an onslaught by national magazines and media pundits on political correctness, the supposed left-wing and multicultural orthodoxy in American universities.

Here we encounter a number of puzzling paradoxes about "reading" in America today. As reading diminishes — not in absolute terms but in relation to other ways of receiving information — as reading loses its hold on people, the metaphor of reading constantly expands. Molecular biologists like Robert Pollack talk about "reading DNA," the structure of genetic transmission in each living cell. Students of urban life discuss "the city as text" and how to read it, as they did at a conference I attended in 1989. Film scholars publish books about "how to read a film" reflecting on our constantly expanding (and increasingly undifferentiated) notion of what constitutes a text. And literary critics over the past sixty years have developed ever more subtle and complex ways of reading those texts, often using obscure, specialized language that itself resists being read.

As educators worry about the role of video and electronic media in displacing the written word, as the skills of ordinary readers seem to languish, the sophistication and territorial ambition of academic readers continue to grow, widening a split that has been one of the hallmarks of the modern period. The common reader still exists, but many professional readers dissociate themselves on principle from the habits of the tribe: they deliberately read against the grain of the text, against common sense, against most people's way of reading — indeed, against their own way of reading in their ordinary lives. If the reader of *Scarlett* or *Gone with the Wind* reads passively, wanting to be possessed and carried away by a book, as by an old-fashioned movie or piece of music, the critical reader, influenced by theory and by the new historicism, has developed an active, aggressive, even adversarial approach to writing. What Paul Ricoeur in his book on Freud calls the "hermeneutics of suspicion" has become a primary feature of academic criticism, which aims above all to disclose the institutional pressures and ideological formations that speak through texts and influence us as we read.°. . .

Our advanced criticism is especially marked by the suspicion and the hostility with which it performs such operations: its failure to distinguish art from propaganda, literature from advertising; its fierce resistance to the mental frame-

---

What . . . read: Paul Ricoeur (b. 1913), a French philosopher and critic, author of *Freud and Philosophy: An Essay on Interpretation* (1970). Hermeneutics refers to the theory and method of perceiving and interpreting texts.

work of the works it examines. "All right, what's wrong with this book?" asks one programmatically suspicious instructor of the students in her humanities class, to make sure they don't get taken in by those "great" books. Some of our recent ideological criticism turns the social understanding of literature, which can be intrinsically valuable, into an all too predictable exercise in debunking and demystification. . . .

The role of the critic is not to read notionally and cleverly, and certainly not to castigate writers for their politics, but to raise ordinary reading to its highest power — to make it more insightful, more acute, without losing touch with our deepest personal responses. It is ironic to speak for the social responsibility of the writer while betraying the public sphere of reading. Criticism, even academic criticism, is neither a sect nor a priesthood but ultimately a public trust, mediating between artists or writers and their often puzzled audience. . . .

A naive reading, anchored in wonder, must remain an indispensable moment of a more self-conscious reading, not just a piece of scaffolding to be kicked away as our suspicion and professionalism take over. We need a better balance between the naive and suspicious readers in ourselves: between the willing suspension of disbelief and our ability to withhold ourselves and read skeptically; between our appreciation of art and our wary knowledge of its persuasive power; between a sympathy for the author as an individual like ourselves — working out creative problems, making contingent choices — and our critical sense of a literary work as the discursive formation of a cultural moment.

From "Damaged Literacy: The Decay of Reading," *Profession 93*

Considerations for Critical Thinking and Writing

1. Do you think video and electronic media are "displacing the written word"? What evidence can you point to in your own experience that refutes or supports this claim?

2. What do you think Dickstein means when he refers to academic criticism as "a public trust"? What should the function of criticism be, according to Dickstein? In what sense is the role of the critic "to raise ordinary reading to its highest power"?

3. What criticism does Dickstein level against contemporary literary criticism? Explain why you agree or disagree with his perspective.

16. Reading and Writing

THE PURPOSE AND VALUE
OF WRITING ABOUT LITERATURE

Introductory literature courses typically include three components: reading, discussion, and writing. Students usually find the readings a pleasure, the class discussions a revelation, and the writing assignments — at least initially — a little intimidating. Writing an analysis of the symbolic use of a wall in Robert Frost's "Mending Wall" (p. 304) or in Herman Melville's "Bartleby, the Scrivener," for example, may seem considerably more daunting than making a case for animal rights or analyzing a campus newspaper editorial that calls for grade reforms. Like Bartleby, you might want to respond with "I would prefer not to." Literary topics are not, however, all that different from the kinds of papers assigned in English composition courses; many of the same skills are required for both. Regardless of the type of paper, you must develop a thesis and support it with evidence in language that is clear and persuasive.

Whether the subject matter is a marketing survey, a political issue, or a literary work, writing is a method of communicating information and perceptions. Writing teaches. But before writing becomes an instrument for informing the reader, it serves as a means of learning for the writer. An essay is a process of discovery as well as a record of what has been discovered. One of the chief benefits of writing is that we frequently realize what we want to say only after trying out ideas on a page and seeing our thoughts take shape in language.

More specifically, writing about a literary work encourages us to be better readers, because it requires a close examination of the elements of a short story, poem, or play. To determine how plot, character, setting, point of view, style, tone, irony, or any number of other literary elements function in a work, we must study them in relation to one another as well as separately. Speed-reading won't do. To read a text accurately and validly — neither ignoring nor distorting significant details — we must return to the work repeatedly to test our responses and interpretations. By paying attention to details and being sensitive to the author's use of language, we develop a clearer understanding of how the work conveys its effects and meanings.

Nevertheless, students sometimes ask why it is necessary or desirable to write about a literary work. Why not allow stories, poems, and plays to speak for themselves? Isn't it presumptuous to interpret Hemingway, Dickinson, or Shakespeare? These writers do, of course, speak for themselves, but they do so indirectly. Literary criticism does not seek to replace the text by explaining it but to enhance our readings of works by calling attention to elements that we might have overlooked or only vaguely sensed.

Another misunderstanding about the purpose of literary criticism is that it crankily restricts itself to finding faults in a work. Critical essays are sometimes mistakenly equated with newspaper and magazine reviews of recently published works. Reviews typically include summaries and evaluations to inform readers about a work's nature and quality, but critical essays assume that readers are already familiar with a work. Although a critical essay may point out limitations and flaws, most criticism — and certainly the kind of essay usually written in an introductory literature course — is designed to explain, analyze, and reveal the complexities of a work. Such sensitive consideration increases our appreciation of the writer's achievement and significantly adds to our enjoyment of a short story, poem, or play. In short, the purpose and value of writing about literature are that doing so leads to greater understanding and pleasure.

READING THE WORK CLOSELY

Know the piece of literature you are writing about before you begin your essay. Think about how the work makes you feel and how it is put together. The more familiar you are with how the various elements of the text convey effects and meanings, the more confident you will be explaining whatever perspective on it you ultimately choose. Do not insist that everything make sense on a first reading. Relax and enjoy yourself; you can be attentive and still allow the author's words to work their magic on you. With subsequent readings, however, go more slowly and analytically as you try to establish relations between characters, actions, images, or whatever else seems important. Ask yourself why you respond as you do. Think as you read, and notice how the parts of a work contribute to its overall nature. Whether the work is a short story, poem, or play, you will read relevant portions of it over and over, and you will very likely find more to discuss in each review if the work is rich.

It's best to avoid reading other critical discussions of a work before you are thoroughly familiar with it. There are several good reasons for following this advice. By reading interpretations before you know a work, you deny yourself the pleasure of discovery. That is a bit like starting with the last chapter in a mystery novel. But perhaps even more important than protecting the surprise and delight that a work might offer is that a premature reading of a critical discussion will probably short-circuit your own responses. You will see the work through the critic's eyes and have to struggle with someone else's perceptions and ideas before you can develop your own.

Reading criticism can be useful, but not until you have thought through your own impressions of the text. A guide should not be permitted to become a tyrant. This does not mean, however, that you should avoid background information about a work, for example, that the title of Diane Ackerman's "A Fine, a Private Place" (p. 61) alludes to Andrew Marvell's earlier *carpe diem* poem, "To His Coy Mistress" (p. 57). Knowing something about the author as well as historic and literary contexts can help to create expectations that enhance your reading.

ANNOTATING THE TEXT
AND JOURNAL NOTE TAKING

As you read, get in the habit of making marginal notations in your textbook. If you are working with a library book, use notecards and write down page or line numbers so that you can easily return to annotated passages. Use these cards to record reactions, raise questions, and make comments. They will freshen your memory and allow you to keep track of what goes on in the text.

Whatever method you use to annotate your texts — whether by writing marginal notes, highlighting, underlining, or drawing boxes and circles around important words and phrases — you'll eventually develop a system that allows you to retrieve significant ideas and elements from the text. Another way to record your impressions of a work — as with any other experience — is to keep a journal. By writing down your reactions to characters, images, language, actions, and other matters in a reading journal, you can often determine why you like or dislike a work or feel sympathetic or antagonistic to an author or discover paths into a work that might have eluded you if you hadn't preserved your impressions. Your journal notes and annotations may take whatever form you find useful; full sentences and grammatical correctness are not essential (unless they are to be handed in and your instructor requires that), though they might allow you to make better sense of your own reflections days later. The point is simply to put in writing thoughts that you can retrieve when you need them for class discussion or a writing assignment. Consider the following student annotation of the first twenty-four lines of Andrew Marvell's "To His Coy Mistress" and the journal entry that follows it:

Annotated Text

If we had time...

(Had we but world enough, and time,
This coyness, lady, were no (crime).   *Waste life and you steal from yourself.*
We would sit down, and think which way
To walk, and pass our long love's day.
Thou by the Indian (Ganges) side   5
Shouldst rubies find; I by the tide
Of (Humber) would complain.° I would
Love you ten years before the Flood,   *write love songs*
And you should, if you please, refuse   **Measurements of time**
Till the conversion of the Jews.   10

My vegetable love should grow,°   *slow, unconscious growth*
Vaster than empires, and more slow;
An hundred years should go to praise
Thine eyes and on thy forehead gaze,
Two hundred to adore each breast,   15
But thirty thousand to the rest:
An age at least to every part,
And the last age should show your heart.
For, lady, you deserve this state,
Nor would I love at lower rate.   20
But at my back I always hear
Time's wingèd chariot hurrying near;
And yonder all before us lie
Deserts of vast eternity.

[Handwritten annotations: "contrast river and desert images"; "Lines move faster here— tone changes"; "This eternity rushes in."]

Journal Note

```
     He'd be patient and wait for his "mistress" if they
had the time--sing songs, praise her, adore her, etc.
But they don't have that much time according to him.  He
seems to be patient but he actually begins by calling
patience--her coyness--a "crime."  Looks to me like he's
got his mind made up from the beginning of the poem.
Where's her response?  I'm not sure about him.
```

This journal note responds to some of the effects noted in the annotations of the poem; it's an excellent beginning for making sense of the speaker's argument in the poem.

Taking notes will preserve your initial reactions to the work. Many times first impressions are the best. Your response to a peculiar character, a striking phrase, or a subtle pun might lead to larger perceptions. The student paper on "The Love Song of J. Alfred Prufrock" (p. 590), for example, began with the student making notes in the margins of the text about the disembodied images of eyes and arms that appear in the poem. This, along with the fragmentary thoughts and style of the speaker eventually led her to examine the significance of the images and how they served to characterize Prufrock.

You should take detailed notes only after you've read through the work. If you write too many notes during the first reading, you're likely to disrupt your response. Moreover, until you have a sense of the entire work, it will be difficult to determine how connections can be made among its various elements. In addition to recording your first impressions and noting significant passages, images, diction, and so on, you should consult the Questions for Responsive Reading and Writing on page 248. These questions can assist you in getting inside a work as well as organizing your notes.

Inevitably, you will take more notes than you finally use in the paper. Note taking is a form of thinking aloud, but because your ideas are on paper you don't have to worry about forgetting them. As you develop a better sense of a potential topic, your notes will become more focused and detailed.

CHOOSING A TOPIC

If your instructor assigns a topic or offers a choice from among an approved list of topics, some of your work is already completed. Instead of being asked to come up with a topic about Emily Dickinson's poems in this anthology, you may be assigned a three-page essay that specifically discusses "Dickinson's Treatment of Grief in 'The Bustle in a House.' " You also have the assurance that a specified topic will be manageable within the suggested number of pages. Unless you ask your instructor for permission to write on a different or related topic, be certain to address yourself to the assignment. An essay that does not discuss grief but instead describes Dickinson's relationship with her father would be missing the point. Notice too that there is room even in an assigned topic to develop your own approach. One question that immediately comes to mind is whether grief defeats or helps the speaker in the poem. Assigned topics do not relieve you of thinking about an aspect of a work, but they do focus your thinking.

At some point during the course, you may have to begin an essay from scratch. You might, for example, be asked to write about a poem that somehow impressed you or that seemed particularly well written or filled with insights. Before you start considering a topic, you should have a sense of how long the paper will be, because the assigned length can help to determine the extent to which you should develop your topic. Ideally, the paper's length should be based on how much space you deem necessary to present your discussion clearly and convincingly, but if you have any doubts and no specific guidelines have been indicated, ask. The question is important; a topic that might be appropriate for a three-page paper could be too narrow for ten pages. Three pages would probably be adequate for a discussion of the speaker's view of death in John Keats's "To Autumn." Conversely, it would be futile to try to summarize Keats's use of sensuality in his poetry in even ten pages; the topic would have to be narrowed to something like "Images of Sensuality in 'The Eve of St. Agnes.' " Be sure that the topic you choose can be adequately covered in the assigned number of pages.

Once you have a firm sense of how much you are expected to write, you can begin to decide on your topic. If you are to choose what work to write about, select one that genuinely interests you. Too often students pick a poem, because it is mercifully short or seems simple. Such works can certainly be the subjects of fine essays, but simplicity should not be the major reason for selecting them. Choose a work that has moved you so that you have something to say about it. The student who wrote about "The Love Song of J. Alfred Prufrock" was initially attracted to the poem's imagery because she had heard a friend (no doubt an English major) jokingly quote Prufrock's famous lament that "I should have a pair of ragged claws / Scuttling across the floors of silent seas." Her paper then grew out of her curiosity about the meaning of the images. When a writer is engaged in a topic, the paper has a better chance of being interesting to a reader.

After you have settled on a particular work, your notes and annotations of the text should prove useful for generating a topic. The student paper on Prufrock developed naturally from the notes (p. 588) that the student jotted down about the images. If you think with a pen in your hand, you are likely to find when you review your notes that your thoughts have clustered into one or more topics. Perhaps there are patterns of imagery that seem to make a point about life. There may be symbols that are ironically paired or levels of diction that reveal certain qualities about the speaker. Your notes and annotations on such aspects can lead you to a particular effect or impression. Having chuckled your way through Meinke's "The ABC of Aerobics" (p. 245), you may discover that your notations about the poem's humor point to a serious satire of society's values.

DEVELOPING A THESIS

When you are satisfied that you have something interesting to say about a work and that your notes have led you to a focused topic, you can formulate a *thesis,* the central idea of the paper. Whereas the topic indicates what the paper focuses on (the disembodied images in "Prufrock," for example), the thesis explains what you have to say about the topic (the frightening images of eyes, arms, and claws reflect Prufrock's disjointed, fragmentary response to life). The thesis should be a complete sentence (though sometimes it may require more than one sentence) that establishes your topic in clear, unambiguous language. The thesis may be revised as you get further into the topic and discover what you want to say about it, but once the thesis is firmly established it will serve as a guide for you and your reader, because all the information and observations in your essay should be related to the thesis.

One student on an initial reading of Andrew Marvell's "To His Coy Mistress" (p. 57) saw that the male speaker of the poem urges a woman to love now before time runs out for them. This reading gave him the impression that the poem is a simple celebration of the pleasures of the flesh, but on subsequent readings he underlined or noted these images: "Time's wingèd chariot hurrying near"; "Deserts of vast eternity"; "marble vault"; "worms"; "dust"; "ashes"; and these two lines: "The grave's a fine and private place, / But none, I think, do there embrace."

By listing these images associated with time and death, he established an inventory that could be separated from the rest of his notes on point of view, character, sounds, and other subjects. Inventorying notes allows patterns to emerge that you might have only vaguely perceived otherwise. Once these images are grouped, they call attention to something darker and more complex in Marvell's poem than a first impression might suggest.

These images may create a different feeling about the poem, but they still don't explain very much. One simple way to generate a thesis about a literary work is to ask the question "why?" Why do these images appear in the poem? Why does the speaker in William Stafford's "Traveling through the Dark" (p. 141) push the dead deer into the river? Why does disorder appeal so much to the speaker in Robert Herrick's "Delight in Disorder" (p. 193)? Your responses to these kinds of questions can lead to a thesis.

Writers sometimes use free writing to help themselves explore possible answers to such questions. It can be an effective way of generating ideas. Free writing is exactly that: the technique calls for nonstop writing without concern for mechanics or editing of any kind. Free writing for ten minutes or so on a question will result in fragments and repetitions, but it can also produce some ideas. Here's an example of a student's response to the question about the images in "To His Coy Mistress":

> He wants her to make love. Love poem. There's little time. Her crime. He exaggerates. Sincere? Sly? What's he want? She says nothing--he says it all. What about deserts, ashes, graves, and worms? Some love poem. Sounds like an old Vincent Price movie. Full of sweetness but death creeps in. Death--hurry hurry! Tear pleasures. What passion! Where's death in this? How can a love poem be so ghoulish? She does nothing. Maybe frightened? Convinced? Why death? Love and death--time--death.

This free writing contains several ideas; it begins by alluding to the poem's plot and speaker, but the central idea seems to be death. This emphasis led the student to five potential thesis statements for his essay about the poem:

1. "To His Coy Mistress" is a difficult poem.
2. Death in "To His Coy Mistress."
3. There are many images of death in "To His Coy Mistress."
4. "To His Coy Mistress" celebrates the pleasures of the flesh but it also recognizes the power of death to end that pleasure.
5. On the surface, "To His Coy Mistress" is a celebration of the pleasures of the flesh, but this witty seduction is tempered by a chilling recognition of the reality of death.

The first statement is too vague to be useful. In what sense is the poem difficult? A more precise phrasing, indicating the nature of the difficulty, is needed. The second statement is a topic rather than a thesis. Because it is not a sentence, it does not express a complete idea about how the poem treats death. Although this could be an appropriate title, it is inadequate as a thesis statement. The third statement, like the first one, identifies the topic, but even though it is a sentence, it is not a complete idea that tells us anything significant beyond the fact it states. After these preliminary attempts to develop a thesis, the student remembered his first impression of the poem and incorporated it into his thesis statement. The fourth thesis is a useful approach to the poem because it limits the topic and indicates how it will be treated in the paper: the writer will begin with an initial impression of the poem and then go on to qualify it. However, the fifth thesis is better than the fourth because it indicates a shift in tone produced by the ironic relationship between death and flesh. An effective thesis, like this one, makes a clear statement about a manageable topic and provides a firm sense of direction for the paper.

Most writing assignments in a literature course require you to persuade readers that your thesis is reasonable and supported with evidence. Papers that report information without comment or evaluation are simply summaries. Similarly, a paper that merely pointed out the death images in "To His Coy Mistress" would not contain a thesis, but a paper that attempted to make a case for the death imagery as a grim reminder of how vulnerable flesh is would involve persuasion. In developing a thesis, remember that you are expected not merely to present information but to argue a point.

ARGUING ABOUT LITERATURE

An argumentative essay is designed to make persuasive your interpretation of a work. Arguing about literature doesn't mean that you're engaged in an angry, antagonistic dispute (though controversial topics do sometimes engender heated debates). Instead, argumentation requires that you present your interpretation of a work (or a portion of it) by supporting your discussion with clearly defined terms, ample evidence, and a detailed analysis of relevant portions of the text.

If you have a choice, it's generally best to write about a topic that you feel strongly about. Even if you don't like cats you might find Jane Kenyon's "The Blue Bowl" (p. 99) just the sort of treatment that helps explain why you don't want one. On the other hand, if you're a cat fan, the poem may suggest something essential about cats that you've experienced but have never quite put your finger on. If your essay is to be interesting and convincing, what is important is that it be written from a strong point of view that persuasively argues your evaluation, analysis, and interpretation of a work. It is not enough to say that you like or dislike a work; instead you must give your reader some ideas and evidence that can be accepted or rejected based on the quality of the answers to the questions you raise.

One way to come up with persuasive answers is to generate good questions that will lead you further into the text and to critical issues related to it. Notice how the Perspectives, Complementary Readings, and Critical Case Study in this anthology raise significant questions and issues about texts from a variety of points of view. Moreover, the critical strategies for reading summarized in Chapter 15 can be a resource for raising questions that can be shaped into an argument. The following lists of questions for the critical approaches covered in Chapter 15 should be useful for discovering arguments you might make about a short story, poem, or play. The page number that follows each heading refers to the discussion in the anthology for that particular approach.

Formalist Questions (p. 529)

1. How do various elements of the work — character, point of view, setting, tone, diction, images, symbol, etc. — reinforce its meanings?
2. How are the elements related to the whole?
3. What is the work's major organizing principle? How is its structure unified?
4. What issues does the work raise? How does the work's structure resolve those issues?

Biographical Questions (p. 531)

1. Are there facts about the writer's life relevant to your understanding of the work?
2. Are characters and incidents in the work versions of the writer's own experiences? Are they treated factually or imaginatively?
3. How do you think the writer's values are reflected in the work?

Psychological Questions (p. 533)

1. How does the work reflect the author's personal psychology?
2. What do the speaker's emotions and behavior reveal about his or her psychological state? What type of personality is the speaker?
3. Are psychological matters such as repression, dreams, and desire presented consciously or unconsciously by the author?

Historical Questions (p. 535)

1. How does the work reflect the period in which it is written?
2. How does the work reflect the period it represents?
3. What literary or historical influences helped to shape the form and content of the work?
4. How important is the historical context (both the work's and your own) to interpreting the work?

Marxist Questions (p. 537)

1. How are class differences presented in the work? Are characters aware or unaware of the economic and social forces that affect their lives?
2. How do economic conditions determine the characters' lives?
3. What ideological values are explicit or implicit?
4. Does the work challenge or affirm the social order it describes?

Feminist Questions (p. 537)

1. How are women's lives portrayed in the work? Do the women in the work accept or reject these roles?
2. Is the form and content of the work influenced by the author's gender?

3. What are the relationships between men and women? Are these relationships sources of conflict? Do they provide resolutions to conflicts?
4. Does the work challenge or affirm traditional ideas about women?

Mythological Questions (p. 539)

1. How does the poem resemble other poems in diction, character, setting, or use of symbols?
2. Are archetypes presented, such as quests, initiations, scapegoats, or withdrawals and returns?
3. Does the protagonist or the speaker undergo any kind of transformation such as a movement from innocence to experience that seems archetypal?
4. Are there any specific allusions to myth that shed light on the text?

Reader-Response Questions (p. 541)

1. How do you respond to the work?
2. How do your own experiences and expectations affect your reading and interpretation?
3. What is the work's original or intended audience? To what extent are you similar to or different from that audience?
4. Do you respond in the same way to the work after more than one reading?

Deconstructionist Questions (p. 543)

1. How are contradictory or opposing meanings expressed in the work?
2. How does meaning break down or deconstruct itself in the language of the text?
3. Would you say that ultimate definitive meanings are impossible to determine and establish in the text? Why? How does that affect your interpretation?
4. How are implicit ideological values revealed in the work?

These questions will not apply to all texts; and they are not mutually exclusive. They can be combined to explore a text from several critical perspectives simultaneously. A feminist approach to Anne Bradstreet's "The Author to Her Book" (p. 110) could also use Marxist concerns about class to make observations about the oppression of women's lives in the historical context of the seventeenth century. Your use of these questions should allow you to discover significant issues from which you can develop an argumentative essay that is organized around clearly defined terms, relevant evidence, and a persuasive analysis.

ORGANIZING A PAPER

After you have chosen a manageable topic and developed a thesis, a central idea about it, you can begin to organize your paper. Your thesis, even if it is still somewhat tentative, should help you decide what information will need to be included and provide you with a sense of direction.

Consider again the sample thesis in the section on developing a thesis:

```
On the surface, "To His Coy Mistress" is a celebration of
the pleasures of the flesh, but this witty seduction is
tempered by a chilling recognition of the reality of death.
```

This thesis indicates that the paper can be divided into two parts: the pleasures of the flesh and the reality of death. It also indicates an order: Because the central point is to show that the poem is more than a simple celebration, the pleasures of the flesh should be discussed first so that another, more complex, reading of the poem can follow. If the paper began with the reality of death, its point would be anticlimactic.

Having established such a broad and informal outline, you can draw upon your underlinings, margin notations, and notecards for the subheadings and evidence required to explain the major sections of your paper. This next level of detail would look like the following:

```
1. Pleasures of the flesh
   Part of the traditional tone of love poetry
2. Recognition of death
   Ironic treatment of love
      Diction
      Images
      Figures of speech
      Symbols
      Tone
```

This list was initially a jumble of terms, but the student arranged the items so that each of the two major sections leads to a discussion of tone. (The student also found it necessary to drop some biographical information from his notes because it was irrelevant to the thesis.) The list indicates that the first part of the paper will establish the traditional tone of love poetry that celebrates the pleasures of the flesh, while the second part will present a more detailed discussion about the ironic recognition of death. The emphasis is on the latter because that is the point to be argued in the paper. Hence, the thesis has helped to organize the parts of the paper, establish an order, and indicate the paper's proper proportions.

The next step is to fill in the subheadings with information from your notes. Many experienced writers find that making lists of information to be included under each subheading is an efficient way to develop paragraphs. For a longer paper (perhaps a research paper), you should be able to develop a paragraph or more on each subheading. On the other hand, a shorter paper may require that you combine several subheadings in a paragraph. You may also discover that while an informal list is adequate for a brief paper, a ten-page assignment could require a more detailed outline. Use the method that is most productive for you. Whatever the length of the essay, your presentation must be in a coherent and logical order that allows your reader to follow the argument and evaluate the evidence. The quality of your reading can be demonstrated only by the quality of your writing.

WRITING A DRAFT

The time for sharpening pencils, arranging your desk, and doing almost anything else instead of writing has ended. The first draft will appear on the page only if you stop avoiding the inevitable and sit, stand up, or lie down to write. It makes no difference how you write, just so you do. Now that you have developed a topic into a tentative thesis, you can assemble your notes and begin to flesh out whatever outline you have made.

Be flexible. Your outline should smoothly conduct you from one point to the next, but do not permit it to railroad you. If a relevant and important idea occurs to you now, work it into the draft. By using the first draft as a means of thinking about what you want to say, you will very likely discover more than your notes originally suggested. Plenty of good writers don't use outlines at all but discover ordering principles as they write. Do not attempt to compose a perfectly correct draft the first time around. Grammar, punctuation, and spelling can wait until you revise. Concentrate on what you are saying. Good writing most often occurs when you are in hot pursuit of an idea rather than in a nervous search for errors.

To make revising easier, leave wide margins and extra space between lines so that you can easily add words, sentences, and corrections. Write on only one side of the paper. Your pages will be easier to keep track of that way, and, if you have to clip a paragraph to place it elsewhere, you will not lose any writing on the other side.

If you are working on a word processor, you can take advantage of its capacity to make additions and deletions as well as move entire paragraphs by making just a few simple keyboard commands. Some software programs can also check spelling and certain grammatical elements in your writing. It's worth remembering, however, that though a clean copy fresh off a printer may look terrific, it will read only as well as the thinking and writing that have gone into it. Many writers prudently store their data on disks and print their pages each time they finish a draft to avoid losing any material because of power failures or other problems. These printouts are also easier to read than the screen when you work on revisions.

Once you have a first draft on paper, you can delete material that is unrelated to your thesis and add material necessary to illustrate your points and make your paper convincing. The student who wrote "Disembodied Images in 'The Love Song of J. Alfred Prufrock'" (p. 590) wisely dropped a paragraph that questioned whether Prufrock displays chauvinistic attitudes toward women. Although this could be an interesting issue, it has nothing to do with the thesis, which explains how the images reflect Prufrock's inability to make a meaningful connection to his world.

Remember that your initial draft is only that. You should go through the paper many times — and then again — working to substantiate and clarify your ideas. You may even end up with several entire versions of the paper. Rewrite. The sentences within each paragraph should be related to a single topic. Transitions should connect one paragraph to the next so that there are no abrupt or confusing shifts. Awkward or wordy phrasing or unclear sentences and paragraphs should be mercilessly poked and prodded into shape.

Writing the Introduction and Conclusion

After you have clearly and adequately developed the body of your paper, pay particular attention to the introductory and concluding paragraphs. It's probably best to write the introduction — at least the final version of it — last, after you know precisely what you are introducing. Because this paragraph is crucial for generating interest in the topic, it should engage the reader and provide a sense of what the paper is about. There is no formula for writing effective introductory paragraphs, because each writing situation is different — depending on the audience, topic, and approach — but if you pay attention to the introductions of the essays you read, you will notice a variety of possibilities. The introductory paragraph to the Prufrock paper, for example, is a straightforward explanation of why the disembodied images are important for understanding Prufrock's character. The rest of the paper then offers evidence to support this point.

Concluding paragraphs demand equal attention because they leave the reader with a final impression. The conclusion should provide a sense of closure instead of starting a new topic or ending abruptly. In the final paragraph about the disembodied images in "Prufrock" the student explains their significance in characterizing Prufrock's inability to think of himself or others as complete and whole human beings. We now see that the images of eyes, arms, and claws are reflections of the fragmentary nature of Prufrock and his world. Of course, the body of your paper is the most important part of your presentation, but do remember that first and last impressions have a powerful impact on readers.

Using Quotations

Quotations can be a valuable means of marshaling evidence to illustrate and support your ideas. A judicious use of quoted material will make your points clearer and more convincing. Here are some guidelines that should help you use quotations effectively.

1. Brief quotations (four lines or fewer of prose or three lines or fewer of poetry) should be carefully introduced and integrated into the text of your paper with quotation marks around them.

```
According to the narrator, Bertha "had a reputation for
strictness." He tells us that she always "wore dark
clothes, dressed her hair simply, and expected contrition
and obedience from her pupils."
```

For brief poetry quotations, use a slash to indicate a division between lines.

```
The concluding lines of Blake's "The Tyger" pose a disturb-
ing question: "What immortal hand or eye / Dare frame thy
fearful symmetry?"
```

Lengthy quotations should be separated from the text of your paper. More than three lines of poetry should be double spaced and centered on the page. More than four lines of prose should be double spaced and indented ten spaces from the left margin, with the right margin the same as for the text. Do *not* use quotation marks for the passage; the indentation indicates that the passage is a quotation. Lengthy quotations should not be used in place of your own writing. Use them only if they are absolutely necessary.

2. If any words are added to a quotation, use brackets to distinguish your addition from the original source.

```
"He [Young Goodman Brown] is portrayed as self-righteous
and disillusioned."
```

Any words inside quotation marks and not in brackets must be precisely those of the author. Brackets can also be used to change the grammatical structure of a quotation so that it fits into your sentence.

```
Smith argues that Chekhov "present[s] the narrator in an
ambivalent light."
```

If you drop any words from the source, use an ellipsis (three spaced periods) to indicate the omission.

```
"Early to bed . . . makes a man healthy, wealthy, and wise."
```

Use an ellipsis following a period to indicate an omission at the end of a sentence.

```
"Early to bed and early to rise makes a man healthy. . . ."
```

Use a single line of spaced periods to indicate the omission of a line or more of poetry or more than one paragraph of prose.

```
Nothing would sleep in that cellar, dank as a ditch,
Bulbs broke out of boxes hunting for chinks in the dark,
. . . . . . . . . . . . . . . . . . . . . . . . . . . .
```

```
Nothing would give up life:
Even the dirt kept breathing a small breath.
```

   3. You will be able to punctuate quoted material accurately and confidently if you observe these conventions.
Place commas and periods inside quotation marks.

```
"Even the dirt," Roethke insists, "kept breathing a small
breath."
```

Even though a comma does not appear after "dirt" in the original quotation, it is placed inside the quotation mark. The exception to this rule occurs when a parenthetical reference to a source follows the quotation.

```
"Even the dirt," Roethke insists, "kept breathing a small
breath" (11).
```

Punctuation marks other than commas or periods go outside the quotation marks unless they are part of the material quoted.

```
What does Roethke mean when he writes that "the dirt kept
breathing a small breath"?

Yeats asked, "How can we know the dancer from the dance?"
```

REVISING AND EDITING

   Put some distance — a day or so if you can — between yourself and each draft of your paper. The phrase that seemed just right on Wednesday may be revealed as all wrong on Friday. You'll have a better chance of detecting lumbering sentences and thin paragraphs if you plan ahead and give yourself the time to read your paper from a fresh perspective. Through the process of revision, you can transform a competent paper into an excellent one.

   Begin by asking yourself if your approach to the topic requires any rethinking. Is the argument carefully thought out and logically presented? Are there any gaps in the presentation? How well is the paper organized? Do the paragraphs lead into one another? Does the body of the paper deliver what the thesis promises? Is the interpretation sound? Are any relevant and important elements of the work ignored or distorted to advance the thesis? Are the points supported with evidence? These large questions should be addressed before you focus on more detailed matters. If you uncover serious problems as a result of considering these questions, you'll probably have quite a lot of rewriting to do, but at least you will have the opportunity to correct the problems — even if doing so takes several drafts.

   A useful technique for spotting awkward or unclear moments in the paper is to read it aloud. You might also try having a friend read it aloud to you. If your handwriting is legible, your friend's reading — perhaps accompanied by hesitations and puzzled expressions — could alert you to passages that need reworking. Having identified problems, you can readily correct them on a word processor or on the draft provided you've skipped lines and used wide margins. The final draft you hand in should be neat and carefully proofread for any inadvertent errors.

The following checklist offers questions to ask about your paper as you revise and edit it. Most of these questions will be familiar to you; however, if you need help with any of them, ask your instructor or review the appropriate section in a composition handbook.

Revision Checklist

1. Is the topic manageable? Is it too narrow or too broad?
2. Is the thesis clear? Is it based on a careful reading of the work?
3. Is the paper logically organized? Does it have a firm sense of direction?
4. Is your argument persuasive? Do you use evidence from the text to support your main points?
5. Should any material be deleted? Do any important points require further illustration or evidence?
6. Does the opening paragraph introduce the topic in an interesting manner?
7. Are the paragraphs developed, unified, and coherent? Are any too short or long?
8. Are there transitions linking the paragraphs?
9. Does the concluding paragraph provide a sense of closure?
10. Is the tone appropriate? Is it unduly flippant or pretentious?
11. Is the title engaging and suggestive?
12. Are the sentences clear, concise, and complete?
13. Are simple, complex, and compound sentences used for variety?
14. Have technical terms been used correctly? Are you certain of the meanings of all the words in the paper? Are they spelled correctly?
15. Have you documented any information borrowed from books, articles, or other sources? Have you quoted too much instead of summarizing or paraphrasing secondary material?
16. Have you used a standard format for citing sources (see p. 606)?
17. Have you followed your instructor's guidelines for the manuscript format of the final draft?
18. Have you carefully proofread the final draft?

When you proofread your final draft, you may find a few typographical errors that must be corrected but do not warrant retyping an entire page. Provided there are not more than a handful of such errors throughout the page, they can be corrected as shown in the following passage. This example condenses a short paper's worth of errors; no single passage should be this shabby in your essay.

To add a letter or word, use a caret on the line where the
addition is needed. To delete a word draw a single line
                ^
through ~~through~~ it. Run-on words are separated by a verti-
cal|line, and inadvertent spaces are closed like t͜his.
Transposed letters are indicated this wa̷y̷ New paragraphs
are noted with the sign ¶ in front of where the next
paragraph is to begin.¶Unless you . . .

These sorts of errors can be minimized by using correction fluid or tape while you type. If you use a word processor, you can eliminate such errors completely by simply entering corrections as you proofread on the screen.

MANUSCRIPT FORM

The novelist and poet Peter De Vries once observed in his characteristically humorous way that he very much enjoyed writing but that he couldn't bear the "paper work." Behind this playful pun is a half-serious impatience with the mechanics of it all. You may feel some of that too, but this is not the time to allow a thoughtful, carefully revised paper to trip over minor details that can be easily accommodated. The final draft you hand in to your instructor should not only read well but look neat. If your instructor does not provide specific instructions concerning the format for the paper, follow these guidelines.

1. Papers (particularly long ones) should be typed on 8½ × 11-inch paper in double space. Avoid transparent paper such as onionskin; it is difficult to read and write comments on. The ribbon should be dark and the letters on the machine clear. If you compose on a word processor with a dot-matrix printer, be certain that the dots are close enough together to be legible. And don't forget to separate your pages and remove the strips of holes on each side of the pages if your printer uses a continuous paper feed. If your instructor accepts handwritten papers, write legibly in ink on only one side of a wide-lined page.

2. Use a one-inch margin at the top, bottom, and sides of each page. Unless you are instructed to include a separate title page, type your name, instructor's name, course number and section, and date on separate lines one inch below the upper-left corner of the first page. Double space between these lines and then center the title below the date. Do not underline or put quotation marks around your paper's title, but do use quotation marks around the titles of poems, short stories, or other brief works, and underline the titles of books and plays (a sample paper title: "Mending Wall" and Other Boundaries in Frost's North of Boston). Begin the text of your paper two spaces below the title. If you have used secondary sources, center the heading "Notes" or "Works Cited" one inch from the top of a separate page and then double space between it and the entries.

3. Number each page consecutively, beginning with page 2, a half inch from the top of the page in the upper-right corner.

4. Gather the pages with a paper clip rather than staples, folders, or some other device. That will make it easier for your instructor to handle the paper.

TYPES OF WRITING ASSIGNMENTS

The types of papers most frequently assigned in literature classes are explication, analysis, and comparison and contrast. Most writing about literature involves some combination of these skills. This section includes a sample explication, an analysis, and a comparison and contrast paper. For a sample research paper that demonstrates a variety of strategies for documenting outside sources, see page 613. For other examples of student papers, see pages 585, 590, and 596.

Explication

The purpose of this approach to a literary work is to make the implicit explicit. *Explication* is a detailed explanation of a passage of poetry or prose. Because explication is an intensive examination of a text line by line, it is mostly used to interpret a short poem in its entirety or a brief passage from a long poem, short story, or play. Explication can be used in any kind of paper when you want to be specific about how a writer achieves a certain effect. An explication pays careful attention to language: the connotations of words, allusions, figurative language, irony, symbol, rhythm, sound, and so on. These elements are examined in relation to one another and to the overall effect and meaning of the work.

The simplest way to organize an explication is to move through the passage line by line, explaining whatever seems significant. It is wise to avoid, however, an assembly-line approach that begins each sentence with "In line one. . . ." Instead, organize your paper in whatever way best serves your thesis. You might find that the right place to start is with the final lines, working your way back to the beginning of the poem or passage. The following sample explication on Emily Dickinson's "There's a certain Slant of light" does just that. The student's opening paragraph refers to the final line of the poem in order to present her thesis. She explains that though the poem begins with an image of light, it is not a bright or cheery poem but one concerned with "the look of Death." Since the last line prompted her thesis, that is where she begins the explication.

You might also find it useful to structure a paper by discussing various elements of literature, so that you have a paragraph on connotative words followed by one on figurative language and so on. However your paper is organized, keep in mind that the aim of an explication is not simply to summarize the passage but to comment on the effects and meanings produced by the author's use of language in it. An effective explication (the Latin word *explicare* means "to unfold") displays a text to reveal how it works and what it signifies. Although writing an explication requires some patience and sensitivity, it is an excellent method for coming to understand and appreciate the elements and qualities that constitute literary art.

A STUDENT EXPLICATION

The sample paper by Bonnie Katz is the result of an assignment calling for an explication of about 750 words on any poem by Emily Dickinson. Katz selected "There's a certain Slant of light."

EMILY DICKINSON (1830–1886)
There's a certain Slant of light

c. 1861

There's a certain Slant of light,
Winter Afternoons —
That oppresses, like the Heft
Of Cathedral Tunes —

Heavenly Hurt, it gives us — 5
We can find no scar,
But internal difference,
Where the Meanings, are —

None may teach it — Any —
'Tis the Seal Despair — 10
An imperial affliction
Sent us of the Air —

When it comes, the Landscape listens —
Shadows — hold their breath —
When it goes, 'tis like the Distance 15
On the look of Death —

This essay comments on every line of the poem and provides a coherent reading that relates each line to the speaker's intense awareness of death. Although the essay discusses each stanza in the order that it appears, the introductory paragraph provides a brief overview explaining how the poem's images contribute to its total meaning. In addition, the student does not hesitate to discuss a line out of sequence when it can be usefully connected to another phrase. This is especially apparent in the third paragraph, in her discussion of stanzas 2 and 3. The final paragraph describes some of the formal elements of the poem. It might be argued that this discussion could have been integrated into the previous paragraphs rather than placed at the end, but the student does make a connection in her concluding sentence between the pattern of language and its meaning.

Several other matters are worth noticing. The student works quotations into her own sentences to support her points. She quotes exactly as the words appear in the poem, even Dickinson's irregular use of capital letters.

(Text continues on page 588.)

Bonnie Katz

Professor Quiello

English 109-2

October 26, 19--

A Reading of Dickinson's

"There's a certain Slant of light"

Because Emily Dickinson did not provide titles for her poetry, editors follow the customary practice of using the first line of a poem as its title. However, a more appropriate title for "There's a certain Slant of light," one that suggests what the speaker in the poem is most concerned about, can be drawn from the poem's last line, which ends with "the look of Death." Although the first line begins with an image of light, nothing bright, carefree, or cheerful appears in the poem. Instead, the predominant mood and images are darkened by a sense of despair resulting from the speaker's awareness of death.

In the first stanza, the "certain Slant of light" is associated with "Winter Afternoons," a phrase that connotes the end of a day, a season, and even life itself. Such light is hardly warm or comforting. Not a ray or beam, this slanting light suggests something unusual or distorted and creates in the speaker a certain slant on life that is consistent with the cold, dark mood that winter afternoons can produce. Like the speaker, most of us have seen and felt this sort of light: it "oppresses" and pervades our sense of things when we encounter it. Dickinson uses the senses of hearing and touch as well as sight to describe the overwhelming oppressiveness that the speaker experiences. The light is transformed into sound by a simile that tells us it is "like the Heft / Of Cathedral Tunes." Moreover, the "Heft" of that sound--the

slow, solemn measures of tolling church bells and organ
music--weighs heavily on our spirits. Through the use of
shifting imagery, Dickinson evokes a kind of spiritual
numbness that we keenly feel and perceive through our
senses.

By associating the winter light with "Cathedral
Tunes," Dickinson lets us know that the speaker is concerned about more than the weather. Whatever it is that
"oppresses" is related by connotation to faith, mortality,
and God. The second and third stanzas offer several suggestions about this connection. The pain caused by the
light is a "Heavenly Hurt." This "imperial affliction /
Sent us of the Air" apparently comes from God above, and
yet it seems to be part of the very nature of life. The
oppressiveness we feel is in the air, and it can neither
be specifically identified at this point in the poem nor
be eliminated, for "None may teach it--Any." All we can
know is that existence itself seems depressing under the
weight of this "Seal [of] Despair." The impression left
by this "Seal" is stamped within the mind or soul rather
than externally. "We can find no scar," but once experienced this oppressiveness challenges our faith in life and
its "Meanings."

The final stanza does not explain what those "Meanings" are, but it does make clear that the speaker is
acutely aware of death. As the winter daylight fades,
Dickinson projects the speaker's anxiety onto the surrounding landscape and shadows, which will soon be
engulfed by the darkness that follows this light: "The
Landscape listens-- / Shadows--hold their breath." This
image firmly aligns the winter light in the first stanza
with darkness. Paradoxically, the light in this poem

illuminates the nature of darkness. Tension is released when the light is completely gone, but what remains is the despair that the "imperial affliction" has imprinted on the speaker's sensibilities, for it is "like the Distance / On the look of Death." There can be no relief from what that "certain Slant of light" has revealed, because what has been experienced is permanent--like the fixed stare in the eyes of someone who is dead.

The speaker's awareness of death is conveyed in a thoughtful, hushed tone. The lines are filled with fluid l and smooth s sounds that are appropriate for the quiet, meditative voice in the poem. The voice sounds tentative and uncertain--perhaps a little frightened. This seems to be reflected in the slightly irregular meter of the lines. The stanzas are trochaic with the second and fourth lines of each stanza having five syllables, but no stanza is identical because each works a slight variation on the first stanza's seven syllables in the first and third lines. The rhymes also combine exact patterns with variations. The first and third lines of each stanza are not exact rhymes, but the second and fourth lines are exact so that the paired words are more closely related: Afternoons, Tunes; scar, are; Despair, Air; and breath, Death. There is a pattern to the poem, but it is unobtrusively woven into the speaker's voice in much the same way that "the look of Death" is subtly present in the images and language of the poem.

When something is added to a quotation to clarify it, it is enclosed in brackets so that the essayist's words will not be mistaken for the poet's: "Seal [of] Despair." A slash is used to separate line divisions as in "imperial affliction / Sent us of the Air." And, finally, because the essay focuses on a short poem, it is not necessary to include line numbers, though they would be required in a study of a longer work.

Analysis

The preceding sample essay shows how an explication examines in detail the important elements in a work and relates them to the whole. An analysis, however, usually examines only a single element — such as diction, character, point of view, symbol, tone, or irony — and relates it to the entire work. An analytic topic separates the work into parts and focuses on a specific one; you might consider "Point of View in 'The Love Song of J. Alfred Prufrock,' " "Patterns of Rhythm in Robert Browning's 'My Last Duchess,' " or "Irony in 'The Road Not Taken.' " The specific element must be related to the work as a whole or it will appear irrelevant. It is not enough to point out that there are many death images in Andrew Marvell's "To His Coy Mistress"; the images must somehow be connected to the poem's overall effect.

Whether an analytic paper is just a few pages or many, it cannot attempt to discuss everything about the work it is considering. Only those elements that are relevant to the topic can be treated. This kind of focusing makes the topic manageable; this is why most papers that you write will probably be some form of analysis. Explications are useful for a short passage, but a line-by-line commentary on a story, play, or long poem simply isn't practical. Because analysis allows you to consider the central effect or meaning of an entire work by studying a single important element, it is a useful and common approach to longer works.

A SAMPLE ANALYSIS: DISEMBODIED IMAGES IN "THE LOVE SONG OF J. ALFRED PRUFROCK"

Beth Hart's paper analyzes some of the images in T. S. Eliot's "The Love Song of J. Alfred Prufrock" (the poem appears on p. 371). The assignment simply called for an essay of approximately 750 words on a poem written in the twentieth century. The approach was left to the student.

The idea for this essay began with Hart asking herself why there are so many fragmentary, disjointed images in the poem. The initial answer to this question was that "The disjointed images are important for understanding Prufrock's character." This answer was the rough beginning of a tentative thesis. What still had to be explained, though, was how the images are important. To determine the significance of the disjointed images, Hart jotted down some notes based on her underlinings and marginal notations.

Prufrock	Images
odd name--nervous, timid?	fog
"indecisions," "revisions"	lost, wandering
confessional tone, self	watching eyes
conscious	ladies arms
"bald spot"	polite talk, meaningless talk
"afraid"	"ragged claws" that scuttle
questioning, tentative	oppressive
"I am not Prince Hamlet"	distorted
"I grow old"	weary longing
wake--to drown	entrapped--staircase

From these notes Hart saw that the images — mostly fragmented and disjointed — suggested something about Prufrock's way of describing himself and his world. This insight led eventually to the final version of her thesis statement: "Eliot's use of frightening disembodied images such as eyes, arms, and claws reflects Prufrock's terror at having to face a world to which he feels no meaningful connection." Her introductory paragraph concludes with this sentence so that her reader can fully comprehend why she then discusses the images of eyes, arms, and claws that follow.

The remaining paragraphs present details that explain the significance of the images of eyes in the second paragraph, the arms in the third, the claws in the fourth, and in the final paragraph all three images are the basis for concluding that Prufrock's vision of the world is disconnected and disjointed.

Hart's notes certainly do not constitute a formal outline, but they were useful to her in establishing a thesis and recognizing what elements of the poem she needed to cover in her discussion. Her essay is sharply focused, well-organized, and generally well written (though some readers might wish for a more engaging introductory paragraph that captures a glint of Prufrock's "bald spot" or some other small detail in order to generate some immediate interest in his character).

(Text continues on page 593.)

Beth Hart

Professor Lucas

English 110-3

March 30, 19--

Disembodied Images in

"The Love Song of J. Alfred Prufrock"

T. S. Eliot's poem "The Love Song of J. Alfred

Prufrock," addresses the dilemma of a man who finds himself

trapped on the margins of the social world, unable to make

any meaningful interpersonal contact because of his deep-

seated fear of rejection and misunderstanding. Prufrock

feels acutely disconnected from society, which makes him so

self-conscious that he is frightened into a state of social

paralysis. His overwhelming self-consciousness, disillu-

sionment with social circles, and lack of connection with

those around him are revealed through Eliot's use of frag-

mented imagery. Many of the predominant images are disem-

bodied pieces of a whole, revealing that Prufrock sees the

world not as fully whole or complete, but as disjointed,

fragmented parts of the whole. Eliot's use of frightening

disembodied images such as eyes, arms, and claws reflects

Prufrock's terror at having to face a world to which he

feels no meaningful connection.

Eliot suggests Prufrock's acute self-consciousness

through the fragmentary image of "eyes." Literally, these

eyes merely represent the people who surround Prufrock,

but this disembodied image reveals his obsessive fear of

being watched and judged by others. His confession that "I

have known the eyes already, known them all-- / The eyes

that fix you in a formulated phrase" (lines 55-56) sug-

gests how deeply he resists being watched, and how uncom-

fortable he is with himself, both externally--referring in

part to his sensitivity to the "bald spot in the middle
of my hair" (40)--and internally--his relentless self-
questioning " 'Do I dare?' and, 'Do I dare?' " (38).
The disembodied eyes force the reader to recognize the
oppression of being closely watched, and so to share in
Prufrock's painful self-awareness. Prufrock's belief that
the eyes have the terrifying and violent power to trap him
like a specimen insect "pinned and wriggling on the wall"
(58), to be scrutinized in its agony, further reveals the
terror of the floating, accusatory image of the eyes.

   The disembodied image of "arms" also reflects
Prufrock's distorted vision of both himself and others
around him. His acknowledgment that he has "known the arms
already, known them all-- / Arms that are braceleted and
white and bare" (62-63) relates to the image of the eyes,
yet focuses on a very different aspect of the people surrounding Prufrock. Clearly, the braceleted arms belong to
women, and that these arms are attached to a perfumed dress
(65) suggests that these arms belong to upper-class, privileged women. This is partially what makes the disembodied
image of the arms so frightening for Prufrock: he is incapable of connecting with a woman the way he, as a man, is
expected to. The image of the arms, close enough to Prufrock
to reveal their down of "light brown hair" (64), suggests
the potential for reaching out and possibly touching
Prufrock. The terrified self-consciousness that the image
elicits in him leads Prufrock to wish that he could leave
his own body and take on the characteristics of yet another
disembodied image.

   Prufrock's despairing declaration, "I should have been
a pair of ragged claws / Scuttling across the floors of
silent seas" (73-74), offers yet another example of his

vision of the world as fragmented and incomplete. The "pair of claws" that he longs to be not only connotes a complete separation from the earthly life that he finds so threatening, so painful, and so meaningless, but also suggests an isolation from others that would allow Prufrock some freedom and relief from social pressures. However, this image of the claws as a form of salvation for Prufrock in fact offers little suggestion of actual progress from his present circumstances; crabs can only "scuttle" from side to side and are incapable of moving directly forward or backward. Similarly, Prufrock is trapped in a situation in which he feels incapable of moving either up or down the staircase (39). Thus, this disembodied image of the claws serves to remind the reader that Prufrock is genuinely trapped in a life that offers him virtually no hope of real connection or wholeness.

The fragmented imagery that pervades "The Love Song of J. Alfred Prufrock" emphasizes and clarifies Prufrock's vision of the world as disconnected and disjointed. The fact that Prufrock thinks of people in terms of their individual component parts (specifically, eyes and arms) suggests his lack of understanding of people as whole and complete beings. This reflects his vision of himself as a fragmentary self, culminating in his wish to be not a whole crab, but merely a pair of disembodied claws. By use of these troubling images Eliot infuses the poem with the pain of Prufrock's self-awareness and his confusion at the lack of wholeness he feels, in his world.

Hart's essay suggests a number of useful guidelines for analytic papers.

1. Only those points related to the thesis are included. In another type of paper the significance of Eliot's epigraph from Dante, for example, might have been more important than the imagery.
2. The analysis keeps the images in focus while at the same time indicating how they are significant in revealing Prufrock's character.
3. The title is a useful lead into the paper; it provides a sense of what the topic is.
4. The introductory paragraph is direct and clearly indicates the paper will argue that the images serve to reveal Prufrock's character.
5. Brief quotations are deftly incorporated into the text of the paper to illustrate points. We are told what we need to know about the poem as evidence is provided to support ideas. There is no unnecessary summary.
6. The paragraphs are well developed, unified, and coherent. They flow naturally from one to another. Notice, for example, the smooth transition worked into the final sentence of the third paragraph and the first sentence of the fourth paragraph.
7. Hart makes excellent use of her careful reading and notes by finding revealing connections among the details she has observed.
8. As events in the poem are described, the present tense is used. This avoids awkward tense shifts and lends an immediacy to the discussion.
9. The concluding paragraph establishes the significance of why the images should be seen as a reflection of Prufrock's character and provides a sense of closure by relating the images of Prufrock's disjointed world with the images of his fragmentary self.
10. In short, Hart has demonstrated that she has read the work closely, has understood the function of the images in the revelation of Prufrock's sensibilities, and has argued her thesis convincingly by using evidence from the poem.

Comparison and Contrast

Another essay assignment in literature courses often combined with analytic topics is the type that requires you to write about similarities and differences between or within works. You might be asked to discuss "How Sounds Express Meanings in May Swenson's 'A Nosty Fright' and Lewis Carroll's 'Jabberwocky,' " or "Love and Hate in Sylvia Plath's 'Daddy.' " A *comparison* of either topic would emphasize their similarities, while a *contrast* would stress their differences. It is possible, of course, to include both perspectives in a paper if you find significant likenesses and differences. A comparison of Andrew Marvell's "To His Coy Mistress" and Richard Wilbur's "A Late Aubade" would, for example, yield similarities, because each poem describes a man urging his lover to make the most of their precious time together; however, important differences also exist in the tone and theme of each poem that would constitute a contrast. (You should, incidentally, be aware that the term *comparison* is sometimes used inclusively to refer to both similarities and differences. If you are assigned a comparison of two works, be sure that you understand what your instructor's expectations are; you may be required to include both approaches in the essay.)

When you choose your own topic, the paper will be more successful — more manageable — if you write on works that can be meaningfully related to each other. Although Robert Herrick's "To the Virgins, to Make Much of Time" and T. S. Eliot's "The Love Song of J. Alfred Prufrock" both have something to do with hesitation, the likelihood of anyone making a connection between the two that reveals something interesting and important is remote — though perhaps not impossible if the topic were conceived imaginatively and tactfully. Choose a topic that encourages you to ask significant questions about each work; the purpose of a comparison or contrast is to understand the works more clearly for having examined them together.

Choose works to compare or contrast that intersect with each other in some significant way. They may, for example, be written by the same author or about the same subject. Perhaps you can compare their use of some technique, such as irony or point of view. Regardless of the specific topic, be sure to have a thesis that allows you to organize your paper around a central idea that argues a point about the two works. If you merely draw up a list of similarities or differences without a thesis in mind, your paper will be little more than a series of observations with no apparent purpose. Keep in the foreground of your thinking what the comparison or contrast reveals about the works.

There is no single way to organize comparative papers since each topic is likely to have its own particular issues to resolve, but it is useful to be aware of two basic patterns that can be helpful with a comparison, a contrast, or a combination of both. One method that can be effective for relatively short papers consists of dividing the paper in half, first discussing one work and then the other. Here, for example, is a partial informal outline for a discussion of Hughes's "Let America Be America Again" and Laviera's "AmeRícan"; the topic is a comparison and contrast:

```
"Two Views of America by Hughes and Laviera"
1. "Let America Be America Again"
     a. Diction
     b. Images
     c. Allusions
     d. Themes
2. "AmeRícan"
     a. Diction
     b. Images
     c. Allusions
     d. Themes
```

This organizational strategy can be effective provided that the second part of the paper combines the discussion of "AmeRícan" with references to "Let

America Be America Again" so that the thesis is made clear and the paper unified without being repetitive. If the two poems were treated entirely separately, then the discussion would be merely parallel rather than integrated. In a lengthy paper, this organization probably would not work well because a reader would have difficulty remembering the points made in the first half as he or she reads on.

Thus for a longer paper it is usually better to create a more integrated structure that discusses both works as you take up each item in your outline. Here is the second basic pattern using the elements in partial outline just cited.

```
1. Diction
     a. "Let America Be America Again"
     b. "AmeRícan"
2. Images
     a. "Let America Be America Again"
     b. "AmeRícan"
3. Allusions
     a. "Let America Be America Again"
     b. "AmeRícan"
4. Themes
     a. "Let America Be America Again"
     b. "AmeRícan"
```

This pattern allows you to discuss any number of topics without requiring that your reader recall what you first said about the diction of "America" before you discuss the diction of "AmeRícan" many pages later. However you structure your comparison or contrast paper, make certain that a reader can follow its elements and keep track of its thesis.

A SAMPLE COMPARISON: MARVELL AND ACKERMAN SEIZE THE DAY

The following paper is in response to an assignment that required a comparison and contrast — about 1,000 words — of two assigned poems. The student chose to write an analysis of two very different *carpe diem* poems.

Although these two poems are fairly lengthy, Stephanie Smith's brief analysis of them is satisfying because she focuses on the male and female *carpe diem* voices of Andrew Marvell's "To His Coy Mistress" (p. 57) and Diane Ackerman's "A Fine, a Private Place" (p. 61). After introducing the topic in the first paragraph, she takes up the two poems in a pattern similar to the first outline suggested for "Two Views of America by Hughes and Laviera." Notice how Smith works in subsequent references to Marvell's poem as she discusses Ackerman's so that her treatment is integrated and we are reminded why she is comparing and contrasting the two works. Her final paragraph sums up her points without being repetitive and reiterates the thesis with which she began.

Stephanie Smith

English 109-10

Professor Monroe

April 2, 19--

Marvell and Ackerman Seize the Day

In her 1983 poem "A Fine, A Private Place," Diane Ackerman never mentions Andrew Marvell's 1681 poem "To His
Coy Mistress." However, her one-line allusion to Marvell's famous argument to his lover is all the reference
she needs. Through a contemporary lens, she firmly qualifies Marvell's seventeenth-century masculine perspective.
Marvell's speaker attempts to woo a young woman and convince her to have sexual relations with him. His seize-
the-day rhetoric argues that "his mistress" should let
down her conventional purity and enjoy the moment, his
logic being that we are grave-bound anyway, so why not?
Although his poetic pleading is effective, both stylisti-
cally and argumentatively, Marvell's speaker obviously
assumes that the coy mistress will succumb to his grasps
at her sexuality. Further, and most important for Ackerman, the speaker takes for granted that the female must be
persuaded to love. His smooth talk leaves no room for a
feminine perspective, be it a slap in the face or a sharing of his carpe diem attitudes. Ackerman accommodates
Marvell's masculine speaker but also deftly takes poetic
license in the cause of female freedom and sensuously lays
out her own fine and private place. Through describing a
personal sexual encounter both sensually and erotically,
Ackerman's female speaker demonstrates that women have
just as many lustful urges as the men who would seduce
them; she presents sex as neither solely a male quest nor
a female sacrifice. "A Fine, A Private Place" takes a

female perspective on sex, and enthusiastically enjoys the pleasure of it.

"To His Coy Mistress" is in a regular rhyme scheme, as each line rhymes with the next--almost like a compilation of couplets. And this, accompanied by traditional iambic tetrameter, lays the foundation for a forcefully flowing speech, a command for the couple to just do it. By the end of the poem the speaker seems to expect his mistress to capitulate. Marvell's speaker declares at the start that if eternity were upon them, he would not mind putting sex aside and paying her unending homage. "Had we but world enough, and time, / This coyness, lady, were no crime. / We would sit down, and think which way / To walk, and pass our long love's day" (lines 1-4). He proclaims he would love her "ten years before the Flood" (8) and concedes that she "should, if you please, refuse / Till the conversion of the Jews" (9-10). This eternal love-land expands as Marvell asserts that his "vegetable love should grow / Vaster than empires, and more slow" (11-12). Every part of her body would be admired for an entire "age" because "lady, you deserve this state, / Nor would I love at lower rate" (19-20). He would willingly wait but, alas, circumstances won't let him. She'll have to settle for the here and now, and he must show her that life is not an eternity but rather an alarm clock.

The speaker laments that "at my back I always hear / Time's wingèd chariot hurrying near" (21-22). He then cleverly draws a picture of what exactly eternity does have in store for them, namely barren "Deserts" where her "beauty shall no more be found" (25) while "worms shall try / That long preserved virginity" (27-28) and her "quaint honor turn to dust" (29). This death imagery is

meant to frighten her for not having lived enough. He
astutely concedes that "The grave's a fine and private
place, / But none, I think, do there embrace" (31-32),
thereby making even more vivid the nightmare he has just
laid before her. Although he must make his grim argument,
he does not want to dampen the mood, so he quickly returns
to her fair features.

    "Now," the speaker proclaims, "while the youthful hue /
Sits on thy skin like morning dew, / And while thy willing soul transpires / At every pore with instant fires, /
Now let us sport us while we may" (33-37). The speaker
has already made the decision for her. Through sex,
their energies will become one--they will "roll" their
"strength" and "sweetness up into one ball" (41) as they
"tear" their "pleasures with rough strife" (43). If the
two of them cannot have eternity and make the "sun /
Stand still" (45-46), then they will seize the day, combine and
celebrate their humanity, and "make [the sun] run" (46).
The speaker makes a vivid case in favor of living for the
moment. His elaborate images of the devotion his mistress
deserves, the inevitability of death, and the vivacious-
ness of human life are compelling. Three hundred years
later, however, Diane Ackerman demonstrates that women no
longer need this lesson, because they share the same
desires.

    Ackerman's title is taken directly from "To His Coy
Mistress." This poet's fine and private place is not the
grave, as it was in Marvell's poetic persuasion, but
rather her underwater sexual encounter. Ackerman's familiarity with Marvell informs us that she knows about death
and its implications. More importantly, her speaker needs

no rationale to live fully, she just does. She has sex on her own, willingly, knowingly, and thoroughly.

Unlike "To His Coy Mistress," the poem has no rhyme scheme and has little meter or conventional form. The free verse tells the sexual story in an unconfined, open way. The poem flows together with sensual, sexual images drawn from the mystical, vibrant, undersea world. The speaker and her lover float "under the blue horizon / where long sea fingers / parted like beads / hitched in the doorway / of an opium den" (2-6). Whereas Marvell's lovers race against time, Ackerman's seem to bathe in it. Within this sultry setting the "canyons mazed the deep / reef with hollows, / cul-de-sacs, and narrow boudoirs" (7-10) that evoke erotic images. Her lover's "stroking her arm / with a marine feather / slobbery as aloe pulp" (12-14) constitutes foreplay, and when "the octopus / in his swimsuit / stretch[es] one tentacle / ripple[s] its silky bag" (15-18), she becomes a willing partner. In this "lusty dream" (58), "her hips rolled" (59), "her eyes swam / and chest began to heave" (61-62), and the sea also becomes a willing partner in their love-making as the underwater waves help "drive [his brine] / through petals / delicate as anemone veils / to the dark purpose / of a conch-shaped womb" (68-72).

After "panting ebbed" (75), they return to "shallower realms, / heading back toward / the boat's even keel" (81-83), away from the sensual, wild, sea-world in which they reveled. However, the speaker has not literally or figuratively exhausted the waters yet. The "ocean still petted her / cell by cell, murmuring / along her legs and neck / caressing her / with pale, endless arms" (84-88).

Though she emerges from the water and the encounter, the experience stays with her as a satisfying memory.

Her sensual memories of the encounter allow her to savor the moment, in contrast to Marvell's speaker, whose desperate, urgent tone is filled with tension rather than the relief of consummation. In the final section of the poem (106-15), we see that the speaker's sexual encounter is an experience that stays with her "miles / and fathoms away." The erotic language of the sea is in her own voice as she looks out at "minnow snowflakes" while "holding a sponge / idly under [a] tap-gush." As water seems to cascade all around her, the memory of her underwater experience surfaces in the sensuous image of "sinking her teeth / into the cleft / of a voluptuous peach." Ackerman's subject does not have to be persuaded by an excited man to be a sexual being; her sexuality seeps into every day of her life, and we marvel at the depth of her sensuality. Unlike Marvell's speaker, who remains eternally poised to "tear our pleasures," Ackerman's speaker is steeped in those pleasures.

17. The Literary Research Paper

A close reading of a primary source such as a short story, poem, or play can give insights into a work's themes and effects, but sometimes you will want to know more. A published commentary by a critic who knows the work well and is familiar with the author's life and times can provide insights that otherwise may not be available. Such comments and interpretations — known as *secondary sources* — are, of course, not a substitute for the work itself, but they often can take you into a work further than if you made the journey by yourself.

After imagination, good sense, and energy, perhaps the next most important quality for writing a research paper is the ability to organize material. A research paper on a literary topic requires a writer to take account of quite a lot at once: the text, ideas, sources, and documentation techniques all make demands on one's efforts to present a topic clearly and convincingly.

The following list should give you a sense of what goes into creating a research paper. Although some steps on the list can be folded into one another, they offer an overview of the work that will involve you.

1. Choosing a topic
2. Finding sources
3. Evaluating sources
4. Taking notes
5. Developing a thesis
6. Organizing an outline
7. Writing drafts
8. Revising
9. Documenting sources
10. Preparing the final draft and proofreading

Even if you have never written a research paper, you most likely have already had experience choosing a topic, developing a thesis, organizing an outline, and writing a draft that you then revised, proofread, and handed in. Those skills represent six of the ten items on the list. This chapter briefly reviews some of these steps and focuses on the remaining tasks, unique to research paper assignments.

CHOOSING A TOPIC

Chapter 16 discussed the importance of reading a work closely and taking careful notes as a means of generating topics for writing about literature. If you know a work well and record your understanding of it in notes, you'll have impressions and ideas to choose from for potential topics. You may find it useful to review the information on pages 567–570 before reading the advice about putting together a research paper in this chapter.

The student author of the sample research paper "Defining Identity in 'Mending Wall' " (p. 613) was asked to write a five-page paper that demonstrated some familiarity with published critical perspectives on a Robert Frost poem of her choice. Before looking into critical discussions of the poem, she read "Mending Wall" several times, taking notes and making comments in the margin of her textbook on each reading.

What prompted her choice of "Mending Wall" was a class discussion that focused on the poem's speaker's questioning the value and necessity of the wall in contrast to his neighbor's insistence upon it. At one point, however, the boundaries of the discussion opened up to the possibility that the wall is important to both characters in the poem rather than only the neighbor. It is, after all, the speaker, not the neighbor, who repairs the damage to the wall caused by hunters and who initiates the rebuilding of the wall. Why would he do that if he wanted the wall down? Only after having thoroughly examined the poem did the student go to the library to see what professional critics had to say about this question.

FINDING SOURCES

Whether your college library is large or small, its reference librarians can usually help you locate secondary sources about a particular work or author. Unless you choose a very recently published poem about which little or nothing has been written, you should be able to find commentaries about a literary work efficiently and quickly. Here are some useful reference sources that can help you to establish both an overview of a potential topic and a list of relevant books and articles. They are useful for topics on fiction and drama as well as poetry.

Annotated List of References

Baker, Nancy L. *A Research Guide for Undergraduate Students: English and American Literature.* 2nd ed. New York: MLA, 1985. Especially designed for students; a useful guide to reference sources.

Bryer, Jackson, ed. *Sixteen Modern American Authors: A Survey of Research and Criticism.* New York: Norton, 1973. Extensive bibliographic essays on Sherwood Anderson, Willa Cather, Hart Crane, Theodore Dreiser, T. S. Eliot, William Faulkner, F. Scott Fitzgerald, Robert Frost, Ernest Hemingway, Eugene O'Neill, Ezra Pound, Edwin Arlington Robinson, John Steinbeck, Wallace Stevens, William Carlos Williams, and Thomas Wolfe.

Corse, Larry B., and Sandra B. Corse. *Articles on American and British Literature: An Index to Selected Periodicals, 1950–1977.* Athens, OH: Swallow Press, 1981. Specifically designed for students using small college libraries.

Eddleman, Floyd E., ed. *American Drama Criticism: Interpretations, 1890–1977.* 2nd ed. Hamden, CT: Shoe String Press, 1979. Supplement 1984.

Elliot, Emory, et al. *Columbia Literary History of the United States.* New York: Columbia UP, 1988. This updates the discussions in Spiller (below) and reflects recent changes in the canon.

Harner, James L. *Literary Research Guide: A Guide to Reference Sources for the Study of Literature in English and Related Topics.* 2nd ed. New York: MLA, 1993. A selective but extensive annotated guide to important bibliographies, abstracts, data bases, histories, surveys, dictionaries, encyclopedias, and handbooks; an invaluable research tool with extensive, useful indexes.

Holman, C. Hugh, and William Harmon, *A Handbook to Literature.* 6th ed. New York: Macmillan, 1992. A thorough dictionary of literary terms that also provides brief, clear overviews of literary movements such as Romanticism.

Kuntz, Joseph M., and Nancy C. Martinez. *Poetry Explication: A Checklist of Interpretation since 1925 of British and American Poems Past and Present.* Boston: Hall, 1980.

MLA International Bibliography of Books and Articles on Modern Language and Literature. New York: MLA, 1921–. Compiled annually; a major source for articles and books.

The New Cambridge Bibliography of English Literature. 5 vols. Cambridge, Eng.: Cambridge UP, 1967–77. An important source on the literature from A.D. 600 to 1950.

The Oxford History of English Literature. 13 vols. Oxford, Eng.: Oxford UP, 1945–, in progress. The most comprehensive literary history.

The Penguin Companion to World Literature. 4 vols. New York: McGraw-Hill, 1969–71. Covers classical, Oriental, African, European, English, and American literature.

Preminger, Alex, and T. V. F. Brogan, eds. *The New Princeton Encyclopedia of Poetry and Poetics.* Princeton, NJ: Princeton UP, 1993. Includes entries on technical terms and poetic movements.

Rees, Robert, and Earl N. Harbert. *Fifteen American Authors before 1900: Bibliographic Essays on Research and Criticism.* Madison: U of Wisconsin P, 1971. Among the writers covered are Stephen Crane and Emily Dickinson.

Spiller, Robert E., et al. *Literary History of the United States.* 4th ed. 2 vols. New York: Macmillan, 1974. Coverage of literary movements and individual writers from colonial times to the 1960s.

Walker, Warren S. *Twentieth-Century Short Story Explication.* 3rd ed. Hamden, CT: Shoe String Press, 1977. A bibliography of criticism on short stories written since 1800; supplements appear every few years.

These sources are available in the reference sections of most college libraries; ask a reference librarian to help you locate them.

Computer Searches

Researchers can locate materials in a variety of sources, including card catalogues, specialized encyclopedias, bibliographies, and indexes to periodicals. Many libraries now also provide computer searches that are linked to a data base of the libraries' holdings. This can be an efficient way to establish a bibliography on a specific topic. If your library has such a service, consult a reference librarian about how to use it and to determine if it is feasible for your topic. If a computer service is not accessible at your library, you can still collect the same information from printed sources.

EVALUATING SOURCES AND TAKING NOTES

Evaluate your sources for their reliability and the quality of their evidence. Check to see if an article or book has been superseded by later studies; try to use up-to-date sources. A popular magazine article will probably not be as authoritative as an article in a scholarly journal. Sources that are well documented with primary and secondary materials usually indicate that the author has done his or her homework. Books printed by university presses and established trade presses are preferable to books privately printed. But there are always exceptions. If you are uncertain about how to assess a book, try to find out something about the author. Are there any other books listed in the catalogue that indicate the author's expertise? What do book reviews say about the work? Three valuable indexes to book reviews of literary studies are *Book Review Digest, Book Review Index,* and *Index to Book Reviews in the Humanities.* Your reference librarian can show you how to use these important tools for evaluating books. Reviews can be a quick means to get a broad perspective on writers and their works because reviewers often survey previous approaches to the topic under discussion.

As you prepare a list of reliable sources relevant to your topic, record the necessary bibliographic information so that it will be available when you make up the list of works cited for your paper. (See the illustration of a sample bibliography card.) For a book include the author, complete title, place of publication, publisher, and date. For an article include author, complete title, name of periodical, volume number, date of issue, and inclusive page numbers.

Once you have assembled a tentative bibliography, you will need to take notes on your readings. If you are not using a word processor, use 3 × 5-, 4 × 6-, or 5 × 8-inch cards for note taking. They are easy to manipulate and can be readily sorted later on when you establish subheadings for your paper. Be sure to keep track of where the information comes from by writing the author's name and page number on each notecard. If you use more than one work by the same author include a brief title as well as the author's name. (See the illustration of the sample notecard.)

Lynen, John F. *The Pastoral Art of Robert Frost.* New Haven: Yale UP, 1960.

Sample Bibliography Card for a Book

Symbolic value of the wall   Lynen 29

*Lynen describes the wall as
"the symbol for all kinds of
man-made barriers."*

*[Do these barriers have any
positive value?]*

Sample Notecard

The sample notecard records the source of information (the complete publishing information is on the bibliography card) and provides a heading that will allow easy sorting later on. Notice that the information is summarized rather than quoted in large chunks. The student also includes a short note asking herself if Lynen's reading could be expanded upon.

Notecards can combine quotations, paraphrases, and summaries; you can also use them to cite your own ideas and give them headings so that you don't lose track of them. As you take notes try to record only points relevant to your topic, though, inevitably, you'll end up not using some of your notes.

DEVELOPING A THESIS AND ORGANIZING THE PAPER

As the notes on "Mending Wall" accumulated, the student sorted them into topics including

```
1. Publication history of the poem
2. Frost's experiences as a farmer
3. Critics' readings of the poem
4. The speaker's attitude toward the wall
5. The neighbor's attitude toward the wall
6. Mythic elements in the poem
7. Does the wall have any positive value?
8. How do the speaker and neighbor characterize themselves?
9. Humor in the poem
10. Frost as a regional poet
```

The student quickly saw that items 1, 2, 6, and 10 were not directly related to her topic concerning why the speaker initiates the rebuilding of the wall. The remaining numbers (3–5, 7–9) are the topics taken up in the paper. The student had begun her reading of secondary sources with a tentative thesis that stemmed from her question about why the poem's speaker helps his neighbor to rebuild the wall. That "why" shaped itself into the expectation that she would have a thesis something like this: "The speaker helps to rebuild the wall because. . . ."

She assumed she would find information that indicated some specific reason. But the more she read the more she discovered that there was no single explanation provided by the poem or by critics' readings of the poem. Instead, through the insights provided by her sources, she began to see that the wall had several important functions in the poem. The perspective she developed into her thesis — that the wall "provided a foundation upon which the men build a personal sense of identity" — allowed her to incorporate a number of the critics' insights into her paper in order to shed light on why the speaker helps to rebuild the wall.

Because the assignment was relatively brief, the student did not write up a formal outline but instead organized her stacks of usable notecards and proceeded to write the first draft from them.

REVISING

After writing your first draft, you should review the advice and revision checklist on pp. 581–582 so that you can read your paper with an objective eye. Two days after writing her next-to-last draft, the writer of "Defining Identity in 'Mending Wall' " realized that she had allotted too much space for critical discussions of the humor in the poem that were not directly related to her approach. She realized that it was not essential to point out and discuss the puns in the poem; hence she corrected this by simply deleting most references to the poem's humor. The point is that she saw this herself after she took some time to approach the paper from a fresh perspective.

DOCUMENTING SOURCES

You must acknowledge the use of a source when you (1) quote someone's exact words, (2) summarize or borrow someone's opinions or ideas, or (3) use information and facts that are not considered to be common knowledge. The purpose of this documentation is to acknowledge your sources, to demonstrate that you are familiar with what others have thought about the topic, and to provide your reader access to the same sources. If your paper is not adequately documented, it will be vulnerable to a charge of *plagiarism* — the presentation of someone else's work as your own. Conscious plagiarism is easy to avoid; honesty takes care of that for most people. However, there is a more problematic form of plagiarism that is often inadvertent. Whether inadequate documentation is conscious or not, plagiarism is a serious matter and must be avoided. Papers can be evaluated only by what is on the page, not by their writers' intentions.

Let's look more closely at what constitutes plagiarism. Consider the following passage quoted from A. R. Coulthard, "Frost's 'Mending Wall,' " *Explicator* 45 (Winter 1987): 40:

> "Mending Wall" has many of the features of an "easy" poem aimed at high-minded readers. Its central symbol is the accessible stone wall to represent separation, and it appears to oppose isolating barriers and favor love and trust, the stuff of Golden Treasury of Inspirational Verse.

Now read this plagiarized version:

```
"Mending Wall" is an easy poem that appeals to high-minded
readers who take inspiration from its symbolism of the stone
wall, which seems to oppose isolating barriers and support
trusting love.
```

Though the writer has shortened the passage and made some changes in the wording, this paragraph is basically the same as Coulthard's. Indeed, several of his phrases are lifted almost intact. (Notice, however, that the plagiarized version seems to have missed Coulthard's irony and, therefore, misinterpreted and misrepresented the passage.) Even if a parenthetical reference had been included at the end of the passage and the source included in "Works Cited," the language of this passage would still be plagiarism because it is presented as the writer's own. Both language and ideas must be acknowledged.

Here is an adequately documented version of the passage:

```
A. R. Coulthard points out that "high-minded readers" mistak-
enly assume that "Mending Wall" is a simple inspirational poem
that uses the symbolic wall to reject isolationism and to sup-
port, instead, a sense of human community (40).
```

This passage makes absolutely clear that the observation is Coulthard's, and it is written in the student's own language with the exception of one quoted phrase. Had Coulthard not been named in the passage, the parenthetical reference would have included his name: (Coulthard 40).

Some mention should be made of the notion of common knowledge before we turn to the standard format for documenting sources. Observations and facts that are widely known and routinely included in many of your sources do not require documentation. It is not necessary to cite a source for the fact that Alfred, Lord Tennyson, was born in 1809 or that Frost writes about New England. Sometimes it will be difficult for you to determine what common knowledge is for a topic that you know little about. If you are in doubt, the best strategy is to supply a reference.

There are two basic ways to document sources. Traditionally, sources have been cited in footnotes at the bottom of each page or in endnotes grouped together at the end of the paper. Here is how a portion of the sample paper on "Mending Wall" would look if footnotes were used instead of parenthetical documentation:

It remains one of Frost's more popular poems, and, as
Douglas Wilson notes, "one of the most famous in all
of American poetry."[1]

[1]Douglas L. Wilson, "The Other Side of the Wall," Iowa
Review 10 (Winter 1979): 65.

Unlike endnotes, which are double spaced throughout under the title of "Notes" on separate pages at the end of the paper, footnotes appear four spaces below the text. They are single spaced with double spaces between notes.

No doubt you will have encountered these documentation methods in your reading. A different style is recommended, however, in the third edition of the Modern Language Association's *MLA Handbook for Writers of Research Papers* (1988). The new style employs parenthetical references within the text of the paper; these are keyed to an alphabetical list of works cited at the end of the paper. This method is designed to be less distracting for the reader. Unless you are instructed to follow the footnote or endnote style for documentation, use the new parenthetical method explained in the next section.

The List of Works Cited

Items in the list of works cited are arranged alphabetically according to the author's last name and indented five spaces after the first line. This allows the reader to locate quickly the complete bibliographic information for the author's name cited within the parenthetical reference in the text. The following are common entries for literature papers and should be used as models. If some of your sources are of a different nature, consult Joseph Gibaldi and Walter S. Achtert, *MLA Handbook for Writers of Research Papers,* 3rd ed. (New York: MLA, 1988); many of the bibliographic possibilities you are likely to need are included in this source.

A Book by One Author

Hendrickson, Robert. The Literary Life and Other Curiosi-
ties. New York: Viking, 1981.

Notice that the author's name is in reverse order. This information, along with the full title, place of publication, publisher, and date should be taken from the title and copyright pages of the book. The title is underlined to indicate italics and is also followed by a period. If the city of publication is well known, it is unnecessary to include the state. Use the publication date on the title page; if none appears there use the copyright date (after ©) on the back of the title page.

A Book by Two Authors

```
Horton, Rod W., and Herbert W. Edwards.  Backgrounds of
     American Literary Thought.  3rd ed. Englewood Cliffs:
     Prentice, 1974.
```

Only the first author's name is given in reverse order. The edition number appears after the title.

A Book with More than Three Authors

```
Abrams, M. H., et al., eds.  The Norton Anthology of
     English Literature.  5th ed. 2 vols. New York:
     Norton, 1986.  Vol. 1.
```

The abbreviation *et al.* means "and others." It is used to avoid having to list all fourteen editors of this first volume of a two-volume work.

A Work in a Collection by the Same Author

```
O'Connor, Flannery.  "Greenleaf."  The Complete Stories.
     By O'Connor.  New York: Farrar, 1971.  311-34.
```

Page numbers are given because the reference is to only a single story in the collection.

A Work in a Collection by Different Writers

```
Frost, Robert.  "Design."  Poetry: An Introduction.  2nd ed.
     Ed. Michael Meyer.  Boston: Bedford-St. Martin's P,
     1998.  318.
```

The hyphenated publisher's name indicates a publisher's imprint: Bedford Books of St. Martin's Press.

A Translated Book

```
Grass, Günter.  The Tin Drum.  Trans. Ralph Manheim.  New
     York: Vintage-Random, 1962.
```

An Introduction, Preface, Foreword, or Afterword

```
Johnson, Thomas H.  Introduction.  Final Harvest: Emily
     Dickinson's Poems.  By Emily Dickinson.  Boston:
     Little, Brown, 1961.  vii-xiv.
```

This cites the introduction by Johnson. Notice that a colon is used between the book's main title and subtitle. To cite a poem in this book use this method:

```
Dickinson, Emily.  "A Tooth upon Our Peace."  Final
     Harvest: Emily Dickinson's Poems.  Ed. Thomas H. John-
     son. Boston: Little, Brown, 1961.  110.
```

An Encyclopedia

"Wordsworth, William." The New Encyclopedia Britannica.
1984 ed.

Because this encyclopedia is organized alphabetically, no page number or other information is given, only the edition number (if available) and date.

An Article in a Magazine

Morrow, Lance. "Scribble, Scribble, Eh, Mr. Toad." Time
24 Feb. 1986: 84.

The citation for an unsigned article would begin with the title and be alphabetized by the first word of the title other than "a," "an," or "the."

An Article in a Scholarly Journal with Continuous Pagination beyond a Single Issue

Mahar, William J. "Black English in Early Blackface
Minstrelsy: A New Interpretation of the Sources of
Minstrel Show Dialect." American Quarterly 37 (1985):
260-85.

Because this journal uses continuous pagination instead of separate pagination for each issue, it is not necessary to include the month, season, or number of the issue. Only one of the quarterly issues will have pages numbered 260–85. If you are not certain whether a journal's pages are numbered continuously throughout a volume, supply the month, season, or issue number, as in the next entry.

An Article in a Scholarly Journal with Separate Pagination for Each Issue

Updike, John. "The Cultural Situation of the American
Writer." American Studies International 15 (Spring
1977): 19-28.

By noting the spring issue, the entry saves a reader looking through each issue of the 1977 volume for the correct article on pages 19–28.

An Article in a Newspaper

Ziegler, Philip. "The Lure of Gossip, the Rules of History." New York Times 23 Feb. 1986: sec. 7: 1+.

This citation indicates that the article appears on page 1 of section 7 and continues onto another page.

A Lecture

```
Stern, Milton.  "Melville's View of Law."  English 270
     class lecture.  University of Connecticut, Storrs,
     12 Mar. 1996.
```

Parenthetical References

A list of works cited is not an adequate indication of how you have used sources in your paper. You must also provide the precise location of quotations and other information by using parenthetical references within the text of the paper. You do this by citing the author's name (or the source's title if the work is anonymous) and the page number.

```
Collins points out that "Nabokov was misunderstood by early
reviewers of his work" (28).
```

or

```
Nabokov's first critics misinterpreted his stories
(Collins 28).
```

Either way a reader will find the complete bibliographic entry in the list of works cited under Collins's name and know that the information cited in the paper appears on page 28. Notice that the end punctuation comes after the parentheses.

If you have listed more than one work by the same author, you would add a brief title to the parenthetical reference to distinguish between them. You could also include the full title in your text.

```
Nabokov's first critics misinterpreted his stories (Collins
"Early Reviews" 28).
```

or

```
Collins points out in "Early Reviews of Nabokov's Fiction"
that his early work was misinterpreted by reviewers (28).
```

There can be many variations on what is included in a parenthetical reference, depending on the nature of the entry in the list of works cited. But the general principle is simple enough: provide enough parenthetical information for a reader to find the work in "Works Cited." Examine the sample research paper for more examples of works cited and strategies for including parenthetical references. If you are puzzled by a given situation, ask your reference librarian to show you the *MLA Handbook*.

A SAMPLE STUDENT RESEARCH PAPER:
DEFINING IDENTITY IN "MENDING WALL"

The following research paper by Juliana Daniels follows the format described in the *MLA Handbook for Writers of Research Papers,* Fourth Edition (1995). This format is discussed in the preceding section on Documentation and in Chapter 16, in the section "Manuscript Form" (pp. 582–583). Though the sample paper is short, it illustrates many of the techniques and strategies useful for writing an essay that includes secondary sources. Notice that when you cite poetry lines no abbreviation is used in the parenthetical documentation. Simply use the word *line* or *lines* in that first citation along with the number(s), and then just use the number(s) in subsequent citations after having established that the number(s) refers to lines ("Mending Wall" is reprinted on p. 304).

Juliana Daniels

Professor Caron

English 109-11

December 6, 19--

Defining Identity in "Mending Wall"

Robert Frost's poem "Mending Wall" has been the object of much critical scrutiny since its publication in 1914. It remains one of Frost's more popular poems, and, as Douglas L. Wilson notes, "one of the most famous in all of American poetry" (65). Perhaps partly as a result of its widespread popularity and frequent inclusion in literature anthologies, critics have tended to treat "Mending Wall" as a fairly straightforward poem that is easily accessible to high school students as well as professional scholars. But over the years there have been decided trends in the critical interpretations of this poem. These trends manifest themselves mostly in debates over which character, the speaker or his neighbor, has a clearer understanding of the real significance of the crumbling stone wall they endeavor to mend. However, scholars have overlooked the important ways that the wall helps each man to define himself in relation to the other. The wall not only offers the men a tangible way to demarcate their property but also affords them a way to clearly define their relationship with each other. Thus the wall does far more than just, as the neighbor asserts, make "good neighbors" (line 27)--it provides a foundation upon which the men may build a personal sense of identity.

This notion of identity as a significant theme in the poem has often been ignored by critics in favor of discussions of the meaning of the wall itself. Many previous interpretations of "Mending Wall" have focused on the

speaker's supposed insight, crediting him with the wisdom
to recognize the unnaturally limiting and divisive qualities inherent in the wall. After all, it is the speaker
who twice mentions that "Something there is that doesn't
love a wall" (35), thereby challenging his neighbor's firm
defense of the wall as the means of creating "good neighbors" (27). Charles Watson acknowledges the common tendency of readers to interpret the poem as "the meditation
of a right-minded man who, even as he participates in the
annual wall-mending rite, indulges privately in some
gently mocking reflections on his neighbor's mindless
adherence to his father's belief in walls" (653). The
speaker's apparent "right-mindedness," as well as the
appeal of joining him in his supposed aversion to artificial boundaries between people, effectively lulls readers
into a mistaken faith in the speaker's negative perception
of both the wall and his "recalcitrant and plodding neighbor [who] is a slave to the rituals of the quotidian"
(Lentricchia 11).

This original critical trend of favoring the speaker's
vision of the wall as meaningless and the neighbor as
mindless has been countered by numerous readings of the
poem in which the neighbor's point of view is deemed the
wiser and more valuable. Fritz Oehlschlaeger, among others, suggests the possibility of interpreting "Mending
Wall" in favor of the neighbor's perspective, maintaining
that it is the neighbor "who understands both the intran-
sigence of natural fact and the need to limit human ego.
This understanding makes the Yankee farmer, not the
speaker, the truly neighborly figure in the poem" (244).
In this case the neighbor is credited with the understanding that established boundaries provide the necessary

foundations for strong and successful relationships between people. His repeated assertion that "Good fences make good neighbors" (27, 45) suggests that walls are "the essential barriers that must exist between man and man if the individual is to preserve his own soul, and mutual understanding is to survive and flourish" (Ward 428).

However, the real wisdom in "Mending Wall" lies not in deciding whose point of view is more admirable but in recognizing that although the wall is perceived differently by the two men, it is essential in defining both of them. That is, the sense of identity that each man has in relation to the other deeply depends upon the existence of the wall that divides them and the way that they conceive of the wall. The neighbor can more readily acknowledge and articulate his desire for the wall to remain in place, but the speaker also does his part to ensure that the wall dividing their property does not crumble. For they each realize, on some level, that if the wall that defines the limits of their land were to disappear, then their sense of the established social order would also disappear, along with their identity as a part of that social order. As James R. Dawes points out, these "men can only interact when reassured by the constructed alienation of the wall" (300). So they work together to keep the wall firmly in place, keeping themselves separated in order to maintain their individual sense of self.

Part of the speaker's sense of identity lies in his role as a questioner, a challenger, a rebel thinker. He twice mentions his recognition that "Something there is that doesn't love a wall" (35), and seems pleased to ally himself with the forces of nature that conspire to destroy that wall which becomes, as John Lynen notes, "the symbol

for all kinds of man-made barriers" (29). Yet the
speaker's pleasure at minimizing the importance of the
wall results less from any inherent properties of the
actual wall than it does from the sense of superiority
over his neighbor which this belief affords him. The
speaker's created sense of identity as an insightful,
clever "free-thinker" is corroborated by his belief that
"the neighbor's adherence to his father's saying suggests
the narrowness and blind habit of the primitive" (Lynen
28); it is his opposition to the neighbor which defines
the speaker in the poem. The speaker declares that he can
think of no good reason for maintaining the wall, as there
are no cows to contain and his "apple trees will never get
across / And eat the cones under his [neighbor's] pines"
(25-26). Clearly, his belief in his own wisdom leads to
his sense of superiority over his neighbor, the "old-stone
savage" (40) who "moves in darkness" (41). Thus, the
existence of the wall provides the speaker with the means
to identify himself as superior to his neighbor.

It is revealing to note that in spite of the speaker's
superfluous objections to the rebuilding of the wall, it
is he who initiates its repair each spring. He acknowledges that "I let my neighbor know beyond the hill; / And
on a day we meet to walk the line / And set the wall
between us once again" (12-14). He also explains how he
repeatedly replaces the stones on the wall after hunters
dislodge them: "I have come after them and made repair /
Where they have left not one stone on a stone, / But they
would have the rabbit out of hiding" (6-8). Thus, the
speaker's behavior indicates that he does in fact believe
in the importance of the wall, diligently restoring it
whenever the stones are knocked out of place. This appar-

ent contradiction between the speaker's actions and his purported beliefs suggests a subtle recognition of the importance of maintaining the wall. The speaker fancies himself a genuine liberal, responding to his neighbor's conservative refrain "Good fences make good neighbors" (27) with the question "Why do they make good neighbors?" (30). The answer lies in the reader's understanding that the wall is crucial to maintaining the speaker's own self image. Perhaps the wall is not needed to fence in cows or trees, but it is necessary in order for the speaker to define himself in relation to the way his neighbor conceives of the wall. The speaker's superfluous objections to the wall are nothing more than fancy, for without the wall the speaker would be unable to define himself in opposition to his neighbor.

While the speaker defines his neighbor as a close-minded primitive, thereby validating his notion of himself as much superior to him, the neighbor defines himself as someone who, unlike the speaker, can acknowledge the importance of the wall. He finds it necessary to tell the speaker two separate times that "Good fences make good neighbors" (27, 45), suggesting his recognition that the speaker resists acknowledging the merit of his father's saying. Thus the neighbor is able to define himself in relation to the speaker, believing himself to clearly possess more valuable knowledge about fences and about relationships than his seemingly flighty neighbor does. The humor of this poem lies in the irony that both men consider themselves to have sharper perceptions and broader knowledge than the other, thus contributing to their individual sense of superiority.

Marion Montgomery explains that a "wise person knows

that a wall is a point of reference, a touchstone of sanity, and that it must be not only maintained but respected as well" (147). But the wall in "Mending Wall" goes beyond a reference point that protects merely one's privacy and individuality; it actually offers two people the foundation they need in order to be able to relate to each other and to understand themselves. Without the ritual of rebuilding the wall, neither the speaker nor the neighbor would have a way to compare himself to the other and thus reaffirm his own vision of himself. The confrontation between the two men in "Mending Wall" is as much of a ritual as the actual mending of the wall and is maintained as the poem "concludes with the fence having been mended and with the reader expecting the same movement to take place in succeeding years" (Bowen 14). Both the speaker and his neighbor "walk the line" (13) together, each complicit in the rebuilding and re-enforcing of the established barrier that allows them to maintain a sense of personal identity.

Works Cited

Bowen, J. K. "The Persona in Frost's 'Mending Wall':
     Mended or Amended." CEA Critic 31 (November 1968):
     14.

Dawes, James R. "Masculinity and Transgression in Robert
     Frost." American Literature 65 (June 1993): 297-312.

Frost, Robert. "Mending Wall." Poetry: An Introduction.
     2nd ed. Ed. Michael Meyer. Boston: Bedford-St.
     Martin's, 1998. 304.

Lentricchia, Frank. "Experience as Meaning: Robert
     Frost's 'Mending Wall.'" CEA Critic 34 (May 1972):
     8-12.

Lynen, John F. The Pastoral Art of Robert Frost. New
     Haven: Yale UP, 1960. 27-31.

Montgomery, Marion. "Robert Frost and His Use of Barri-
     ers: Man vs. Nature toward God." Robert Frost: A
     Collection of Critical Essays. Ed. James M. Cox.
     Englewood Cliffs: Prentice, 1962. 138-150.

Oehlschlaeger, Fritz. "Fences Make Neighbors: Process,
     Identity, and Ego in Robert Frost's 'Mending Wall.'"
     Arizona Quarterly 40 (Autumn 1984): 242-54.

Ward, William S. "Lifted Pot Lids and Unmended Walls."
     College English 27 (February 1966): 428-29.

Watson, Charles N. "Frost's Wall: The View from the Other
     Side." New England Quarterly 44 (December 1971):
     653-56.

Wilson, Douglas L. "The Other Side of the Wall." Iowa
     Review 10 (Winter, 1979): 65-75.

18. Taking Essay Examinations

PREPARING FOR AN ESSAY EXAM

Keep Up with the Reading

The best way to prepare for an examination is to keep up with the reading. If you begin the course with a commitment to completing the reading assignments on time, you will not have to read in a frenzy and cram just days before the test. The readings will be a pleasure, not a frantic ordeal. Moreover, you will find that your instructor's comments and class discussion will make more sense to you and that you'll be able to participate in class discussion. As you prepare for the exam you should be rereading texts rather than reading for the first time. It may not be possible to reread everything but you'll at least be able to scan a familiar text and reread passages that are particularly important.

Take Notes and Annotate the Text

Don't rely exclusively on your memory. The typical literature class includes a hefty amount of reading, so unless you take notes, annotate the text with your own comments, and underline important passages, you're likely to forget material that could be useful for responding to an examination question (see pp. 568–570 for a discussion of these matters). The more you can retrieve from your reading the more prepared you'll be for reviewing significant material for the exam. Your notes can be used to illustrate points that were made in class. By briefly quoting an important phrase or line from the text you can provide supporting evidence that will make your argument convincing. Consider, for example, the difference between writing that "Marvell's speaker in 'To His Coy Mistress' says that they won't be able to love after they die" and writing that "the speaker intones that 'The grave's a fine and private place / But none, I think, do there embrace.' " No one expects you to memorize the entire poem, but recalling a few lines here and there can transform a sleepy generality into an illustrative, persuasive argument.

Anticipate Questions

As you review the readings keep in mind the class discussions and the focus provided by your instructor. Very often class discussions and the instructor's emphasis become the basis for essay questions. You may not see the exact same topics on the exam, but you might find that the matters you've discussed in class will serve as a means of responding to an essay question. If, for example, class discussion of Robert Frost's "Mending Wall" (see p. 304) centered on the poem's rural New England setting, you could use that conservative, traditional setting to answer a question such as "Discuss how the conflicts between the speaker and his neighbor are related to the poem's theme." A discussion of the neighbor's rigidity and his firmly entrenched conservative New England attitudes could be connected to his impulse to rebuild the wall between himself and the poem's speaker. The point is that you'll be well prepared for an essay exam when you can shape the material you've studied so that it is responsive to whatever kinds of reasonable questions you encounter on the exam. Reasonable questions? Yes, your instructor is more likely to offer you an opportunity to demonstrate your familiarity with and understanding of the text than to set a trap that, for instance, demands you discuss how Frost's work experience as an adolescent informs the poem when no mention was ever made of that in class or in your reading.

You can also anticipate questions by considering the generic Questions for Responsive Reading and Writing about poetry (p. 248), and the questions in Arguing About Literature (p. 573), along with the Questions for Writing About an Author in Depth (p. 292). Not all of these questions will necessarily be relevant to every work that you read, but they cover a wide range of concerns that should allow you to organize your reading, note taking, and reviewing so that you're not taken by surprise during the exam.

Studying with a classmate or a small group from class can be a stimulating and fruitful means of discovering and organizing the major topics and themes of the course. This method of brainstorming can be useful not only for studying for exams, but through the semester as a way to understand and review course readings. And, finally, you needn't be shy about asking your instructor what types of questions might appear on the exam and how best to study for them. You may not get a very specific reply but almost any information is more useful than none.

TYPES OF EXAMS

Closed-Book versus Open-Book Exams

Closed-book exams require more memorization and recall than open-book exams, which permit you to use your text and perhaps even your notes to answer questions. Obviously, dates, names, definitions, and other details play less of a role in an open-book exam. An open-book exam requires no less preparation, however, because you'll need to be intimately familiar with the texts and the major ideas, themes, and issues that you've studied in order to quickly and efficiently support your points with relevant, specific evidence.

Since every student has the same advantage of having access to the text, preparation remains the key to answering the questions. Some students find open-book exams more difficult than closed-book tests, because they risk spending too much time reading, scanning, and searching for material and not enough time writing a response that draws upon the knowledge and understanding that their reading and studying has provided them. It's best to limit the time you allow yourself to review the text and/or notes, so that you devote an adequate amount of time to getting your ideas down on paper.

Essay Questions

Essay questions generally fall within one of the following categories. If you can recognize quickly what is being asked of you, you will be able to respond to them more efficiently.

1. Explication. Explication calls for a line-by-line explanation of a passage of poetry or prose that considers, for example, diction, figures of speech, symbolism, sound, form, and theme in an effort to describe how language creates meaning. (For a more detailed discussion of explication see p. 583.)

2. Definition. Defining a term and then applying it to a writer or work is a frequent exam exercise. Consider: "Define *romanticism.* To what extent can Keats's "Ode on a Grecian Urn" (p. 69) be regarded as a romantic poem?" This sort of question requires that you first describe what constitutes a romantic literary work and then explain how "Ode on a Grecian Urn" does (or doesn't) fit the bill.

3. Analysis. An analytical question focuses on a particular part of a literary work. You might be asked, for example, to analyze the significance of images in Diane Ackerman's poem "A Fine, a Private Place" (p. 61). This sort of question requires you to discuss not only a specific element of the poem but to explain also how that element contributes to the poem's overall effect. (For a more detailed discussion of analysis, see p. 588.)

4. Comparison and Contrast. Comparison and contrast calls for a discussion of the similarities and/or differences between writers, works, or elements of works, for example, "Compare and contrast the tone of the *carpe diem* arguments made by the speaker in Richard Wilbur's 'A Late Aubade' (p. 60) and in Andrew Marvell's 'To His Coy Mistress' (p. 57)." Despite the nearly three hundred years that separate these two poems in setting and circumstances, a discussion of the tone of the speakers' arguments reveals some intriguing similarities and differences. (For a more detailed discussion of comparison and contrast, see p. 593.)

5. Discussion of a Critical Perspective. A brief quotation by a critic about a work is usually designed to stimulate a response that requires you to agree with, disagree with, or qualify a critic's perspective. Usually it is not so important whether you agree or disagree with the critic; what matters is the quality of your argument. Think about how you might wrestle with this assessment of Robert Frost written by Lionel Trilling: "The manifest America of Mr. Frost's poems may be pastoral; the actual America is tragic." With some qualifications (surely not all of Frost's poems are "tragic") this could provide a useful way of talking about a poem such as "Mending Wall" (p. 304).

6. Imaginative Questions. To a degree every question requires imagination regardless of whether it's being asked or answered. However, some questions require more imaginative leaps to arrive at the center of an issue than others do. Consider, for example, the intellectual agility needed to respond to this question: "Discuss the speakers' attitudes toward the power of imagination in Emily Dickinson's 'To make a prairie it takes a clover and one bee' (p. 259), Frost's 'Mending Wall' (p. 304), and Philip Larkin's 'A Study of Reading Habits' (p. 22)." As tricky as this thematic triangulation may seem, there is plenty to discuss concerning the speakers' varied, complicated, and contradictory attitudes toward the power of an individual's imagination. Or try a simpler but no less interesting version: "How do you think Frost would review Marvell's 'To His Coy Mistress' and Ackerman's 'A Fine, a Private Place'?" Such questions certainly require detailed, reasoned responses, but they also leave room for creativity and even wit.

STRATEGIES FOR WRITING ESSAY EXAMS

Your hands may be sweaty and your heart pounding as you begin the exam, but as long as you're prepared and you keep in mind some basic strategies for writing essay exams, you should be able to respond to questions with confidence and a genuine sense of accomplishment.

1. Before you begin writing, read through the entire exam. If there are choices to be made, make certain you know how many questions must be answered (for instance, only one out of four, not two). Note how many points each question is worth; spend more time on the two worth forty points each and perhaps leave the twenty-point question for last.

2. Budget your time. If there are short-answer questions do not allow them to absorb you so that you cannot do justice to the longer essay questions. Follow the suggested time limits for each question; if none is offered, then create your own schedule in proportion to the points allotted for each question.

3. Depending upon your own sensibilities, you may want to begin with the easiest or hardest questions. It doesn't really matter which you begin with as long as you pace yourself to avoid running out of time.

4. Be sure that you understand the question. Does it ask you to compare and/or contrast, define, analyze, explicate, or use some other approach? Determine how many elements there are to the question so that you don't inadvertently miss part of the question. Do not spend time copying the question.

5. Make some brief notes about how you plan to answer the question; even a simple list of what you'll need to cover can serve as a useful outline.

6. Address the question; avoid unnecessary summaries or irrelevant asides. Focus on the particular elements enumerated or implied by the question.

7. After beginning the essay, write a clear thesis that describes the major topics you will discuss: "Mending Wall" is typical of Frost's concerns as a writer owing to its treatment of setting, tone, and theme.

8. Support and illustrate your answer with specific, relevant references to the text. The more specificity — the more you demonstrate a familiarity with the text (rather than simply providing a summary) — the better the answer.

9. Don't overlap and repeat responses to questions; your instructor will recognize such padding. If two different questions are about the same work or writer, demonstrate the breadth and depth of your knowledge of the subject.

10. Allow time to proofread and to qualify and to add more supporting material if necessary. At this final stage, too, it's worth remembering that Mark Twain liked to remind his readers that the difference between the right word and the almost right word is the difference between lightning and the lightning bug.

Glossary of Literary Terms

Accent The emphasis, or STRESS, given a syllable in pronunciation. We say *"syl*lable" not "syl*lable*," *"em*phasis" not "em*pha*sis." Accents can also be used to emphasize a particular word in a sentence: *Is* she con*tent* with the con*tents* of the *yel*low *pack*age? See also METER.

Allegory A narration or description usually restricted to a single meaning because its events, actions, characters, settings, and objects represent specific abstractions or ideas. Although the elements in an allegory may be interesting in themselves, the emphasis tends to be on what they ultimately mean. Characters may be given names such as Hope, Pride, Youth, and Charity; they have few if any personal qualities beyond their abstract meanings. These personifications are not symbols because, for instance, the meaning of a character named Charity is precisely that virtue. See also SYMBOL.

Alliteration The repetition of the same consonant sounds in a sequence of words, usually at the beginning of a word or stressed syllable: *"d*escending *d*ew *d*rops"; *"l*uscious *l*emons." Alliteration is based on the sounds of letters, rather than the spelling of words; for example, *"k*een" and *"c*ar" alliterate, but *"c*ar" and *"c*ite" do not. Used sparingly, alliteration can intensify ideas by emphasizing key words, but when used too self-consciously, it can be distracting, even ridiculous, rather than effective. See also ASSONANCE, CONSONANCE.

Allusion A brief reference to a person, place, thing, event, or idea in history or literature. Allusions conjure up biblical authority, scenes from Shakespeare's plays, historic figures, wars, great love stories, and anything else that might enrich an author's work. Allusions imply reading and cultural experiences shared by the writer and reader, functioning as a kind of shorthand whereby the recalling of something outside the work supplies an emotional or intellectual context, such as a poem about current racial struggles calling up the memory of Abraham Lincoln.

Ambiguity Allows for two or more simultaneous interpretations of a word, phrase, action, or situation, all of which can be supported by the context of a work. Deliberate ambiguity can contribute to the effectiveness and richness of a work. However, unintentional ambiguity obscures meaning and can confuse readers.

Anagram A word or phrase made from the letters of another word or phrase, as "heart" is an anagram of "earth." Anagrams have often been considered merely an exercise of one's ingenuity, but sometimes writers use anagrams to conceal proper names or veiled messages, or to suggest important connections between words, as in "hated" and "death."

Anapestic meter See FOOT.

Apostrophe An address, either to someone who is absent and therefore cannot hear the speaker or to something nonhuman that cannot comprehend. Apostrophe often provides a speaker the opportunity to think aloud.

Approximate rhyme See RHYME.

Archetype A term used to describe universal symbols that evoke deep and sometimes unconscious responses in a reader. In literature, characters, images, and themes that symbolically embody universal meanings and basic human experiences, regardless of when or where they live, are considered archetypes. Common literary archetypes include stories of quests, initiations, scapegoats, descents to the underworld, and ascents to heaven. See also MYTHOLOGICAL CRITICISM.

Assonance The repetition of internal vowel sounds in nearby words that do not end the same, for example, "as*lee*p under a tr*ee*," or "*ea*ch *e*vening." Similar endings result in rhyme, as in as*lee*p in the d*ee*p. Assonance is a strong means of emphasizing important words in a line. See also ALLITERATION, CONSONANCE.

Ballad Traditionally, a ballad is a song, transmitted orally from generation to generation, that tells a story and that eventually is written down. As such, ballads usually cannot be traced to a particular author or group of authors. Typically, ballads are dramatic, condensed, and impersonal narratives, such as "Bonny Barbara Allan." A **literary ballad** is a narrative poem that is written in deliberate imitation of the language, form, and spirit of the traditional ballad, such as Keats's "La Belle Dame sans Merci." See also BALLAD STANZA, QUATRAIN.

Ballad stanza A four-line stanza, known as a QUATRAIN, consisting of alternating eight- and six-syllable lines. Usually only the second and fourth lines rhyme (an *abcb* pattern). Coleridge adopted the ballad stanza in "The Rime of the Ancient Mariner."

> All in a hot and copper sky
> The bloody Sun, at noon,
> Right up above the mast did stand,
> No bigger than the Moon.

See also BALLAD, QUATRAIN.

Biographical criticism An approach to literature that suggests that knowledge of the author's life experiences can aid in the understanding of his or her work. While biographical information can sometimes complicate one's interpretation of a work, and some formalist critics (such as the New Critics) disparage the use of the author's biography as a tool for textual interpretation, learning about the life of the author can often enrich a reader's appreciation for that author's work. See also FORMAL-IST CRITICISM, NEW CRITICISM.

Blank verse Unrhymed iambic pentameter. Blank verse is the English verse form closest to the natural rhythms of English speech and therefore is the most common pattern found in traditional English narrative and dramatic poetry from Shakespeare to the early twentieth century. Shakespeare's plays use blank verse extensively. See also IAMBIC PENTAMETER.

Cacophony Language that is discordant and difficult to pronounce, such as this line from John Updike's "Player Piano": "never my numb plunker fumbles." Cacophony ("bad sound") may be unintentional in the writer's sense of music, or it may be used consciously for deliberate dramatic effect. See also EUPHONY.

Caesura A pause within a line of poetry that contributes to the rhythm of the line. A caesura can occur anywhere within a line and need not be indicated by punctuation. In scanning a line, caesuras are indicated by a double vertical line (‖). See also METER, RHYTHM, SCANSION.

Canon Those works generally considered by scholars, critics, and teachers to be the most important to read and study, which collectively constitute the "masterpieces" of literature. Since the 1960s, the traditional English and American literary canon, consisting mostly of works by white male writers, has been rapidly expanding to include many female writers and writers of varying ethnic backgrounds.

Carpe diem The Latin phrase meaning "seize the day." This is a very common literary theme, especially in lyric poetry, which emphasizes that life is short, time is fleeting, and that one should make the most of present pleasures. Robert Herrick's poem "To the Virgins, to Make Much of Time" employs the *carpe diem* theme.

Cliché An idea or expression that has become tired and trite from overuse, its freshness and clarity having worn off. Clichés often anesthetize readers, and are usually a sign of weak writing. See also SENTIMENTALITY, STOCK RESPONSES.

Colloquial Refers to a type of informal diction that reflects casual, conversational language and often includes slang expressions. See also DICTION.

Connotation Associations and implications that go beyond the literal meaning of a word, which derive from how the word has been commonly used and the associations people make with it. For example, the word *eagle* connotes ideas of liberty and freedom that have little to do with the word's literal meaning. See also DENOTATION.

Consonance A common type of near rhyme that consists of identical consonant sounds preceded by different vowel sounds: *home, same; worth, breath.* See also RHYME.

Contextual symbol See SYMBOL.

Controlling metaphor See METAPHOR.

Convention A characteristic of a literary genre (often unrealistic) that is understood and accepted by readers because it has come, through usage and time, to be recognized as a familiar technique. For example, the use of meter and rhyme are poetic conventions.

Conventional symbol See SYMBOL.

Cosmic irony See IRONY.

Couplet Two consecutive lines of poetry that usually rhyme and have the same meter. A **heroic couplet** is a couplet written in rhymed iambic pentameter.

Dactylic meter See FOOT.

Deconstructionism An approach to literature that suggests that literary works do not yield fixed, single meanings, because language can never say exactly what we intend it to mean. Deconstructionism seeks to destabilize meaning by examining the gaps and ambiguities of the language of a text. Deconstructionists pay close attention to language in order to discover and describe how a variety of possible readings are generated by the elements of a text. See also NEW CRITICISM.

Denotation The dictionary meaning of a word. See also CONNOTATION.

Dialect A type of informational diction. Dialects are spoken by definable groups of people from a particular geographic region, economic group, or social class. Writers use dialect to contrast and express differences in educational, class, social, and regional backgrounds of their characters. See also DICTION.

Diction A writer's choice of words, phrases, sentence structures, and figurative language, which combine to help create meaning. **Formal diction** consists of a dignified, impersonal, and elevated use of language; it follows the rules of syntax exactly and is often characterized by complex words and lofty tone. **Middle diction** maintains correct language usage, but is less elevated than formal diction; it reflects the way most educated people speak. **Informal diction** represents the plain language of everyday use, and often includes idiomatic expressions, slang, contractions, and many simple, common words. **Poetic diction** refers to the way poets sometimes employ an elevated diction that deviates significantly from the common speech and writing of their time, choosing words for their supposedly inherent poetic qualities. Since the eighteenth century, however, poets have been incorporating all kinds of diction in their work and so there is no longer an automatic distinction between the language of a poet and the language of everyday speech. See also DIALECT.

Didactic poetry Poetry designed to teach an ethical, moral, or religious lesson. Michael Wigglesworth's Puritan poem *Day of Doom* is an example of didactic poetry.

Doggerel A derogatory term used to describe poetry whose subject is trite and whose rhythm and sounds are monotonously heavy-handed.

Dramatic irony See IRONY.

Dramatic monologue A type of lyric poem in which a character (the speaker) addresses a distinct but silent audience imagined to be present in the poem in such a way as to reveal a dramatic situation and, often unintentionally, some aspect of his or her temperament or personality. See also LYRIC.

Electra complex The female version of the Oedipus complex. *Electra complex* is a term used to describe the psychological conflict of a daughter's unconscious rivalry with her mother for her father's attention. The name comes from the Greek legend of Electra, who avenged the death of her father, Agamemnon, by plotting the death of her mother. See also OEDIPUS COMPLEX, PSYCHOLOGICAL CRITICISM.

Elegy A mournful, contemplative lyric poem written to commemorate someone who is dead, often ending in a consolation. Tennyson's *In Memoriam,* written on the death of Arthur Hallam, is an elegy. *Elegy* may also refer to a serious meditative poem produced to express the speaker's melancholy thoughts. See also LYRIC.

End rhyme See RHYME.

End-stopped line A poetic line that has a pause at the end. End-stopped lines reflect normal speech patterns and are often marked by punctuation. The first line of Keats's "Endymion" is an example of an end-stopped line; the natural pause coincides with the end of the line, and is marked by a period:

A thing of beauty is a joy forever.

English sonnet See SONNET.

Enjambment In poetry, when one line ends without a pause and continues into the next line for its meaning. This is also called a **run-on line.** The transition between the first two lines of Wordsworth's poem "My Heart Leaps Up" demonstrates enjambment:

My heart leaps up when I behold
A rainbow in the sky:

Envoy See SESTINA.

Epic A long narrative poem, told in a formal, elevated style, that focuses on a serious subject and chronicles heroic deeds and events important to a culture or nation. Milton's *Paradise Lost,* which attempts to "justify the ways of God to man," is an epic. See also NARRATIVE POEM.

Epigram A brief, pointed, and witty poem that usually makes a satiric or humorous point. Epigrams are most often written in couplets, but take no prescribed form.

Euphony *Euphony* ("good sound") refers to language that is smooth and musically pleasant to the ear. See also CACOPHONY.

Exact rhyme See RHYME.

Extended metaphor See METAPHOR.

Eye rhyme See RHYME.

Falling meter See METER.

Feminine rhyme See RHYME.

Feminist criticism An approach to literature that seeks to correct or supplement what may be regarded as a predominantly male-dominated critical perspective with a feminist consciousness. Feminist criticism places literature in a social context and uses a broad range of disciplines, including history, sociology, psychology, and linguistics, to provide a perspective sensitive to feminist issues. Feminist theories also attempt to understand representation from a woman's point of view and to explain women's writing strategies as specific to their social conditions. See also SOCIOLOGICAL CRITICISM.

Figures of speech Ways of using language that deviate from the literal, denotative meanings of words in order to suggest additional meanings or effects. Figures of speech say one thing in terms of something else, such as when an eager funeral director is described as a vulture. See also METAPHOR, SIMILE.

Fixed form A poem that may be categorized by the pattern of its lines, meter, rhythm, or stanzas. A sonnet is a fixed form of poetry because by definition it must have fourteen lines. Other fixed forms include LIMERICK, SESTINA, and VILLANELLE. However, poems written in a fixed form may not always fit into categories precisely, because writers sometimes vary traditional forms to create innovative effects. See also OPEN FORM.

Foot The metrical unit by which a line of poetry is measured. A foot usually consists of one stressed and one or two unstressed syllables. An *iambic foot,* which consists of one unstressed syllable followed by one stressed syllable ("away"), is the most common metrical foot in English poetry. A *trochaic foot* consists of one stressed syllable followed by an unstressed syllable ("lovely"). An *anapestic foot* is two unstressed syllables followed by one stressed one ("understand"). A *dactylic foot* is one stressed syllable followed by two unstressed ones ("desperate"). A *spondee* is a foot consisting of two stressed syllables ("dead set"), but is not a sustained metrical foot and is used mainly for variety or emphasis. See also IAMBIC PENTAMETER, LINE, METER.

Form The overall structure or shape of a work, which frequently follows an established design. Forms may refer to a literary type (narrative form, lyric form) or to patterns of meter, lines, and rhymes (stanza form, verse form). See also FIXED FORM, OPEN FORM.

Formal diction See DICTION.

Formalist criticism An approach to literature that focuses on the formal elements of a work, such as its language, structure, and tone. Formalist critics offer intense examinations of the relationship between form and meaning in a work, emphasizing the subtle complexity in how a work is arranged. Formalists pay special attention to diction, irony, paradox, metaphor, and symbol, as well as larger elements such as plot, characterization, and narrative technique. Formalist critics read literature as an independent work of art rather than as a reflection of the author's state of mind or as a representation of a moment in history.

Therefore, anything outside of the work, including historical influences and authorial intent, is generally not examined by formalist critics. See also NEW CRITICISM.

Found poem An unintentional poem discovered in a nonpoetic context, such as a conversation, news story, or advertisement. Found poems serve as reminders that everyday language often contains what can be considered poetry, or that poetry is definable as any text read as a poem.

Free verse Also called *open form poetry,* free verse refers to poems characterized by their nonconformity to established patterns of meter, rhyme, and stanza. Free verse uses elements such as speech patterns, grammar, emphasis, and breath pauses to decide line breaks, and usually does not rhyme. See OPEN FORM.

Genre A French word meaning kind or type. The major genres in literature are poetry, fiction, drama, and essays. Genre can also refer to more specific types of literature such as comedy, tragedy, epic poetry, or science fiction.

Haiku A style of lyric poetry borrowed from the Japanese that typically presents an intense emotion or vivid image of nature, which, traditionally, is designed to lead to a spiritual insight. Haiku is a fixed poetic form, consisting of seventeen syllables organized into three unrhymed lines of five, seven, and five syllables. Today, however, many poets vary the syllabic count in their haiku. See also FIXED FORM.

Heroic couplet See COUPLET.

Historical criticism An approach to literature that uses history as a means of understanding a literary work more clearly. Such criticism moves beyond both the facts of an author's personal life and the text itself in order to examine the social and intellectual currents in which the author composed the work. See also NEW HISTORICISM.

Hyperbole A boldly exaggerated statement that adds emphasis without intending to be literally true, as in the statement "He ate everything in the house." Hyperbole (also called *overstatement*) may be used for serious, comic, or ironic effect. See also FIGURES OF SPEECH.

Iambic meter See FOOT.

Iambic pentameter A metrical pattern in poetry that consists of five iambic feet per line. (An iamb, or iambic foot, consists of one unstressed syllable followed by a stressed syllable.) See also FOOT, METER.

Image A word, phrase, or figure of speech (especially a SIMILE or a METAPHOR) that addresses the senses, suggesting mental pictures of sights, sounds, smells, tastes, feelings, or actions. Images offer sensory impressions to the reader and also convey emotions and moods through their verbal pictures. See also FIGURES OF SPEECH.

Implied metaphor See METAPHOR.

Informal diction See DICTION.

Internal rhyme See RHYME.

Irony A literary device that uses contradictory statements or situations to reveal a reality different from what appears to be true. It is ironic for a firehouse to burn down, or for a police station to be burglarized. **Verbal irony** is a figure of speech that occurs when a person says one thing but means the opposite. **Sarcasm** is a strong form of verbal irony that is calculated to hurt someone through, for example, false praise. **Dramatic irony** creates a discrepancy between what a character believes or says and what the reader or audience member knows to be true. **Situational irony** exists when there is an incongruity between what is expected to happen and what actually happens due to forces beyond human comprehension or control. The suicide of the seemingly successful main character in Edwin Arlington Robinson's poem "Richard Cory" is an example of situational irony. **Cosmic irony** occurs when a writer uses God, destiny, or fate to dash the hopes and expectations of a character or of humankind in general. In cosmic irony, a discrepancy exists between what a character aspires to and what universal forces provide. Stephen Crane's poem "A Man Said to the Universe" is a good example of cosmic irony, because the universe acknowledges no obligation to the man's assertion of his own existence.

Italian sonnet See SONNET.

Limerick A light, humorous style of fixed form poetry. Its usual form consists of five lines with the rhyme scheme *aabba;* lines 1, 2, and 5 contain three feet, while lines 3 and 4 usually contain two feet. Limericks range in subject matter from the silly to the obscene, and since Edward Lear popularized them in the nineteenth century, children and adults have enjoyed these comic poems. See also FIXED FORM.

Line A sequence of words printed as a separate entity on the page. In poetry, lines are usually measured by the number of feet they contain. The names for various line lengths are as follows:

monometer: one foot	pentameter: five feet
dimeter: two feet	hexameter: six feet
trimeter: three feet	heptameter: seven feet
tetrameter: four feet	octameter: eight feet

The number of feet in a line, coupled with the name of the foot, describes the metrical qualities of that line. See also END-STOPPED LINE, ENJAMBMENT, FOOT, METER.

Literary ballad See BALLAD.

Literary symbol See SYMBOL.

Litotes See UNDERSTATEMENT.

Lyric A type of brief poem that expresses the personal emotions and thoughts of a single speaker. It is important to realize, however, that although the lyric is uttered in the first person, the speaker is not necessarily the poet. There are many varieties of lyric poetry, including the DRAMATIC MONOLOGUE, ELEGY, HAIKU, ODE, and SONNET forms.

Marxist criticism An approach to literature that focuses on the ideological content of a work — its explicit and implicit assumptions and values about matters such as culture, race, class, and power. Marxist criticism, based largely on the writings of Karl Marx, typically aims at not only revealing and clarifying ideological issues but also correcting social injustices. Some Marxist critics use literature to describe the competing socioeconomic interests that too often advance capitalist interests such as money and power rather than socialist interests such as morality and justice. They argue that literature and literary criticism are essentially political because they either challenge or support economic oppression. Because of this strong emphasis on the political aspects of texts, Marxist criticism focuses more on the content and themes of literature than on its form. See also SOCIOLOGICAL CRITICISM.

Masculine rhyme See RHYME.

Metaphor A metaphor is a figure of speech that makes a comparison between two unlike things, without using the words *like* or *as*. Metaphors assert the identity of dissimilar things, as when Macbeth asserts that life *is* a "brief candle." Metaphors can be subtle and powerful, and can transform people, places, objects, and ideas into whatever the writer imagines them to be. An **implied metaphor** is a more subtle comparison; the terms being compared are not so specifically explained. For example, to describe a stubborn man unwilling to leave, one could say that he was "a mule standing his ground." This is a fairly explicit metaphor; the man is being compared to a mule. But to say that the man "brayed his refusal to leave" is to create an implied metaphor, because the subject (the man) is never overtly identified as a mule. Braying is associated with the mule, a notoriously stubborn creature, and so the comparison between the stubborn man and the mule is sustained. Implied metaphors can slip by inattentive readers who are not sensitive to such carefully chosen, highly concentrated language. An **extended metaphor** is a sustained comparison in which part or all of a poem consists of a series of related metaphors. Robert Francis's poem "Catch" relies on an extended metaphor that compares poetry to playing catch. A **controlling metaphor** runs through an entire work and determines the form or nature of that work. The controlling metaphor in Anne Bradstreet's poem "The Author to Her Book" likens her book to a child. **Synecdoche** is a kind of metaphor in which a part of something is used to signify the whole, as when a gossip is called a "wagging tongue," or when ten ships are called "ten sails." Sometimes, synecdoche refers to the whole being used to signify the part, as in the phrase "Boston won the baseball game." Clearly, the entire city of Boston did not participate in the game; the whole of Boston is being used to signify the individuals who played and won the game. **Metonymy** is a type of metaphor in which something closely associated with a subject is substituted for it. In this way, we speak of the "silver screen" to mean motion pictures, "the crown" to stand for the king, "the White House" to stand for the activities of the president. See also FIGURES OF SPEECH, PERSONIFICATION, SIMILE.

Meter When a rhythmic pattern of stresses recurs in a poem, it is called *meter*. Metrical patterns are determined by the type and number of feet in a line of verse; combining the name of a line length with the name of a foot concisely describes the meter of the line. **Rising meter** refers to metrical feet that move from unstressed to stressed sounds, such as the iambic foot and the anapestic foot. **Falling meter** refers to metrical feet that move from stressed to unstressed sounds, such as the trochaic foot and the dactylic foot. See also ACCENT, FOOT, IAMBIC PENTAMETER, LINE.

Metonymy See METAPHOR.

Middle diction See DICTION.

Mythological criticism An approach to literature that seeks to identify what in a work creates deep universal responses in readers, by paying close attention to the hopes, fears, and expectations of entire cultures. Mythological critics (sometimes called *archetypal critics*) look for underlying, recurrent patterns in literature that reveal universal meanings and basic human experiences for readers regardless of when and where they live. These critics attempt to explain how archetypes (the characters, images, and themes that symbolically embody universal meanings and experiences) are embodied in literary works in order to make larger connections that explain a particular work's lasting appeal. Mythological critics may specialize in areas such as classical literature, philology, anthropology, psychology, and cultural history, but they all emphasize the assumptions and values of various cultures. See also ARCHETYPE.

Narrative poem A poem that tells a story. A narrative poem may be short or long, and the story it relates may be simple or complex. See also BALLAD, EPIC.

Near rhyme See RHYME.

New Criticism An approach to literature made popular between the 1940s and the 1960s that evolved out of formalist criticism. New Critics suggest that detailed analysis of the language of a literary text can uncover important layers of meaning in that work. New Criticism consciously downplays the historical influences, authorial intentions, and social contexts that surround texts in order to focus on explication — extremely close textual analysis. See also FORMALIST CRITICISM.

New Historicism An approach to literature that emphasizes the interaction between the historic context of the work and a modern reader's understanding and interpretation of the work. New Historicists attempt to describe the culture of a period by reading many different kinds of texts and paying close attention to many different dimensions of a culture, including political, economic, social, and aesthetic concerns. They regard texts not simply as a reflection of the culture that produced them but also as productive of that culture playing an active role in the social and political conflicts of an age. New Historicism acknowledges and then explores various versions of "history," sensitizing us to the fact that the history on which we choose to focus is colored by being reconstructed from our present circumstances. See also HISTORICAL CRITICISM.

Octave A poetic stanza of eight lines, usually forming one part of a sonnet. See also SONNET, STANZA.

Ode A relatively lengthy lyric poem that often expresses lofty emotions in a dignified style. Odes are characterized by a serious topic, such as truth, art, freedom, justice, or the meaning of life; their tone tends to be formal. There is no prescribed pattern that defines an ode; some odes repeat the same pattern in each stanza, while others introduce a new pattern in each stanza. See also LYRIC.

Oedipus complex A Freudian term derived from Sophocles' tragedy *Oedipus the King*. It describes a psychological complex that is predicated on a boy's unconscious rivalry with his father for his mother's love and his desire to eliminate his father in order to take his father's place with his mother. The female equivalent of this complex is called the *Electra complex*. See also ELECTRA COMPLEX, PSYCHOLOGICAL CRITICISM.

Off rhyme See RHYME.

Onomatopoeia A term referring to the use of a word that resembles the sound it denotes. *Buzz, rattle, bang,* and *sizzle* all reflect onomatopoeia. Onomatopoeia can also consist of more than one word; writers sometimes create lines or whole passages in which the sound of the words helps to convey their meanings.

Open form Sometimes called *free verse*, open form poetry does not conform to established patterns of METER, RHYME, and STANZA. Such poetry derives its rhythmic qualities from the repetition of words, phrases, or grammatical structures, the arrangement of words on the printed page, or by some other means. The poet E. E. Cummings wrote open form poetry; his poems do not have measurable meters, but they do have RHYTHM. See also FIXED FORM.

Organic form Refers to works whose formal characteristics are not rigidly predetermined but follow the movement of thought or emotion being expressed. Such works are said to grow like living organisms, following their own individual patterns rather than external fixed rules that govern, for example, the form of a SONNET.

Overstatement See HYPERBOLE.

Oxymoron A condensed form of paradox in which two contradictory words are used together, as in "sweet sorrow" or "jumbo shrimp." See also PARADOX.

Paradox A statement that initially appears to be contradictory but then, on closer inspection, turns out to make sense. For example, John Donne ends his sonnet "Death, Be Not Proud" with the paradoxical statement "Death, thou shalt die." To solve the paradox, it is necessary to discover the sense that underlies the statement. Paradox is useful in poetry because it arrests a reader's attention by its seemingly stubborn refusal to make sense.

Paraphrase A prose restatement of the central ideas of a poem, in your own language.

Parody A humorous imitation of another, usually serious, work. It can take any fixed or open form, because parodists imitate the tone, language, and shape of the original in order to deflate the subject matter, making the original work seem absurd. Anthony Hecht's poem "Dover Bitch" is a famous parody of Matthew Arnold's well-known "Dover Beach." Parody may also be used as a form of literary criticism to expose the defects in a work. But sometimes parody becomes an affectionate acknowledgment that a well-known work has become both institutionalized in our culture and fair game for some fun. For example, Peter De Vries's "To His Importunate Mistress" gently mocks Andrew Marvell's "To His Coy Mistress."

Persona Literally, a *persona* is a mask. In literature, a *persona* is a speaker created by a writer to tell a story or to speak in a poem. A persona is not a character in a story or narrative, nor does a persona necessarily directly reflect the author's personal voice. A persona is a separate self, created by and distinct from the author, through which he or she speaks.

Personification A form of metaphor in which human characteristics are attributed to nonhuman things. Personification offers the writer a way to give the world life and motion by assigning familiar human behaviors and emotions to animals, inanimate objects, and abstract ideas. For example, in Keats's "Ode on a Grecian Urn," the speaker refers to the urn as an "unravished bride of quietness." See also METAPHOR.

Petrarchan sonnet See SONNET.

Picture poem A type of open form poetry in which the poet arranges the lines of the poem so as to create a particular shape on the page. The shape of the poem embodies its subject; the poem becomes a picture of what the poem is describing. Michael McFee's "In Medias Res" is an example of a picture poem. See also OPEN FORM.

Poetic diction See DICTION.

Prose poem A kind of open form poetry that is printed as prose and represents the most clear opposite of fixed form poetry. Prose poems are densely compact and often make use of striking imagery and figures of speech. See also FIXED FORM, OPEN FORM.

Psychological criticism An approach to literature that draws upon psychoanalytic theories, especially those of Sigmund Freud or Jacques Lacan, to understand more fully the text, the writer, and the reader. The basis of this approach is the idea of the existence of a human unconscious — those impulses, desires, and feelings about which a person is unaware but which influence emotions and behavior. Critics use psychological approaches to explore the motivations of characters and the symbolic meanings of events, while biographers speculate about a writer's own motivations — conscious or unconscious — in a literary work. Psychological approaches are also used to describe and analyze the reader's personal responses to a text.

Pun A play on words that relies on a word's having more than one meaning or sounding like another word. Shakespeare and other writers use puns extensively, for serious and comic purposes; in *Romeo and Juliet* (III.i.101), the dying Mercutio puns, "Ask for me tomorrow and you shall find me a grave man." Puns have serious literary uses, but since the eighteenth century, puns have been used almost purely for humorous effect. See also COMEDY.

Quatrain A four-line stanza. Quatrains are the most common stanzaic form in the English language; they can have various meters and rhyme schemes. See also METER, RHYME, STANZA.

Reader-response criticism An approach to literature that focuses on the reader rather than the work itself, by attempting to describe what goes on in the reader's mind during the reading of a text. Hence, the consciousness of the reader — produced by reading the work — is the actual subject of reader-response criticism. These critics are not after a "correct" reading of the text or what the author presumably intended; instead, they are interested in the reader's individual experience with the text. Thus, there is no single definitive reading of a work, because readers create rather than discover absolute meanings in texts. However, this approach is not a rationale for mistaken or bizarre readings, but an exploration of the possibilities for a plurality of readings. This kind of strategy calls attention to how we read and what influences our readings, and what that reveals about ourselves.

Rhyme The repetition of identical or similar concluding syllables in different words, most often at the ends of lines. Rhyme is predominantly a function of sound rather than spelling; thus, words that end with the same vowel sounds rhyme, for instance, *day, prey, bouquet, weigh,* and words with the same consonant ending rhyme, for instance *vain, feign, rein, lane.* Words do not have to be spelled the same way or look alike to rhyme. In fact, words may look alike but not rhyme at all. This is called **eye rhyme,** as with *bough* and *cough,* or *brow* and *blow.*
End rhyme is the most common form of rhyme in poetry; the rhyme comes at the end of the lines.

It runs through the reeds
　And away it proceeds,
Through meadow and glade,
　In sun and in shade.

The **rhyme scheme** of a poem describes the pattern of end rhymes. Rhyme schemes are mapped out by noting patterns of rhyme with small letters: the first rhyme sound is designated *a,* the second becomes *b,* the third *c,* and so on. Thus, the rhyme scheme of the stanza above is *aabb.* **Internal rhyme** places at least one of the rhymed words within the line, as in "Dividing and gliding and sliding" or "In mist or cloud, on mast or shroud." **Masculine rhyme** describes the rhyming of single-syllable words, such as *grade* or *shade.* Masculine rhyme also occurs when rhyming words of more than one syllable, when the same sound occurs in a final stressed syllable, as in *defend* and *contend, betray* and *away.* **Feminine rhyme** consists of a rhymed stressed syllable followed by one or more identical unstressed syllables, as in *butter, clutter; gratitude, attitude; quivering, shivering.* All the examples so far have illustrated **exact rhymes,** because they share the same stressed vowel sounds as well as sharing sounds that follow the vowel. In **near rhyme** (also called **off rhyme, slant rhyme,** and **approximate rhyme**), the sounds are almost but not exactly alike. A common form of near rhyme is CONSONANCE, which consists of identical consonant sounds preceded by different vowel sounds: *home, same; worth, breath.*

Rhyme scheme See RHYME.

Rhythm A term used to refer to the recurrence of stressed and unstressed sounds in poetry. Depending on how sounds are arranged, the rhythm of a poem may be fast or slow, choppy or smooth. Poets use rhythm to create pleasurable sound patterns and to reinforce meanings. Rhythm in prose arises from pattern repetitions of sounds and pauses that create looser rhythmic effects. See also METER.

Rising meter See METER.

Run-on line See ENJAMBMENT.

Sarcasm See IRONY.

Satire The literary art of ridiculing a folly or vice in order to expose or correct it. The object of satire is usually some human frailty; people, institutions, ideas, and things are all fair game for satirists. Satire evokes attitudes of amusement, contempt, scorn, or indignation toward its faulty subject in the hope of somehow improving it. See also IRONY, PARODY.

Scansion The process of measuring the stresses in a line of verse to determine the metrical pattern of the line. See also LINE, METER.

Sentimentality A pejorative term used to describe the effort by an author to induce emotional responses in the reader that exceed what the situation warrants. Sentimentality especially pertains to such emotions as pathos and sympathy; it cons readers into falling for the mass murderer who is devoted to stray cats, and it requires that readers do not examine such illogical responses. Clichés and stock responses are the key ingredients of sentimentality in literature. See also CLICHÉ, STOCK RESPONSES.

Sestet A stanza consisting of exactly six lines. See also STANZA.

Sestina A type of fixed form poetry consisting of thirty-six lines of any length divided into six sestets and a three-line concluding stanza called an **envoy.** The six words at the end of the first sestet's lines must also appear at the ends of the other five sestets, in varying order. These six words must also appear in the envoy, where they often resonate important themes. An example of this highly demanding form of poetry is Elizabeth Bishop's "Sestina." See also SESTET.

Setting The physical and social context in which the action of a poem occurs. The major elements of setting are the time, the place, and the social environment that frames the poem. Setting can be used to evoke a mood or atmosphere that will prepare the reader for what is to come, as in Robert Frost's "Home Burial."

Shakespearean sonnet See SONNET.

Simile A common figure of speech that makes an explicit comparison between two things by using words such as *like, as, than, appears,* and *seems:* "A sip of Mrs. Cook's coffee is like a punch in the stomach." The effectiveness of this simile is created by the differences between the two things compared. There would be no simile if the comparison were stated this way: "Mrs. Cook's coffee is as strong as the cafeteria's coffee." This is a literal translation because Mrs. Cook's coffee is compared with something like it — another kind of coffee. See also FIGURES OF SPEECH, METAPHOR.

Situational irony See IRONY.

Slant rhyme See RHYME.

Sociological criticism An approach to literature that examines social groups, relationships, and values as they are manifested in literature. Sociological approaches emphasize the nature and effect of the social forces that shape power relationships between groups or classes of people. Such readings treat literature as either a document reflecting social conditions or a product of those conditions. The former view brings into focus the social milieu; the latter emphasizes the work. Two important forms of sociological criticism are Marxist and feminist approaches. See also FEMINIST CRITICISM, MARXIST CRITICISM.

Sonnet A fixed form of lyric poetry that consists of fourteen lines, usually written in iambic pentameter. There are two basic types of sonnets, the Italian and the English. The **Italian sonnet,** also known as the **Petrarchan sonnet,** is divided into an octave, which typically rhymes *abbaabba,* and a sestet, which may have varying rhyme schemes. Common rhyme patterns in the sestet are *cdecde, cdcdcd,* and *cdccdc.* Very often the octave presents a situation, attitude, or problem that the sestet comments upon or resolves, as in John Keats's "On First Looking into Chapman's Homer." The **English sonnet,** also known as the **Shakespearean sonnet,** is organized into three quatrains and a couplet, which typically rhyme *abab cdcd efef gg.* This rhyme scheme is more suited to English poetry because English has fewer rhyming words than Italian. English sonnets, because of their four-part organization, also have more flexibility with respect to where thematic breaks can occur. Frequently, however, the most pronounced break or turn comes with the concluding couplet, as in Shakespeare's "Shall I compare thee to a summer's day?" See also COUPLET, IAMBIC PENTAMETER, LINE, OCTAVE, QUATRAIN, SESTET.

Speaker The voice used by an author to tell a story or speak a poem. The speaker is often a created identity, and should not automatically be equated with the author's self. See also PERSONA.

Spondee See FOOT.

Stanza In poetry, *stanza* refers to a grouping of lines, set off by a space, that usually has a set pattern of meter and rhyme. See also LINE, METER, RHYME.

Stock responses Predictable, conventional reactions to language, characters, symbols, or situations. The flag, motherhood, puppies, God, and peace are common objects used to elicit stock responses from unsophisticated audiences. See also CLICHÉ, SENTIMENTALITY.

Stress The emphasis, or accent, given a syllable in pronunciation. See also ACCENT.

Style The distinctive and unique manner in which a writer arranges words to achieve particular effects. Style essentially combines the idea to be expressed with the individuality of the author. These arrangements include individual word choices as well as matters such as the length of sentences, their structure, tone, and use of irony. See also DICTION, IRONY, TONE.

Symbol A person, object, image, word, or event that evokes a range of additional meaning beyond and usually more abstract than its literal significance. Symbols are educational devices for evoking complex ideas without having to resort to painstaking explanations that would make a story more like an essay than an experience. **Conventional symbols** have meanings that are widely recognized by a society or culture. Some conventional symbols are the Christian cross, the Star of David, a swastika, or a nation's flag. Writers use conventional symbols to reinforce meanings. E. E. Cummings, for example, emphasizes the spring setting in "in Just —" as a way of suggesting a renewed sense of life. A **literary** or **contextual symbol** can be a setting, character, action, object, name, or anything else in a work that maintains its literal significance while suggesting other meanings. Such symbols go beyond conventional symbols; they gain their symbolic meaning within the context of a specific story. For example, the urn in Keats's "Ode on a Grecian Urn" takes on multiple symbolic meanings in the work, but these meanings do not automatically carry over into other poems about urns. The meanings suggested by Keats's urn are specific to that text; therefore, it becomes a contextual symbol. See also ALLEGORY.

Synecdoche See METAPHOR.

Syntax The ordering of words into meaningful verbal patterns such as phrases, clauses, and sentences. Poets often manipulate syntax, changing conventional word order, to place certain emphasis on particular words. Emily Dickinson, for instance, writes about being surprised by a snake in her poem "A narrow Fellow in the Grass," and includes this line: "His notice sudden is." In addition to the alliterative hissing *s*-sounds here, Dickinson also effectively manipulates the line's syntax so that the verb *is* appears unexpectedly at the end, making the snake's hissing presence all the more "sudden."

Tercet A three-line stanza. See also STANZA, TRIPLET.

Terza rima An interlocking three-line rhyme scheme: *aba, bcb, cdc, ded,* and so on. Dante's *The Divine Comedy* and Frost's "Acquainted with the Night" are written in terza rima. See also RHYME, TERCET.

Theme The central meaning or dominant idea in a literary work. A theme provides a unifying point around which the plot, characters, setting, point of view, symbols, and other elements of a work are organized. It is important not to mistake the theme for the actual subject of the work; the theme refers to the abstract concept that is made concrete through the images, characterization, and action of the text. In nonfiction, however, the theme generally refers to the main topic of the discourse.

Thesis The central idea of an essay. The thesis is a complete sentence (although sometimes it may require more than one sentence) that establishes the topic of the essay in clear, unambiguous language.

Tone The author's implicit attitude toward the reader or the people, places, and events in a work as revealed by the elements of the author's style. Tone may be characterized as serious or ironic, sad or happy, private or public, angry or affectionate, bitter or nostalgic, or any other attitudes and feelings that human beings experience. See also STYLE.

Triplet A tercet in which all three lines rhyme. See also TERCET.

Trochaic meter See FOOT.

Understatement The opposite of hyperbole, *understatement* (or litotes) refers to a figure of speech that says less than is intended. Understatement usually has an ironic effect, and sometimes may be used for comic purposes, as in Mark Twain's statement, "The reports of my death are greatly exaggerated." See also HYPERBOLE, IRONY.

Verbal irony See IRONY.

Verse A generic term used to describe poetic lines composed in a measured rhythmical pattern, that are often, but not necessarily, rhymed. See also LINE, METER, RHYME, RHYTHM.

Villanelle A type of fixed form poetry consisting of nineteen lines of any length divided into six stanzas: five tercets and a concluding quatrain. The first and third lines of the initial tercet rhyme; these rhymes are repeated in each subsequent tercet *(aba)* and in the final two lines of the quatrain *(abaa)*. Line 1 appears in its entirety as lines 6, 12, and 18, while line 3 reappears as lines 9, 15, and 19. Dylan Thomas's "Do not go gentle into that good night" is a villanelle. See also FIXED FORM, QUATRAIN, RHYME, TERCET.

Acknowledgments (*continued from p. iv*)

Amiri Baraka. "SOS" from *Selected Poetry of Amiri Baraka/Leroi Jones*. Copyright © 1979 by Amiri Baraka.

Richard K. Barksdale. "On Censoring 'Ballad of the Landlord' " from *Langston Hughes: The Poet and His Critics* by Richard K. Barksdale. American Library Association, 1977.

Regina Barreca. "Nighttime Fires" from *The Minnesota Review* (Fall, 1986). Reprinted by permission of the author.

Matsuo Bashō. "Under cherry trees" from *Japanese Haiku*, trans. by Peter Beilenson, Series I. Copyright © 1955–56, Peter Beilenson, Editor. Reprinted by permission of Peter Pauper Press.

Michael L. Baumann. "The 'Overwhelming Question' for Prufrock" excerpted from "Let Us Ask What Is It?" *Arizona Quarterly* 37 (Spring 1981): 47–58.

Robin Becker. "Shopping" from *All American Girl* by Robin Becker. Copyright © 1996. Reprinted by permission of the University of Pittsburgh Press.

Paula Bennett. "On 'I heard a Fly buzz — when I died — ' " excerpt from *Emily Dickinson: Woman Poet* by Paula Bennett. Reprinted with permission of the University of Iowa Press.

Faith Berry. "On Hughes's Repudiation of 'Goodbye Christ' " from *Langston Hughes: Before and Beyond Harlem* by Faith Berry. Published by arrangement with Carol Publishing Group. A Citadel Press Book.

John Berryman. "Dream Song 14" from *The Dream Songs* by John Berryman. Copyright © 1969 by John Berryman. Reprinted by permission of Farrar, Straus & Giroux, Inc.

Elizabeth Bishop. "Manners," "Sestina," and "The Fish" from *The Complete Poems 1927–1979* by Elizabeth Bishop. Copyright © 1979, 1983 by Alice Helen Methfessel. Reprinted by permission of Farrar, Straus & Giroux, Inc.

Sophie Cabot Black. "August" copyright © 1994 by Sophie Cabot Black. Reprinted from *The Misunderstanding of Nature* with the permission of Graywolf Press, Saint Paul, Minnesota.

Robert Bly. "Sitting Down to Dinner" and "Snowbanks North of the House" from *The Man in the Black Coat Turns* by Robert Bly. Copyright © 1981, 1988 by Robert Bly. Used by permission of Georges Borchardt, Inc., for the author, and Doubleday, a division of Bantam Doubleday Dell Publishing Group, Inc. "Snowfall in the Afternoon" and "Waking from Sleep" reprinted from *Silence in the Snowy Fields*, by Robert Bly, Wesleyan University Press, Middletown, CT, 1962. Copyright © 1962 by Robert Bly. Reprinted with his permission. "On 'Snowbanks North of the House'" reprinted by permission of the author. "Youth" (translation of Neruda's "Juventud") from *Neruda & Vallejo: Selected Poems*. Ed. Robert Bly. Beacon Press, 1993. Copyright © 1993 by Robert Bly.

Marilyn Bowering. "Wishing Africa" from *Sleeping with Lambs* by Marilyn Bowering.

Anne Bradstreet. "Before the Birth of One of Her Children" from *The Works of Anne Bradstreet*, ed. by Jeannine Hensley. Cambridge, Mass: Harvard University Press, Copyright © 1967 by the President and Fellows of Harvard College.

Joseph Brodsky. "Love Song" from *So Forth* by Joseph Brodsky. Copyright © 1996 by the Estate of Joseph Brodsky. Reprinted by permission of Farrar, Straus & Giroux, Inc.

Gwendolyn Brooks. "The Bean Eaters," "The Mother" and "We Real Cool" from *Blacks* (Chicago, IL: Third World Press, 1987). Copyright © 1987 and 1991 by Gwendolyn Brooks.

Joseph Bruchac. "Ellis Island." Reprinted by permission of the Barbara S. Kouts Literary Agency.

Rosario Castellanos. "Chess" translated by Maureen Ahern from *A Rosario Castellanos Reader*, ed. and trans. by Maureen Ahern. Fondo de Cultura Econimica. Copyright © 1988. Reprinted by permission of the University of Texas Press.

Helen Chasin. "The Word *Plum*" from *Coming Close and Other Poems* by Helen Chasin. Copyright © 1968 by Yale University Press.

David Chinitz. "The Romanticization of Africa in the 1920s" excerpted from "Rejuvenation through Joy: Langston Hughes, Primitivism, and Jazz" by David Chinitz from *American Literary History* Spring 1997, vol. 9, no. 1, pp. 60–78. Reprinted by permission of Oxford University Press.

John Ciardi. "Suburban" from *For Instance* by John Ciardi. Copyright © 1979 by Jon Ciardi. Reprinted by permission of W. W. Norton & Company, Inc.

Amy Clampitt. "Dancers Exercising" from *The Kingfisher* by Amy Clampitt. Copyright © 1983 by Amy Clampitt. Reprinted by permission of Alfred A. Knopf, Inc.

Lucille Clifton. "come home from the movies" and "for deLawd" copyright © 1986 by Lucille Clifton. Reprinted from *Good Woman: Poems and a Memoir 1969-1990*, by Lucille Clifton, with the permission of BOA Editions, Ltd., Rochester, NY.

Edmund Conti. "Pragmatist" from *Light Year '86*. Reprinted by permission of the author.

Wendy Cope. "Lonely Hearts" from *Making Cocoa for Kingsley Amis* by Wendy Cope. Reprinted by permission of Faber & Faber, Ltd.

Herbert R. Coursen Jr. "A Parodic Interpretation of 'Stopping by Woods on a Snowy Evening'" excerpted from "The Ghost of Christmas Past: 'Stopping by Woods on a Snowy Evening'" by Herbert R. Coursen Jr. from *College English*, December 1962. Originally published by the National Council of Teachers of English.

Sally Croft. "Home-Baked Bread" from *Light Year '86*. Reprinted by permission of the author.

Victor Hernandez Cruz. "Anonymous" from *Rhythm, Content and Flavor* by Victor Hernandez Cruz, © 1969. Reprinted by permission of the author.

Countee Cullen. "On Racial Poetry" from *Opportunity: A Journal of Negro Life*, February 1926 issue. Copyright © 1926 by *Opportunity Magazine*; copyright renewed 1954 by Ida M. Cullen. "Saturday's Child" and " Yet Do I Marvel " from *Color* by Countee Cullen. Copyright © 1925 by Harper & Brothers; copyright renewed 1953 by Ida M. Cullen. Reprinted by permission of GRM Associates, Inc., Agents for the Estate of Ida M. Cullen.

E. E. Cummings. "anyone lived in a pretty how town," "Buffalo Bill's," "in Just-," "l(a," "next to of course god america i," "she being Brand," and "since feeling is first" from *Complete Poems: 1904–1962* by E. E. Cummings, edited by George J. Firmage. Copyright 1923, 1925, 1926, 1931, 1935, 1938, 1939, 1940, 1944, 1945, 1946, 1947, 1948, 1949, 1950, 1951, 1952, 1953, 1954. Copyright © 1955, 1956, 1957, 1958, 1959, 1960, 1961, 1962, 1963, 1966, 1967, 1968, 1972, 1973, 1974, 1975, 1976, 1977, 1978, 1979, 1980, 1981, 1982, 1983, 1984, 1985, 1956, 1987, 1988, 1989, 1990, 1991 by the Trustees for the E. E. Cummings Trust. Copyright © 1973, 1976, 1978, 1979, 1981, 1983, 1985, 1991 by George James Firmage. Reprinted by permission of Liveright Publishing Corporation. "On the Artist's Responsibility" from *i: six non lectures* by e. e. cummings, Cambridge, Mass: Harvard University Press, Copyright © 1953 by e. e. cummings. Copyright © 1981 by e. e. cummings trust.

Jim Daniels. "Short-Order Cook" from *Places/Everyone*. Copyright © 1985. Winner of the 1985 Brittingham Prize in Poetry. Reprinted by permission of The University of Wisconsin Press.

Peter De Vries. "To His Importunate Mistress." Reprinted by permission of the Estate of Peter De Vries and the Watkins/Loomis Agency. Originally published in *The New Yorker*.

Andrew P. Debicki. "New Criticism and Deconstructionism: Two Attitudes in Teaching Poetry" from *Writing and Reading Differently: Deconstruction and the Teaching of Composition and Literature*, eds. G. Douglas Atkins and Michael L. Johnson. Copyright © 1985 by the Unviversity Press of Kansas. Reprinted by permission.

James Dickey. "Deer Among Cattle" from *Poems, 1957–1967* by James Dickey. Wesleyan UP, 1978.

Emily Dickinson. "A Bird came down the Walk — ," "A light exists in Spring," "After great pain, a formal feeling comes — ," "Because I could not stop for Death — ," "From all the Jails the Boys and Girls," "I cannot dance upon my Toes," "I dwell in Possibility — ," "I felt a Cleaving in my Mind — ," "I heard a Fly buzz — when I died — ," "I never saw a Moor — ," "I read my sentence — steadily," "I taste a liquor never brewed — ," "If I shouldn't be alive," "I'm Nobody! Who are you?," "Much Madness is divinest Sense — ," "Of Bronze — and Blaze," "One need not be a Chamber — to be Haunted — ," "Safe in their Alabaster Chambers — (1859 version)," "Safe in their Alabaster Chambers — (1861 version)," "Success is counted sweetest," "Tell all the Truth but tell it slant — ," "The Grass so little has to do — ," "The Lightning is a yellow Fork," "The Soul selects her own Society — ," "The Thought beneath so slight a film — ," "There's a certain Slant of light," "This is my letter to the World," "This was a Poet — it Is That," "What Soft — Cherubic Creatures — ," and " 'Heaven' — is what I cannot 'reach!" Reprinted by permission of the publishers and the Trustees of Amherst College from *The Poems of Emily Dickinson*, Thomas H. Johnson, ed., Cambridge, Mass.: The Belknap Press of Harvard University Press, Copyright © 1951, 1955, 1979, 1983 by the President and fellows of Harvard College.

Emily Dickinson. "After great pain a formal feeling comes — " and "I dwell in Possibility — " from *The Complete Poems of Emily Dickinson* by Thomas H. Johnson. Copyright © 1929, 1935 by Martha Dickinson Bianchi. Copyright © renewed 1957, 1963 by Mary L. Hampson. By permission of Little, Brown and Company.

Emily Dickinson. "Description of Herself" and excerpt from a letter to Thomas Wentworth Higginson from August 20, 1862 reprinted by permission of the publishers from *The Letters of Emily Dickinson,* edited by Thomas J. Johnson. Cambridge, Mass.: The Belknap Press of Harvard University Press, Copyright © 1958, 1986 by the President and Fellows of Harvard College.

Morris Dickstein. "On the Social Responsibility of the Critic." Reprinted by permission of the Modern Language Association of America from "Damaged Literacy: The Decay of Reading." Originally appeared in *Profession 93.* Copyright © 1993 by the Modern Language Association.

Chitra Banerjee Divakaruni. "Indian Movie New Jersey" from the *Indiana Review,* 1990. Copyright © by Chitra Banerjee Divakaruni. Reprinted by permission of the author.

Gregory Djanikian. "When I First Saw Snow" Reprinted from *Gregory Djanikian: Falling Deeply Into America* by permission of Carnegie Mellon University Press. Copyright © 1989 by Gregory Djanikian.

Bernard Duyfhuizen. " 'To His Coy Mistress': On How a Female Might Respond" excerpted from "Textual Harassment of Marvell's Coy Mistress: The Institutionalization of Masculine Criticism," *College English* (April 1988). Copyright © 1988 by the National Council of Teachers of English.

Cornelius Eady. "The Supremes." Reprinted from *Cornelius Eady: The Gathering of my Name* by permission of Carnegie Mellon University Press. Copyright © 1991 by Cornelius Eady.

George Eliot. "In a London Drawing Room" from *George Eliot, Collected Poems,* Ed. Lucien Jenkins. Skoob Books Publishing LTD, London, 1989. Reprinted by permission.

James A. Emanuel. "Hughes's Attitudes toward Religion" from "Christ in Alabama: Religion in the Poetry of Langston Hughes" in *Modern Black Poets,* Ed. Donald B. Gibson.

Louise Erdrich. "Windigo" from *Jacklight* by Louise Erdrich. Copyright © 1984 by Louise Erdrich. Reprinted by permission of Henry Holt & Co., Inc.

Martín Espada. "Coca-Cola and Coca Frío" from *City of Coughing and Dead Radiators* by Martín Espada. Copyright © 1993 by Martín Espada. Reprinted by permission of W. W. Norton & Company, Inc. "Latin Night at the Pawn Shop" from *Rebellion is the Circle of a Lover's Hands* by Martín Espada. Curbstone Press, 1990. Reprinted by permission of Curbstone Press, Inc.

Barbara Everett. "The Problem of Tone in Prufrock" excerpted from "In Search of Prufrock," *Critical Quarterly* 16 (Summer, 1974).

Ruth Fainlight. "Flower Feet." Copyright © Ruth Fainlight. Originally in The New Yorker, July 10, 1989.

Faiz Ahmed Faiz. "If You Look at the City from Here" from *Faiz Ahmed Faiz, The True Subject,* trans. Naomi Lazard. Copyright © 1988 Princeton UP.

Blanche Farley. "The Lover Not Taken" from *Light Year '86.* Reprinted by permission of the author.

Kenneth Fearing. "AD" from *New and Collected Poems* by Kenneth Fearing (Indiana University Press, 1956).

Judith Fetterley. "A Feminist Reading of 'A Rose for Emily'" from *The Resisting Reader: A Feminist Approach to American Fiction* by Judith Fetterlyey. Copyright © 1978.

Stanley Fish. "On What Makes an Interpretation Acceptable" from *Is There a Text In This Class?* by Stanley Fish. Cambridge, Mass.: Harvard University Press. Copyright © 1988 by the President and Fellows of Harvard College.

Robert J. Fogelin. "A Case against Metaphors" from *Figuratively Speaking,* Yale University Press, copyright © 1988. Reprinted by permission of Yale University Press.

Carolyn Forché. "The Colonel" from *The Country Between Us* by Carolyn Forché. Copyright © 1981 by Carolyn Forché. Reprinted by permission of The Virginia Barber Literary Agency.

Robert Francis. "Catch" and "The Pitcher" copyright © 1950, 1953 by Robert Francis. From *The Orb Weaver,* copyright © 1950, 1953 by Robert Francis. Wesleyan University Press. Reprinted by permission of the University Press of New England. "On 'Hard' Poetry" reprinted from *The Satirical Rogue of Poetry* by Robert Francis (Amherst: University of Massachusetts Press, 1968), copyright © 1968 by Robert Francis.

Robert Frost. "Acquainted with the Night," "Away," "Come In," "Design," "Fire and Ice," "Neither Out Far nor In Deep," "Nothing Gold Can Stay," "Once by the Pacific," "Stopping by Woods on a Snowy Evening," "The Most of It," "The Silken Tent," and "Two Tramps in Mudtime" from *The Poetry of Robert Frost* by Robert Frost. Copyright © 1936, 1942, 1951, © 1956 by Robert Frost. Copyright © 1964, 1970 by Lesley Frost Ballantine. Copyright © 1923, 1928, © 1969 by Henry Holt & Co., Inc. Reprinted by permission of Henry Holt & Co., Inc. "In White" from *The Dimensions of Robert Frost* by Reginald L. Cook. Copyright © 1958 by Reginald L. Cook. "On the Living Part of a Poem" from *A Swinger of Birches: A Portrait of Robert Frost* by Sidney Cox. Copyright © 1957 by New York University Press. Reprinted with permission of New York University Press. "On the Way to Read a Poem " from "Poetry and School" by Robert Frost in *The Atlantic Monthly,* June 1951. Reprinted by permission of the Estate of Robert Frost. "The Figure a Poem Makes" from *The Selected Prose of Robert Frost,* edited by Hyde Cox and Edward Connery Lathem. Copyright © 1946, 1956, 1959 by Robert Frost. Copyright © 1949, 1954, © 1966 by Henry Holt & Co., Inc. Reprinted by permission of Henry Holt & Co., Inc.

Alice Fulton. "On the Validity of Free Verse" from *Ecstatic Occasions, Expedient Forms,* David Lehman, ed. Copyright © 1983, 1987, 1993, 1994, 1995, 1996, 1997 by Alice Fulton. Reprinted by permission of the author.

Deborah Garrison. "She Was Waiting to Be Told." Copyright © 1990 by Deborah Garrison. Originally appeared in *The New Yorker.* Reprinted by permission of the author.

Donald B. Gibson. "The Essential Optimism of Hughes and Whitman," excerpt from "The Good Black Poet and the Good Gray Poet: The Poetry of Hughes and Whitman" in *Langston Hughes — Black Genius: A Critical Evaluation* by Donald B. Gibson. William Morrow, 1971. Reprinted with permission of the author.

Sandra M. and Susan Gubar Gilbert. "On Dickinson's White Dress" excerpted from *The Madwoman in the Attic,* Yale University Press, 1979. Reprinted by permission of Yale University Press.

Allen Ginsberg. "First Party at Ken Kesey's with Hell's Angels" from *Collected Poems 1947-1980* by Allen Ginsberg. Copyright © 1965 by Allen Ginsberg. Reprinted by permission of HarperCollins Publishers, Inc.

Henry A. Giroux. "The Canon and Liberal Arts Education" excerpted from "Liberal Arts Education and the Struggle for Public Life: Dreaming about Democracy." *South Atlantic Quarterly* 89:1 (1990) and Glenn and Herrnstein Smith, *The Politics of Liberal Education* (1992), copyright © Duke University Press, 1988. Reprinted by permission of Duke University Press.

Louise Glück. "The School Children" from *The House on Marshland.* Copyright © 1971, 1972, 1973, 1974, 1975 by Louise Glück. First published by The Ecco Press in 1989. Reprinted by permission of The Ecco Press.

Donald J. Greiner. "On What Comes 'After Apple-Picking'" from "The Indispensable Robert Frost" by Donald J. Greiner. Excerpted with permission of G. K. Hall & Co., an imprint of Simon & Schuster Macmillan, from *Critical Essays on Robert Frost,* edited by Philip L. Gerber. Copyright © 1982 by Philip L. Gerber.

H. D. [Hilda Doolittle]. "Heat" from H.D., from *Collected Poems, 1912-1944.* Copyright © 1982 by The Estate of Hilda Doolittle. Reprinted by permission of New Directions Publishing Corp.

Marilyn Hacker. "Groves of Academe" from *Winter Numbers* by Marilyn Hacker. Copyright © 1994 by Marilyn Hacker. Originally published in *Open Places.* Reprinted with permission of Marilyn Hacker and W. W. Norton & Co., Inc.

Rachel Hadas. "The Red Hat" from *Halfway Down the Hall: New and Selected Poems.* Copyright © 1997 by Rachel Hadas. Reprinted by permission of The University Press of New England.

Donald Hall. "My Son My Executioner" from *Old and New Poems* by Donald Hall. Copyright © 1990 by Donald Hall. Reprinted by permission of Ticknor & Fields/Houghton Mifflin Company. All rights reserved. "Scenic View" from *The Happy Man* by Donald Hall. Copyright © 1981, 1982, 1983, 1984, 1985, 1986 by Donald Hall. Reprinted by permission of Random House, Inc. An earlier version of "Letter with No Address" appeared in *Ploughshares,* Winter 1996-97, vol. 22, no. 4, pp. 109–113. Reprinted with permission of the author.

Mark Halliday. "Graded Paper" from *The Michigan Quarterly Review.* Reprinted by permission of the author.

Joy Harjo. "Fishing" from June 21, 1991 Op-Ed page of the *New York Times.* Copyright © 1991 by The New York Times Company. Reprinted by permission.

Michael S. Harper. "Grandfather." Reprinted by permission of the author.

Robert Hass. "A Story About the Body" from *Human Wishes* by Robert Hass. Copyright © 1989 by Robert Hass. First published by The Ecco Press in 1989. Reprinted by permission of The Ecco Press. "Happiness" from *Sun Under Wood* by Robert Hass. Copyright © 1996 by Robert Hass. First Published by The Ecco Press in 1989. Reprinted by permission of The Ecco Press.

William Hathaway. "Oh Oh" from Light Year '86. This poem was originally published in *The Cincinnati Poetry Review.*

Harriet Hawkins. "Should We Study *King Kong* or *King Lear*?" from "From King Lear to King Kong and Back: Shakespeare in Popular Modern Genres" in *"Bad" Shakespeare: Revelations of the Shakespeare Cannon,* ed. Maurice Cherney, Fairleigh Dickinson University Press, 1988.

Robert Hayden. "Those Winter Sundays" copyright © 1966 by Robert Hayden, from *Angle of Ascent: New and Selected Poems* by Robert Hayden. Reprinted by permission of Liveright Publishing Corporation.

Seamus Heaney. "Mid-term Break" from *Poems 1965–1975* by Seamus Heaney. Copyright © 1980 by Seamus Heaney. Reprinted by permission of Farrar, Straus & Giroux, Inc. "The Pitchfork" from *Seeing Things* by Seamus Heaney. Copyright © 1991 by Seamus Heaney. Reprinted by permission of Farrar, Straus & Giroux, Inc.

Anthony Hecht. "The Dover Bitch" from *Collected Earlier Poems* by Anthony Hecht. Copyright © 1990 by Anthony D. Hecht. Reprinted by permission of Alfred A. Knopf., Inc.

Judy Page Heitzman. "The Schoolroom on the Second Floor of the Knitting Mill." Copyright © 1991 by Judy Page Heitzman. Originally in *The New Yorker,* December 2, 1992, p. 102.

William Heyen. "The Trains" from *The Host: Selected Poems 1965-1990,* by William Heyen. Reprinted by permission of Time Being Books. Copyright © 1994 by Time Being Press. All Rights Reserved.

Thomas Wentworth Higginson. "On Meeting Dickinson for the First Time" from *The Letters of Emily Dickinson,* ed. Thomas H. Johnson. Cambridge, Mass.: The Belknap Press of Harvard University Press, Copyright © 1958, 1986 by the President and Fellows of Harvard University.

Conrad Hilberry. "The Frying Pan" first appeared in *Field 19* (Fall, 1978). Reprinted by permission of Oberlin College Press.

Edward Hirsch. "Fast Break" from *Wild Gratitude* by Edward Hirsch. Reprinted by permission of Alfred A. Knopf, Inc.

Jane Hirshfield. "The Lives of the Heart" from *The Lives of the Heart* published by HarperCollins. Copyright © 1997 by Jane Hirshfield. First appeared in *The Yale Review,* January, 1997, vol. 85, no. 1. Used by permission.

Linda Hogan. "Hunger" from *The Book of Medicines* by Linda Hogan, Coffee House Press, 1993. Copyright © 1993 by Linda Hogan. Used by permission of the publisher. "Song for My Name" from *Calling Myself Home* by Linda Hogan (Greenfield Review Press).

Margaret Holley. "Peepers" from *Morning Star* by Margaret Holley. Copyright © 1992 by Margaret Holley. Reprinted by permission of Copper Beach Press.

M. Carl Holman. "Mr. Z." Reprinted by permission of the Estate of M. Carl Holman.

Garrett Kaoru Hongo. "The Cadence of Silk" from *The River of Heaven* by Garrett Hongo. Copyright © 1988 by Garrett Hongo. Reprinted by permission of Alfred A. Knopf., Inc.

A. E. Housman. "Is my team ploughing," "Loveliest of trees, the cherry now," "To an Athlete Dying Young," and "When I was one-and-twenty" from *The Collected Poems of A. E. Housman.* Copyright © 1939, 1949 © 1965 by Holt, Rinehart and Winston. Copyright © 1967, 1968 by Robert E Symons. Reprinted by permission of The Society of Authors as the literary representative of the Estate of A. E. Housman.

Carolynn Hoy. "In the Summer Kitchen" from *Ariel,* vol. 24:2, April 1993. Reprinted with permission of The Board of Governors, University of Calgary.

Andrew Hudgins. "Seventeen" from *The Glass Hammer.* Copyright © 1994 by Andrew Hudgins. Reprinted by permission of Houghton Mifflin Company. All rights reserved. "Elegy for My Father, Who is Not Dead" from *The Never-Ending.* Copyright © 1991 by Andrew Hudgins. Reprinted by permission of Houghton Mifflin Company. All rights reserved.

Langston Hughes. "Ballad of the Landlord," "Cross," "Danse Africaine," "Dinner Guest: Me," "Doorknobs," "Dream Boogie," "Dream Variations," "Formula," "Frederick Douglass: 1817–1895," "Harlem," "I, Too," "Jazzonia," "Johannesburg Mines," "Juke-Box Love Song," "Lenox Avenue: Midnight," "Let America Be America Again," "Midnight Raffle," "Negro," "Note on Commercial Theatre," "Old Walt," "Red Silk Stockings" "Rent-Party Shout: For a Lady Dancer," "The English," "The Negro Speaks of Rivers," "The Weary Blues," "Theme for English B," and "Un-American Investigators," from *Collected Poems* by Langston Hughes. Copyright © 1994 by the Estate of Langston Hughes. Reprinted by permission of Alfred A. Knopf., Inc. "On Harlem Rent Parties" text excerpt from "When the Negro Was in Vogue" from *The Big Sea* by Langston Hughes. Copyright © 1940 by Langston Hughes. Copyright renewed © 1968 by Arna Bontemps and George Houston Bass. Reprinted by permission of Hill and Wang, a division of Farrar, Straus & Giroux, Inc. "On Racial Shame and Pride" excerpt from "The Negro Artist and the Racial Mountain" by Langston Hughes. Reprinted with permission from the June 23, 1926 issue of *The Nation.*

Ted Hughes. "Thistles" from *Wodwo* by Ted Hughes. Copyright © 1961 by Ted Hughes. Reprinted by permission of HarperCollins Publishers, Inc.

Paul Humphrey. "Blow" from *Light Year '86.* Reprinted with permission of the author.

Bonnie Jacobsen. "On Being Served Apples" from *Stopping for Time.* Reprinted by permission of Green Tower Press.

Mark Jarman. "Unholy Sonnet" from *The New Criterion,* April 1993. Reprinted by permission of the author.

Randall Jarrell. "Next Day" and "The Death of the Ball Turret Gunner" from *The Complete Poems.* Copyright © 1969 by Mrs. Randall Jarrell. Reprinted by permisison of Farrar, Straus & Giroux, Inc.

Onwuchekwa Jemie. "On Universal Poetry" from *Langston Hughes* by Onwuchekwa Jemie. Copyright © 1985 by Columbia University Press. Reprinted with permission of the publisher.

Alice Jones. "The Foot." Reprinted by permission of the author.

Donald Justice. "Order in the Streets " from *Losers Weepers* by Donald Justice. Reprinted by permission of the author.

Katherine Kearns. "On the Symbolic Setting of 'Home Burial'" excerpt from "The Place Is the Asylum: Women and Nature in Robert Frost's Poetry" in *American Literature 59* (May 1987). Copyright © 1991 by Duke University Press. Reprinted by permission of Duke University Press.

Aron Keesbury. "Song to a Waitress." Copyright 1997 by Aron Keesbury, Boston, MA. Reprinted by permission of the author.

Karl Keller. "Robert Frost on Dickinson" from *The Only Kangaroo among the Beauty: Emily Dickinson in America.* Copyright © 1979. The Johns Hopkins University Press.

X. J. Kennedy. "A Visit from St. Sigmund." Copyright © 1993 by X. J. Kennedy. Originally published in *Light, The Quarterly of Light Verse.* Reprinted by permission of the author and *Light.*

Jane Kenyon. "Blue Bowl" and "Surprise" copyright © 1996 by Jane Kenyon. Reprinted from *Otherwise: New & Selected Poems* with the permission of Graywolf Press, Saint Paul, Minnesota.

Maxine Hong Kingston. "Restaurant" from *The Iowa Review 12* (Spring/Summer, 1981). Reprinted by permission of the author.

Galway Kinnell. "After Making Love We Hear Footsteps" and "Blackberry Eating" from *Three Books.* Copyright © 1993 by Galway Kinnell. Originally published in *Mortal Acts, Mortal Words* (1980). Reprinted by permission of Houghton Mifflin Company. All rights reserved. "The Deconstruction of Emily Dickinson" from *Imperfect Thirst.* Copyright © 1994 by Galway Kinnell. Reprinted by permission of Houghton Mifflin Company. All rights reserved.

Joan Kirkby. "On the Fragility of Language in Dickinson's Poetry" from *Emily Dickinson* by Joan Kirkby. Reprinted by permission of the author.

Carolyn Kizer. "Food for Love" copyright © 1984 by Carolyn Kizer. Reprinted from *Yin,* by Carolyn Kizer, with the permission of BOA Editions, Ltd., Rochester, NY.

Etheridge Knight. "A Watts Mother Mourns While Boiling Beans" from *Belly Song and Other Poems* by Etheridge Knight. Copyright © 1973 by Broadside Press. Reprinted with their permission. "Eastern Guard Tower" from *Poems from Prison* by Etheridge Knight. Copyright © 1968 by Etheridge Knight. Reprinted by permission of Broadside Press.

Annette Kolodny. "On the Commitments of Feminist Criticism" from "Dancing Through the Minefield: Some Observations on the Theory, Practice and Politics of a Feminist Literary Criticism," *Feminist Studies 6,* 1980. Copyright © 1979 by Annette Kolodny: all rights reserved. Reprinted by permission of the author.

Yusef Komunyakaa. "Facing It" from *Dien Cai Dau.* Copyright © 1988 by Yusef Komunyakaa, Wesleyan University Press. Reprinted by permission of The University Press of New England.

Ted Kooser. "The Urine Specimen" from *One World at a Time* by Ted Kooser. Copyright © 1985. Reprinted by permission of the University of Pittsburgh Press.

Maxine Kumin. "Woodchucks" from *Maxine Kumin: Selected Poems 1960–1990* by Maxine Kumin. Copyright © 1971 by Maxine Kumin. Reprinted by permission of W. W. Norton & Co., Inc.

Philip Larkin. "A Study of Reading Habits" and "This Be the Verse" from *Collected Poems* by Philip Larkin. Copyright © 1988, 1989 by the Estate of Philip Larkin. Reprinted by permission of Farrar, Straus & Giroux, Inc.

Queen Latifah. "The Evil That Men Do." T-Boy Music Publishing, Inc. and Queen Latifah Music. All rights reserved. International copyright secured.

Richard Lattimore. "Invocation to Aphrodite (translation of Sappho)" from *Greek Lyrics* tr. by Richard Lattimore, 2 ed. University of Chicago Press, pp. 38–39. Reprinted by permission of the University of Chicago Press.

Tato Laviera. "AmeRican" from *AmeRican*. Copyright © 1985. Reprinted by permission of Arte Publico Press–University of Houston.

D. H. Lawrence. "Snake" and "The English Are So Nice" from *The Complete Poems of D.H. Lawrence* by D. H. Lawrence, edited by V. de Sola Pinto & F. W. Roberts. Copyright © 1964, 1971 by Angelo Ravagli and C. M. Weekley, Executors of the Estate of Frieda Lawrence Ravagli. Used by permission of Viking Penguin, a division of Penguin Books USA Inc.

Li-Young Lee. "Eating Together." Copyright © 1986 by Li-Young Lee. Reprinted from *Rose*, by Li-Young Lee, with the permission of BOA Editions, Ltd, Rochester, NY.

David Lenson. "On the Contemporary Use of Rhyme" from *The Chronicle of Higher Education* (February 24, 1988). Reprinted by permission of the author.

Denise Levertov. "Gathered at the River" by Denise Levertov from *Oblique Prayers*. Copyright © 1984 by Denise Levertov. Reprinted by permission of New Directions Publishing Corp. "News Items " from *The Freeing of the Dust*. Copyright © 1975 by Denise Levertov. Reprinted by permission of New Directions Publishing Corporation. "On 'Gathered at the River'" from *Gathered at the River*. Copyright © 1997 by Denise Levertov. Reprinted by permission of New Directions Publishing Corp.

Philip Levine. "The Simple Truth" from *The Simple Truth* by Philip Levine. Copyright © 1994 by Phillip Levine. Reprinted by permission of Alfred A. Knopf., Inc.

J. Patrick Lewis. "The Unkindest Cut" from *Light 5* (Spring 1993). Reprinted with permission of the author and *Light*.

Li Ho. "A Beautiful Girl Combs Her Hair" translated by David Young, from *Four T'ang Poets: Field Translation Series #4.* Copyright © 1980 Oberlin College Press. Reprinted by permission of Oberlin College Press.

Audre Lorde. "Hanging Fire" from *The Black Unicorn* by Audre Lorde. Copyright © 1978 by Audre Lorde. Reprinted by permission of W. W. Norton & Company, Inc. "Poems Are Not Luxuries" reprinted with permission by Audre Lorde.

Katharyn Howd Machan. "Hazel Tells LaVerne" from *Light Year '85*. Reprinted by permission of the author.

Archibald MacLeish. "Ars Poetica" from *Collected Poems 1917-1982* by Archibald MacLeish. Copyright © 1985 by The Estate of Archibald MacLeish. Reprinted by permission of Houghton Mifflin Company. All rights reserved.

Elaine Magarrell. "The Joy of Cooking" from *Sometime the Cow Kick Your Head, Light Year 88/89*. Reprinted with permission of the author.

Charles Martin. "Victoria's Secret" from *What the Darkness Proposes*, p. 7 by Charles Martin. Copyright © by Charles Martin. Reprinted by permission of Johns Hopkins University Press.

Julio Marzán. "Ethnic Poetry." Originally appeared in *Parnassus: Poetry In Review*. Reprinted by permission of the author.

Florence Cassen Mayers. "All-American Sestina." Copyright © 1996 Florence Cassen Mayers, as first published in *The Atlantic Monthly*. Reprinted with permission of the author.

David McCord. "Epitaph on a Waiter" from *Odds without Ends* by David McCord. Reprinted by permission of Arthur B. Page, executor of the estate of David McCord.

Michael McFee. "In Medias Res" from *Light Year '86*. Reprinted with permission of the author.

Peter Meinke. "The ABC of Aerobics" from *Night Watch on the Chesapeake*, by Peter Meinke. Copyright © 1987. Reprinted by permission of the University of Pittsburgh Press.

James Merrill. "Casual Wear" from *Selected Poems 1946-1985* by James Merrill. Copyright © 1992 by James Merrill. Reprinted by permission of Alfred A. Knopf Inc.

Edna St. Vincent Millay. "I will put Chaos into fourteen lines" and "What Lips My Lips Have Kissed" from *Collected Poems,* HarperCollins. Copyright © 1923, 1951, 1954, 1982 by Edna St. Vincent Millay and Norma Millay Ellis. All rights reserved. Reprinted by permission of Elizabeth Barnett, literary executor.

Janice Mirikitani. "Recipe" excerpted from *Shedding Silence*, copyright © 1987 by Janice Mirikitani. Reprinted by permission of Celestial Arts, P.O. Box 7123, Berkeley, CA 94707.

Elaine Mitchell. "Form" from *Light 9* (Spring 1994). Reprinted by permission of the author.

N. Scott Momaday. "The Bear" Copyright © 1992 by N. Scott Momaday. From *In the Presence of The Sun* by N. Scott Momaday. Reprinted by permission of St. Martin's Press Incorporated.

Janice Townley Moore. "To a Wasp." Reprinted by permission of the author.

Marianne Moore. "Poetry." Reprinted with the permission of Simon & Schuster from *Collected Poems of Marianne Moore*. Copyright © 1935 by Marianne Moore. Copyright renewed © 1963 by Marianne Moore and T. S. Eliot.

Robert Morgan. "Mountain Graveyard" from *Sigodlin*, copyright © 1990 by Robert Morgan. Wesleyan University Press. Reprinted by permission of the University Press of New England. "On the Shape of a Poem" from *Epoch* (Fall/Winter 1983). Reprinted by permission of the author.

Jon Mukand. "Lullaby" from *Articulations: The Body and Illness in Poetry*, ed. John Mukand (University of Iowa Press, 1994). Copyright © John Mukand. Originally published in *The Journal of the American Medical Association*, 4/1/83.

Joan Murray. "Play-By-Play." Reprinted by permission from *The Hudson Review*, Vol. XLIX, No. 4 (Winter 1997). Copyright © 1997 by Joan Murray.

Susan Musgrave. "Right through the Heart" from *Tarts and Muggers: Poems New and Selected (1982)*. Reprinted by permission of the author.

Pablo Neruda. "Juventud (to be printed in spanish)" from *Neruda & Vallejo: Selected Poems*. Ed. Robert Bly. Beacon Press, 1993. "Youth" from *Canto General* by Pablo Neruda, tr. Jack Schmitt, University of California Press, 1991. "Sweetness Always" from *Extravagaria* by Pablo Neruda, translated by Alastair Reid. English translation copyright © 1974, by Alastair Reid. Reprinted by permission of Farrar, Straus & Giroux, Inc.

John Frederick Nims. "Love Poem" from *Selected Poems*. Copyright © 1982 by the University of Chicago. Reprinted by permission of the Publisher.

Alden Nowlan. "The Bull Moose" from *An Exchange of Gifts* by Alden Nowlan. Reprinted with the permission of Stoddart Publishing Co. Limited, Canada.

Frank O'Hara. "Autobiographia Literaria" from *Collected Poems* by Frank O'Hara. Copyright © 1958 by Maureen Granville-Smith, Administrator of the Estate of Frank O'Hara. Reprinted by permission of Alfred A. Knopf Inc.

Sharon Olds. "Rite of Passage" and "Sex without Love" from *The Dead And The Living* by Sharon Olds. Copyright © 1983 by Sharon Olds. Reprinted by permission of Alfred A. Knopf., Inc.

Mary Oliver. "The Black Snake" from *Twelve Moons* by Mary Oliver. Copyright © 1972, 1973, 1974, 1976, 1977, 1978, 1979 by Mary Oliver. By permission of Little, Brown and Company.

Wilfred Owen. "Arms and the Boy" and "Dulce et Decorum Est" by Wilfred Owen from *The Collected Poems of Wilfred Owen*. Copyright © 1963 by Chatto & Windus, Ltd. Reprinted by permission of New Directions Publishing Corp.

Dorothy Parker. "One Perfect Rose" copyright 1929, renewed © 1957 by Dorothy Parker, from *The Portable Dorothy Parker* by Dorothy Parker, Introduction by Brenda Gill. Used by permission of Viking Penguin, a division of Penguin Books USA Inc.

Linda Pastan. "Marks" and "after minor surgery" copyright © 1978 and 1981 by Linda Pastan from *PM/AM: New and Selected Poems* by Linda Pastan. Reprinted by permission of W. W. Norton & Co., Inc.

Octavio Paz. "The Street" from *Early Poems 1935-1955*. Reprinted with permission of Indiana University Press.

Molly Peacock. "Desire" from Molly Peacock, *Raw Heaven* Random House, 1984.

Laurence Perrine. "The limerick's never averse" from *A Limerick's Always A Verse: 200 Original Limericks* by Laurence Perrine. Copyright © 1990 by Harcourt Brace & Company.

Stephen Perry. "The Blue Spruce." Copyright © 1991 by Stephen Perry. Originally in *The New Yorker*, January 28, 1991, pp. 34–35.

Marge Piercy. "Barbie Doll" and "The Secretary Chant" from *Circles on the Water* by Marge Piercy. Copyright © 1982 by Marge Piercy. Reprinted by permission of Alfred A. Knopf, Inc.

Sylvia Plath. "Daddy" from *The Collected Poems* by Sylvia Plath, ed. Ted Hughes. "Mirror" from *The Collected Poems* by Sylvia Plath, ed. Ted Hughes. Originally appeared in *The New Yorker*. Reprinted by permission of Faber & Faber, Ltd. and

HarperCollins Publishers, Inc. "Mushrooms" from *The Colossus and Other Poems* by Sylvia Plath. Copyright © 1960 by Sylvia Plath. Reprinted by permission of Alfred A. Knopf, Inc.

Ezra Pound. "In a Station of the Metro" and "The River-Merchant's Wife: A Letter" from *Personae*. Copyright © 1926 by Ezra Pound. Reprinted by permission of New Directions Publishing Corp. "On Free Verse" by Ezra Pound from *The Literary Essays of Ezra Pound*. Copyright © 1935 by Ezra Pound. Reprinted by permission of New Directions Publishing Corp.

Jim Powell. "[Artfully adorned Aphrodite, deathless]" from *Sappho A Garland: The Poems and Fragments of Sappho*. Copyright © by Jim Powell. Reprinted by permission of Farrar, Straus & Giroux, Inc.

Wyatt Prunty. "Elderly Lady Crossing on Green" from *The Run of the House*, page 18. Copyright © 1993. The Johns Hopkins University Press.

Peter Rabinowitz. "On Close Readings" excerpted from *Pedagogy Is Politics: Literary Theory and Critical Thinking*, ed. by Marina-Regina Kecht. Copyright © 1992 by the Board of Trustees of the University of Illinois. Reprinted with permission of the University of Illinois Press.

Henry Reed. "Naming of Parts" and "Lessons of War" (1. Naming of the Parts) from *Henry Reed: Collected Poems*, ed. Jon Stallworthy. Copyright © 1991 by the Executor of Henry Reed's Estate.

David S. Reynolds. "Popular Literature and 'Wild Nights — Wild Nights!" from *Beneath the American Renaissance* by David S. Reynolds. Copyright © 1988 by David S. Reynolds. Reprinted by permission of Alfred A. Knopf, Inc.

Adrienne Rich. "Living in Sin." Copyright © 1993, 1955 by Adrienne Rich from *Collected Early Poems: 1950-1970* by Adrienne Rich. Reprinted by permission of W. W. Norton & Company, Inc.

Rainer Maria Rilke. "The Panther" from *The Selected Poetry of Rainer Maria Rilke* by Rainer Maria Rilke, edited & translated by Stephen Mitchell. Copyright © 1982 by Stephen Mitchell. Reprinted by permission of Random House, Inc.

Alberto Ríos. "Seniors" from *Five Indiscretions*. Copyright © 1985 by Alberto Ríos. Reprinted by permission of the author.

Edwin Arlington Robinson. "Mr. Flood's Party." Reprinted with the permission of Simon & Schuster from *The Collected Poems of Edwin Arlington Robinson*. Copyright © 1921 by Macmillan Publishing Company, renewed 1949 by Ruth Nivision.

Theodore Roethke. "I Knew a Woman" "My Papa's Waltz," and "Root Cellar" copyright © 1954 by Theodore Roethke. From *The Collected Poems of Theodore Roethke* by Theodore Roethke. Used by permission of Doubleday, a division of Bantam Doubleday Dell Publishing Group, Inc.

Frederik L. Rusch. "Society and Character in " 'The Love Song of J. Alfred Prufrock' " from "Approaching Literature through the Social Psychology of Erich Fromm" in *Psychological Perspectives on Literature: Freudian Dissidents and Non-Freudians*, edited by Joseph Natoli. Copyright © 1984.

Vern Rutsala. "Words." Reprinted from *Vern Rutsala: Walking Home from the Icehouse* by permission of Carnegie Mellon University Press. Copyright © 1981 by Vern Rutsala.

Ira Sadoff. "Nazis." Copyright © 1989 by Ira Sadoff. Reprinted by permission of David R. Godine, Publisher, Inc.

Mary Jo Salter. "Welcome to Hiroshima" from *Henry Purcell in Japan* by Mary Jo Salter. Copyright © 1984 by Mary Jo Slater. Reprinted by permission of Alfred A. Knopf, Inc.

Indira Sant. "Household Fires" from *Sixteen Modern Indian Poems*, eds. A. K. Ramanujan and Vinay Dharwadker, copyright © 1989. Reprinted by permission of *Daedalus, Journal of the American Academy of Arts and Sciences* from the issue entitled "Another India," Fall 1989, vol. 118, No. 4.

Jack Schmitt. "Youth (translation of Neruda's 'Juventud')" from *Pablo Neruda, Canto General* tr. Jack Schmitt, University of California Press, 1991.

Elisabeth Schneider. "Hints of Eliot in Prufrock" from "Prufrock and After: The Theme of Change," *PMLA 87* (1982): 1103–1117.

Anne Sexton. "Lobster" from *45 Mercy Street* by Anne Sexton. Copyright © 1976 by Linda Gray Sexton and Loring Conant, Jr. Reprinted by permission of Houghton Mifflin Co. All rights reserved.

Louis Simpson. "In the Suburbs" from *At the End of the Open Road* by Louis Simpson. Wesleyan UP, 1963. Reprinted by permission of the University Press of New England.

David R. Slavitt. "Titanic" from *Big Nose* by David R. Slavitt. Copyright © 1983 by David R. Slavitt. Reprinted by permission of Louisiana State University Press.

Ernest Slyman. "Lightning Bugs" from *Sometime the Cow Kick Your Head, Light Year 88/89*. Reprinted by permission of the author.

Gary Snyder. "How Poetry Comes to Me" from *No Nature* by Gary Snyder. Copyright © 1992 by Gary Snyder. Reprinted by permission of Random House, Inc.

David Solway. "Windsurfing." Reprinted by permission of the author.

Cathy Song. "The White Porch (moved from collection)" from *Picture Bride*. Copyright © 1983 by Yale University Press.

Susan Sontag. "Against Interpretation" excerpt from "Against Interpretation" by Susan Sontag from *Against Interpretation* by Susan Sontag. Copyright © 1964; 1966 and copyright renewed © 1994 by Susan Sontag. Reprinted by permission of Farrar, Straus & Giroux, Inc.

Gary Soto. "Behind Grandma's House," "Black Hair," and "Mexicans Begin Jogging" from *New and Selected Works* by Gary Soto. Copyright © 1995, published by Chronicle Books. Reprinted by permission of the publisher.

Wole Soyinka. "Future Plans" from *A Shuttle in the Crypt* by Wole Soyinka. Copyright © 1972 by Wole Soyinka. Reprinted by permission of Hill and Wang, a division of Farrar, Straus & Giroux, Inc. "Telephone Conversation" from *Ibadan*, volume 10, November 1960, p. 34.

Bruce Springsteen. "The Streets of Philadelphia." Reprinted with permission.

William Stafford. "Traveling through the Dark." Copyright © 1977 William Stafford from *Stories That Could Be True* (Harper & Row). Reprinted by permission of The Estate of William Stafford.

Timothy Steele. "An Aubade" and " Waiting for the Storm" from *Sapphics and Uncertainties: Poems, 1970-1986* by Timothy Steele. University of Arkansas Press, 1995. Reprinted by permission of the University of Arkansas Press

Jim Stevens. "Schizophrenia" originally appeared in *Light: The Quarterly of Light Verse* (Spring 1992). Copyright © 1992 by Jim Stevens. Reprinted by permission of the author.

Wallace Stevens. "The Emperor of Ice-Cream" from *Collected Poems* by Wallace Stevens. Copyright © 1923 and renewed 1951 by Wallace Stevens. Reprinted by permission of Alfred A. Knopf, Inc.

Mark Strand. "Sleeping with One Eye Open" from *Selected Poems* by Mark Strand. Copyright © 1979, 1980 by Mark Strand. Reprinted by permission of Alfred A. Knopf, Inc.

Robert Sward. "A Personal Analysis of 'The Love Song of J. Alfred Prufrock'" from *Touchstones: American Poets on a Favorite Poem*, eds. Robert Pack and Jay Parini, Middlebury College Press. Published by UP New England.

May Swenson. "A Nosty Fright." Copyright © 1984 by May Swenson. Reprinted by permission of the Estate of May Swenson.

Wislawa Szymborska. "End and Beginning" translated by Joseph Brodsky. Originally appeared in *The Times Literary Supplement* (December 31, 1993). Copyright © 1993, Times Supplements, Limited. "The Joy of Writing" from *Sounds, Feelings, Thoughts: Seventy Poems* by Wislawa Szymborska. tr. Magnus J. Krynski and Robert A. Maguire. Copyright © 1981 by Princeton University Press. "The Joy of Writing, translated by Stanislaw Barańczak and Clare Cavanagh" from *View with a Grain of Sand: Selected Poems*, copyright © 1993 by Wislawa Szymborska, English translation copyright © 1995 by Harcourt Brace & Company. Reprinted by permission of the publisher. "Hatred" from *View with a Grain of Sand: Selected Poems*, copyright © 1993 by Wislawa Szymborska. English translation copyright © 1995 by Harcourt Brace & Company.

Brook Thomas. "A New Historical Approach to Keats's 'Ode on a Grecian Urn'" excerpted from "The Historical Necessities for — and Difficulties with — New Historical Analysis in Introductory Literature Courses," *College English*, September 1987. Copyright © 1987 by the National Council of Teachers of English. Reprinted with permission.

Dylan Thomas. "Do not go gentle into that good night" " Fern Hill," and "The Hand That Signed the Paper" by Dylan Thomas from *Poems of Dylan Thomas*. Copyright © 1952 by the Trustees for the Copyrights of Dylan Thomas. Reprinted by permission of New Directions Publishing Corp. "On the Words in Poetry" by Dylan Thomas from *Quite Early One Morning*. Copyright © 1964 by New Directions Publishing Corp. Reprinted by permission of New Directions Publishing Corp.

Mabel Loomis Todd. "The Character of Amherst" from *The Years and Hours of Emily Dickinson*, volume 2, by Jay Leda. Copyright © 1960 by Yale University Press.

Jean Toomer. "Reapers" from *Cane* by Jean Toomer. Copyright © 1923 by Boni & Liveright, renewed 1951 by Jean Toomer. Reprinted by permission of Liveright Publishing Corporation.

Steven C. Tracy. "A Reading of 'The Weary Blues'" from *Langston Hughes and the Blues* by Steven C. Tracy. Copyright © 1988 by the Board of Trustees of the University of Illinois. Reprinted with permission of The University of Illinois Press.

Tomas Transtromer. "April and Silence" translated by Robin Fulton. First published in *The Kenyon Review New Series*, Summer 1991, vol. 12, no. 3. Copyright © Robin Fulton. Reprinted by permission.

Lionel Trilling. "On Frost as a Terrifying Poet." Copyright © 1959 by Lionel Trilling, reprinted by permission of the Wylie Agency, Inc.

John Updike. "Dog's Death" from *Midpoint and Other Poems* by John Updike. Copyright © 1969 by John Updike. Reprinted by permission of Alfred A. Knopf, Inc.. "Player Piano" from *Collected Poems 1953-1993* by John Updike. Copyright © 1993 by John Updike. Reprinted by permission of Alfred A. Knopf., Inc.

Diane Wakoski. "Belly Dancer." Copyright © 1988 by Diane Wakoski. Reprinted from *Emerald Ice: Selected Poems 1962-1987* with the permission of Black Sparrow Press.

Derek Walcott. "The Virgins" from *Sea Grapes* by Derek Walcott. Copyright © 1976 by Derek Walcott. "The Road Taken" excerpt from "The Road Taken" by Derek Walcott from *Homage to Robert Frost* by Joseph Brodsky, Seamus Heaney, and Derek Walcott. Copyright © 1996 by the Estate of Joseph Brodsky. Reprinted by permission of Farrar, Straus & Giroux, Inc.

Alice Walker. "a woman is not a potted plant" from *Her Blue Body Everything We Know: Earthling Poems, 1965–1990*. Copyright © 1991 by Alice Walker, reprinted by permission of Harcourt Brace & Company.

Robert Wallace. "The Double-Play" copyright © 1961 by Robert Wallace. From *Views of a Ferris Wheel*. Reprinted by permission of the author.

Ronald Wallace. "Dogs" from *The Yale Review*, Jan, 1997, vol. 85, no. 1. Reprinted by permission of the author.

Marilyn Nelson Waniek. "Emily Dickinson's Defunct" from *For the Body* by Marilyn Nelson Waniek. Copyright © 1978 by Marilyn Nelson Waniek. Reprinted by permission of Louisiana State University Press.

Thom Ward. "Vasectomy." Copyright © 1996 Thom Ward, as first published in *The Atlantic Monthly*.

Richard Wilbur. "A Late Aubade" from *Walking to Sleep: New Poems and Translations*. Copyright © 1968 by Richard Wilbur, originally published in *The New Yorker*, reprinted by permission of Harcourt Brace & Company. "Love Calls Us to the Things of This World" from *Things of This World*. Copyright © 1956 and renewed 1984 by Richard Wilbur, reprinted by permission of Harcourt Brace & Company.

Miller Williams. "Excuse Me." Reprinted from *Adjusting to the Light: Poems* by Miller Williams, by permission of the University of Missouri Press. Copyright © 1992 by Miller Williams. "Thinking About Bill Dead of AIDS" from *Living on the Surface: New and Selected Poems* by Miller Williams. Copyright © 1972, 1975, 1976, 1979, 1980, 1987, 1988, 1989 by Miller Williams. Reprinted by permission of Louisiana State University Press.

Willam Carlos Williams. "Poem," "Spring and All," "The Red Wheelbarrow," and "This Is Just to Say " by William Carlos Williams from *Collected Poems: 1909-1939*, Volume I. Copyright © 1938 by New Directions Publishing Corp. Reprinted by permission of New Directions Publishing Corp.

Greg Williamson. "Waterfall" from *The Silent Partner* by Greg Williamson, 1995. Reprinted by permission of Story Line Press.

Cynthia Griffin Wolff. "On the Many Voices in Dickinson's Poetry" from *Emily Dickinson* by Cynthia Griffin Wolff. Copyright © 1986 by Cynthia Griffin Wolff. Reprinted by permission of Alfred A. Knopf, Inc.

James Wright. "A Blessing" from James Wright, *The Branch Will Not Break*, Wesleyan UP 1961. Reprinted by permission of the University Press of New England.

Mitsuye Yamada. "A Bedtime Story" from *Camp Notes and Other Poems*. Copyright © 1992 by Mitsuye Yamada. Reprinted by permission of the author and of Kitchen Table: Women of Color Press, P.O. Box 40-490, Brooklyn, NY 11240-4920.

William Butler Yeats. "Crazy Jane Talks with the Bishop," "Leda and the Swan," "Sailing to Byzantium," and "The Second Coming" reprinted with the permission of Simon & Schuster from *The Poems of W.B. Yeats: A New Edition*, edited by Richard J. Finneran. Copyright © 1933 by Macmillan Publishing Company. Copyright renewed © 1961 by Bertha Georgie Yeats.

Xu Gang. "Red Azalea on the Cliff" from *Three Hundred Lyric Poems by Modern Young Poets in The Red Azalea: Chinese Poetry Since the Cultural Revolution*, ed. Edward Morin. Trans. Fang Dai, Dennis Ding, and Edwin Morin. Copyright © 1990 by U of Hawaii Press.

Index of First Lines

Index of Authors and Titles

Index of Terms

Boldface numbers refer to the Glossary of Literary Terms